Teaching Notes

ELEMENTS OF LITERATURE

FIFTH COURSE

Literature of the United States

Teaching Notes

ELEMENTS OF
LITERATURE

FIFTH COURSE

Literature of the United States

Barbara Freiberg
English Department
Louisiana State University
  Laboratory School
Baton Rouge, Louisiana

Patricia Brundage-Rude
English Department
North High School
Bakersfield, California

Andyce Orde
formerly, English Department
North High School
Bakersfield, California

Holt, Rinehart and Winston, Inc.

Harcourt Brace Jovanovich, Inc.

Austin • Orlando • San Diego • Chicago • Dallas • Toronto

ACKNOWLEDGMENTS

For permission to reprint copyrighted material, grateful acknowledgment is made to the following sources:

Edward J. Acton: From Introduction entitled ''Sweet Lorraine'' by James Baldwin from *To Be Young, Gifted and Black: Lorraine Hansberry in Her Own Words,* adapted by Robert Nemiroff. Copyright © 1969 by James Baldwin.

The Atlantic: From ''Farewell to Europe'' by Richard Aldington from *The Atlantic Monthly,* CLXVI, 1940.

Elizabeth Barnett, Literary Executor of the Estate of Edna St. Vincent Millay: From ''Dirge Without Music'' from *Collected Poems* by Edna St. Vincent Millay. Copyright © 1922, 1928, 1950, © 1955 by Edna St. Vincent Millay and Norma Millay Ellis. Published by Harper & Row Publishers, Inc.

The Continuum Publishing Company: From *The Literary History of the American Revolution, 1763–1783: Volume I, 1763–1776* by Moses Coit Tyler. Published by Frederick Ungar Publishing Co., NY, 1957.

Delacorte Press/Seymour Lawrence, a division of Bantam Doubleday Dell Publishing Group, Inc.: From ''Tamar'' from *Ellis Island & Other Stories* by Mark Helprin. Copyright © 1976, 1977, 1979, 1980, 1981 by Mark Helprin.

Farrar, Straus & Giroux, Inc.: From ''First Death in Nova Scotia'' from *The Complete Poems 1927–1979* by Elizabeth Bishop. Copyright © 1946, 1955, 1962 and renewed © 1973 by Elizabeth Bishop; copyright © 1983 by Alice Helen Methfessel. From ''Randall Jarrell'' from *Babel to Byzantium: Poets and Poetry Now* by James Dickey. Copyright © 1968 by James Dickey. From ''The Death of the Ball Turret Gunner'' from *The Complete Poems* by Randall Jarrell. Copyright © 1945, 1969 and renewed © 1973 by Mrs. Randall Jarrell. From ''For the Union Dead'' from *For the Union Dead* by Robert Lowell. Copyright © 1960, 1964 by Robert Lowell.

Harcourt Brace Jovanovich, Inc.: From ''The Love Song of J. Alfred Prufrock'' and from ''Preludes'' from *Collected Poems 1909–1962* by T. S. Eliot. Copyright 1936 by Harcourt Brace Jovanovich, Inc.; copyright © 1963, 1964, by T. S. Eliot. From Preface to *The Book of American Negro Poetry* by James Weldon Johnson. Copyright 1922, 1931 by Harcourt Brace Jovanovich, Inc.; copyright 1950 by Grace Johnson; copyright © 1958 by Mrs. Grace Nail Johnson. From ''Notes for a Preface'' from *The Complete Poems of Carl Sandburg.* Copyright 1950 by Carl Sandburg; copyright renewed © 1978 by Margaret Sandburg, Helga Sandburg Crile and Janet Sandburg. From ''Year's-End'' from *Ceremony and Other Poems* by Richard Wilbur. Copyright 1949 and renewed © 1977 by Richard Wilbur.

HarperCollins Publishers: From ''Homework'' from *Collected Poems, 1947–1980* by Allen Ginsberg. Copyright © 1989 by Allen Ginsberg.

Holt, Rinehart and Winston, Inc.: From ''Puritan Poetry'' by Michael L. Lasser from *Major American Authors,* edited by D. Bruce Lockerbie. Copyright © 1970 by Holt, Rinehart and Winston, Inc.

Houghton Mifflin Company: From *James Russell Lowell* by Martin Duberman. Copyright © 1966 by Martin Duberman.

Alfred A. Knopf, Inc.: From ''I, Too'' and from ''The Negro Speaks of Rivers'' from *Selected Poems of Langston Hughes.* Copyright 1926, 1948 by Alfred A. Knopf, Inc.; copyright renewed 1954 by Langston Hughes. From ''Anecdote of the Jar'' from *The Collected Poems of Wallace Stevens.* Copyright 1923 and renewed 1951 by Wallace Stevens.

Liveright Publishing Corporation: From ''what if a much of a which of a wind'' from *Collected Poems, 1913–1962* by E. E. Cummings. Copyright © 1923, 1925, 1931, 1935, 1938, 1939, 1940, 1944, 1945, 1946, 1947, 1948, 1949, 1950, 1951, 1952, 1953, 1954, 1955, 1956, 1957, 1958, 1959, 1960, 1961, 1962 by the Trustees for the E. E. Cummings Trust; copyright © 1961, 1963, 1968 by Marion Morehouse Cummings. From ''nobody loses all the time'' from *IS 5, poems* by E. E. Cummings. Copyright 1926 by Horace Liveright; copyright renewed 1954 by E. E. Cummings. From ''Summertime and the Living . . .'' from *Angle of Ascent, New and Selected Poems* by Robert Hayden. Copyright © 1966, 1970, 1972, 1975 by Robert Hayden.

James Merrill: From ''Kite Poem'' from *First Poems* by James Merrill. Copyright 1950 by Alfred A. Knopf, Inc.; copyright renewed © 1978 by James Merrill.

National Council of Teachers of English: From ''What I Wish I Had Known About Peer-Response Groups But Didn't'' by Ronald Barron from *English Journal,* September 1991. Copyright © 1991 by the National Council of Teachers of English. ''Using Portfolios to Empower Student Writers'' by Winfield Cooper and B. J. Brown from *English Journal,* February 1992. Copyright © 1992 by the National Council of Teachers of English. ''Readers Responding to 'Rappaccini's Daughter' '' by Jane Carlson from *English Journal,* January 1988. Copyright © 1988 by the National Council of Teachers of English. ''Twenty (Better) Questions'' by Kris L. Myers from *English Journal,* January 1988. Copyright © 1988 by the National Council of Teachers of English. From ''Hill-Climbing with Thoreau: Creating Meaningful Carry-over'' by Mary Jo Schaars from *English Journal,* November 1990. Copyright © 1990 by the National Council of Teachers of English.

Estate of Robert Nemiroff: From *To Be Young, Gifted and Black: Lorraine Hansberry in Her Own Words,* adapted by Robert Nemiroff, with an Introduction by James Baldwin. Copyright © 1969 by Robert Nemiroff and Robert Nemiroff as Executor of the Estate of Lorraine Hansberry.

New Directions Publishing Corporation: From ''Dulce et Decorum Est'' from *Collected Poems of Wilfred Owen.* Copyright © 1963 by Chatto & Windus. From ''The Garden'' from *Personae* by Ezra Pound. Copyright 1926 by Ezra Pound. From ''December at Yase'' from *The Back Country* by Gary Snyder. Copyright © 1957, 1958, 1959, 1960, 1962, 1963, 1964, 1965, 1966, 1967, 1968 by Gary Snyder.

The New York Times Company: From ''Little Red Riding Hood Revisited'' by Russell Baker from *The New York Times,* January 13, 1980. Copyright © 1980 by The New York Times Company. From

Acknowledgments continue on page 372, which is an extension of the copyright page.

CONTENTS

USING THE
TEACHING NOTES

Part One of the Teaching Notes contains student objectives and teaching strategies for each unit and selection in the text. Part One provides complete coverage of the text's instructional features as well as extension activities and reading and reference lists. Following the teaching guides, in Part Two you will find articles on teaching writing, on assessment, use of portfolios, peer-response groups, questioning strategies, reading development, critical thinking, reading rates, vocabulary growth, and various teaching techniques. The reference section includes several interesting research articles on new pedagogy and teaching strategies.

For each literary selection, the Teaching Notes include, as appropriate, an outline of major elements, suggestions for introducing the selection, and helpful background information. The teaching strategies focus on discussions of how to cope with cultural differences; teaching approaches for students of different ability levels as well as for students learning English as a second language; approaches to reading the selection, including prereading activities, oral reading, method of assignment, and audiovisual presentation; and reteaching alternatives. See page 324 in Part Two of these Teaching Notes for an annotated bibliography of general reference works for both students and teachers. A bibliography of books and articles appears in Part One at the end of each unit. These annotated bibliographies will be useful in providing additional resources for you and for students.

The Teaching Notes also provide answers for the language and vocabulary exercises in the text as well as ideas for presenting the writing assignments. Evaluation criteria for every writing assignment suggest the major points you will want to look for in assessing students' writing.

Part One

TEACHING STRATEGIES

THE COLONIAL PERIOD
THE AGE OF FAITH

Teaching the Colonial Period Unit

A nation's literature is most often studied in the order in which it was written. A key word in that sentence is *written.* Although Native Americans had outstanding public speakers and long oral traditions, they lacked a method of writing down their speeches, poems, stories, and legends. Colonial explorers and settlers were therefore the first people in what is now the United States to create written records of what they observed, thought, and experienced.

Teaching American literature chronologically—beginning at the beginning—presents an obvious challenge. The nation's earliest literature is not the fast-paced prose or engaging poetry of later years. Instead, it consists mainly of serious-minded journals, sermons, personal narratives, religious poetry and histories, written in a language that may seem archaic and difficult to your students. In spite of these obstacles, the literature of the Colonial period is important to students, for it introduces them to a way of thinking and living—the Puritan ethic—that has shaped many of our values and that continues to affect our lives. With this unit, it is especially important to provide a historical context for the literature students will read. The unit introduction in the student text (pages 2–10) and the background information on the authors and the selections provide students with a much needed overview of Puritan history and beliefs.

This unit concentrates on the Puritans of New England, because the Puritans, inward-looking and industrious, were America's principal writers of the pre-Revolutionary period. Their religion encouraged written self-examination as a manifestation of the workings of God. Even their poetry had a devout purpose, as critic Michael L. Lasser explains in *Major American Authors:*

> Most important and most rewarding to the Puritans was poetry's moral significance: beyond its capacity to delight, poetry must offer its readers profound spiritual insights. To the Puritans, then, the subject matter of poetry was primary, regardless of the didacticism of the presentation. While they readily accepted poetic expression, it would nonetheless be incorrect to say that the Puritans cared particularly about literary theory, about matters of style, about the development of cultivated literary judgment. Like scientific investigation, political maneuvering, and all other secular activities of Puritan New England, poetry was a means to an end. And that end was spiritual.

Of the seven writers featured in this unit, six are New Englanders, five of whom are deeply religious Puritans. Well-educated Southern planters, sophisticated though they were, produced little writing of permanent interest. A notable exception was the Virginia planter William Byrd, whose witty and graceful journals were published after his death.

Objectives of the Colonial Period Unit

1. To improve reading proficiency and expand vocabulary
2. To gain exposure to notable Colonial writers and their works
3. To define and identify significant literary techniques
4. To define and identify elements of poetry and nonfiction
5. To interpret and respond to poetry and nonfiction, orally and in writing
6. To practice the following critical thinking and writing skills
   a. Analyzing a writer's attitude
   b. Comparing and contrasting historical accounts
   c. Interpreting an allusion
   d. Analyzing character
   e. Comparing and contrasting the use of metaphors
   f. Analyzing the use of imagery and the conceit
   g. Interpreting metaphor

Introducing the Colonial Period Unit

Your students will already have some knowledge of European exploration and colonization of America. Be sure they understand the meaning of "Colonial period"—the years (1607–1776) during which England governed a group of colonies on the east coast of North America. After the Revolutionary War, these colonies became the thirteen original states. Although students are unlikely to have studied Puritan life and thought in any detail, most will know the stories of the *Mayflower,* Miles Standish, and the first Thanksgiving. To get an indication of what else they know about the Puritans, you may want to begin with a series of questions:

1. Who are the Puritans?
2. Why are some of them called Pilgrims?
3. Where did the *Mayflower* Pilgrims come from?
4. Where did they settle?
5. How many were there?
6. What were they seeking?
7. Why was the first winter so hard?
8. What was their relationship with the Native Americans?
9. Who were the two or three most prominent leaders?
10. What were the Puritans' fundamental beliefs about God and the Bible?

These questions are answered in the unit introduction, text pages 2–10.

William Bradford

Text page 11

FROM OF PLYMOUTH PLANTATION

Text page 13

Objectives

1. To respond to an account of the settlement of Plymouth Plantation
2. To write narration from a different point of view
3. To write an essay comparing and contrasting two historical accounts

Introducing the History

Of Bradford's history, the British critic and author A. L. Rowse observed, "It is indeed the qualities that give enduring life to a book: absolute fidelity, lifelikeness, and trustworthiness; its moral purity—the selflessness, submission, and control—shines through. Its tones are russet and gray and white. . . . Perhaps there is a sober, subdued poetry in Bradford. . . ." (*American Heritage,* October 1959).

BACKGROUND ON THE HISTORY   Bradford's history was never intended for publication. It was probably written to remain in his family as a tribute to the founders of this colony. The manuscript came to rest in the library of the Old South Church in Boston and was lost after the church was plundered by British troops in the Revolutionary War. Thought to have been destroyed, it was found in 1855 in the library of the Bishop of London and first published the following year.

SUMMARY   In Chapter 9 of his history, Bradford tells of the death of a profane sailor who earlier condemned the sick Pilgrims. Bradford explains the repair of the main mast and the landing at what is now Provincetown. He gives his own thoughts on the Pilgrims' situation. In Chapter 10 Bradford relates the incidents that occurred during the search for a harbor and a permanent place to settle. At the end of the chapter, he notes the landing at Plymouth Rock. In Chapter 11 he narrates the events of the "Starving Time" and discusses Indian relations, including the treaty with Massasoit. The chapter concludes with a paragraph about the first Thanksgiving.

Teaching Strategies

PROVIDING FOR CULTURAL DIFFERENCES   Native American students may be especially interested in the tribes that met the new settlers. In Virginia, Captain John Smith was met by the Powhatans, the tribe to which Pocahontas belonged. In Massachusetts, the Pilgrims were met by the Wampanoags, Massasoit's tribe. Squanto, a Pawtuxet, was not a native of the Plymouth region.

Note that everyone in America—except, of course, Native Americans—either immigrated to this country from other lands or is a descendant of those who immigrated here. Ask students if they know any stories about their families' arrival in this country. You may want to try to elicit some of these stories.

PROVIDING FOR DIFFERENT LEVELS OF ABILITY   LEP readers will need help in understanding Bradford's difficult sentence structure and archaic wording. Capable volunteers might explain orally each of the main incidents that Bradford describes. Also, students familiar with Bible stories can expand on some of the Biblical allusions that are briefly identified in the footnotes; there is usually more to be said about them.

READING THE HISTORY   Before students read, ask them to discuss what they already know about the Pilgrims. Why were they willing to leave the security of Europe and travel 3,000 miles across turbulent seas? What dangers and hardships did they endure during the voyage and as they settled in their new home? Help students to understand that these first settlers were arriving in what to them was a totally new world. It was a vast, unexplored continent thinly populated with unknown people of whom they had heard sometimes frightening reports. At the same time, the settlers had broken free from the political and religious bonds of Europe. They were truly on their own.

RETEACHING ALTERNATIVES   Ask students to compile on the chalkboard a chronology of the incidents in Bradford's history, beginning with the account of the profane seaman and ending with the first Thanksgiving. Have one student start the chronology and a different student add each next event.

Responding to the History   Text page 21

Answers to the questions in the Pupil's Edition appear in the Annotated Teacher's Edition.

Writing About the History

For help in revising their compositions, refer students to **Grammar, Usage, and Mechanics: A Reference Guide** on text pages 1183–1228 at the back of their books.

A CREATIVE RESPONSE

1. Using Another Point of View   Students might work on this assignment in pairs or small groups. Have students list the events in Chapter 10, and then determine which ones the Native Americans could have observed. Next have them discuss what the Native American observers might have found strange about the English scouts' appearance and behavior. Discuss especially how they might have interpreted the scouts' following them and taking some of their corn and beans. For further help in completing this assignment, refer students to the **Literature and Language Exercise** on page 1161, Using the Descriptive and Narrative Modes.

▶ CRITERIA FOR EVALUATING THE ASSIGNMENT   The point of view is that of a Native American of that time. The narrator might mention the scouts' landing, their strange appearance and clothing, the theft of the Indians' corn, etc. Feelings attributed to the narrator are appropriate. Any additional creative details fit both the narrator and the situation.

A CRITICAL RESPONSE

2. Contrasting Two Historical Accounts   Read aloud the excerpt from Smith's pamphlet, checking for literal comprehension, and the assignment in the text. Call students' attention to the fact that the assignment (last paragraph, text page 21) outlines the expected content and organization of their essays.

▶ CRITERIA FOR EVALUATING THE ASSIGNMENT   Students should note that Smith is trying to persuade people (probably poor, uneducated) to settle in the New World. Bradford is describing actual events to preserve a record for posterity. His audience is probably educated and religious. Smith promises abundance of food, liberty, wealth, and leisure but doesn't mention hardships, danger, disease.

Extending the History

Bradford did not write his history to attract new settlers, nor was most of it even published until long after his death. Yet prospective settlers did need honest information on what to expect if they came to the New World. Have students role play a group of young men and women living in London several years after the settlement of Plymouth Plantation. They would like to move permanently to New England, but do not know what to expect and are meeting with representatives from Plymouth Plantation who are trying to recruit new settlers. Have the prospective recruits ask questions that the Plymouth residents answer. For example: How dangerous is the voyage? How friendly are the Indians? What kind of work is available in Plymouth? What skills are needed? What should a settler bring from England? What is life like for women and children? Encourage students to do additional reading to answer such questions.

Primary Sources   Text page 22

THE FIRST THANKSGIVING

Explain to students that a primary source is an original, or firsthand, source. Since Edward Winslow was present at the first Thanksgiving, his letter about the event is a primary source. You might mention that a primary source may leave out something the reader wishes to know, such as the date of the first Thanksgiving. It may also be inaccurate or biased, although historians generally regard a primary source as more trustworthy than a secondary source—an account that is not original, but rather is based on other, earlier sources. The introduction to Unit One, for example, is a secondary source. Ask students whether Bradford's history is a primary source. (It is.)

ELEMENTS OF LITERATURE   Text page 22

THE PLAIN STYLE

Students may find it hard to see why a style as difficult as Bradford's is called "plain." Remind them that its plainness is in contrast to the style then popular in England, a style filled with figurative language and classical allusions. Bradford uses allusions, but they are Biblical. When students recast the beginning of Chapter 10 into simple modern prose, they are almost sure to find that the sound of older Biblical translations (such as the King James version) is indeed lost.

Before students begin writing, refer them to Elements of a Sentence (text page 1185) in **Grammar, Usage, and Mechanics: A Reference Guide** at the back of the Pupil's Edition. Have them review items 1–3, the essential elements of a complete sentence.

Mary Rowlandson

Text page 23

FROM A NARRATIVE OF HER CAPTIVITY

Text page 24

Objectives

1. To respond to a personal narrative
2. To identify examples of subjective reporting
3. To interpret allegorical meanings
4. To write a journal entry from a different point of view
5. To write an essay explaining an allusion

Introducing the Journal

At the start of King Philip's War—55 years after the Pilgrims had landed—there were about 40,000 English settlers in New England and about 20,000 Native Americans. According to an English friend of his, King Philip (Metacomet) said, ". . . little remains of my ancestor's domain. I am resolved not to see the day when I have no country." King Philip was killed a few months after the events in Rowlandson's narrative.

SUMMARY   Rowlandson and her six-year-old daughter Sarah, both of them wounded, accompany their Indian captors into the wilderness. Although Rowlandson's faith is strong, she realizes that her life and Sarah's are in deadly peril. They travel from place to place, under constant threat, in bitter weather, and with little food. On the ninth day of captivity, Sarah dies and is buried by the Indians. Rowlandson's son, also a captive, visits her. One Indian gives her a Bible taken in a raid. The traveling continues, still with virtually no food, but Rowlandson discovers she can eat the "filthy trash" that the Indians have also been forced to eat.

Rowlandson meets King Philip (Metacomet), who asks her to make his son a shirt, which she does and for which he gives her a shilling. After that, other Indians ask her to make shirts, one in exchange for some bear meat, another for a knife. The Indians' travel never ceases, nor does the quest for food. A friendly squaw gives her a piece of bear and some goundnuts. Throughout the ordeal, Rowlandson is sustained by her faith in God.

Teaching Strategies

PROVIDING FOR CULTURAL DIFFERENCES   Students who do not have a strong background in early American history would benefit from some additional background on the relationship between the early Colonists and Indians. You may also wish to use the Annotated Teacher's Edition Humanities Connections to help present a more balanced sense of Colonial life in Mary Rowlandson's time.

PROVIDING FOR DIFFERENT LEVELS OF ABILITY
For less advanced classes grouped homogeneously, divide students into six groups before assigning the entire selection. (With mixed classes do the same, distributing more advanced students among all groups.) Have each group read, discuss, and summarize on paper a separate section of the Rowlandson narrative. One student can then present each group's summary orally, with the rest of the class taking notes. Finally, assign the entire selection as homework.

READING THE JOURNAL   You may want to ask students what modern experiences might compare to Mrs. Rowlandson's experience. (Students may suggest kidnapping, capture by terrorists or by enemy forces during a war.)

RETEACHING ALTERNATIVES   Have students compile a list of Mary Rowlandson's grievances against her captors, arranging them in the order in which the events occurred. Then have them list the kindnesses she mentions. (The captors buried her dead child; one Indian gave her a Bible; an Indian woman gave her bear meat and groundnuts; another woman gave her shelter; etc.)

Responding to the Journal

Text page 30

Answers to the questions in the Pupil's Edition appear in the Annotated Teacher's Edition.

Writing About the Journal

For help in revising their compositions, refer students to **Grammar, Usage, and Mechanics: A Reference Guide** on text pages 1183–1228 at the back of their books.

A CREATIVE RESPONSE
1. Using Another Point of View   Groups of three or four students may work together to do research, pool their information, and collaborate on a joint paper. Research should lead students to a greater understanding of the difficulty of determining responsibility for the war and to

a grasp of how the expansion of settlements contributed to depletion of Wampanoag food sources.

▶ CRITERIA FOR EVALUATING THE ASSIGNMENT The point of view is that of a member of the Wampanoag tribe. The explanation is supported by factual details.

A CRITICAL RESPONSE
2. Explaining an Allusion Read aloud the writing assignment and Psalm 137, checking for literal comprehension. Before students begin their essays, have them identify the verses Rowlandson quotes (text page 28) and the events that brought them to mind.

▶ CRITERIA FOR EVALUATING THE ASSIGNMENT The essay cites several parallels Rowlandson would have seen between her own and the psalmist's experiences: e.g., the destruction of her town (''Jerusalem''); homesickness; the sheer fact of being a captive; strange villages as a kind of ''Babylon.'' Students may think of other parallels.

Extending the Journal

When students think of the frontier, they are likely to think of the American West. Remind them that when European settlers arrived in the New World, the frontier began at Plymouth, Massachusetts, and Jamestown, Virginia. Mary Rowlandson was a true frontierswoman, living in the outpost settlement of Lancaster, about thirty miles west of Boston.

Have students discuss the meaning of the word *frontier.* When did the traditional frontier disappear? (Most historians say 1890.) What is today's frontier, if there is one? (The usual answer is space, although the word is often applied metaphorically to science, technology, medicine, and other fields in which advances continue to be made.) Have students work in pairs to describe to each other the kinds of frontiers they would like to explore. Ask each listener to summarize in a few sentences what his or her partner has said.

Sarah Kemble Knight Text page 31

FROM **THE JOURNAL OF MADAM KNIGHT** Text page 32

Objectives

1. To appreciate style and wit in an early eighteenth-century journal
2. To contrast the use of metaphor in two writers
3. To analyze differences in tone among three writers
4. To write a journal entry narrating a trip
5. To write an essay analyzing two characters

Introducing the Journal

Mrs. Knight was thirty-eight years old when she made her famous trip. Her journal, although delightfully written, was not intended for publication. It first appeared in print in 1825, published by Theodore Dwight in New York, and has been reprinted many times since then. The original handwritten journal has been lost.

You may wish to ask student volunteers to tell the class about any travel experiences, including camping or hiking, they have had in wilderness locations. How do such experiences resemble Colonial travel, and how do they differ from it?

SUMMARY On October 3, Knight, on horseback, pauses first at a post stop, where she finds the meal very unappealing. At a river her guide (a mail carrier) gets a boy with a canoe to take her across. After dark her horse carries her across a second, hazardous river. They stop at a public house. After drinking some chocolate milk, she tries to sleep, but two ''town topers'' keep her awake with their arguing. She composes a verse, imploring the rum to ''still their tongues.'' On October 6, she gets a new guide to accompany her to New Haven. They proceed along bad roads to Saybrook ferry, cross the river, and stop at an inn. Once again the food is inedible.

Teaching Strategies

PROVIDING FOR CULTURAL DIFFERENCES LEP/ESL students may have difficulty with Knight's journal. The language is unusual, the sentence structure complex, the vocabulary somewhat archaic. You may wish to assign each of the seven paragraphs to a student who is proficient in English. The seven students can read and study their paragraphs, and then paraphrase them orally in class. In this way, all students will have some understanding of the events in the narrative before attempting to read it on their own.

PROVIDING FOR DIFFERENT LEVELS OF ABILITY

To provide groundwork for students, assign the selection to everyone and ask one student to read it with special care. On the day you discuss it in class, have this student, pretending to be the feisty Mrs. Knight, relate her series of adventures orally in class. She (or he) should use note cards to keep the sequence of events in order. This oral paraphrasing will help students and should also provide a springboard for discussion.

READING THE JOURNAL

Be sure students read the biography of Sarah Kemble Knight on text page 31 before reading the narrative itself. In introducing this selection, ask students to try to visualize what travel must have been like in the early 1700's. Were there roads? (Yes, but not paved roads) Was there any motorized transportation? (No) Were there road signs? (Perhaps, but not many) Were there bridges? (Only over smaller streams) Were there inns and public houses? (Yes, quite a few because of the short distances that could be covered) Were there hostile Indians? (Yes, but not along the Boston to New York route)

RETEACHING ALTERNATIVES

Have students use a large wall map to trace the general route that Sarah Kemble Knight followed from Boston to New York. They should be able to find one specific place that Mrs. Knight mentions for October 3 (Providence, Rhode Island) and two that she mentions for October 6 (New Haven and [Old] Saybrook, Connecticut).

Responding to the Journal   Text page 35

Answers to the questions in the Pupil's Edition appear in the Annotated Teacher's Edition.

Writing About the Journal

For help in revising their compositions, refer students to **Grammar, Usage, and Mechanics: A Reference Guide** on text pages 1183–1228 at the back of their books.

A CREATIVE RESPONSE

1. Writing a Journal Entry   Read the assignment aloud and, with the students, list on the chalkboard several kinds of trips that would lend themselves to the purposes of this assignment. Discuss how the same event could be treated humorously (as in Knight's journal) or seriously (as in Rowlandson's) by changing the style and tone.

For help in completing this assignment, refer students to pages 1197–1199 (Using Pronouns Correctly) in **Grammar, Usage, and Mechanics: A Reference Guide** at the back of the Pupil's Edition.

▶ CRITERIA FOR EVALUATING THE ASSIGNMENT   The tone is consistent. The journal entry comments on methods of travel, length of the trip, discomforts or dangers encountered, and the types and quality of food and accommodations.

A CRITICAL RESPONSE

2. Analyzing Character   Have students first brainstorm events or situations they recall which show, for both Rowlandson and Knight, the character traits mentioned in the writing assignment. Have them check their accuracy by locating suitable journal passages before they write their essays.

▶ CRITERIA FOR EVALUATING THE ASSIGNMENT   The essay is clearly organized and quotes from the journals to support its major points. (Rowlandson is stoic and deeply religious. She is resourceful; eats Indian food to survive. Knight is fearful and anxious; not as religious as Rowlandson; picky about food; witty.)

Extending the Journal

Unlike Bradford's history and Rowlandson's journal, Knight's journal is not filled with religious references. Ask students to play the part of context detectives and see if they can find one statement that suggests each of the following traits: (a) Knight's familiarity with at least one Bible story; (b) Knight's acceptance and probable tolerance of a different religion; (c) Knight's faith in God, expressed in a way that sounds rather like Rowlandson. *Suggested answers:* (a) text page 32: "not so much as think of Lot's wife" (b) text page 33: "at the best, like a holy sister just come out of a spiritual bath in dripping garments" (c) text page 34: "through God's goodness I met with no harm."

SINNERS IN THE HANDS OF AN ANGRY GOD

Objectives

1. To listen and respond to a powerful Colonial sermon

2. To analyze the writer's use of figures of speech, imagery, and emotional appeals

3. To rewrite two paragraphs for a modern audience

4. To rewrite a paragraph from another point of view

Introducing the Sermon

The series of religious revivals known as the Great Awakening aroused tremendous enthusiasm, although it could not restore Puritanism to its former status. It did have other important effects, however. It led to increased missionary work among the Indians, early antislavery activity, and the founding of a number of colleges, including Princeton, Brown, Rutgers, and Dartmouth.

Today's charismatic religious leaders are the successors to Jonathan Edwards and other revivalist preachers of the Great Awakening. You may want to introduce this selection with a discussion of what tendencies in society make today's evangelical movement popular. What do evangelists offer the people who see and hear them? What influence do they have on the rest of society?

SUMMARY "Natural men"—those who have not accepted Christ as their Savior—deserve hellfire and will get it. The purpose of this sermon is to awaken such unconverted people by letting them see the horror of their fate should the wrath of God be let loose upon them. Only the pleasure of God prevents His vengeance from being wreaked at this very moment. God's pure eyes are angered by wickedness; He abhors the unconverted. Their punishment will be frightful and infinite. Some members of the congregation will no doubt meet this fate, and perhaps soon. The time to obtain salvation is now.

Teaching Strategies

PROVIDING FOR CULTURAL DIFFERENCES Students who are familiar with modern evangelism, either from television or personal experience, might share their insights with the class. Have them discuss the intense emotionalism that can accompany evangelical sermons. If your class has no experience with Biblical evangelism, you may wish to have students do some library research on the Great Awakening and give oral reports on the subject prior to reading "Sinners in the Hands of an Angry God."

PROVIDING FOR DIFFERENT LEVELS OF ABILITY
Edwards's sermon should be presented orally and dramatically in all classes. ESL and LEP students will have a difficult time reading the sermon but all should gain a general impression of its style, content, and tone from hearing it read aloud.

READING THE SERMON In your most fiery manner, read aloud the first four paragraphs as students follow in their books. Ask students to imagine how they would *feel* if they thought Edwards was preaching directly to them. After they talk about their responses, continue reading aloud, focusing especially on the three passages containing the figures of speech of the dam, bow and arrow, and spider.

RETEACHING ALTERNATIVES Since Edwards's fire-and-brimstone sermon is based on the Bible—on people being "out of Christ"—you may find it worthwhile to read one or more passages on wrath and hellfire from the New Testament. See Luke 3:1–9 (John's preaching) and Revelation 6:8–17 (breaking of the fifth through seventh seals) in particular. Have students compare the content and style of these passages with Edwards's sermon.

Responding to the Sermon Text page 40

Answers to the questions in the Pupil's Edition appear in the Annotated Teacher's Edition.

Writing About the Sermon

For help in revising their compositions, refer students to **Grammar, Usage, and Mechanics: A Reference Guide** on text pages 1183–1228 at the back of their books.

A CREATIVE RESPONSE

1. Adapting the Sermon As a replacement for Edwards's ''O sinner!'' ask students to suggest some forms of address a television evangelist might use today. What kinds of language and images are most effective for modern audiences? For further help in completing this assignment, refer students to the **Literature and Language Exercise** on page 1165, Using the Persuasive Aim.

▶ CRITERIA FOR EVALUATING THE ASSIGNMENT The paper adapts two paragraphs of Edwards's sermon. The parallels with Edwards's sermon are clear, but the language and imagery are designed to stir a contemporary American audience.

2. Using Another Point of View The assignment implies a first-person reaction. Students might think of the paragraph as a journal entry or segment of a conversation or letter. Remind students that the sermon so affected the original congregation that the minister had to ask for quiet several times.

▶ CRITERIA FOR EVALUATING THE ASSIGNMENT The paragraph is written in the first-person and reveals the effect of the sermon personally on a member of the congregation. The paragraph may also describe observations of the words, behavior, and facial expressions of others present.

Extending the Sermon

In *The Minister's Wooing,* an all but forgotten novel published in 1859, Harriet Beecher Stowe, daughter of the famous minister Lyman Beecher, describes a mother lamenting the death of her unreligious son. Have students comment on the mother's reaction:

> I cannot, will not be resigned. It is all so unjust, cruel! To all eternity I will say so. To me there is no goodness, no justice, no mercy. . . . Think of all those awful ages of eternity! And then think of all God's power and knowledge used on the lost to make them suffer! . . . Frightful, unspeakable . . . !

Primary Sources   Text page 41

JOURNALS

Students may be asked to read these journal entries aloud. Point out that journals, as highly personal primary sources, often reveal the character of the writer. Ask students how they would characterize Jonathan Edwards based on these three journal entries. Have them note that (just as in fiction) the character of a person (Jonathan Edwards) can be revealed by the observations of another person (Esther).

Anne Bradstreet   Text page 42

HERE FOLLOW SOME VERSES . . .   Text page 43

Objectives

1. To respond to an autobiographical poem about a personal loss
2. To identify and explain an extended metaphor
3. To analyze word choice
4. To write a paragraph analyzing the writer's attitude
5. To analyze the use of inversions to accommodate meter

Introducing the Poem

Here are the major elements in the poem:

- **Rhythm:** iambic tetrameter

- **Rhyme:** aabbcc

- **Significant techniques:** extended metaphor, Biblical allusion

BACKGROUND ON THE POEM Even though Anne Bradstreet was recognized in her own time as a significant poet, the Puritans did not celebrate earthly glory. There is no portrait of Anne Bradstreet, no grave marker for her, and no Bradstreet house still standing. Her poetry is her monument. It reveals her as a talented poet and a charming woman.

THE LITERAL MEANING Awakened by shouts of ''Fire!,'' Bradstreet escapes from her house, then watches the flames consume it. When she passes the ruins, she thinks about her lost possessions, her memories, and the events that will never occur there. She chides herself for contemplating ''wealth on earth,'' knowing that it is God who laid her worldly goods ''in the dust.'' She realizes that her true house, hope, and treasure lie in heaven.

Teaching Strategies

PROVIDING FOR CULTURAL DIFFERENCES Students from different backgrounds will be able to identify more easily with Bradstreet's sorrow than with many other Puritan sentiments. Discuss how cultures differ in the emphasis they place on material things.

PROVIDING FOR DIFFERENT LEVELS OF ABILITY With less able readers, you may want to go through the poem line by line, paraphrasing each line—especially those with inversions—into language that all students can understand. LEP/ESL students will need some help in translating archaic contractions *(e'er, 'gin)* and words *(repine, bereft)*. Make sure students know that *Adieu* (line 36) is French for ''goodbye.''

READING THE POEM A week before you read this poem, assign it to a small group of students for an oral interpretation. Let them divide the lines and practice their parts before presenting it to the class.

Before the presentation, remind students that although the Puritans were industrious and often acquired material goods (the Bradstreets lost 800 books in this fire), they were not supposed to desire possessions. Bradstreet's emotional conflict between the loss of a comfortable, memory-filled house and her Puritan belief that such a loss does not matter is what gives this poem its poignancy. It is what prompts the extended metaphor at the end.

RETEACHING ALTERNATIVES The last verse of the 23rd Psalm is one of many Biblical references to a home in heaven: ''Surely goodness and mercy shall follow me all the days of my life: and I will dwell in the house of the Lord forever.'' You may wish to read that verse in class and have students discuss how it applies to Bradstreet's poem.

Responding to the Poem   Text page 44

Answers to the questions in the Pupil's Edition appear in the Annotated Teacher's Edition.

Writing About the Poem

For help in revising their compositions, refer students to **Grammar, Usage, and Mechanics: A Reference Guide** on text pages 1183–1228 at the back of their books.

A CRITICAL RESPONSE
Analyzing the Writer's Attitude Review the information on Puritan thought (A Comment on the Poem, text page 44) before students do the assignment.

▶ CRITERIA FOR EVALUATING THE ASSIGNMENT Paraphrased, lines 14–20 should read something like this:

I blessed God, who gave and took away,
Who reduced everything I owned to dust.
That's the way it was, and it was fair:
My property was His anyway, not mine,
So it's not my place to complain.
It would have been fair for Him to take everything,
But He left us with enough.

Students' paragraphs should interpret the lines as revealing a belief that God has a purpose for everything. Students should note that this belief could be especially comforting to an immigrant, who would face many hard times.

Analyzing Language and Style

THE "POETIC" STYLE
Students should note that the iambic beat disappears when lines are written in normal order, even if they are not paraphrased. For example, lines 27–30 would scan as follows:

My pleăsănt thíngs líe ĭn ashĕs,
Ănd Í shăll behŏld them no móre.
No guĕst shăll sít undĕr thy roof,
Nŏr eat ă bít ăt thy tablĕ.

UPON A SPIDER CATCHING A FLY

Text page 46

FROM GOD'S DETERMINATIONS TOUCHING HIS ELECT

Text page 49

Objectives

1. To respond to two Puritan poems

2. To interpret a complex metaphor

3. To identify and analyze poetic elements

4. To rewrite a poem as prose

Introducing the Poems

Here are the major elements of ''Upon a Spider Catching a Fly'':

- **Rhythm:** iambic with lines of varying length (stanzas of 3, 2, 4, 2, 1 feet)
- **Rhyme:** ababb
- **Significant techniques:** internal rhyme, alliteration, parable

Here are the major elements of from ''God's Determinations Touching His Elect'':

- **Rhythm:** iambic pentameter
- **Rhyme:** aabbcc
- **Significant techniques:** slant rhyme, imagery, puns, paradoxes, series of questions

BACKGROUND ON THE POEMS The editors of *The American Tradition in Literature* (Random House, 1985) sum up Taylor's poetry in this way:

> Taylor's work was uneven; yet at his best he produced lines and passages of startling vitality, fusing lofty concept and homely detail in the memorable fashion of great poetry. He was a true mystic, whose experience still convinces us, and one of four or five American Puritans whose writings retain the liveliness of genuine literature.

THE LITERAL MEANING *''Upon a Spider Catching a Fly''* In the first five stanzas, a spider weaves a web to catch a fly. Instead it catches a wasp. Because the wasp can match the spider's powers and ruin the web, the spider treats the wasp gently. A trapped fly is less fortunate; the spider bites its head, killing it. The last five stanzas explain the meaning of this parable. The spider represents Satan. The wasp represents a person with grace, one who therefore has the power to destroy Satan's web. The fly is a sinful person, destined to be destroyed by the power of Satan.

From ''God's Determinations—the Preface'' In a series of metaphorical questions, the speaker asks who created the world and ''hung the twinkling lanthorns [lanterns/stars] in the sky.'' His answer is God—the ''Might Almighty.'' God's power is infinite. He created ''nothing man'' and gave him ''all.'' But ''nothing man'' threw it all away by sinning and now, burdened with evil, is darker than coal.

Teaching Strategies

PROVIDING FOR CULTURAL DIFFERENCES Both of these poems deal with the relationship of humans to God. For ''Upon a Spider Catching a Fly,'' briefly review the Christian concepts of Satan, sin, and hell. Students should also be familiar with the story of Job in the Bible.

PROVIDING FOR DIFFERENT LEVELS OF ABILITY ''Upon a Spider Catching a Fly'' looks easier to read than it is. LEP/ESL students will have trouble with the archaic words (*Thou, thy, Lest, Didst,* etc.), contractions, and idioms. You may want to explain the meaning of each stanza, and then have one student read the poem aloud. Advise all students to read the accompanying explanatory material carefully. It helps clarify both this poem and the next one.

READING THE POEMS For both poems, students may find it helpful to go over the questions at the end before reading the poems. Most students probably know how and why a spider spins a web, but before reading the first poem, it may be a good idea to reinforce that knowledge.

Before reading the second poem, students might try to name five kinds of seventeenth-century crafts. In reading the poem, they can see whether Taylor includes these crafts when marveling at God's creation of the world. Play the audiocassette recording of the excerpt from ''God's Determinations Touching His Elect'' that accompanies the student text.

RETEACHING ALTERNATIVES Have all students write a one-sentence statement of the theme (or message) of each of the Taylor poems. Read five of the statements aloud for each poem, and have students select the one they think best. Put the two statements on the chalkboard. See if further improvements or refinements can be made in either of them.

UPON A SPIDER CATCHING A FLY   Text page 46

Responding to the Poem   Text page 47

Answers to the questions in the Pupil's Edition appear in the Annotated Teacher's Edition.

Writing About the Poem

For help in revising their compositions, refer students to **Grammar, Usage, and Mechanics: A Reference Guide** on text pages 1183–1228 at the back of their books.

A CREATIVE RESPONSE
1. Rewriting the Poem   Before students begin to write, review the concepts of word inversion and paraphrasing. Suggest that students read Elements of Literature: The Conceit (text page 48) in order to be able to paraphrase ''glory's cage'' (line 48).

▶ CRITERIA FOR EVALUATING THE ASSIGNMENT   Students' paragraphs should begin by addressing the spider. Sentences should be clear and easy to understand. A sample paraphrase follows:

You sad, poisoning thing. Is this your game—spinning webs out of yourself to catch a fly? Why do you do it? Once I saw an agitated wasp fall into your web. Fearing its sting, you didn't grab it. You stroked it gently so that it wouldn't get angry and wreck your web. But when a stupid fly got caught by one leg, you quickly bit it to death. Just as that fly was doomed, so are people who don't follow natural reason. Reader, don't try to go beyond your own strength or you too will lose the fight. The battle looks like this to me. The devil spins out tough cords, weaving tricky nets to entangle us descendants of Adam and lead us into sin. Please Lord, send your grace to break the cords and lead us through your heavenly gates. When we sit on high in glorious sanctuary with you, we will sing your praise as joyfully and gratefully as nightingales.

A CRITICAL RESPONSE
2. Comparing Spiders   Have students reread the paragraph in which Jonathan Edwards uses a spider image (text page 39). Elicit from students that his spider stands not for the devil, as in Taylor's poem, but for the loathsome (human) sinner.

▶ CRITERIA FOR EVALUATING THE ASSIGNMENT   The paragraph notes a resemblance (both Edwards and Taylor connect the spider with sin) but also a difference (Edwards uses the spider to represent a sinful human being fit only to be cast into hell; Taylor uses the spider to represent the cruel, clever devil who traps human beings into sinning).

ELEMENTS OF LITERATURE   Text page 48

THE CONCEIT
You might tell students to think of a conceit as a ''far-out'' metaphor. Because it *is* ''far-out,'' the associations the writer is making often require careful thought on the part of the reader. Students are asked how Taylor can compare salvation to being caged. The text explains the paradox and complexity involved in the answer.

When students write their own conceit, remind them of the ''far-out'' requirement. An original metaphor, even a good one, is not enough—the metaphor must be unusual or fanciful. Students who find this assignment daunting will benefit from brainstorming in small groups and collaborating to create and extend a conceit. Ask students to be prepared to explain their conceits.

Responding to the Poem   Text page 51

Answers to the questions in the Pupil's Edition appear in the Annotated Teacher's Edition.

Writing About the Poem

For help in revising their compositions, refer students to **Grammar, Usage, and Mechanics: A Reference Guide** on text pages 1183–1228 at the back of their books.

A CRITICAL RESPONSE
Comparing the Poem with Job   Read aloud the excerpt from the Book of Job and provide the students with copies of Chapters 38–41. Call to their attention the organization outlined in the last paragraph of the writing assignment.

▶ CRITERIA FOR EVALUATING THE ASSIGNMENT   The essay cites the question-answer format as a structural similarity; cites, as the answer used by both writers, ''See what God can do!''; lists ''homely'' images and metaphors from both Taylor and Job, such as ''foundations,'' ''doors,'' ''quilts,'' and ''bowling alley''; and concludes that each passage suggests that man is nothing compared with God.

Analyzing Language and Style

IMAGERY
A few of the sights are a marked globe, a vast furnace, a mold for making the world, pillars, rivers like green ribbons, a silver box, a bowling alley, and twinkling lanterns. Some sounds include God's voice, rocking of the hills, and quaking aspen leaves. Textures are implied by the ''laced and filleted'' earth, the touch of a little finger, ''spun'' curtains, ''imbossed'' gems.

Students will vary in selection of the images they find most fantastic and most successful in describing the world and its creation. Crafts and occupations Taylor might use today could range from the microchip industry to laser surgery or the piloting of space ships.

Extending the Poems

Students may be asked to interpret the following two stanzas from Edward Taylor's ''Sacramental Meditations, XXXVIII.''

> I JOHN II: 1: And if any man sin, we have an
> advocate with the Father.
>
> God's Judge himselfe, and Christ Atturny is;
>   The Holy Ghost Regesterer is founde.
> Angells the sergeants are, all Creatures kiss
>   The booke, and doe as Evidence abounde,
>   All Cases pass according to pure Law,
>   And in the sentence is no Fret nor flaw.
>
> My Case is Bad, Lord, be my Advocate.
>   My sin is red: I'me under Gods Arrest.
> Thou has the Hit of Pleading; plead my state.
>   Although it's bad, thy Plea will make it best.
>   If thou wilt plead my Case before the King,
>   I'le Waggon Loads of Love and Glory bring.

William Byrd

Text page 53

FROM THE HISTORY OF THE DIVIDING LINE

Text page 54

Objectives

1. To respond to an excerpt from a Colonial history by a non-Puritan

2. To interpet elements of satire

3. To analyze the writer's diction and point of view

4. To write an essay contrasting purpose, tone, and style in two selections

5. To write a paragraph analyzing the position of women

Introducing the History

Although Byrd's journal reads as if it were written for publication, it was not. The manuscript was found among Byrd's papers at Westover and was first published in 1841, nearly a hundred years after his death.

SUMMARY   Byrd discusses the aims and character of the early settlers, calling Jamestown's founders "about a hundred . . . reprobates of good families." He praises John Smith's bravery and leadership. He argues that English settlers should have intermarried with the Native Americans, comments somewhat sarcastically on the Puritans of New England, and describes in detail the religion of Bearskin, the expedition's Native American guide.

Teaching Strategies

PROVIDING FOR CULTURAL DIFFERENCES   Students who are newcomers to this country will need a brief review of Jamestown and the early settlements. Review the time line on text pages 6–7; Jamestown was founded in 1607.

PROVIDING FOR DIFFERENT LEVELS OF ABILITY
This is a much easier selection to read than preceding ones. If you discuss with students the biographical material on

text page 53 and then have students work with the vocabulary before beginning to read the selection, they should have few problems. More advanced students can be asked to point out examples of satire in the history.

READING THE HISTORY   Before students read the selection, you might ask them to assume the identity of a Puritan and write a journal entry expressing a Puritan viewpoint toward the worldly and sophisticated Southern plantation life in Virginia, as described in published accounts and rumors. Assign the selection as homework. After students have read the selection, have them compare their journal accounts with the views Byrd expresses.

RETEACHING ALTERNATIVES   Ask four volunteers to role play the part of William Byrd. Have each of them take one of the four excerpts—"Early Virginia Colonies," "Intermarriage," "The New England Colonies," "The Native Religion"—and present Byrd's ideas orally, putting them entirely in modern conversational English. Ask the listeners to comment on each speaker's accuracy, thoroughness, and persuasiveness.

Responding to the History   Text page 58

Answers to the questions in the Pupil's Edition appear in the Annotated Teacher's Edition.

Writing About the History

For help in revising their compositions, refer students to **Grammar, Usage, and Mechanics: A Reference Guide** on text pages 1183–1228 at the back of their books.

A CRITICAL RESPONSE
1. Contrasting Two Histories   Briefly review the content, tone, purpose, and style of Bradford's account of the Puritan landing before students begin to write.

▶ CRITERIA FOR EVALUATING THE ASSIGNMENT   Students should contrast the sober historical purposes of Bradford with the entertaining, informative purposes of Byrd; the serious, religious tone of Bradford with the light, mocking tone of Byrd; and the Biblical allusions of Bradford with the literary allusions of Byrd.

2. *Analyzing the History*　Before students begin writing, have the class find and list on the board the passages that explicitly mention women. (They are not even explicitly mentioned in the section on ''Intermarriage''; they are mentioned only in paragraph 2 of ''Early Virginia Colonies,'' text page 54, and passages from ''The Native Religion,'' text page 58.) Students should conclude that women are not important in Byrd's world view.

▶ CRITERIA FOR EVALUATING THE ASSIGNMENT　Students mention specific references and comment on their scarcity as well as the negative images conveyed in those passages.

Extending the History

William Byrd's Westover, one of the first large plantation houses on the James River, is a notable example of Georgian architecture. Built in the 1730's, it still stands and is privately owned, as are a number of the elegant plantation houses of Tidewater Virginia. For a research project, you may want to have students report on one or more of the prominent families or great estates of colonial Virginia.

Family	Estate
Byrd	Westover
Mason	Gunston Hall
Harrison	Berkeley *and* Brandon
Carter	Carter's Grove *and* Shirley
Lee	Stratford
Tyler	Sherwood Forest

Feature

A SAMPLE OF NATIVE AMERICAN MYTHS AND RITUAL SONGS

Text page 59

Objectives

1. To respond to some examples of Native American literature

2. To recognize elements of mythology common to many cultures

Introducing the Feature

This feature introduces students to Native American literature with two myth-based stories and two ritual songs. Be sure that students know that these myths and stories represent deeply held religious or philosophical beliefs. At the heart of Native American culture is a spiritual relationship with the earth that goes back thousands of years. Indians express this relationship in rituals, songs, and myths. Encourage students to talk about other creation myths and trickster tales they have read and about the archetypes of Earth Mother and Sky Father. They should recognize that some of the ideas and values expressed in the four selections in the text are central to today's environmental movement.

Before students read the selections, make sure they understand these important concepts:

1. Native American literature was handed down through the ages in the oral tradition. The selections in the text were not written until many centuries after their first telling or singing. Anthropologists in the late 1800's began collecting and writing down the oral literature, much in the way that the Grimm brothers set down folk tales in Europe—by locating the storytellers and recording the tales they spoke.

2. The purpose of early Native American literature was not literary. Rather, the songs and stories were religious in nature and transmitted the values and wisdom of a people. Until recent years, Native American literature was largely ignored in courses of American literature. But since the 1960's and 1970's, Native American literature has enhanced American literature anthologies and textbooks.

GRANDMOTHER SPIDER STEALS THE SUN

Text page 60

BACKGROUND ON THE MYTH The Cherokee, the largest tribe in the Southeast, lived in southern Virginia, North and South Carolina, Georgia, and Ohio. Their name means "cave people" or "real people." Students may have heard of the "Trail of Tears." In 1838 and 1839, despite a Supreme Court ruling upholding Cherokee rights to their lands in the Southeast, federal troops under orders from President Andrew Jackson uprooted the Cherokee and marched them westward to a reservation in Oklahoma.

No provisions were made for food or shelter during the forced march, and more than 4,000 Cherokee (nearly a fourth of those who began the march) died along the way.

A Cherokee named Sequoyah invented a system of writing in 1821. Sequoyah's alphabet, made up of new symbols and Roman characters, enabled the Indians to communicate in writing in their own languages and to write down their oral literature.

COYOTE FINISHES HIS WORK

Text page 61

BACKGROUND ON THE MYTH Coyote is a popular trickster hero in Native American folklore. In tales that vary from tribe to tribe, Coyote creates the Indians, gives them different languages, and teaches them to hunt buffalo and to dance. Coyote represents imaginative, creative powers and exhibits a wide range of characteristics; he is compassionate, helpful, irresponsible, and rebellious. (See " 'Old Man Coyote Makes the World': Using Native American Tales" by Francis E. Kazemek, Muriel Radebaugh, and Pat Rigg in *English Journal,* February 1987, for suggestions for using coyote tales in reading, writing, storytelling, dramatic, and singing activities.)

The Nez Percé (literally, French "pierced nose") lived in the Northwest. The first white men the Nez Percé saw were the Lewis and Clark Expedition (1804–1806) in Idaho and Oregon. White fur traders and trappers in the Northwest lived peacefully with the Northwest tribes. But when the United States acquired Oregon in 1846, a flood of settlers threatened the lands. The discovery of gold further threatened the Nez Percé lands, and the federal government coerced the Nez Percé onto smaller reservations.

The most famous Nez Percé is Chief Joseph, who resisted attempts to get his people to leave their homeland in the Wallowa area of northeastern Oregon. In 1877, Chief Joseph led a band of his people, fleeing from federal troops, toward Canada. Only thirty miles from the Canadian border where they would have found refuge, Chief Joseph surrendered, saying:

I am tired of fighting. Our chiefs are killed. Looking Glass is dead. Toohulhulsote is dead. The old men are all dead. It is the young men who say no and yes. He who led the young men is dead. It is cold and we have no blankets. The little children are freezing to death. My people, some of them, have run away to the hills and have no blankets, no food. No one knows where they are—perhaps they are freezing to death. I want to have time to look for my children and see how many of them I can find. Maybe I shall find them among the dead. Hear me, my chiefs, I am tired. My heart is sad and sick. From where the sun now stands I will fight no more.

SONG OF THE SKY LOOM

Text page 62

BACKGROUND ON THE SONG The Tewa people of New Mexico live in Pueblo villages and speak the Tanoan language. They call themselves "the moccasin people." They grow corn, beans, squash, and peaches, and also raise sheep and cattle. They are known for their beautiful pottery, especially in the village of San Ildefonso.

BREATH OF LIFE

Text page 62

BACKGROUND ON THE SONG The Zuñi, who have a distinctive language unrelated to that of any other tribe, live in western New Mexico near the Arizona border. Theirs is the largest pueblo with more than 2,500 people. According to the Zuñi religion, Earth Mother is one of the deities (raw persons) who can change form. Trees and bushes are her arms and hands. Her summer robe is made of yellow flowers (pollen) and her winter robe of white flowers (snowflakes). In songs and ceremonial dances, the Zuñi pray for rain and the growth of crops.

Teaching Strategies

PROVIDING FOR CULTURAL DIFFERENCES Depending on their backgrounds, students may have experience with stories that transmit the values of their particular heritage. Invite students to share their own people's stories or songs.

PROVIDING FOR DIFFERENT LEVELS OF ABILITY These myths and songs are simple, yet they raise complex questions about the origin of life. You may want to discuss creation myths in general as people's attempt to make sense of their world. Note that "Grandmother Spider Steals the Sun" not only explains why the sun exists in our world, but also why Possum's tail and Buzzard's head are bald.

READING THE MYTHS AND RITUAL SONGS Encourage students to read each of the two myths aloud, as if they, the narrators, were respected storytellers with admiring audiences. Remind students that the songs are translations and may not carry the same rhythms as the originals. Encourage students to write music appropriate to the songs and perform them for the class. Or the songs might be simply spoken as a prayer.

RETEACHING ALTERNATIVES If students are having trouble keeping the various mythological characters straight, have them make a chart listing each character (by multiple names if appropriate) and that character's traits and actions.

Extending the Feature

Encourage students to research Native American Indian dance. Groups of students might choose one dance to learn about and present their findings to the class. They may wish to perform parts of the dance, while a narrator describes the various movements and what they mean.

Bring to class some collections of Native American stories and songs for classroom browsing. Ask your librarian to help you create a Center for Native American Studies, with a library of books on art and history as well. Some students may have Indian stories or artifacts they would like to share with the class.

EXERCISES IN CRITICAL THINKING AND WRITING

Text page 63

DETERMINING THE PRECISE MEANINGS OF WORDS
For this exercise, it is important that students use an unabridged dictionary, such as the ones mentioned in the student text, since abridged dictionaries may not give complete etymologies, nor do they indicate archaic meanings. If students need help in reading etymologies, go over several sample etymologies at the chalkboard. All abbreviations and symbols used in etymologies are explained in the front matter of the dictionary.

As a prewriting exercise, you might select one word from the excerpts on text page 64 and complete the chart during a class discussion.

▶ CRITERIA FOR EVALUATING THE ASSIGNMENT Student essays should include the etymology of the word and its meaning in the context of the excerpt. If the word implies a value judgment, adequate evidence should be cited to support that judgment.

UNIT ONE: The Colonial Period **19**

Further Reading

Works listed are suitable for both students and teachers unless the annotation ends with the note [Teachers].

Davis, William T., ed. *Bradford's History of Plymouth Plantation, 1606–1646* (Barnes & Noble, 1946). Complete text from which excerpts in the student text are drawn. Spellings are from Bradford's original manuscript.

Dillon, Francis. *The Pilgrims* (Doubleday, 1975). A lively social history of the Pilgrims. [Teachers]

Erodes, Richard, and Alfonso Ortiz. *American Indian Myths and Legends* (Pantheon, 1984). A comprehensive collection of 160 stories from 80 tribal groups.

Fishwick, Marshall. "The Pepys of the Old Dominion," *American Heritage,* December 1959. A fascinating look at William Byrd through his private diaries.

"1491—America Before Columbus," *National Geographic,* October 1991. A hundred pages of photos and text on creation myths, the land, and a close look at life in four Native American villages (California, Georgia, New York, and New Mexico) as reconstructed from archaeological findings.

Gunn, Sidney. "Knight, Sarah Kemble," *Dictionary of American Biography,* vol. 5 (Scribner's, 1933). A good general introduction to Knight's life.

Heaton, Vernon. *The Mayflower* (Mayflower Books, 1980). A clearly organized, well-illustrated book on the European background of Puritanism, the Atlantic crossing, and life in the New World.

Heimert, Alan, and Nicholas Delbanco, eds. *The Puritans in America: A Narrative Anthology* (Harvard University Press, 1985). A good collection of additional readings by writers in this unit and other Puritan writers.

Leach, Douglas Edward. *Flintlock and Tomahawk: New England in King Philip's War* (Macmillan, 1958). Full, readable history of the two-year war in which Mary Rowlandson was taken captive, mentioning her from time to time.

Levin, David, ed. *Jonathan Edwards: A Profile* (Hill and Wang, 1969). An excellent collection of biographical and critical readings, including a brief biography by Samuel Hopkins first published in 1765, essays by noted critics, and two relevant poems by Robert Lowell.

Miller, Arthur. *The Crucible* in *Collected Plays,* vol. 1 (Viking, 1957). Miller's powerful play about the Salem witch trials, inspired by the McCarthy hearings.

Miller, John C. *The First Frontier: Life in Colonial America* (Dell, 1966). An excellent source of information on all aspects of Colonial life—recreation, health, housing, and education. [Teachers]

Miller, Perry. *The New England Mind: The Seventeenth Century.* (Harvard University Press, 1939). The classic study of the period, the first of two volumes. The second volume is Miller's *The New England Mind: From Colony to Province* (1953). [Teachers]

Miller, Perry. *Jonathan Edwards* (Greenwood Press, 1973). Originally published in 1949, this book skillfully intersperses the "external biography" of Edwards with his "life of the mind." The Great Awakening in New England is well described.

Morgan, Edmund S. *The Puritan Dilemma: The Story of John Winthrop* (Little, Brown, 1958). Biography of the Puritan leader John Winthrop and also a brief, clear explanation of Puritan beliefs.

Preston, Richard M. "William Byrd II," *Dictionary of Literary Biography,* vol. 24 (Gale Research Company, 1984). A seven-page article plus a list of all of Byrd's writings and references about him.

Stanford, Ann. *Images of Women in Early American Literature* (New York University Press, 1977). Perceptive discussion of Knight and her *Journal,* and interesting commentary on Mary Rowlandson, Anne Bradstreet, and other Colonial women writers.

VanDerBeets, Richard, ed. *Held Captive by Indians: Selected Narratives, 1642–1836* (University of Tennessee Press, 1973). An outstanding collection of ten captivity narratives, including an informative preface and map for Mary Rowlandson's narrative. [Teachers]

Waters, Frank. *Book of the Hopi* (Viking, 1963). Carefully researched collection of Hopi creation myths, legends, mystery plays, history, illustrated with photographs and Hopi art.

Westbrook, Perry D. *William Bradford* (Twayne, 1978). Discussion of Bradford as a man of letters; a good introduction to Bradford, the writer and historian. [Teachers]

Wright, L.B., ed. *The American Heritage History of the Thirteen Colonies* (American Heritage, 1967). Beautifully illustrated, concise overview of the Colonial period.

THE REVOLUTIONARY PERIOD
THE AGE OF REASON

Text page 65

Teaching the Revolutionary Period Unit

This unit focuses on the founding of the American nation and the development of a distinct American character and philosophy. The literary style of this period swings from the plain prose and sly wit of Benjamin Franklin's *Autobiography* to the impassioned oratory of Patrick Henry's speech to the Virginia Convention. Despite the varieties of style, students will recognize two themes that link these selections: the moral progress both of the individual and of the state. The selections emphasize self-examination and self-improvement, most notably in Benjamin Franklin's autobiography, in Thomas Jefferson's letter to his daughter, and in Thomas Paine's and Patrick Henry's exhortations to fellow citizens to search themselves for the strength and spirit to support the Revolution. You may want to emphasize the similarities among the selections, for students may not always recognize the common themes in a speech, pamphlet, letter, and autobiography.

As the unit introduction in the student text notes, some of these early American writings have equivalents in such contemporary forms as the popular autobiography and the self-help book. The popularity of these genres, then and now, makes for some interesting literary and social comparisons. Then, as now, America has been, in the words of the art critic Harold Rosenberg, "the civilization of people engaged in attempting to transform themselves." You might ask students what they think of this description of the American spirit. Does it match their own perception and experiences?

This unit introduces literary devices and forms such as persuasion, propaganda, allusion, imagery, metaphor, first-person point of view, and the aphorism, or maxim. Discussions of rhetorical devices are particularly suited to this unit because eighteenth-century prose was often propagandistic in nature and marked by fluency and balance derived from classical models.

Most of the writings in this unit are by men who were closely associated with the American Enlightenment. They lived in a time of turbulence and change that America did not experience again until the Civil War. They used the written word almost as a weapon, to rail against Great Britain and to gain support for the Revolution. These men gave shape to our country—to a society that did not have the social, political, or cultural establishment of Great Britain or Europe to rest upon. They had to make a society and culture, build towns and banks and schools, wring a government from the conflicting needs of the great variety of peoples who emigrated to America. They sought to create and define an American character that could encompass the manifold religions and cultures that made up the colonies. A hundred years later Walt Whitman addressed this idea in "Song of Myself," when he wrote, "Very well then, I contradict myself, I contain multitudes." From the first, American thought was as divergent as the many nationalities that today make up the country.

It might be useful for students to look ahead to the Enlightenment's influence on the philosophies, attitudes, and writing styles in nineteenth- and twentieth-century American literature. In this regard, you could cite the wit of Mark Twain, the democratic embrace of Walt Whitman, and the vitalization of the "American idiom" by William Carlos Williams. It would be interesting to test later American literature against the deism and humanistic ideas that are the foundation of this country. Encourage your students to keep in mind such a comparison of theme and style as they progress through the text.

The Enlightenment of the Age of Reason as an international movement was spread throughout the western world, most noticeably in England, France, and Germany. It was an age that believed that there was virtually no limit to what well-intentioned people could accomplish when guided by reason. Reason could alter a corrupt environment and even—as in Adam Smith's version of a free marketplace, guided by an "Invisible Hand"—harmonize competing self-interests. Ignorance, prejudice, and unchecked power were considered primary factors in the corruption and sinfulness of human beings. Such concepts of the Enlightenment, many derived from the British philosopher John Locke, were put directly into the Declaration of Independence and are reflected in much of the other literature in this unit.

Objectives of the Revolutionary Period Unit

1. To improve reading proficiency and expand vocabulary
2. To gain exposure to notable Revolutionary writers
3. To define and identify significant literary techniques
4. To interpret and respond to forms of nonfiction, orally and in writing, through analysis of their elements
5. To recognize the growth of American English
6. To practice the following critical thinking and writing skills
   a. Comparing and contrasting writers
   b. Responding to critical comments
   c. Evaluating word connotations
   d. Comparing and contrasting speeches
   e. Evaluating a generalization
   f. Analyzing reasoning
   g. Responding to a point of view

Introducing the Revolutionary Period Unit

Before beginning the unit, you might want to discuss how Americans before the Revolution generally felt about Great Britain, how their attitudes changed over time, and how that change was reflected in the writings of the period. This excerpt from Moses Coit Tyler's *The Literary History of the American Revolution, 1763–1783, Volume I* (1897, 1957) gives some of the flavor of that change:

The deep, true love of Americans for the mother country, their pride in the British empire, their sincerity in the belief that all their political demands were compatible with their own loyalty and with the honor of England, their desire that the solution of every vexing problem should be reached in peace,— all these were realities, realities as genuine as they were pathetic. In the transactions of the nineteenth of April, 1775, at the hands of official representatives of the mother country, all these sacred realities were foully dealt with,—they were stamped upon, were spit upon, they were stabbed and shot at and covered with blood and cast into the mire. Accordingly, reaching this fatal point in his journey across the period of the Revolution, the student of its literature becomes then and there conscious of crossing a great spiritual chasm—of moving from one world of ideas and sentiments to a world of ideas and sentiments quite other and very different.

You might want to discuss briefly with your students how they imagine they would have felt if they had lived in these times. Would they have wanted to remain within the protection of a great empire whose language, culture, and values they shared, or rebelliously declare their independence and face the task of building a new kind of nation? The best reasons for doing the latter can be found in the writings of the authors in this unit, who combined fiery spirit with towering nationality.

Benjamin Franklin

FROM THE AUTOBIOGRAPHY

Objectives

1. To respond to a famous autobiography
2. To write an essay comparing and contrasting two writers
3. To write an essay evaluating a critical commentary
4. To recognize varieties of English

Introducing the Autobiography

As the text indicates, Benjamin Franklin's life story is a great and various one. Yet for all he accomplished and all that is known about him, he remains difficult to define. He is for some readers the ideal American. He achieved material success at a young age. He took risks, tried his hand and succeeded at many endeavors, and constantly strove to better himself.

Other readers find Franklin's emphasis on moralism and materialism restrictive. He wrote a brilliant and fascinating autobiography, but many critics believe Franklin has removed his personal self from the work and given us instead an idealized life, or, at least, a self-created one. According to these critics, Franklin has created in his *Autobiography* a Benjamin persona, just as he created the persona of Silence Dogwood for his first essay, and later Richard Saunders of *Poor Richard's Almanack*, Father Abraham of *The Way to Wealth,* the Busy Body in the *American Weekly Mercury*, and many others. On the other hand, Frederick Tolles, in an essay on Franklin, writes, "Not only his final *Autobiography* but also a large part of his written work . . . followed the steps of his life, recording it." Tolles believes the personae Franklin created were mere masks for autobiographical writing.

BACKGROUND ON THE AUTOBIOGRAPHY   Franklin wrote his autobiography with an eye toward reporting his life for the benefit of those who wished to learn from it. Just as he attempted to improve his writing style by imitating Addison and others, so the readers of his book might improve themselves by imitating or studying his life. Franklin says just this on the first page of *The Autobiography*:

> Having emerg'd from the Poverty & Obscurity in which I was born & bred, to a State of Affluence &

some Degree of Reputation in the World, and having gone so far thro' Life with a considerable Share of Felicity, the conducing Means I made use of, which, with the Blessing of God, so well succeeded, my Posterity may like to know, as they may find some of them suitable to their own Situations, & therefore fit to be imitated.

You might use this ideal of Franklin's to discuss the concept of learning by imitation. Do students think they learn this way?

SUMMARY   In "Leaving Boston," young Franklin decides to leave his brother's service. He goes to New York seeking work as a printer, and finds nothing. He next ventures to Philadelphia and has quite an adventure getting there. He gets caught in a storm, saves a drunken man who had fallen overboard, and becomes ill. He walks fifty miles to Burlington, Pennsylvania, stopping at an inn where he is befriended by a retired doctor. He is given shelter by a woman who would have him set up a print shop in Burlington, but instead he finds a boat that will give him passage for Philadelphia.

In "Arrival in Philadelphia," Franklin describes his first day in the city. He has trouble communicating with a baker and on Market Street he passes his future wife, who notices his awkward appearance. He follows a group of Quakers to their meeting house, where he falls asleep.

"Arriving at Moral Perfection" describes Franklin's plan for achieving moral perfection. He includes his list and definitions of the important virtues, the most important of which is temperance because it is the first step towards self-discipline. This section concludes with a description of his plan for mastering each virtue.

Teaching Strategies

PROVIDING FOR CULTURAL DIFFERENCES   Note that travel between cities was extremely difficult in Franklin's day. Students born in other countries may relate to Franklin's arduous journey—by boat and foot—from Boston to Philadelphia. He arrives in Philadelphia with no money, knowing no one, almost an archetypal immigrant, who goes on to achieve success through hard work and right living. Ask students from other cultures how Franklin's list of virtues compares with the values of their heritage.

PROVIDING FOR DIFFERENT LEVELS OF ABILITY
Because of the difficult language and sentence structure, you might find it helpful to list for LEP/ESL students the events that Franklin describes. More advanced students might evaluate the slightly ironic tone of the autobiography and consider whether Franklin is directing it toward himself. All students will be interested in discussing Franklin's plan for moral perfection.

READING THE AUTOBIOGRAPHY   To prepare students for reading the selection, you might first explain that Franklin's first intent was to teach or edify. Students should be encouraged to read first for the story and then for insight into Franklin's character. You might also ask students to imagine themselves in Franklin's position at age sixteen or seventeen.

RETEACHING ALTERNATIVES   To ensure that students understand Franklin's method of attaining moral perfection, you might have them paraphrase the paragraph directly following the list of virtues. You might also have students write their own definitions of Franklin's virtues.

Responding to the Autobiography
Text page 80

Answers to the questions in the Pupil's Edition appear in the Annotated Teacher's Edition.

Writing About the Autobiography

For help in revising their compositions, refer students to **Grammar, Usage, and Mechanics: A Reference Guide** on text pages 1183–1228 at the back of their books.

A CRITICAL RESPONSE
1. Comparing and Contrasting Two Writers   The students' writing assignment contains helpful suggestions on how students should prepare to write, but clarify how you want them to organize their papers. You might suggest that they first state how Edwards and Franklin are alike, and then how they differ. They should cite examples from Edwards's sermon and from Franklin's *Autobiography* to support all major points.

For help in planning this comparison/contrast essay, refer students to the **Exercises in Critical Thinking and**

Writing (text page 373). Although the exercise deals with poems, the directions it provides apply to all comparison/contrast essays.

▶ CRITERIA FOR EVALUATING THE ASSIGNMENT   The essay states one way in which Franklin and Edwards are alike, and three or more ways in which they differ. (Both believe that people can control their behavior to change for the better; both advocate avoiding certain "bad" behaviors. Franklin aims at moral perfection and material success to achieve a fulfilling life on earth. God and religion play no part in his plan. Edwards advocates embracing Christ and avoiding sinful behavior to escape eternal damnation. Edwards finds joy and God in Nature; Franklin makes no mention of Nature.)

2. Responding to Critical Comments   Read aloud the excerpt from Mark Twain, checking students' literal comprehension. Call students' attention to the fact that the assignment clearly outlines the content and organization of their essays.

▶ CRITERIA FOR EVALUATING THE ASSIGNMENT   The essay consists of three paragraphs. The first paragraph states in the student's own words how Twain felt about Franklin and why he felt that way. The second paragraph correctly describes Twain's tone as satiric (or humorous). The third paragraph gives the student's own reaction to Twain's comments.

Analyzing Language and Style

AMERICAN ENGLISH
1. Answers will vary by region of the United States.
2. An English "biscuit" is an American "cookie."
3. Answers will vary by region of the United States.

Extending the Autobiography

Have interested students read more of Franklin's *Autobiography* or *Ben Franklin Laughing* edited by P. M. Zall (University of California Press, 1980), an entertaining book that also provides a good picture of life in the eighteenth century. Students can discuss whether or not these books changed the image of Franklin they formed from the selections in the text.

SAYINGS OF POOR RICHARD

Objectives

1. To respond to a series of eighteenth-century maxims

2. To identify irony

3. To identify contemporary maxims and create some original ones

Introducing the Maxims

The sayings have affected the lives of countless young Americans, among them Mark Twain, who once wrote, "It has taken me many years and countless smarts to get out of that barbed wire moral enclosure that Poor Richard rigged up." What Twain and others object to is the moral strictures that Franklin imposed (seemingly) on himself, and, through the force of his writing, on his readers. In response to such criticism, Theodore Hornberger, in a pamphlet titled *Benjamin Franklin,* argues that "Franklin often acted upon rasher impulses and nobler principles than those which he publicly avowed." This seems a fair assessment when considering the hundreds of projects in which Franklin involved himself. It seems he immersed himself in every passing societal need or idea.

BACKGROUND ON THE MAXIMS To give students an idea of the personality Franklin originally created for Richard Saunders, you might read part of the preface to the first *Poor Richard's Almanack* in 1733.

COURTEOUS READER,

I might, in this place attempt to gain thy Favour, by declaring that I write Almanacks with no other View than that of the publick Good; but in this I should not be sincere; and Men are now adays too wise to be deceived by Pretences how specious soever. The plain Truth of the Matter is, I am excessive poor, and my Wife, good Woman, is, I tell her, excessive proud; she cannot bear, she says, to sit spinning her Shift of Tow, while I do nothing but gaze at the Stars; and has threatned more than once to burn all my Books and Rattling-Traps (as she calls my Instruments) if I do not make some profitable Use of them for the Good of my Family. The Printer has offer'd me some considerable share of the Profits, and I have thus begun to comply with Dame's Desire.

Critics have different attitudes toward the persona of Poor Richard. Some see him as an autobiographical mask, some as a playful and useful creation. Students will want to judge for themselves whether the sayings reflect the character of Franklin as revealed in the excerpts from his *Autobiography,* his letter to Samuel Mather, and the biography on text pages 72–73. The Richard Saunders in the 1733 passage quoted above appears cynical and oppressed at home. Many of the maxims certainly convey a similar message and tone. You might lead students to consider whether Poor Richard is more a pragmatist or opportunist. Do they see evidence of either quality in other writings?

Teaching Strategies

PROVIDING FOR CULTURAL DIFFERENCES Some students may be unfamiliar with ideas expressed in proverb form. Explain to them that proverbs, or maxims, take generally accepted truths or common experiences and condense them into concise and often terse language. Proverbs, which were very common in Franklin's time, were passed on from one person to another as jokes and gossip are today. Every culture and ethnic group passes on its wisdom in proverbs. Ask students to share some of the sayings they know from older family members or friends.

The second maxim uses the image of a man emptying his purse into his head as a metaphor for pursuing knowledge. Students should know that men carried small purses rather than wallets in the eighteenth century.

PROVIDING FOR DIFFERENT LEVELS OF ABILITY The parallel form of many maxims might confuse some students. To clear up any confusion, you might explain the structure of one or two of the maxims. For instance, maxim number 12 uses the word *composes* in its two clauses. To some students the parallel senses of composing oneself and composing or writing a book will be clear. Other students may need help in understanding that the use of *composing* is a metaphor for developing one's life as carefully as one would write a book. *Compose* in the first part of the sentence also has a second meaning: "to make oneself calm."

READING THE MAXIMS Before students read the maxims, you might explore the ideas of cynicism and practicality. You can suggest that what appears to be cynicism on first glance can prove to be practical wisdom on subsequent readings. Similarly, a reader might mistake for wisdom what is actually cynicism. More often a maxim is open to various interpretation. Suggest that students consider carefully maxims whose meanings seem obvious on first reading.

As students read the maxims, ask them to decide which ones they think are true—based on their own observations and experiences. Which ones do they think are not true?

RETEACHING ALTERNATIVES You might bring to class a facsimile of *Poor Richard's Almanack* or another almanac from the period to give students a clearer picture of the uses of the almanac and to provide insight into the daily life of the times.

Also, you might read to the class Robert Frost's poem ''The Mending Wall,'' which addresses more fully the idea expressed in the first maxim in the text.

Responding to the Maxims   Text page 82

Answers to the questions in the Pupil's Edition appear in the Annotated Teacher's Edition.

Writing About the Maxims

For help in revising their compositions, refer students to **Grammar, Usage, and Mechanics: A Reference Guide** on text pages 1183–1228 at the back of their books.

A CREATIVE RESPONSE
Analyzing Contemporary Maxims Students will have fun with this assignment, especially if they work in small groups. To help them get started you might read a few selections from Paul Dickson's *The Official Rules* (Delacorte Press, 1978), or these modern sayings or bumper stickers:

1. If anything can go wrong, it will. (Murphy's Law)
2. There's no such thing as a free lunch.
3. In the fight between you and the world, back the world. (Franz Kafka)
4. Nice guys finish last. (Leo Durocher)
5. It works better if you plug it in.

If students collaborate in small groups, tell them to make up at least six new maxims. Have each group present its original maxims to the class. Students may choose the best class maxims and create a booklet or poster.

▶ CRITERIA FOR EVALUATING THE ASSIGNMENT The student has listed ten popular sayings or slogans and has made up three new maxims. Each is a complete sentence and rings true in its literal or ironic comment on contemporary life.

Extending the Maxims

Share a modern almanac, such as *The Farmer's Almanac,* and then have students collaborate to create a class almanac for one month. In addition to astrological forecasts and weather, tides, sunrise, sunset, and so on, suggest to students that the almanac include special school and community events and their own sayings, or maxims. Newspapers and calendars will provide much of the information that students will need. Encourage students to include original drawings and cartoons.

Primary Sources   Text page 83

A LETTER TO SAMUEL MATHER
In this letter Franklin relates a personal anecdote of a lesson learned when he was young. He also expresses homesickness for Boston, which he has not seen for twenty-two years. The letter is tender and even sentimental, showing a side of Franklin not seen in other selections. Read aloud the letter in class, and ask students what they think of Cotton Mather's advice to young Franklin and Franklin's comments on pride.

THE MIDDLE PASSAGE: A NARRATIVE BY OLAUDAH EQUIANO

Text page 84

Objectives

1. To respond to a personal narrative about slavery
2. To share information in a brief oral report

Introducing the Feature

This feature is an excerpt from the autobiography of Olaudah Equiano, who was kidnapped from his African family at a young age and sold into slavery. His autobiography was published first in Great Britain in 1789, when slavery still existed in the United States. Only two years earlier, in 1787, delegates to the Constitutional Convention had hotly debated the issue of slavery. Though many Northerners wanted it abolished, they accepted its continuance as an economic necessity in the South. England had formally abolished slavery in 1772 and in 1807 put an end to all slave trade with its colonies.

BACKGROUND ON THE FEATURE Equiano's narrative focuses on the brutal treatment of slaves aboard ship during what was called the middle passage. At the time, many sea captains traveled a triangular trade route. On the first leg of a typical journey, they carried goods such as cotton cloth and firearms from England to Africa, trading them for slaves. The second leg of their trip was called the middle passage. They sailed to the West Indies or to the United States, where the cargo of slaves was sold to the highest bidder. The third leg was the return voyage to England.

Equiano's personal narrative introduces several ideas about slavery that have only recently appeared in history textbooks. First, slave captains did not simply sail to Africa and kidnap every African they met. They established a business relationship—albeit an abhorrent one—with strong African leaders, who captured the slaves and brought them to the African coast. Second, the enslavement of enemy peoples was common in Africa and the rest of the world at the time. Slavery was part of a far-flung trading system in existence for a thousand years. In fact, traders shipped goods and slaves from Africa's east coast all the way to India and China. However, no earlier traders could match the eighteenth- and nineteenth-century European and American slave traders in the number of Africans taken and in their brutal treatment of the captured Africans.

Teaching Strategies

PROVIDING FOR CULTURAL DIFFERENCES African American students may have facts to add to this narrative or stories of their own ancestors to share with the class. Alex Haley's *Roots* raised the consciousness of many Americans, who began a search for information about their own family histories.

PROVIDING FOR DIFFERENT LEVELS OF ABILITY Students should have a fairly easy time with this narrative, though it is essentially a series of descriptive scenes without a plot. Students might imagine the narrative as part of a longer story. They might suggest an appropriate beginning and an ending that would draw a reader into Equiano's narrative and also offer some plausible resolution. After reaching America, Equiano was sold as a slave in Virginia, where he eventually managed to purchase his freedom. He settled in England and worked in the movement to abolish the slave trade.

READING THE FEATURE Tell students that Equiano was just eleven years old when he was torn away from his family. They can all think back to that age, to the kind of life they had, and imagine how they would have coped with being uprooted, dragged away, and forced to suffer the brutalities of the middle passage.

Students may already be familiar with the story of Olaudah Equiano—it is often included in history textbooks.

RETEACHING ALTERNATIVES Students should understand that this narrative is what historians call a primary source, and its value for them lies in documenting the events and conditions on board a slave ship. You might ask students to play the historian and isolate the various appalling practices of the ship's crew. They might then create a story board—rough sketches of each scene in the narrative. Students might draw or write their sketches.

Extending the Feature

Have students compare this simple, rich narrative with other slave narratives of the same era. Encourage students to look into primary source materials not only in print, but now available on videodiscs and videocassettes. Seeing the actual documents can help students appreciate the personalities of those who experienced the events which are recounted.

Collect some books on African and African American art, literature, and history. Let each student choose one thing to read. Then ask each student to give a very brief oral report on something he or she learned. Limit reports to just a minute or two.

Patrick Henry
Text page 87

SPEECH TO THE VIRGINIA CONVENTION
Text page 88

Objectives

1. To listen and respond to a great American speech

2. To analyze a persuasive speech

3. To analyze the use of metaphor as a tool of persuasion

4. To identify rhetorical questions and explain their uses

5. To interpret allusions

6. To write a newspaper article

Introducing the Speech

The introductory material on Patrick Henry (text page 87) discusses Henry's personal background as well as the historical setting in which the speech was delivered. Although Henry's 1765 speech to the Virginia House of Burgesses in reaction to the Stamp Act did secure Henry's political future (he was later elected to five successive terms as governor of Virginia), he was at the time declared an outlaw by the Virginia governor. Students should also know that in 1787 Henry was one of many distinguished dissenters (James Monroe was another) to the Constitution who claimed that it did not protect the rights of large numbers of the community, including the poor. Henry became instrumental in the fight to add the first ten amendments to the Constitution, the Bill of Rights.

BACKGROUND ON THE SPEECH To understand why Henry's speech had to be powerful and convincing, it is important for students to understand the colonists' hesitancy to bear arms against Great Britain. As the following excerpt from a Congressional declaration on July 6, 1775, makes clear, even after fighting broke out, leaders in America still hoped for reconciliation with the "mother country."

Lest this declaration should disquiet the minds of our friends and fellow-subjects in any part of the empire, we assure them that we mean not to dissolve that union which has so long and so happily subsisted between us, and which we sincerely wish to see restored. . . . We have not raised armies with ambitious designs of separating from Great Britain, and establishing Independent States.

Moses Coit Tyler puts the conflict and Henry's crucial role into the clearest perspective when he writes, "After ten years of words, the disputants come at last to blows. Prior to this day, the Revolutionary controversy was a political debate: after that it was a civil war. [And an] immense transformation then and there [was] made in the very character and atmosphere of the struggle—in its ideas, its purposes, its spirit, its tone. . . ." Patrick Henry was at the apex of this transformation. Through the power of words and ideas he helped move the controversy away from ideas into armed resistance.

SUMMARY Henry opens the speech by paying respect to previous speakers. He then begs to differ with the desire to compromise, and states that the decision to arm or not to arm is a matter of slavery or freedom. He understands the desire to reconcile, but the facts do not warrant such a hope. He asks members of the House to judge from experience, not words, and experience demonstrates that the king means to subjugate. In the third paragraph of his speech, Henry uses a series of rhetorical questions regarding British military forces and American attempts at reconciliation. The next paragraph, beginning with another series of questions, defends the strength and unity of the Colonies and states that war is inevitable. Henry concludes with a statement that war has already begun and that it is time to rise and fight for liberty.

Teaching Strategies

PROVIDING FOR CULTURAL DIFFERENCES There will probably be few difficulties caused by cultural differences. However, the concept of "patriotism" should be discussed briefly. In the period just before the Revolutionary War, "patriotism" could refer to patriotism to Great Britain as well as to America. Students whose families fled oppressive governments (Vietnamese, Cambodian, Holocaust survivors) may be baffled by the strong allegiance to Britain.

PROVIDING FOR DIFFERENT LEVELS OF ABILITY With ESL/LEP students, concentrate on having students understand Henry's political ideas rather than analyze his use of language. For these students, you may want to read the speech paragraph by paragraph, summarizing as you go.

More advanced students will profit from studying the structure of the speech and the literary devices Henry employs so profusely. Guide students through the speech by referring them to specific allusions, metaphors, and rhetorical questions. They can deduce for themselves the intended purpose (such as emotional hook, appeal to common sense, appeal to safety) and determine the effectiveness of Henry's language.

READING THE SPEECH The speech warrants a number of readings. You might first ask students to envision the surroundings in which the speech was delivered (see headnote, text page 88). Students should imagine a 26-year-old man, delivering an impassioned, urgent, yet controlled speech before a distinguished group of men. Then play the accompanying audiocassette recording of the speech. This professional reading gives students an indication of the tone, rhythm, and passion with which the speech was likely delivered.

RETEACHING ALTERNATIVES Have students imagine themselves as listeners to Henry's speech in 1775. Ask students to discuss their response to Henry's speech. If they had been members of the Virginia Convention, would they have been persuaded by Henry's speech? What would they have found most convincing?

Responding to the Speech   Text page 91

Answers to the questions in the Pupil's Edition appear in the Annotated Teacher's Edition.

Writing About the Speech

For help in revising their compositions, refer students to **Grammar, Usage, and Mechanics: A Reference Guide** on text pages 1183–1228 at the back of their books.

A CREATIVE RESPONSE
1. Reporting on the Speech Review the fact that a news story presents information but does not offer the reporter's opinions. Review also the news story's "inverted pyramid" format: The first or *lead* sentence catches the reader's attention and succinctly covers as many as possible of the five *W's—Who, What, When, Where,* and *Why.* Remaining information is given in the order of descending importance so that cuts (from bottom up) will not destroy the story. Elicit one or two sample leads, and alert students to the need to draw information from text introductory pages 87–88.

▶ CRITERIA FOR EVALUATING THE ASSIGNMENT The paper reports; it does not editorialize. The lead includes all or most of the five *W*'s. Subsequent sentences state the assembly's response to the speech, summarize Henry's major points, and describe how Henry made his points. Additional sentences may quote others present.

A CRITICAL RESPONSE
2. Comparing and Contrasting Speeches Urge students to make a chart on the two episodes, like the one suggested in the writing assignment, before they write their essays. Students can work with a partner or small group to complete the prewriting chart.

▶ CRITERIA FOR EVALUATING THE ASSIGNMENT The essay notes specific similarities and differences in the speeches of Edwards and Henry. (Both aim to persuade and use metaphors. Edwards addresses churchgoers; Henry a governing body. Henry uses Biblical and classical allusions; Edwards doesn't. Both appeal to emotion rather than reason. Both use repetition; Henry uses many rhetorical questions. Edwards wants sinners in his audience to embrace Christ; Henry wants his audience to declare war against Britain.)

Extending the Speech

Have students compare the rhetorical devices of noted twentieth-century speeches to Patrick Henry's speech. As examples of orators whose speeches stirred the nation, you might refer the class to John F. Kennedy, Martin Luther King, Jr., or Franklin Delano Roosevelt. As you play a recording of one or more of these speeches, have students **listen** for the speaker's main points. As soon as the speech ends, have them do a quick-write of their responses.

PERSUASION

Students will be able to find a great many examples of heightened style, including the following ones:

"of awful moment to this country" (text page 88)

"nothing less than a question of freedom or slavery" (text page 88)

"the implements of war and subjugation" (text page 90)

"preserve inviolate those inestimable privileges" (text page 90)

"the glorious object of our contest" (text page 90)

"the delusive phantom of hope" (text page 90)

Thomas Paine   Text page 93

THE CRISIS, NO. 1   Text page 94

Objectives

1. To respond to a pamphlet's persuasive arguments

2. To analyze the use of analogy, metaphor, and imagery

3. To write a response to the pamphlet by someone who heard it in 1776

4. To write an essay evaluating a generalization

Introducing the Pamphlet

The introduction to Paine in the student text notes his condemnation and exile from England after the publication of *The Rights of Man.* He fled to France where he was at first lionized but then imprisoned. The direct cause of his imprisonment was that Paine spoke against the executions of the French Revolution, and, more specifically, he advocated the exile rather than execution of King Louis XVI. When Paine returned to the United States, he was ostracized because his great work, *The Age of Reason,* was misinterpreted as an attack on Christianity. Use these biographical facts to help students understand that Paine was never able to find a place for himself in the world.

BACKGROUND ON THE PAMPHLET   After finishing work on the selection, you may want to read the excerpt below from *The Crisis, No. 13.* It can be interpreted as a companion piece to *Crisis, No. 1,* and is very moving. It will take students full swing, from the call to arms of *The Crisis, No. 1* to the winding down of the war. Paine calls on his countrymen to exert reason over an exuberant release of emotion. Note the grace and poetry of the prose. Note also his reference to *Crisis, No. 1* in the first sentence.

The times that tried men's souls are over—and the greatest and completest Revolution the world ever knew, gloriously and happily accomplished.

But to pass from the extremes of danger to safety—from the tumult of war to the tranquility of peace—though sweet in contemplation, requires gradual composure of the senses to receive it. Even calmness has the power of stunning, when it opens too instantly upon us. . . .

In the present case, the mighty magnitude of the object, the various uncertainties of fate which it has undergone, the numerous and complicated dangers we have suffered or escaped, the eminence we now stand on, and the vast prospect before us, must all conspire to impress us with contemplation.

To see it in our power to make a world happy, to teach mankind the art of being so, to exhibit on the theatre of the universe a character hitherto unknown, and to have, as it were, a new creation entrusted in our hands, are honors that command reflection, and can neither be too highly estimated, nor too gratefully received.

In this pause, then, of reflection, while the storm is ceasing, and the long-agitated mind vibrating to a rest, let us look back on the scenes we have passed, and learn from experience what is to be done.

SUMMARY   Paine begins by exhorting Americans to fight the tyranny of Great Britain. Fighting should have begun earlier, but victory can still be attained. He argues that God is on the side of the just and compares George III with a thief. To counter the American panic after numerous battle defeats, Paine relates a story of the weakness of Britain. He describes the courageous retreat of militiamen from Fort Lee to the Delaware and provides a character study of Washington. He berates the behavior of the Tories and tells an anecdote of the selfishness of a Tory tavern owner. Paine again describes the strengths and courage of American forces and the harm Tories will bring on themselves from both Americans and British. He persuades the uncommitted and fearful sympathizers to commit themselves. He argues that a victorious Britain will be brutal and pictures a ravaged country if the people do not join the fight for liberty.

Teaching Strategies

PROVIDING FOR CULTURAL DIFFERENCES Some students may have emigrated from a country whose government was more restrictive than that of England, perhaps even oppressive. Thomas Paine's ideas may seem as revolutionary or radical to them as they did for many of Paine's contemporaries in England and America. Discuss with students the fact that Paine and others fought for the freedom of the individual at a time when the king of England had absolute power over an individual's life.

PROVIDING FOR DIFFERENT LEVELS OF ABILITY Although Paine's language is reasonably clear, some students may become confused by the string of aphorisms that run through the essay, particularly in the first paragraph. You might want to spend some time discussing these aphorisms. If students become lost in Paine's persuasive argument, you might want to break the pamphlet into four parts: (1) Setting the emotional tone for the appeal to Tories and uncommitted supporters; (2) Describing the soundness of the military retreat, mostly to encourage militiamen; (3) Haranguing Tories and appealing to the consciences of sympathizers; (4) Exhibiting faith in the cause and conviction that the Revolution will succeed. Ask students to find the place where each part begins and ends.

READING THE PAMPHLET Clarify further to the class the dire conditions under which the pamphlet was written. The writing is plain, strong, and clear, and yet the essay was written while on retreat from a battle. The fate of America was at stake, and Paine rose to the occasion. The pamphlet was an inspiration to thousands, many of whom joined the Continental Army after reading or hearing it.

Have a student read *The Crisis, No. 1* aloud, as it was read to the troops and later to the general populace. Then refer students to Patrick Henry's speech (text page 88). Ask students to consider why Paine's essay might be more appealing to the general public than Henry's speech.

RETEACHING ALTERNATIVES Point out specific ideas and sentences that reflect Enlightenment beliefs. One such idea is that a king does not have the right to impose unjust laws on the people. The appeal to the general population, Tory and Whig alike, suggests that the people's fate is in their own hands.

You could also explore further the use of analogies and examples in the essay. Have students look for all analogies to hell and devils, and then note whether they apply to the British or Americans. Ask students how the anecdote of the tavern owner and his child (text page 96) demonstrates the immorality of the Tory position, and whether the example was likely to win over Tories.

Responding to the Pamphlet   Text page 99

Answers to the questions in the Pupil's Edition appear in the Annotated Teacher's Edition.

Writing About the Pamphlet

For help in revising their compositions, refer students to **Grammar, Usage, and Mechanics: A Reference Guide** on text pages 1183–1228 at the back of their books.

A CREATIVE RESPONSE
1. Writing a Firsthand Account Read the writing assignment aloud and discuss probable reactions of the volunteer soldiers who heard this pamphlet read aloud. Clarify directions as necessary.

▶ CRITERIA FOR EVALUATING THE ASSIGNMENT The paragraph is written in first person. As the writer describes his feelings and the responses of the people around him, the writer reveals his own attitude toward the war.

A CRITICAL RESPONSE
2. Evaluating a Generalization Define *generalization* as a general statement that is true for the most part, but to which there may be exceptions. Read the quote from Paine and ask students to explain what makes it a generalization. When they begin to move into arguing about whether or not Paine is right, they are ready to write their essays. Tell students that they should include reasons and evidence to back up their opinions.

▶ CRITERIA FOR EVALUATING THE ASSIGNMENT The essay, while brief, consists of at least one paragraph. It clearly states either agreement or disagreement with Paine's words, and offers clear reasons or evidence to support the writer's position.

Objectives

1. To understand and appreciate one of the great documents in American history and writing

2. To identify examples of parallelism

3. To write an essay analyzing the persuasive arguments of the Declaration of Independence

4. To write an essay evaluating changes in the document

5. To define precisely two general words and phrases

Introducing the Autobiography

Critic Adrienne Koch calls Jefferson the greatest of the "philosopher-statesmen," the others being Alexander Hamilton, James Madison, and John Adams. She assesses that these four men "taken together almost define the range of our national ideology—our objectives, our character as a people, our economic and social patterns, our 'Americanism.'" She states that Jefferson's prime contribution was his faith that the common people could be educated and were capable of governing themselves. Contrary to Alexander Hamilton, he saw that the people could govern themselves, or, at least, choose responsible representation.

BACKGROUND ON THE AUTOBIOGRAPHY The Declaration of Independence has been criticized on many fronts for its lack of originality. John Adams said it was an amalgamation of ideas and statements considered for two years in the Continental Congress. Jefferson himself was acutely aware that the work's ideas were not original, but it was neither his intent nor duty to be original. The originality of the Declaration is in the quality of its expression: its moral strength, its phrasing, the inspirational tone of the aphorisms, and in its timeless and passionate appeal to the "rights of man."

The Declaration of Independence was a source of strength and inspiration to the French in the days before and during the French Revolution. It continues to be inspirational to peoples seeking liberty and justice from oppressive governments. Be sure to point out that the Declaration makes clear that revolution is not a frivolous act, but must only be enacted under the extreme threat of loss of liberty.

Teaching Strategies

PROVIDING FOR CULTURAL DIFFERENCES For students newly arrived in America, emphasize the prime importance of the Declaration of Independence in America's history and clarify the different purposes of the Declaration of Independence, the Constitution, and the Bill of Rights.

PROVIDING FOR DIFFERENT LEVELS OF ABILITY The long sentences and sometimes elaborate phrasing will cause difficulty for some students; however, hearing parts of the Declaration read aloud will be helpful. The significance of the passages omitted and/or replaced will be particularly difficult for some students to understand. You may want to clarify the reasons for the deletions and insertions. Question 4 in Identifying Facts, and question 3 in A Critical Response (text page 107) deal with this issue.

READING THE AUTOBIOGRAPHY Have students read aloud the opening two paragraphs of the Declaration. The first of these paragraphs establishes the intention of the document and states why independence is being declared. The second establishes the relationship between a people and their government. Call attention to the radical, yet seemingly reasonable, words, "whenever any form of government becomes destructive of these ends [the rights of man], it is the right of the people to alter or abolish it." This idea will seem revolutionary to many students and so it still is. The remainder of the paragraph defines specifically the situation in which revolt is justified. Explain that the rights of human beings were most crucial to Jefferson and that he was later instrumental in having the Bill of Rights added to the Constitution. The remainder of the Declaration works as a support for the first and second paragraphs.

RETEACHING ALTERNATIVES Have students pay particular attention to the omissions and additions to the Declaration. Have them note on a paper while rereading, places where omissions were made for the sake of clarity and where they were made for political reasons, such as in the passage on slavery. Point out also the delegates' concern for meaning and precision. For example, the Congress made several substitutions of *colonies* for *states,* because the colonies were not yet states. Ask students to consider while reading if most of the changes clarify and strengthen sentences and passages, or whether, as Jefferson felt, the changes were detrimental to the document.

Students are asked to write an opinion on the changes in A Critical Response, page 107 in the student text.

Responding to the Declaration

Answers to the questions in the Pupil's Edition appear in the Annotated Teacher's Edition.

Writing About the Declaration

For help in revising their compositions, refer students to **Grammar, Usage, and Mechanics: A Reference Guide** on text pages 1183–1228 at the back of their books.

A CRITICAL RESPONSE
1. Analyzing Its Reasoning   Call to students' attention the three questions in the writing assignment. These questions suggest the organization of their essays with one paragraph devoted to each question.

▶ CRITERIA FOR EVALUATING THE ASSIGNMENT   The essay lists Jefferson's major arguments, cites examples of the evidence Jefferson uses to support his points, and explains which elements of Jefferson's conclusion summarize and justify his arguments. Students' ideas should be clearly stated and supported with quotations or references to the text.

2. Responding to a Point of View   Read the excerpt from Abigail Adams's letter aloud, and elicit from students their first reactions. Students may write either an essay or a letter. If they choose the letter form, have them use a style as personal and informal as Abigail Adams's.

▶ CRITERIA FOR EVALUATING THE ASSIGNMENT   The essay or letter is clearly a response to Abigail Adams's letter. it offers the writer's own opinion on "remember[ing] the ladies." If it is a letter, it is informal in tone and style.

3. Responding to Changes in the Document   Clarify with students how deleted passages are identified in the text, and discuss which deleted passages Abigail Adams might have been referring to as "manly" but wiser to remove. Note that this assignment calls for an *essay*—not a letter response.

▶ CRITERIA FOR EVALUATING THE ASSIGNMENT   The essay discusses two appropriate deleted passages. Students state their opinion as to whether deletion of the passages made the document stronger or weaker, and explain why.

Analyzing Language and Style

PRECISE MEANINGS
While answers will vary, these are examples of suitable responses:

1. *Equal:* alike in nature or status; having the same rights
2. *Pursuit of happiness:* efforts to achieve a comfortable standard of living; efforts to achieve political freedom; efforts to achieve satisfying relationships with other people
3. *Equal* does not mean alike in talent or ability.
4. *Pursuit of happiness* does not imply a right to ignore the rights of everyone else in order to please oneself.

Extending the Autobiography

Students will enjoy watching the video of *1776,* the award-winning musical by Sherman Edwards and Peter Stone about the writing of the Declaration of Independence (Columbia Pictures, 1972).

Primary Sources

A LETTER FROM JEFFERSON TO HIS DAUGHTER
The letter can be approached in various ways. It is a fountain of Enlightenment ideals—fortitude, industry, self-improvement, and self-reliance. You might ask students what they would know of this period, the American Age of Reason, if the letter were the only piece of writing left from the period. Another approach would be to compare the virtues described in the letter with Franklin's list of virtues for achieving moral perfection. Finally, you might ask students what they think of Jefferson's advice. Does any of it still apply to modern life? Which parts seem dated?

UNIT TWO: The Revolutionary Period   **35**

This essay on "Revolutionary" English gives students a historical perspective on the nature of changes in the English language in the "New World," the reasons for these changes, and the political impact of such developments. The essay provides background to support students' growing understanding and appreciation of the fact that American English has always changed according to the way it is used, not the way authorities say it should be used.

Assign the essay for homework. Then have students work collaboratively on the Analyzing Language assignment that follows the essay.

Analyzing Language

Text page 112

1. Students should use an unabridged dictionary to find the English meaning of the italicized words. Reasons for the disappearance of these meanings will vary.

   chase: private game preserve

   bog: lavatory, bathroom

   common: tract of land owned jointly by the residents of a community

   shire: a British county

2. Students' definitions and dates may vary somewhat.

   cold snap: sudden onset of cold weather (1770–1780)

   dude: fellow, chap (1880–1885)

   everglade: tract of low, swampy land (1815–1825)

   Indian summer: period of mild, dry weather in late October or early November (1770–1780)

   pot pie: deep-dish pie with a pastry crust, containing meat or chicken (1785–1795)

   ranch: large farm (1800–1810)

   salt lick: place to which animals go to lick natural salt deposits (1735–1745)

   snowshoe: shoe for walking in snow (1655–1665)

   Comments on the words will vary. Possible areas of comment may include distinctively American elements of climate, diet, geography, topography, agriculture, and development of the economy.

3. For each of the italicized words, the origin is given first, followed by the common meaning in America. Students should note that except for *daughter,* the common meaning differs from the original meaning of the root.

   clue: variant of *clew,* < Middle English *clewe:* "a ball of thread or yarn"; "a hint leading to the solution of a mystery"

   companion: < Middle English, Old French, Late Latin, "messmate, someone you eat bread with"; "associate"

   daughter: < Middle English, German, "female offspring"

   expedite: < Latin, "set the feet free"; "hasten"

   precocious: < Latin, "early ripening"; "unusually advanced or mature"

   steward: < Old English, "house" or "hall"; "manager of a household"

   town: < Old English, "walled or fenced place"; "populated area"

4. Pronunciation keys will vary. Ask students to say the words aloud and see if they agree on pronunciations. Note also that there may be some regional differences in American pronunciations.

   been: bēn in England, bin in America

clerk: klark in England, klerk in America

lieutenant: lef te′ nent in England, lo͞o ten′ ent in America

schedule: shed′ yo͞ol in England, skej′ ool in America

Exercises in Critical Thinking and Writing

Text page 113

Analyzing and Evaluating Persuasion: Logic

To help students evaluate the underlying logic of Patrick Henry's "Speech to the Virginia Convention," discuss the highly charged emotional language that may make Henry's use of logical appeals hard to see. Students should understand, for example, that Henry carefully chooses his language to make an "either-or" choice seem logical. He begins in the first paragraph by saying that the House must choose between freedom or slavery. Later in the speech he opposes the British "chains which the British ministry have so long been forging" and the "tyrannical hands of the ministry and Parliament" against the Colonists' "appeal to arms and to the God of Hosts" and the "holy cause of liberty."

You might elicit a brief summary of each paragraph, which will outline Henry's argument.

Paragraph 1: It is a question of freedom or slavery. Freedom of debate lets us arrive at the truth and fulfill our responsibility to God and country.

Paragraph 2: Hope closes eyes to the truth, which is what common men do. Wise men must know "whole truth," no matter the anguish.

Paragraph 3: The experience of the last ten years has shown us that British have denied all our requests. Why believe they mean to change? Note the warlike preparations.

Paragraph 4: Why else would they send armies except to subjugate Colonists? Argument has been ineffective past ten years. There is nothing left to do but fight; no hope. If we wish to be free, we must fight.

Paragraph 5: We are not weak. We are strong enough to fight. Three million people in "holy cause" are invincible, and God is on our side. Besides, we have no choice—we must fight now.

Paragraph 6: The war is actually begun. We must join our brothers who are fighting.

▶ Criteria for Evaluating the Assignment Students' essays should follow the plan for writing outlined on text page 114. Look for a clearly worded thesis statement. Students should be aware that in evaluating Henry's argument, they are developing an argument of their own. Their opinions about Henry's logic should be supported with specific evidence from the speech.

Students should note the *either-or* fallacy.

Further Reading

Works listed are suitable for both students and teachers unless the annotation ends with the note [Teachers].

Commager, Henry Steele. *The Empire of Reason* (Anchor Press/Doubleday, 1977). Excellent overview of the Enlightenment in America from both European and American perspectives.

Crevecoeur, J. Hector St. John de. *Eighteenth Century America,* ed. Albert E. Stone (Penguin, 1981). Continues Crevecoeur's descriptive commentary on the American landscape and people begun in *Letters from an American Farmer.*

Edwards, Sherman, and Peter Stone. *1776,* a video (Columbia Pictures, 1972). A prize-winning, high-spirited musical about the Founding Fathers and the writing of the Declaration of Independence.

Malone, Dumas. *Jefferson and His Time,* five volumes (Little, Brown, 1948–1974). The most complete biography of Jefferson.

Miller, Perry. *The New England Mind: From Colony to Province* (Harvard University Press, 1953). A classic literary history of the period, still considered the best. [Teachers]

Tyler, Moses Coit. *The Literary History of the American Revolution,* two volumes (Frederick Ungar, 1957). Considered an outstanding critical history despite subsequent revival of authors not available to Tyler. [Teachers]

Van Doren, Carl. *Benjamin Franklin and Jonathan Edwards* (Arden Library, 1979). The classic biography of Franklin.

AMERICAN ROMANTICISM

Teaching the American Romanticism Unit

The literature of Romanticism differs decisively from earlier American literature. Before Irving began publishing his *Sketch Book* serially in 1819, American writing was primarily religious, economic, and political. Writers like Franklin and Jefferson were only secondarily men of letters; they were primarily builders of a nation. The entire nation's attention, in fact, was on practical accomplishment—the opposite of Romanticism.

As the text suggests, Romanticism, which began in Europe, developed distinct American characteristics out of our Colonial past and the development of the new nation. As students read the works in this and the following units, ask them to keep in mind the two principal ways that the Romantic sensibility sought to rise above "dull realities": by exploring exotic settings, past and present; and by contemplating the natural world. Both activities were well suited to the luxuriant new land that faced Americans. It was perhaps inevitable that the first celebrated American novelist, James Fenimore Cooper, would be a Romantic celebrator of wilderness virtues.

Even while Cooper was taking Natty Bumppo into the frontier and celebrating American skill and initiative, the Fireside Poets, as the text points out, "looked backward . . . at established European models." The first two poems in the unit, "To a Waterfowl" and "Thanatopsis," lend themselves to a discussion of this question of whether poets such as Bryant were distinctively American. Students might agree that "Thanatopsis" could more easily be mistaken for a British poem, whereas they may see the barrenness of the setting of "To a Waterfowl" as more suggestive of early New England.

The Romantic period fostered the beginning of what we consider today to be distinctively American literature. Pathfinders such as Irving, Cooper, and Bryant were to make way for such giants as Hawthorne, Melville, and Poe. But, more significantly, as time went on, it was not only the writers but also their themes that attracted readers in Europe as well as in America.

Objectives of the American Romanticism Unit

1. To improve reading proficiency and expand vocabulary

2. To gain exposure to notable authors and their works

3. To define and identify the elements of the story and poem

4. To define and identify significant literary techniques

5. To respond orally and in writing to stories and poetry

6. To analyze the language and style of notable authors

7. To write original works

8. To practice the following critical thinking and writing skills:
   a. Analyzing conflict, style, and imagery
   b. Interpreting tone
   c. Comparing and contrasting poems
   d. Analyzing a poem
   e. Analyzing the appeal of a literary work
   f. Responding to a poem's message
   g. Paraphrasing a poem

Introducing the American Romanticism Unit

The names of some of the Romantics will be familiar to students: Longfellow, Cooper, Irving. But students may have an inexact idea about when they lived and wrote, and what was happening in America in their lifetimes. Use the time line on text pages 120–121 to help students get a sense of the period of Romanticism, usually thought of as flourishing in the half century before the Civil War. Discussing the time line in class will also help students see themselves in relation to American history as well as literature. The time line will remind students of how short a time America has been a nation. Some will recall the 200th anniversary of the Constitution in 1987. While two centuries in the past seems like ancient history to forward-looking teenagers, suggest that their great-grandparents might conceivably have known someone who saw George Washington. This should give them some idea of the relative youth of our nation.

Remind students as they look at the time line that when the Romantics were at the height of their careers, America had been a nation for only a few years. You might ask them to imagine that they were aspiring American writers living in 1815, when Bryant wrote "To a Waterfowl." If they had been embarking upon literary careers at that time, what would they have chosen to write about? Where would they have sought their material? In the western frontier? In the established civilization of Europe? Or in their own imaginations? The American Romantics, you can inform students, drew from all these sources.

Washington Irving

Text page 123

RIP VAN WINKLE

Text page 125

Objectives

1. To enjoy one of the classic American short stories

2. To analyze characters, theme, and tone in a short story

3. To define Romantic aspects of setting

4. To write an epilogue to the story

5. To write an essay explaining parallels between the story and the awakening of the American nation

6. To write an essay analyzing conflict

Introducing the Story

Here are the major elements of the story:

- **Protagonist:** Rip Van Winkle
- **Antagonists:** Dame Van Winkle, his wife; the little men
- **Setting:** a remote village in the Catskills before and after the American Revolution
- **Point of view:** third-person, with a note by Diedrich Knickerbocker at the story's end
- **Conflict:** husband vs. wife; individual vs. environment; youth vs. age; past vs. present

BACKGROUND ON THE STORY Even to its first readers, the story was set in the past (first published in 1819, thirty years after George Washington's first inaugural). Rip's village was founded "just about the beginning of the government of the good Peter Stuyvesant" (1646). Readers in the early 1800's had a natural interest in the early history and legends of their new nation. Irving's interest in the past suggests that he was an early American Romantic.

The remoteness of the village in the Catskill Mountains also helps us see the story as folklore, not intended to be realistic. Because the writer is known, this story can be called a *literary folktale.* Irving consciously included elements of the folk tale: the supernatural, mysterious setting, "little people."

THE PLOT When Rip's wife scolds him for not helping around the house, Rip leaves home and takes an afternoon ramble in the mountains with his dog Wolf. He is beguiled into a mystical ravine, where several little people dressed in "the antique Dutch fashion" are playing at ninepins. Rip sneaks a good deal of the little people's drink and falls into a deep sleep. When he wakes up, he finds his gun rusted and his dog gone. He returns to his village and is surprised to find no faces he recognizes. His house is empty and the village all changed. Gradually Rip discovers that twenty years have passed and his wife is dead. He discovers his son and daughter, now grown, and enters into the life of the village in its new era.

Teaching Strategies

PROVIDING FOR CULTURAL DIFFERENCES Students may want to talk about the stereotype Rip's wife represents. Do students from other cultures recognize the shrewish, angry wife from stories they know?

PROVIDING FOR DIFFERENT LEVELS OF ABILITY It is a good idea to read the first three paragraphs of the story aloud in class (or have a student reader do it) so that students will get used to Irving's style and have a chance to ask questions about meaning. You might also point out that Irving is establishing a tone of legend through his use of such words as *noble, lording, magical, fairy,* and *chivalrous.* Help students through the last three sentences of the third paragraph, which for many will be a stumbling block.

READING THE STORY Some students will be familiar with the plot of Irving's tale from other sources, such as television cartoons, without having read the original version. You might ask whether any of your students can recount the story line before the class reads the story. This will ease some of the burden of comprehension for less advanced students, and help the more advanced students explore some of the subtleties of the work.

RETEACHING ALTERNATIVES You might concentrate on a limited part of the story—for example, Rip's experience in the mountains (text pages 129–130). Ask students to note the natural setting, described in the second paragraph on text page 129, and the imagined setting of the amphitheater in the next column. Students might ask if the amphitheater itself was a dream, since Rip couldn't find it when he woke up. But they should realize that one does not ask a question like this of a folktale, any more than one asks how Jack could climb up a beanstalk.

Responding to the Story   Text page 137

Answers to the questions in the Pupil's Edition appear in the Annotated Teacher's Edition.

Writing About the Story

For help in revising their compositions, refer students to **Grammar, Usage, and Mechanics: A Reference Guide** on text pages 1183–1228 at the back of their books.

A CREATIVE RESPONSE
1. *Writing an Epilogue*   An *epilogue* is an addition to a literary work that rounds out the story. Discuss with students the point at which the Dame Van Winkle epilogue would fit into the story as a whole, and the advantages and disadvantages of choosing her or Knickerbocker as narrator. Suggest that students include dialogue. Students may collaborate with a small group to plot the story and take turns writing sections. Have them spend some time editing and revising their first draft before writing a final copy. Each group should read aloud its story while classmates listen and respond.

▶ CRITERIA FOR EVALUATING THE ASSIGNMENT   The epilogue tells what happened to Dame Van Winkle after Rip disappeared. The tone is consistent and the events are believable.

A CRITICAL RESPONSE
2. *Modernizing the Story*   Make sure students understand that their task is to explain *how* to modernize the story—not actually to do so. Some students will find it easier to work with a partner or small group to brainstorm ideas.

▶ CRITERIA FOR EVALUATING THE ASSIGNMENT   The paragraph comments on changes necessary in setting, characters, and conflict to reset the story in the late twentieth century. Have students read aloud their paragraphs and encourage individuals or small groups to write the updated version they have described.

3. Explaining a Parallel Before students write their essays, read with them A Comment on the Story, text page 136. Note that the writing assignment suggests three specific topics: independence, peace, and maturity. Students do not need to cover all three.

▶ CRITERIA FOR EVALUATING THE ASSIGNMENT The essay cites several parallels between Rip's emancipation and that of the United States. Details from the story support points made about parallels in independence, peace, and maturity.

4. Analyzing a Conflict Discuss other comedies, such as Shakespeare's *The Taming of the Shrew* and various TV series (*I Love Lucy*), that focus on "the battle of the sexes." Point out that the writing assignment asks for a three-part essay.

▶ CRITERIA FOR EVALUATING THE ASSIGNMENT The essay briefly summarizes the conflict between Rip Van Winkle and his wife, names at least two other comedies that use the "battle of the sexes," and gives the student's personal reaction to the theme.

Analyzing Language and Style

INFLATED LANGUAGE
1. Two of the possible answers: Rip's farm "was the most pestilent little piece of ground in the whole country . . . weeds were sure to grow quicker in his fields than anywhere else . . ."; Rip's dog Wolf "sneaked about with a gallows air, casting many a sidelong glance at Dame Van Winkle, and at the least flourish of a broomstick or ladle he would fly to the door with yelping precipitation."
2. "Rip's farm was a terrible piece of ground where weeds grew easily." "Rip's dog watched Mrs. Van Winkle carefully, and yelped and ran every time she used a broom or a ladle."
3. Most students will have enjoyed the hyperbole.

Extending the Story

Students who enjoyed the story should be encouraged to read "The Legend of Sleepy Hollow" if they have not already done so. Or they might find other works by Irving in the library. Students who read more by Irving should give a brief, informal oral report. They should identify what they read, summarize it in a few sentences, and talk about their responses to the work.

Primary Sources   Text page 137

A TRAVELER COMMENTS ON AMERICAN MANNERS
Students may be amused by Mrs. Trollope's comments on American manners. Be sure that they understand that more than politeness is meant by the term *manners*. Mrs. Trollope was commenting on the impressions Americans made on her through their attitudes and everyday behavior.

It is, of course, impossible to judge how good a reporter Mrs. Trollope was from this brief account. You might ask students to trust her reporting and to suggest some specific ways in which Americans might have seemed to lack enthusiasm or to have been, like Rip Van Winkle, in a long sleep. Ask students to consider how Americans have changed since 1832. Is the Fourth of July the only holiday celebrated with enthusiasm? Is it still celebrated with extravagance and splendor? What parts do women today play in celebrating American holidays like Fourth of July and Thanksgiving?

William Cullen Bryant   Text page 138

TO A WATERFOWL   Text page 139

Objectives

1. To respond to a Romantic poem

2. To recognize onomatopoeia

3. To interpret symbols and theme

4. To write a paragraph analyzing the poem

Introducing the Poem

Here are the major elements of the poem:

- **Rhyme:** abab
- **Rhythm:** iambic tetrameter and pentameter
- **Significant techniques:** alliteration, onomatopeia, imagery, varied line length

BACKGROUND ON THE POEM   Bryant was a child prodigy but had the same youthful doubts that your own students have probably experienced. He was inspired to write "To a Waterfowl" after taking a seven-mile walk one December twilight in 1817, "forlorn and desolate, not knowing what was to become of him in the big world," according to his biographer Parke Godwin. While communing with his own soul, he watched a solitary bird flying along the sunset horizon and asked himself where it had come from and where it was going.

THE LITERAL MEANING   The narrator observes a waterfowl flying far off in the "rosy depths" of the sunset. He imagines that it will soon find its destination, having flown all day in "the cold, thin atmosphere." The narrator reflects that the "Power" that has guided the bird will also guide him "in the long way" ahead of him.

that the poet assumes and that need not be the poet's own voice. Thus, in the background statement we learn that Bryant wrote the poem in December, but the poem is set in the summer; the speaker talks about the bird's soon finding "a summer home." Students need to recognize the apostrophe starting with the first line and extending through the poem. The effect is to establish a bond between the narrator and the bird.

RETEACHING ALTERNATIVES   You might have students work individually or with a partner to create a sequence of eight drawings, one for each stanza, in comic-strip format. Artistic ability isn't necessary; students can use stick figures. When the drawings have been completed, let students share them and discover how close they have come to agreeing on the story line implied in the poem and on the feeling it evokes.

Teaching Strategies

PROVIDING FOR CULTURAL DIFFERENCES   The poem is more accessible to students who have lived in the country than to city dwellers, if only because of its setting. However, everyone at one time or another has been alone, and much of the poem's appeal derives from our ability to share with the narrator the sense of being alone with nature.

PROVIDING FOR DIFFERENT LEVELS OF ABILITY
LEP students will benefit from reducing the poem to its simplest terms. A little help with the stylized diction would be appropriate ("Seek'st thou . . ." could be translated, "Are you looking for . . ."), and students will need to notice that stanzas one and three are questions. The first stanza can be reduced to, "Where are you going?" and the second to "The hunter won't be able to shoot you."

To accustom students to the idea of apostrophe, encourage them to think of times when they have talked to their pets or even to an inanimate object like a bicycle. They may understand better how the narrator feels as he addresses the bird.

READING THE POEM   Before discussing the poem, students may need help in understanding the vocabulary and diction. It is useful to speak of a narrator, a persona

Responding to the Poem   Text page 141

Answers to the questions in the Pupil's Edition appear in the Annotated Teacher's Edition.

Writing About the Poem

For help in revising their compositions, refer students to **Grammar, Usage, and Mechanics: A Reference Guide** on text pages 1183–1228 at the back of their books.

A CRITICAL RESPONSE
Analyzing the Poem   Divide the class into small groups to discuss the questions raised in the writing assignment. After five or ten minutes of group discussion, ask students to write a single paragraph that answers all three questions. Give students time to revise their papers for clarity and coherence.

▶ CRITERIA FOR EVALUATING THE ASSIGNMENT   Students should address all three questions. Look for clarity of expression. Students should recognize that Bryant's purpose (as expressed in the headnote) is to recognize the divine in nature and to give comfort to readers by acknowledging a divine plan. The long description of the bird's lone migration is beautiful in itself and is also a moving, apt comparison with the human journey through life.

Objectives

1. To respond to a poem about death and nature

2. To analyze the use of imagery to create tone

3. To identify metaphors and imagery

4. To recognize iambic pentameter

5. To write a letter from the point of view of a Puritan reading the poem

6. To write an essay comparing and contrasting two poems

7. To write an essay analyzing imagery and meaning

8. To recognize inverted syntax and archaic diction

Introducing the Poem

Here are the major elements of the poem:

- **Rhythm:** blank verse
- **Rhyme:** none
- **Theme:** Death is not to be feared; it is everyone's destiny, a union with nature and all who have already died.
- **Significant techniques:** variation of meter, inversion of word order, shifts of tone, personification, metaphor, imagery

BACKGROUND ON THE POEM   Bryant left Williams College in his sophomore year in 1811. He had been reading eighteenth-century British poems, including Robert Blair's "The Grave." In this and other poems of the period, blank verse had replaced the heroic couplet and for the first time since Milton was a widely used verse form.

Of the genesis of "Thanatopsis" Bryant himself later wrote: "I cannot give you any information of the occasion which suggested to my mind the idea of my poem Thanatopsis. It was written when I was seventeen or eighteen years old . . . and I believe it was composed in my solitary rambles in the woods."

THE LITERAL MEANING   The narrator reflects on what nature means to a person who "holds communion" with her: she confirms his glad hours and heals his "darker musings." When you fear death, go out and observe nature. Death is not to be feared. Rather, when death comes, we will "mix forever with the elements" and lie down with kings and all who have died before us. We will have the entire world of nature as our sepulcher. The dead are everywhere. The narrator draws this lesson from his "musings": Live in such a way that when your time comes to die, you will go trustfully, looking forward to pleasant dreams.

Teaching Strategies

PROVIDING FOR CULTURAL DIFFERENCES   You might ask students to research and discuss attitudes toward death in different cultures (perhaps ancient Greek, Hindu, Native American, and others). Volunteers may want to talk about their own attitudes and experiences with funerals.

PROVIDING FOR DIFFERENT LEVELS OF ABILITY For some readers, the language of the poem may be difficult, and they will need the help of paraphrasing. Lines 17–30 are among those that may cause difficulty.

READING THE POEM   Ask students to write freely for ten minutes about some experience they have had that is associated with death. It might be visiting a cemetery, taking part in a Memorial Day ceremony, attending a funeral, or simply reading a novel or play in which a death occurs. Encourage students to write their recollection of the experience in some detail and to examine their feelings about it. (Suggest that they will not have to share their writing unless they wish to.) A brief discussion and some voluntary sharing of the writing should develop the sense that death is a subject everyone has thought about and that people have different attitudes and views.

Tell students that "Thanatopsis" expresses one view of death, and that Bryant wrote it when he was about their age or perhaps a year or two older.

RETEACHING ALTERNATIVES   You might select a group of students to give a dramatic reading of the poem. Have them divide the reading themselves. Some lines could be read by individuals, some by the entire group. Students may want to experiment with various readings— including the use of all-female or all-male voices in parts. Have them decide which interpretation is the most successful and present it to the class.

Responding to the Poem Text page 145

Answers to the questions in the Pupil's Edition appear in the Annotated Teacher's Edition.

Writing About the Poem

For help in revising their compositions, refer students to **Grammar, Usage, and Mechanics: A Reference Guide** on text pages 1183–1228 at the back of their books.

A CREATIVE RESPONSE

1. Writing a Letter Before students begin to write, review the Puritans' world view, text pages 5–10, and elicit from students some possible reactions a Puritan might have. Students should note (on text page 10) that they believed God reveals his purpose through Nature, so that a Puritan would be likely to approve of Bryant's seeking solace and meaning in Nature. Some students may also point out that because Puritans could not tell if they were saved or damned (text page 6) and believed in eternal damnation, many would indeed fear death.

▶ CRITERIA FOR EVALUATING THE ASSIGNMENT The paper is in formal letter form and accurately reflects reactions to "Thanatopsis" appropriate to a Puritan reader.

A CRITICAL RESPONSE

2. Comparing and Contrasting Poems On the board with students' help, fill in a prewriting chart like the one on page 91. Students will have two basic points to cover: how Nature speaks and the lessons Nature delivers.

▶ CRITERIA FOR EVALUATING THE ASSIGNMENT The essay explains similarities and differences in the two Bryant poems in terms of how Nature speaks and the messages delivered.

3. Analyzing Imagery and Meaning Have students work together to list on the board all phrases referring to death as sleep (for example, "thine eternal resting place," line 31; "couch," line 33; "last sleep," line 57). When all the images are identified, students can meet in small groups to focus on the poem as a whole and discuss whether or not Bryant suggests an afterlife.

▶ CRITERIA FOR EVALUATING THE ASSIGNMENT The essay traces the sleep images in "Thanatopsis" and uses specific details from the poem to support the opinion that Bryant does or does not suggest an awakening into an afterlife. Lines 24–26 suggest that dead bodies break down to become one with the elements. Other lines (33–37, 54–58) support the notion of an afterlife of individuals who are in an eternal sleep.

Analyzing Language and Style

INVERSIONS AND ARCHAIC LANGUAGE

1. These are five of the many examples of inversion:
   a. "To him who in the love of Nature holds / Communion with her visible forms, she speaks / A various language. . . ."
   b. ". . . while from all around . . . / Comes a still voice. . . ."
   c. "Yet not to thine eternal resting place / Shalt thou retire alone. . . ."
   d. "Are but the solemn decorations all. . . ."
   e. "Where rolls the Oregon. . . ."

   Altering the syntax destroys the regular iambic rhythm, despite the many iambic stresses natural to English speech:

   "Náture spéaks ă várious lánguăge tŏ hím
   Whŏ, ĭn lóve ŏf Náture, hólds commúnion
   Wĭth her vísĭble fórms."

2. Some of the archaic phrases (and their modern equivalents) are "holds communion" (communicates), "visible forms" (appearances), "shroud and pall" (burial clothes), "rude swain" (hick, country bumpkin), "hoary seers" (old prophets), "the drapery of his couch" (bedclothes), etc.

3. Archaic diction (and their modern equivalents) in "To a Waterfowl" (text pages 139, 141): *Whither* (where to), *dost* (does), *thou* and *thy* (you, your), *fowler* (hunter), *seek'st* (seek), *plashy* (splashing), *marge* (edge), *stoop* (descend), *toil* (work, labor), *shalt* (shall or will), *o'er* (over), *thou'rt* (you are), *hath* and *hast* (has), *tread* (walk), and *aright* (correctly). Substituting the modern words destroys the tone of the poem.

Henry Wadsworth Longfellow

THE CROSS OF SNOW

Objectives

1. To respond to a sonnet about grief
2. To identify tone
3. To interpret symbolism
4. To write a paragraph responding to the poem

Introducing the Poem

Here are the major elements of the poem:

- **Form:** Petrarchan sonnet
- **Rhythm:** iambic pentameter
- **Rhyme:** abba abba cde cde
- **Significant technique:** figurative language

BACKGROUND ON THE POEM   This poem is as close as one can get to being able to say that the poet and the speaker are the same person. "Eighteen years" (line 13) did in fact pass between the death of Longfellow's wife, Frances Appleton (Fanny) Longfellow, and the writing of this sonnet. The biographer Edward Wagenknecht calls the death of Fanny Longfellow "the great crisis of his life."

THE LITERAL MEANING   The narrator, unable to sleep, contemplates the picture of his wife, who died from burns in the same room eighteen years before. He remembers what an exceptional person his wife was. He then tells of a mountain which, because of its sheltered ravines, keeps a "cross of snow" all year long: and he likens this "changeless" cross to the cross he wears in memory of his wife.

Teaching Strategies

PROVIDING FOR CULTURAL DIFFERENCES   To understand the poem, students must know the significance of the cross as a Christian symbol. You might ask volunteers to explain very briefly some symbols associated with other religions (e.g., star of David, yin and yang).

PROVIDING FOR DIFFERENT LEVELS OF ABILITY   All students should be able to analyze the rhyme of the sonnet by assigning letters to each end rhyme and discovering the abba abba cde cde pattern.

READING THE POEM   You may choose to play the tape recording of this poem that accompanies the text, or have a student read the poem aloud. Then lead students to examine each quatrain and tercet more closely.

In the first line, the two stressed syllables (*long sleepless*) slow the reading to accentuate their meaning. The contrast between the night and the halo created by the night lamp gives a remarkable visual image. The second quatrain emphasizes the exceptional qualities of the dead woman. The word *legend* reminds us of the Romantic's interest in the past. In the first tercet, "sun-defying" provides a visual contrast of the white snow with the darker surroundings. Having evoked feelings of darkness broken by shifting patterns of light, the narrator in the final tercet introduces the symbol of the cross to make us understand why his tone is so unsettling and his night sleepless.

RETEACHING ALTERNATIVES   Divide the poem up into its quatrains and tercets and have students paraphrase each group of lines. Next, ask students to suggest a word or two that describes the feelings the poem evokes in each section. Students with artistic talent may wish to draw a sketch for each group of lines.

Responding to the Poem   Text page 148

Answers to the questions in the Pupil's Edition appear in the Annotated Teacher's Edition.

Writing About the Poem

For help in revising their compositions, refer students to **Grammar, Usage, and Mechanics: A Reference Guide** on text pages 1183–1228 at the back of their books.

A CRITICAL RESPONSE
Responding to the Poem   Remind students that a response paper has no "right" or "wrong" answers. They should write about their personal reactions and associations and tell what specific details from the poem aroused their responses.

► CRITERIA FOR EVALUATING THE ASSIGNMENT The paragraph states the writer's general response to "The Cross of Snow" and cites specific examples of message, language, rhyme, rhythm, and tone that aroused that response.

ELEMENTS OF LITERATURE
Text page 148

THE SONNET
The subject (in the octave) is that Longfellow's wife is dead and he still misses her. The comment (in the sestet) is that the pain of his loss is as enduring as the cross of snow in a certain mountain ravine which is never touched by sunlight. The rhyme scheme is abba abba cde cde.

Extending the Poem

Writing an Italian sonnet may seem more difficult than it really is. Suggest that students find a picture or some symbol that has special meaning for them, and write about it in the form of a sonnet, possibly taking clues from the Longfellow sonnet on how they might structure their work. For a more detailed discussion about the form, refer students to the *sonnet* entry in the **Handbook of Literary Terms,** text page 1180. Many students will prefer to collaborate with two or three others in writing a sonnet. Others may prefer to work alone or with a writing partner.

THE ROPEWALK
Text page 149

Objectives

1. To respond to a poem's images and figurative language
2. To recognize trochaic meter
3. To write a paragraph describing a scene and its mood

Introducing the Poem

Here are the major elements of the poem:

- **Rhythm:** trochaic tetrameter
- **Rhyme:** aabccb
- **Themes:** the dehumanization of factory life; the varied human condition
- **Significant techniques:** imagery, series of imagined scenes, metaphor, internal rhyme, shifts in tone

BACKGROUND ON THE POEM Longfellow's journal entry for May 20, 1854, was very brief: "A lovely morning. Wrote a poem—'The Ropewalk.'" Longfellow's broad sympathies are hinted at in the poem: his love for children; his associations with Europe, where bellringing was more common than in this country (though Cambridge would have had its bellringers in his time); his interest in the farm and the sea typical of the Romantics.

THE LITERAL MEANING The speaker describes a ropewalk and presents different pictures of the uses that he imagines the rope being manufactured will be put to: stanza four, "two fair maidens" swinging; stanza five, a girl on a tightrope; stanza six, a woman drawing water from a well; stanza seven, a ringer in a bell tower; stanza eight, a gallows; stanza nine, multiple pictures: a boy flying a kite, a roundup, trappers with their snares, and a fisherman; and stanza ten, ships at sea with ropes being used not only for anchors and rigging, but for sounding the depths.

Teaching Strategies

PROVIDING FOR CULTURAL DIFFERENCES Tell students that when this poem was written, children often worked long hours in crowded factories and sweatshops. In India today 10-year-old girls assemble matches; their quick, small hands make them more efficient workers than adults. Ask students to tell what they know of factories today in other countries. Do children work? Are there labor unions?

PROVIDING FOR DIFFERENT LEVELS OF ABILITY
LEP and ESL students may find the syntax, particularly the inversions, confusing. Read the poem aloud and stop to paraphrase each stanza.

For students who do not find the connections that the poem makes between the manufacture of rope and its uses, ask them to concentrate on the central metaphor. What does mention of a spider make them think of? What words do they associate with *thread* and *cobweb*? What does a spider look like while it is spinning a web? How would you describe the way a spider works? Their answers will help students see the similarity between a ropewalker and a spider.

READING THE POEM   For the first three poems of this unit, the focus has been on nature and death; now we have a poem that seems to have as its focus manufacturing. Students will become aware, however, that though this poem starts as a description of the manufacture of rope, it soon shifts through the dream that begins at the end of stanza 2 to descriptions of other scenes that are more typical of the Romantics. Once students have understood the structure of the poem, call their attention to such poetic elements as alliteration, repetition, metaphor, and imagery. Ask students to describe how the tone and feeling change from one stanza to the next.

RETEACHING ALTERNATIVES   Stanzas four to ten are self-contained descriptions. Ask students to try to explain the order of these stanzas. They might try shifting the order and reading the poem with the stanzas rearranged, to see if this makes any difference to the tone or feeling. They will note that such rearranging cannot be done with the last stanza.

Even if they do not notice much difference between the original and their new version of the poem, students will better understand the poem's structure and how it contributes to the total effect.

Responding to the Poem   Text page 151

Answers to the questions in the Pupil's Edition appear in the Annotated Teacher's Edition.

Writing About the Poem

For help in revising their compositions, refer students to **Grammar, Usage, and Mechanics: A Reference Guide** on text pages 1183–1228 at the back of their books.

A CREATIVE RESPONSE
Describing an Idyllic Scene   Question 3 (Analyzing the Poem) will have given students a list of scenes from which to choose, but clarify the meaning of *idyllic*.

▶ CRITERIA FOR EVALUATING THE ASSIGNMENT   The paragraph cites a scene from "The Ropewalk" that would make an apt Currier & Ives subject, and describes the scene and its mood. Students are likely to choose one of the following stanzas as idyllic: 4, 6, 7, and 9. Stanzas 5, 8, and 10 (with its wrecks) are definitely *not* idyllic.

Analyzing Language and Style

TROCHAIC METER
Longfellow does repeat his count faithfully. The only exception is one use of two unaccented syllables—the last two syllables of "lessening" in line 59. The carrying power of the rhythm would, however, induce one to pronounce even this word as a trochee: "less'ning."

Extending the Poem

You might suggest that students describe a process that they are familiar with and that affects the lives of other people, as rope manufacture does. For example, a boy who works as a cashier might imagine how the goods he sells will be used; or a girl who pumps gas could imagine where the cars she services are going. Encourage volunteers to write about these, using the same short descriptive technique that Longfellow does. Students may choose to write free verse; maintaining Longfellow's rhyme and rhythm is not necessary.

THE TIDE RISES, THE TIDE FALLS

Objectives

1. To respond to the sound and meaning of a famous American lyric poem

2. To identify the poem's theme

3. To recognize personification and onomatopoeia

4. To write an essay comparing and contrasting two poems

Introducing the Poem

This short poem is generally considered one of Longfellow's finest lyrics. The "traveler" of line four may be taken as one traveling through life. The facts that Longfellow wrote the poem near the end of his own life (three years before his death) and that the traveler returns to the shore "nevermore" suggests that the poem is about the end of life's journey. The restrained diction, the concrete images, and the absence of moralizing keep the tone from becoming sentimental. Longfellow used water imagery in an earlier poem, "My Lost Youth," and the figure "footprints in the sands" in his "Psalm of Life."

Here are the major elements of the poem:

- **Rhythm:** iambic tetrameter with many variations to mimic the sea's rhythms

- **Rhyme:** aabba aacca aadda

- **Theme:** Though human lives end, the sea and its tides are eternal.

- **Significant techniques:** repetition, alliteration, assonance, imagery

THE LITERAL MEANING   The speaker stands at the shore near evening. He notices a traveler hastening "toward the town," darkness settling on the town, and the "little waves" effacing the footprints, the last signs of the traveler. The next morning the horses are ready, but the traveler does not return to the shore. Through it all, the tide rises and falls.

Teaching Strategies

PROVIDING FOR CULTURAL DIFFERENCES   The rising and falling of the tide is universal—in all cultures and generations. Some students, however, will have ex-perienced the tides more than others. Students who have lived at the shore can describe what the shore is like as the tide rises and falls, and can perhaps relate the feeling of having a sandcastle or other creation disappear with the tide.

PROVIDING FOR DIFFERENT LEVELS OF ABILITY
Some readers may have trouble understanding the repetition in the poem. After all, there are only fifteen lines, and four of them are the same. If the question comes up, ask students to tell you the lyrics of their favorite songs. They may discover that the repetition in this poem serves somewhat the same purpose as it does in song lyrics. More advanced readers should be able to note other musical devices such as alliteration and assonance.

READING THE POEM   A good reading of this poem will reveal the alliteration, the softness of the sounds, and the steady and regular movement of the rhythm. Play the audiocassette recording that accompanies the poem.

RETEACHING ALTERNATIVES   You might have the class decide on a thematic statement they would like to make about school, and follow the pattern of "The tide rises . . ." to create a class poem developing this theme. It will be most meaningful if they think of something that, like the tide, keeps coming and going, like the bell, school books, or lunch period. The purpose of this exercise is to help students understand how the elements of a poem come together to develop a theme and create a feeling. Having tried it themselves, they may appreciate more fully what Longfellow has achieved.

Responding to the Poem

Answers to the questions in the Pupil's Edition appear in the Annotated Teacher's Edition.

Writing About the Poem

For help in revising their compositions, refer students to **Grammar, Usage, and Mechanics: A Reference Guide** on text pages 1183–1228 at the back of their books.

A CRITICAL RESPONSE
Comparing and Contrasting Poems   Read both "The Tide Rises, the Tide Falls" and "Break, Break, Break," aloud. As a prewriting activity, help students complete the chart at the bottom of page 154.

The essay cites differences between the poems in mood (Longfellow's has a trace of sadness, while Tennyson's is filled with grief), meter (Longfellow uses iambic / anapestic tetrameter; Tennyson, a mix of iambic / anapestic trimeter and tetrameter, with the opening line consisting of three stresses), rhyme patterns (Longfellow's is aabba; Tennyson's, abcb). For Longfellow the sea represents time; for Tennyson, heartless nature. But the paper notes the similarity of the message—the sea washes away the past: ''The day returns, but nevermore / Returns the traveler to the shore'' (Longfellow); ''the tender grace of a day that is dead / Will never come back to me'' (Tennyson).

Extending the Poem

This is a good poem to ask students to memorize. For further reading and thinking, you might ask students to compare the poem with Robert Frost's ''Neither Out Far nor In Deep'' (text page 656), another deceptively simple poem about watching the sea.

Primary Sources   Text page 155

VISITING MR. LONGFELLOW
This brief extract, from a biography by a prominent contemporary critic, lends a note of humor to your class's study of the Romantics. It should lead them to see early nineteenth-century people as being lively and sometimes irreverent. You might, if time permits, ask students if they can compare the ''bloopers'' uttered by Longfellow's visitors with ones they have heard about present-day celebrities.

John Greenleaf Whittier   Text page 156

FROM SNOW-BOUND: A WINTER IDYLL   Text page 157

Objectives

1. To sample a popular poem about eighteenth-century rural life
2. To identify allusions in the poem
3. To write a paper analyzing the poem's appeal
4. To analyze the poem's imagery

Introducing the Poem

This poem is autobiographical, written when the poet was nearing sixty and inclined to reminisce about his youth. Whittier lived in northern Massachusetts, where in those days a snowstorm could completely isolate a family for days. Whittier describes the storm and its aftermath in realistic but imaginative terms. There is humor in the descriptions, but the details of the cold and darkness create a tone of loneliness, almost of horror. Thus, while the poem has the quality of an idyll and evokes a warm and for some a nostalgic response, it has a dark side too.

Few people in our industrial and electronic world have had an experience comparable to the one described in the poem, regardless of their cultural background. However, students may relate *Snow-Bound* to their own experiences if they recall a time when the family had to fall back on its own resources: a car breakdown on a trip, a power outage, a storm during a camping trip, or some other unusual and unexpected occurrence. What did the family do on such an occasion?

Here are the major elements of the poem:

- **Rhythm:** iambic tetrameter
- **Rhyme:** aabbcc
- **Significant techniques:** alliteration, personification, imagery, allusions

BACKGROUND ON THE POEM   The first part of the poem, which appears in the text, sets the stage for the nearly six hundred lines that follow. There we learn of the family and guests: father, mother, two sisters, aunt, uncle, the school-master, another guest, and the two boys themselves. The descriptions of these people and the accounts of the stories they told when the family was snowbound touched a responsive chord in American readers, who needed just such a romantic and nostalgic idyll to help them recover from the Civil War. The poem sold thousands of copies and gave Whittier financial security for the first time in his life.

THE LITERAL MEANING   The poet recalls a December day in his youth when all the signs pointed to an approaching snowstorm. The family lived on a farm, removed from the nearest neighbors, so a heavy storm meant total isolation. After bringing in wood and bedding down the animals, the two boys went to bed early, when it was already snowing. After the storm, the boys dug a path to the barn—tunneling where the drifts were deepest—and were welcomed by the animals. That evening the family gathered at the hearth and enjoyed a roaring fire, warm cider, apples, and "nuts from brown October's wood."

Teaching Strategies

PROVIDING FOR CULTURAL DIFFERENCES   Students from Southern states and tropical countries may never have experienced snow. Ask them what they imagine being stuck in a snowstorm would be like and how they think they'd react to the experience.

PROVIDING FOR DIFFERENT LEVELS OF ABILITY   There should not be much difficulty for any readers in following the narrative line of the poem. Some students, however, may need help with allusions and imagery. You might encourage them to sketch their interpretations of a few objects or scenes: for example, the "clothesline posts" (lines 39–40); the tunnel (line 75); or the fire being laid (lines 120–126).

READING THE POEM   After you have introduced the poem, play the audiocassette recording or read the poem aloud. Have students listen for the details that make the storm vivid. Check for understanding by giving some line numbers and asking students to tell in their own words what picture is being presented in those lines. The sentence in lines 9–14 may be especially troublesome. Written in the normal prose fashion, the sentence would read: "A chill which no coat could shut out . . . (fore)told the coming of the snowstorm."

RETEACHING ALTERNATIVES   You might give students a group of words or phrases and ask them to state whether they describe something pleasant or something unpleasant. Then ask them to think of a word with comparable meaning that would have the opposite connotation. Substituting the new word for the old word should change the tone of the poem. For example, in line 54, "the old, familiar sight" could be changed to "the decrepit, boring sight." Refer students ahead to the section on connotations (text page 163) before starting the activity.

Responding to the Poem   Text page 160

Answers to the questions in the Pupil's Edition appear in the Annotated Teacher's Edition.

Writing About the Poem

For help in revising their compositions, refer students to **Grammar, Usage, and Mechanics: A Reference Guide** on text pages 1183–1228 at the back of their books.

A CRITICAL RESPONSE
Analyzing the Poem's Appeal   Before students begin to write, discuss the appeal of the clean, wholesome, simple, "romantic past" presented in *Snow-Bound*.

▶ CRITERIA FOR EVALUATING THE ASSIGNMENT   The paper gives at least one reason to explain the poem's popularity. Ideas are clearly stated and developed. Students address the question of whether today's media appeal to a "romantic past."

Analyzing Language and Style

ALLUSIONS
(1) Allusions to architecture appear in lines 62 and 65 ("a Chinese roof," "Pisa's leaning miracle"); (2) to literature in lines 75–80 ("Aladdin's wondrous cave"); (3) to history in line 90 ("Egypt's Amun"). Such allusions suggest that Whittier assumed his audience was educated and had a broad knowledge of world history and literature.

Extending the Poem

Students who enjoy the poem should be encouraged to read the complete version. They might report to the class, each student reading aloud a small section from later in the poem. Or students may describe one of the characters at the hearthside.

Objectives

1. To respond to the poem and interpret its message

2. To write a paragraph applying the shipwreck symbol to a human situation

3. To write an essay about contemporary parallels to the poem's message and purpose

4. To recognize the effects of word connotations

Introducing the Poem

This poem was written for the specific purpose of arousing readers to persuade the government to preserve the frigate *Constitution*. Thus its tone is important. The poem catches the reader's attention immediately and builds to the end, without letting up. Many strong accents in the poem create a tone of strong emotion, possibly even anger. The vowel sounds and the alliteration of "beneath," "battle," and "burst" sustain the intensity of the sound.

The emotional pitch is kept high through to the end, where the poem verges on the melodramatic with its "shattered hulk," its "nail to the mast her holy flag" (at the time the ship had no masts), and its calling on the "god of storms."

Here are the major elements of the poem:

- **Rhythm:** iambic tetrameter and trimeter
- **Rhyme:** abcbdefe
- **Significant techniques:** metaphor, symbolism, alliteration

BACKGROUND ON THE POEM In August 1830, the *Constitution* was thirty years old—more than twice the lifespan of the average wooden warship. A Navy report indicated it had a sound frame but needed "very extensive repairs." However, the Boston *Advertiser* on September 14, erroneously reported that the Navy had condemned the ship. What happened in the Holmes household on that day or the next is dramatically recreated by Catherine Drinker Bowen in her biography of Holmes, *Yankee from Olympus:*

> . . . Oliver, bursting in the door one afternoon, found [Abiel Holmes, his father] sitting moodily at his desk, trying to compose a letter to the *Boston Daily Advertiser*. . . .

Oliver went upstairs and, sitting down by the western window, got out pen and paper. The lines poured from him, swept from him in a tide. It was as though he were writing someone else's poem, dictated carefully by its author and transcribed by Oliver Holmes. . . .

It was late when he took the poem downstairs . . . . His father was still at his desk. . . . Silently Oliver laid the poem on the desk and left the room.

A moment later his father called him. When Oliver came in, Abiel Holmes was standing by the desk, the poem in his hand. He began to speak, and his voice choked. With enormous surprise and a great lift of the heart. Oliver, looking up, saw tears in his father's eyes, saw that the hand holding his verses was trembling.

THE LITERAL MEANING In lines 1–12 the narrator reviews in generalized but heroic terms the noble history of the frigate. In the next four lines he acknowledges that the ship will have no further victories. In the final stanza he says that it is better that she should be given "to the god of storms" and have an ending befitting her victorious career, rather than be broken up.

Teaching Strategies

PROVIDING FOR CULTURAL DIFFERENCES Students from military, especially Navy, families will respond most immediately to the emotional pull of the poem. Other students may be able to find in their own background, or in present-day America, something comparable to "Old Ironsides" which they would fight to save from destruction. Ask them to suggest something that means as much to them as the frigate meant to the people of Boston, and to explain why it does.

PROVIDING FOR DIFFERENT LEVELS OF ABILITY Students may have difficulty understanding that the diction of the poem is deliberately elevated for purposes of arousing the reader's emotions and keeping them at a high pitch. You might have them replace some of the phrases with others less emotionally loaded. "Tattered ensign" might be replaced with "ragged flag." The second line might be changed to "It's been up there for a while." Reading a stanza or two in the new version will help to convince students that the diction in the original does, in fact, contribute greatly to the success of the poem.

More advanced readers may want to examine the history of the *Constitution* and try to connect some of the imagery, such as ''the vanquished foe,'' with actual events.

READING THE POEM Students may be interested to know that this poem was written rapidly in a burst of emotion. Understanding the circumstances, they will be prepared to find examples of hyperbole, and diction that arouses a high pitch of emotion.

After reading the poem aloud, start off the discussion by asking students how the famous first line gets its impact. They may point to the alliteration, the strongly stressed first two syllables, the image of the ''tattered ensign'' (not just any old flag!), and above all to the verbal irony.

Keep the students' attention focused on the flag through discussion of the first stanza; it becomes a ''banner in the sky.'' Finally, it becomes a ''meteor of the ocean air'' sweeping the clouds—or, if you interpret ''meteor'' to mean the ship itself, the flag is the topmost part of her.

RETEACHING ALTERNATIVES Some students may respond emotionally to the poem and enjoy it without wanting to analyze its structure or its technique. You might point out that at the time Holmes wrote the poem, Old Ironsides lay in Boston Harbor with no masts or rigging, and presumably no ensign, and in need of a great deal of new planking as well as new sails and anchor cable. Have them look once more at the specific descriptions that Holmes gives of the ship, and compare them with the reality of the ship's decrepit appearance.

Responding to the Poem   Text page 163

Answers to the questions in the Pupil's Edition appear in the Annotated Teacher's Edition.

Writing About the Poem

For help in revising their compositions, refer students to **Grammar, Usage, and Mechanics: A Reference Guide** on text pages 1183–1228 at the back of their books.

A CREATIVE RESPONSE
1. Applying the Poem to Other Situations Read and briefly discuss the writing assignment with students before they begin to write. Clarify parts of the ship as necessary.

▶ CRITERIA FOR EVALUATING THE ASSIGNMENT The paragraph makes logical use of a ship's parts in human terms; for example, flag for hair/a hat, thunders for a voice, sails for garments, and so on. The situation might involve providing care and rehabilitation for a person who is injured, ill, or elderly.

A CRITICAL RESPONSE
2. Finding Contemporary Parallels You might discuss restoration of the Statue of Liberty or appeals of the 1980's related to paying belated honor to Vietnam War soldiers. Students may brainstorm contemporary forms of expression in such appeals (TV ads, songs, letters to the editor and to Congressional representatives).

▶ CRITERIA FOR EVALUATING THE ASSIGNMENT The essay is at least one paragraph long. It names at least two issues (local or national) that have inspired appeals to honor the past, and describes the methods of communication used rather than poetry to make the appeals.

Analyzing Language and Style

CONNOTATIONS
The original phrases, and some possible responses:

1. *meteor of the ocean air:* shrapnel of the ocean air
2. *red with heroes' blood:* red with children's blood
3. *harpies of the shore:* realists of the shore
4. *eagle of the sea:* old hulk of the sea
5. *shattered hulk:* worthless hulk
6. *holy flag:* meaningless flag
7. *threadbare sail:* ragged sail

Extending the Poem

Old Ironsides lies today in Boston Harbor. Some of your students may have visited Boston and had a tour of the ship and a look at the museum on the grounds. Ask them to share their impressions and any literature they may have brought back with them. Students who enjoyed the poem will be interested in knowing more about the history and present status of the frigate. You might recommend they read *A Most Fortunate Ship, A Narrative History of ''Old Ironsides''* by Tyrone G. Martin, who was captain of the frigate from 1974 to 1978 (The Globe Pequot Press, Chester, CT 06412, 1982).

THE CHAMBERED NAUTILUS

Text page 164

Objectives

1. To interpret and respond to the poem's metaphor and imagery

2. To write an essay responding to the poem's message

3. To write a paragraph analyzing the poem's appeal

4. To identify archaic language and inverted syntax and recast them into contemporary English

Introducing the Poem

Here are the major elements of the poem:

- **Rhythm:** iambic pentameter, trimeter, and hexameter
- **Rhyme:** aabbbcc
- **Figures of speech:** allusion (sirens, Triton); metaphor (the nautilus for growth of the human spirit)
- **Significant techniques:** alliteration, apostrophe

BACKGROUND ON THE POEM The poem first appeared at the close of a section of *The Autocrat of the Breakfast Table* in 1858. Holmes seemed to have been proud of the poem.

THE LITERAL MEANING The narrator reminds the reader of the legendary quality of the nautilus, which is now "wrecked" and "rent." He tells in the third stanza how the animal passed each year from one chamber to a larger one. In the fourth stanza, he thanks the dead nautilus for the lesson its shell teaches. In the final stanza he draws the lesson: that his soul should leave its "low-vaulted past" and "build . . . more stately mansions" until it casts off its "outgrown shell" and becomes free.

Teaching Strategies

PROVIDING FOR CULTURAL DIFFERENCES The poem's archaic words will cause difficulties for LEP/ESL students. Go over some of the vocabulary (the glossed words and *wont, crypt, thee, thou, thine*) before reading the poem aloud.

PROVIDING FOR DIFFERENT LEVELS OF ABILITY For less advanced readers, you might read the headnote aloud and discuss the photograph, which shows the pearly,

chambered *inside* of a nautilus shell. Perhaps a student can add some facts in a brief oral report from information gathered from an encyclopedia or science text. More advanced readers will enjoy analyzing the rhythm and rhyme scheme of the poem and discussing how it supports the sense and tone of the poem.

READING THE POEM Before you read the poem aloud, tell students what to listen for in the structure of the poem and in its imagery.

In discussing the poem, ask students how its sounds and imagery affect the reader. Alliteration and assonance give the first two stanzas a soft musical quality in keeping with the imagery from myth and folklore.

The movement from long to short lines and back again surprises and pleases the listener by introducing a rhyme sooner than anticipated at first and then prolonging the wait for a rhyme while introducing alliteration (dim-dreaming; was-wont; irised-ceiling-sunless).

Ask students to describe, in terms of their own experience, what they think Holmes may have had in mind in the last stanza. Can they make the analogy between the nautilus's leaving its "low-vaulted past" and some progress they have made in the last year—something they have learned or achieved, perhaps?

Students may object to the moralizing of the last two stanzas, and be reminded of the Bryant poetry they have read earlier; or they may like it. You might point out that the best modern poets often imply a moral without making it explicit.

RETEACHING ALTERNATIVES You might have students in groups or individually "translate" the language of the poem, keeping the meaning the same, but getting rid of archaic language, dropping some of the modifiers that may complicate the sentences, and reducing the statements of the poem to simplified contemporary English. Then have the entire new version of the poem read aloud. Students will see that it has lost its poetry; but they may more easily understand what is literal and what is metaphor, what is observed scientific description and what is imagined. The poetic value of the original version may then be more apparent to them.

Responding to the Poem

Text page 166

Answers to the questions in the Pupil's Edition appear in the Annotated Teacher's Edition.

Writing About the Poem

For help in revising their compositions, refer students to **Grammar, Usage, and Mechanics: A Reference Guide** on text pages 1183–1228 at the back of their books.

A CREATIVE RESPONSE

1. Taking Another Point of View Have students look up "chambered nautilus" in a dictionary or science text before they write the paragraph. This is an abstract assignment that should be optional. More advanced students may enjoy its challenge; others may be stymied by it.

▶ CRITERIA FOR EVALUATING THE ASSIGNMENT The paragraph should contain some appropriate scientific impressions, questions, and conclusions—e.g., The spiral seems to develop according to a mathematical formula. How do you know what size to make your chambers? Nautiluses are somehow "programmed" to fulfill their destiny.

A CRITICAL RESPONSE

2. Responding to a "Message" In discussion, lead students to see how carefully Holmes builds toward his moral, but do not force your view. Students should feel free to choose either opinion as long as they support their view.

▶ CRITERIA FOR EVALUATING THE ASSIGNMENT The paragraph states a clear opinion as to whether the poem has a tacked-on moral or is "all of a piece," and uses specific details from the poem to support this opinion.

3. Analyzing the Poem's Appeal Before students begin to write, discuss what they find attractive about the poem in terms of both its message and its sounds. Most students will say that the poem has endured because of its message. Ask for a clearly worded paragraph with a topic sentence.

▶ CRITERIA FOR EVALUATING THE ASSIGNMENT The paper is a coherent paragraph with topic sentence and supporting details explaining why the poem still appeals to readers.

Analyzing Language and Style

POETIC AND ARCHAIC LANGUAGE

Here are some archaic words and modern substitutes:

feign (imagine)	*thine* (yours)
main (sea)	*thou* (you)
bark (boat)	*beheld* (saw)
wont (accustomed)	*art* (are)
thee (you)	

Putting the substitutions into the poem makes it sound more modern, but the poem loses some of its appeal.

Normal English sentence order for sample lines with inverted syntax:

"Its webs of living gauze unfurl no more" (line 8)

"The ship of pearl is wrecked" (line 9)

"Lies revealed before thee" (line 13)

"Stole through its shining archway with soft step" (line 19)

Rephrasing to normal sentence order reduces the archaic effect; the rhyme pattern of the poem is, however, lost.

Four of the archaic words listed in the exercise are used today in other senses:

feign: pretend
main: principal
bark: tree covering, dog's vocalization
art: skill; creativity

Extending the Poem

Have students compare the last twelve lines of Robert Frost's "Birches" (text page 658) with this poem. In both poems the poets use natural objects as metaphors for aspects of life. Ask students to decide if the message each poet gives is similar or different. (In the Holmes poem the end is freedom from being earthbound, whereas in "Birches," Frost says "Earth's the right place for love.") Allow students to explore differences and similarities in theme and technique. Would they agree, for example, that the message is more explicit in "The Chambered Nautilus," or do they feel that both poets are making their message quite clear?

James Russell Lowell

SHE CAME AND WENT

Objectives

1. To respond to a poem about a child's death

2. To identify similes and images

3. To write an essay comparing and contrasting two poems

Introducing the Poem

Here are the major elements of the poem:

- **Rhythm:** four-line stanzas, iambic tetrameter
- **Rhyme:** abab cbcb dbdb ebeb fbfb
- **Figures of speech:** similes, metaphor (life's last oil), symbolism (angel, tent)
- **Significant techniques:** use of a repeated line as a refrain in the first four stanzas, slightly varied in the final stanza

BACKGROUND ON THE POEM   Blanche, born on the last day of 1845, was the Lowells's first child. Biographer Martin Duberman says, "Lowell vowed to bring Blanche up as independent as possible of all mankind . . . a great, strong, vulgar, mud-pudding-baking, tree-climbing, little wench." Fifteen months later, Blanche died, according to Mrs. Longfellow of "rapid teething." Soon after the child's death, Lowell wrote this poem.

THE LITERAL MEANING   The speaker tells of his grief at the brief life of his daughter. In the final stanza he declares that even when death approaches and his eyes grow dim, he will be brightened by her memory.

Teaching Strategies

PROVIDING FOR CULTURAL DIFFERENCES   Students from all backgrounds can relate to the death of a child.

PROVIDING FOR DIFFERENT LEVELS OF ABILITY   You might ask students to find substitutes for *came* and *went* in the middle three stanzas. While this may disrupt the rhythm and destroy the rhyme, it should help them to understand the force of the simple diction and of the repetition, if they read their new version aloud. Examples,

"was born and died," "arrived and departed," "appeared and disappeared," etc.

READING THE POEM   Read the poem aloud as students follow in their books. You might want to examine the similes in the first three stanzas with the students, since these can be difficult to follow. They may not all understand, for example, that "then leaves unbent" (line 2) means "when the bird leaves, the twig no longer bends." Ask students why Lowell uses *twig* instead of *branch*, and why he has the bird *sing*. How good a simile is this to explain his memory? In the second stanza students may not understand that the syntax reverses subject and verb, so that in simplified prose the lines would read: "As some lake, unruffled by the breeze, mirrors the peacefulness of the sky."

RETEACHING ALTERNATIVES   Students who continue to have difficulty with the poem are probably confused by the vocabulary or the syntax. You might have them work in small groups to paraphrase each stanza.

Responding to the Poem   Text page 168

Answers to the questions in the Pupil's Edition appear in the Annotated Teacher's Edition.

Writing About the Poem

For help in revising their compositions, refer students to **Grammar, Usage, and Mechanics: A Reference Guide** on text pages 1183–1228 at the back of their books.

A CRITICAL RESPONSE

Comparing Two Poems on the Same Theme   As preparation for writing, review the central image in Longfellow's poem (a white cross of snow in a mountain ravine) and Lowell's similes that begin stanzas 1–3 (a trembling twig, the way a mountain lake holds the sky, the suddenness of spring and blossoms). Note Longfellow's use of sonnet form while Lowell chose four-line stanzas.

▶ CRITERIA FOR EVALUATING THE ASSIGNMENT   The paragraph identifies the images and notes that all are images of Nature. Lowell adds the image of a dying lamp. Students comment on structure (a sonnet vs. five four-line stanzas) and tell which poem evokes a more vivid image of the loved one who was lost.

Extending the Poem

Read aloud John Crowe Ransom's ''Bells for John White-side's Daughter'' (text page 673). Ask students to compare the two poems (both are about the death of a young girl) and to consider some of their differences. (Ransom's poem has a much less mournful, almost a light tone. Ransom's diction is more that of natural-sounding prose. Lowell uses the same pattern of rhyme, figurative language, and repetition in each stanza; Ransom only repeats the rhyme. The predominant figure of speech in Lowell's poem is simile; in Ransom's, metaphor.)

FROM A FABLE FOR CRITICS

Text page 170

Objectives

1. To respond to a satirical poem
2. To identify and interpret paradoxes
3. To interpret allusions
4. To write a summary of a verse and an evaluation of writers

Introducing the Poem

It is sometimes difficult for adolescents to see shades of gray. Often they see their peers, their parents, and other adults in extreme ways, either all good or all bad. Tell them that in this poem Lowell criticizes his peers, saying both good and bad things about them, and expects them to like it.

Here are the major elements of the poem:

- **Rhyme:** rhymed couplets with an occasional extra rhymed line
- **Rhythm:** anapestic tetrameter
- **Significant techniques:** paradox (lines 1–18 dealing with Hawthorne, the image of the rough oak blooming with ''a single anemone,'' or the image of Nature fashioning him with clay but also using ''finer-grained stuff''); allusion; humor

BACKGROUND ON THE POEM   Once published, the ''Fable'' was widely read and admired and became immensely popular. Even today it is thought to be one of Lowell's finest works. The section on Hawthorne was particularly praised. Predictably, Poe was not so enthusiastic.

THE LITERAL MEANING   Lowell aims well-meaning satire at Hawthorne and Poe, and chides Poe and Cornelius Mathews for their harshness toward Longfellow.

Teaching Strategies

PROVIDING FOR CULTURAL DIFFERENCES   Make sure students use the glosses to identify unfamiliar names. Have someone explain ''a descent from Olympus'' (line 5) to students unfamiliar with ancient Greek mythology.

PROVIDING FOR DIFFERENT LEVELS OF ABILITY ESL and LEP students, who usually have trouble identifying meters, will enjoy line 38, since many of them, like readers of ''common sense'' in the nineteenth century, would be likely to ''damn meters.'' When you read Poe in Unit Four, you might ask your students to decide how true Lowell's criticism is in lines 35–40. You might also call attention to Lowell's own meter in this poem. Anapestic tetrameter tends to be singsong. Do students think that while Lowell was ridiculing Poe for his use of rhythm, he might have had his tongue in his cheek because of his own?

More advanced readers might wish to read more of the ''Fable'' and report to the class or read aloud short passages they particularly like.

READING THE POEM   You might want to start by telling students that Lowell deals first in his criticism with Hawthorne, then with Poe, and finally, briefly, with Longfellow. Read the poem aloud, and ask students to listen for Lowell's opinion of all three poets.

Discuss the metaphor in lines 6–9, and have them note that the rhythm and diction lend themselves to a tone that is not altogether serious. But be sure they observe the paradoxes, especially in the Hawthorne section, and that they note the marked contrast in the Poe section between lines 39 and 40, where the tone changes from modest approval to criticism a good deal more serious than ''two-fifths sheer fudge.''

RETEACHING ALTERNATIVES   Since the poem moves quite rapidly from one idea to another, with adequate but not strong transition, students who have had a difficult time understanding it might try to paraphrase it.

Have them work with a partner or small group. Each group can be responsible for paraphrasing one section: lines 1–5, lines 6–9 (or lines 6–12), lines 10–12, lines 13–18, lines 35–40, and lines 41–46, or 41 to the end. In their paraphrasing, help students determine whether their section is mainly serious or humorous, figurative or literal, or a combination. This exercise will help you discover and address any problems the students have with vocabulary, syntax, or allusions. Also, it should help students understand the shifting tone of the poem.

Responding to the Poem   Text page 171

Answers to the questions in the Pupil's Edition appear in the Annotated Teacher's Edition.

Writing About the Poem

For help in revising their compositions, refer students to **Grammar, Usage, and Mechanics: A Reference Guide** on text pages 1183–1228 at the back of their books.

A CRITICAL RESPONSE
Summarizing a Verse   Read Lowell's self-assessment aloud, checking for literal understanding. Discuss other writers the students feel have not learned the distinction between singing and preaching, but ask students to focus their writing on summarizing Lowell's self-criticism.

▶ CRITERIA FOR EVALUATING THE ASSIGNMENT   The summary notes that Lowell's attempts to use meter and rhyme sometimes weigh down his work and that he must learn to make his work sound less forced (to "sing" instead of "preach").

Extending the Poem

Lowell acknowledged that he wrote the poem rapidly. You might suggest that students try their hand at anapestic tetrameter couplets. Their subjects might be a humorous criticism of a book they have had to read in English class or a speaker they have heard at an assembly. Or perhaps they can just tell a brief story or anecdote. Many students will feel more confident about this assignment if they collaborate with a partner to think of a topic and something to say, and to brainstorm ideas for rhymes.

Warn students who have not tried to write rhyming couplets that it is important to end the first line of the couplet with a word which can easily be rhymed. Those students who are serious about the effort might want to buy an inexpensive rhyming dictionary at the local bookstore or use one at the library.

THE AMERICAN LANGUAGE   Text page 172

This special essay focuses on the creation of Webster's dictionary and the *American Spelling Book* as early attempts to provide some reasonable guidelines for accuracy in the spelling, pronunciation, and usage of American English. Students will gain insight into the reasons for the "schoolmastering of English" and the personality of the man whose name still appears in the titles of dictionaries in homes, libraries, and classrooms across the nation.

Assign the essay for students to read as homework. Encourage students to think about the pros and cons of regulating language: its impact on every form of communication from the labels on favorite products, or their favorite television and movie features, newspapers and the mass media, to simple communication between friends. Then have students collaborate in small groups to complete the Analyzing Language activity that follows the essay. You can assign one activity to each group, who will present their findings to the class.

Analyzing Language

Text page 176

1. Answers will vary. Possibilities include the following:

writers	essays
introduced	spelling
preference	possible
force	reezon
influence	offered
ancestors	full

2. Lists will vary. Possibilities for *a* included *late, hat,* and *ball;* possibilities for *e* include *let* and *equal;* possibilities for *i* include *if* and *ice.*
3. Student lists will vary. Possibilities for the first list include *now* and *slow, rough* and *bough, read* and *bread.* Possibilities for the second list include *higher* and *fire, soul* and *mole, kite* and *night.*
4. Answers will vary. Some examples include: *quik, rite* (right), *brite, slo, tonite.*
5. Answers will vary. Possibilities for school subjects include Fizikle Edukashun, Inglish, Jermin, Aljibruh, Kalkulus. Possibilities for jobs include riter, enjineer, plummer, karpenter, shef. List other suggestions on the board. Also, check to see whether students can understand the simplified spellings in their partners' paragraphs.

EXERCISES IN CRITICAL THINKING AND WRITING   Text page 177

RESPONDING TO LITERATURE
After students have read the prewriting instructions and have written thesis statements, you might want to have them share their comments and questions with each other in class discussion. You may also want to have some students read their thesis statements aloud before they go on to write the body of the essay. Assure students that they need not cover all five topics under Background. However, they should try to explain their responses by referring to details in the poem or quoting lines or phrases.

▶ CRITERIA FOR EVALUATING THE ASSIGNMENT   Students' essays should express their own personal responses to the poem. Responses should be supported by citing details from the poem.

Further Reading

Works listed are suitable for both students and teachers unless the annotation ends with the note [Teachers].

Bowen, Catherine Drinker. *Yankee from Olympus* (Houghton Mifflin, 1962). A detailed biography of Justice Oliver Wendell Holmes, Jr., which also deals with many other figures of the period.

Brooks, Van Wyck. *The Flowering of New England: 1815–1865* (Houghton Mifflin, 1981). A noted history containing chapters on Longfellow, Lowell, Holmes, and others. [Teachers]

Duberman, Martin. *James Russell Lowell* (Houghton Mifflin, 1966). A biography presenting Lowell not only as a poet, but also as an intellectual leader, reformer, and diplomat.

Holberg, Ruth Langland. *John Greenleaf Whittier* (Thomas Y. Crowell, 1958) A small volume geared toward young readers (short chapters, large print, appealing drawings by Aldren A. Watson).

Parrington, Vernon L. *The Romantic Revolution in America, 1800–1860,* Volume II of *Main Currents in American Thought* (Harcourt Brace Jovanovich, 1955). Definitive account of the Romantic Period, with chapters on Irving, Bryant, Holmes, and others in this unit. [Teachers]

Sullivan, Wilson. *New England Men of Letters* (Macmillan, 1972). Chapters devoted to ten writers: Emerson, Thoreau, Hawthorne, Dana, Melville, Prescott, Parkman, Longfellow, Lowell, and Holmes.

THE AMERICAN RENAISSANCE
FIVE MAJOR WRITERS

Text page 179

Teaching the American Renaissance Unit

The range of the five writers represented in this unit is considerable, yet each is essentially Romantic, developed within the cultural climate of the bold, new, wilderness-exploring American nation. None of them deals very much with ordinary life. Hawthorne, of the five, dwells most upon male/female relationships, but almost always in a historical or supernatural setting, highly charged with symbolism. Poe employs the emotion of love—usually lost love—primarily as a catalyst to terror. Women scarcely figure in Melville's work at all. And while Thoreau writes about the most humdrum daily occupations—hoeing beans, counting pennies—he is decidedly not writing about the life of the average Concord citizen; he is elevating the humdrum to the level of meditative bliss.

The similarities and differences among these writers can be seen in their different relationships to Transcendentalism. Transcendentalism was, according to the scholar Perry Miller, primarily a religious rather than a literary movement, but two of its prominent adherents were among the greatest of American prose stylists, and the documents of the movement have survived in literary form. Essentially, Transcendentalists sought to create a new religious consciousness that would exhibit the freedom and democracy of the new nation, as opposed to conventional religion, which they felt to be an ossified European product, or to science, which they distrusted as dehumanizing. Emerson and the others felt that the way to God led through the self: contemplation of one's own thoughts would lead one to a perception of the Infinite. Donald N. Koster, in *Transcendentalism in America* (Twayne, 1975), finds four major historical influences contributing to this philosophy: (1) Platonism, which held that there exists a universal Good, of which the things of the material world are a mere shadow, and which can be reached through intellectual contemplation; (2) Romanticism, which glorified the self and the emotions rather than society and reason; (3) Asian religious works such as the *Vedas* and the *Upanishads,* which teach that the individual self contains a piece of the universal Self; and (4) the Puritan heritage, which made Transcendentalists into ethical idealists deeply concerned with questions of good and evil.

Emerson is the central Transcendentalist, perpetually seeking the God within himself. Thoreau, his protégé, shares Emerson's main beliefs and his aphoristic quality, but takes to its furthest point the search for an ecstatic experience in the outer world of nature, while Emerson mostly contemplates his own mind. Of the three fiction writers in the unit, none embraced Transcendentalism (perhaps because good fiction requires intellectual flexibility), yet all show its influence, since it was a major element of the intellectual climate of the times. Hawthorne, who was closest to the movement, was ambivalent about it. He lived for a while at the Utopian community Brook Farm, but soured on it, and satirized it in *The Blithedale Romance.* Melville outwardly mocked Transcendentalism, yet nothing is more Transcendentalist than Ahab's great line, "Strike through the mask!" The difference was that what Emerson and Thoreau found behind the mask of the external world was benign, while what Melville found was malign or, at best, indifferent and unfathomable. Melville, the ex-sailor, quested outward for the truth, while the Transcendentalists quested inward. Poe, more removed from the New England scene, expressed scorn for the movement, but a late philosophical essay of his, *Eureka,* comes to the rather Transcendentalist conclusion that everything is part of God and that God is reflected in the human mind.

The contrast between Hawthorne and Poe is striking. Both wrote symbolic, often supernatural, tales filled with atmosphere, but Hawthorne was burdened by a sense of sin that was a bequest from the Puritan ethic. Poe was burdened not by history or morality but by the sheer terror of the lonely human soul facing the fact of death, by the sheer power of his own imagination. Poe's settings are often vague, more like mere window-dressing, while the background of Puritan New England is central to Hawthorne. Alfred Kazin, in *An American Procession* (Knopf, 1984), identifies Hawthorne with the sense of guilt and Poe with the sense of anxiety. Kazin considers Poe a supremely skillful professional, a virtuoso audience-manipulator, while Hawthorne, who probably possessed less verbal and imaginative talent, went deeper. In *The Scarlet Letter,* Kazin says, Hawthorne achieved the "unity of effect" that Poe preached.

Objectives of the American Renaissance Unit

1. To improve reading proficiency and expand vocabulary
2. To gain exposure to notable authors and their works
3. To define and identify significant literary techniques
4. To define and identify elements of nonfiction, fiction, and poetry
5. To interpret and respond to nonfiction, fiction, and poetry, orally and in writing
6. To practice the following critical thinking and writing skills:
   a. Comparing and contrasting literary forms
   b. Responding to a writer's views
   c. Paraphrasing a poem
   d. Analyzing and interpreting poetic elements
   e. Analyzing a poem
   f. Analyzing and evaluating persuasive writing

Introducing the American Renaissance Unit

It will be useful to devote some attention to the philosophy of Transcendentalism before reading the selections from Emerson and Thoreau. Students are usually quite receptive to the ideas of the movement when they are couched in simple twentieth-century English. Thoreau's individualism and "back to nature" creed are traditional favorites with young people, and while Emerson can seem a bit musty nowadays, his rebellion against old institutions places him on the side of youth.

Since Emerson, Thoreau, and Hawthorne were great believers in the value of keeping journals, this unit provides ample opportunities for students to write in journals of their own. You might suggest, as a journal entry in keeping with the spirit of this unit, that students write down their thoughts as to what material goods in the lives of Americans today seem truly essential, and what goods seem nonessential or dispensable.

Or you might ask them to do a quickwrite (see page 366 of these Teaching Notes) on the following topic: Imagine that they have the power to change their own lives completely, with no pre-existing social conditions. How would they choose to live? Some of their answers may reflect values similar to those of the Transcendentalists; others may be at the opposite end of the spectrum. The important thing, the Transcendentalists believed, is that each individual should think about the deepest questions of how to live, and should choose his or her own way of life through an act of individual freedom.

Ralph Waldo Emerson

Text page 187

FROM NATURE

Text page 191

Objectives

1. To interpret and respond to an essay's message

2. To identify and analyze images

3. To write an essay comparing two descriptions

4. To discuss the use of paradoxes

Introducing the Essay

The basic assumptions underlying Emerson's view of nature are described in this essay. These include Emerson's belief that God is always near to us and reveals Himself everywhere and at all times in nature. Within the individual lies a divinity that allows human intuition to behold God's spirit in nature. Also, there is a correspondence between natural law and moral law; by use of intuition, humans can see God's laws revealed in nature.

BACKGROUND ON THE ESSAY   The year 1836 was memorable in Emerson's life; it saw the birth of his first son, the initial meetings of the Transcendentalist Club, and the publication of his book *Nature,* which would become the "bible of American Transcendentalists." Emerson completed the first draft of the book in the same room in which Hawthorne would later write *Mosses from an Old Manse.*

SUMMARY   Emerson says that in nature, we are able to feel "the perpetual presence of the sublime." In the presence of nature, we can feel real delight in spite of sorrow. Nature gives us better, "higher" thoughts and emotions.

Teaching Strategies

PROVIDING FOR CULTURAL DIFFERENCES   Students' feelings about nature may vary depending on their backgrounds. Students from large urban centers may be unfamiliar with nature except in parks or resorts; they may feel that nature is glamorous but frightening. In contrast, students from rural areas may be so familiar with nature that they rarely pause to see its beauty. Even students' perceptions of what constitutes nature may vary. The same community, seen by people from three different backgrounds, could be called "the city," "the suburbs," or "the country." Point out that Emerson's view of nature, too, was at least partly the result of his background as a member of a highly cultured, leisured, landed gentry.

PROVIDING FOR DIFFERENT LEVELS OF ABILITY   Even advanced students will have some difficulty with Emerson's mystical concepts and rather antiquated diction. You might want to guide the class in composing paraphrases of passages that prove troublesome. For the thornier sentences and vocabulary words (such as *maugre*), paraphrases or definitions could be written on the board. You may want to divide the essay into smaller passages, each of which can be analyzed by a group of students. (The opening paragraph itself can be divided between two groups.)

READING THE ESSAY   The sermonlike quality of Emerson's style lends itself to oral reading, but the subtleties of his ideas are more suited to silent reading and re-reading. It is difficult to listen to an Emerson essay and comprehend it fully. You might want to read aloud only certain key passages, such as the one about the "transparent eyeball" (text page 192). Use paraphrase and discussion to clarify any passages that students find confusing.

RETEACHING ALTERNATIVES   In a review discussion session, let the students who have grasped Emerson's ideas explain them to those who have not. This might be done in small groups with students asking questions of an expert. Or an expert group of students can take on the challenge of reviewing Emerson's ideas.

Many students have difficulty with Emerson's philosophical metaphors. Ask them, as a quickwrite, to state as simply as possible what they think Emerson felt when he stood on a hill and looked at the sky.

Responding to the Essay

Text page 193

Answers to the questions in the Pupil's Edition appear in the Annotated Teacher's Edition.

Writing About the Essay

For help in revising their compositions, refer students to **Grammar, Usage, and Mechanics: A Reference Guide** on text pages 1183–1228 at the back of their books.

Comparing Two Descriptions   Encourage students, either individually or in groups, to make a prewriting chart of similarities (e.g., feelings of exhilaration) and differences (e.g., Emerson's focus on nature as a whole vs. Edwards's focus on a thunderstorm) before they write their essays. Remind students to refer to specific details in the essays.

▶ CRITERIA FOR EVALUATING THE ASSIGNMENT   The essay is arranged in a logical, coherent manner. It uses specific details from the essays of Edwards and Emerson to support points made about similarities and differences between the two writers' views of God, nature, and human beings.

Analyzing Language and Style

PARADOXES
Answers will vary. The following statements are representative responses.

1. I'm not alone when I read and write because I am sharing ideas with people who aren't in the room.
2. Every night the beauty and light of the stars remind us really to see the universe.
3. Most people take the sun for granted.
4. I'm so happy that the intensity almost makes me afraid.

Extending the Essay

Socrates said, "Flowers and trees teach me nothing, but people in a city do." Ask students what they think of this idea. What would Emerson reply to Socrates? A pair of volunteers might do a dialogue as the rest of the class listens to decide if they are accurately portraying Socrates's and Emerson's views. Listeners may also think of questions they'd like to ask Emerson or Socrates.

FROM **SELF-RELIANCE**   Text page 194

Objectives

1. To respond to a famous essay about individualism
2. To write an essay on a limited topic
3. To write an essay responding to the writer's views
4. To analyze figures of speech

Introducing the Essay

Here are the main ideas of the essay:

- Imitation of others is ignorance; we must take ourselves "for better, for worse."
- Only as individuals do we know what is best for us or what we are capable of doing.
- People only "half express" themselves because they fear that what they have to say is not great.
- We must put our hearts into our work if we are to feel relieved and satisfied with it.
- We must trust ourselves and trust the divinity within each of us.
- Society is "in conspiracy" against the individual and demands that we conform to its "names" and "customs."
- To be fully human, one must be a nonconformist.

- The person who is always consistent has nothing to do in life but follow others.
- To be great is to be misunderstood.

BACKGROUND ON THE ESSAY   It will help students appreciate Emerson's philosophy if they know that it arose, to some extent, out of his experiences in his own life. His father's death, when Emerson was eight, forced him to look to himself as a spiritual guide, and to seek role models in more remote sources, such as the Hindu sages who wrote the *Upanishads*. (Emerson's theory is to some extent a transplanting, into individualistic America, of Hindu ideas about the relationship between the individual soul, or "atman," and the world-soul.) Emerson practiced what he preached, in that he resigned his ministry at the Second Church of Boston over a matter of conscience.

SUMMARY   Emerson speaks of an individualism and goodness that have always been part of the American character. He espouses nonconformity and self-reliance, finds sanctity in the individual mind, and calls upon us to express ourselves strongly rather than diffidently.

Teaching Strategies

PROVIDING FOR CULTURAL DIFFERENCES   Students should become aware that different cultures place different values on nonconformity versus conformity and individuality versus community. Anglo-American cultures are generally more individual-oriented than other cultures, so students from other ethnic backgrounds may have grown up with strong pressures to fulfill the expectations of their communities. On the other hand, their families' decision to emigrate to a new country demands a high degree of self-reliance. It might be fruitful to discuss the various forms of conformity and nonconformity students have experienced or observed. Ask them to describe examples of self-reliance in the lives of their families, neighbors, and friends.

PROVIDING FOR DIFFERENT LEVELS OF ABILITY
After the complexities of ''Nature,'' ''Self-Reliance'' is relatively clear and straightforward in style. Students who have trouble with the abstract concepts in the essay will be more comfortable if the discussion is shifted to a more concrete level. Draw students into a discussion of specific examples of self-reliant behavior that they know from life. You might also play the audiocassette recording that is available for this selection.

READING THE ESSAY
Have students define the word *self*, writing suggested definitions on the board. Then have students think of words that begin with *self* and list these on the board under two columns—words with positive meanings or connotations and words with negative ones. You might conclude the discussion with a close look at the word *self-reliance*. What are the meanings of this word? When are people called upon to exhibit self-reliance? Have students been self-reliant? If so, when and why? What was the result of their self-reliance? Was it a positive or a negative experience? Do we tend too much to ''follow the crowd,'' and what happens when we do (or don't)?

RETEACHING ALTERNATIVES
Students who still have trouble understanding Emerson's view of self-reliance might benefit from a quickwrite. Ask them to write, in their own words and without reference to Emerson's essays, their own views on nonconformity and on the importance of being true to oneself. Since Emerson's vision of self-reliance has helped shape the values of contemporary America, there are likely to be significant points of agreement between his vision and the students' own.

Responding to the Essay   Text page 195

Answers to the questions in the Pupil's Edition appear in the Annotated Teacher's Edition.

Writing About the Essay

For help in revising their compositions, refer students to **Grammar, Usage, and Mechanics: A Reference Guide** on text pages 1183–1228 at the back of their books.

A CREATIVE RESPONSE
1. Writing an Essay   Help students choose the topic on which they have the strongest views by discussing the meaning of Emerson's five statements and eliciting examples that illustrate each.

▶ CRITERIA FOR EVALUATING THE ASSIGNMENT   The essay reflects the writer's personal views on the selected topic. The essay uses examples or reasons to support its theme. It does not stray to other topics.

A CRITICAL RESPONSE
2. Writing a Response   Read through the writing assignment with the students. Point out that its three basic questions suggest a way to organize the three-paragraph essay. Emphasize that there are no ''right'' or ''wrong'' responses.

▶ CRITERIA FOR EVALUATING THE ASSIGNMENT   The essay addresses the three questions in the assignment. Students express their opinions clearly and support their opinions with examples and reasons.

Analyzing Language and Style

FIGURATIVE LANGUAGE
1. **a.** making the best of one's own self
   b. the heart
   c. human beings in the hands of the Almighty
   d. society
   e. hard, clear words
2. It is a string made for strength rather than beauty. *Silken, golden*, or *silver* suggests beauty or value, but not the strength for daily life that *iron* suggests.
3. The metaphor suggests that fear or embarrassment at changing one's mind is like a mental hobgoblin. A hobgoblin is a sort of ''bogeyman,'' a mischievous spirit or elf. A ''little'' mind is one too limited to see a new point of view. An example of a ''wise'' consistency is for a teacher to use consistent, announced grading practices. An example of a ''foolish'' consistency is to stick to one's first position on a ballot issue when new information shows that the opposite position fits the facts better.

Extending the Essay

The decade of the 1970's was properly called the ''Me Decade,'' after the title of an essay by Tom Wolfe. Some social critics feel that unbridled self-interest has been largely responsible for insider-trading scandals and other manifestations of a decline in social cohesion in America today. What would Emerson say to these critics? How would he react to the modern social environment? For purposes of an informal debate, you might divide the class into two groups, one supporting Emersonian self-reliance in light of modern developments, and one opposing it.

CONCORD HYMN

Objectives

1. To respond to a famous poem about the American Revolution
2. To identify and analyze apostrophe, hyperbole, and personification
3. To write a letter responding to the poem
4. To write a paraphrase of the poem

Introducing the Poem

This poem was written to commemorate the bravery of the Minutemen who fought the British troops at Concord in April 1775.

Here are the major elements of the poem:

- **Rhythm:** iambic tetrameter
- **Rhyme:** abab cdcd
- **Significant techniques:** alliteration, internal rhyme, apostrophe, hyperbole

THE LITERAL MEANING   The first stanza recalls the events of April 1775 and praises the heroic spirit of the "embattled farmers." The second stanza says that both foe and conqueror are dead and that the bridge is now gone. The third stanza states the occasion for the poem, the dedication of a stone marker to the memory of these men of Concord. The fourth stanza asks God to see that time and nature protect the marker.

Teaching Strategies

PROVIDING FOR CULTURAL DIFFERENCES   Students whose families arrived in America recently, or whose ancestors were enslaved, may wish to discuss what their people's struggles for freedom have in common with the struggles of the American Colonists.

PROVIDING FOR DIFFERENT LEVELS OF ABILITY Some students will need careful explanations of such phrases as "embattled farmers," "votive stone," and "spare the shaft," as well as of Emerson's rhetorical devices. You might also need to emphasize that the poem describes two separate historical events: the battle at Concord and the later commemoration of the memorial stone.

READING THE POEM   Most students will have already heard the fourth line of this poem. After this line you may want to stop to discuss the meaning of the phrase, "the shot heard round the world." This is a good poem to have a student read aloud. Or you might ask a different student to read each stanza.

RETEACHING ALTERNATIVES   Students who still have trouble visualizing the setting of the poem or understanding Emerson's plea to "Time and Nature" may gain understanding if you ask them to paraphrase, either orally or in a quickwrite, the scene of the poem and the speaker's relationship to that scene.

You might have students work in small groups to create a collage or poster that commemorates some event in American history. For a collage, they might include photographs, poems, song lyrics, maps, objects—anything that suggests the event in a patriotic way, as "Concord Hymn" does.

Responding to the Poem

Answers to the questions in the Pupil's Edition appear in the Annotated Teacher's Edition.

Writing About the Poem

For help in revising their compositions, refer students to **Grammar, Usage, and Mechanics: A Reference Guide** on text pages 1183–1228 at the back of their books.

A CREATIVE RESPONSE
1. Writing a Letter   Discuss with the class the words and phrases that would be especially moving for a veteran of Concord, and the added effect created by hearing the poem sung to a solemn melody. If any student knows the melody, ask him or her to teach it to the class so students may sing it through before they write.

▶ CRITERIA FOR EVALUATING THE ASSIGNMENT   The paper is written in first person and in letter form. It reveals the writer's emotions and memories.

A CRITICAL RESPONSE
2. Paraphrasing the Poem   As a prewriting activity, have students list the archaic or old-fashioned words to replace, missing words to supply, inverted words to rearrange, and figurative expressions to rephrase literally.

▶ CRITERIA FOR EVALUATING THE ASSIGNMENT   Paraphrases will vary. Here is a sample paraphrase:

Stanza 1: The fighting farmers once stood beside the crude bridge across this river and fired shots reported worldwide.

Stanza 2: Since then the fighters on both sides have died, and the ruined bridge has been swept away by the river.

Stanza 3: Today we are placing a stone marker on the riverbank so the memory of that battle will last even when our children are dead, like our ancestors.

Stanza 4: God, you gave these men the courage to die for our freedom. Please see that time and weather spare this monument we erect in honor of them and you.

THE RHODORA

Text page 198

Objectives

1. To respond to the sound effects and message of the poem
2. To identify and interpret personification and apostrophe
3. To analyze the poem's metrical structure and rhyme scheme
4. To write an essay comparing and contrasting two philosophies of nature
5. To rewrite inverted lines in normal word order

Introducing the Poem

In this poem Emerson says that beauty needs no excuse for being. He uses the rhodora, a New England forest flower, to exemplify beauty. Ask students to think of some object that exemplifies beauty to them.

Here are the major elements of the poem:

- **Rhythm:** iambic pentameter
- **Rhyme:** aabbcdcd eeffghgh
- **Theme:** Everything in Nature is God's creation.
- **Significant techniques:** apostrophe, personification, alliteration

THE LITERAL MEANING The speaker of the poem says that in May, while walking in the woods, he found the fresh rhodora in a secluded spot. He notes its purple color and its beauty, which is greater than the redbird's. He says that if people ask the flower why its beauty is wasted in this hidden spot, it should reply that beauty is its own excuse for being. The speaker does not wonder why the flower was there but believes that the same power that brought him to that spot also placed the flower.

Teaching Strategies

PROVIDING FOR CULTURAL DIFFERENCES You might ask students from other countries (or regions of America) to name the flower, bird, or natural feature of their native lands that they consider most beautiful.

PROVIDING FOR DIFFERENT LEVELS OF ABILITY The use of apostrophe may be the single largest point of difficulty in this poem. Be sure students understand that the speaker describes an experience in lines 1–8, and in lines 9–16 addresses the flower.

READING THE POEM Before students read the poem, define for them the word *apostrophe*. Be sure to distinguish it from its much more familiar homonym, the punctuation mark.

RETEACHING ALTERNATIVES Have students work with a partner to express the poem's theme in one sentence. Then share some of the statements to see if the class agrees.

Responding to the Poem Text page 199

Answers to the questions in the Pupil's Edition appear in the Annotated Teacher's Edition.

Writing About the Poem

For help in revising their compositions, refer students to **Grammar, Usage, and Mechanics: A Reference Guide** on text pages 1183–1228 at the back of their books.

A CRITICAL RESPONSE
1. Analyzing the Poem Give students a head start by helping them identify the rhyme scheme (aabbcdcd eeffghgh), and note that the first two lines employ "slant rhyme" (slightly off). Then scan the entire poem (using

the chalkboard). Students should note that lines 3, 6, 7, and 11 begin with trochees rather than iambs (DUMda, not daDUM). Note also that in other places the iambic meter requires stress on such minor words as *in* (lines 2, 5, 15) and *on* (line 10).

Students' personal response at the end of the essay can be simply a statement of whether they liked the metrics and rhyme and why. They may be more specific also—giving their opinion as to whether Emerson's variations enhanced the poem, prevented a sing-song quality, detracted from the poem, or had some other effect on the student.

▶ CRITERIA FOR EVALUATING THE ASSIGNMENT The essay notes where Emerson alters the iambic pattern and how he uses rhyme, and gives the student's response to the metrics and rhyme.

2. *Comparing Philosophies*   Read aloud and clarify the meaning of the quotation from *As You Like It*. Call students' attention to the fact that in their papers they should comment specifically on how Emerson and Shakespeare deal with the idea that nature contains signs of divinity.

▶ CRITERIA FOR EVALUATING THE ASSIGNMENT The essay summarizes the philosophies of Emerson and of Shakespeare that can be deduced from the sources. Most students will say that both find God in nature. In the Shakespeare quotation, the stones speak sermons, religious teachings; and nature is not neutral, but filled with "good."

Analyzing Language and Style

INVERSIONS

Line 6: *Gay* is moved to the end instead of following *water*. Line 7: *Here* is moved from mid-sentence to the beginning, *might* and *come* are separated, and *to cool* should precede *plumes*. Lines 5 and 8 are in normal word order.

The sentence written in normal word order appears as follows:

5   The purple petals, fallen in the pool,
6   Made the black water gay with their beauty;
7   The redbird might come here to cool his plumes,
8   And court the flower that cheapens his array.

THE SNOW-STORM

Text page 200

Objectives

1. To enjoy a poem describing a winter scene

2. To explain personification

3. To compare and contrast the moods of two poems

Introducing the Poem

Here are the major elements of the poem:

- **Rhythm:** iambic pentameter with many variations
- **Rhyme:** none
- **Theme:** awe at the power and beauty of nature
- **Significant techniques:** personification, imagery

BACKGROUND ON THE POEM   This was one of Emerson's earliest successful poems. In it he praises the turbulent, creative efforts of nature as the "fierce artificer" who creates a "frolic architecture." Subject matter is once again transcendentalized.

THE LITERAL MEANING   "Announced by all the trumpets of the sky," the snow covers the farmhouse and garden and keeps "all friends shut out" as the family within the house sit around the fireplace. The poet speaks of the north wind as a skilled craftsman whose labor has left a work of art built in one night. Art (architecture) mimics nature by building "in an age" what the north wind accomplishes in one night.

Teaching Strategies

PROVIDING FOR CULTURAL DIFFERENCES   Depending on your area of the country and the composition of your class, students may have different experiences and attitudes toward snow. Discuss these with them, and ask them how they feel about Emerson's awed pleasure at seeing snow.

PROVIDING FOR DIFFERENT LEVELS OF ABILITY   Emerson's vocabulary and syntax may be difficult for some students. You might want to use class discussion to do a line-by-line paraphrase of the poem.

READING THE POEM For purposes of oral reading, assign the poem to three students and let them decide how to divide the lines. (Some lines may be spoken by all three.) Suggest that the oral interpretation should be calm and straightforward, rather than oratorical.

RETEACHING ALTERNATIVES Have students go back over the poem, looking for images that describe how the snow arrives and what the snow does to transform the farm. Students might work with a partner to find these images and decide which ones they think are most effective.

Responding to the Poem   Text page 201

Answers to the questions in the Pupil's Edition appear in the Annotated Teacher's Edition.

Writing About the Poem

For help in revising their compositions, refer students to **Grammar, Usage, and Mechanics: A Reference Guide** on text pages 1183–1228 at the back of their books.

A CRITICAL RESPONSE
Comparing Poems Questions 1–4 (Analyzing the Poem) will have called students' attention to figurative language in Emerson's ''The Snow-Storm''; students should reread Whittier's ''Snow-Bound'' with special attention to figurative and sensory language. Suggest that *compare* in this assignment means that students are to concentrate only on similarities.

▶ CRITERIA FOR EVALUATING THE ASSIGNMENT The essay cites specific examples from Emerson's and Whittier's poems. Emerson personifies the snow as a fierce artist who leaves behind ''frolic architecture.'' Lines 41–65 in Whittier's poem resemble Emerson's lines 17–28, describing details of the snow. Students may say Whittier's outdoor mood (dark, bitter cold) is gloomier than Emerson's; both portray the indoor mood as warm, happy with the family round the radiant fire. Whittier gives more sensory details of indoors than Emerson.

Extending the Poem

Another poet studied in this text, T.S. Eliot provides a very different description of a winter storm in the first of his four ''Preludes'':

> The winter evening settles down
> With smell of steaks in passageways.
> Six o'clock
> The burnt-out ends of smoky days.
> 5   And now a gusty shower wraps
> The grimy scraps
> Of withered leaves about your feet
> And newspapers from vacant lots;
> The showers beat
> 10   On broken blinds and chimney-pots,
> And at the corner of the street
> A lonely cab-horse steams and stamps.
>
> And then the lighting of the lamps.

You might guide student discussion with the following questions: How are Eliot's images different from those in Emerson's and Whittier's snow poems? (They are urban, have almost nothing to do with nature, and are less beautiful.) How does the Eliot poem make you feel? What words evoke this feeling?

EMERSON'S APHORISMS   Text page 202

Objectives

1. To respond to some of Emerson's aphorisms
2. To write paraphrases of several aphorisms

Teaching Strategies

You might divide the class into small groups and have each group work on paraphrasing one aphorism. Discuss the meaning of the aphorisms before students attempt to write paraphrases. Or you might read aloud one or two of these paraphrases to give students the idea:

> Maybe I'm a little cynical, but I question it when everybody's yelling about their patriotism. It seems to me that, as a rule, really serious citizens don't shout about their patriotism. Instead they quietly act like citizens, by doing things like voting.—*Journals*, 1824

> We say, ''Don't give children sharp objects.'' Please, God, don't trust us with more power until we've learned

to make better use of what we have. What a wreck we'd make of the world if we could do whatever we wanted! Put safeguards on our knowledge until we've learned not to hurt each other with it.—*Journals*, 1832 (Students may be especially interested in applying this aphorism to contemporary life. What would Emerson say about nuclear power, environmental issues, war?)

Just as God used words to create a universe out of chaos and darkness, so the writer of a well-made sentence creates something delightful.—*Journals*, 1834

Poetry should bring fresh, new words to solid, old ideas.—*Journals*, 1844

It's true wisdom to recognize everyday wonders.—*Nature*

A human being is a god with faults.—*Nature*

Peace can come only from living according to your principles.—"Self-Reliance"

Prayer should not be for individual desires. Humans should feel unified with nature, each other, and God. Then every action is a prayer.—"Self-Reliance"

These *are* "the good old days" if we use them right.—"Self-Reliance"

Knowledge in itself is wonderful, but it becomes terrible if it is used wrongly.—"The American Scholar"

The greed of individuals and whole societies corrupts the very atmosphere.—"The American Scholar"

Extending the Aphorisms

Have students suggest aphorisms—either original ones or ones they've heard and believe are true. Perhaps a committee can collect these to produce a poster or illustrated booklet.

Primary Sources   Text page 203

HAWTHORNE TALKS ABOUT EMERSON
In this excerpt from "The Old Manse," Hawthorne describes Emerson as a "poet of deep beauty and austere tenderness" and as a philosopher with a "pure intellectual gleam." Using the selections by Emerson in the text as evidence, students might discuss how Hawthorne arrived at this evaluation of Emerson.

Henry David Thoreau   Text page 204

WALDEN, OR LIFE IN THE WOODS   Text page 207

Objectives

1. To respond to the ideas in the essays

2. To write a personal journal entry

3. To write a journal entry expressing Franklin's view of life at Walden Pond

4. To write an essay on how Thoreau finds "the miraculous" in everyday life

5. To write an essay comparing Thoreau's essays and a poem by Yeats

6. To identify and interpret metaphors and similes

Introducing the Essays

Summaries of the essays' main ideas appear in the Annotated Teacher's Edition.

Teacher Mary Jo Schaars describes how she introduces *Walden* to her American literature class (see "Hill-Climbing with Thoreau: Creating Meaningful Carryover," *English Journal,* November 1990, pp. 52–57):

. . . In my class, students never catch a glimpse of *Walden* before they find out how they feel about materialism, moral commitment, goals, lifestyle, and the like. First, we talk about each student's answers to the following questionnaire:

1. If you didn't have to worry about making a lot of money, what occupation would you choose? Why?
2. What do you like best about autumn? Spring?
3. Are clothes and your appearance important to you? Explain.
4. What do you consider your highest achievement so far in life?
5. What do you consider to be your greatest failure?
6. Do you ever take a walk with no destination in mind?
7. When during a routine day do you find yourself the happiest? Most bored?
8. Do you believe you have too many, just enough, too few conveniences in your life? Explain.
9. Would you go to jail rather than conform to a law that went against your conscience? Explain.
10. Check one: (explain, if necessary)
    a. Money can buy most things I want in life.
    b. Money can buy few things I want in life.
11. Do you express your opinions even when they aren't popular?
12. Circle ''A'' if you agree with the statement and ''D'' if you disagree. Explain your answers if you feel it is necessary.
    A D Every person is basically good.
    A D I try to depend on myself and be independent.
    A D I want to simplify my life.
    A D It is possible to have a life filled with both material things and spiritual ideals.

Next, if the weather cooperates, we take a class period to get what I call ''A Breath of Nature'' and tone up the senses. Students take a brief walk, paying close attention to the smells inside and outside the building; they examine closely a small plot of ground and then a larger landscape. They respond in journal entries. The following excerpts show a variety of honest observations:

Inside

The air is hard and dull—it has many different lingering odors. They all mix at times and go into my lungs with a heavy fall. It isn't the most enjoyable air.

Outside

The air is sharp, clear. There is no smell, just an ease off my chest as my lungs fill easily. I guess a word to sum it up is refreshing.

My patch of earth contains three sun stripes where a tree holds back the nurturing rays. There are two yellow flowers, each with a group of toothedge weeds around them. One is glowing as the light shines on it. The other is shaded behind the tree.

Cars go by and I hear the rumble of their engines, the sound of their jolts as they hit a bump. I suddenly hear a sharp, sawing sound, then a radio playing in the distance . . . a handyman stands on a ladder and hammers on a roof panel of some sort. The trees are all different colors now that the weather has become cool. They are starting to look lonely and bleak—getting ready for the white fluffs to submerge them.

Steph

The poet emerges:

The grass is starting to wither and turn yellow with frost.
  The trees are looking bare and naked like when you step out of the shower, waiting for the towel of spring's leaves.

Tom

Here, the thinking clusters and branches. Thoreau would like that . . . .
  ''Around school, real nature is foiled by humanity, but that is *Truth;* Thoreau would have to deal with that if he were writing today. The sounds of trucks and cars and ventilator fans and the smell of grease wafting toward us from the burger joints a quarter of a mile away make us realize how tenacious nature must be to survive. Thus Thoreau's lessons are updated and realized.

BACKGROUND ON THE ESSAYS The privacy at Walden Pond gave Thoreau an opportunity to put his theories of plain, simple living to the test. He was not trying to be a hermit, however, and spent much time visiting. The Transcendalist philosopher Bronson Alcott spent every Sunday evening at Walden during Thoreau's second year there.

Teaching Strategies

PROVIDING FOR CULTURAL DIFFERENCES Students' responses to Thoreau's attitudes may be in part influenced by their socioeconomic backgrounds. Students from blue-collar backgrounds may feel that Thoreau's antagonism to the work ethic is a luxury they could not afford. Students from low-income families may resent Thoreau's voluntary poverty and can justifiably complain that his family and friends cushioned him from real want. These responses are valid critiques that can lead to stimulating discussion of such topics as the nature of independence, the necessity of money-making labor, and the socioeconomic role of philosophers. Thoreau himself would doubtless welcome such a discussion. In addition, you should alert students to the fact that Thoreau's remarks about the Irish were not always complimentary and were unfortunately typical of the prejudices of his era.

PROVIDING FOR DIFFERENT LEVELS OF ABILITY
You might want to divide the class into small groups, making each group responsible for summarizing and reporting to the class about one section of *Walden*. ''Economy'' and ''Brute Neighbors'' can each be divided between two groups. ''Brute Neighbors'' is easier; ''Conclusion'' is suitable for a group of more advanced students.

READING THE ESSAYS You might begin by asking where students go when they want to be alone with their thoughts. Discussion can continue with some of the following questions: Why have they selected this particular place? Does it help them to ''escape'' for a time? Why is this sort of ''escape'' necessary? How much solitude is good for people? At what point does solitude become harmful? What sorts of material comforts are absolutely necessary? If students were to live for two years in a cabin in the woods, what items would they feel they had to bring—TVs? Stereos? What do they feel they could live without?

RETEACHING ALTERNATIVES Ask students to imagine that they are textbook editors. If they could choose only one of these six excerpts from *Walden* to give readers a sample of Thoreau's writing and ideas, which excerpt would they choose, and why? Suggest that students look quickly at the excerpts before they make their choice.

Responding to the Essays   Text page 218

Answers to the questions in the Pupil's Edition appear in the Annotated Teacher's Edition.

Writing About the Essays

For help in revising their compositions, refer students to **Grammar, Usage, and Mechanics: A Reference Guide** on text pages 1183–1228 at the back of their books.

A CREATIVE RESPONSE

1. Writing a Journal Entry The key point in the writing assignment is ''Try to think like Thoreau for a day.'' Discuss with students how Thoreau's mind worked—the connections he saw between events and literary works, and the messages or lessons he drew from what he observed or experienced.

▶ CRITERIA FOR EVALUATING THE ASSIGNMENT The journal entry records what the writer saw, heard, and thought, in a manner reminiscent of Thoreau in its use of allusions and its attention to lessons to be learned.

2. Writing from Another Point of View Review especially the final column on text page 73, on Benjamin Franklin's mind set. Discuss how Franklin's thinking differed from Thoreau's.

▶ CRITERIA FOR EVALUATING THE ASSIGNMENT The journal entry records what the writer saw, heard, and thought, in a manner reminiscent of Franklin in its emphasis on the scientific and the rational.

A CRITICAL RESPONSE

3. Developing a Topic The writing assignment establishes the organization and content for the essays. Discuss with students the scenes from *Walden* best suited to the assignment—e.g., baking bread in the rain, weeding the beans, the battle of the ants, Thoreau and the loon, or other scenes. Tell students to use specific details and to include at least two quotations.

▶ CRITERIA FOR EVALUATING THE ASSIGNMENT The essay uses Emerson's statement as its topic sentence, supports this sentence with specific details, and uses quotations from *Walden*.

4. Comparing a Poem with Walden Read aloud Yeats's ''The Lake Isle of Innisfree,'' and with no discussion, have students immediately jot down similarities to *Walden* in terms of imagery, tone, and subject matter. Then discuss students' lists.

▶ CRITERIA FOR EVALUATING THE ASSIGNMENT Students should mention similarities in situation and mood (peaceful isolation, building one's own house); imagery (beans, lake, sky and evening); and tone (peace, joy, satisfaction). Yeats adds other images of nature not found in the *Walden* excerpts. For Yeats, the venture lies in the future (he is still on the pavements) but Thoreau writes of something already accomplished.

Analyzing Language and Style

A METAPHORICAL STYLE
1. *Metaphor*: Ideas are compared with a coat. *Rephrased:* Readers should take only the ideas that fit them, and not try to ''put on'' ideas that fit others well, but don't fit them.
2. *Metaphor*: Life is compared with a bone. *Rephrased*: I wanted to live deeply and get everything I could out of life.
3. *Simile*: A person's life is compared with the unsettled German Confederacy. *Rephrased*: Our life is like the map of the world, with new nations popping up every day.
4. *Metaphor*: Life is compared with a journey by ship. *Rephrased*: I didn't want to live a comfortable, sheltered life, but rather work hard and experience everything to the fullest. I don't want to live that sheltered life now either.
5. *Metaphor*: Ideas are compared with a drumbeat. *Rephrased*: If people don't go along with the crowd, maybe it's because they are being faithful to their personal vision.
6. *Simile*: One's life is compared with a river that sometimes floods. *Rephrased*: Our inner life has its ups and downs. Maybe this will be the year we are full of ideas that enrich the barren places in our lives and clear out the problems.

Extending the Essays

Many contemporary American nature essayists owe a deep debt to Thoreau. Among the best examples of this genre are Annie Dillard's *Pilgrim at Tinker Creek*, Edward Hoagland's *Walking the Dead Diamond Desert*, Peter Matthiessen's *The Snow Leopard*, Barry Lopez's *Arctic Dreams*, and Ivan Doig's *This House of Sky*. Students interested in the outdoors, or in fine writing, might want to read these or similar books and report on them to the class.

FROM RESISTANCE TO CIVIL GOVERNMENT

Text page 220

Objectives

1. To respond to an essay whose ideas have influenced contemporary American history

2. To interpret paradoxes

3. To write a short speech stating an opposing view

4. To write an essay responding to a political statement

5. To write an essay comparing and contrasting two political statements

6. To determine precise meanings of words

Introducing the Essay

Here are the main ideas of the essay:

• Government is an expedient, a means to an end.

• The majority will inevitably, in some instances, harm the minority.

• People must do what they feel is right; they have an obligation not to support what they feel is wrong.

• The "free and enlightened state" is one that will "recognize the individual as a higher power."

BACKGROUND ON THE ESSAY   Thoreau's influence on the development of the theory and practice of civil disobedience—and thus on a great deal of twentieth-century history—can perhaps best be seen in Mahatma Gandhi's protests in India and in the civil rights movement in America. In "A Legacy of Creative Protest," Dr. Martin Luther King, Jr., wrote of Thoreau: As a result of his writings and personal witness we are heirs of a legacy of creative protest. The Mexican War was unpopular in New England in its day, sparking more than one protest. Thoreau's protest against the poll tax was perhaps inspired by Bronson Alcott's refusal three years earlier to pay taxes to a government that tolerated slavery.

SUMMARY   Thoreau expounds his ideas about government and the dangers of majority rule. Then he relates his experiences in being taken to Concord jail for nonpayment of poll taxes.

Teaching Strategies

PROVIDING FOR CULTURAL DIFFERENCES   Students' attitudes toward civil disobedience will vary with their backgrounds and experiences. Ask your students whether their lives, their families' lives, or their ethnic or racial groups have been affected by acts of political protest.

PROVIDING FOR DIFFERENT LEVELS OF ABILITY   "Resistance to Civil Government" is more important as a position paper than as a stylistic achievement. The historical examples of Gandhi, King, and others who have practiced civil disobedience are valid points of entry to Thoreau's text. Real historical events serve as "paraphrases," so to speak, of Thoreau's ideas. Once students have become familiar with the practical application of the ideas, they will find Thoreau's essay easier to understand.

READING THE ESSAY   Before reading this essay, you might discuss some of the following questions: Why do we have laws? Do we really need them? What would happen if there were no laws? What options do Americans have when they believe a law is unjust? How, in the course of our history, did these options arise? Point out that Thoreau, among many others, helped create a strategy for changing unjust laws.

RETEACHING ALTERNATIVES   While civil disobedience is a familiar idea in the modern world, some students may have trouble seeing it in the context of the issues of the 1840's. You might ask the class to do a quickwrite in which they discuss some rule that they have encountered that they consider unjust. Ask them to describe how they might go about protesting it. Since Thoreau's ideas have largely shaped the nature of protest in American culture as a whole, it is likely that the students' responses will incorporate Thoreau's approach.

Responding to the Essay   Text page 224

Answers to the questions in the Pupil's Edition appear in the Annotated Teacher's Edition.

Writing About the Essay

For help in revising their compositions, refer students to **Grammar, Usage, and Mechanics: A Reference Guide** on text pages 1183–1228 at the back of their books.

A CREATIVE RESPONSE
1. Taking Another Point of View   Have students write the speech as if they were speaking either to Thoreau himself or to his neighbors.

▶ CRITERIA FOR EVALUATING THE ASSIGNMENT   The paper is in first-person language and in the form of a speech. Arguments are appropriate for a specific audience, and reasons are given for Thoreau's arrest. (For example, the police officer might argue that all citizens have responsibilities as well as rights, that a prime responsibility is to obey all laws, that a citizen cannot pick and choose which laws to obey, that citizens have peaceful means to change laws, etc.) The speaker also expresses a personal response to Thoreau's strategy.

A CRITICAL RESPONSE
2. Supporting a Statement   You might briefly discuss *anarchy* and contemporary terms such as *deregulation*. Students should express their opinion and support it with convincing reasons and evidence.

▶ CRITERIA FOR EVALUATING THE ASSIGNMENT   The paper is logical and forceful in making points that support or attack Thoreau's concept.

3. Comparing or Contrasting Two Political Statements   In class, ask students to volunteer a few statements from the Declaration that might serve as a starting point. (See the second paragraph, which asserts that no government has the right to destroy the inherent and inalienable rights of "life, liberty, and the pursuit of happiness.") Note that the assignment calls for similarities or differences—not both. This would be a good assignment for students to collaborate in groups of three or four.

▶ CRITERIA FOR EVALUATING THE ASSIGNMENT   The essay cites some specific details from both sources concerning resistance to law and authority. Most students will find differences both in the situation and resolution of the conflict. Ideas should be clearly stated. Look for a thesis statement.

Analyzing Language and Style
PRECISE MEANINGS
1. *Neutrality* means "taking no stand." *Apathy* means "simply not caring." In Thoreau, *indifference* means "apathy."
2. *Unmoral* means "having nothing at all to do with ethics." *Immoral* means "ethically wrong."
3. The final sentence, quoted in part above, could be paraphrased as follows:
   Once you get used to sinning you quit caring about sin; and instead of seeming wrong, it just seems irrelevant, unconnected with life in general.
4. Text page 222, footnote 5, has already defined "poll tax." Students who missed the note might guess that it is a special "head of household" tax or something similar.
5. *Poll:* an opinion survey. *Pollster:* compiler of data. *Poll booth:* a place to register or take part in a poll. All three deal with "heads" in the sense of counting "heads" or individuals.

Extending the Essay

In Plato's dialogue "Phaedo," Socrates, who has been unjustly condemned to death by an Athenian court, refuses to try to escape his punishment. He says that he has no right to rebel against the decisions of a state that has nurtured him and whose laws, by living in that state, he has implicitly agreed to obey. Socrates's view is diametrically opposed to Thoreau's. Have students take the parts of Socrates and Thoreau and debate the individual's right to disobey the law for reasons of conscience. You might divide the class roughly in half—with half taking Socrates's viewpoint and half Thoreau's. Students should gain experience in arguing *any* position.

Primary Sources   Text page 225

TWO JOURNALS
In his journal entry, Nathaniel Hawthorne describes "Mr. Thorow," who dined at Hawthorne's home. Among his comments, Hawthorne says that Thoreau is a "keen and delicate observer of nature" and that he has "more than a tincture of literature." Based on what they have read of Thoreau, ask students what they think of how accurate an assessment of the young man Hawthorne has made.

Edgar Allan Poe

THE MASQUE OF THE RED DEATH

Objectives

1. To respond to a famous American short story
2. To interpret symbolism, allegory, and allusion
3. To state the story's theme
4. To describe the opening scene of a movie or stage adaptation
5. To write three opening sentences for original stories
6. To write an essay commenting on a criticism
7. To analyze the emotional effects of language

Introducing the Story

Here are the major elements of the story:

- **Protagonist:** Prince Prospero and his guests
- **Antagonist:** the Red Death
- **Conflict:** person vs. the supernatural (death)
- **Point of view:** third-person, partially omniscient
- **Significant techniques:** unity of effect, tone, allegory
- **Setting:** Prince Prospero's palace, probably in southern Europe in the sixteenth or seventeenth century
- **Theme:** Death is inescapable regardless of human vanity.

BACKGROUND ON THE STORY   Poe completed this story in 1842, just three months after Virginia Clemm, his young wife, had suffered a tubercular attack, which had caused her to hemorrhage from her lungs. (This may explain Poe's preoccupation with blood in this story.) His wife's illness was devastating to Poe, whose nervous disposition left him unable to continue with his work as an editor at *Graham's Magazine*.

THE PLOT   Prince Prospero invites a thousand of his friends to his palace to escape the plague that is ravaging the land. They hold a ball to celebrate, but the Red Death enters the palace in costume and kills all the people.

Teaching Strategies

PROVIDING FOR CULTURAL DIFFERENCES   Poe's story requires some familiarity with medieval architecture, weapons, and court life. Make a list of terms (*knights, dames, abbey, buffoons, Gothic, tapestries,* etc.) and assign each word to a student to teach the class.

PROVIDING FOR DIFFERENT LEVELS OF ABILITY   Because of the story's difficult vocabulary, careful review of the vocabulary list will be helpful. LEP and ESL students will benefit from listening to the story being read aloud. Use the audiocasette recording that accompanies the text.

READING THE STORY   The ending of the story—from the first entrance of the Red Death at midnight—is the most effective portion for reading aloud, and contains all of Poe's verbal and atmospheric effects in full measure. If your students have already read the story at home, you might want to have them read aloud from that point for heightened appreciation of Poe's language. For fullest dramatic effect, play the entire tape recording that accompanies the story.

RETEACHING ALTERNATIVES   Have students work with a partner to retell Poe's story in another form. They might consider a fairy tale, a rap, a comic strip, a newspaper story, a TV news report. Have them try to capture the story's emotional effects—of horror and fear. You might suggest that they review the story to see how Poe manages to create those feelings in the reader.

Responding to the Story

Answers to the questions in the Pupil's Edition appear in the Annotated Teacher's Edition.

Writing About the Story

For help in revising their compositions, refer students to **Grammar, Usage, and Mechanics: A Reference Guide** on text pages 1183–1228 at the back of their books.

A CREATIVE RESPONSE

1. Staging the Story Brainstorm a number of possible "first things" the audience would see and hear—a dying, shrieking plague victim; a violent thunderstorm; the "castellated abbey" with a clock tolling in the background; etc. Discuss which ones are best for stage and which for screen.

▶ CRITERIA FOR EVALUATING THE ASSIGNMENT The paragraph vividly describes the first thing the audience would see and hear. The scene and the sounds are suitable for setting the mood of terror.

2. Writing an Opening Sentence Clarify the intent of the assignment: Students should not try to imitate Poe. Rather, they should write sentences aimed at effects of their choice. To convey the possible range, read aloud the opening sentence from several different stories in the text.

▶ CRITERIA FOR EVALUATING THE ASSIGNMENT There are three sentences, each of which could open a story. Each sentence sets an identifiable mood.

A CRITICAL RESPONSE

3. Commenting on a Criticism Read and discuss Wilbur's comment on the dream world in Poe's stories, clarifying Wilbur's meaning as necessary. When students begin to argue for or against Wilbur's theory, they are ready to write.

▶ CRITERIA FOR EVALUATING THE ASSIGNMENT The essay clearly supports or opposes Wilbur's interpretation of Prince Prospero's costume ball as a dream sequence, and explains fully why the writer agrees or disagrees with Wilbur.

Analyzing Language and Style

EMOTIONAL EFFECTS

1. Blood is used to describe the color red in "the panes here were scarlet—a deep blood color" (p. 229); "... the blood-tinted panes ..." (p. 229); "... light through the blood-colored panes ..." (p. 230). Alternative choices that would create a different effect: "a deep neon red color"; "scarlet-tinted panes"; "strawberry-colored panes."

2. The plague called "the Red Death" caused profuse bleeding.

3. Some possible choices include "... the duke's love of the *exotic* ..." and "there was much of the ... *intricate*. ..."

4. Words adding to the emotional tone of repulsiveness and irrationality are *delirious, madman, wanton, terrible, disgust.* Poe aims to provoke a sense of horror.

5. The sentence conveys despair and devastation. *Decay* is associated with death, rottenness, and foulness. Opposites are *grow, bloom, increase.*

Extending the Story

Plagues have long stimulated the literary imagination. The greatest examples are Defoe's *A Journal of the Plague Year*, Camus's *The Plague*, and Manzoni's *The Betrothed*. You might suggest that students think of story ideas describing the reactions of contemporary Americans in their own community to a plague. Many will see AIDS as a modern plague; some may write about drug addiction. Have students meet in small groups to discuss and brainstorm story ideas. Some members of the group may want to collaborate on actually writing a story to share with the class.

Primary Sources   Text page 233

A VISIT TO THE POES

In this excerpt from a biography of Poe, Mrs. Gove Nichols describes a visit to Poe's cottage. Mrs. Nichols's account of the unfurnished cottage and of the distress caused by Poe's bursting his gaiters during a leaping game illustrates the grinding poverty that Poe faced throughout his life. The anecdote about the leaping game gives students the opportunity to see the human side of Poe. Students will be interested in the two contemporary views of Poe's poetry. The English poet Elizabeth Barrett Browning was enthusiastic; Mrs. Gove Nichols "could not make head or tail of it." Yet Poe knew his own worth and, despite his failures, would not be discouraged from writing. Ask students what other artists and writers they know of who persisted despite failure.

THE FALL OF THE HOUSE OF USHER

Text page 234

Objectives

1. To respond to a classic horror story

2. To analyze imagery, point of view, and allegory

3. To retell an incident from another point of view

4. To analyze the use of detail to create mood

5. To write an essay comparing and contrasting the themes of two stories

6. To write an essay developing a statement about the story's meaning

7. To analyze the use of words for emotional effect

8. To identify and interpret symbols in a story

Introducing the Story

Here are the major elements in the story:

- **Main characters:** the narrator; Roderick Usher; Madeline Usher, twin sister of Roderick

- **Conflict:** person vs. self (fear)

- **Point of view:** first-person (the narrator, a friend of Usher's)

- **Setting:** the House of Usher, whose location is never given or even hinted at

BACKGROUND ON THE STORY   While serving as the editor of *Burton's Gentleman's Magazine* in Philadelphia, Poe published "The Fall of the House of Usher" in the September 18, 1839, edition of the magazine. He was an extremely successful editor; however, his often unconventional methods and his unacceptable habits of drink and absenteeism lost him his job in the summer of 1840.

"The Haunted Palace," a poem that the narrator and Roderick read together in the story, is a poem by Poe that was published in the *Baltimore Museum* just five months before it appeared as part of his story. Poe wrote to the editor, "By 'The Haunted Palace' I mean to imply a mind haunted by phantoms—a disordered brain."

THE PLOT   The narrator visits the home of his boyhood friend Roderick Usher, after receiving a desperate letter from him. He finds both Roderick and his sister Madeline in a state of depression and physical decline. The narrator tries to relieve Roderick's melancholy, to no avail. Madeline apparently dies, and the two men place her body in a dungeon vault, but it is a premature burial. On her reappearance, days later, Madeline falls upon her brother and dies. Roderick also dies of shock. As the narrator flees, the house itself collapses into ruins.

Teaching Strategies

PROVIDING FOR CULTURAL DIFFERENCES   Students from all cultures enjoy reading and listening to ghost stories and stories of horror and fear. You might have one or two volunteers retell an especially scary tale to get students in the mood for reading Poe's story.

PROVIDING FOR DIFFERENT LEVELS OF ABILITY   Careful attention to vocabulary study can make the descriptions, in particular, more comprehensible to students. Students who might be baffled by the idea of a *tarn* may be relieved to learn that it is simply a lake, and that a "valet of stealthy step" is simply a servant walking sneakily. For specific passages that give students trouble, encourage paraphrasing in the course of discussion.

READING THE STORY   Read aloud the story's beginning through the end of the paragraph that begins "The room in which I found. . . ." Make sure students understand the story situation and setting. Pause to discuss the mood, and ask for predictions of what will happen in the story. Assign the rest of the story as homework.

Few, if any, American students today would be able to identify with the frailties of a decaying landed aristocracy. Some may well be impatient with the problems of such people. Point out that the setting of the story, while important in establishing its mood, is not really indispensable to Poe's theme of emotional collapse. You might ask the class to imagine the same theme of emotional collapse set in the present day, or in some more familiar setting.

RETEACHING ALTERNATIVES   Have students meet in small groups to plan a horror film based on this story. Who would they choose to play each role? Have them describe the sets, lighting, music, and special effects. Do they think Poe's story could be a popular movie today? Why, or why not?

Responding to the Story Text page 246

Answers to the questions in the Pupil's Edition appear in the Annotated Teacher's Edition.

Writing About the Story

For help in revising their compositions, refer students to **Grammar, Usage, and Mechanics: A Reference Guide** on text pages 1183–1228 at the back of their books.

A CREATIVE RESPONSE

1. Using Another Point of View   Have the class list incidents which could be retold from Madeline's point of view (e.g., arrival of the narrator).

▶ CRITERIA FOR EVALUATING THE ASSIGNMENT   The story is done in first person and reveals the character of Madeline as she narrates an event or comments on other characters.

A CRITICAL RESPONSE

Since the three critical writing assignments achieve different objectives, you may wish to discuss all three, but allow students to choose *one* for writing a critical essay. You may choose to make this a collaborative writing assignment (in groups of three or four) rather than an individual one.

2. Analyzing the Story's Effect   Read the quotation from Poe and make clear to students that this assignment requires a careful analysis of details and word choices that build the mood of terror.

▶ CRITERIA FOR EVALUATING THE ASSIGNMENT   The essay demonstrates, through a large number of examples, how Poe uses details and word choice to build the mood of terror.

3. Comparing Two Stories   Refer back to Richard Wilbur's comment in the third writing assignment on text page 232, on imagination and reality in the stories of Poe. Students should proceed as if they agree with Wilbur if they choose to write on this topic.

▶ CRITERIA FOR EVALUATING THE ASSIGNMENT   The essay uses examples from ''The Masque of the Red Death'' and ''The Fall of the House of Usher'' to support the thesis that it is impossible to achieve the Romantic ideal of imagination transcending reality.

4. Analyzing the Story's Meaning   Discuss the three statements about the theme of the story, clarifying the meaning of each as necessary, before students begin to write.

▶ CRITERIA FOR EVALUATING THE ASSIGNMENT   The essay adopts one of the three statements as its thesis statement and uses examples and quotations from ''The Fall of the House of Usher'' to support it.

Analyzing Language and Style

SUGGESTIVE WORDS

1. dull, dark, soundless, oppressively, dreary, shades of the evening, melancholy, insufferable gloom, sternest, desolate, terrible, bleak, vacant, rank, decayed, depression, hideous, iciness, sinking, sickening, unredeemed dreariness, unnerved, insoluble, shadowy fancies, annihilate, sorrowful, precipitous brink, black and lurid tarn, unruffled luster, gray sedge, ghastly tree stems, vacant and eyelike windows

2. The first sentence and several others repeat the *d* sound: ''*D*uring the whole of a *d*ull, *d*ark, and soun*d*less *d*ay. . . .'' The *s* sound is also used often: ''an ici*ne*s*s, a *s*inking, a *s*ickening of the heart. . . .'' The sounds could be those of a dull, repeated thud or a hissing snake.

3. Adverbs and adjectives characterizing the mind of the narrator and revealing his feelings include oppressively, melancholy, insufferable, desolate, terrible, bleak, sickening, sorrowful.

4. The main detail that personifies the house is ''vacant eyelike windows,'' used twice.

5. The entire mood and atmosphere of the story would be different. You would expect a more light-hearted story.

6. A rewritten sentence can alter the sentence's emotional effect entirely: ''During the morning of a bright, sunshiny day filled with birdsong in the spring of the year, when white clouds floated benignly, high in the heavens, I had been passing alone, on horseback, through an unusually picturesque tract of country; and at length found myself, as noon approached, within view of the intriguing House of Usher.''

ELEMENTS OF LITERATURE Text page 247

SYMBOLS

This is an important feature, crucial to students' understanding of many poems and stories to come. Read and discuss the feature in class. The last question suggests an additional critical writing topic for students to explore.

Extending the Story

''The Fall of the House of Usher'' is a model of descriptive prose, particularly through the subtle—though overelaborate by today's standards—use of adjectives. You might want to have students list all the adjectives in the renowned first paragraph. (Refer students to the section on Adjectives, text page 1184, in **Grammar, Usage, and Mechanics: A Reference Guide.**) Then have students read the passage, first with the adjectives, and then without them. You might continue item 6 in Analyzing Language and Style. Ask students to rewrite the entire first paragraph to express a happier mood, merely by substituting different adjectives.

ELDORADO

Objectives

1. To respond to a poem about a quest
2. To analyze meter, word connotations, and tone
3. To interpret symbolic meaning

Introducing the Poem

Here are the major elements of the poem:

- **Rhythm:** iambic dimeter and trimeter
- **Rhyme:** aabccb
- **Significant techniques:** rhyme, meter, symbolism, and tone
- **Theme:** Though some may spend a lifetime searching, the land of their heart's desire is always beyond reach.

BACKGROUND ON THE POEM This poem was written in 1849, shortly before Poe's death. In October of that year, Poe was found lying in the rain outside Ryan's Public House (a bar) and was taken to Washington College Hospital in a coma. He remained delirious for three and a half days, and on Sunday, October 7, at only forty years of age, died, saying, "Lord help my poor soul."

Students should recognize the year 1849 as the year of the California Gold Rush. The search for gold was current news and the American frontier was still being explored and settled.

THE LITERAL MEANING A gaily clad knight journeys in search of Eldorado. As the quest continues, he is saddened and grows old, and his strength begins to fail him. Meeting a pilgrim traveler—a shadow—he asks the way to Eldorado. The pilgrim tells him that he must "ride, boldly ride" over the Mountains of the Moon and through the Valley of the Shadow if he wishes to find Eldorado.

Teaching Strategies

PROVIDING FOR CULTURAL DIFFERENCES Students may vary in their ability to identify with the character of a questing knight. You might want to ask your students to discuss what their forebears' lives were like in 1849. Lead them to understand that, despite differences in circumstances, the hopeful quest for a better life unites people from all backgrounds. Those who immigrate to America from other lands are in search of a kind of Eldorado. In fact, some immigrants from Europe toward the end of the nineteenth century believed America's streets were literally paved with gold.

PROVIDING FOR DIFFERENT LEVELS OF ABILITY Because of its brevity, lively action, colorful setting, bouncy rhythm, and strong rhymes, everyone should be able to read and enjoy this poem. More advanced students will probably want to concentrate on the symbolic implications.

READING THE POEM The entire poem can be read aloud. (An audiocassette recording accompanies the selection.) You might want to have three different students read the parts of narrator, knight, and shadow.

RETEACHING ALTERNATIVES If your students have trouble with the symbolic meanings of the story, you might focus on key words such as *Eldorado, pilgrim,* and especially, because of its shifting meanings, *shadow.* Have students brainstorm the connotations of these words. Then discuss what each word means and suggests in the poem.

Responding to the Poem　　Text page 249

Answers to the questions in the Pupil's Edition appear in the Annotated Teacher's Edition.

ANNABEL LEE

Objectives

1. To respond to a poem's sound effects and story

2. To analyze the use of rhyme and meter

3. To write a stanza imitating the poem

4. To write a paragraph comparing and contrasting two poems

Introducing the Poem

Here are the major elements of the poem:

- **Rhythm:** anapestic tetrameter and trimeter
- **Rhyme:** ababcb dbebfb
- **Theme:** An obsessive love continues even after the death of the beloved.
- **Significant techniques:** internal rhyme, repetition

BACKGROUND ON THE POEM   Poe suffered greatly, descending into alcoholism and mental illness, during the repeated, nearly fatal crises of his tubercular young wife Virginia. For weeks after her death, he would wander off to her tomb and spend hours there, weeping hysterically. The remaining two years of his life were his most melancholy. ''Annabel Lee'' first appeared in the New York *Tribune* of October 9, 1849, just two days after Poe's death.

THE LITERAL MEANING   The speaker, remembering his youth, says that long ago in a kingdom by the sea, he loved a young girl named Annabel Lee. Their love was so great that even the angels were jealous of their relationship, and this was the real cause of her death, though she died from a chill. After her death, her ''highborn kinsmen'' buried her by the sea. Each night the speaker dreams of Annabel Lee and lies by her side in the tomb. Though physically separated, their souls are united, for love is stronger than death.

Teaching Strategies

PROVIDING FOR CULTURAL DIFFERENCES   Idealized romantic love is particularly a Western notion and was at its most fashionable in Poe's day. To modern American teenagers, highly romantic ideals and anti-sentimental

ones often co-exist. This poem provides a good opportunity to discuss changing ideas of love over time and in different cultures.

PROVIDING FOR DIFFERENT LEVELS OF ABILITY
Be sure that students read the headnote (text page 250) and A Comment on the Poem (text page 252). This simple love poem is as straightforward as a popular song.

READING THE POEM   This is an excellent poem for students to read aloud. A certain amount of lightheartedness will not hurt.

RETEACHING ALTERNATIVES   Have students paraphrase the poem orally.

Responding to the Poem

Answers to the questions in the Pupil's Edition appear in the Annotated Teacher's Edition.

Writing About the Poem

For help in revising their compositions, refer students to **Grammar, Usage, and Mechanics: A Reference Guide** on text pages 1183–1228 at the back of their books.

A CREATIVE RESPONSE
1. Imitating the Poem   Give students the option of working with a group or partner or alone. This is a challenging task. Suggest word-for-word substitution that exactly matches Poe's accented and unaccented syllables as a way to begin. Go over the first stanza's rhyme scheme (ababcb) before students begin.

▶ CRITERIA FOR EVALUATING THE ASSIGNMENT
Rhymes should be exact but make allowances for variations in meter (it's hard to imitate Poe's stanza). The stanza should contain at least one sentence.

A CRITICAL RESPONSE
2. Comparing Poems   Read and discuss the lines from Wordsworth (A Comment on the Poem, text page 252). Elicit some similarities and differences.

▶ CRITERIA FOR EVALUATING THE ASSIGNMENT   Paragraph 1 names both poems and cites at least one similarity. Paragraph 2 discusses at least one difference. (Poe tells a whole story; Wordsworth does not. Poe imagines love and loss through death; Wordsworth speaks only of early infancy.)

TO HELEN

Objectives

1. To respond to a poem about ideal beauty

2. To identify an extended simile, alliteration, and rhyme

3. To analyze an allusion

4. To write a brief evaluation and analysis of the poem

Introducing the Poem

Here are the major elements of the poem:

- **Rhythm:** iambic tetrameter
- **Rhyme:** ababb cdcdc effef
- **Theme:** Idealized, classical beauty is a timeless source of comfort.
- **Significant techniques:** alliteration, literary allusion, apostrophe, extended simile

BACKGROUND ON THE POEM The initial inspiration for the poem, which was published in 1831, may have been Jane Stith Stanard, the mother of one of Poe's boyhood friends in Richmond. A revised version was printed in 1845. Some critics believe that the Helen of this version was Sarah Helen Whitman, a widow Poe planned to marry.

THE LITERAL MEANING The speaker begins with a simile: Helen's beauty is like that of the ships of ancient Greece that took the "way-worn wanderer" home. Helen's beauty has brought the narrator home to the grandeur of Greece and Rome, to a renewed awareness of beauty.

Teaching Strategies

PROVIDING FOR CULTURAL DIFFERENCES Students today are not nearly so familiar with classical Greece as students of previous generations. Make sure you read and discuss A Comment on the Poem (text page 254) before they read or listen to the poem. Also, ideals of beauty have changed over time. Let students discuss their ideas about what makes a person (male or female) beautiful. Does everyone agree? Do people in different cultures and times have varying notions of beauty?

PROVIDING FOR DIFFERENT LEVELS OF ABILITY Many students may have trouble with the classical allusions and particularly with the third stanza. Assure them that understanding each classical reference is much less important than an overall appreciation of Poe's feelings about ancient Greece, and of why a woman's beauty brings it to mind.

READING THE POEM It will be helpful to review briefly the story of Helen of Troy, the most beautiful woman of the ancient world, who ran off with Paris, a prince of Troy. When her husband, King Menelaus of Sparta, went to get her, the ten-year-long Trojan War began. A Comment on the Poem, text page 254, is an excellent source of information on the allusions in the poem. Read the poem aloud or play the audiocassette recording that accompanies this selection.

RETEACHING ALTERNATIVES Ask students to restate, in their own words, the speaker's feelings about Helen.

Responding to the Poem

Answers to the questions in the Pupil's Edition appear in the Annotated Teacher's Edition.

Writing About the Poem

For help in revising their compositions, refer students to **Grammar, Usage, and Mechanics: A Reference Guide** on text pages 1183–1228 at the back of their books.

A CRITICAL RESPONSE
Analyzing the Poem Read the writing assignment with the class, clarifying directions and discussing its content as needed. Refer students also to "A Comment on the Poem" (text page 254).

▶ CRITERIA FOR EVALUATING THE ASSIGNMENT The essay on Poe's "To Helen" consists of at least three paragraphs. Answers may vary. Students may indeed find Poe's comparison of a woman's beauty to ships strained unless they appreciate the extended simile as a conceit describing how beauty can "transport" the speaker to his long-sought destination.

The seas are not *desperate,* but the way-worn speaker is; he is desperate to reach home.

Helen is probably standing very still, looking as beautiful as an ancient statue.

THE RAVEN

Text page 255

Objectives

1. To respond to one of the most famous poems in American literature

2. To analyze the poem's imagery, tone, and symbols

3. To describe an alternate setting for the poem

4. To write two verses imitating the poet's rhyme scheme and meter

5. To write an essay comparing and contrasting two poems

6. To write a paragraph analyzing Poe's statement about the poem

Introducing the Poem

Here are the major elements of the poem:

- **Rhythm:** trochaic with lines of varying length (see text page 262)
- **Rhyme:** abcbbb
- **Speaker:** a scholar and bereaved lover of Lenore
- **Significant techniques:** alliteration, rhyme, repetition, tone, symbolism, narrative verse
- **Theme:** Death is irrevocable, but memory and grief linger.

BACKGROUND ON THE POEM   In early versions of the poem, the bird was an owl, the bird associated with Athena, ancient Greek goddess of wisdom. Perhaps the idea to use the raven came from Poe's reading of Dickens's *Barnaby Rudge.* In reviewing the novel, Poe was critical of Dickens's failure to make more use of the bird: "Its croakings might have been *prophetically* heard in the course of the drama." The "lost Lenore" of the poem has variously been identified as Elmyra Royster, a sweetheart from Poe's youth, and as Virginia Clemm, Poe's wife. "The Raven" brought Poe immediate fame, but its printing in the January 29, 1845, New York *Evening Post,* earned him only ten dollars. In 1929 a manuscript of the poem was sold for $100,000.

THE LITERAL MEANING   Reading old books at midnight, the speaker in the poem is sorrowing over his lost love Lenore. He hears a tapping at his chamber door, flings it open, but sees nothing. Then flinging open the shutter,

he is greeted by a stately raven that enters the room and settles on the bust of Pallas Athena, the goddess of wisdom. When the speaker asks the bird its name, the raven's only reply is, "Nevermore." The gloomy, grave, and ungainly bird causes the speaker to experience momentary amusement, but the bird's repetition of the word *nevermore*, especially when it is the answer to the speaker's desire to know about being reunited with Lenore, drives him into a state of frenzied despair.

Teaching Strategies

PROVIDING FOR CULTURAL DIFFERENCES   Students from all cultures can relate to this mysterious narrative poem. Remind them to use the footnotes for the Biblical and classical allusions.

PROVIDING FOR DIFFERENT LEVELS OF ABILITY   The rhythm and rhyme of this poem are so strong and so jaunty that for some students they may obscure the meaning of the poem. The poem is also so familiar that students who have encountered it before may be more taken with its jingle-like sound effects than with its depiction of frenzied despair. Try to break through these barriers to understanding by clear, direct paraphrase. Also, discuss the poem's sound as a symptom of the speaker's state of mind.

READING THE POEM   Students will enjoy doing an oral interpretation of this dramatic narrative, and the poem is long enough for everyone to read some lines. Let a group of students assign roles, and give students time to practice before their final reading. Students may perform before another class, or you may videotape their reading.

RETEACHING ALTERNATIVES   If the antique trappings deter some of your students from enjoying this extremely vivid poem, you might ask the class to offer possible updated paraphrases of key words such as *nevermore*. A class vote could determine the winner among competing synonyms. Reassure your students that even in Poe's day, the classical lore the narrator studied was "quaint and curious" and "forgotten."

Responding to the Poem   Text page 260

Answers to the questions in the Pupil's Edition appear in the Annotated Teacher's Edition.

Writng About the Poem

For help in revising their compositions, refer students to **Grammar, Usage, and Mechanics: A Reference Guide** on text pages 1183–1228 at the back of their books.

A CREATIVE RESPONSE

1. Describing an Alternate Setting Clarify for students that they are to write a descriptive paragraph, not a poem. Have the class brainstorm some settings that would work for the assignment.

▶ CRITERIA FOR EVALUATING THE ASSIGNMENT The vividly described scene is one that would allow the events in ''The Raven'' to remain as disturbing as they are.

2. Imitating Poe's Techniques Brainstorm a list of names (to replace Lenore) for which there are many rhymes. Then analyze Poe's rhyme scheme (abcbbb, with an internal rhyme in the third line) and meter (see Sound Effects, text page 262). Suggest that students try word-for-word substitution until they feel the meter. Some students will feel more confident if they can collaborate with a partner or small group. Ask for volunteers to read their stanzas aloud.

▶ CRITERIA FOR EVALUATING THE ASSIGNMENT The opening line is ''Once upon a midnight dreary, while I pondered, weak and weary.'' Another name is substituted for Lenore. The two stanzas imitate Poe's meter and rhyme scheme.

A CRITICAL RESPONSE

3. Comparing Poems Note with students that they are expected to *compare* (state similarities) and to *contrast* (state differences). The writing assignment suggests the content and organization of students' essay.

▶ CRITERIA FOR EVALUATING THE ASSIGNMENT Both poems have speakers mourning a lost love. The tone of ''The Raven'' is mysterious and wild; the tone of ''Annabel Lee'' is mournful but much more serene. Students should mention specifics about rhyme, metrics, alliteration, repetition, and their overall effects.

4. Analyzing the Poem Read Poe's essay (Primary Sources, text pages 260–261) and discuss the concept of ''the human thirst for self-torture.'' To be sure that students understand Poe's phrase, ask them for examples they have observed either personally or in movies, books, plays, and TV shows.

▶ CRITERIA FOR EVALUATING THE ASSIGNMENT The essay explains the meaning of Poe's phrase and cites details and quotations from the poem to support the writer's opinion. Either view may be supported adequately, and students will disagree. Have students with opposing views read their papers aloud while the class listens to evaluate the ''proof.''

Primary Sources — Text page 260

POE'S ESSAY ON THE WRITING PROCESS

According to the text, Poe describes the writing process in reverse, first deciding on the effect he wants to achieve, and then choosing a subject. In a class discussion, you might have students describe their own writing process and discuss how it compares with Poe's. Also, students might consider the point made by *The New Yorker* cartoon on text page 261. What is it about ''The Raven'' that has inspired so many parodies and so much humorous commentary?

ELEMENTS OF LITERATURE — Text page 262

SOUND EFFECTS

This section analyzes the meter, internal rhyme, and alliteration Poe uses in ''The Raven.'' Read and discuss it before students attempt their imitations of Poe for creative writing assignment 2.

Extending the Poem

A contemporary American poet, Gary Snyder, wrote the following poem about the teenage love he parted from. Read the poem aloud, and ask students to listen to decide how love in Snyder's poem compares with the love in ''The Raven.'' Before you read, ask someone to explain *karma*, a Buddhist and Hindu concept that means ''fate'' or ''destiny.''

From ''Four Poems for Robin''

December at Yase

You said, that October,
In the tall dry grass by the orchard
When you chose to be free,
''Again someday, maybe ten years.''

5   After college I saw you
One time. You were strange.
And I was obsessed with a plan.

Now ten years and more have
Gone by: I've always known
10   where you were—
I might have gone to you
Hoping to win your love back.
You still are single.

I didn't.
15   I thought I must make it alone. I
Have done that.

Only in dream, like this dawn,
Does the grave, awed intensity
Of our young love
20 Return to my mind, to my flesh.

We had what the others
All crave and seek for;
We left it behind at nineteen.

I feel ancient, as though I had
25 Lived many lives.

And may never now know
If I am a fool
Or have done what my
    karma demands.

Note that Snyder uses the word *never* in his final stanza, in a context similar to Poe's, with less dramatic effect but greater emotional reality.

Nathaniel Hawthorne

Text page 263

THE MINISTER'S BLACK VEIL

Text page 265

Objectives

1. To respond to a short story

2. To analyze character, symbol, tone, and theme

3. To rewrite a paragraph of the story from another point of view

4. To write an essay comparing and/or contrasting the story with Edwards's sermon

5. To write an essay comparing and contrasting the story with Emerson's essay

6. To use context clues to understand archaic and old-fashioned words

Introducing the Story

Here are the major elements of the story:

- **Main characters:** Mr. Hooper, a ''gentlemanly'' bachelor and minister; Elizabeth, Mr. Hooper's fiancée; parishioners of the Milford church
- **Conflicts:** person vs. self (guilt); person vs. society
- **Point of view:** limited third-person
- **Significant techniques:** allegory and symbolism, parable, and characterization
- **Setting:** Milford, Massachusetts, the early 1700's
- **Theme:** Secret sin is universal, but people are unwilling and afraid to acknowledge it.

BACKGROUND ON THE STORY Hawthorne's use of allegory, where characters embody abstract qualities, is complex. Poe, among others, advised him to give up allegory in his otherwise favorable review of *Twice-Told Tales,* but moral symbolism and allegory were unalterable parts of Hawthorne's view of life. Of his own style, Hawthorne wrote the following comment in a letter to a friend in 1858:

My own individual taste is for quite another class of works than those which I myself am able to write. If I were to meet with such books as mine, by another writer, I don't believe I should be able to get through them.

THE PLOT The Reverend Mr. Hooper astonishes his congregation in the village of Milford by preaching to them one Sunday wearing a black veil. He explains, to his parishioners and later to his fiancée Elizabeth, that it is a symbol of universal secret sin, and that he will wear it for the rest of his life. The veil alienates his congregation and causes Elizabeth to break their engagement. Hooper grows old and dies, isolated and unloved, but a respected, powerful minister.

Teaching Strategies

PROVIDING FOR CULTURAL DIFFERENCES Hawthorne's Puritan background made him especially concerned with the concept of sin. You might ask students how they would define *sin* according to the values and traditions of their cultural heritage.

Providing for Different Levels of Ability

Somber and doleful on the surface, Hawthorne's stories are vividly dramatic at the core; the difficulty for many students is to cut through to that core. Paraphrasing of Hawthorne's old-fashioned, musty diction will help.

Reading the Story It may also be helpful to highlight the dramatic qualities of the story by having students take the roles of the various characters, and read aloud their lines of dialogue.

Reteaching Alternatives If some of your students have trouble grasping the themes of the story, you might ask them to write in their own words, or deliver orally, a brief character description of Reverend Hooper. Ask them why such a mild, law-abiding man would be so obsessed with sin. Guide them toward understanding that Hooper is concerned with both his own unspecified sinfulness and with universal secret guilt.

Responding to the Story   Text page 274

Answers to the questions in the Pupil's Edition appear in the Annotated Teacher's Edition.

Writing About the Story

For help in revising their compositions, refer students to **Grammar, Usage, and Mechanics: A Reference Guide** on text pages 1183–1228 at the back of their books.

A CREATIVE RESPONSE
1. Using Another Point of View Discuss passages from "The Minister's Black Veil" (e.g., on pages 270, 271, and 273) that hint at Reverend Hooper's intent. Students might write their paragraph as an entry in Reverend Hooper's diary or journal.

▶ CRITERIA FOR EVALUATING THE ASSIGNMENT Building on remarks of Reverend Hooper, the first-person paragraph believably explains what the veil means to Hooper, how he first thought of wearing it, and how wearing it all the time makes him feel.

A CRITICAL RESPONSE
2. Comparing the Story to a Sermon In class, have students devise and fill in a prewriting chart on sin, hypocrisy, and conditions for salvation in Edwards's sermon

and Hawthorne's story. Students may deal only with similarities, only with differences, or both. Have them cite details to support their points.

▶ CRITERIA FOR EVALUATING THE ASSIGNMENT The essay compares or contrasts what Edwards's sermon and Hawthorne's story say about sin, hypocrisy, and conditions needed for salvation. Examples support all major points.

3. Comparing the Story to an Essay A prewriting chart or a sheet of paper divided into columns headed "Emerson" and "Hawthorne" will help students organize and gather details for this assignment.

▶ CRITERIA FOR EVALUATING THE ASSIGNMENT The essay explains the similarities or differences between Emerson's optimistic and Hawthorne's darker opinion of human nature. It cites examples from both writers to support points made. It states whether the student agrees with either writer, or has a different view.

Analyzing Language and Style

ARCHAIC AND OLD-FASHIONED WORDS
1. Words that are rarely used today include *crape, prodigy, well-nigh, waggery, wrought.*
2. Here are some modern substitutes. Students' answers may vary.
   crape: a light, crinkled fabric
   prodigy: extraordinary phenomenon
   well-nigh, waggery: nearly, mischief
   wrought: worked
3. These words have different meanings today:
   crape: (crepe) a light, crinkled paper
   prodigy: a highly talented child
   wrought: in set phrases—"wrought iron," "all wrought up over nothing"

Extending the Story

Ask your students to imagine what this story might have been like if Poe had written it. What might have been gained? What lost? Would they have enjoyed it more? Would they have gotten as much of a glimpse into human nature?

RAPPACCINI'S DAUGHTER

Objectives

1. To respond to a short story with several themes
2. To analyze character, climax, setting, and irony
3. To interpret the story's message
4. To extend the story by writing a new ending
5. To analyze the story's Romantic elements
6. To write an essay comparing and contrasting two stories
7. To write an essay describing Biblical parallels
8. To identify word connotations and figures of speech

Introducing the Story

Here are the major elements of the story:

- **Protagonists:** Giovanni, a young student at the University of Padua; Beatrice Rappaccini, beautiful daughter of Dr. Rappaccini
- **Antagonist:** Dr. Giacomo Rappaccini, a scientist experimenting with plants
- **Conflicts:** science vs. nature; love vs. intellect
- **Point of view:** third-person
- **Significant techniques:** symbolism and allegory, setting, character foils
- **Setting:** long ago in Padua, Italy
- **Themes:** the arrogant overdevelopment of the intellect at the expense of the heart; the tragic destruction of innocence; the perverted use of science

BACKGROUND ON THE STORY The major literary product of Hawthorne's stay in Concord was the 1846 publication of *Mosses from an Old Manse,* a book whose stories had been written in the same room in which Emerson had written "Nature." "Rappaccini's Daughter," first published in *Democratic Review,* December 1844, appears in this collection of stories. In 1846 Hawthorne took a job at the Salem Custom House and left Concord for good. While preparing the second edition of *Mosses from an Old Manse* in 1854, Hawthorne wrote to his publisher this comment on his work:

> I am not quite sure that I entirely comprehend my own meanings in some of these blasted allegories; but I remember that [when I wrote them] I always had a meaning, or at least thought I had.

THE PLOT Staying in a room overlooking Rappaccini's garden of poisonous plants, Giovanni becomes infatuated with Beatrice Rappaccini, but is warned against her by Baglioni. Rappaccini has infused a poisonous nature into his own daughter by rearing her among his plants. Giovanni then discovers that he himself has acquired the same poisonous touch. He tries to free Beatrice with the aid of Baglioni's antidote, but it kills her, and she dies reproaching the men around her.

Teaching Strategies

PROVIDING FOR CULTURAL DIFFERENCES Many students may find it hard to believe that a father could experiment with his daugher's life. Ask them to talk about parents' roles as they know them from their own backgrounds. What do they think are the parents' responsibilities to their children? Are these roles the same in all cultures?

PROVIDING FOR DIFFERENT LEVELS OF ABILITY The Italian Renaissance setting, which gave the story a fashionably antique atmosphere in its own day, may now be a barrier for some students. All they need really know about it is that (as in Shakespeare) Renaissance Italy represented a vague, glowing atmosphere of bygone romance.

The length of the story may also make it a challenge for your less advanced students. Class discussion can be used to elicit paraphrases. Students who may not be very interested in a story about a desiccated Paduan apothecary may become more interested upon realizing that the story is about a mad scientist; his beautiful, sheltered daughter; a handsome young suitor; and a meddling neighbor.

READING THE STORY Because this is a rather long story, you may want to assign it as homework, and, afterward, read only the beginning in class. If you read at least through the Baglioni-Giovanni scene on text pages 278–279, you will have introduced the four major characters and foreshadowed the major conflict. Or you may play the audiocassette recording of Hawthorne's exposition, which runs from the beginning of the story through Giovanni's dream after his first sight of Beatrice in the garden.

RETEACHING ALTERNATIVES The mad-scientist aspect of this story will probably be easier for your students to grasp than the interpersonal-relations aspect, which is stronger here than in any of the other works in this unit. Using the board and class discussion, you might want to list the characters' traits and the ways they manipulate each other. You might also divide the class into four groups, each taking the side of one of the characters against the other three.

Responding to the Story   Text page 292

Answers to the questions in the Pupil's Edition appear in the Annotated Teacher's Edition.

Writing About the Story

For help in revising their compositions, refer students to **Grammar, Usage, and Mechanics: A Reference Guide** on text pages 1183–1228 at the back of their books.

A CREATIVE RESPONSE
1. Ending the Story   Have students meet in small groups to brainstorm some possible endings. Students can collaborate on writing an ending or work alone. Have each group read its ending aloud, while students listen to decide which ending they like best.

▶ CRITERIA FOR EVALUATING THE ASSIGNMENT   The paper is at least one paragraph long. It explains what happens to Giovanni, Rappaccini, and the garden. It contains specific details and is consistent with the rest of the story.

A CRITICAL RESPONSE
2. Analyzing the Story's Romantic Elements   The writing assignment defines the Romantic outlook and suggests a plan of organization for the essay.

▶ CRITERIA FOR EVALUATING THE ASSIGNMENT   The essay refers to details in the text and covers all four topics in the assignment. Each subject should be covered in a separate paragraph.

3. Comparing Stories   Briefly discuss what isolates Reverend Hooper (''The Minister's Black Veil'') and Beatrice (''Rappaccini's Daughter'') from others, and why. Hooper takes upon himself the expression of universal secret sin. People fear that he is mad, a sinner, or both. Beatrice's isolation is involuntary. She is a victim of her father's love of science, poisonous to others.

▶ CRITERIA FOR EVALUATING THE ASSIGNMENT   The paragraph explains what isolates Reverend Hooper and what isolates Beatrice, and the purpose in each case.

4. Comparing Stories   Students may leap to the conclusion that it is the minister's veil and Beatrice's beauty which conceal evil. Discuss the concept until they discover the facade of the people around Hooper, and the scientific facade of Rappaccini and the beauty of his plants.

▶ CRITERIA FOR EVALUATING THE ASSIGNMENT   The paper explains the different ways in which both stories reveal that evil can exist behind a facade of normalcy or beauty. Students end with their response to this idea.

5. Describing Biblical Parallels   Read Genesis 1–3 aloud as students listen for parallels. Divide the class into six groups and assign one of the questions to each group. After discussing the question, a spokesperson for each group should present the group's conclusions. Listeners should have the opportunity to question and further discuss any conclusion. Ask students to identify direct allusions to Genesis in Hawthorne's story.

▶ CRITERIA FOR EVALUATING THE ASSIGNMENT   The paper explains the six points requested: How the gardens are (1) similar and (2) different; and what or whom Hawthorne presents as equivalent to (3) the forbidden tree, (4) Adam, (5) Eve, and (6) the serpent. The paper also cites passages from the story that allude to elements of the Biblical account.

Analyzing Language and Style

CONNOTATIONS
1. Students' answers may vary; these are possibilities:
   a. *emaciated:* feeble, skeletal, bones almost visible, sickly
   b. *sallow:* sickly, yellowish
   c. *sickly looking:* thin, pale, bent over, weak
   d. *scholar's garb of black:* ceremonial gown, funeral gown

2. Rappaccini approaches the shrubs and flowers as if they were ''savage beasts, or deadly snakes, or evil spirits.'' The figure of speech makes the reader want to recoil, and suggests that the doctor deals in evil, deadly matters.

3. *Deadlier malice, inward disease*

4. The words *rich and youthful voice;* figures of speech about a tropical sunset and delectable perfumes.

5. The words *beautiful, life, energy, health, fair;* figures of speech comparing her with a flower.

6. The fact that Beatrice freely handles deadly things her father must avoid suggests evil within her. The emotional effect is to make one back off from Beatrice in fear or awe.

7. The description of Beatrice on text pages 279–280 reinforces the impression of beauty that conceals something deadly. The description of Dr. Rappaccini on page 281 suggests that inner energy is more powerful than the wasted appearance. See also text pages 283, 285, 288 (Beatrice) and 290 (Dr. Rappaccini). Only at its end (text pages 290–291) does the story restore one's original impression that Beatrice is good and her father is evil.

Extending the Story

Gothic horror tales, including mad-scientist tales such as Mary Shelley's *Frankenstein,* were at their height of popularity in the early nineteenth century. They have remained popular ever since: from turn-of-the-century science fiction like Wells's *The Invisible Man,* to classic horror movies like *Bride of Frankenstein,* to updated remakes like *The Fly.* Your students have probably enjoyed some examples of the genre and might enjoy discussing the reasons for the appeal of the genre, the similarities and differences among earlier and later works, and the particular relevance of the subject matter to our highly technological age.

Primary Sources   Text page 293

HAWTHORNE AND THE MONUMENT AT CONCORD
In this excerpt from ''The Old Manse,'' Hawthorne relates a story about the Revolutionary War in which a young man (not a soldier) who is chopping wood goes to see what is happening when he hears the noise of battle. He finds the battlefield deserted. A wounded Briton stares at the boy, who kills him with an axe blow to his head.

Hawthorne says that ''The story comes home to me like truth'' and that he often wonders what happened to the boy. Read the excerpt aloud in class, and ask students to use what they know about Hawthorne to consider why the author was so attracted to this story and what he felt that he learned from it. Ask them to speculate on what happened to the boy during the war and after the war. How would students have reacted had they been the boy on that battlefield?

A Reader-Response Approach

Jane Carlson of Boulder High School in Boulder, Colorado, reports on her success in using a reader-response approach with this story (''Readers Responding to 'Rappaccini's Daughter,' '' *English Journal,* January 1988, pp. 49–53):

Recently I put a reader-response approach to the test in teaching Nathaniel Hawthorne's ''Rappaccini's Daughter'' to a sophomore writing class. I was brought to this drastic change by studying literary theory, especially reader-response criticism, and by the teaching styles of two professors who opened up my response to literature. One of them, Marty Bickman, in his monograph, *Active Learning,* shows how students construct meaning, without his agenda subverting ''the open market place of class reaction'' (36). This monograph became the guidebook for my experiment with reader-response and his teaching a model to follow. We began

our study by talking about story telling: stories our grandparents and relatives tell us and stories teenagers tell one another. I gave the students a handout of lists:

Characters
Dr. Rappaccini, a physician and a scientist
Beatrice, Dr. Rappaccini's daughter
Giovanni, a student
Lisbetta, the old landlady
Professor Pietro Baglioni

Places
The University of Padua (in Italy)
An old rooming house
A garden

Things
A shrub with many purple blossoms
A silver vase
An insect
A small orange chameleon

The goal was to make up a story using as many of the clues as possible. They begged to work in pairs, and that idea appealed to me also. As far as they knew they were the original narrators; no one had heard of Hawthorne's ''Rappaccini's Daughter,'' and I didn't mention it. The next day the students read their stories aloud. Some were sci-fi with a high-tech emphasis; others were variations of Italian soap operas: Giovanni loved Beatrice who was having an affair with Baglioni whose affection was reserved for Lisbetta.

I had misgivings about teaching ''Rappaccini's Daughter'' to sophomores. The story is filled with subtle innuendos, the characters and scenes are often mysterious (qualities that could also be advantages), and the vocabulary is difficult. I wanted to do some sort of prereading exercise but not to skew the students' meanings by anything I said or implied before their reading. I could justify a creative story to familiarize the class with people's names, places, and a few significant objects; I could also rationalize going over difficult words presented in context and reading the introduction aloud to get the students into the first pages. But that, I decided, was enough for activating schema. They found out, of course, when we began going over the vocabulary that the story ''Rappaccini's Daughter'' had already been told by Nathaniel Hawthorne. Their own stories made them eager to see how Hawthorne's story was similar to or different from theirs.

The second stage of the reader-response experiment began as I gave each student a packet of paper. The cover page was my letter to them:

You will do four free writings during your reading of ''Rappaccini's Daughter.'' The writings will come at specific times: at the end of pages 98, 107, 116, and 128. In each writing try to put together the meaning of what you have read. Ask yourself these questions:

What has happened?

How does that fit/not fit in with the meaning as I understand it now?

What phrases, lines, paragraphs are confusing?

Why are they confusing?

What am I learning about the places, the characters, the events?

What are my reactions, and why am I reacting in this way?

It is possible that you will not answer all of these questions each time you write. Maybe other questions will occur to you, and that's okay too. These writings and other in-class free writings will substitute for an analysis paper.

I had reasons for breaking up the reading with free writings. First, I wanted to see how their meanings developed. Where did they begin to put the pieces together? In what specific places did they falter? Also, I had in mind testing the approach of Steven Mailloux, who has based his reader-oriented analysis of "Rappaccini's Daughter" on a temporal model, for as he explains, "A temporal model interprets American fiction (in this case "Rappaccini's Daughter") by bringing to the foreground the author's rhetoric of entanglement, a rhetoric resulting in sequential responses from the reader" (90).

My read-then-write, read-then-write assignments, I theorized, should reveal these sequential responses and, in addition, should be helpful to the reader in clarifying and articulating the meanings. Mailloux identifies three enigmas the reader encounters: (1) Who (and soon what) is Rappaccini's daughter? (2) What is the garden? (3) What exactly is the relation between Beatrice and the garden? As these enigmas are slowly solved, explains Mailloux, the text introduces two related plot conflicts—the thwarted affair of the young lovers and the rivalry between Rappaccini and Baglioni—plots that are resolved by the death of Beatrice. A second text is initiated and disguised by the first text (enigmas and conflicts). Disguised, Mailloux explains, by the narrator's misleading and undercutting comments. This second reading scenario tests the reader's moral judgment: which source of information is to be trusted, and finally, who is really responsible for Beatrice's death? (74–85) I assume that Mailloux posited these possibilities for "Rappaccini's Daughter" after he himself had read the story and holistically synthesized the meaning. Another reason, then, for the four free writings was to support or disprove his hypotheses.

The free writings were, for me, the most exciting part of the study. Each day the students read, then wrote, then handed their journals in to me. I checked them but did not write comments, again waiting to see when they would answer the questions they asked, how they would put everything together. Often they responded to the enigmas Mailloux proposed.

Jena: I don't understand why Dr. Rappaccini avoids touching and smelling the flowers and Beatrice inhales the odor of the plants.

Eric: Could it be that the plant might kill Dr. Rappaccini while it gives life to Beatrice?

Roger: Giovanni has a scar on his arm where Beatrice grabbed him. Is she a mutant or something? I think she is a demon.

Jill: There is some mystery in the relationship of Dr. Rappaccini, Beatrice, and the flowers. I'm curious as to how Giovanni will be involved, as participant or observer.

Although I had not asked that they make predictions, many of them did.

Amy: I think Giovanni will become like Beatrice.

Clay: From what I have read so far, it sounds like a *Romeo and Juliet* type of story.

Several comments surprised me. Phrases I had barely noticed became extremely important to some of the students. For instance, Nyssa, whose interest is science, wrote, "I like the way Giovanni refers to science as an art."

Brian picked up on the misleading narrator: "The author keeps contradicting himself." And Jena was not sure which person to trust: "Because Hawthorne said that Giovanni couldn't have seen the chameleon die, I wonder how he (Giovanni) knew. Did he just sense it? I don't think so."

Clearly the most confusing part of the story was Baglioni's role and also his final statement, "Rappaccini, Rappaccini! And is this the upshot of your experiment?" Many journals registered confusion:

What does Baglioni's last statement mean?

Is he bad or good?

I'm not sure if Professor Baglioni is helping or doing harm.

They were working hard to assign the moral responsibility Mailloux includes as the second text.

Each day the journals improved in quality. From fairly general observations, student responses became more detailed and specific. Of course, the mystery became more engrossing, and students became involved. Michelle wrote, "The story is becoming more interesting now. I feel sympathy toward Giovanni, and I have mixed emotions about Beatrice."

Even though I did not comment in the journals, I offered encouragement each day, telling the students they were competent readers, fully capable of constructing meaning. We discussed their reading strategies and started listing them each day on the board:

Readers read some sections several times to grasp the meaning.

Readers sometimes skip and an explanation comes later.

Readers ask questions.

Readers make predictions.

Readers paraphrase and then check to see if their words make sense.

Sometimes one word or one phrase stumps a reader, and it's hard to get back on track.

Readers become frustrated, lose concentration.

Readers like to figure things out.

Their list reminds me of Iser's explanation of recreation:

> The act of recreation is not a smooth or continuous process, but one which, in its essence, relies on interruptions of the flow to render it efficacious. We look forward, we look back, we decide, we change our decisions, we form expectations, we are shocked by their nonfulfillment, we question, we muse, we accept, we reject; this is the dynamic process of recreation. (Tompkins 62)

The next step in this process was sharing questions and possible answers, first in small groups, then with the entire class. Robert Crosman describes the communal process:

> Reading is both a solitary and a communal enterprise; we read both for self-discovery and to learn about the world; and we go on learning, after we have read a text, by sharing our interpretation with others, and by letting their interpretations enrich our own. (214)

By this time the students were hungry to discuss their ideas. Alyssa noted in her journal after her small group session. "We thought about our questions and didn't really come up with for-sure answers. We came up with many possibilities, though. We made up more 'what-if' questions."

The whole class discussion was organized this way: each student asked a question, and any other student could answer (or try to answer it). On that day students continued to work out Baglioni's role and the moral responsibility for Beatrice's death. I gave no explanations but continually reminded them to find the specific place in the text. The two words on the last page, "in triumph," which Malcolm spotted, were crucial to the understanding of the rivalry between the two older men. The students reread aloud the scenes where Giovanni meets Baglioni and the entire last scene in the garden.

The final writing assignment was a worksheet I made up following the pattern suggested by Bickman's monograph: "The greatest challenge is to have the worksheets structured but still open-ended" (27). My New Critical background at first hindered me from following Bickman's suggestions; I began writing questions about symbols. Unconsciously I was slipping back into "the role of custodian and informed explicator" (Corcoran

and Evans 2). At 11:00 p.m. I threw away what I had written. "What are the students most interested in?" I asked myself. "What still baffles them?"

The answers came easily: the relationship between the characters and their motives and Dr. Baglioni's role. For fun, a little divergent thinking, I threw in a question on poison. As it turned out, this one was the most frustrating for the students. "What do you want us to do?" they asked. "Should we write a paragraph about poison with a topic sentence?" "Ah," thought I, feeling smug in my new reader-response wisdom, "this is the way form inhibits content."

Worksheet on "Rappaccini's Daughter"

Include specific examples from the story as you write on these questions:

1. The word "poison" appears often in this story. And words related to poison also occur frequently—"venom," "antidote," "deadly malice," and "virulent." What do you make of all these references to poison in RD?

2. What does Professor Baglioni's final statement mean to you? How do his words relate to the story?

3. Several of you worked out complicated relationships between the characters in your original stories. What are the relationships in Hawthorne's story, and what are the feelings behind these relationships?

Choose *one* of the following options:

Option 1. Begin with the Professor's last statement and continue the last scene until we know what happens to the remaining characters. Follow Hawthorne's intent in his characterizations, as you understand it, as you write your ending.

Option 2. Write a poem that synthesizes the meaning of the story. Explore your interpretation in a concise form, a haiku, for instance.
    5 syllables in the first line
    7 syllables in the second line
    5 syllables in the third line

Option 3. You are a director of the film *Rappaccini's Daughter*. Take one scene (be sure to say which one you are choosing) and write director's notes. Include how the characters will be dressed, how they will speak, move about the stage, depict their parts. Also, what props and scenery will be used, what type of lighting.

"Just play with the idea," I answered. "Do a free writing on poison. Use your own ideas."

They had the most fun with the three options—a poem, a continuation of the story, or a director's notes. Jeff took great care with the colors in his scene. Beatrice was to wear a lavender gown to symbolize (his word, not mine) her identification with the purple blossoms. Heidi's haiku revealed her understanding of the victimization (my word, not hers) of Beatrice:

Destruction is wreaked
Upon the innocent by
The power moguls

Most students wrote a continuation of the last scene. I particularly admired Clay's simulation of Hawthorne's style. He began, "Giovanni looked at Baglioni, then fell to his knees in front of the hapless body." "Hapless" seemed a rather unusual word choice for a fifteen-year-old boy!

The next day I asked the students to share an idea from their worksheets. We began in an organized way with each one reading a personal insight but ended in one of the most energetic, committed discussions I have heard. Jill asked the question, "Why did Lisbetta lead Giovanni into the garden?" This was the enigma neither Mailloux nor the class had discussed. The students reacted with fervor:

Lisbetta was just an old busy-body.

No, I think she was being paid off by Rappaccini.

Yeah, she probably put Giovanni in that room next to the garden on purpose.

No way. How could she have known that Giovanni was going to fall in love with Beatrice?

And on and on. I sat in the classroom as an observer, listening to the opinions. Obviously, I was no longer the resident authority with the students passively accepting my judgments. They were the critics responding to the entanglements of the text.

I kept a journal of my teaching of "Rappaccini's Daughter." Sometimes the entries show frustration: "Today the class is figuring out the relationships between the characters. Each student seems to say in different words what another has just stated. It is endless."

Maybe I was just tired that day, or maybe I was chafing inwardly at my loss of control. Whatever the case, this kind of teaching does take time. Again, Bickman's advice helped allay my anxieties: "What may seem banal or intuitively obvious for the teacher, who may have passed this way decades ago and forgotten his own learning processes, may need to be stated, clarified, reiterated, explicated by students for each other" (38).

Most of the time, though, I was elated. Students who ordinarily did not pay attention felt challenged to come up with their own meanings. Although the reading competency of the students varied, everyone made an effort to read, understand, write responses, and listen to each other. At the end of our last discussion I asked them what they liked the most in our study of "Rappaccini's Daughter."

You spend each day listening to us.

We could work in pairs and small groups.

You never told us what you thought the meaning was.

You let us figure it out.

I think this feeling of respect, mine for my students, was an important "upshot" of my experiment with a reader-response approach. Although I faltered occasionally (especially in the first draft of the worksheet questions), I did listen to my students. Each one brought a unique background to the story. Jill had lived in Italy for a year and had visited Padua; for her the story recaptured memories of ancient Italian mansions and courtyard gardens. Mason had read many stories, some in comic book format, of macabre poisonings by means of exotic herbs and plants. Their reactions, as well as the perceptions of other students—puzzled, humorous, and creative—enhanced the understanding of the story for us all. Instead of a passive audience dutifully taking notes from the teacher's lecture, this tenth grade class was in charge. A sense of discovery and adventure revitalized the air space in room 151 while twenty-five students participated individually and collectively as co-creators with Hawthorne of "Dr. Rappaccini's Daughter."

Works Cited

Bickman, Martin. *Active Learning in the University: Faculty Teaching Excellence Program.* Boulder: U of Colorado, 1986.

Corcoran, Bill, and Emrys Evans, eds. *Readers, Texts, Teachers.* Upper Montclair, NJ: Boynton/Cook, 1987.

Crosman, Robert. "How Readers Make Meaning." *College Literature* 9.3 (1982): 207–15.

Mailloux, Steven. *Interpretive Conventions.* Ithaca: Cornell UP, 1982.

Probst, Robert. "Mom, Wolfgang and Me: Adolescent Literature, Critical Theory and the English Classroom." *English Journal* 75.6 (1986): 33–39.

———. "Three Relationships in the Teaching of Literature." *English Journal* 75.1 (1986): 60–68.

Tompkins, Jane, ed. *Reader Response Criticism: From Formalism to Post-Structuralism.* Baltimore: Johns Hopkins UP, 1980.

Herman Melville

FROM MOBY-DICK

Objectives

1. To respond to excerpts from one of the most important novels in American literature

2. To analyze significant elements of the novel: point of view, foreshadowing, characterization, personification, imagery, and symbolism

3. To identify and interpret similes and metaphors

4. To describe an event from another point of view

5. To write an essay comparing and contrasting a speech with Transcendentalist ideas

6. To write a paragraph analyzing a character

7. To write an essay interpreting a symbol

8. To discuss the significance of characters' names

Introducing the Novel

Here are the major elements of the novel:

- **Protagonist:** Ishmael, the narrator, a young man who ships out on the *Pequod*

- **Antagonist:** Ahab, the one-legged captain of the *Pequod*

- **Conflicts:** person vs. self (Ahab), person vs. nature (the whale)

- **Point of view:** first-person (Ishmael)

- **Significant techniques:** symbolism, allegory, allusion, metaphor, foreshadowing, parody, and characterization

- **Setting:** a whaling ship, out of Nantucket, sailing the south Atlantic, Pacific, and Indian oceans in the 1800's

- **Themes:** human self-destructiveness in the quest for the unrealizable; the ability of an idealistic, self-reliant leader to gain absolute power; the cruelty and unfathomability of surrounding forces

BACKGROUND ON THE NOVEL   Melville is the classic example of an author whose career suffered when his work deepened. He began *Moby-Dick* as a factual account of life in the whaling industry, and by late summer of 1850 was finished with the book. In September, however, he moved to Arrowhead, a farm near Pittsfield, Massachusetts, which was his home for the next twelve years.

It was during this time, when *Moby-Dick* was being "broiled in the hell-fire" of his brain, that Melville became friends with Hawthorne, who lived in nearby Lenox. The two novelists shared an interest in the darker side of human nature and destiny, and both took an intellectually skeptical view of doctrines of human progress that were popular at the time. Both men were fascinated by the complexities of human psychology, especially the effects of alienation and distortions of the ego. Association with Hawthorne and other writers and critics during this time helped Melville express, in his sea story, his own quest for the ultimate truth of human existence.

Plot summaries for each chapter also appear in the Annotated Teacher's Edition.

THE PLOT OF "LOOMINGS"   (Chapter 1 in the novel) *Moby-Dick* begins with the three words, "Call me Ishmael." Ishmael says that some years ago, having no money and nothing on shore to interest him, when life seemed to cause "a damp, drizzly November in my soul," he sought escape at sea. He went as an ordinary seaman, having no desire for the responsibilities of an officer. He claims that people in all times and places have been drawn to the magic of the sea. What he is unable to understand or explain is why he chose a whaling ship. Directed by "the stage managers, the Fates," he assumes that he has been selected for some role in a grand performance they are staging.

THE PLOT OF "AHAB"   (Chapter 28 in the novel) For several days after leaving Nantucket, nothing is seen of the ship's captain, who remains in seclusion in his cabin. One gray, gloomy morning as he goes to take his watch at noon, Ishmael glances toward the ship's stern. He shivers with foreboding as he realizes he is looking at Ahab. Ishmael is so shocked by Ahab's appearance that he initially fails to realize that part of the reason the captain appears so grim is "owing to the barbaric white leg upon which he stood." Ahab stands erect, his leg anchored in one of two small holes drilled into either side of the deck. Neither Ahab nor the officers speak as the captain looks forward over the prow of the boat. His look is one of "firmest fortitude" and "unsurrenderable willfulness." Before long Ahab retreats to his cabin but is seen every day thereafter, seated, walking unsteadily on the deck, or standing with his leg anchored in the deck.

THE PLOT OF "THE QUARTER-DECK" (Chapter 36 in the novel) Ahab intensely paces the deck, lost in thought. Even after he returns to his cabin, the sound of Ahab's ferocious pacing continues. Just before sunset, Ahab appears again on the deck and orders Starbuck to assemble the entire crew. When the crew stands before him, Ahab uses oratory to excite their passion for whale-killing. Then he nails a doubloon, a Spanish ounce of gold, to the main mast, and promises it to the first man who spots "that white-headed whale, with three holes punctured in his starboard fluke." He reveals that the quest for Moby-Dick is the true purpose of this voyage. The men are enthusiastic, except for the level-headed first mate, Starbuck, who objects to Ahab's seeking vengeance on a "dumb brute," an animal that acts instinctively and without malice. At the end of the chapter, the crew drinks to their quest, and Ahab pours grog into the inverted heads of the harpooners' shafts, in a blasphemous mock-communion.

THE PLOT OF "MOBY-DICK" (Chapter 41 in the novel) In this chapter the reader learns more of the character of the whale and also comes to realize that Ahab is insane.

Teaching Strategies

PROVIDING FOR CULTURAL DIFFERENCES Students with strong religious beliefs may be troubled by the mock-communion and by Melville's emphasis on the destructive or indifferent, rather than creative and loving, aspect of cosmic forces. Point out that in portraying evil, Melville is not endorsing it, and that in challenging God on the question of evil, he is directly in line with—and doubtless modeling himself on—Job and the Biblical prophets.

PROVIDING FOR DIFFERENT LEVELS OF ABILITY Your more advanced students will quickly devour these four tidbits from an immense feast, and should be encouraged to read the entire novel on their own. Other students may be intimidated by Melville's lofty rhetoric and use of archaic allusions (Seneca, Cato, Cellini). Discuss problems of vocabulary and syntax as they arise; paraphrase freely. You may want to give your students a very brief synopsis of each chapter before they read it; this will be of considerable help in overcoming barriers to their understanding.

READING THE NOVEL "Loomings" is accompanied by a thirteen-minute audiocassette recording. Few, if any, passages in American literature are worthier of being spoken aloud than this prologue in the voice of Ishmael. The other chapters can be read aloud by students. In the scenes featuring the crew, a different student can be assigned to speak each sailor's lines.

RETEACHING ALTERNATIVES Divide the class into four groups, one for each of the four chapters, and have each group present an oral report or a creative presentation to the class. "The Quarter-Deck" is ideal for dramatization. For "Moby-Dick," the students might actually want to present the whale's point of view.

Alternatively, divide the class by characters rather than by chapters. (You might include some of the minor but revealing characters such as Starbuck and Queequeg.) This will allow students to arrive at insights they might not have reached through Ishmael's first-person narration alone.

Responding to the Novel   Text page 316

Answers to the questions in the Pupil's Edition appear in the Annotated Teacher's Edition.

Writing About the Novel

For help in revising their compositions, refer students to **Grammar, Usage, and Mechanics: A Reference Guide** on text pages 1183–1228 at the back of their books.

A CREATIVE RESPONSE
1. *Describing an Event from Another Point of View* Discuss the questions at the end of the assignment to help students get ideas for their entries. Caution them to make their entries consistent with everything they've learned about Ahab's character. You may want to review his traits briefly—perhaps with the chart in writing assignment 3. Have students choose a specific event in the voyage to write about.

▶ CRITERIA FOR EVALUATING THE ASSIGNMENT Through comments on an event, the log entry reveals Ahab's fears, desires, and feelings. Ask for volunteers to read aloud their log entries. Listeners should evaluate whether the entry is consistent with Ahab's character.

A CRITICAL RESPONSE
2. *Comparing Ahab's Speech with Transcendental Ideas* Direct students to "The Transcendentalists" (text pages 183–184), "Emerson and Transcendentalism: The American Roots" (text pages 184–185), and especially text page 186, which comments specifically on Melville and Transcendentalism.

▶ CRITERIA FOR EVALUATING THE ASSIGNMENT The essay presents in an orderly manner the ways in which Captain Ahab's speech agrees with Transcendentalist thought and the ways in which it rejects Transcendentalism. Students should observe that both look beyond physical reality to find a spiritual reality. For the Transcendalists, the meaning in Nature is God and human perfectibility. Ahab, in contrast, sees evil in the natural world and seeks vengeance. The Transcendalists strive for union with Nature and God.

3. *Analyzing a Character* Have students work together to complete the suggested chart before they begin writing.

▶ CRITERIA FOR EVALUATING THE ASSIGNMENT The paragraph offers several conclusions about Captain Ahab that can logically be deduced from his speech, actions, appearance, and thoughts.

4. *Explaining a Symbol* Read aloud D. H. Lawrence's comments about *Moby-Dick* and discuss the symbolism students see in the great white whale. Students may suggest evil, Nature, death, fear. Assure them there is no one "right" answer and that you want them to respond by telling what the whale means to them personally. Remind them that their essay should cite passages that have suggested this interpretation to them.

▶ CRITERIA FOR EVALUATING THE ASSIGNMENT The essay briefly explains what the whale Moby-Dick symbolizes to the student and cites supportive passages from the text.

Analyzing Language and Style

NAMES AND THEIR SIGNIFICANCE

Ahab was the king of Israel from 869 to 850 B.C. He knew right, but failed to do it. Encouraged by his wicked wife Jezebel, he built temples to her foreign gods and offered them sacrificial pagan worship. Melville's Ahab is similarly willing to sacrifice everything to his "god," the pursuit of Moby-Dick. Although the Biblical King Ahab was an excellent soldier, he was killed in battle, and when he was buried, dogs drank his blood.

In the Bible, Ishmael was the son of Abraham and Hagar, a serving maid of Abraham's wife, Sarah. Since Sarah did not have a son yet, the custom of the time made Ishmael the heir to Abraham's estate. When Isaac was born to Sarah, the two mothers became jealous rivals, and Abraham was compelled to send Ishmael and Hagar away into the wilderness in accordance with Sarah's wishes. God told the hesitant Abraham to do as Sarah desired. Although Ishmael grew up to be an archer and married an Egyptian woman who bore him many sons, he was an outcast whose name has come to be symbolic of a displaced person or wanderer. In *Moby-Dick*, Ishmael is not only a wanderer in the physical world of the sea, but also a spiritual wanderer in search of the real meaning in life.

Extending the Novel

1. Melville and Poe might seem to be opposites in many ways: the former, an artist on the broadest canvas, grandiloquent and somewhat heedless of form, the latter a craftsman of exquisite miniatures on rather claustrophobic subjects. Your students may be surprised to learn that Poe's only book-length work of fiction, *The Narrative of Arthur Gordon Pym*, is about a bizarre sea voyage in which the color white has symbolic meaning. Many critics feel that it influenced Melville. Students might enjoy reading this work and comparing it with *Moby-Dick*.

2. Your students have now encountered the fiction of Hawthorne, Melville, and Poe, and have some ideas of the similarities and differences among the three. This may be a good time to place these writers in a larger context, and to get an idea of the extent of their particular range, which resulted from the mind-set of their cultures. You might initiate discussion by asking, "What kinds of things *didn't* Hawthorne, Poe, and Melville write about?" (Social issues, heroic heroes, marriage, children, hopeful views of life)

3. Students playing the roles of Hawthorne, Poe, Melville, Emerson, and Thoreau might present a panel discussion. Each author should address three points: what's most important in life, why they write what they write, how they hope they will be remembered.

Primary Sources   Text page 317

A LETTER AND A JOURNAL ENTRY

Melville's letter to Hawthorne and Hawthorne's journal entry about Melville reveal much about Melville's character. Ask students what they can infer from these primary sources. (Melville's letter shows him to be absent-minded, self-absorbed, humorous. Hawthorne calls him grave and reserved; not caring much for material things—like clothing and clean underwear; restless in spirit. Hawthorne clearly admires Melville's noble nature.)

SHILOH

ART

Objectives

1. To respond to the poems
2. To paraphrase lines from a poem
3. To recognize situational irony
4. To write an essay comparing and contrasting the ideas about art in two poems

Introducing the Poems

Melville's style anticipated twentieth-century versification techniques. However, his poems are often flawed by archaic words, forced rhymes, and awkward, inverted word order.

Here are the major elements of "Shiloh":

- **Rhythm:** iambic tetrameter and trimeter
- **Rhyme:** abcbddeebffgghghbib
- **Significant techniques:** internal rhyme, alliteration, imagery, irony

Here are the major elements of "Art":

- **Rhythm:** iambic tetrameter
- **Rhyme:** aabbccdeeff
- **Significant techniques:** alliteration, personification

THE LITERAL MEANING OF SHILOH This song-like poem reminds readers that the waste of life in battle can never be undone. The poet describes the swallows that fly over the field at Shiloh, where the log-built church once served as a hospital for the dying men of both sides. As they lay dying, fame and country were of little concern to the soldiers, who now lie buried in the hushed fields of Shiloh.

Art Creation of a work of art requires wrestling with unknown forces. Patience and energy, humility and pride, love and hate, and instinct and study are some of the dissimilar qualities that must be fused together if one is to be able to "wrestle with the angel—Art."

Teaching Strategies

PROVIDING FOR CULTURAL DIFFERENCES The Civil War scene in "Shiloh" will seem more remote to students in some sections of the country than in others. You may want to draw an analogy with more recent wars and point out that Melville's requiem could be for soldiers of any war. Melville's view of art, in "Art," arises from a highly individualistic culture. Much great art, in various cultures, has been produced as part of an informal process, or a group religious effort, or an individual fusion with—rather than wrestling with—spiritual forces. Additionally, Melville's reference to Jacob may be unfamiliar to students who are not from Judeo-Christian backgrounds. It may be clarified by reading the headnote to "Art" on text page 319.

PROVIDING FOR DIFFERENT LEVELS OF ABILITY Paraphrase "Shiloh" before students read it, so that they can have in mind a picture of the aftermath of a battle, with swallows flying over the field on which twenty thousand dead soldiers lie—enough to fill an arena. Because of its highly compressed syntax and mystical imagery, paraphrase of "Art" is essential for all students. More advanced students can work toward such a paraphrase on their own.

READING THE POEMS "Shiloh," a tranquil, descriptive piece, can be read aloud by a single student. Because it is more difficult, you might want to read "Art" aloud yourself. On a second reading, stop where necessary to paraphrase and clarify.

RETEACHING ALTERNATIVES After students have read and discussed each poem, you might ask them to write in their own words, in a sentence or two, the poem's literal meaning.

Or have them go back over both poems and choose the one they like better. Have them meet with a partner to explain why they prefer one poem to the other.

Responding to the Poem

Answers to the questions in the Pupil's Edition appear in the Annotated Teacher's Edition.

Writing About the Poem

For help in revising their compositions, refer students to **Grammar, Usage, and Mechanics: A Reference Guide** on text pages 1183–1228 at the back of their books.

A CRITICAL RESPONSE

Comparing Poems   Have students first attempt to summarize the advice Melville and Emerson offer to the artist in their poems. Then discuss each of the questions in the writing assignment.

▶ CRITERIA FOR EVALUATING THE ASSIGNMENT   Students should write well-organized paragraphs noting the similarities and differences. Both poets write about merging opposites. Emerson mentions art as restoring the past; his sunny, romantic message would appeal to sentimental or traditional artists. Melville focuses on the agony of the act of creating new, imaginative works. His advice would appeal to boldly experimental artists.

Extending the Poem

Several poems in this textbook are natural candidates for comparison with "Shiloh": Whitman's "A Sight in Camp" (text page 348), Crane's "War Is Kind" (text page 463), and Stevens's "The Death of a Soldier" (text page 752). You might have students compare and contrast Whitman's, Crane's, and Stevens's poems with Melville's.

EXERCISES IN CRITICAL THINKING AND WRITING

Text page 321

ANALYZING AND EVALUATING PERSUASIVE WRITING: RHETORIC

Although student answers may vary somewhat, the following responses to questions 1–4 on the Emerson excerpt are representative. Answers to questions 5 and 6 will vary. Have students discuss those questions in class or share their written answers.

1. Emerson's purpose is to convince his audience that they should learn to recognize their spontaneous thoughts and speak what they think.

2. I read some verses by a painter the other day that represented his original thought. This speaking your own thought is genius. The greatness of Moses, Plato, and Milton, in fact, is that they spoke what they truly thought. We should learn to recognize our spontaneous thoughts, lest they come back to us later when someone else speaks them. Every person learns, at some time, that he or she has something new in the universe and that only he or she can make something of it. Each of us represents a divine idea that can be trusted, so we must speak our own thoughts.

3. Emerson develops his argument with several reasons, including the fact that our rejected thoughts may show up in works of genius and that each of us represents the divine idea.

4. Examples of rhetorical devices:
   a. hyperbole: "Speak your latent conviction, and it shall be the universal sense."
   b. connotations: "that is genius"; "trumpets of the Last Judgment"; "gleam of light"; "suicide"
   c. parallelism and repetition: "To believe is your own thought, to believe that what is true for you in your private heart"; "that envy is ignorance; that imitation is suicide . . ."

   ▶ CRITERIA FOR EVALUATING THE ASSIGNMENT   The essay should define Emerson's purpose and briefly state his argument. In a thesis statement, students should summarize their evaluation of Emerson's use of rhetorical devices. The evaluation should be supported with specific examples and quotations.

Further Reading

Works listed are suitable for both students and teachers unless the annotation ends with the note [Teachers].

Allen, Gay Wilson. "Plain Talk from Ralph Waldo Emerson," *American Heritage,* July 1986. Allen suggests that Emerson was not the "solemn prig" that Hemingway and others thought him to be.

Allen, Hervey. *Israfel: The Life and Times of Edgar Allan Poe,* two volumes (Doran, 1926). A popular, thorough study. [Teachers]

Arvin, Newton. *Herman Melville* (Greenwood, 1973). A good critical biography of Melville, especially the chapters through the writing of *Moby-Dick.*

Barbour, Brian, ed. *American Transcendentalism* (University of Notre Dame Press, 1973). A useful collection of studies. [Teachers]

Bloom, Harold, ed. Several anthologies of contemporary criticism, published by Chelsea House:
Modern Critical Views: Edgar Allan Poe (1985)
Modern Critical Views: Henry David Thoreau (1986)
Modern Critical Views: Nathaniel Hawthorne (1986)
Modern Critical Views: Ralph Waldo Emerson (1985)

Brown, Martha C. "Henry David Thoreau and the Best Pencils in America," *American History Illustrated,* May 1980. Article on the family pencil business and its influence on Thoreau's life and writing, with excellent photographs.

Carlson, Eric W., ed. *The Recognition of Edgar Allan Poe* (University of Michigan Press, 1966). A collection of Poe criticism. [Teachers]

Cortage, Andy. "Self-Reliance in Today's World," *Ideas Plus: Book II* (National Council of Teachers of English, 1985). Activities encouraging close reading of Emerson and application of his philosophy to today's problems. [Teachers]

Crawley, Thomas Edward. *Four Masters of the American Mind: Emerson, Thoreau, Whitman, and Melville* (Duke University Press, 1976). Good analysis of the work of these authors. [Teachers]

Gura, Philip F., and Joel Myerson, eds. *Critical Essays on American Transcendentalism* (G.K. Vesel, 1982). A collection of critical essays. [Teachers]

Harding, Walter, ed. *Thoreau: A Century of Criticism* (Southern Methodist University Press, 1954). A collection of critical essays on Thoreau, from his publication to contemporary times. [Teachers]

Howard, Leon. *Herman Melville: A Biography* (University of California Press, 1951). The best critical biography of Melville.

Howarth, William. *The Book of Concord: Thoreau's Life as a Writer* (Penguin, 1983). Perceptive account of how Thoreau's inner thought and experiences motivated his writing.

Howarth, William. "Following the Tracks of a Different Man—Thoreau," *National Geographic,* March 1981. Informative article with excellent photographs by Farrell Grehan.

James, Henry. *Hawthorne* (Cornell University Press, 1956). A major study. [Teachers]

Krutch, Joseph Wood. *Henry David Thoreau* (Greenwood, 1973). A good biography.

Lawrence, Jerome, and Robert E. Lee. *The Night Thoreau Spent in Jail* (Bantam, 1972). An excellent drama, parts of which could be acted in class.

Lewis, R.W.B. *The American Adam: Innocence, Tragedy, and Tradition in the Nineteenth Century* (University of Chicago Press, 1968). A classic study. [Teachers]

Matthiesen, F.O. *American Renaissance: Art and Expression in the Age of Emerson and Whitman* (Oxford University Press, 1968). A good critical study. [Teachers]

Morrow, Lance. "The Bishop of Our Possibilities," *Time,* 10 May 1982, 124. Stimulating essay on the relevance of Emerson to the twentieth century.

Parrington, Vernon L. *The Romantic Revolution in America, 1800-1860,* Volume II of *Main Currents in American Thought* (Harcourt Brace Jovanovich, 1955). Definitive account of the Romantic Period, with chapters on writers from this unit.

Paul, Sherman, ed. *Thoreau: A Collection of Critical Essays* (Prentice-Hall, 1962). A varied selection. [Teachers]

Regan, Robert, ed. *Poe: A Collection of Critical Essays* (Prentice-Hall, 1967). Collection of modern criticism through the mid-1960's. [Teachers]

Turner, Arlin. *Nathaniel Hawthorne: An Introduction and Interpretation* (Barnes and Noble, 1961). The literary work and style of Nathaniel Hawthorne.

Van Doren, Mark. *Nathaniel Hawthorne: A Critical Biography* (William Sloane Associates, 1949). Hawthorne's life and works.

Wagenknecht, Edward C. Biographies for the general reader published by Oxford University Press:
> *Edgar Allan Poe—The Man Behind the Legend* (1963)
> *Henry Wadsworth Longfellow: Portrait of an American Humanist* (1966)
> *Nathaniel Hawthorne, Man and Writer* (1961)
> *Ralph Waldo Emerson: Portrait of a Balanced Soul* (1974)

Williams, Harold, ed. "Whaling Life," *American Heritage,* June 1964. A journal kept by Eliza Williams during a three-year voyage on a New Bedford whaler; interesting for use with selections from Melville's *Moby-Dick.*

Woodson, Thomas, ed. *Twentieth Century Interpretations of "The Fall of the House of Usher"* (Prentice-Hall, 1969). Excellent background for the short story. [Teachers]

A NEW AMERICAN POETRY
WHITMAN AND DICKINSON

Text page 323

Teaching the New American Poetry Unit

You will find that Unit Five breaks naturally into three sections: Walt Whitman, Emily Dickinson, and review. Throughout, assignments in the text help students relate poems to their historical context and connect them with earlier American literature. Your challenge is simultaneously to present Whitman and Dickinson as unique individuals and to "place" them within the ongoing flow of American literature.

The unit introduction (text pages 324–325) can help students focus both on the poets' uniqueness and on their places in American literature. The first part of the introduction presents Whitman and Dickinson as representing "two distinct seams in the fabric of American poetry." Help students note the contrasts between the two poets by having them prepare a chart summary such as the following one:

	WHITMAN	**DICKINSON**
Personality	sociable, gregarious	private, shy
Expectations	his message to be carried to the future	her message to die in oblivion
When Famous	during his lifetime	after her death
Poetic Style	sweeping catalogs and the cadences of free verse	meticulous word choice, rhyme, and hymnbook meters

The seventh paragraph of the unit introduction ("As the history of our poetry shows . . . ," text page 325) makes generalizations on American poetry subsequent to Whitman and Dickinson. Alert students to the fact that understanding Whitman and Dickinson will prepare them for Units Eight, Nine, and Thirteen, where they will encounter poets representing every facet of American life from the 1890's to recent times—poets who owe to Whitman and Dickinson their freedom and range of subjects and style. Have students preview the table of contents for a list of later poets and skim the unit introductions for a preview of their subjects and styles. They will note several poets who follow Whitman's free verse path and others who emulate Dickinson's traditional forms while adopting Whitman's range of subject matter.

Finally, the concluding paragraph of the unit introduction and the poem by Ezra Pound stress the "co-equal importance" of free verse and traditional forms. You may need to stress "co-equal" as you check students' understanding of the paragraph—some may be biased for or against one of the verse forms. If some students have no idea what *free verse* is, Miller Williams's definition can serve for now: "Poetry in which line length and rhyme (if any) to come [are] not predictable from what has gone before nor prescribed by tradition." You might end by reading aloud Pound's poem and asking students to jot down in their journals or notebooks their immediate interpretation of Pound's meaning—a "best guess." After a few minutes, ask two or three students to share what they have written. Make no judgments at this time, but ask students to leave space to write a second response to Pound's poem after they have completed the unit.

Objectives of the New American Poetry Unit

1. To improve reading proficiency and expand vocabulary
2. To gain exposure to notable poets and their works
3. To define and identify elements of poetry
4. To express and explain responses to poetry, orally and in writing
5. To practice the following critical thinking and writing skills
   a. Comparing and contrasting poetry and other forms
   b. Rewriting a paragraph as a poem
   c. Comparing and contrasting poems
   d. Analyzing responses to poetry
   e. Evaluating a title
   f. Commenting on criticism
   g. Interpreting metaphors
   h. Interpreting poems

Walt Whitman

The biography of Whitman (text pages 326–329) refers repeatedly to Whitman's personality and poetic innovations—references with little meaning unless students have in mind both some of Whitman's poems and some of his contemporaries. You may therefore wish first to assign two Whitman poems (''I Hear America Singing'' and ''Song of Myself,'' text pages 331–332), and a quick review of two poems by his contemporary, Herman Melville (''Shiloh'' and ''Art,'' text pages 318–319). Have students list both what the poems reveal about their authors' lives and personalities and differences they notice in the style of the two poems. (Text questions on Whitman's poems can wait until later.) Students should find that Whitman's poems speak of his age, parentage, and so on, while Melville's poems reveal no directly biographical data; and that Whitman's style is loose and difficult to define in comparison with Melville's more predictable rhymes and meters. You may then wish to assign the biography of Whitman (text pages 326–329), asking students to keep in mind the fact that Whitman and Melville, born the same year, were writing for approximately the same audience.

After students have read the biographical material, you may wish to organize discussion around these four questions:

1. How would Whitman's unexpectedly deep American roots have contributed to self-confidence? (Some of your own students may be able to speak from experience as first- or second-generation Americans.)
2. What would it have been like to have Whitman as a friend—exciting? boring? frustrating?

3. How would Whitman's background have helped or hindered him in applying for a (hypothetical) ''Poet in Residence'' job at a university of his time?
4. How do today's critics and readers evaluate Whitman's contributions to literature?

During or after this discussion you may wish to expand upon Whitman's teen-age years and the fact that ''for a time he taught school'' (text page 326). As a boy he was enthralled by the novels of Sir Walter Scott, and in his mid-teens was already contributing ''pieces'' (most likely correct, conventional poems) to a Manhattan paper, crossing the ferry from Brooklyn to attend debating societies, and using his journalist's pass to hear singers at Manhattan theaters. At fifteen he had reached physical maturity, and at sixteen was a journeyman printer in Manhattan.

When two great fires disrupted the printing industry as he turned seventeen, he rejoined his family (irritating his father by refusing to do farmwork) and began five years of intermittent teaching at country and small-town schools. He interrupted teaching to start a newspaper of his own in 1838 and to work briefly on another Long Island newspaper. Whitman was an innovative teacher, but the farm families he boarded with considered him lazy: instead of helping with chores, he preferred taking part in debates, writing poems, writing articles about teaching, or continuing his studies of Shakespeare, Scott, Dante, Homer, other Greek poets, Hindu and German poetry. His teaching ended just before he turned twenty-one, when he began the life in New York described in the text.

You may wish to establish a historical context for Whitman's work by listing other events of the half-decade of

100   UNIT FIVE: A New American Poetry

1850–1855. American literature saw the appearance of Hawthorne's *The Scarlet Letter,* Melville's *Moby-Dick,* Thoreau's *Walden,* and Whitman's *Leaves of Grass.* During the same five years the following events took place: the Sioux ceded their lands in Iowa and most of Minnesota to the United States government, Senator Charles Sumner emerged as a leader in the fight against slavery, Florence Nightingale departed for Turkey to treat British soldiers fighting in the Crimean War, and Commodore Matthew C. Perry opened trade with Japan. Stephen Foster published "Old Folks at Home," Verdi was producing popular operas in Italy, and two Dickens novels appeared in England. In science and technology during the same years, Bunsen introduced use of the Bunsen burner (he didn't invent it), Isaac Singer of New York patented a continuous-stitch sewing machine, Elisha Otis of Vermont designed a passenger elevator, and Kier built America's first oil refinery in Pittsburgh.

Finally, give students some reactions from Whitman's contemporaries. Early readers either hated *Leaves of Grass* or were fascinated by it—often simultaneously. It was bad enough that the first edition carried a "shocking" engraving of Whitman—a young man with a short beard, dressed in an open-collared shirt that revealed the top of his colored underwear, with one hand resting on a hip and the other thrust into a pocket of his work jeans. (Recall that this was a time when the stovepipe hat and formal, long-tailed coat we identify with Lincoln were a more expected standard of dress.) Even more provocative were the poems themselves. Edward Everett Hale, writing in a leading literary magazine, *Putnam's Monthly,* spoke of Whitman's "scorn for the wonted usages of good writing," use of "words usually banished from polite society," and a style "which may briefly be described as a compound of the New England transcendentalism and New York rowdy."

Many readers assumed that Whitman's eccentricities resulted from ignorance—that he was barely literate. In fact he *was* self-taught, but fully aware of conventional forms. Another myth, Whitman as con-man, arose at least in part because he (anonymously) wrote some of his own reviews. In fact, he believed strongly enough in himself to advertise his message. A third myth was that Whitman's American emphasis was equivalent to paranoid suspicion of foreigners. In reality he was challenging the class-conscious resentment of the recent immigrants who were crowding the New York slums and surrounding areas.

Mixed feelings blend with an ultimately favorable judgment in a *New York Times* review of the second (1856) edition of *Leaves of Grass:*

> As we read it again and again, . . . a singular order seems to arise out of its chaotic verses. Out of the mire and slough[,] . . . keen philosophy starts suddenly. . . . A lofty purpose still dominates the ridiculous self-conceit in which the author, led astray by ignorance[,] indulges.

As you turn next to the poems of Whitman, you might give students the ongoing challenge of responding to these early critics with their own interpretations.

I HEAR AMERICA SINGING

Text page 331

Objectives

1. To explain and support a response to the poem
2. To recognize the use of the *catalogue*

Introducing the Poem

Like traditional forms of verse, free verse may be lyric or narrative. Whitman's poem is a lyric poem, one evoking an emotional response. Read it aloud, after reminding students to note how a natural cadence (rhythmic fall of words) dictates where lines break.

BACKGROUND ON THE POEM   The poem is a prime example of *cataloging,* use of a list. In this case the list ultimately shows the equality of people whatever their occupation. The word *intermission* means "break." The word *carol* is evocative in two senses: its original meaning of a round dance accompanied by singing, and the meaning (as with Christmas carols) of joyous praise as if in song.

Teaching Strategies

PROVIDING FOR CULTURAL DIFFERENCES   Students from all cultures should have no problem relating to this poem about the pride of workers.

Elicit from the class a brief description of the precise work performed by a person of each occupation. Although some of the occupations are now rare (e.g., hatter), the poem poses no problems to understanding.

READING THE POEM   Have a student who reads well prepare in advance to read the poem in class, or read it aloud yourself. Lead a class discussion of the five Re-sponding to the Poem questions (text page 331). Later in the unit, when students are more familiar with Whitman, you may wish to have students work individually or in small groups to respond to these questions.

RETEACHING ALTERNATIVES   Have students re-read the poem to look at the use of repetition and parallel structure. Point out that all of the images make up a single sentence.

FROM **SONG OF MYSELF**
SONG **1. I CELEBRATE MYSELF . . .**   Text page 332

Objectives

1. To respond to the style and ideas of the poem
2. To recognize the technique of incremental repetition
3. To recognize the poet's use of autobiographical data
4. To analyze word connotations

Introducing the Poem

You might ask, "When is loafing not laziness?" Through-out his life Whitman ignored schedules set by other people and baffled his friends and relatives by appearing to loaf away his time in purposeless strolls, random reading, and aimless writing. We, however, realize that he was absorb-ing sights, sounds, and details which later emerged in his poetry.

This selection uses the phrase "a spear of summer grass," making this a good time to examine the book title, *Leaves of Grass.* Lead students to see that *leaves* may pun both upon *leaves, blades,* or *spears* of grass, and upon the *leaves* or *pages* of books.

Read and discuss Elements of Literature: Free Verse (text page 333). Students should understand that Whit-man's verse form is a major departure from the metrics of poets they have studied in preceding units.

BACKGROUND ON THE POEM   The poem presents the philosophical notion that everyone is part of the whole of nature and that poet and reader are somehow one—a concept not specifically addressed in the response ques-tions, but one that you may wish to explore. The opening lines also suggest that Whitman sees his book as an arche-typal journey—a voyage of discovery he invites the reader to share with him. Throughout the poem the repetition is *incremental:* that is, more is added in the repetition. Note with students how line 5 repeats, then expands upon line 4.

Teaching Strategies

PROVIDING   FOR   CULTURAL   DIFFERENCES
Strongly religious students may find Whitman's hedonis-tic joy and setting aside of "creeds and schools" offen-sive. Invite them to study his views as representing a type of American optimism about the goodness of human na-ture that is a theme in many pieces of American literature. They don't have to agree with Whitman to see his point.

PROVIDING FOR DIFFERENT LEVELS OF ABILITY
After studying the vocabulary for this lesson, have stu-dents paraphrase the difficult last four lines. Suggest that they begin by inserting *with* ahead of *Creeds and schools,* and *Nature* after *harbor* and *permit.*

READING THE POEM   The complexity of thought in this poem requires a sensitive reading, such as that on the accompanying audiocassette. "Song 1" introduces the entire series of Whitman poems. Play the cassette, or have a student prepare a reading.

RETEACHING ALTERNATIVES   Suppose students had a chance to meet and talk with Walt Whitman. Based on their reading of this poem, what questions would they ask him?

THE ELEMENTS
OF LITERATURE   Text page 333

FREE VERSE
Pause for a detailed discussion of this section with your students before they continue reading Whitman. Spend enough time to be sure that students are comfortable with the major terms presented: *free verse, assonance, alliter-* ation, onomatopoeia, parallel structure, imagery, cadence, *and* trochaic tetrameter.

In answer to the questions posed in the final paragraph: There are thirty-three repetitions of a sibilant consonant sound (*s* or *z*). Examples of parallel structure include the use of *I* plus a verb to open several lines and second halves of lines, and the parallel use of verbs connected by *and* (as in "loaf and invite," "lean and loaf").

SONG 10. ALONE FAR IN THE WILDS . . .   Text page 334

Objectives

1. To respond to the use of images in a free-verse poem

2. To analyze the cadence of a poem

3. To identify a poem's tone

4. To analyze the speaker's attitude toward the subjects

Introducing the Poem

This selection is also available on audiocassette that will help students identify the change in tone at line 15. The recording should also help students formulate impressions of the speaker's personality as portrayed in the final stanza (see Responding question 6 on text page 335). Again encourage students to listen for Whitman's repetition and rhythmical cadences.

BACKGROUND ON THE POEM   Historical context is important to "Song 10." By 1848 Whitman was a "Free-soiler"—a member of a political party opposed to the acquisition of more slave territory. In 1848 he was a delegate to the Buffalo, New York, Free-Soil convention, which shows that his views on slavery were well-formed before the Civil War.

Teaching Strategies

PROVIDING FOR CULTURAL DIFFERENCES   If you have students who are recent immigrants to this country, you may need to explain that now, as in Whitman's day, the "wild frontier" holds a perennial attraction for Americans. Racial issues addressed by the poem—treatment of Native Americans and African Americans—have divided Americans since earliest times. During Whitman's time, abolitionists (people in favor of abolishing slavery in America) provided runaway slaves with a series of "safe houses" we call "the underground railroad."

PROVIDING FOR DIFFERENT LEVELS OF ABILITY
Present the vocabulary before reading the poem.

READING THE POEM   Use the audiocassette that is available for this selection or prepare your own reading in advance. Go to the questions in the text when you are satisfied that students have grasped Whitman's literal meaning.

RETEACHING ALTERNATIVES   Assign readers who read well to prepare a Readers' Theater presentation for the class. Audio- or videotape their presentation for use with students who are absent.

SONG **26.** NOW I WILL DO NOTHING BUT LISTEN . . .

Text page 336

Objectives

1. To respond to a poem about sounds
2. To identify examples of parallel sentence construction
3. To identify onomatopoeia

Introducing the Poem

The song "My Favorite Things," from the frequently televised Rodgers and Hammerstein musical *The Sound of Music* (1965), consists of catalogues followed by the refrain, "These are a few of my favorite things." As an introduction to "Song 26," you might ask students to create a similar list of their own favorite sounds. Have students meet in small groups to share and compare their lists and to see which sounds are named most often.

BACKGROUND ON THE POEM   The major literary techniques to note in "Song 26" are use of the catalogue, evocative sensory images, parallel construction, and onomatopoeia—words with sounds that echo their meaning.

Teaching Strategies

PROVIDING FOR CULTURAL DIFFERENCES   The images catalogued are common to cultures worldwide, with the possible exception of grand opera. If students have little acquaintance with opera, you might play a brief operatic selection that offers at least two or three of the elements mentioned by Whitman: violoncello, cornet, choral song, tenor solo, soprano solo.

PROVIDING FOR DIFFERENT LEVELS OF ABILITY   Discuss vocabulary and the allusion to the planet Uranus (see headnote on text page 336) before reading the poem.

READING THE POEM   A good oral reading will go far in helping students interpret the poem. This selection lends itself to oral interpretation as Readers' Theater by several students. Whoever reads the poem should convey the emotional tone of the various lines. Encourage listeners to note repetition and evocative images of sight and sound.

RETEACHING ALTERNATIVES   Direct students to study text page 333 on free verse, with special attention to the definitions of *alliteration, onomatopoeia,* and *imagery,* and then to reread the poem aloud.

FROM SONG **33.** I UNDERSTAND THE LARGE HEARTS . . .

Text page 338

Objectives

1. To respond to a poem about heroism and empathy
2. To analyze the use of sensory images and repetition
3. To note changes of tone

Introducing the Poem

The themes of this selection are heroism and empathy. You might ask students to jot down two or three examples of "everyday" heroism that they can identify with.

BACKGROUND ON THE POEM   Note especially the evocative sensory images of the selection. You may also wish to elicit information about the "underground railroad" of the mid-1800's.

Teaching Strategies

PROVIDING FOR CULTURAL DIFFERENCES   All cultures have heroes and some notion of what makes everyday people heroic. If you have students from a variety of ethnic backgrounds, have them compose short lists of heroic acts, real or fictional, that they know from stories they have heard or read. Have students share their lists with the class.

PROVIDING FOR DIFFERENT LEVELS OF ABILITY
Discuss vocabulary before students listen to the poem, following along in the text as it is read.

READING THE POEM   Use the audiocassette recording that accompanies the selection, followed by a class discussion. The speaker/reader *becomes* each hero conjured up—the sea captain, the hounded slave, the mashed fireman, the old artillerist. This selection is also an especially good one to use in asking students to account for Whitman's line breaks and line lengths.

RETEACHING ALTERNATIVES   Have small groups of students paraphrase the poem in prose paragraphs.

SONG 52. THE SPOTTED HAWK SWOOPS BY . . .

Text page 341

Objectives

1. To describe a response to the poet's language

2. To write a paragraph as a poem

3. To write an essay comparing and contrasting Whitman's poems with Emerson's essay "Nature"

4. To write an essay comparing and contrasting "Song 33" with Psalm 22

Introducing the Poem

This is the final poem of the 1855 edition of *Leaves of Grass,* Whitman's valedictory to the reader. Have students go back to look at "Song 1" (text page 332) before reading "Song 52."

BACKGROUND ON THE POEM   Whitman shows his awareness of the newness of his kind of poetry, alluding to it as "barbaric yawp." He characterizes his own oneness with nature through his identifying himself with the dirt under his readers' boot soles.

Teaching Strategies

PROVIDING FOR CULTURAL DIFFERENCES   Students from Native American and Eastern religious backgrounds may find the concepts of this poem (union, harmony, and oneness with nature) even easier to grasp than students in the Judeo-Christian tradition. Clarify vocabulary, however.

PROVIDING FOR DIFFERENT LEVELS OF ABILITY
Again, the only difficulty may be with vocabulary. Also, have students follow along in the text as the poem is read.

READING THE POEM   Use the audiocassette reading that accompanies the poem, or prepare your own reading. Check for understanding after the first reading by using the questions on text page 342, and then reread the poem or replay the cassette.

RETEACHING ALTERNATIVES   Have students listen to the audiocassette or paraphrase the poem with the aid of another student.

Responding to the Poem

Text page 342

Answers to the questions in the Pupil's Edition appear in the Annotated Teacher's Edition.

Writing About "Song of Myself"

For help in revising their compositions, refer students to **Grammar, Usage, and Mechanics: A Reference Guide** on text pages 1183–1228 at the back of their books.

A CREATIVE RESPONSE
1. Writing an Essay as a Poem   Suitable sections from Emerson include "I become a transparent eyeball" ("Nature," text page 192); and "Trust thyself" and "A foolish consistency" ("Self-Reliance," text page 194). Have students experiment until they find a paragraph that works well for them. Give students the option of collaborating with a partner.

▶ CRITERIA FOR EVALUATING THE ASSIGNMENT   The student has arranged the lines from Emerson as a poem and broken lines to reveal their cadence and units of thought.

A CRITICAL RESPONSE
2. Comparing Whitman to Emerson   Note that students can draw from any of the selections from "Song of Myself" in comparing Whitman's message and style with

that of Emerson in "Nature." Before they write their individual essays, students can work in small groups to discuss the messages, style, and diction of each writer. Have them find passages that exemplify their points.

▶ CRITERIA FOR EVALUATING THE ASSIGNMENT The essay compares Emerson's and Whitman's messages about people and their relationship to nature. Points about the writers' styles and diction are supported by quotes.

3. *Comparing a Poem to a Psalm* Give students copies of Psalm 22 ("My God, my God, why hast thou forsaken me . . . ?") for reference, and read the psalm aloud. This psalm, sometimes called a "Suffering Servant" psalm and applied to the crucified Christ, can also apply to any sufferer. Complete the prewriting chart on the board as students suggest similarities. They should find many.

▶ CRITERIA FOR EVALUATING THE ASSIGNMENT The essay cites similarities between Psalm 22 and "Song 33" in terms of parallel structure, cadences, message, and tone. Quotes from the psalm and from the poem support the essay's major points.

ON THE BEACH AT NIGHT

Text page 343

Objectives

1. To respond to a poem about immortality
2. To recognize vivid imagery

Introducing the Poem

Ask students if they can recall what they thought about the moon, stars, and clouds when they were very small. Did they ever worry, for instance, that the stars were being covered forever by the clouds?

This poem may be read on both a literal level (a child on the beach with her father is crying) and on a symbolic level (all life passes except—perhaps—the stars, or maybe the human spirit).

Ask students how they understand the term "immortality." You might also ask them to name some things thought to be immortal by various groups of people.

Teaching Strategies

PROVIDING FOR CULTURAL DIFFERENCES According to Greek mythology, the seven stars we call the Pleiades were the seven daughters of Atlas and Pleione, whom Zeus placed in the sky. Students from different cultures may be able to tell other myths about the constellations or planets.

PROVIDING FOR DIFFERENT LEVELS OF ABILITY Have students study the vocabulary words before reading the poem aloud. Students should take notes on words that are new to them.

READING THE POEM Read the poem aloud or have several good readers present the poem as students follow in their textbooks. After checking for literal comprehension, have students answer the questions on text page 344.

RETEACHING ALTERNATIVES Have students discuss the poem line by line in small groups.

ON THE BEACH AT NIGHT ALONE

Objectives

1. To respond to a poem about the relationship of all things and people in the universe

2. To recognize a catalogue of parallel phrases

3. To write an essay comparing two poems

Introducing the Poem

The sea is used here as an archetype—a pattern basic to literature of every culture in every age. In this poem the sea is a creative force, "the old mother." Ask students why peoples of all cultures have come to view the sea both as life-giver and as destroyer—the two main uses of the archetype.

Teaching Strategies

PROVIDING FOR CULTURAL DIFFERENCES Sea imagery is common to all cultures, although some students may never have seen an ocean. Allow those who have done so, or who have experienced the sea's danger, to describe their experiences.

PROVIDING FOR DIFFERENT LEVELS OF ABILITY Review the vocabulary before reading the poem. Have students take notes on words that are new to them.

READING THE POEM Rehearse the poem yourself (or have a student who reads well do so) and read it aloud, with students following in their textbooks. Check for literal comprehension, and then discuss with students the questions on text page 345.

RETEACHING ALTERNATIVES Ask students to imagine themselves alone at the shore on a starry night. What thoughts might they have about living beings in general, and how earthbound creatures relate to the universe? When students have jotted down at least one idea, send them back to the poem to see how Whitman responded in the same circumstances.

Responding to the Poem

Answers to the questions in the Pupil's Edition appear in the Annotated Teacher's Edition.

Writing About the Poem

For help in revising their compositions, refer students to **Grammar, Usage, and Mechanics: A Reference Guide** on text pages 1183–1228 at the back of their books.

A CRITICAL RESPONSE
Comparing the Poem to "Thanatopsis" Briefly review William Cullen Bryant's "Thanatopsis" (text pages 142–144), and discuss similarities the students see. They should note that in both poems the speaker, observing nature, thinks about the unity of all things. Like Bryant, Whitman senses a unity with all who have lived on earth and are to come. Whitman talks about the unity of all things in the universe; Bryant talks about people. Some students may say that Whitman's "vast similitude" is God, suggested also in line 79 of Bryant's poem (see the Comment on text page 144).

▶ CRITERIA FOR EVALUATING THE ASSIGNMENT The essay is brief, but notes similarities in views of the universe. Quotes from the poems support the essay's points.

WHEN I HEARD THE LEARNED ASTRONOMER

Text page 347

Objectives

1. To respond to a poem about science vs. the imagination

2. To write an essay comparing two poems

Introducing the Poem

The poem contrasts the aesthetic and the scientific approach to the stars. To anticipate this contrast, ask students to explain the different ways in which an artist and a surgeon would think about the human body.

Teaching Strategies

PROVIDING FOR CULTURAL DIFFERENCES   Students from all backgrounds should be able to understand this poem.

PROVIDING FOR DIFFERENT LEVELS OF ABILITY Review the vocabulary before reading the poem. Have students take notes on words that are new to them.

READING THE POEM   Read the poem aloud with students following in their textbooks. Call to students' attention the fact that the poem consists of a single sentence, and ask them to note how the sentence builds to its climax as they hear the poem read.

RETEACHING ALTERNATIVES   If possible, bring to class a copy of Antoine de Saint-Exupéry's *The Little Prince.* Read students the first eleven paragraphs of Part IV. The Little Prince's reaction to a lecturing astronomer exactly parallels that of Whitman's speaker. Then send students back to the poem.

Responding to the Poem   Text page 347

Answers to the questions in the Pupil's Edition appear in the Annotated Teacher's Edition.

Writing About the Poem

For help in revising their compositions, refer students to **Grammar, Usage, and Mechanics: A Reference Guide** on text pages 1183–1228 at the back of their books.

A CRITICAL RESPONSE
Comparing Poems   Note that the assignment asks students to use the speaker from "On the Beach at Night" (text page 343) rather than the speaker of ". . . Learned Astronomer."

▶ CRITERIA FOR EVALUATING THE ASSIGNMENT   The essay is brief, but notes that for the speaker of "On the Beach at Night," the stars lead to thoughts not of orbits and measurements but of the unity of all creation.

A SIGHT IN CAMP IN THE DAYBREAK GRAY AND DIM

Text page 348

Objectives

1. To respond to a poem and interpret its message

2. To identify details of setting

3. To analyze the speaker's tone

4. To describe responses to rhythms, diction, catalogues, subject matter, and tone in Whitman's poetry as a whole

Introducing the Poem

Ask students to describe the view of war conveyed in the more serious episodes of the television series *M*A*S*H* or films such as *Platoon* or *The Killing Fields.* Like this poem, such war films depict the horrible reality of individual deaths obscured by phrases like "casualty rate."

BACKGROUND ON THE POEM   Field hospitals during the Civil War were places of horror since they predated antiseptic practices. Amputation served as the most common solution if an arm or leg were injured. Soldiers were as likely to die from infections acquired in the hospital as from their actual wounds. Note, too, the headnote on text page 348—Whitman wrote from personal experience.

Teaching Strategies

PROVIDING FOR CULTURAL DIFFERENCES Cultural differences should cause no problems with this poem.

PROVIDING FOR DIFFERENT LEVELS OF ABILITY Point out the inversion that occurs in some sentences (line 3, for example) before reading the poem aloud.

READING THE POEM Give three students a chance to practice an oral interpretation, and have them read it aloud, with students following in their textbooks. Ask students to listen for the vivid description of the setting.

RETEACHING ALTERNATIVES Locate a copy of Wilfred Owen's World War I poem, ''Dulce et Decorum Est.'' Read and discuss it with any student who had difficulty with Whitman's poem, or use it as an enrichment of Whitman's poem for the entire class. (The Latin motto ending Owen's poem, ''Dulce et decorum est / Pro patria mori'' means ''It is sweet and right / To die for one's fatherland.'' Owen, too, shows this motto to be a false image of war.)

You might also ask students to bring to class and read aloud other poems and brief prose pieces about war.

Responding to the Poem   Text page 349

Answers to the questions in the Pupil's Edition appear in the Annotated Teacher's Edition.

Writing About the Poems

For help in revising their compositions, refer students to **Grammar, Usage, and Mechanics: A Reference Guide** on text pages 1183–1228 at the back of their books.

A CREATIVE RESPONSE
1. Writing a Free-Verse Poem   Note that students are to select *one* of the lines given (not all four) and use the poetic elements listed in the writing assignment. This would be a good assignment for a small group (three or four) to collaborate in writing a joint poem.

▶ CRITERIA FOR EVALUATING THE ASSIGNMENT   The poem opens with one of Whitman's lines, and achieves its effect through imagery, sound effects, and at least one form of repetition. Ask for volunteers to read their poems to the class.

A CRITICAL RESPONSE
You may wish to have students write only *one* of the following assignments, but discuss all five in class.

2. Analyzing the Ideas in the Poems   Elicit a listing of the poems in which Whitman most clearly expresses these three ideas. The list will provide students with appropriate sources.

▶ CRITERIA FOR EVALUATING THE ASSIGNMENT   The essay cites examples and quotations to support all three points.

3. Explaining the Poet's Statement   Discuss the aspects of Whitman's poems that definitively mark them as American. Tell students to mention specific poems, details, and quotes.

▶ CRITERIA FOR EVALUATING THE ASSIGNMENT   The essay cites examples and quotes from Whitman's poems. Students should mention the democratic sense of being at one with all Americans, details about slavery and Native Americans, references to specific events in American history (e.g., the Civil War).

4. Contrasting Whitman with a Fireside Poet   The ''Fireside Poets'' (text page 122) are the Boston group of Longfellow, Holmes, Lowell, and Whittier. Make sure students understand Whitman's statement before they review poems by the Fireside group to seek support for Whitman's own assessment of his poetry. In their essays, they should replace ''I'' with ''Whitman'' to use his statement as their thesis statement.

▶ CRITERIA FOR EVALUATING THE ASSIGNMENT   The essay contrasts the conventional themes and style of the Fireside Poets with the themes and style of Whitman. Examples from the Fireside Poets and from Whitman support the essay's major points.

5. Comparing Whitman to Taylor and Emerson   Review Taylor's ''Upon a Spider Catching a Fly'' (text page 46) and Emerson's ''Nature'' (text page 191), having students take notes on how each man ''reads'' nature. Then discuss how Whitman ''reads'' nature.

▶ CRITERIA FOR EVALUATING THE ASSIGNMENT   The essay shows similarities and differences in how Taylor, Emerson, and Whitman ''read'' nature. Examples from the writings of all three men support the essay's major points.

6. Analyzing the Prose   Read and discuss ''Primary Sources'' (text pages 350–351) in class. Have students work together to complete the chart suggested in the writing prompt.

▶ CRITERIA FOR EVALUATING THE ASSIGNMENT   The essay briefly compares Whitman's prose with his poetry in terms of tone, democratic feelings, use of lists and catalogues, and use of vigorous language.

Extending the Poems

Students who are good oral interpreters may wish to locate, prepare, present, and interpret for the class another Whitman poem: ''When lilacs last in the dooryard bloom'd,'' parts of ''Out of the cradle endlessly rocking,'' or Songs 4, 6, or 8 from ''Song of Myself.''

Students with an interest in classical music may enjoy Ralph Vaughan Williams's *A Sea Symphony,* based on several of Whitman's sea poems, including ''On the Beach at Night Alone.'' The contemporary American composer John Adams used Whitman's Civil War poem ''The Wound-Dresser'' in a moving 1989 piece for baritone, violin, and trumpet. Students might listen to this work in conjunction with their reading of ''A Sight in Camp in the Daybreak Gray and Dim.''

Research topics associated with Whitman's era include the Free-Soil political party (of which Whitman was a member), the Underground Railroad, and medical practices during the Civil War period.

In addition to works on Whitman, some students may wish to gain a fuller appreciation of the practicalities of life in the 1860's, as well as the political issues, by reading Gore Vidal's fictional account of Lincoln's presidency, *Lincoln,* and preparing a written or oral report.

Primary Sources   Text page 350

FROM SPECIMEN DAYS

You may wish to have students compare the last two paragraphs beginning ''Such was the war . . .'' with Lincoln's ''Gettysburg Address'' (text page 444), for tone, vivid language, overall impact. Or, some students might be interested in comparing the excerpt to a contemporary article by a war correspondent. Students might give an oral presentation in which they share brief quotes that exemplify tone, word choice, and point of view.

Emily Dickinson   Text page 352

The challenge with Emily Dickinson is to strike a balance between myth and fact. You might assign reading of the biography (text pages 352–353) and Primary Sources (text pages 371–372), and open class discussion the following day by asking why the following quotation from *The Norton Anthology of American Literature* (Volume 1: New York, 1985, 1979) is appropriate to Emily Dickinson:

[To] think of Emily Dickinson only as an eccentric recluse is a serious mistake. Like Thoreau, she lived simply and deliberately; she fronted the essential facts of life. In Henry James's phrase, she was one of those on whom nothing was lost.

During discussion, you may wish to supplement the text with some additional information.

Dickinson's frailty has often been exaggerated. She repeatedly insisted that it was not invalidism that led to her seclusion. (It may, nevertheless, interest students to know that in her lifetime, in Massachusetts alone, more than forty percent of all children died of diseases like diphtheria, tuberculosis, ''brain fever,'' and malaria before the age of twelve.) In adulthood Dickinson developed Bright's disease, a kidney disease which eventually caused her death and may also have caused the eye problems that led to two minimally successful operations during her early thirties. Her vision problems directly affected her penmanship.

In childhood Dickinson was a tomboy, much happier romping with her brother Austin (a year older than she; their sister Lavinia was three years younger than Emily) than practicing the domestic and hostessing tasks expected of nineteenth-century women. In her first school she was mischievous enough to be shut up in a dark closet for punishment at least once. In her teens she loved reading forbidden romantic novels, and was part of a chattering group of girls. At Amherst Academy she had the usual schoolgirl crushes on male teachers and enjoyed her curriculum of classical languages, philosophy, history and rhetoric. In addition, she often joined other girls in trekking up the hill to Amherst College, where they were allowed to sit in on college lectures in geology, astronomy, and biology.

After graduation from Amherst Academy, Dickinson so adamantly refused to turn to domestic interests that in 1847 her father sent her to South Hadley Seminary for Women (later Mount Holyoke College). Her career there lasted less than a year. Regardless of her scores in academic subjects, she was not allowed to return because she repeatedly and publicly refused to accept the tenets of the Calvinistic Christian faith.

There is, nevertheless, a deeply religious quality to Dickinson's work. She was influenced by the Puritan philosophy of her times, and metaphysical topics—the origin of the universe, whether or not there is an afterlife, the true nature of God and of the soul—equaled slavery as a topic of everyday discussion. Dickinson, though religious, simply would not yield to any efforts to force her acceptance of a specific body of religious doctrine.

Like religion, literature was a formative influence for Dickinson, as suggested by her letter to Higginson (''Primary Sources,'' text page 371). Her father believed in giving his children books rather than toys, and his home library contained law books, English classics, and a smattering of travel, religious, and natural science books. Dickinson was especially familiar with the Bible, the classics, and Shakespeare, but also valued the work of her contemporaries—Tennyson, the Brontë sisters, the Brownings, Thoreau, and Emerson.

Biographers have repeatedly attempted to explain Dickinson's seclusion as resulting from a thwarted love affair. In fact, when Dickinson was fourteen, the death of a girlfriend, Sophia Holland, led to so deep a depression that she had to be taken out of school for a time. Dominating her life was her father, Edward (a stern Calvinist, a lawyer who later served a term in Congress). He did drive off some men, including Benjamin Newton, a law student who apprenticed in his office and who later died of tuberculosis (it was he who introduced Emily to the works of Emerson); and college students with whom she shared the excitement of poetry. Overall, however, it appears that after the death of her girlfriend, Dickinson found all partings so traumatic that she chose to withdraw. Others of whom she was fond were Susan Gilbert, who married her brother Austin; the Reverend Charles Wadsworth (see text), to whom she turned for spiritual guidance; and various editors and critics of her poetry, including Higginson and Todd, who edited the first editions of Dickinson's poems after her death.

Some of the problems experienced by Dickinson's early editors were of her making. She wrote on any scrap of paper available—the fish wrapper, an envelope, the grocery list—and filled drawers and bags with these scraps. Sometimes she sewed the scraps together into little books. Another difficulty was her poor handwriting. At other times she could not decide on the exact word and would list several possibilities, making it necessary for the editors to select one. Then, too, her use of ''slant'' or ''off'' rhyme, imperfect grammar and spelling, and made-up words made her poems somewhat shocking in her own day.

When Dickinson died, several clergymen participated in a service described as ''poetical,'' and workmen who had served the Dickinsons carried her casket. The cemetery was not the end of Dickinson, however. Her sister Vinnie took bundles of poems (she left some 1,775 poems) to Higginson and Todd, and the small gold and white first volume, published in November 1890, astonished Amherst.

The Boston *Herald*, while commenting that ''Madder rhymes one has seldom seen,'' nevertheless reported that there was in the poems ''a fascination, a power, a vision . . . that draws you back.'' Higginson himself remained ''bewildered'' by Dickinson's work. William Dean Howells, distinguished novelist and editor, praised the poems as being ''true as the grave and certain as mortality. They are each a compressed whole, a sharply finished point . . . If nothing else had come out of our life but this strange poetry, we should feel that in the work of Emily Dickinson, America . . . had made a distinctive addition to the literature of the world.''

It was really not until 1955, however, when Dickinson's complete work as made available, that her accomplishment could be fully assessed. She is now seen as a distinctively modern poet who tackles the deepest puzzles of human consciousness and whose work is remarkable for its variety, subtlety, and richness, despite its apparent simplicity. She has been praised by poets as varied as Hart Crane, Allen Tate, and Adrienne Rich; and William Carlos Williams, whose work students will read in Unit Nine, claimed her as his ''patron saint.''

HEART! WE WILL FORGET HIM! Text page 355

Objectives

1. To respond to a poem about love
2. To paraphrase lines from the poem
3. To identify feeling or tone

Introducing the Poem

You might ask students whether they've ever been so emotionally involved with someone or something that they couldn't stop thinking about the person or issue no matter how hard they tried. Students can give some general responses about the situation, how they felt, how it ended. Keep the discussion from being too personal or intrusive.

The poem is written in iambic tetrameter and trimeter with many variations. The rhyme scheme is abcb defe with slant rhyme in the second stanza. Significant techniques include the use of apostrophe and exclamatory sentences.

BACKGROUND ON THE POEM The poem uses apostrophe (direct address to an absent person or to something abstract or inanimate) and slant rhyme (off rhyme, as with *begin/him*). Critics and the public have speculated endlessly on Dickinson's love life, encouraged in part by this poem. It is more important, however, to remind students that the speaker in a literary work is a creation of the writer—not automatically the writer herself. The audio-cassette accompanying this selection reinforces this point by having four different readers interpret Dickinson's poems. All twelve of the Dickinson poems included in the textbook are recorded on the audiocassette.

Teaching Strategies

PROVIDING FOR CULTURAL DIFFERENCES The theme of loving and losing someone is universal, as is the conflict between mind and heart.

PROVIDING FOR DIFFERENT LEVELS OF ABILITY The general concept of the poem is accessible to all, including the symbolic uses of warmth and light.

READING THE POEM Discuss the headnote on text page 355 and then read the poem aloud. Discuss the response questions, and then read the poem aloud again or play the audiocassette. You may wish to discuss all twelve of Dickinson's poems in the text before replaying all of them on the audiocassette.

RETEACHING ALTERNATIVES Ask students to name a popular song (perhaps in the country-western tradition) about trying to forget someone. Discuss it briefly, and then reread the Dickinson poem.

SUCCESS IS COUNTED SWEETEST
Text page 356

Objectives

1. To respond to a poem and interpret its meaning
2. To identify imagery

Introducing the Poem

Ask students whether they have ever achieved something they had wanted very much—buying a desired object, winning a certain contest, being invited to a special party—only to find that success did not make them feel as good as they had expected. In retrospect, is there any sense in which they would have appreciated the goal more if they *hadn't* achieved it?

The poem is written in iambic tetrameter and trimeter with an abcb rhyme scheme in each stanza.

BACKGROUND ON THE POEM Concentrate on the message. You might note that Dickinson's use of war imagery doesn't have the immediacy of Whitman's in "A Sight in Camp in the Daybreak Gray and Dim" (text page 348), since she uses war imagery symbolically to convey a different point.

Teaching Strategies

PROVIDING FOR CULTURAL DIFFERENCES Winning and losing are familiar concepts in every culture.

PROVIDING FOR DIFFERENT LEVELS OF ABILITY Dickinson's compression of language and inversion of usual word order (lines 7–8, for example, would normally be expressed "Can so clear[ly] tell the definition of victory") may confuse some students. Check for literal comprehension by asking students to paraphrase the poem orally before you assign the response questions.

READING THE POEM After brief introductory discussion, read and discuss the headnote on text page 356 and then read the poem aloud. Ask students to paraphrase the poem orally before you assign or discuss the response questions. You may then wish to read the poem aloud again or play the audiocassette.

RETEACHING ALTERNATIVES Do a line-by-line, thought-by-thought paraphrase with the students.

THE SOUL SELECTS HER OWN SOCIETY Text page 357

Objectives

1. To respond to the poem and its images
2. To analyze changes in meter
3. To write an essay evaluating a title

Introducing the Poem

Read and discuss the headnote on text page 357. The idea that each of us has internal "rules" for selecting friends may be new to some students and should arouse discussion.

The poem's meter is basically iambic with lines of varying length and many variations. In each stanza the rhyme scheme is abab with some slant rhyme.

BACKGROUND ON THE POEM   This poem is particularly compressed, and students may benefit from inserting omitted words such as "[even if] an Emperor [should] be kneeling" (line 7) or "[She is] Present no more" (line 4).

Teaching Strategies

PROVIDING FOR CULTURAL DIFFERENCES   The theme is universal.

PROVIDING FOR DIFFERENT LEVELS OF ABILITY
Word choice may present some difficulty. Use text notes and response questions 6–8 on text page 357.

READING THE POEM   Read the poem aloud, discuss the response questions, and then reread the poem (or play the audiocassette).

RETEACHING ALTERNATIVES   Have students work in small groups to paraphrase the poem, with a very capable student assigned to each group. Or read aloud Robert

Frost's "Mending Wall" (text page 660, lines 32–33). Then lead students to see a connection between Frost's idea and Dickinson's poem.

Responding to the Poem Text page 357

Answers to the questions in the Pupil's Edition appear in the Annotated Teacher's Edition.

Writing About the Poem

For help in revising their compositions, refer students to **Grammar, Usage, and Mechanics: A Reference Guide** on text pages 1183–1228 at the back of their books.

A CRITICAL RESPONSE
Evaluating a Title   Discuss the early editors' choice of "Exclusion" to title the poem, in terms of both its applicability and its limitations. Brainstorm a list of other possible titles (e.g., Choice of the Heart, Choice, It's Personal) which students may use as a starting point for selecting or offering a new title of their own.

▶ CRITERIA FOR EVALUATING THE ASSIGNMENT   The paragraph evaluates the applicability and limitations of "Exclusion" as a title for "The Soul selects . . . ," and suggests an alternative title that addresses the message of the poem.

THE ELEMENTS OF LITERATURE Text page 358

SLANT RHYME
Read and discuss this section, and have students look for slant rhymes in the three Dickinson poems already read. Questions are asked of the students in the final two paragraphs. Answers are matters of opinion, except for the slant rhymes employed in "The Soul selects . . ." on text page 358. The slant rhymes in that poem are Society/Majority, Gate/Mat, nation/attention, and One/Stone.

A BIRD CAME DOWN THE WALK

Objectives

1. To respond to the poem and its images
2. To analyze figures of speech

Introducing the Poem

William Carlos Williams, some of whose poems (such as "The Red Wheelbarrow," text page 718) are pure images, claimed Dickinson as his "patron saint." The sharp images of this poem suggest why.

The poem has a basic iambic meter with lines of varying length. In each stanza the rhyme scheme is abcb, but the last three stanzas use slant rhyme. Students should note the poem's vivid imagery, similes, and metaphors.

BACKGROUND ON THE POEM Concentrate on figures of speech and images with this poem. You may also wish to check to see whether students are now catching on to the slant rhyme.

Teaching Strategies

PROVIDING FOR CULTURAL DIFFERENCES Students from all backgrounds will be able to understand this poem.

PROVIDING FOR DIFFERENT LEVELS OF ABILITY The figures of speech may be difficult for some students to grasp. Handle the response questions either in a full-class discussion or in small-group discussions.

READING THE POEM Read the poem aloud, have a student who reads well do so, or play the audiocassette. Briefly check for grasp of the main idea—that the poet is describing an encounter with a bird—and *then* discuss the headnote on text page 358. Follow up with discussion of the response questions.

RETEACHING ALTERNATIVES Ask students to watch a bird and then give a brief description (orally or in writing) of how it moves and what happens when someone tries to offer it food. Then return to the poem with pauses after each stanza to help students visualize the scene.

I DIED FOR BEAUTY—BUT WAS SCARCE

Objectives

1. To respond to a poem about beauty and truth
2. To analyze the use of slant rhymes
3. To identify the poet's message

Introducing the Poem

Read the headnote above the poem and ask students to paraphrase Keats's words. Note that Keats was one of Dickinson's favorite poets.

The poem has alternating lines of iambic tetrameter and trimeter with a rhyme scheme of abcb (slant rhymes in stanzas 2 and 3). Students should note Dickinson's use of dialogue and metaphor.

BACKGROUND ON THE POEM Until now slant rhyme has merely been identified. In this poem its importance in emphasizing meaning is addressed by response question 4 on text page 360.

Teaching Strategies

PROVIDING FOR CULTURAL DIFFERENCES Students who are unfamiliar with Keats's poem will benefit from hearing the whole poem read aloud before they read Dickinson's poem.

PROVIDING FOR DIFFERENT LEVELS OF ABILITY Have students work in small groups (with at least one very able student per group) to answer the response questions.

READING THE POEM Read the poem through, and then go back to identify the imaginary setting and the main message of the poem. Does Dickinson agree or disagree with the words of Keats in the headnote? Then send students to the response questions on text page 360.

RETEACHING ALTERNATIVES Have students listen to the poem on the audiocassette and then write a prose paraphrase of the poem.

I HEARD A FLY BUZZ—WHEN I DIED— Text page 362

Objectives

1. To respond to a poem about the moment of death

2. To analyze word choice

3. To paraphrase lines from the poem

Introducing the Poem

What child—or adult, for that matter—hasn't at some time or other imagined all the people who would come to his or her funeral? Dickinson does the same, but focuses imaginatively on a fly that invades the room.

The lines of alternating iambic tetrameter and trimeter have a rhyme scheme of abcb (slant rhymes) in each stanza. Have students note the importance of images of light and sound.

BACKGROUND ON THE POEM You may wish to ask students what they have heard to be the common elements of near-death experiences. According to researchers such as Dr. Elisabeth Kubler-Ross, people who have almost died often report a joyful feeling, seeing their bodies on the bed, a journey through a tunnel toward a bright light,

reunion with loved ones who have died. Make sure students understand, however, that this poem creates an *imaginary* experience.

Teaching Strategies

PROVIDING FOR CULTURAL DIFFERENCES Students from all cultures should have no problem relating to the poem; its theme is universal.

PROVIDING FOR DIFFERENT LEVELS OF ABILITY Students are unlikely to have difficulty with this poem.

READING THE POEM Be sure to read and discuss the headnote (text page 362) before students read the poem. You might ask two students to rehearse the poem, assuring them that their interpretations may differ. Have one student read the poem to the class before discussion of the response questions; the other, after.

RETEACHING ALTERNATIVES Ask students what Dickinson has done to make this such a ''brilliantly original'' poem about death. Then play the audiocassette recording.

IF YOU WERE COMING IN THE FALL

Objectives

1. To respond to a metaphysical poem
2. To identify similes
3. To paraphrase a stanza

Introducing the Poem

Like most people, teenagers are impatient: they can't wait until Friday, they can't wait until the dance, they can't wait until so-and-so arrives. Discuss with them the added strain of not knowing the exact arrival time of the event or the person you are awaiting, or if the event or person will ever arrive.

The poem has alternating lines of iambic tetrameter and trimeter with an abcb rhyme scheme (slant rhyme in most stanzas). Like most of Dickinson's poems, this one contains startling similes and metaphors.

BACKGROUND ON THE POEM This is a metaphysical poem, one with far-fetched intellectual imagery. A conceit is an extended concept or image that gives structure to a metaphysical poem—in this poem, extensions of the time period the speaker can bear to wait. The headnote (text

page 363) explains metaphysical poetry. See also text page 48 to review conceits.

Teaching Strategies

PROVIDING FOR CULTURAL DIFFERENCES Before students read the poem, have them look at the definitions of *Van Dieman's Land* (line 12) and *goblin* (line 19) in questions 3 and 7.

PROVIDING FOR DIFFERENT LEVELS OF ABILITY Discuss the poem slowly, stanza by stanza.

READING THE POEM Read the poem through entirely once, and then go back over it stanza by stanza, interpreting each stanza yourself if students are unable to do so. Then reread the entire poem and move on to the response questions on text page 363.

RETEACHING ALTERNATIVES Assist students in writing a prose paraphrase of each stanza. You might divide the class into five groups with each group working together to paraphrase one of the five stanzas. Have a spokesperson from each group present its paraphrase, and ask the listeners to comment if they still have questions.

BECAUSE I COULD NOT STOP FOR DEATH—

Objectives

1. To respond to the poem and its extended metaphor
2. To analyze irony
3. To write a paragraph interpreting a phrase from the poem

Introducing the Poem

Read the headnote (text page 364) aloud in class. You may wish to assign reading of the poem as homework, to be followed by class discussion of the poem and the response questions.

The poem is written in iambic tetrameter and trimeter with a rhyme scheme of abcb (slant rhyme). Students should notice the use of personification, metaphor, alliteration, and repetition.

BACKGROUND ON THE POEM The poem depends on an extended metaphor. Death comes for the speaker in a carriage.

Teaching Strategies

PROVIDING FOR CULTURAL DIFFERENCES You might discuss the ways different cultures personify death—as a "grim reaper," a rider of a black horse, or something else.

PROVIDING FOR DIFFERENT LEVELS OF ABILITY

Discuss the vocabulary and identify the basic metaphor of the poem before reading and discussing the poem in class.

READING THE POEM

Have students read the headnote and the poem itself before class. Then read it aloud in class, discuss the response questions, and assign the writing topic on text page 365.

RETEACHING ALTERNATIVES

Dickinson's punctuation is a source of difficulty to some students. Have students listen to the accompanying audiocassette and punctuate the poem as the reader interprets it. Give the students a copy with altered punctuation and go through the poem again, thought unit by thought unit.

Or read an entirely different poem which also personifies death, such as James Weldon Johnson's "Go Down Death" (text page 681). Have students recall how Poe personified death in "The Masque of the Red Death" (text page 228), and then return to Dickinson's poem.

Responding to the Poem   Text page 365

Answers to the questions in the Pupil's Edition appear in the Annotated Teacher's Edition.

Writing About the Poem

For help in revising their compositions, refer students to **Grammar, Usage, and Mechanics: A Reference Guide** on text pages 1183–1228 at the back of their books.

A CRITICAL RESPONSE

Commenting on a Critic   Discuss Kazin's comment and students' ideas on what Dickinson meant by the Eternity the horses were going toward in "Because I could not stop for Death—." Caution students to focus on interpreting the lines in the context of the poem.

▶ CRITERIA FOR EVALUATING THE ASSIGNMENT   The paragraph offers a reasonable explanation of what Dickinson could have meant by the Eternity toward which the horses were going.

I NEVER SAW A MOOR—   Text page 366

Objectives

1. To respond to the poem and interpret its meaning
2. To analyze word choice

Introducing the Poem

Use the text headnote. You might also quote Blaise Pascal, the seventeenth-century French philosopher: "The heart has its reasons which Reason does not know." Ask students to apply Pascal's words to the poem—particularly the second stanza.

The poem is written in iambic tetrameter and trimeter with an abab rhyme scheme. In both stanzas, the second and fourth lines are exact rhymes; the first and third are slant rhymes.

Teaching Strategies

PROVIDING FOR CULTURAL DIFFERENCES

Make sure students know the meanings of *Moor* (line 1) and *Checks* (line 8) as they are used in the poem. Students also need to know what heather is—a low plant with feathery flowers shown in the photograph.

PROVIDING FOR DIFFERENT LEVELS OF ABILITY

Without changing any of the words, rewrite the poem as short prose paragraphs, restoring normal English word order and observing current rules of capitalization and punctuation. Have students read this prose version and then return to the poem.

READING THE POEM

Read and discuss the headnote, poem, and response questions in class, or assign the entire page as homework. Emphasize grasp of Dickinson's theme or message in this poem.

RETEACHING ALTERNATIVES

Suggest that students collaborate in small groups to think of other examples that fit the first stanza. Have each group share its examples with the whole class, and then reread Dickinson's poem.

TELL ALL THE TRUTH

TELL ALL THE TRUTH

Text page 367

Objectives

1. To respond to the poem and its message
2. To paraphrase lines from the poem
3. To interpret a metaphor

Introducing the Poem

The poem is written in alternating lines of iambic tetrameter and trimeter with an abcb rhyme scheme in each stanza. In lines 3–4 and 5–6 you may wish to restore normal English word order and supply appropriate words for ones Dickinson omits, for comprehension's sake. Note also the simile (truth is like lightning) with which Dickinson expresses her message.

Teaching Strategies

PROVIDING FOR CULTURAL DIFFERENCES Students from different cultures should have no special problem; the theme is universal.

PROVIDING FOR DIFFERENT LEVELS OF ABILITY If you provide missing words and restore normal English word order, students should have no difficulty understanding the poem.

READING THE POEM Call students' attention to the headnote and first line of the poem. What is their immediate impression of how the line applies to Dickinson's poetry? Read the poem aloud, and discuss the response questions. Ask students to respond to the headnote: Does this poem describe how "all poetry works," or does it apply more specifically to Dickinson's poetry?

RETEACHING ALTERNATIVES Ask students to reread the poem to determine what kind of truth they think the poet is talking about. Does "scientific truth" fit these lines? Or is it some other kind of truth?

APPARENTLY WITH NO SURPRISE

Text page 368

Objectives

1. To respond to a lyric about nature
2. To analyze the theme
3. To identify tone

Introducing the Poem

Discuss the headnote on text page 368 and play the poem on the accompanying audiocassette.

BACKGROUND ON THE POEM Remind students of the definitions of tone, theme, and personification.

Teaching Strategies

PROVIDING FOR CULTURAL DIFFERENCES Students from tropical regions may not know what frost is. Have another student explain what an unseasonal frost does to flowers, young plants, and fruit.

PROVIDING FOR DIFFERENT LEVELS OF ABILITY If you paraphrase the poem, students should have no difficulty understanding it.

READING THE POEM Call attention to the headnote, play the audiocassette, or have a student read the poem. Then discuss the questions.

RETEACHING ALTERNATIVES Although the poem is about death and nature, Dickinson never uses those words. Have students reread the poem to find the words and phrases she uses instead.

TO MAKE A PRAIRIE IT TAKES
A CLOVER AND ONE BEE

Objectives

1. To respond to a five-line poem about imagination
2. To interpret the poet's message

Introducing the Poem

Have students look up the word *revery* as suggested in the headnote. Take a few minutes to get students to talk about daydreams in general—if they can ever be "useful," if they can cause problems, etc.

Dickinson uses iambic rhythm in lines of varying length with an aaabb rhyme scheme. Have students notice the repetition and extreme compression.

Teaching Strategies

PROVIDING FOR CULTURAL DIFFERENCES Make sure all students know that a prairie (a vast, flat grassland) is covered with clover (a wild, common plant with small flowers).

PROVIDING FOR DIFFERENT LEVELS OF ABILITY This short lyric poem should be easily understood by students of all ability levels.

READING THE POEM Have students define *revery*, read the poem, and discuss the questions.

RETEACHING ALTERNATIVES Read the poem once more and ask students what the second sentence (lines 4–5) adds to the poem's message.

Responding to the Poem Text page 370

Answers to the questions in the Pupil's Edition appear in the Annotated Teacher's Edition.

Writing About the Poem

For help in revising their compositions, refer students to **Grammar, Usage, and Mechanics: A Reference Guide** on text pages 1183–1228 at the back of their books.

A CREATIVE RESPONSE

1. Writing Quatrains Discuss the possible rhyme schemes (abab, abba, abcb) and then list some rhyming words for the starter lines suggested in the writing assignments. Note that students should consider using slant rhyme and irregular meter, like Dickinson, to prevent the quatrain's being mechanical. Students who think they may have trouble with the assignment should choose a partner to work with.

▶ CRITERIA FOR EVALUATING THE ASSIGNMENT The quatrain has a definite pattern of rhyme and meter, but does not sound sing-song or mechanical. Have students share their quatrains with the whole class or in small groups.

A CRITICAL RESPONSE

Discuss all of the critical writing assignments, although you may wish to permit students to select *one* to write.

2. Analyzing a Poem Use the first stanzas of "Tell all the Truth" (text page 367) to demonstrate, respectively, the 8, 6, 8, 6 syllable count (note: *syllables,* not accents). Then have students turn to "I never saw a Moor" (text page 366) to demonstrate the 6, 6, 8, 6 syllable count. Tell students that they can use both of these poems in their essays. They will need to find one more in the 8, 6, 8, 6 pattern.

▶ CRITERIA FOR EVALUATING THE ASSIGNMENT The essay correctly cites two Dickinson poems employing the 8, 6, 8, 6 count of syllables; and at least one using the 6, 6, 8, 6 pattern.

3. Analyzing an Edited Version "If you were coming in the Fall" is printed here as it was on text page 363. Make sure students understand that the blue marks show the editors' changes. Discuss the effects of these changes before students write the essay.

▶ CRITERIA FOR EVALUATING THE ASSIGNMENT The essay offers logical reasons for the editors' changes and describes the effect of the changes on the poem.

4. Comparing Poems You might divide the class into three groups. Have each group review one of the poems and briefly present their findings to the class. They should review Bryant's "Thanatopsis" (text page 142) and Taylor's "Upon a Spider Catching a Fly" (text page 46) and "God's Determinations Touching His Elect" (text page 49) in terms of subject matter, message, tone, metaphor, rhythms, and rhymes. This is a challenging assignment.

Students may also collaborate in discussing a Dickinson poem before they begin writing.

▶ CRITERIA FOR EVALUATING THE ASSIGNMENT The essay cites examples from the poems of Dickinson, Bryant, and Taylor to support its major points about how the poems are alike and how they differ in terms of subject matter, message, tone, metaphors, rhythms, and rhymes.

Analyzing Language and Style

DICTION AND SYNTAX

As students identify each case of rule-breaking, discuss the effects, and also whether or not Dickinson's eccentric punctuation affects the poem's meaning.

1. No example appears in the poems in the text.
2. Ask students to supply the subject of the verb *feels,* line 22 (text page 364).
3. See ''Goblin Bee'' on text page 363. Dickinson does not make up new words in these poems but startles the reader by combining words in a new way.
4. Nearly every poem provides examples of nonstandard punctuation.
5. Most poems also provide examples of omission of articles.
6. For example, *Bretheren* on text page 360.

Extending the Poems

Students with a dramatic flair may wish to select from Dickinson's collected works a series of poems on a theme of their choice, and present these poems to the class in Readers' Theater format.

Harmonium, a large orchestral and choral work by the contemporary American composer John Adams, includes a haunting setting of ''Because I could not stop for Death'' as well as a thundering setting of ''Wild Nights.'' After listening to a recording, students can discuss how well Adams captures the spirit of Dickinson's poems.

More-advanced students may do some research to explore further the influence of the philosophies of Ralph Waldo Emerson and Henry David Thoreau on Emily Dickinson.

Students intrigued with Dickinson's solitary life may wish to read about the poet herself and about three other unmarried women writers of the same era, the Brontë sisters (Anne, Charlotte, and Emily). Suggest that they compare their lives in an oral or written report.

Primary Sources   Text page 371

HIGGINSON'S ACCOUNT OF DICKINSON

If you did not assign this section in conjunction with reading the biography of Dickinson (text pages 352–353), assign it now. It further demonstrates Dickinson's personal eccentricities, comments on her handwriting and appearance. It also provides reliable, first-hand evidence that in 1862, when she was 32, she sought critical evaluation of her work, experienced illness, and as yet possessed no photograph of herself.

Now that students have completed the sections on both Whitman and Dickinson, return to Ezra Pound's poem in the unit introduction (text page 325). Ask them to write in their journals an interpretation of Pound's meaning.

EXERCISES IN CRITICAL THINKING AND WRITING   Text page 373

COMPARING AND CONTRASTING POEMS

Be sure students are familiar with the elements of poetry cited in the Background notes. Students should read the poems aloud and think about their task before beginning to organize their essays. More able students may wish to begin writing at this point. Others should follow the plan that is outlined for them, choosing one of the suggested ways of organizing their essays and then making notes before beginning to write. For additional support, you may wish to refer students to the text feature, Writing Answers to Essay Questions, beginning on page 1148.

▶ CRITERIA FOR EVALUATING THE ASSIGNMENT   The essay is effectively organized so that the various elements of each are clearly compared and contrasted. The main idea is summarized in the form of a thesis statement. The essay concludes with a subjective response to the poems and gives details to support that response.

Further Reading

Works listed are suitable for both students and teachers unless the annotation ends with the note [Teachers].

Allen, Gay Wilson. *A Reader's Guide to Walt Whitman* (Farrar, Straus & Giroux, 1970). A guide to Whitman bibliography, scholarship, and criticism. [Teachers]

Dickinson, Emily. *The Complete Poems of Emily Dickinson,* ed. Thomas H. Johnson (Little, Brown, 1960). The first one-volume definitive edition of all of Dickinson's poems.

Johnson, Thomas H. *Emily Dickinson: An Interpretive Biography* (Harvard University Press, 1955). An extensive discussion of Dickinson's life and an analysis of the themes and structure of her poetry.

Johnson, Thomas H., and Theodora W. Ward, eds. *The Letters of Emily Dickinson* (Harvard University Press, 1958). Emily Dickinson's letters to her friends and family.

Leyda, Jay. *The Years and Hours of Emily Dickinson* (1960). A biographical study.

Pearce, Roy Harvey, ed. *Whitman: A Collection of Critical Essays* (Prentice-Hall, 1962). Scholarly essays by fourteen writers including Ezra Pound. [Teachers]

Voices & Visions (Annenberg/CPB Project, 1987). Fifty-minute documentaries on Walt Whitman and Emily Dickinson shown on PBS television with readings of poems, biographical information, and interviews with critics, available on videocassettes.

White, Hilda. *Truth Is My Country: Portraits of Eight New England Authors* (Doubleday, 1971). Informative, readable biographical essays on Dickinson, Hawthorne, Emerson, Thoreau, Stone, Robinson, Millay, and Frost.

Whitman, Walt, ed. Emory Holloway. *Leaves of Grass,* (Doubleday, 1926; Book League of America, 1942); or *Leaves of Grass,* ed. Harold W. Blodgett and Sculley Bradly (Norton, 1973). Comprehensive editions of Whitman's poems.

THE RISE OF REALISM
THE CIVIL WAR AND POST-WAR PERIOD

Text page 375

Teaching the Rise of Realism Unit

The change from romanticism to realism in American fiction was in large part due to historical and social changes. The Civil War, the growth of the railroads, the telegraph, mass immigration, and rapid industrialization all combined in the latter half of the nineteenth century to transform the United States from a mostly agrarian, decentralized nation to an urbanized, more centralized one. Transportation and communication brought people into closer contact with the various regions of the country at precisely the same time that regional differences began to fade away. The result was nostalgia, a feeling that expressed itself in fiction as regionalism, or local color.

The hardships of the Civil War and its aftermath, and the grim conditions that prevailed in the burgeoning urban slums, factories, railroad camps, and mines impressed themselves upon writers. Many of them believed that the depiction of the human suffering they observed was an important artistic end in itself.

The influence of foreign literature was also important in the development of realism in American writing. American romanticism had followed in the footsteps of its European models. When European writers turned to realism, Americans, who at that time still represented the "junior" nation, followed suit. Frank Norris studied Emile Zola, Henry James was influenced by Gustave Flaubert and Ivan Turgenev in his striving toward ever more subtle psychological realism. Stephen Crane and Joseph Conrad, who knew each other in England, strengthened each other in their development of an impressionistic descriptive style. Rudyard Kipling was another strong influence on Crane, who took his famous "wafer" simile from a line in *The Light That Failed*: ". . . the sun shone, a blood-red wafer. . . ." And the journalistic, sentimental, comic melodrama of Charles Dickens influenced a whole generation of writers, from Feodor Dostoevski in Russia to Mark Twain and Bret Harte in the United States.

Objectives of the Rise of Realism Unit

1. To increase proficiency and expand vocabulary

2. To gain exposure to notable authors and their works

3. To define and identify elements of nonfiction, fiction, and spirituals

4. To define and identify significant literary techniques

5. To interpret and respond to autobiography, spirituals, stories, and novels, through analysis of their elements

6. To practice the following critical thinking and writing skills:
   a. Responding to an idea
   b. Comparing and contrasting forms of literature
   c. Comparing and contrasting writers
   d. Analyzing euphemism and irony
   e. Comparing and contrasting tone and theme
   f. Analyzing features of impressionistic style
   g. Analyzing inferences and point of view

The introduction to the unit in the student text can be divided naturally into two sections: a discussion of the Civil War and its effect on American literature (text pages 376–379) and a discussion of realism and regionalism as literary styles contrasted with romanticism (text pages 380–384). It might be fruitful to study Frederick Douglass's "The Battle with Mr. Covey" immediately after the first part of the introduction, since its subject, slavery, has a strong historical bearing on the Civil War. Also, as a nonfictional memoir, it doesn't strictly belong to a fiction-oriented classification of realism versus romanticism. After the Douglass piece, you can then go on to finish the introduction, following it up with Bret Harte's "The Outcasts of Poker Flat," a representative work of regionalism.

Your students have already, in their history courses, studied such topics as the Civil War, slavery, Reconstruction, the expansion and settlement of the frontier, and the rise of industrialism and urbanization after the Civil War. Encourage them to apply this knowledge during your discussion of the unit introduction.

Frederick Douglass Text page 385

THE BATTLE WITH MR. COVEY Text page 386

Objectives

1. To respond to a personal narrative about slavery

2. To analyze character and motivation

3. To relate an essay's ideas to the narrative

4. To write a paragraph responding to an idea

5. To analyze metaphors

Introducing the Autobiography

Here are the major elements of the autobiography:

- **Protagonist:** Frederick Douglass, a young slave

- **Antagonists:** Covey, a slaveowner to whom Douglass has been "rented" for a year; Thomas, Douglass's owner

- **Themes:** The spirit of freedom rises up against slavery, and inner strength results from fighting injustice. Slavery is degrading to slaveowners as well as slaves.

- **Point of view:** first-person

- **Significant techniques:** narrative combined with exposition, metaphor

- **Setting:** a slaveowner's farm on the eastern shore of Maryland in the 1830's

BACKGROUND ON THE AUTOBIOGRAPHY Frederick Douglass was far more than a single-issue crusader. His personal sufferings led him to identify with, and fight for, the rights of the downtrodden in many areas of the world. He was a leader of the women's rights movement, and on the day he died, he spoke at a women's rights meeting with Susan B. Anthony. After escaping to the North, he learned about the kinds of discrimination faced by free African Americans. In an early example of nonviolent civil disobedience, he desegregated the trains in New England by refusing to leave the all-white section until physically carried off. During his career as a writer and lecturer, he spoke out for world peace, temperance, Irish freedom, repeal of the corn laws oppressing English farm laborers, free speech, the abolition of capital punishment, and prison reform.

SUMMARY After passing out from exhaustion while fanning wheat, Douglass is beaten by Covey and given a severe head wound. He flees seven miles to Thomas's farm, but Thomas refuses to give him sanctuary and orders him to return to Covey. Covey treats him decently at first, because it is Sunday when Douglass returns. Later, however, Covey and a hired hand, Hughes, try to beat and tie Douglass, but Douglass fights back and gets the better of them. For the duration of Douglass's stay, Covey treats him cautiously and nonviolently.

Teaching Strategies

PROVIDING FOR CULTURAL DIFFERENCES Depending on your area, your class may have students whose family histories include the experience of slavery, as well as students whose ancestors were refugees from various kinds of political, economic, or religious persecution. Encourage students to share their knowledge and feelings about these historical experiences. The goal of such a discussion is to help students empathize with the ordeals of peoples of all kinds.

PROVIDING FOR DIFFERENT LEVELS OF ABILITY This is a forceful, straightforward narrative, but some students may have a little trouble with vocabulary, as in the word *intimated* in the first sentence. The custom of slaveowners' ''renting'' slaves to each other will need to be explained at the outset. The episode concerning Sandy Jenkins's ''magic'' root is clearly narrated, but its significance and tone will probably puzzle some students and require a bit of discussion.

READING THE AUTOBIOGRAPHY The selection is short and vivid enough to read at one sitting, either at home or in class. Ask for volunteers to read it aloud, and pause frequently to let students respond to the narrative.

RETEACHING ALTERNATIVES Some students may be slow to grasp the historical particulars of Douglass's experience: the renting of a slave by one farmer to another, the belief in magical talismans, and so forth. These can be clarified during class discussion, but reassure your students that these details are not the essence of the narrative: Douglass's battle for his own dignity is. You might ask your students to write in-class paragraphs describing how they would feel if they were slaves and were subjected to the kind of treatment Douglass describes.

Responding to the Autobiography
Text page 390

Answers to the questions in the Pupil's Edition appear in the Annotated Teacher's Edition.

Writing About the Autobiography

For help in revising their compositions, refer students to **Grammar, Usage, and Mechanics: A Reference Guide** on text pages 1183–1228 at the back of their books.

A CREATIVE RESPONSE
1. Applying Meanings Skim ''Self-Reliance'' with your students. They may at first see a contradiction between Douglass's behavior and Emerson's ''Accept the place the divine Providence has found for you.'' Through discussion, they should realize that Douglass's narrative exemplifies Emerson's principles: a man ''must take himself . . . as his portion''; ''Trust thyself''; ''Society everywhere is in conspiracy against the manhood of every one of its members''; ''Whoso would be a man must be a nonconformist.''

▶ CRITERIA FOR EVALUATING THE ASSIGNMENT By citing examples and quotations from both Douglass and Emerson, the essay briefly demonstrates that Douglass's realizations and actions support Emerson's philosophy.

A CRITICAL RESPONSE
2. Responding to an Idea Students' responses to the quotation from Douglass will vary. Note the three questions students are to cover in their essays. They should mention at least one way the idea might be true and one way it might not.

▶ CRITERIA FOR EVALUATING THE ASSIGNMENT The paragraph expresses the student's personal response to Douglass's words, explores the implications of the quotation, and suggests at least one way in which it is true and one in which it might not be true.

Analyzing Language and Style

METAPHORS
1. A fading ambition for freedom is compared with the embers of a dying fire; the battle is compared with a spark or puff of air that rekindles the fire. Any new fire offers warmth and light—a source of rebirth. Fire is also central to the image of the phoenix, said to die on a pyre and be reborn again from the ashes.
2. The word *arm* personifies slavery as a cruel taskmaster who inflicts death, wounds or pain (the word *bloody*).
3. ''It was a glorious resurrection, from the tomb of slavery, to the heaven of freedom'' (text page 389). Slavery is compared with death; freedom is compared with a new life in heaven.

Extending the Autobiography

Several of the writers in previous units have espoused or exemplified freedom, but Douglass is the only one who was actually a slave. Jefferson, in fact, was a slaveowner. Ask your students how they think Douglass would respond to the writings and lives of Bradford, Byrd, Jefferson, Paine, Franklin, Emerson, Thoreau, or Whitman, and how those writers would respond to him. A panel discussion or student-created dramatic sketch might be appropriate.

Objectives

1. To respond to African American spirituals

2. To write an original stanza for a code song

3. To analyze allusions

4. To write an essay comparing the spirituals with the Puritans' writings

5. To write a paragraph describing code songs

Introducing the Songs

BACKGROUND ON THE SONGS   Douglass, in the passage on text page 391, emphasizes the melancholy nature of the slaves' songs. Another great African American leader, W. E. B. Du Bois (1868–1963), called them "sorrow songs" but thought they always contained an element of hope that transcended the sorrow:

> Through all the sorrow of the Sorrow Songs there breathes a hope—a faith in the ultimate justice of things. . . . Sometimes it is faith in life, sometimes a faith in death, sometimes assurances of boundless justice in some fair world beyond. But whichever it is, the meaning is always clear: that sometime, somewhere, men will judge men by their souls and not by their skins.

SUMMARY   *Go Down Moses* The song retells the story of Moses leading the Hebrews out of slavery in Egypt. It calls on Moses to "go down" to Egypt and to tell Pharaoh, "Let my people go."

Follow the Drinking Gourd This code song gives directions for escape along a river bank, and tells the listener, "For the old man is a-waiting for to carry you to freedom / If you follow the drinking gourd."

Teaching Strategies

PROVIDING FOR CULTURAL DIFFERENCES   Many spirituals have entered the general heritage of American culture, and some students may be familiar with them as folk songs performed in modern versions. If some of your students have recordings of these or other spirituals at home, you might play them for the class. Some students may be more familiar than others with the Biblical story of Moses, and may be able to retell the story for the class.

PROVIDING FOR DIFFERENT LEVELS OF ABILITY   The line, "Left foot, peg foot, traveling on" is possibly the most obscure in the two songs. Some folk versions, such as the Weavers's, include an introduction explaining that a peg-legged sailor was supposedly walking along a levee near the fields, singing this song, and that his "peg-foot" left a trail for the slaves to follow. In most respects, though, the songs are clear and straightforward.

READING THE SONGS   As the word *songs* implies, these pieces of folk poetry are best appreciated when set to music. Instruments are not necessary, though—they were intended to be sung by unaccompanied voice. Play the audiocassette recording of "Go Down, Moses," and encourage students to bring in other recordings of spirituals or songs of slavery. Your school library may have some as well.

RETEACHING ALTERNATIVES   The major problem some students may have with these songs is that the lyrics have double meanings. You might ask them to draw a line down the middle of a sheet of paper and paraphrase the songs' literal meaning on one side and their "code" meaning on the other. This can also be done on the chalkboard.

Responding to the Songs   Text page 392

Writing About the Songs

For help in revising their compositions, refer students to **Grammar, Usage, and Mechanics: A Reference Guide** on text pages 1183–1228 at the back of their books.

A CREATIVE RESPONSE
1. Writing a Stanza   After students have analyzed codes as explained in assignment 5, they should write an original stanza that echoes the pattern of the song and continues or supplements the directions in its existing stanzas. Students may work on the assignment with a partner or small group. Tell them to try to imitate as closely as possible the stanza form, refrain, and meter of the original.

▶ CRITERIA FOR EVALUATING THE ASSIGNMENT   The four-line stanza uses "Follow the drinking gourd" as the fourth line, fits the meter of the original, and gives directions that follow or fit between the directions already given. Have students read or sing their stanzas to the class.

A CRITICAL RESPONSE

2. *Analyzing Allusions*   Allusions not mentioned in the assignment are ''Israel'' and ''smite your first-born dead.'' ''Israel'' was the alternate name of Jacob, whose twelve sons fathered the twelve Hebrew tribes; by extension it means the entire Hebrew people. ''Smite'' alludes to ten plagues God inflicts on the hardhearted Egyptians so they will release Israel. The tenth plague is the death of every Egyptian's firstborn child (Exodus 11:1–10 and 12:29–30).

▶ CRITERIA FOR EVALUATING THE ASSIGNMENT   The essay identifies allusions to Israel and the plagues, and explains the parallels a slave would have seen: Moses and a rescuer, Pharaoh and slaveowners, Egypt and states where slavery was legal.

3. *Reporting on Other Spirituals*   You may wish to give students the Biblical chapters containing the allusions, allowing them to focus on interpretation: (a) When Pharaoh's army pursues the Israelites, the Red Sea closes and drowns them (Exodus 14:23–31). (b) The prophet Elijah ascends to heaven in a flaming chariot shortly after parting the Jordan (2 Kings 2: 7–11). (c) After the death of Moses, the Israelites cross the parted Jordan and enter the Promised Land, led by Joshua (Joshua 3).

▶ CRITERIA FOR EVALUATING THE ASSIGNMENT   The essay explains the Biblical allusions and interprets them in a manner consistent with slaves' experiences.

4. *Comparing the Spirituals to the Puritans' Writings*   You may wish to guide students especially to William Bradford's history (text pages 13–20) and Mary Rowlandson's account of her captivity (text pages 24–29).

▶ CRITERIA FOR EVALUATING THE ASSIGNMENT   The essay cites similarities between any two spirituals and the writing of one Puritan writer in use of Biblical narratives and images as ''types'' of human experiences.

5. *Analyzing a Code Song*   Review ''Follow the Drinking Gourd'' and let students identify some of the code phrases that are really directions.

▶ CRITERIA FOR EVALUATING THE ASSIGNMENT   The paragraph cites repeated references to ''the old man'' (an underground railroad guide), and lines about following the riverbank (line 9), passing dead trees (line 10), coming to the end of a river between two hills (line 13), and reaching the place where a small river joins a larger one (line 16).

Extending the Songs

Douglass compared the slaves' songs with those of the oppressed Irish of his day. Others have compared their soulful quality to the music of Russian serfs before their emancipation in 1862 or to Yiddish music of the ghettoes of Europe. There are also similarities and differences between American slavery and other forms of servitude and oppression in other parts of the world and in other eras. Some of your students may be interested in reporting on such institutions as South American peonage, Russian serfdom, feudal European peasanthood, ancient Greek and Roman slavery, and the like.

Bret Harte

Text page 393

THE OUTCASTS OF POKER FLAT

Text page 394

Objectives

1. To respond to a story about the West

2. To state the theme of a short story

3. To write paragraphs explaining casting choices for actors in a movie adaptation

4. To write a report comparing Harte's characters and themes with those in a modern Western novel

5. To analyze the use of euphemism and irony as a source of humor

Introducing the Story

Here are the major elements of the story:

- **Characters:** Oakhurst, a gambler; "The Duchess," "Mother Shipton," and Uncle Billy, deportees from the town of Poker Flat; Tom Simson and Piney Woods, a pair of innocent young lovers

- **Conflicts:** people vs. nature, conventional morality vs. inner goodness

- **Point of view:** third-person, omniscient

- **Significant techniques:** euphemism, comic irony, sentimentalism

- **Setting:** California, November and December 1850

BACKGROUND ON THE STORY Harte was one of the earliest in a long tradition of American newspapermen-turned-fiction-writers, which continued with Twain, Crane, Hemingway, and John O'Hara. This was a parallel literary tradition to the more genteel, philosophical New England tradition that produced Hawthorne and the Transcendentalists. Newspapers carried reports from the frontier back to the cities, and writers such as Harte, aiming at a predominantly white male audience, told stories that were considered racy at the time. The use of dialect was favored for its air of authenticity. The exaggeration of the glories of the Old West in these tales caused many a settler from back East to move West, drawn by the ringing words of newspaper reports and "dime store novels."

THE PLOT The law-abiding citizens of Poker Flat cast out a group of people they consider immoral. Making camp in the mountains, the outcasts are joined by a pair of innocent young lovers. Then Uncle Billy steals the mules and leaves camp, and the remaining characters are trapped by a snowstorm, which directly or indirectly kills all of them except young Tom Simson, who returns with help, but too late.

Teaching Strategies

PROVIDING FOR CULTURAL DIFFERENCES Most students' ideas about the Old West have been formed from watching Western movies. (You might discuss some of the stereotypes of "good guy," "bad guy," and Native American.) Students whose families come from Old West backgrounds may be able to provide bits of local or family history that may help illuminate Harte's subject from a different angle.

Female students may be troubled by Harte's use of stereotypes, such as the prostitute with the heart of gold and the comically innocent young backwoods bride. Remind them that this story was written a long time ago and that its portrayal of the good side of "fallen" women actually seemed forward-thinking in its day.

PROVIDING FOR DIFFERENT LEVELS OF ABILITY Harte's use of euphemistic humor makes careful vocabulary study important. Students who have trouble with the story's antiquated diction will find a brief synopsis of the plot helpful. The plot events and characters are vividly and schematically drawn. You might want to make a list of the major characters on the chalkboard, and have students discuss brief descriptions of the characters' traits.

READING THE STORY The difficult vocabulary and arch, sentimental tone of this story may make it difficult for some students to read aloud in a convincing tone. You might want to assign the story as homework and then go over it in class, scene by scene, stopping at points where students have questions.

RETEACHING ALTERNATIVES Class discussion will probably help clear up any remaining questions about plot and character, but students may still have reservations about Harte's style, tone, and themes. You might point out that this story is essentially a precursor of the more realistic works of Twain and Crane. One way of assessing the story might be to have each student draw up a list of what aspects of the story are realistic and what aspects are not. Students' individual reactions can then be compared and refined. This activity can also be done on the chalkboard.

Responding to the Story   Text page 400

Answers to the questions in the Pupil's Edition appear in the Annotated Teacher's Edition.

Writing About the Story

For help in revising their compositions, refer students to **Grammar, Usage, and Mechanics: A Reference Guide** on text pages 1183–1228 at the back of their books.

A CREATIVE RESPONSE
1. Casting a Film   You might list the characters on the chalkboard and brainstorm lists of actors for each part.

▶ CRITERIA FOR EVALUATING THE ASSIGNMENT   The essay consists of one paragraph per character, each paragraph naming an actor and giving reasons for the choice. Essays should also show a grasp of key traits for the characters in the story.

A CRITICAL RESPONSE
2. Comparing Depictions of the Frontier   Students may already be familiar with Clark's *The Ox-Bow Incident* and with Schaefer's *Shane,* Western classics. Ask your librarian to recommend specific works by Johnson and the prolific L'Amour that are appropriate for students.

▶ CRITERIA FOR EVALUATING THE ASSIGNMENT   The report analyzes the realism or romanticism with which each writer depicts themes and characters of the Old West. The essay also explains whether the novel by the modern writer is more or less realistic than Harte's.

Analyzing Language and Style

EUPHEMISMS AND COMIC IRONY
1. **a.** The hanged women had made a career of an "improper" line of work.
   b. They were prostitutes.
2. **a.** *Regenerating* means "to form or grow again." In a context such as this, it usually refers to spiritual renewal.
   b. He uses *regenerating* ironically to mean a false, hypocritical type of moral rebirth.
3. **a.** A *profession* is usually a respectable career in law, medicine, or the like.
   b. He is a gambler.
4. **a.** They are frailer in morality and in the physical strength of youth.
   b. The "celestial guardians," or angels, are prostitutes.
5. **a.** The women are making the cabin habitable.
   b. Her experience would be with bordellos, usually considered gaudy and extremely tasteless in décor.
6. **a.** He is referring to rouge on the Duchess's cheeks.
   b. Prostitutes used makeup, but "virtuous" women of the time did not.

Extending the Story

Harte's fiction looks backward to Dickens and forward to Twain and Crane. From Dickens, Harte learned a sentimental style of melodrama, leavened by humor, and eccentric characters. Harte, however, did not have Dickens's verbal and psychological genius.

From Harte, the later American realists learned an appreciation of the value of stark incident and realistic local detail. Your more advanced students might be interested in reading Stephen Crane's two best Western stories, "The Blue Hotel" and "The Bride Comes to Yellow Sky." Ask them to choose one of the stories, discuss it in a group, and come to some consensus about how the story compares to Harte's "The Outcasts of Poker Flat."

Mark Twain

Text page 402

FROM LIFE ON THE MISSISSIPPI

Text page 404

Objectives

1. To sample and enjoy Mark Twain's humor

2. To analyze hyperbole, metaphor, and boasts

3. To write an exaggerated boast

4. To rewrite regional dialect into standard English

Introducing the Story

Here are the major elements of the story:

- **Characters:** Huck Finn, Jim, and a group of raftsmen on the Mississippi

- **Conflicts:** boast vs. actuality, fantasy vs. reality, fear vs. bravery

- **Point of view:** first-person introduction and conclusion in Twain's own voice, as frame story to a first-person narrative with Huck Finn as narrator

- **Significant techniques:** dialect, hyperbole, comic metaphor, incongruity, boasts, digression

- **Setting:** the Mississippi River, just south of Cairo, Illinois, before the Civil War

BACKGROUND ON THE STORY Twain worked on *Life on the Mississippi* and *Huckleberry Finn* at the same time, and his notes for the two books overlapped. Indeed, after finishing both, Twain at one time contemplated writing a sequel in which Huck would become a cabin boy on a Mississippi steamboat.

Twain's books were published on the subscription system, rather than being sold in bookstores and published by the usual trade publishing houses. Traveling salesmen for the subscription publishing company went from door to door, usually in rural areas, selling subscriptions to the book before it came out. The audience for subscription books demanded massive volumes for their money, which explains why *Life on the Mississipi* is padded, not only with an excerpt from one of Twain's other books, but with quotations from earlier travel writers.

The subscription sales for *Life on the Mississippi* were disappointing, but nevertheless the book was the fruit of the greatest creative period of Twain's life.

THE PLOT Twain begins by describing the history of Mississippi River raftsmen and their times in his own words. Then he introduces a chapter written for *Huckleberry Finn* in which Jim sends Huck, at night, to swim over to a raft so he can overhear the raftsmen talking, and thus find out how close they are to Cairo, Illinois. Huck doesn't find out that information, but overhears the raftsmen boasting, fighting, and telling a ghost story. The raftsmen discover and threaten him, but let him go after he talks his way winningly out of the jam.

Teaching Strategies

PROVIDING FOR CULTURAL DIFFERENCES The amount of explanation you may have to give about the way of life on the Mississippi River will vary depending on your region of the country. Of course, all regions of America today are very distant from the antebellum era on the Mississippi.

This selection is very much a boyish adventure episode. You might point out that in comparison to the life of the average American boy on the Mississippi in the early 1800's, Huck's adventures are an exaggeration, a heightening of reality—not a documented, factual report of reality. And it is not difficult to imagine a girl participating in adventures similar to Huck's. (A modern work showing a girl of the 1800's crossing the country with a pet wolf is the Disney movie *The Journey of Natty Gann*.)

PROVIDING FOR DIFFERENT LEVELS OF ABILITY For LEP and ESL students it will probably be necessary to paraphrase the dialect into standard English to at least some extent, even though some of the flavor will be lost. Ask the ESL students if they can identify or describe some dialect differences in their native language. What, for example, are some of the differences in Puerto Rican, Cuban, and Mexican Spanish?

The history of rafting at the beginning of the chapter may be a bit heavy for some students. It can be readily summarized; the crucial paragraphs are the ones that directly describe the river trade and the boatmen. In the excerpt from *Huckleberry Finn*, the events themselves are quite vivid, but the use of dialect and some padding may put a veil between the action and the reader.

READING THE STORY The raftsmen's boasts (from the bottom of text page 405 through the first paragraph on text page 408) cry out for oral reading. The surrounding passages describing the fight can be read aloud too. The ghost story (text pages 409–411) has some effective and humorous moments, but it may be too long and too thick with dialect to be profitably read aloud in its entirety. After having the class read the story on their own, you might choose specific passages (such as the comparison of Mississippi and Ohio River waters, from the bottom of text page 408 to the top of text page 409) for oral reading by volunteers.

RETEACHING ALTERNATIVES Extensive paraphrasing will probably be necessary for the central portions of this selection. It would probably be best to divide the class into small groups and have each group paraphrase a portion. The selection breaks naturally into separate units: the introduction in Twain's voice; Huck's eavesdropping on the boasts and the fight; the raftsmen's recreations, including singing and conversation; the ghost story, which can be divided into two or three parts; and the raftsmen's discovery of Huck. A spokesperson for each group can present its paraphrase to the whole class.

Responding to the Story   Text page 413

Answers to the questions in the Pupil's Edition appear in the Annotated Teacher's Edition.

Writing About the Story

For help in revising their compositions, refer students to **Grammar, Usage, and Mechanics: A Reference Guide** on text pages 1183–1228 at the back of their books.

A CREATIVE RESPONSE
1. Writing an Exaggerated Boast A review of the rivermen's boasts which begin at the bottom of text page 405 and continues through the first paragraph of text page 407 and a look ahead to text page 486 (Davy Crockett) should

establish the idea. You might also brainstorm a list of *types* of braggarts—he-men, scholars, artists, politicians, etc.

▶ CRITERIA FOR EVALUATING THE ASSIGNMENT The boast contains the following elements: name, metaphors, humor, and highly exaggerated claims.

2. Rewriting Dialect Suitable exchanges begin to appear on text page 405. Call students' attention to the fact that they are also to comment on what is lost when standard English is substituted in the specific context.

▶ CRITERIA FOR EVALUATING THE ASSIGNMENT The selection is accurately rendered in standard English, and the student comments on the resultant loss of liveliness, verve, immediacy, or realism.

Analyzing Language and Style

DIALECT AND FRONTIER HUMOR
1. The assignment is to find five examples each of variation from standard English in (1) vocabulary, (2) pronunciation, and (3) grammar. There are numerous examples throughout Huck Finn's narrative.
2. Students' examples of hyperbole, metaphors, incongruity, boasts, and digressions will vary. You might, however, suggest starting with the shouting match on page 407.
3. All are used, but metaphor and hyperbole stand out.
4. Students should be able to come up with many examples of hyperbole, incongruity, and digressions. They may have a harder time finding current examples of metaphor and boasts.

Extending the Story

Interested students should be encouraged to read more of the book on their own. The first thirty-one chapters are generally considered the high point of *Life on the Mississippi,* containing Twain's classic descriptions of river commerce and steamboat piloting. The later chapters tend to be somewhat padded.

FROM THE ADVENTURES OF HUCKLEBERRY FINN

Objectives

1. To respond to an excerpt from a great American novel
2. To analyze images, figures of speech, and tone
3. To write a paragraph imitating a writer's technique
4. To write a journal entry
5. To write an essay responding to a critical statement
6. To write an essay analyzing the selection
7. To write an essay evaluating voice
8. To analyze descriptive language

Introducing the Story

Here are the major elements of the story:

- **Protagonists:** Huck Finn, the narrator, a fourteen-year-old boy; Jim, a runaway slave
- **Antagonist:** Pap, Huck's father
- **Conflicts:** the individual vs. authority, personal morality vs. social morality, freedom vs. confinement
- **Theme:** Through a series of ordeals that test his ingenuity and spirit, a youth develops emotionally and morally into an adult.
- **Significant techniques:** "voice," dialect, comic irony, colloquial lyricism
- **Point of view:** first-person, major character
- **Setting:** the Mississippi River and environs, 1845

BACKGROUND ON THE STORY Twain worked on his masterpiece for six years or more, on and off. His method of composition for all his books was to work on a project when he was inspired and to set it aside when inspiration flagged. In the summer of 1883, he experienced the greatest creative surge of his life. He finished a draft of *Huckleberry Finn* and began revising it. "This summer it is no more trouble for me to write than it is to lie," he told his mother. At the same time he was working on another book, which never panned out, and several of his characteristic, wrong-headed business schemes. Students will be interested to learn that among his failed business ventures was a game, "Mark Twain's Memory-Builder," which was similar to today's "Trivial Pursuit."

Although Twain was a world-famous writer and lecturer at the time, the pre-publication outlook for *Huckleberry Finn* was gloomy, because of bad planning, bad luck, and generally hard economic conditions. During the first month after publication, there was little critical response of any kind, and what did appear was often negative. The genteel establishment was offended by the book's gritty, vernacular realism. What propelled the book toward success, in fact, was further negative reaction. The Concord, Massachusetts, public library banned the book from its shelves. Louisa May Alcott said, "If Mr. Clemens cannot think of something better to tell our pure-minded lads and lasses, he had best stop writing for them." The resulting publicity turned the book's fortunes around. Twain wrote to his publisher: "They have expelled Huck from their library as 'trash and suitable only for the slums.' That will sell 25,000 copies for us sure."

THE PLOT Pap appears in Huck's room one night in search of the money he heard Huck received. He abuses Huck verbally and physically. Later we see Pap, whom a new judge had tried to reform, lapse into delirium tremens. Huck decides to run away, and covers his trail with pig's blood and other signs of violence so people will think he has been killed. He escapes to Jackson's Island, where he encounters the runaway slave Jim, and promises not to turn him in.

Teaching Strategies

PROVIDING FOR CULTURAL DIFFERENCES The obviously sensitive area is that of race. Jim's dialect may be something of a problem. While it's true that Twain carefully records several different dialects in the book, it's also true that the African American dialect is made to seem substantially thicker. And Jim's reaction to what he thinks is Huck's "ghost" is an unfortunate piece of stereotypical humor. Nevertheless, Twain depicts Jim as an intelligent, level-headed, and dignified human being, and the book as a whole is a sustained argument against prejudice and inhumanity. Twain, both as an individual and a writer, was essentially fair-minded and decent, and the elements of racism that we detect more than a century later were vestiges of the times he was brought up in.

PROVIDING FOR DIFFERENT LEVELS OF ABILITY ESL and LEP students may have trouble with the dialect, and also with the rather dense descriptive detail concerning Huck's escape. You might want to introduce each section with a brief paraphrase so the students will recognize the "landmarks" as they come to them. If students find particular passages to be stumbling blocks, you might have them read the passages out loud and work out their own paraphrases. To ease their frustration, have students work with partners who read the passages more easily.

READING THE STORY The accompanying audiocassette for "Pap starts in on a New Life" will accustom students to the "sound" and "feel" of Huck's colloquial narration. It might be a good idea to play this recording on the first day you study the selection, even if students have already read it at home. Depending on time constraints, you may want to ask your class to read other portions aloud as well.

RETEACHING ALTERNATIVES You might ask students to write brief descriptions of Pap, Huck, and Jim, and summarize the important events in these four chapters. If some students are confused as to why Jim is so frightened of Huck, remind them that Jim is a fugitive slave and subject to the death penalty.

Responding to the Story   Text page 428

Answers to the questions in the Pupil's Edition appear in the Annotated Teacher's Edition.

Writing About the Story

For help in revising their compositions, refer students to **Grammar, Usage, and Mechanics: A Reference Guide** on text pages 1183–1228 at the back of their books.

A CREATIVE RESPONSE

1. Imitating a Writer's Technique Carefully analyze the description of Pap on text page 414 ("He was most fifty . . ."). Review word connotations (see text page 1172) and note Twain's blend of physical description and words conveying attitude. For further help in completing this assignment, refer students to the **Literature and Language Exercise** on text page 1161, Using the Descriptive and Narrative Modes.

▶ CRITERIA FOR EVALUATING THE ASSIGNMENT The paragraph reveals both a person's appearance (hair, eyes, color, face, and clothes) and how the speaker feels about the person.

2. Writing a Journal Entry Twain's comment ("Primary Sources," text page 429) reveals the later respectability of his model for Huck Finn. It may help students decide what Huck will be like as an old man, but they need not make their own Huck a justice of the peace in Montana.

▶ CRITERIA FOR EVALUATING THE ASSIGNMENT The journal entry is a plausible one for a much older Huck Finn. It reveals his age, where he lives, the form of his name he prefers, and his adult interpretation of his boyhood escapades.

A CRITICAL RESPONSE

3. Responding to a Critic Read Young's comment aloud in class (text page 427) and discuss it until students are able to cite specific reasons for agreeing or disagreeing with Young.

▶ CRITERIA FOR EVALUATING THE ASSIGNMENT The essay argues for or against Young's claim and cites specific details to support the writer's opinion.

4. Analyzing the Selection Review the concepts of realistic and romantic writing (text pages 380–381) and "The American Hero in Romantic Fiction" (text pages 120–121). Before students begin writing, have them brainstorm some ideas for how Washington Irving might have handled the story. (How might Irving have used nature, supernatural elements, a quest?)

▶ CRITERIA FOR EVALUATING THE ASSIGNMENT The essay cites several elements making Twain's novel realistic, and proposes the romantic solutions Washington Irving might have used.

5. Evaluating "Voice" Review the concept of *voice*. As an example, ask students for instances where they understood more quickly than Huck what was happening.

▶ CRITERIA FOR EVALUATING THE ASSIGNMENT The essay briefly analyzes the narrative voice of *Huckleberry Finn* and lists elements Twain would have had to change for an older Huck.

Analyzing Language and Style

DESCRIPTIVE LANGUAGE
1. The word *smelt* is an extremely effective choice.
2. Choices will vary, but images should clearly appeal to at least one of the senses. See, for instance, the paragraph on text page 425 beginning, "My heart jumped up. . . ."

Extending the Story

What if Bret Harte had written this excerpt from *Huckleberry Finn*? Have students discuss what aspects of Twain's characters, story line, and style might have been changed. What aspects might have remained the same?

Primary Sources   Text page 429

THE "ORIGINAL" HUCKLEBERRY FINN
Students may be asked to read Twain's reply aloud. Point out that an autobiography is a highly personal primary source that often reveals the character of the writer. (Although journals are most personal, an autobiography gives the writer a chance to create his public persona.) Ask students how they would characterize Mark Twain based on his reply to the man from Hannibal.

AN OCCURRENCE AT OWL CREEK BRIDGE

Objectives

1. To respond to a suspenseful story

2. To evaluate the story's theme

3. To analyze the use of cinematic techniques in a story

4. To imitate a writer's technique

5. To write an essay analyzing the use of suspense

6. To write an essay responding to a critical comment

Introducing the Story

Here are the major elements of the story:

- **Protagonist:** Peyton Farquhar, a Southern planter
- **Antagonists:** some Union soldiers
- **Conflicts:** illusion vs. reality; subjective time vs. objective time
- **Themes:** The intensity of the stream of consciousness within a very few seconds; the disappointment of human dreams by inevitable fate
- **Point of view:** third-person limited, major character
- **Significant techniques:** cinematic style, controlled point of view, suspense, flashback, surprise ending
- **Setting:** Alabama during the Civil War

BACKGROUND ON THE STORY This very famous story has perhaps had more influence on genre fiction, such as science fiction, than on "serious" literature. Indeed, it was made into an episode of the original (black and white, half-hour) *Twilight Zone* television series. Genre writers have often imitated Bierce's psychological surprise ending, changing the setting and the costumes. The fact that virtually all of the externals of this story can be altered and its essence still retained may say something about its limitations as a work of literature. To some extent the story is built around a mere contrivance, but, there is no doubt that embedded in this contrivance is a forceful psychological truth.

THE PLOT Peyton Farquhar, a well-to-do Alabama planter, has been captured by Union forces for attempting to sabotage a bridge. As the story opens, Farquhar is about to be hanged. We see him, through his own point of view, escaping and returning to his home, but at the ending we learn that the escape has been a fantasy, taking place in the few moments during which he has, in reality, been hanged.

Teaching Strategies

PROVIDING FOR CULTURAL DIFFERENCES The story's point of view makes it seem sympathetic to the Confederate side, but Bierce himself was a much-decorated Union veteran. It seems likely, therefore, that Bierce was expressing his bitterness at the idea of war in general as a waste of human life.

PROVIDING FOR DIFFERENT LEVELS OF ABILITY Some students may not be able to catch on to the surprise ending at first. After a first reading and discussion, you may want to guide them through the selection again, pointing out the specific places where clues and foreshadowings are presented. Advanced students may already be familiar with the story and therefore not surprised. They will probably enjoy analyzing Bierce's techniques.

READING THE STORY The last four paragraphs contain all the essential elements of the contrast between Farquhar's fantasy and the reality of his hanging, as well as Bierce's techniques of foreshadowing and cinematic cutting. You might want to select this passage for reading aloud, but only after the students have read the story in its entirety by themselves. Otherwise the surprise ending will be given away.

RETEACHING ALTERNATIVES If some students have trouble locating the changes from reality to fantasy in the story, you might have them go over the story paragraph by paragraph, or passage by passage, jotting down, in each case, whether the description is of an external fact or an internal fancy. (Part III of the story is the section where most of the fantasy occurs; the first two parts are rather straightforward.) You might draw a line down the middle of the chalkboard, and for each paragraph in Part III, ask the class to determine whether it belongs on the "fantasy" or "reality" side of the line.

Responding to the Story
Text page 438

Answers to the questions in the Pupil's Edition appear in the Annotated Teacher's Edition.

Writing About the Story

For help in revising their compositions, refer students to **Grammar, Usage, and Mechanics: A Reference Guide** on text pages 1183–1228 at the back of their books.

A CREATIVE RESPONSE

1. Imitating a Technique   It may be helpful for small groups or the class as a whole to brainstorm several situations students could use as starting points. (For example, having a heart attack, a baby being born, a person falling from a great height, someone in a car accident, etc.)

▶ CRITERIA FOR EVALUATING THE ASSIGNMENT   The account plausibly yet suspensefully narrates the thoughts inside a character's mind over a very short but intensely stressful period of time.

A CRITICAL RESPONSE

2. Analyzing Suspense   Elicit from the class several examples of how Bierce builds suspense. (At the end of Part II we learn that the Confederate soldier who suggests the scheme to destroy the bridge is really a Federal scout. In Part III, the details of the escape are plausible, and it seems ever more likely that Farquhar will make his escape.)

▶ CRITERIA FOR EVALUATING THE ASSIGNMENT   The essay cites two different methods Bierce uses to increase the reader's suspense in the second and third parts of the story.

3. Responding to a Critical Comment   Read Brooks and Warren's comment and make sure students understand their point. Direct students to use details from the story to support their opinion.

▶ CRITERIA FOR EVALUATING THE ASSIGNMENT   The essay agrees with the comment that the story is not true fiction, or argues that the story uses psychology to reveal something important about Farquhar or human nature in general. In either case, the writer's opinion is supported by details from the story.

Extending the Story

Surprise endings were, in the past, a staple of popular fiction: a few decades ago, *Collier's* magazine relied almost exclusively on stories with surprise or twist endings. Your students may have read such old chestnuts of the genre as O. Henry's "The Last Leaf" and Maupassant's "The Necklace." Ask them what other examples of surprise-ending stories they know, and discuss the advantages and limitations of the device. Such stories have gone out of fashion, but an excellent, very brief one from fairly recent years is the third of John Cheever's "Three Stories" in *The Stories of John Cheever*. J. D. Salinger's "A Perfect Day for Bananafish" and "Pretty Mouth and Green My Eyes" both have surprise endings. Ann Beattie's "Janus" is an excellent, fairly short example of a contemporary story in which the surprise is that there is *no* gimmick ending. The story proceeds as if it might be foreshadowing such an ending, but instead gives us a richer emotional truth.

Feature

VOICES FROM THE CIVIL WAR
Text page 439

Objectives

1. To react to some personal responses to the Civil War

2. To analyze differences in tone among writers

3. To write a summary of content

4. To write a character sketch

Introducing the Feature

This feature is a varied collection of Civil War writings, including letters, speeches, and journal entries. Together they give a strong personal sense of history in the making. The focus of these writings is on people—from the Presidents and generals who led the Union and Confederacy to the soldiers who fought with uncommon bravery.

We see them as real people doing a dirty job that had few rewards. The writings begin with the opening of hostilities at Fort Sumter and end with the surrender of Lee's army. In between there is enough anguish and sorrow to persuade the hardest-hearted reader that the Civil War was indeed, as Lincoln said, a "horrid nightmare."

Many students may express shock at the violence and suffering that resulted from the Civil War. They may wonder how such a thing could have happened. Did Americans of that era not know what they were getting into when the first shot was fired? You might ask students to apply the same question to more recent American wars, and consider how difficult they were to stop once they had begun. What do we learn about war from reading personal accounts such as these? Is a war ever worth fighting?

BACKGROUND ON THE FEATURE   These writings reveal the innate goodness of the people on both sides of the battle line. Once the war was under way, there was little personal animosity between the enemies. Rather, soldiers on both sides respected each other, perhaps because they understood what agony the other fellow was going through. When Lee's men surrendered their arms at Appomattox Court House, there were no hoots and hollers from the victorious Union soldiers. Instead, they greeted their Confederate counterparts with a small salute. Thus the healing process began.

Students might be interested to know that Lincoln was not the main speaker at the Gettysburg cemetery that summer day in 1863. A famous orator, Edward Everett, gave the major speech—a sophisticated discourse that went on for two hours. Lincoln's "Gettysburg Address," considered to be one of the most eloquent speeches in American history, lasted just two minutes. It is not true, as is sometimes reported, that Lincoln's speech was universally scorned for its brevity or that Lincoln dashed it off on the back of an envelope. Lincoln worked long and hard on his speech, and most people recognized it immediately as a masterpiece.

Teaching Strategies

PROVIDING FOR CULTURAL DIFFERENCES   Students who have recently arrived from other countries will need a brief review of the basic facts about the American Civil War. They may be able to tell stories about civil wars in countries they have emigrated from.

PROVIDING FOR DIFFERENT LEVELS OF ABILITY   Some students, especially ESL students unfamiliar with American history, will benefit from seeing a time line of the Civil War. They could consult a history textbook to discover the major events of the war, and you might draw a time line on the chalkboard. Another helpful organizational tool for a feature with so many parts is an outline or a chart that lists each writer and title along with a brief summary of the content.

READING THE FEATURE   Ask students to read aloud excerpts from the longer selections and some of the shorter ones in their entirety. Give each student time to prepare the reading, to establish the proper tone and compose an appropriate voice. If possible, tape-record their readings and play them back for comment. Also, you might wish to find and play a recording of "The Battle Hymn of the Republic."

RETEACHING ALTERNATIVES   Most of these selections introduce the reader to a strong character—either the writer or the person who is the subject of the writing. Have students compose five brief character sketches of people they met in this feature. Some students may wish to try drawing these characters too. All sketches should reveal the essence of that character.

Extending the Feature

Have students consider what effect the existence of television might have had on the course of the Civil War. Ask groups of students to choose one of the selections in this feature or one event from a selection and prepare a television news report on it. Students should share the responsibility for researching, writing, and reporting. If they have access to video equipment, they might even prepare a film of the recreated event. Otherwise, they might sketch the scene, or simply leave it to the viewers' imagination.

Students will enjoy looking at the photographs and text in *The Civil War*, a book based on the documentary filmscript by Geoffrey C. Ward, Ric Burns, and Ken Burns (Knopf, 1990). Or you can play all or part of one of the videos of this nine-part award-winning PBS documentary (Pacific Arts Video Publication, 1990).

Stephen Crane

A MYSTERY OF HEROISM

Objectives

1. To respond to a story and poem about war

2. To evaluate the use of imagery

3. To identify a character's motivation

4. To interpret the ambiguous ending of a story

5. To evaluate the use of personification

6. To write an essay comparing a story with a poem

7. To write an essay evaluating a critic's statement

Introducing the Story

Here are the major elements of the story:

- **Protagonist:** Fred Collins, a private in the army

- **Conflict:** self-doubt vs. heroism, self-perception vs. society's perception

- **Theme:** War is irrational and ignoble, and causes men to behave in strange ways.

- **Point of view:** third-person omniscient

- **Significant techniques:** personification, dialogue, imagery, characterization

- **Setting:** an unnamed battle of the Civil War, possibly either Chancellorsville or Fredericksburg

BACKGROUND ON THE STORY   Like Crane's novel *The Red Badge of Courage*, this story is quintessential, realistic fiction. Reading Crane's battle scenes, one can almost smell the gunpowder and feel the concussion of shells hitting the earth. Yet Crane had never even seen a battle—he relied on his imagination. (Crane was born in 1871 and wrote "A Mystery of Heroism" in 1895.) Crane was a journalist by trade, so he knew how to piece together facts. By augmenting his research with visits to Civil War battle sites, Crane was able to impart a sense of authenticity to his story's setting and plot.

SUMMARY   In the midst of a heated Civil War battle, private Fred Collins decides he is willing to risk death to get some water. Egged on by his comrades, he sets out across a meadow that is being bombarded, fills an old bucket at a well, and with shells landing all about, makes his way back to his company's position. On the trip back, a dying officer asks for a drink. Collins runs on, but turns back to give the officer some water. Upon his safe return, two joking lieutenants get first crack at the water. Somehow, the bucket ends up on the ground, empty.

Teaching Strategies

PROVIDING FOR CULTURAL DIFFERENCES   Different regions and cultures have disparate views of the military and dissimilar responses to military behavior. Some of your students may react negatively to Crane's realistic depiction of war, while others may believe that it is important to show that war is an often frightening and inhuman activity rather than a glorious one. Some students might see themselves as potential future heroes, and Crane's portrayal may undermine their ideas of heroism. Such students need to understand that not all heroic acts are foolhardy.

PROVIDING FOR DIFFERENT LEVELS OF ABILITY   Crane's style of intercutting dialogue with description may be difficult for some students. You may wish to highlight the paragraphs that move the plot from those that paint a picture of the scene so that students can follow the story smoothly from start to finish. However, they should not ignore descriptive details, for they are essential to the story.

READING THE STORY   Students can easily read the story in one sitting. Before they read, remind students that they will be asked to judge the actions of the main character, Fred Collins. You may wish to have students read aloud the seven paragraphs on text pages 460–461 that describe Collins's thoughts about his actions and their heroic nature. You may also want students to read aloud some of the many colorful descriptive passages to appreciate the story's atmosphere.

RETEACHING ALTERNATIVES   Since Collins's motivation is, in some ways, a mystery, students might benefit from offering answers to several "Why?" questions: Why did he want to go after water? (He was thirsty.) Why did his comrades urge him to go get the water in the midst of heavy shelling? (They were kidding at first; later, after arguing with Collins, their taunts became more severe.)

Why did Collins go, knowing how dangerous it was? (He was rising to the challenge of his comrades. His colonel, who could have prevented him from going, instead told him he could go if he wanted to. He had no fear at first. Once he started, with six of the company's canteens, his mission took on more importance in his own eyes than it had assumed earlier.)

Responding to the Story   Text page 462

Answers to the questions in the Pupil's Edition appear in the Annotated Teacher's Edition.

Writing About the Story

For help in revising their compositions, refer students to **Grammar, Usage, and Mechanics: A Reference Guide** on text pages 1183–1228 at the back of their books.

A CRITICAL RESPONSE
1. Comparing a Poem and a Story   Divide students into small groups to read and discuss the poem. Have them identify any passages in the poem that express ideas found in the story. Students can work in groups to complete the chart, answering each question for both the poem and the story.

▶ CRITERIA FOR EVALUATING THE ASSIGNMENT   The essay summarizes Crane's attitude toward war and offers details from both the story and the poem to back up the summary statement. The essay touches on the theme of heroism, explains the irony in Crane's line ''War is kind,'' and applies those words to the story as well.

2. Responding to a Critic   Discuss the terms *touchstone* (criterion; way of telling if something is authentic) and *parable* (moral tale). Review the definition of *naturalism* in the fourth paragraph of Crane's biography (text page 455). *Naturalistic* in the quotation refers to an analysis of what causes people to behave the way they do.

▶ CRITERIA FOR EVALUATING THE ASSIGNMENT   The essay examines the story for instances of fear or the lack of it and for examples of brotherly love. It explains the irony of finding brotherhood within a war that pitted brother against brother in a struggle to the death. The essay draws a conclusion about whether or not the critic's statement applies fully to the story.

Extending the Story

You might want to assign each student to locate, read, and do a brief oral report on another story, memoir, or novel about war. Some excellent ones are Walt Whitman, *Specimen Days* (Civil War); Robert Graves, *Goodbye to All That* (World War I); E. E. Cummings, *The Enormous Room* (World War I); John Dos Passos, *Three Soldiers* (World War I); Leo Tolstoy, *Sebastopol Sketches* (Crimean War); Stendhal, *The Charterhouse of Parma*, Chapters 3 and 4 (the Napoleonic wars in Italy); Ernest Hemingway, *For Whom the Bell Tolls* (Spanish Civil War); William Wharton, *A Midnight Clear* (World War II); James Michener, *Tales of the South Pacific* (World War II); Tim O'Brien, *Going After Cacciato* (fiction—Vietnam War); Tim O'Brien, *If I Die in a Combat Zone* (nonfiction—Vietnam War); Philip Caputo, *A Rumor of War* (Vietnam War); Ron Kovic, *Born on the Fourth of July* (Vietnam War); Michael Herr, *Dispatches* (Vietnam War); Joseph Ferrandino, *Firefight* (Vietnam War).

THE OPEN BOAT   Text page 464

Objectives

1. To respond to a story that is an example of naturalism

2. To interpret the meaning of symbols

3. To recognize shifts in point of view

4. To write a news story describing the events in the story

5. To write an essay explaining the theme of a story

6. To write an essay comparing a story with a poem

7. To write an essay contrasting two writers' views of nature

Introducing the Story

Ask students familiar with the ocean's ways to verify Crane's description of the relentless waves and the dangers a small boat faces in the open sea. Any student who has ever rowed a long distance might offer details of the technique required as well as the strain on the body.

You might have a committee prepare in advance a two-dimensional version of the open boat made from newspaper or brown paper bags taped together. The cutout boat should be ten feet long by approximately four feet at its widest. Have four students sit in this paper boat to get an idea of how small it is.

Here are the major elements of the story:

- **Protagonists:** the correspondent; the captain; the cook; the oiler, Billie
- **Antagonist:** the sea
- **Conflict:** man vs. nature
- **Theme:** the gaining of insight through suffering
- **Point of view:** third-person omniscient
- **Significant techniques:** symbolism, foreshadowing, imagery
- **Setting:** the Atlantic Ocean off the Florida coast, two days in January, the late 1890's

BACKGROUND ON THE STORY   Reporter Stephen Crane, twenty-five years old, was off to cover the Cuban revolution for the *New York Journal* when his ship the *Commodore* sank on New Year's Day 1897 off the coast of Jacksonville, Florida. Before it sank, dinghies and rafts were lowered. In a small open boat, Crane, the ship's oiler, the cook, and the captain found themselves fighting for their lives. Crane first wrote a factual reporter's account of the ordeal. Later, in ''The Open Boat,'' he took the facts and wove them into a tale of great symbolic force.

THE PLOT   Four shipwrecked men maneuver a small open boat through rough seas off the coast of Florida. The captain lies injured in the bow, the correspondent and the oiler share rowing duties, and the cook squats in the bottom of the boat, bailing out sea water. Each huge wave, eager to crash the dinghy to bits, is followed by another just as menacing. The crew are well aware of their perilous situation, but they perform their duties with little complaint. Early on, the cook says there is a life-saving station near the Mosquito Inlet lighthouse, which gives the men hope. Some time later, the captain spots the lighthouse. The boat makes progress toward that speck on the horizon, which slowly grows in size. Soon they can see land. Now they expect to be sighted from the lighthouse and saved, but there is no sign of life on shore. They know if they go any closer to shore they will be swamped and have to swim for it, so they decide to move back out to sea and wait. Later, they spy people, even an omnibus, on the beach, but there is no lifeboat. Night falls, and the sea carries them northward. In the morning the captain decides it is time to head for the beach, to take their chances swimming before all are too exhausted. The captain, correspondent, and cook make it to shore alive, but the oiler drowns.

Teaching Strategies

PROVIDING FOR CULTURAL DIFFERENCES   Students from all cultures will be able to relate to the characters' struggle against the sea. Some students may have stories to tell about Vietnamese or Haitian ''boat people'' struggling to keep small boats afloat in heavy seas.

PROVIDING FOR DIFFERENT LEVELS OF ABILITY
Give LEP students some help with this very long story by reading most of it aloud in class. You might read through the end of Part VI and have students read Part VII as homework.

Other students may complain that Crane's story is too long, with too much description, and not enough action. Suggest to them that Crane may have wanted his readers to experience the agony of this seemingly endless floating nightmare. The reader, too, keeps expecting the adventure to end.

READING THE STORY   The story is divided into seven numbered parts. Try having students read one or two parts at a time and then stop to write down what they think will happen next. Students might first read Part I, then Parts II and III together, then Parts IV and V, and finally Parts VI and VII. They should compare their predictions for each segment of the story with what actually happens in the story. In this way students will come to appreciate the suspense, expectations, and reversals of the plot. (Part I ends cautiously, but with a bit of hope. At the end of Part III, the seamen are puffing on cigars, having come within sight of land. Parts IV and V are full of frustrations and end with a new danger—a shark. Part VI drags out the mental anguish, and Part VII finally brings release.)

Have students explain how they felt as they read certain parts of the story. Ask students to find their favorite descriptive sentence or passage in the story and explain what it means and why it is effective.

RETEACHING ALTERNATIVES   Since this story is really a tale of men against nature, ask students to skim the story to find passages that deal directly with this conflict. Have students summarize each of the examples (e.g., various descriptions of the waves, the effect of the wind, the approach of the gull, the visit of the shark, and the strong current that pulled the correspondent as he swam to shore). Ask students to draw a conclusion about the role of nature in the story. How does Crane seem to view nature? Most students will agree that nature in this story, though it can be destructive, is really just indifferent. This discussion will help prepare students for writing assignments 3 and 4 (text page 479).

Responding to the Story   Text page 478

Answers to the questions in the Pupil's Edition appear in the Annotated Teacher's Edition.

Writing About the Story

For help in revising their compositions, refer students to **Grammar, Usage, and Mechanics: A Reference Guide** on text pages 1183–1228 at the back of their books.

A CREATIVE RESPONSE

1. Reporting the Facts Discuss with students where their "facts" can come from. They should exhaust the resources at hand before they begin inventing details. Refer them to the primary source on text page 479 for names of the sailors. Students can find and bring to class Crane's newspaper story ("Stephen Crane's Own Story" published in the *New York Press*, January 7, 1897). It appears in *Stephen Crane: An Omnibus* edited by R. W. Stallman (Knopf, 1952).

▶ CRITERIA FOR EVALUATING THE ASSIGNMENT News stories start with a catchy headline and an opening paragraph that answers the main questions a reader might have. Each succeeding paragraph fills in details drawn from the story, the headnote, and the primary source excerpts. The news story relates such details as where the steamship started, where it was going, what caused it to sink, what the ordeal in the dinghy was like, and how the sailors finally made it to shore.

A CRITICAL RESPONSE

2. Explaining the Theme Read aloud and discuss Stallman's commentary. Then have the students meet in small groups to discuss the questions in the writing assignment. Students may think of additional themes: the comfort and support of the brotherhood, the sense of nature's indifference. Before they begin writing, remind them to support their opinions with details from the story.

▶ CRITERIA FOR EVALUATING THE ASSIGNMENT The essay clearly agrees or disagrees with Stallman's statement of theme. If students disagree, alternate or additional themes are clearly stated. All statements of theme are supported by details from the story.

3. Comparing the Story with a Poem Read the poem aloud in class. Students should easily see that the maiden represents a land-bound, romantic view of the sea, whereas the sailor knows the grim reality of life and death on the ocean. "The Open Boat" clearly reflects the sailor's view and not the maiden's. Students may disagree about whether nature shows "grim hatred" in "The Open Boat" or is merely indifferent. Encourage students to find details in the story to support their view and to add their own response (their view of nature) at the end of the essay.

▶ CRITERIA FOR EVALUATING THE ASSIGNMENT The essay shows the connection between the poem and the story in the details of the shipwreck, the walls of gray water, the view of nature as an enemy. It supports statements about the view of nature in "The Open Boat" with details from the story. Students end with a statement or paragraph on their own feelings about nature.

4. Contrasting Two Views of Nature Have students turn to Emerson's essay and find two or three quotations about nature. (For example, on text page 191: "Nature never wears a mean appearance." "In the presence of nature, a wild delight runs through the man, in spite of real sorrows.") Write the Emerson quotations on the chalkboard as a starting point. Then have students work with a partner or small group to find Crane quotations. (For example, the gull is called an "ugly brute" on text page 467. "When it occurs to a man that nature does not regard him as important. . . . ," top of text page 474.)

▶ CRITERIA FOR EVALUATING THE ASSIGNMENT The essay cites differences in the way Emerson and Crane view nature and supports points with quotations from the writers' work. Students should see that Emerson's view of benign nature as a revelation of God contrasts directly with Crane's view of nature (the sea) as indifferent, even malevolent, ruled by "seven mad gods."

Extending the Story

Have groups of students find, read, and report on other works that deal with the sea, sailing, and shipwrecks, such as Samuel Taylor Coleridge's "The Rime of the Ancient Mariner" and Ernest Hemingway's *The Old Man and the Sea*. Each group of students should discuss among themselves how these books compare with "The Open Boat" in their mood, content, and view of the natural world. Students should present their reports orally, including readings from the chosen works.

Primary Sources   Text page 479

"PLENTY OF GRIT"

In these excerpts from a newspaper article, students learn that the real captain of the steamship *Commodore* respected Stephen Crane as a fine sailor and a brave man. As preparation for writing assignment 1 (text page 478), have students compare details of the story with the actual facts of the shipwreck as related in the excerpts. Crane's newspaper story (see these notes on writing assignment 1) omits all details of the four men's long struggle alone in the open boat. He wrote, "The history of life in an open boat for thirty hours would no doubt be instructive for the young, but none is to be told here and now." Instead, the news story concentrates on what led up to the sinking of the *Commodore* and the crew's leaving the ship.

Kate Chopin

Text page 480

A PAIR OF SILK STOCKINGS

Text page 481

Objectives

1. To respond to a poignant story about a sympathetic character

2. To analyze character

3. To identify a character's motivation

4. To respond to two critical views of the story

5. To write a paragraph predicting the next scene of a story

6. To write an essay comparing two stories

Introducing the Story

Here are the major elements of the story:

- **Protagonist:** Mrs. Sommers
- **Conflict:** personal freedom vs. family obligations
- **Theme:** In a life confined by duty and repression, everyone deserves a day of self-indulgence.
- **Point of view:** third-person omniscient
- **Significant technique:** characterization mainly through character's thoughts
- **Setting:** a downtown shopping area, 1890's

BACKGROUND ON THE STORY   Kate Chopin based her early stories on her experiences in the town of Cloutierville, Louisiana, where her husband owned a general store. She had a keen eye for characters, and through letter writing, she learned to reproduce on paper the language, dress, and other peculiarities of the Creole and Cajun cultures in and around New Orleans. Along with Sarah Orne Jewett, Mary Wilkins Freeman, and Joel Chandler Harris, Chopin created local-color stories published in popular magazines such as *Century, Vogue, Atlantic Monthly*, and *Harper's*. Later, she turned her attention more inward, writing realistic stories about women in Victorian times and their need for freedom. She had more trouble getting these stories published. "A Pair of Silk Stockings" might be thought of as groundwork for her controversial novel *The Awakening*.

SUMMARY   Little Mrs. Sommers finds herself one day in possession of the tidy sum of fifteen dollars. She thinks about all the items she should buy for her four children, and the thought of them in new outfits excites her. Once at the store she feels faint, however, and sits down at a counter to rest. Her hand languishes on a luxurious pair of silk stockings, and so her adventure begins. She buys herself not only the stockings but also shoes, gloves, two high-priced magazines, a meal at a fancy restaurant, and a seat at the theater. After a thoroughly enjoyable day, she boards a cable car for home, wishing that her dream would never end.

Teaching Strategies

PROVIDING FOR CULTURAL DIFFERENCES   Students may need some help with unfamiliar terms, such as *shirtwaists, shirting, figured lawn, ladies' waiting room, damask, cress,* and *cable car*.

PROVIDING FOR DIFFERENT LEVELS OF ABILITY   Some students may miss the subtle way that Mrs. Sommers's adventure starts. Have them tell you, without looking at the story, how she entered that kind of dream world in which she suddenly felt free to indulge herself. Then have them read the two paragraphs that begin on the last line of the first column on text page 482 beginning, "But that day she was a little faint." Now ask them again to describe how the author creates the conditions for Mrs. Sommers's "escape."

READING THE STORY   Remind students, before they begin reading, that the story takes place a hundred years ago. Though Mrs. Sommers's actions seem tame enough by today's standards, they represent the repressed longings of many women of the time. As they read, students should note how skilled the author is at relating the nuances of behavior in her characters.

RETEACHING ALTERNATIVES   Have students make a list of everything that Mrs. Sommers spends her money on, along with a brief description of the circumstances of the purchase. Then have them try to make connections among the purchases, telling how the buying of the silk stockings leads to the purchase of the next item, and so forth.

Responding to the Story   Text page 484

Answers to the questions in the Pupil's Edition appear in the Annotated Teacher's Edition.

Writing About the Story

For help in revising their compositions, refer students to **Grammar, Usage, and Mechanics: A Reference Guide** on text pages 1183–1228 at the back of their books.

A CREATIVE RESPONSE

1. Writing the Next Scene   Have students consider the character as she was introduced at the beginning of the story and recall how she entered her "dream." Students might then reread the last two paragraphs of the story to pick up on the mood as it existed at that point.

▶ CRITERIA FOR EVALUATING THE ASSIGNMENT   The events are plausible and consistent with Mrs. Sommers's character and situation.

2. Comparing Stories   Have students read "A Wagner Matinée" (text page 518). Keeping "A Pair of Silk Stockings" in mind, students should chart their notes as they read. They might also pay special attention to the performance scenes.

▶ CRITERIA FOR EVALUATING THE ASSIGNMENT   The essay cites important elements of both stories, especially as they relate to the two characters and their experiences. It draws a conclusion about how the experiences changed each character.

Extending the Story

Have students research and report to the class on various aspects of city life in the 1890's. Students might form committees and collaborate to present facts on typical jobs (for men and women and children), leisure pursuits (including sports), inventions, immigration, politics, fashion, or another subject that interests them. Encourage students to think of original ways to present their information—perhaps skits, radio or TV talk shows, raps, etc.

Primary Sources   Text page 485

VOGUE STORIES

The passage contains no radically new interpretation of the story, but it does give students a better idea about the magazine market in the 1890's. Have students summarize what they can glean from this passage about the typical woman's magazine and how *Vogue* might have been different.

THE AMERICAN LANGUAGE   Text page 486

Just as it is interesting to almost every young person to learn something about his or her family background, it can be interesting to almost every speaker of American English to learn something of the history of the language. This special essay provides an overview of the influences on American English during the early to mid-nineteenth century. The first section reveals the "backwoods" origins of exuberant phrases and slang—some of which remain in the modern vernacular. This section also describes the flowering of American literature. Subsequent sections discuss how the American vernacular seeped into other areas of American life (e.g., politics and the press) and the impact of immigrant populations and the westward expansion on the vernacular. The essay concludes with an historical discussion on the origin of place names.

The essay will prove entertaining to many students, some of whom might be interested in collaborative presentations of a discussion of popularly used words whose etymologies are traced to their own ethnic backgrounds. A helpful resource is Eugene T. Maleska's book, *A Pleasure in Words* (Simon and Schuster, 1982).

Have students work collaboratively on the Analyzing Language activities (text page 490).

Analyzing Language

Text page 490

1. A sample for each suffix follows:

SUFFIX	EXAMPLE	ORIGIN
-logy	mythology	from the Latin *mythologia,* the interpretation of myths
-ism	hucksterism	from Middle English *hokestere* and Greek *ismos,* the practice of promoting something by showmanship
-ize	weatherize	from Middle English *weder* and Greek *izein,* to cause to be resistant to foul weather
-ish	devilish	from Middle English *devel* and Greek *iskos,* characteristic of the devil

2. Students may collaborate in small groups to select words related to their particular interests and define and explain each word. Here is a sample entry for a dictionary of computer words:

   Computer jargon includes the word *byte*, a tiny amount of information. This word has been picked up by critics of the media, who refer to short, manageable snatches of a speech or interview on the news as a "sound byte."

3. Students' paragraphs should contain the following information:

   juice: from the Sanskrit word *yūsa*
   orange: from the Sanskrit word *nāraṅga*
   tomato: from the Nahuatl Indian word *tomatl*
   cereal: from the Latin word for the goddess of grain, Ceres
   waffles; from the Dutch word *wafel*
   syrup: from the Arabic word *sharāb*
   bacon: from the Old High German word *bahho*
   coffee: from the Arabic word *qahwah*
   tea: from the Chinese word *t'e*

EXERCISES IN CRITICAL THINKING AND WRITING

Text page 491

MAKING INFERENCES AND ANALYZING POINT OF VIEW

In Analyzing the Story question 7 (text page 438), students are asked to identify the point of view from which the third part of "An Occurrence at Owl Creek Bridge" is told. Before students begin this writing assignment, you might want to review with them their response to the question and have them support that response with specific details from the story. Then have students discuss whether this third-person point of view is maintained throughout the story.

▶ CRITERIA FOR EVALUATING THE ASSIGNMENT   Students' essays do not necessarily have to follow the plan outlined in the Writing section. In their essays, however, students should identify the point of view of the story and discuss several inferences the reader must make because of that point of view. Encourage students to use information gathered in the Prewriting section to develop their essays.

Further Reading

Works listed are suitable for both students and teachers unless the annotation ends with the note [Teachers].

Blair, Walter. *Mark Twain and Huck Finn* (University of California Press, 1960). Historical criticism of the novel.

Brooks, Wan Wyck. *The Confident Years* (Dutton, 1952). Good studies of Bierce, Norris, London, Wharton, Howells, Dreiser, James, Crane, and Mencken.

Chopin, Kate. *The Awakening* (Holt, Rinehart & Winston, 1970). Consciousness-raising novel about a woman trapped in her family role.

Delblanco, Nicolas. *Group Portrait* (William Morrow, 1982). Biographical study of the interaction of Crane, James, Conrad, Ford, and Wells when they were living in England.

Dickens, Charles. *American Notes* (St. Martin's Press, 1985). Classic, razor-sharp satirical report of Dickens's impressions during a lecture tour of the United States.

Hazard, Lucy Lockwood. *The Frontier in American Literature* (Frederick Ungar, 1961). Reissue of a penetrating study first published in 1927. Sections on Twain, Harte, Norris, Garland, Dreiser, Cather, and earlier American writers.

Kaplan, Justin. *Mr. Clemens and Mark Twain* (Simon & Schuster, 1966). The standard biography of Mark Twain, emphasizing the dual nature of his identity.

Kazin, Alfred. *An American Procession* (Knopf, 1984). A major study of American literary history with chapters on Twain, James, and Crane.

Parrington, Vernon L. *The Beginnings of Critical Realism in America,* Volume III of *Main Currents in American Thought* (Harcourt Brace Jovanovich, 1930). Still a standard, readable, interesting work.

Stallman, R. W. *Stephen Crane* (George Braziller, 1968). A good solid biography, though Crane scholarship has been updated by discovery of new letters.

Stallman, R. W., ed. *Stephen Crane: An Omnibus* (Knopf, 1952). An excellent collection of Crane's novels, short stories, and poems, with informative introductions by the noted Crane scholar.

Ward, Geoffrey C., and Rick Burns, Ken Burns. *The Civil War, an Illustrated History* (Knopf, 1990). A rich resource filled with photographs, letters, journal entries, maps, and history. Students will enjoy browsing through the book, which accompanies the award-winning PBS documentary on the Civil War.

Wilson, Edmund. *Patriotic Gore* (Oxford University Press, 1962). Excellent study of the relationship of the literature and history of the Civil War era; treats both political and literary figures.

THE MODERNS
THE AMERICAN VOICE IN FICTION

Text page 493

Teaching the Moderns

The event that shaped the era of the writers in this unit is World War I. Although America emerged victorious from that war, and—at least in comparison to the European combatants—virtually unscathed, the experience wrought great changes. Even for those who had no direct involvement in it, the war seemed to sever America's past from its present. The values and traditions of the past no longer seemed to answer. New social, sexual, and aesthetic conventions appeared to challenge old ones.

In the literature of the nineteenth century, a cluster of ideas and values, now collectively known as the American dream, played an important role. One element of the dream was the vision of America as a new Eden—innocent, beautiful, rewarding. Another was the optimistic belief that the future held boundless opportunity—that people's lives were bound to get better. A third element was the importance of the individual. All of these ideas were to be challenged and questioned in the light of new philosophies and political movements in the post-war world.

The ideal of the Edenic land is stated by the old man in "The Leader of the People" but scorned by his son-in-law as no longer applicable to modern life. In Hemingway nature is suppressed by the cold gloom brought on by a cruel war. The optimism that was essential to the American dream is still alive in Wolfe's "His Father's Earth," but it is satirized in Babbitt's soulless activities and, more sympathetically, in Anderson's "The Egg."

Of the original elements of the American dream, the importance of the individual alone remains a serious concern of the writers in this unit. But this idea has changed also. Instead of Emerson's "single man . . . indomitable on his instincts" to whom, in time, "the huge world will come around," Hemingway's soldier, despite his medals, doubts that he is a hero. Anderson's hero probes patiently but blindly for meaning in his life; Willa Cather's and Eudora Welty's heroines are able to prevail because they are "capable of compassion and sacrifice and endurance," as Faulkner puts it in his Nobel Prize acceptance address (text page 601).

Modern American writers have explored the predicament of the individual in many different ways, but despite differences in temperament and style, certain common features can be discerned:

- Stories and novels are generally less concerned with plot than with the exploration of theme.
- A good deal of experimenting is done to find ways of representing the thoughts and feelings of characters without authorial intervention.
- A distinctive intensity and singleness of emotion figure as key elements in character.

The concern with character of modern American authors demonstrates, as Alfred Kazin observed, "that fiction can elicit and prove the world we share . . . and display the unforeseen possibilities of the human—even when everything seems dead set against it."

Objectives of the Moderns Unit

1. To improve reading proficiency and expand vocabulary
2. To gain exposure to notable authors and their works
3. To identify and define major elements in fiction
4. To identify and define significant literary techniques
5. To express and explain responses to fiction
6. To provide practice in the following critical thinking and writing skills
   a. Analyzing character and conflict
   b. Inferring the writer's attitude
   c. Comparing and contrasting works
   d. Responding to a theme and a study
   e. Analyzing a story

Introducing the Moderns

As an alternative to assigning the introductory essay for this unit before students begin reading the fiction, you may want to give a brief account of the era and start students reading the short stories. You can then assign the introductory essay after the Hemingway or Steinbeck selections, when students have a firsthand impression of some of the major writers.

"The Egg," the first story in the unit, has some typical features of the work of this group of authors. It takes an ironic view of the Edenic land (a chicken farm in this story), optimism, and self-reliance—all elements of the American dream of the past. "The Egg" also has the advantage of being a funny story, which will help get the unit off to a good start.

Sherwood Anderson   Text page 501

THE EGG   Text page 502

Objectives

1. To respond to an ironic story
2. To interpet the story's central symbol
3. To state the story's theme
4. To rewrite part of the story using another point of view
5. To write an essay analyzing the story's conflict

Introducing the Story

The father in "The Egg" is driven by his wife's ambition to undertake ventures in which he has little prospect for success. His ludicrous failure as an entertainer—a role he invents for himself—is an attempt to redeem the frustrations and disappointments of years of chicken farming by making the egg the talisman of success.

Sherwood Anderson's concept of a *grotesque,* a person obsessed by a single idea or motive, is essentially a comic idea, even though the obsession may have tragic consequences, as in many of Anderson's stories. The person who rigidly pursues his or her course regardless of altered circumstances or consequences—like the stately walker whose averted gaze does not detect the banana peel in the path—has been a staple of comedy since the Greeks. The father in "The Egg" has only a mild mania: he mistakes his long acquaintance with eggs for mastery over them. The scene with Joe Kane, which really ends with the father gently placing the triumphant egg on the bedside table, demonstrates in simple form the basic situation of comedy.

Here are the major elements of the story:

- **Protagonist:** the narrator's father

- **Antagonist:** intractable nature, symbolized by the egg

- **Conflict:** person vs. intractable nature

- **Point of view:** first-person

- **Significant technique:** development of theme through a single comic anecdote

- **Setting:** rural Ohio, in the early years of this century

BACKGROUND ON THE STORY The frustrations and disappointments of contemporary life play a central role in Anderson's stories and novels. As his concept of the *grotesque* suggests, many of these frustrations result from a character's single-minded pursuit of an idea. So it is with the father in "The Egg." He feels he has paid his dues, through long years of suffering on behalf of eggs and poultry; now he hopes to achieve success through his mastery over the egg. The title of the collection from which this story is taken—*The Triumph of the Egg*—indicates how the father's hopes will be realized.

THE PLOT The narrator's father, an easygoing farmhand, marries an ambitious woman who leads him to undertake several ill-fated ventures. After ten or so years of unsuccessful chicken farming, the couple start a restaurant in a nearby town. There the father conceives the idea of entertaining patrons with masterful tricks involving eggs. He tries his act on Joe Kane, a young man waiting for a train, with comically disastrous results.

Teaching Strategies

PROVIDING FOR CULTURAL DIFFERENCES Although the rural setting and the details of chicken farming will be unfamiliar to most students, their experience with television and movies should enable them to visualize the setting of the story.

Students from some ethnic backgrounds may be disturbed by the narrator's attitude toward his parents, especially his father. After they've read the story, get them to talk about how they feel about that attitude. Is the narrator disrespectful, cruel, sympathetic, objective?

PROVIDING FOR DIFFERENT LEVELS OF ABILITY Most students will have no difficulty reading "The Egg" in a single sitting. Some, however, may need encouragement to get through the somewhat discursive first half of the story. If you anticipate this problem, you might read the story aloud up to the point where Anderson describes the scene in the restaurant (text page 506, bottom right). From that point, the comic action should carry most readers along.

READING THE STORY The reading of this story makes a suitable assignment for reading at home or in class. If you assign it for classroom reading, you might ask students to stop at the sentence "There was something prenatal about the way eggs kept themselves connected with the development of his idea" (about one-third of the way down the right-hand column on text page 506). When students have read to this point, ask a volunteer to explain what this sentence means. Try to elicit the explanation that the writer is saying that eggs had a powerful influence on the father's idea as he was first working it out. Ask what kind of idea for entertaining customers the father might have been thinking of. Ask what the idea seemed to involve. (Eggs)

Before they read on, have students write down a prediction about the kind of entertainment the father has in mind and how successful it will be. Ask volunteers who have not read the story's ending to share their predictions.

RETEACHING ALTERNATIVES Anderson's reflections upon the troubles of chicken farming contain examples of verbal irony that you may want to examine with your class. Direct students' attention to the long paragraph beginning on text page 504, left-hand column. Ask whether the writer is being entirely serious in this passage. Explain that one kind of verbal irony involves exaggeration, and illustrate with a sentence like "A few hens and now and then a rooster . . . struggle through to maturity." Ask students if this passage reminds them of the writing of another American author. Possibly a student will recognize a technique often used by Mark Twain.

As an alternative reteaching strategy, ask whether the father in the story reminds the class of a common type in American literature. Students may recognize the well-meaning but ineffectual husband from television sitcoms and comics. Discuss the ways Anderson manages to make this rather weak character sympathetic.

Responding to the Story   Text page 508

Answers to the questions in the Pupil's Edition appear in the Annotated Teacher's Edition.

Writing About the Story

For help in revising their compositions, refer students to **Grammar, Usage, and Mechanics: A Reference Guide** on text pages 1183–1228 at the back of their books.

A CREATIVE RESPONSE
1. *Using Another Point of View* Before students begin to write, elicit from them a short list of scenes where the mother's role is especially important. Briefly review, as well, the relative advantages and disadvantages of first- and third-person point of view. (See text page 1178 in the **Handbook of Literary Terms**.)

▶ CRITERIA FOR EVALUATING THE ASSIGNMENT The narrative passage develops a scene from "The Egg" from the mother's point of view and reveals her thoughts and feelings. It makes effective use of the point of view selected.

2. *Analyzing Conflict* Briefly review internal and external conflicts (refer students to text page 1171 in the **Handbook of Literary Terms**). Have students list all conflicts they noted in "The Egg." Remind them to cite details from the story to support their points. (Students should identify the external conflicts of the parents' striving to achieve their dreams of success vs. the failure of the chicken farm and restaurant; of the father vs. the egg in the balancing episode. Some may point out an internal conflict; the father's shyness vs. his determination to be entertaining.)

▶ CRITERIA FOR EVALUATING THE ASSIGNMENT The essay consists of three well-developed paragraphs that describe the nature of the conflicts in the story and their resolutions by citing details from the story.

Primary Sources Text page 509

"THEY WERE NOT NICE LITTLE PACKAGES...."
So Sherwood Anderson described his stories, going on to say that they were written by "one who did not know the answers." Anderson believed that the "history of life was but a history of moments"; he was convinced that stories that honestly reflected life could not be bound by principles of form or structure—could not be put into "nice little packages." Instead, they must be free to embody the tentative groping of his characters toward meaning and fulfillment.

Encourage students to think about story ideas based on their own common, everyday experiences or on their observations of the people they see and know. Students can share their ideas with a small group, get others' responses, and someday write a short story. Students can record their ideas in a writer's journal, so that the ideas don't slip away.

Sinclair Lewis Text page 510

BABBITT'S AFTER-DINNER SPEECH Text page 511

Objectives

1. To recognize and appreciate satire

2. To identify clichés

3. To write two speeches: an update of Babbitt's speech and a speech that challenges Babbitt's views

4. To write an essay comparing and contrasting two views of the ideal individual

Introducing the Speech

Since students will lack experience with the kind of civic club speech that Lewis satirizes here, you may want to describe some of the features of this American art form. Babbitt begins with classic bromides—the joking reference to the impromptu speech tucked into his pocket, the ethnic joke of no particular relevance, the protestation that he doesn't expect to do well as a speaker. Students, if they wished to do so, could find handbooks for speakers in public libraries that recommend such "ice-breaking" devices.

BACKGROUND ON THE SPEECH *Babbitt* created a sensation when it appeared in 1922, for at that time businessmen enjoyed a mainly positive image in the public mind. (A few years later, President Coolidge was to say, "The business of America is business," a sentiment that Babbitt would have agreed with wholeheartedly.) Although Babbitt is ridiculed for his beliefs and for his way of expressing himself, Lewis obviously feels some sympathy for him. Babbitt emerges in the novel as a man whose individuality has been destroyed by his slavish adherence to conventional values and ideas.

SUMMARY Here are the major points of Babbitt's speech: He begins by praising Zenith, the city in which he lives and sells real estate, and goes on to eulogize "our Ideal Citizen" (also referred to as "our Standardized Citizen" and the "Solid American Citizen"), whose attributes are aggressiveness as a businessman, reliability as a family man, innate good taste in the arts, and common sense in politics and religion. Babbitt returns briefly to the theme of praising Zenith (which contains "the second highest business building in any inland city in the entire country") and ends with a diatribe against "liberals," "radicals," and other intellectuals whom Babbitt considers cynical and pessimistic. He warns that many of these undesirables are to be found on the faculty of the State University. Babbitt sees the hope of Zenith and the nation in the "two-fisted Regular Guy," another epithet for his "Ideal Citizen."

Teaching Strategies

PROVIDING FOR CULTURAL DIFFERENCES The trouble with satire is that many readers and listeners take it literally. Students from other countries need to be warned that the writer is actually ridiculing Babbitt. While Babbitt's boosterism is exaggerated for satiric purposes, students should understand that it is not outrageously exaggerated. Boosters of towns and cities were less subtle in the early part of this century than they are today, and speeches not unlike this one were probably often heard. Students should note also that in the 1920's, a yearly income of $4,000 to $10,000, which Babbitt's ideal family enjoyed, was a very comfortable one for middle-class families.

PROVIDING FOR DIFFERENT LEVELS OF ABILITY Any speech is better to hear than to read, and Babbitt's is no exception. All of your students, but especially those who have reading problems, will benefit from an oral presentation. Ask several of your better readers to divide the speech among themselves, practice their parts, and present it to the class.

READING THE SPEECH As suggested, your students will benefit more from hearing this speech than from reading it. You may wish to omit the doggerel poem on text pages 514 and 515. It satirizes the kind of poetry that formerly appeared in newspapers and expresses values that Babbitt approves of, but it adds little to the speech and may distract students' attention from it.

RETEACHING ALTERNATIVES Let several volunteers play the role of Babbitt and hold a mock press conference. Each student can think of a question to ask Babbitt, based on his speech. Let each Babbitt-speaker take turns answering questions as they think the fictional Babbitt would answer.

Responding to the Speech   Text page 516

Answers to the questions in the Pupil's Edition appear in the Annotated Teacher's Edition.

Writing About the Speech

For help in revising their compositions, refer students to **Grammar, Usage, and Mechanics: A Reference Guide** on text pages 1183–1228 at the back of their books.

A CREATIVE RESPONSE
1. Answering Babbitt Answering the questions on text page 516 will establish Babbitt's values in students' minds. You may wish to discuss briefly the kinds of counter-arguments and values an opponent would offer. Suggest that volunteers read their papers aloud. For help in completing this assignment, refer students to the **Literature and Language Exercise** on Using the Persuasive Aim (text page 1165). Make sure they can identify and make use of both intellectual arguments and emotional appeals.

▶ CRITERIA FOR EVALUATING THE ASSIGNMENT The speech presents values and visions that contrast with Babbitt's. Students use both arguments and emotional appeals effectively.

2. Updating Babbitt Discuss the kinds of audiences students have in mind. You may wish to give students photocopies of the speech so that they can make initial revisions directly on the copy.

▶ CRITERIA FOR EVALUATING THE ASSIGNMENT The revised speech is appropriate in both language and content for the audience named by the student.

A CRITICAL RESPONSE
3. Comparing and Contrasting the Speech with "Self-Reliance" Briefly review the excerpt from "Self-Reliance" (text page 194) as preparation for students' writing. Focus especially on paragraphs 1 and 2 in the second column. Emerson abhors conformity; Babbitt embraces it.

▶ CRITERIA FOR EVALUATING THE ASSIGNMENT The essay cites both "Self-Reliance" and the excerpt from *Babbitt* in demonstrating that Babbit's speech distorts Emerson's perceptions of the self-reliant individual, particularly in the area of an individual's conformity with society.

Analyzing Language and Style

CLICHÉS
1. Examples abound. On text page 512 alone there appear "lay down the battle-ax," "standing together eye to eye and shoulder to shoulder," "waves of good fellowship," "the wheels of progress," "first and foremost," and "busier than a bird-dog."
2. Babbitt expects unthinking acceptance and approval of his ideas and values.

Objectives

1. To respond to a story about a difficult life
2. To state the story's theme
3. To analyze setting
4. To analyze imagery
5. To write a paragraph describing a character
6. To write an essay comparing two responses to nature
7. To analyze figures of speech

Introducing the Story

The effectiveness of this story depends in large part upon the careful selection and presentation of detail. The hardships of Georgiana's frontier life are suggested by the visual details in the story's last paragraph; Cather literally paints the audience in the last full paragraph on page 521. Most important of all, Georgiana's response to the music is shown through a number of closely observed details—her gripping of the narrator's sleeve, her quick intake of breath, the tears rolling down her cheeks.

Students who have read the *Little House* series by Laura Ingalls Wilder or seen episodes of the television series based on these books will have a general idea of the starkness of pioneer life. It may, however, be hard for them to imagine the full extent of Georgiana's sacrifice. Remind them that in those days there were no radios or phonograph records and no nearby city with an orchestra. Georgiana was totally deprived of the music that she loved.

Here are the major elements of the story:

- **Protagonist:** Aunt Georgiana

- **Antagonist:** her life circumstances

- **Conflict:** person vs. fate (life circumstances)

- **Point of view:** first-person

- **Significant techniques:** careful selection and presentaton of detail

- **Setting:** The story itself is set in Boston, but the bleak frontier setting of Georgiana's home, presented in flashbacks, plays an important role in the story.

BACKGROUND ON THE STORY   This short story reflects several themes that run throughout Cather's work. The tension between the values of home and family and the values of art, paralleled by the contrast between frontier life and the cultured life of Boston, reflects conflicts characters typically experience in Cather's stories and novels. Like the narrator of "A Wagner Matinée," Cather left Nebraska at a fairly early age to experience the thriving cultural life of the city—in her case New York, not Boston.

THE PLOT   Clark, the narrator, receives a letter from his Uncle Howard in Nebraska informing him that his Aunt Georgiana, Howard's wife, will arrive in Boston shortly on family business and asking him to look after her. Clark arranges for her to stay at his landlady's and sets out to meet Georgiana at the railroad station. Because of Georgiana's love of music, which found expression mainly before her marriage, Clark has planned to take her to a symphony concert. Her dowdy clothing and her worn-out appearance almost lead him to change his plan. He fears that he may reawaken the old conflict between her bleak farm life and her taste for music and civilized life. However, Clark does take Georgiana to the concert, to which she listens enthralled.

Teaching Strategies

PROVIDING FOR CULTURAL DIFFERENCES   Students from other countries can empathize with Aunt Georgiana's "culture shock" in moving from sophisticated Boston to 640 barren acres in Nebraska. Encourage them to tell how they felt about moving far from home. You may need to explain *dugout* (a shelter dug into a hillside), *Rameses* (ancient Egyptian kings), and the many allusions to composers and operas.

PROVIDING FOR DIFFERENT LEVELS OF ABILITY Good readers will have no difficulty reading this story at home or in class. However, slow readers will benefit from your reading the story aloud up to the beginning of the first full paragraph in the right-hand column of text page 521. Discuss briefly what they know about Georgiana and her relation to the narrator so far. Call students' attention to the short speech of Georgiana's beginning, "Don't love it so well . . ." (text page 520). Ask what Georgiana's sacrifice was. (Her music) Have students finish the story, or if you prefer, read the last part aloud.

READING THE STORY   Students reading at an average or above-average level should have no problems reading this story at home or in class. As suggested, some students may need a break in the story to sort out what they have learned about Georgiana from the short flashbacks provided. The best place to interrupt the story is just before the concert with the passage beginning, ''From the time we entered the concert hall . . .'' near the top of the right-hand column on text page 521. Breaking at this point also has the advantage of having students practice predicting outcomes. How will Georgiana respond to the concert after all these years of being deprived of music?

RETEACHING ALTERNATIVES   As an alternative to describing a person's appearance (text page 524), suggest that students write an entry Georgiana might make in her diary after attending the Wagner matinée.

Responding to the Story   Text page 524

Answers to the questions in the Pupil's Edition appear in the Annotated Teacher's Edition.

Writing About the Story

For help in revising their compositions, refer students to **Grammar, Usage, and Mechanics: A Reference Guide** on text pages 1183–1228 at the back of their books.

A CREATIVE RESPONSE

1. Describing a Character   Draw from the students an awareness of how the paragraph beginning ''But Mrs. Springer knew nothing of all this'' (text page 519) uses carefully chosen physical details to support a single overall impression. Have students choose a real or fictitious person and the characteristics they wish to emphasize, and then list details that convey those characteristics.

▶ CRITERIA FOR EVALUATING THE ASSIGNMENT   The paragraph conveys specific characteristics of the person described through use of carefully selected details.

A CRITICAL RESPONSE

2. Analyzing Imagery   Write on the chalkboard ''farm life'' and ''city life,'' and have students brainstorm images that stand out in their minds. Then send them back to the story for confirmation and expansion of the lists.

▶ CRITERIA FOR EVALUATING THE ASSIGNMENT   The essay contrasts Cather's most prominent images of farm and city life: for example, ''black stuff dress'' (page 519) vs. ''shimmer of fabrics soft and firm'' (page 521); ''The deluge of sound'' (page 523) vs. ''the inconceivable silence of the plains'' (page 522). It also describes the emotional impact of each set of images.

3. Comparing Responses to Nature   Have students skim pages 208–218 from Thoreau's *Walden*, jotting down events or images revealing Thoreau's experiences with a kindly nature, and ask them how they account for the differences between his experiences and those of Cather's heroine.

▶ CRITERIA FOR EVALUATING THE ASSIGNMENT   The essay compares and contrasts Thoreau's perceptions of nature with those of Cather's heroine, and offers a plausible explanation for the differences.

Analyzing Language and Style

FIGURES OF SPEECH

1. The balconies are like terraced gardens. The balconies are filled with colorful clothing, the gardens with flowers.
2. The moving violin necks and bows are compared to tree branches tossing in the wind. Both move together in waves.
3. Strokes of the violin bow are like movements of a magician's wand. The sounds of the music draw feelings from the narrator's heart, just as the wand pulls ribbons from a hat.
4. Movement of the bows is downward and angled, like rain. The similarity lies in the quick, firm, angular direction of movement.
5. Orchestral sound is compared to a strong current in a body of water. The sound and current are strong forces that overwhelm someone caught up in them.
6. The chairs and stands resemble bare, winter cornfields. The similarity lies in their emptiness.

Thomas Wolfe

HIS FATHER'S EARTH

Objectives

1. To respond to a short story that uses elements of poetry
2. To identify images that appeal to the senses
3. To compare a scene in a story with a similar scene in a Biblical parable
4. To write a description imitating the author's style
5. To write an essay comparing the style and techniques of Wolfe's prose and Whitman's poetry

Introducing the Story

Few, if any, students will know much about the circus as it was in Wolfe's time. Yet many of them may have seen a small traveling circus. Have students share their experiences about the circus.

Here are the major elements of the story:

- **Protagonist:** a boy
- **Theme:** the use of imagination to expand horizons and gain a new perspective on life; the search for self in the search for America
- **Point of view:** third-person, limited
- **Significant techniques:** catalogues of evocative images, alliteration, onomatopoeia, detailed descriptions of imagined events and settings
- **Setting:** various places throughout the United States, probably from fifty to a hundred years ago

BACKGROUND ON THE STORY "His Father's Earth" was first published in the April 1935 issue of *Modern Monthly* magazine. It appeared again in 1939 within the novel *The Web and the Rock*. Like much of Wolfe's writing, the story feeds the appetite of Depression-era Americans for new experiences and for hope. Wolfe's lyrical and often uncontrolled prose has been criticized as adolescent bombast, but it has also been praised for its exultant, lavish depiction of the possibilities of the American experience.

SUMMARY A boy is standing with his brother, looking at the circus, when he lapses into a daydream in which he is traveling with the circus as a ticket seller and procurer of food. His travels with the circus take him all over the United States. The great variety of landscapes that make up the nation is matched only by the mountains and rivers of food the performers devour. This world, isolated from the world outside, is all that the boy knows. Yet he has a memory, deep in his heart, of his father's land, which he has never seen. One day the train stops in the early morning. The boy recognizes the place, jumps off the train, and makes his way to his father's house. His father and brothers instantly recognize the long-wandering boy and welcome him lovingly back into the family.

Teaching Strategies

PROVIDING FOR CULTURAL DIFFERENCES Students who have little experience with country life may have trouble connecting with some of Wolfe's rural images (such as the silence before sunrise, sounds of birds in the early morning, and smell of wet earth). You might have them write brief, evocative descriptions of the early morning sounds that they are more familiar with.

PROVIDING FOR DIFFERENT LEVELS OF ABILITY LEP and ESL students may bog down in Wolfe's long sentences. With these students plan to read the story aloud. Make sure all readers understand that everything following the first paragraph is a daydream. The word *thought* is ambiguous.

Students who learn visually may be helped if they think of Wolfe as an artist. In fact, you might have students imagine these evocative scenes as paintings. For example, if they were going to paint the market scene on text pages 526–527, what colors would they use and how many? What mood would the painting have? How large a canvas would they use?

READING THE STORY The early part of the story contains only a hint (in the first paragraph) that Wolfe is concerned with more than just describing a reverie. You might wish to discuss that first paragraph before students read the rest of the story. Then have them pay special attention to mentions of the earth, for these often have clues to deeper meaning. When students have finished, you might have them discuss the last two paragraphs in which the boy emerges from his reverie, and come to some conclusion about the overall meaning of the story.

RETEACHING ALTERNATIVES Help students to appreciate Wolfe's style by having them read aloud one of the scenes composed of multiple images piled one upon another, such as the paragraph on text page 527 describing the midday meal. After one or more students read the passage aloud, ask students to try to summarize the scene. They will find that the summary of one of Wolfe's long passages is very short, because the passage explodes with details. Help students see how Wolfe's detailed description completely immerses the reader in the scene. Ask students whether or not they enjoy that experience and why.

Responding to the Story   Text page 532

Answers to the questions in the Pupil's Edition appear in the Annotated Teacher's Edition.

Writing About the Story

For help in revising their compositions, refer students to **Grammar, Usage, and Mechanics: A Reference Guide** on text pages 1183–1228 at the back of their books.

A CREATIVE RESPONSE

1. Using Accumulation of Detail in a Description You might get started by reading aloud one of the passages from the story that uses this technique. Have students brainstorm other likely settings besides the two offered in the writing assignment.

▶ CRITERIA FOR EVALUATING THE ASSIGNMENT The description evokes a familiar place by piling up details to explore many aspects of the scene. The description makes use of a variety of sensory images.

A CRITICAL RESPONSE

2. Comparing Styles and Techniques Have students work in small groups to complete the prewriting chart. Remind students to include a thesis statement either at the beginning or end of their essays. For help in organizing their comparison/contrast essays, refer students to **Exercises in Critical Thinking and Writing,** Comparing and Contrasting Poems (text page 373).

▶ CRITERIA FOR EVALUATING THE ASSIGNMENT The essay deals with both writers' use of descriptive catalogues, celebration of the common man, celebration of America, and emotional effects. Look for a thesis statement and clearly organized presentation of ideas.

Extending the Story

Have students research the circus. Some students may study the Roman circus or other aspects of circus history. Others may find out about the state of the circus today. Still others may concentrate on one particular aspect of circus life or one famous performer. Have them choose a manageable area to research and then give a brief oral report to share with the class. The class might then compare the real circus with the romanticized vision of the circus that Wolfe presented.

F. Scott Fitzgerald

Text page 533

WINTER DREAMS

Text page 535

Objectives

1. To respond to the theme of a story

2. To write a diary entry expressing a different point of view

3. To analyze characterization

4. To write an essay comparing and contrasting the story to a fairy tale

Introducing the Story

Here are the major elements of the story:

- **Protagonist:** Dexter Green
- **Antagonist:** Judy Jones
- **Conflict:** chasing a dream vs. accepting reality
- **Theme:** Some dreams are unreachable, yet their loss causes great pain.
- **Point of view:** third-person, limited
- **Significant techniques:** narrator's speaking directly to reader, characterization, atmosphere
- **Setting:** Minnesota, around 1909 and 1916; New York City in 1924

BACKGROUND ON THE STORY ''Winter Dreams,'' published in 1922, was one of many successful stories Fitzgerald wrote early in his career. It is in many ways autobiographical: from its settings to its focus on a beautiful, emotionally unstable woman who craved new experiences. Fitzgerald grew up in Minnesota on the edges of upper-class life, where he learned to value appearances much as Dexter does. He attended a ''famous university in the East'' (Princeton), joined the armed forces at the start of World War I, and afterward took a job in New York City. ''Winter Dreams'' reveals just a taste of what would become, in *The Great Gatsby*, an aversion for the very style of life he had set out to embrace as a youth.

THE PLOT Fourteen-year-old Dexter Green suddenly quits his caddying job at a private golf club when told he must caddy for a smug little rich girl, eleven-year-old Judy Jones. Dexter, fourteen, makes this decision because of an emotional shock related to his observation of Miss Jones

in action—stubborn, aggressive, petulant, and blessed with a mysteriously attractive smile. She then and there becomes part of his winter dreams. By twenty-three Dexter is a success. He has been to college in the East and has returned to Minnesota and made a great deal of money in the laundry business. One day, while playing golf, he meets the grown-up and beautiful Judy Jones, and that evening their romantic relationship begins. Dexter falls madly in love with Judy, who toys with him; he is just one of many men she takes up with for a time. After a year and a half Dexter gives up on Judy, meets and proposes marriage to a staid, traditional woman, Irene Scheerer. A week before their engagement is to be announced, Judy proposes that they get married. Dexter falls for her all over again, though they split again after just a month. When the United States enters World War I, Dexter joins the armed forces. Seven years later he is a successful businessman in New York City. An acquaintance brings him startling news: Judy is married to a man who treats her badly, and her spirit and beauty are gone. Dexter weeps as he realizes that the dream he has been carrying all these years is irretrievably lost.

Teaching Strategies

PROVIDING FOR CULTURAL DIFFERENCES Although most students will have no experience with the country-club lifestyle of the early 1900's described here, they should still be able to appreciate the theme and plot of this story. What may be more problematic is Judy's perplexing behavior. Because she is both aggressive (as on the golf course) and alluring (in a Marilyn Monroe kind of way) with a dash of just plain craziness, some students may be facing an unfamiliar and unbelievable personality type. Make clear to students that Judy Jones is a complex character, not easily categorized. You might advise students not to reject the character without first making an effort to understand her, which calls for patient analysis.

PROVIDING FOR DIFFERENT LEVELS OF ABILITY All students will benefit from dramatizing several sections of the story. Choose parts of the story with dialogue and assign the roles of Dexter, Judy, and the narrator. Students might offer different readings of the same lines in order to determine a consensus as to the proper characterization, especially of the enigmatic Judy. Have students discuss what they learned from this exercise.

READING THE STORY The story is divided into six numbered parts. You might stop at the end of each part, at which point there is often an important statement by the narrator. The story moves chronologically, in and out of three periods of Dexter Green's life: at fourteen, in his early twenties, and at thirty-two. Students might organize the plot in their minds according to these three periods.

RETEACHING ALTERNATIVES Both Dexter and Judy are interesting characters with distinct personalities. However, their actions are often unexpected. Help students understand these two better by asking these two questions about Dexter and Judy: What does each character want? How does each character change? Focus on the three different time periods in the story: (1) Part I, (2) Parts II–V, (3) Part VI.

Responding to the Story   Text page 550

Answers to the questions in the Pupil's Edition appear in the Annotated Teacher's Edition.

Writing About the Story

For help in revising their compositions, refer students to **Grammar, Usage, and Mechanics: A Reference Guide** on text pages 1183–1228 at the back of their books.

A CREATIVE RESPONSE
1. Using Another Point of View Have students review text pages 536–538 for clues to Judy's personality and state of mind. Discuss what tone they plan to use and how they can create that tone.

▶ CRITERIA FOR EVALUATING THE ASSIGNMENT The first-person diary entry includes a description of Dexter and opinions about him that are in character with the rude and unruly child that Judy is. The tone (arrogant, self-centered, spoiled) is apparent and sustained throughout.

A CRITICAL RESPONSE
2. Analyzing Characterization Students can meet in small groups to discuss the prewriting questions in the assignment. Have them suggest at least three adjectives that they think apply to Judy and support each adjective with details from the story. Give each group a ten-minute time limit, and then have a spokesperson from each group present its list of character traits. Students can collaborate in their groups to write one essay.

▶ CRITERIA FOR EVALUATING THE ASSIGNMENT The essay lists at least three traits and supports each trait with details from the story.

3. Responding to a Critic You might help students define the fairy-tale formula as suggested in the assignment:

boy meets girl; they fall in love, but something tragically separates them. They overcome terrific obstacles, prove themselves worthy, eventually get back together, and live happily ever after.

▶ CRITERIA FOR EVALUATING THE ASSIGNMENT The essay clearly defines elements of the fairy tale and explains how ''Winter Dreams'' both uses and deviates from the fairy-tale formula.

Analyzing Language and Style

PARADOX
Additional paradoxes include the following:

a. Judy is described as ''beautifully ugly.'' (page 536)
b. Judy explains why she has escaped in the motorboat: '' . . . there is a man waiting for me. When he drove up at the door I drove out of the dock because he says I'm his ideal.'' (page 540)
c. '' 'What a remark!' Judy laughed sadly—without sadness.'' (page 547)

These paradoxes may suggest that there is more to Judy than what appears on the surface. Much of what she does seems to be an act, suggesting that she is covering up her true feelings. Some students may think that the paradoxes suggest Judy is all sham and pretense, not to be believed or trusted.

Extending the Story

Have groups of students find out more about the Jazz Age in the United States. One group might give brief oral reports on jazz music, perhaps by playing recordings that were popular during that time. Others might report on Prohibition or changes in the art world or the economic circumstances leading up to the stock-market crash. The class as a whole might then discuss whether or not they believe that Judy Jones and Dexter Green exemplify the spirit of the Jazz Age.

Primary Sources   Text page 552

A LETTER TO HIS DAUGHTER
Fitzgerald was always keen on giving improving advice to others, and his only daughter, Scotty, was a natural recipient. The litany of things to worry about or not to worry about that ends this letter to Scotty at camp is basically serious advice, with a few bits of jocular counsel thrown in. Ask students how they would feel if they received such a letter from a parent. Do they agree with his lists of things to worry about and things not to worry about? What would they add to each list, or drop, or change?

Ernest Hemingway

Text page 553

IN ANOTHER COUNTRY

Text page 555

Objectives

1. To respond to a story about the aftermath of war
2. To identify the narrator's attitude
3. To state the story's theme
4. To write a description of a setting
5. To write an essay responding to the theme

Introducing the Story

Hemingway was himself wounded during his tour of duty as an ambulance driver in World War I, and this experience is reflected in several of his novels and stories. In this story, the wounded soldiers are isolated. The war goes on, but they do not "go to it any more." They are honored with citations and receive medical treatment but hold a pessimistic view of the meaning of their sacrifice and the possibility of a cure.

Explain to students that mechanical devices for physical therapy, common today, were quite primitive eighty years ago. Probably the narrator, the major, and the other patients were justified in their skepticism. Students may also wonder about the "communist quarter," which the soldiers pass through on their way to the Café Cova. The quarter was populated mainly by working-class people, among whom were many proponents of Communism. Communists were opposed to the war, a fact that accounts in part for their hostility to the young officers.

Here are the major elements of the story:

- **Protagonists:** unnamed narrator
- **Conflict:** person vs. hopelessness and disillusionment brought on by war
- **Point of view:** first-person
- **Significant technique:** first-person narrative with minimal expression of feeling by the narrator
- **Setting:** Milan, Italy, during World War I

BACKGROUND ON THE STORY   Like *A Farewell to Arms,* this story is set in northern Italy during World War I. Milan is several hundred miles away from the area along the Austro-Hungarian border where most of the fighting was taking place.

THE PLOT   The narrator, a wounded officer in the Italian army, receives physical therapy along with other outpatients at a hospital in Milan. The doctor in charge is enthusiastic about the new machines used in their therapy, but the patients remain skeptical. The narrator becomes friendly with three young Italian officers, who are fellow patients, and with an older officer, a major, who had been a great fencer, but now has a withered hand as a result of his wound. The major helps the narrator with his Italian and is friendly. One day, however, he tells the narrator that he must never marry. Later, weeping, he tells the narrator that his young wife has just died of pneumonia.

Teaching Strategies

PROVIDING FOR CULTURAL DIFFERENCES   Cultural differences will cause no problem; the story's themes are universal.

PROVIDING FOR DIFFERENT LEVELS OF ABILITY   LEP students may need your help in understanding the irony in the selection. For example, the observation that the plastic surgery for the boy with no nose was not successful because "he came from a very old family and they could never get the nose exactly right," is an ironic reference to the importance a notable family places on such hereditary features. Similarly, when the narrator tells the major that he finds Italian very easy, the major's reply, "Why, then, do you not take up the use of grammar?" is an ironic putdown. Situational irony occurs when the major, who has been careful not to marry until he was invalided out of the army, loses his young wife to pneumonia.

READING THE STORY   You might choose several students to read portions of the story aloud. Ask students to listen for Hemingway's distinctive tone and sentence length.

RETEACHING ALTERNATIVES   In a sentence or two, have students summarize the story situation and their responses to the story. How did they feel after they read the story? What does it make them think about? How does the feeling they have relate to other war stories and poems they have read, such as "A Mystery of Heroism" (text page 457) and "War Is Kind" (text page 463)?

Responding to the Story   Text page 557

Answers to the questions in the Pupil's Edition appear in the Annotated Teacher's Edition.

Writing About the Story

For help in revising their compositions, refer students to **Grammar, Usage, and Mechanics: A Reference Guide** on text pages 1183–1228 at the back of their books.

A CREATIVE RESPONSE

1. Describing a Setting   Have students brainstorm individually or in small groups the feelings and images they associate with a particular setting.

► CRITERIA FOR EVALUATING THE ASSIGNMENT   Students have chosen words and specific sensory images that convey an impression of life and hope or death and loss. Look for a mention of the season and details that appeal to senses other than sight.

A CRITICAL RESPONSE

2. Responding to Theme   Elicit from the class several statements of theme, or offer one of your own as a basis for discussion. For example: War and life may cause wounds from which it is not possible to recover.

► CRITERIA FOR EVALUATING THE ASSIGNMENT   The theme is clearly stated and supported by details from the story. The essay explains the student's personal response to that theme.

Primary Sources   Text page 558

NOBEL PRIZE ACCEPTANCE SPEECH, 1954

In this short speech, Hemingway makes this statement: "For a true writer each book should be a new beginning where he tries again for something that is beyond attainment." Many critics think that Hemingway did not follow this precept himself, but stuck to a kind of writing that he knew he could do well. As William Faulkner said of Hemingway: ". . . he stayed within what he knew. He did it fine, but he didn't try for the impossible."

Zora Neale Hurston   Text page 559

HOW THE LION MET THE KING OF THE WORLD   Text page 560

Objectives

1. To listen to an African American folktale and enjoy its humor.

2. To analyze characterization

3. To infer the folktale's message

4. To identify irony

5. To identify colloquialisms, rhyme, and figures of speech

6. To write a folktale in the oral tradition, using rhyme and alliteration

7. To write an essay comparing tall tales

8. To dramatize a folktale and perform it

Introducing the Folktale

Here are the major elements of the folktale:

- **Protagonist:** John
- **Antagonists:** the grizzly bear; the lion
- **Conflict:** man vs. animals in a struggle for supremacy
- **Theme:** Man uses technology to establish his superiority over even the most powerful animals.
- **Point of view:** third-person omniscient
- **Significant techniques:** dialect, characterization, irony, humor

BACKGROUND ON THE FOLKTALE   Anthropologist Franz Boas encouraged his student, Zora Neale Hurston, to collect the folktales that appear in her book *Mules and*

Men, from which this story is taken. Hurston's purpose as an anthropologist was to uncover an important—and largely ignored—segment of African American culture. Hurston's book helped to secure the place of the folktale—and the southern storyteller—in the African American literary tradition. Many of her peers, who were attempting to move forward in the predominantly white culture, wanted nothing to do with literature that conjured up their slave past. According to some critics, however, that was just what the writers of the Harlem Renaissance needed—a reminder of their folk origins, something to keep them true to their heritage as they pursued success in the modern world.

SUMMARY   Dad Boykin and Sack Daddy, two storytellers, argue about who is the king of the world. Dad Boykin tells his tale about how John beat out the lion for this title. First, the grizzly bear challenges John to a fight for the title. John overcomes the bear's deadly hug by slipping his razor between the bear's ribs. The wounded bear tells the lion that he has met the king of the world. The lion is outraged. He also confronts John, and they battle evenly until John pulls out a rifle, which he fires once into the air and once into the lion's hindquarters. The lion runs away and tells the wounded bear to move over—that he too has met the king of the world.

Teaching Strategies

PROVIDING FOR CULTURAL DIFFERENCES   The only difficult aspect of this story is the dialect. To overcome this difficulty, read the story aloud. African American students may balk at reading dialect, which suggests to many the stereotype of a simple, uneducated people. Assure them that Hurston's use of dialect is an honest attempt to reproduce the story as it was told in the South. Hurston believed that these folktales represented ''the greatest cultural wealth of the continent'' and that they were part of a complex system of communication that led to cultural pride and cohesion.

PROVIDING FOR DIFFERENT LEVELS OF ABILITY   Many LEP and ESL students will have trouble recognizing words written in dialect. All students will need practice in order to learn the special rhythm of the speech. Have students read parts of the story aloud but at a slower pace than they normally might. You might want to model a paragraph or two for those who are having difficulty. You might also have some students translate a section of dialogue into standard English to help others catch on. Then have students comment on how different the story would be if it were written entirely in standard English.

READING THE STORY   Read the story aloud. The content of this story should pose no problems, but students will not enjoy the humor of the story unless they can hear the dialect or read it easily.

RETEACHING ALTERNATIVES   Have students create a summary of the story by writing just one sentence for each of the story's three parts: (1) the storytellers' introductory argument, (2) John's fight with the grizzly bear, and (3) John's fight with the lion.

Responding to the Story   Text page 562

Answers to the questions in the Pupil's Edition appear in the Annotated Teacher's Edition.

Writing About the Folktale

For help in revising their compositions, refer students to **Grammar, Usage, and Mechanics: A Reference Guide** on text pages 1183–1228 at the back of their books.

A CREATIVE RESPONSE
1. Writing a Folktale   Begin by identifying some of the characteristics of the oral tradition (conventional beginnings and endings, colorful language, dialect, action-packed plots, simple characters). Have students brainstorm, individually or in small groups, interesting animal characters along with some of their traits. Then have them assign possible natural or technological enemies to each animal. Once they have locked on to an image of animal and enemy, they should start writing. Students can collaborate on a group tale, which they should share with the class.

▶ CRITERIA FOR EVALUATING THE ASSIGNMENT   Look for a plot with a clear conflict and resolution. The folktale makes use of humorous rhymes, alliteration, and some conventions of oral storytelling.

A CRITICAL RESPONSE
2. Comparing Tall Tales   Have students reread the story from *Life on the Mississippi* (text pages 405–412) and then meet in small groups to discuss and complete the chart on page 563. Have the groups share their charts and come to some consensus before students begin to write their essays. For help in organizing their essays, refer students to **Exercises in Critical Thinking and Writing,** Comparing and Contrasting Poems (text page 373).

▶ CRITERIA FOR EVALUATING THE ASSIGNMENT   The essay is clearly organized and includes all three elements on the chart: boasts, exaggeration, and colorful language. The essay cites examples from both stories to support its points.

Performing the Story

A GROUP ACTIVITY

First have students work out the various assignments. You may have to help in assigning certain parts or have competing students draw lots to see who gets certain assignments. You might also help students make decisions about sets, costumes, and music. Encourage all students to be involved in the dramatization.

Primary Sources   Text page 563

COLLECTING FOLKTALES

Hurston reveals the early source for her curiosity about folktales as the ''lying'' sessions the men held on the store porch. Ask students to describe the scene to confirm their understanding of what was going on and how Hurston managed to get an earful.

Extending the Story

Have students retell in their best storytelling manner other folktales from their own ethnic heritage. They may gather stories from older relatives or friends the way Zora Neale Hurston did. Or they may locate a folktale they like in a book and bring it to class to read aloud. Students should begin to see similarities in plot and characters in folktales from different cultures.

Encourage students to interview the oldest people they know to ask for ''old stories'' and ''old songs.'' If students have access to tape recorders or video cameras, have them record the stories and songs they collect to share with the class. Assemble several of the *Foxfire* volumes edited by Eliot Wigginton for classroom browsing. Explain that these books are the result of a high school project in which students gathered all kinds of information by interviewing elderly residents of their community.

John Steinbeck   Text page 564

THE LEADER OF THE PEOPLE   Text page 565

Objectives

1. To respond to a story about the end of the frontier
2. To analyze the story's characters and conflicts
3. To analyze ironies
4. To state the story's theme
5. To write a paragraph using another point of view
6. To write an essay comparing and contrasting characters
7. To write an essay comparing the themes of two stories

Introducing the Story

This story, set in Steinbeck's native Salinas Valley, pits the hunger for heroism and great achievement of an old man and his grandson Jody against banal reality. The Westward movement, in which Jody's grandfather played an important role, was one of the truly heroic chapters in American history. The fact that the old man's life has seemed anticlimactic ever since that long trek ended and that he is eager to relive those days through his stories is understandable and touching. Of course, the irritation of Jody's father at having to hear the same stories over and

over is also understandable—especially since his own life is by comparison prosaic and unheroic.

You may want to tell your students that Steinbeck's most famous book—*The Grapes of Wrath*—is the epic account of another Westward movement—this one undertaken by depression-broken families who hoped to improve their lot in California.

Here are the major elements of the story:

- **Protagonists:** Jody and his grandfather
- **Antagonist:** Jody's father, Carl Tiflin
- **Conflict:** hunger for heroic achievement vs. reality
- **Point of view:** third-person, limited
- **Setting:** Salinas Valley in the early 1900's

THE PLOT When Jody's grandfather plans a visit to the family, Jody eagerly anticipates hearing some of the heroic stories the old man is fond of telling about his experiences as leader of a wagon train across the west to California. Jody's father, Carl, is impatient with the old man's stories, but grudgingly allows him to tell them at dinner. The next morning, however, Carl angrily complains about having to listen to the old man, only to be overheard by the old man as he comes to breakfast. Carl tries to apologize, but the damage is done: the old man realizes that the sense of the heroic that he had hoped to evoke with his stories has died out along with the dream of ''Westering.'' Jody comforts the old man by bringing him a lemonade.

Teaching Strategies

PROVIDING FOR CULTURAL DIFFERENCES The time at which the story takes place is not indicated, except by the fact that Jody's grandfather travels by horse cart and, as we later learn, was a wagon train leader during the Westward movement. Explain to students that a general migration westward took place in the mid-nineteenth century. The old man's advanced age at the time of the story and his reference to the drought of 1887 suggest that the events take place in the early years of this century.

PROVIDING FOR DIFFERENT LEVELS OF ABILITY LEP students will benefit from having the first half of the story (through the bottom of page 568) read aloud. Then you can discuss briefly the differing attitudes toward the old man held by Jody and his mother and father. Once you are sure students understand the general situation, assign the rest of the story for in-class reading.

READING THE STORY Most students will have no difficulty reading this story in a single sitting, either at home or in class.

RETEACHING ALTERNATIVES Have students go back over the story to find passages that foreshadow the conflict between Grandfather and Carl Tiflin. How is this conflict resolved?

Responding to the Story   Text page 574

Answers to the questions in the Pupil's Edition appear in the Annotated Teacher's Edition.

Writing About the Story

For help in revising their compositions, refer students to **Grammar, Usage, and Mechanics: A Reference Guide** on text pages 1183–1228 at the back of their books.

A CREATIVE RESPONSE

1. Using Another Point of View   Note that Jody is to write when he is ten years older than his age in the story. Ask students to talk about what they think Jody, grown up, might think of this experience. The central question is how he will view his father.

▶ CRITERIA FOR EVALUATING THE ASSIGNMENT   The paragraph is written in first-person as Jody, ten years later. It reveals what he learned from his experience in the story.

A CRITICAL RESPONSE

2. Comparing and Contrasting Characters   Students may wish to work together on prewriting charts of what each character looks like and says, how he behaves, and how others feel about him. Discuss with the whole class some ideas for adjectives they would use for each man. Remind students to use details from the story to support each adjective.

▶ CRITERIA FOR EVALUATING THE ASSIGNMENT   The essay characterizes each man on the basis of what he says and does, how he behaves, and how others respond to him. Three key adjectives describe each man. Points are supported by details from the story.

3. Comparing Themes   Have students work in small groups to think of appropriate stories and their themes. Students may suggest "In Another Country" and the Steinbeck story, though a case could also be made for "Winter Dreams" and maybe even "The Egg."

▶ CRITERIA FOR EVALUATING THE ASSIGNMENT   The essay identifies two stories that touch on the theme of lost opportunities for heroism and cites details from the stories that support this interpretation.

Analyzing Language and Style

FIGURES OF SPEECH

Paraphrases will vary. The figures of speech to be identified are as follows:

1. personification
2. metaphor
3. personification
4. oxymoron
5. metaphor
6. hyperbole
7. simile
8. metaphor/hyperbole

Primary Sources   Text page 575

NOBEL PRIZE ACCEPTANCE SPEECH, 1962

Calling man himself "our greatest hazard and our only hope," Steinbeck sees literature as a medium for understanding which he hopes can bring about the perfectibility of humans. Indeed, Steinbeck says that a writer who does not believe that the perfectibility of humans is possible "has no dedication nor any membership in literature." The statement reflects Steinbeck's warm, somewhat sentimental view of human nature, but most will agree that the requirement he sets for "membership in literature" is extreme. It would exclude many great writers—Hawthorne, Melville, and Faulkner, to name only Americans.

James Thurber

Text page 576

THE SECRET LIFE OF WALTER MITTY

Text page 577

Objectives

1. To enjoy and respond to the humor of Thurber's story
2. To analyze the use of free association
3. To identify the central irony of the story
4. To recognize parody and jargon
5. To write an essay analyzing characters
6. To write an essay comparing and contrasting two fictional couples

Introducing the Story

James Thurber had an acute sense of the absurdity of an ordinary, domesticated husband imagining himself in such heroic roles as navy commander, surgeon, and World War I ace. Yet he also had a sympathy for this pathetic longing to be dashing, dramatic, and important. In this story, Walter Mitty's imagination soars the moment it is given a chance. He briefly plans one dramatic role after another, only to be dragged back to reality by his wife, a cocky parking attendant, or an item on his shopping list.

Here are the major elements of the story:

- **Protagonist:** Walter Mitty
- **Antagonist:** his wife
- **Conflict:** daydream vs. reality; husband vs. wife
- **Point of view:** third-person, limited
- **Significant technique:** clever use of free association
- **Setting:** Waterbury, Connecticut, in the 1930's

BACKGROUND ON THE STORY   Explain to students that James Thurber produced many stories and cartoons that feature an anti-hero who finds it difficult to assert himself. Walter Mitty, the protagonist of this story, is such an anti-hero—sneered at by parking lot attendants, ridiculed by a passing pedestrian for muttering "puppy biscuit" out loud, and browbeaten by his wife. Walter is able to escape from uncomfortable reality, at least for a few moments at a time, into fantasies in which he is always dashing, competent, and admired.

THE PLOT   On a shopping expedition with his domineering wife, Walter Mitty escapes from reality from time to time into a fantasy life rich in drama and adventure.

Driving to Waterbury, he imagines himself piloting a giant navy seaplane through a fierce storm, until his wife rebukes him for speeding. Passing a hospital triggers the fantasy that he is Dr. Mitty, the famous surgeon who can do anything, including repairing a complicated life-support system with a borrowed fountain pen. Later adventures find Mitty being tried for his life in a courtroom, flying a crucial mission as a World War I ace, and finally standing with his back to the wall, disdainfully facing a firing squad. Each daydream is triggered by a sight or sound or trivial event, and each is cut short by a rude summons back to reality.

Teaching Strategies

PROVIDING FOR CULTURAL DIFFERENCES   Explain to students that when this story was written in 1932, *hydroplane* was the name for a seaplane, not a boat with hydrofoils, and that fifty-five miles per hour was quite fast. You may want to tell them also that Mitty's fantasies mainly parody radio melodramas popular in the 1930's and 1940's. Because the medium was radio, these dramas depended heavily on sound effects and dialogue to tell their stories. The recurring sound effect, "ta-pocketa-pocketa," in Mitty's daydreams reflects this feature.

PROVIDING FOR DIFFERENT LEVELS OF ABILITY All students should be able to read and enjoy this story either as a homework or in-class assignment.

READING THE STORY   Try reading the first paragraph to the class, as the headnote suggests, and ask students what they think the story will be about. If you have time, read the entire story aloud, or have some of your better readers do the reading. Students will enjoy hearing the story read aloud.

RETEACHING ALTERNATIVES   You might have students meet in small groups to talk about an updated Mitty fantasy, using the jargon from a current television program or movie—e.g., Mitty could be a police lieutenant, a computer expert, or a private eye. Have each group suggest an additional plot along with some details and tell why it "fits" the Mitty story.

Responding to the Story　　　Text page 580

Answers to the questions in the Pupil's Edition appear in the Annotated Teacher's Edition.

Writing About the Story

For help in revising their compositions, refer students to **Grammar, Usage, and Mechanics: A Reference Guide** on text pages 1183–1228 at the back of their books.

A CRITICAL RESPONSE

1. Analyzing Characters　　Brainstorm a list of popular Mr. and Mrs. Mitty types, ranging from Dagwood and Blondie to couples in current movies and TV shows. Identify the key traits of Mr. and Mrs. Mitty, and reevaluate the list of current couples for how well they fit the type.

▶ CRITERIA FOR EVALUATING THE ASSIGNMENT　The essay analyzes the key traits that make Mr. and Mrs. Walter Mitty stock American character types, and cites several couples of that type found in today's popular movies and television shows.

2. Comparing Stories　　On the chalkboard, draw a prewriting chart similar to the one on text page 563 and have students complete it in class discussion.

▶ CRITERIA FOR EVALUATING THE ASSIGNMENT　The essay discusses similarities and differences between the Van Winkle and Mitty stories in terms of the four characters' strengths and weaknesses, sources of the couples' conflicts, how the conflicts are resolved, the husband-wife relationships, and story tone.

Extending the Story

Danny Kaye plays Walter Mitty brilliantly in the hilarious movie version ''The Secret Life of Walter Mitty.'' Watch television listings (it reappears occasionally), and tape it to share with your class. It is also available on video from movie rental stores. Students will also enjoy reading more of Thurber's stories and *The Last Flower*.

Primary Sources　　　Text page 581

THE NEW YORKER'S FAREWELL
The New Yorker is noted for graceful, touching eulogies for deceased workers and staff members, and E.B. White was perhaps the best to attempt this difficult kind of writing. This tribute suggests the scope of Thurber's comic genius without ever falling into extravagance or sentimentality. The last sentence in the third paragraph (about skipping rope and dancing mice) is pure White and one that Thurber would have admired.

Katherine Anne Porter　　　Text page 582

THE JILTING OF GRANNY WEATHERALL　Text page 583

Objectives

1. To respond to a moving story about life and death
2. To interpret ambiguities in the story
3. To recognize and analyze point of view
4. To write a monologue for a character in the story
5. To write an essay comparing Granny Weatherall and Lucinda Matlock

Introducing the Story

Here are the major elements of the story:

- **Protagonist:** Granny Weatherall
- **Antagonist:** memories of her past
- **Conflict:** self-delusion vs. perception of truth
- **Theme:** An elderly, dying woman looks back on her life, revealing the presence of the past in the human mind.

- **Point of view:** omniscient, limited strictly to the major character
- **Significant techniques:** interior monologue, stream of consciousness, epiphany
- **Setting:** Granny's bedroom, the morning and night of a single day

BACKGROUND ON THE STORY "The Jilting of Granny Weatherall" was among the first published stories of Katherine Anne Porter, yet it is an ingenious piece of writing. Full of memories, arranging and rearranging themselves, it calls for a command of story structure and strong observational skills; both are hallmarks of Porter's writing. For the interior monologue to be effective, Porter had to be able to identify closely with her main character, a pioneer farm woman. She could. Born in Texas and the great-great-great-granddaughter of the brother of Daniel Boone, Porter had the frontier spirit in her blood.

SUMMARY Granny Weatherall is in bed, dying, though she does not know yet that this is her final day of life. In the morning, the doctor tends to her. She passes in and out of a semi-conscious state, interacting with her daughter Cornelia and with her memories in a random fashion. She thinks back on her long life, especially to her jilting sixty years earlier by George, who still has a hold on her heart. Her other memories include her childhood home, her hard life, her husband John, and her daughter Hapsy, who evidently died. In the evening the priest gives her the last rites, and her family gathers by her bedside. She realizes that her death is imminent, and she thinks of the things she meant to do before she died. At the moment of her death, she looks for a sign from God, but it does not come. She feels jilted a second time, says she will never forgive it, and dies.

Teaching Strategies

PROVIDING FOR CULTURAL DIFFERENCES Unless they grew up on a farm, students may not be able to sympathize with the hard life Granny Weatherall describes. You may wish to discuss what it takes to dig post holes to fence in a hundred acres or explain what Granny means when she says "such a green day with no threats in it." (Farmers had to be very aware of threatening weather—there were animals and crops to take care of.)

PROVIDING FOR DIFFERENT LEVELS OF ABILITY The stream-of-consciousness technique may be especially confusing to LEP students. You can make clear which are Granny's spoken words and which are her thoughts by having the story read aloud with two different students playing Granny. One should read only the words in quotation marks; the other should read all of Granny's

thoughts. Other students can read the speaking roles of Dr. Harry, Cornelia, and the other children.

There is much in the story that is not quite clear or obvious. (For example, what has become of Hapsy and what is the second jilting suggested at the end of the story.) Emphasize that students are generally free to interpret such ambiguities in their own way, that there is not necessarily one "right" interpretation. However, students should be prepared to make (and argue) interpretations that are consistent with the details of the story.

READING THE STORY Be sure students have a clear understanding of the concept of being jilted, for it plays a vital part in the story. Before they read, you might have students consider what it might be like to be an eighty-year-old country woman who lived in the late 1800's and early 1900's. This might help them adjust to the mood of the story more easily. To sustain the mood, they should read the story in one sitting. Reserve plenty of time for discussion afterward.

RETEACHING ALTERNATIVES You may wish to discuss the story's dramatic irony with students. The other characters know that Granny Weatherall is dying, but she does not, and the reader at first does not. She seems too cantankerous, too full of vinegar to be dying. Ask students to find and read passages that suggest Granny's vitality, at least in her thoughts. Have students review the definition of dramatic irony in **A Handbook of Literary Terms** (text page 1175).

Responding to the Story   Text page 589

Answers to the questions in the Pupil's Edition appear in the Annotated Teacher's Edition.

Writing About the Story

For help in revising their compositions, refer students to **Grammar, Usage, and Mechanics: A Reference Guide** on text pages 1183–1228 at the back of their books.

A CREATIVE RESPONSE
1. Writing a Monologue Before they write, have students imagine what the last sixty years have been like for George and the effect that might have on his present feelings. There are no clues in the story to what became of George or why he jilted Ellen. Students are completely free to make up anything. Have volunteers read aloud their monologues.

▶ CRITERIA FOR EVALUATING THE ASSIGNMENT The monologue uses a first-person point of view and a stream-of-consciousness technique. George expresses his feelings about Ellen and the jilting and tells what his own life has been like.

2. *Comparing a Story and a Poem* Reread the poem aloud, and complete the prewriting chart in class discussion.

▶ CRITERIA FOR EVALUATING THE ASSIGNMENT The essay compares and contrasts Granny Weatherall and Lucinda Matlock, especially in regard to their attitudes and to the kinds of lives that they led.

Analyzing Language and Style

INTERIOR MONOLOGUE

Examples of instances in which Granny's mind shifts away from the present include the following:

1. Thinking about the orderliness of life, she recalls the neatly arranged shelves in the pantry of some former home. (text page 584)
2. Because she hears Cornelia whisper behind her back, she thinks of moving back to her old home, which causes her to remember the hard life she led, raising the children while tending the farm. (text page 584)
3. Cornelia places a cold cloth on her mother's forehead, which reminds her of washing the children's faces. (text page 586)
4. The arrival of Father Connolly sends her mind back to the priest's regular visits in the past. (text page 587)
5. Light flashing on her closed eyelids reminds her of lightning, and she thinks of a past storm and what she had to do to prepare for it. (text page 588)

Extending the Story

Students may wish to examine the novels of English author Virginia Woolf to compare her use of interior monologue with that of Porter. (See especially *Mrs. Dalloway* and *The Waves*.)

William Faulkner

Text page 590

A ROSE FOR EMILY

Text page 592

Objectives

1. To respond to a story with elements of horror
2. To recognize the use of foreshadowing
3. To analyze conflict and setting
4. To reevaluate a traditional symbol
5. To write a horror story
6. To write an essay analyzing the story's main character
7. To analyze plot sequence

Introducing the Story

Unless students have lived in a small southern town, they may have trouble grasping the post-Civil War social traditions that play such an important role in Faulkner's story. Even if they are from such a town, those traditions have probably been diluted by outside forces. You might briefly discuss how Southerners' sense of pride and honor remained strong long after their defeat in the Civil War. So did their sense of social class. Nevertheless, students can relate to the townspeople's need to gossip, to think they know everything about everyone.

Here are the major elements of the story:

- **Protagonist:** Emily Grierson
- **Themes:** the conflict between individual and community, between men and women, and between past and present
- **Point of view:** third-person limited (major character)
- **Significant techniques:** the narrator as a member of the community, characterization, atmosphere
- **Setting:** a small southern town, from the 1890's to the 1930's

BACKGROUND ON THE STORY Critic James B. Carothers claims that "A Rose for Emily" began with the image of a strand of hair on the pillow in an abandoned house. This image, in the context of the small-town southern life that he knew so well, was all Faulkner needed to weave his Gothic tale. Carothers suggests that Faulkner did not set out to write a story with any of the simplistic themes that are popularly attached to this story: "To the contrary, Faulkner seems to have written many of his works without considering the emotional or intellectual effects they might have on the audience."

THE PLOT   After Miss Emily Grierson's father dies, she refuses at first to give up the body for burial. The townspeople find this curious, but accept it. The mayor, a traditional southern gentleman, decides to exempt Miss Emily from having to pay taxes. Many years later, when the next generation of town leaders tries to get her to pay taxes, she refuses and runs them out of her house. This occurs just a short time after her only suitor, a Yankee named Homer Barron, disappears. Their relationship has been the source of much gossip for the townspeople. When Miss Emily buys rat poison, the townspeople are sure she is going to kill herself; when she buys gifts for a man, they are sure she and Homer are getting married. But then he is seen no more. Miss Emily becomes a recluse, grows fat and her hair turns iron-gray. When she finally dies, her house is found to be full of dust and mold. After her burial, townspeople force open a locked room and discover the decayed remains of a man—presumably Homer Barron—in a bed. On the pillow beside him are the indentation left by a head and a long strand of iron-gray hair.

Teaching Strategies

PROVIDING FOR CULTURAL DIFFERENCES   Be sure that students are provided with some background on the small-town southern setting so crucial to this story and many other stories and novels by William Faulkner.

PROVIDING FOR DIFFERENT LEVELS OF ABILITY   Some students may have trouble keeping track of the chronology of the story. Have them go through the story, noting any dates or ages or time spans given, as well as every instance of the story's flashing back or leaping forward in time, along with important events that occurred within each time period. Students might then compare notes and make a summary/time line of the story to resolve any misunderstandings about the order of events.

READING THE STORY   Encourage students to read the story as a detective might, looking for clues to the mystery of where the story is headed. Every time they come across a new piece of puzzling information, they should stop to consider what it might mean in the light of what they already know. By the end of Part IV, students should make a prediction about how the story will end.

RETEACHING ALTERNATIVES   Invite students to write two local newspaper articles concerning Emily

Grierson. The first is her obituary, written the day of her funeral. The second is a review of her life published after the murder is discovered. Suggest to students that they focus on the different ways the two articles would characterize Miss Grierson, based on what they know about the townspeople from the story.

Responding to the Story   Text page 600

Answers to the questions in the Pupil's Edition appear in the Annotated Teacher's Edition.

Writing About the Story

For help in revising their compositions, refer students to **Grammar, Usage, and Mechanics: A Reference Guide** on text pages 1183–1228 at the back of their books.

A CREATIVE RESPONSE
1. Writing a Horror Story   Have students brainstorm ideas with a partner until both have chosen a believable character and a shocking secret. Each student should devise the plot on his or her own. Have students share their stories with the class.

▶ CRITERIA FOR EVALUATING THE ASSIGNMENT   The story concerns a solitary individual with a shocking secret, which is divulged only in the final sentence. The story vividly describes the individual and also provides information about the community.

A CRITICAL RESPONSE
2. Analyzing a Character   Show students how the cluster diagram works: Miss Emily is at the center, character traits branch from the center, and examples of those character traits are the additional branches. Have students gather their details in a similar chart form.

▶ CRITERIA FOR EVALUATING THE ASSIGNMENT   The essay analyzes Miss Emily's character in an organized fashion, suggests three or four of her most striking character traits, and provides details from the story to exemplify those characteristics. The end of the essay reveals student's subjective reaction to the character and suggests Emily's motivation.

3. Analyzing Plot Sequence   You might wish to have students work in pairs or small groups to figure out this complicated chronology.

▶ CRITERIA FOR EVALUATING THE ASSIGNMENT   The analysis is in the form of a chart, with two lists, side by side. The list on the left shows the events in chronological order. The list on the right shows them as they appear in the story (and in the writing assignment).

Research and Discussion Projects

A GROUP ACTIVITY

1. Usher's house is described in the following terms: bleak walls; vacant eyelike windows; unredeemed dreariness; mansion of gloom; a pestilent and mystic vapor; excessive antiquity; minute fungi overspread the whole exterior; neglected; indication of extensive decay; dark and intricate passages; carvings on the ceilings; somber tapestries on the walls; ebony blackness of the floors; phantasmagoric trophies; long, narrow, and pointed windows; dark draperies; profuse, comfortless, antique, and tattered furniture; atmosphere of sorrow; numerous vaults within the main walls. Students might use these details to argue either side of the issue.

2. Students might suggest that Emily Grierson suffers from a different kind of isolation than Richard Cory (text page 612). Though they both are isolated by social class, hers is also physical isolation, while his may be more mental isolation.

3. The dust and the mold and certain objects found in Miss Emily's room certainly remind one of Miss Havisham's apartment.

Primary Sources   Text page 601

NOBEL PRIZE ACCEPTANCE SPEECH, 1950
In this speech, Faulkner, like Steinbeck, sees literature as being important to human survival. But unlike Steinbeck, Faulkner does not expect literature to perfect human beings. He says: ''I believe that man will not merely endure: he will prevail. He is immortal . . . because he has a soul, a spirit capable of compassion and sacrifice and endurance.'' For Faulkner, the writer's duty is to lift man's heart, and literature is one of ''the pillars to help him endure and prevail.'' Ask students to talk about how ''A Rose for Miss Emily'' fits Faulkner's description of what literature does. (Of all the words Faulkner uses to describe the purpose of literature, only *compassion* and *pity* seem to fit Miss Emily.)

Flannery O'Connor   Text page 602

THE LIFE YOU SAVE MAY BE YOUR OWN   Text page 603

Objectives

1. To enjoy an ironic version of a romance

2. To recognize foreshadowing in details of setting, characterization, and dialogue

3. To identify irony and state the story's theme

4. To write a new ending

5. To write an essay expressing an opinion

6. To write an essay analyzing the story

Introducing the Story

This story is one of exploitation. Mr. Shiftlet arrives at the place, looks around to see what he can take, and decides on the old car that hasn't run for years. The old woman sees him as a match for her idiot daughter. Both characters display the selfishness to which the highway slogan in the title appeals.

Here are the major elements of the story:

- **Protagonist:** Mr. Shiftlet
- **Antagonist:** the elder Lucynell Crater
- **Conflict:** one selfish person vs. another
- **Point of view:** third-person, omniscient
- **Setting:** rural Georgia in the 1940's

BACKGROUND ON THE STORY   Flannery O'Connor was a devout Roman Catholic all her life, and her strong beliefs are reflected in all of her stories. She also had a predilection for the grosteque and the violent—features that place most of her writing in the category of Southern Gothic. The violence is absent from this story, but the grotesques are on hand.

THE PLOT   Tom T. Shiftlet appears at the Crater place and accepts meals and a bed (in an out-of-commission car) in return for handyman chores. In a short time, he greatly improves the appearance of the place and teaches Lucynell, the idiot daughter, to say ''bird,'' her first and only word. Lucynell (senior) proposes that Shiftlet marry her daughter Lucynell and he agrees, on condition that the old woman stake him to enough money to stay a night in a good hotel and get something to eat. She agrees, reluctantly, to give him $17.50 for these amenities. Shiftlet and Lucynell are married at the courthouse and drop off her mother. After driving a hundred miles or so, Shiftlet stops at a diner and leaves Lucynell there, asleep at the counter. Shiftlet drives on. At the end of the story, ominous storm clouds descend in front of the car and behind it.

Teaching Strategies

PROVIDING FOR CULTURAL DIFFERENCES Students from all cultures can relate to this story. You might ask what they think of characters who agree that the world is a rotten place and that you can't tell whether a stranger is lying or telling the truth. Do they know people like this?

PROVIDING FOR DIFFERENT LEVELS OF ABILITY Some students may need help in appreciating the ironic humor in the story. Help them focus on specific instances.

READING THE STORY All students will be able to understand the main events in the narrative, but, as suggested above, some may fail to appreciate the humor. Reading at least part of the story aloud will help students become familiar with the tone. If you read from the beginning, the middle of the righthand column on text page 606 offers a good stopping point. An audiocassette recording of this entire story is available. Three performers take the roles of the narrator, Mr. Shiftlet, and Lucynell Crater.

RETEACHING ALTERNATIVES Ask students to go back over the story to write a one-minute television report on the story's events and characters. They might include one or more interviews as part of their report.

Responding to the Story   Text page 610

Answers to the questions in the Pupil's Edition appear in the Annotated Teacher's Edition.

Writing About the Story

For help in revising their compositions, refer students to **Grammar, Usage, and Mechanics: A Reference Guide** on text pages 1183–1228 at the back of their books.

A CREATIVE RESPONSE
1. *Extending the Story* Discuss endings consistent with Lucynell's handicaps and human nature in general. Students may want to continue O'Connor's irony or continue in another vein. Call on volunteers to read aloud their endings.

▶ CRITERIA FOR EVALUATING THE ASSIGNMENT The ending tells what became of Lucynell.

A CRITICAL RESPONSE
2. *Expressing an Opinion* Assign Primary Sources (text page 611) or discuss the page in class. Students should have no problem engaging in lively discussion of the three questions in the writing assignment.

▶ CRITERIA FOR EVALUATING THE ASSIGNMENT The essay shows a grasp both of O'Connor's story and of the realities of schools, movies and television. Students should offer clearly stated reasons to support their answers to the three questions.

3. *Analyzing the Story* Read and discuss Elements of Literature: The Four "Modes" of Fiction (text page 612) before students do this assignment. Lead the class to see that the story is indeed an ironic parody of a romance.

▶ CRITERIA FOR EVALUATING THE ASSIGNMENT The essay identifies O'Connor's story as an ironic parody of a romance. Its three characters are grotesque opposites of the romantic stereotype, though they play the roles of mother, princess, and prince. The setting, too, is grotesque—poor and barren and broken.

Analyzing Language and Style

CONNOTATIONS
1. Answers will vary. Some include "jutting steel-trap jaw" (text page 603), "his clay-colored eyes" (text page 605), "the trigger that moved up and down in his neck" (text page 606), "smile stretched like a weary snake" (text page 608). All of these figures of speech have evil, unpleasant, unnatural connotations. Students may say the words make them feel creepy, nervous, distrustful, frightened.
2. "A cloud . . . shaped like a *turnip*"; "a *guffawing* peal of thunder . . ." (text page 609).
3. The words and phrases suggest that Shiftlet is anything but a knight in shining armor. He seems to be associated with the devil and forces of evil.
4. If students suggest words with positive connotations ("*strong, manly* jaw," "*clear, steady* eyes," "*smooth, strong* neck," "*winning* smile," etc.), Mr. Shiftlet becomes a more princelike character we can view with trust and sympathy.

Primary Sources   Text page 611

THE ADVENTURES OF MR. SHIFTLET
These excerpts from Flannery O'Connor's letters give a goodhumored account of mischances involving "The Life You Save May Be Your Own," including the prospect of Gene Kelly's playing Shiftlet and the discovery that the last paragraph has been omitted when the story was reprinted in a school anthology. Students may enjoy talking about how they would cast the story for a television production.

THE FOUR "MODES" OF FICTION

This section is important and should be read and discussed in class. The definitions and descriptions of the four modes provide a useful way of talking about literature that can be applied to all of world literature. Students should be able to recognize the characteristics of each mode and use the terms easily in talking and writing about literature.

Read and discuss this section before students attempt the third writing assignment on text page 610—analyzing Flannery O'Connor's "The Life You Save May Be Your Own." The final question on this page (What modes do you think the other stories in this unit are written in?) could serve as a general review question. Throughout the rest of the year, you can use these four modes to talk about fiction and drama.

Eudora Welty   Text page 613

A WORN PATH   Text page 614

Objectives

1. To enjoy a moving story about a modern quest

2. To analyze the main character

3. To recognize situational irony and the importance of setting

4. To state the story's theme

5. To write a new ending

6. To write an essay analyzing a character's journey

7. To write an essay analyzing character

Introducing the Story

Tell students that the story they are about to read concerns a very old woman who periodically makes a long journey to a city on foot. You may wish to remind them that from earliest times storytellers have used a journey as a metaphor for life—Ulysses's journey home to Ithaca, Gulliver's travels to strange worlds, and Huck Finn's raft trip down the Mississippi are only a few examples. Have them consider to what extent Phoenix Jackson's journey is a symbolic one.

Here are the major elements of the story:

- **Protagonist:** Phoenix Jackson
- **Antagonist:** obstacles to her journey
- **Conflict:** person vs. obstacle to the journey
- **Point of view:** limited third-person
- **Significant techniques:** development of the theme through journey motif; character talking to herself and addressing the plants and animals
- **Setting:** rural Mississippi in the Depression era

BACKGROUND ON THE STORY   As Eudora Welty explains in the short essay that follows this story, "A Worn Path" was inspired by the sight of an old woman walking slowly across a winter landscape. Welty then invented the errand that would make her go on her journey and the passing adventures that make the story. Be sure to have students read Welty's discussion of her story (text pages 619–620) after they finish reading "A Worn Path."

THE PLOT   Phoenix Jackson makes a long journey on foot through woods, across fields, and along country roads until she reaches Natchez. On her way, she is frightened by a scarecrow and a dog, aided but patronized by a hunter, and patronized again by a receptionist at the doctor's office that is her destination. She has traveled there to obtain medicine for her grandson. With a nickel the receptionist gives her and another the hunter dropped, Phoenix plans to buy a paper windmill for her grandson before she starts back.

Teaching Strategies

PROVIDING FOR CULTURAL DIFFERENCES Reminding students that the story takes place during the Depression, when a nickel went a long way, will help them to understand that the receptionist's gift to Phoenix is not as miserly as it might now appear.

PROVIDING FOR DIFFERENT LEVELS OF ABILITY All students can easily manage this story either as homework or as an in-class assignment.

READING THE STORY Before assigning the story, you may want to read aloud the first three paragraphs, which describe Phoenix Jackson. Ask students to summarize what they know about her and to speculate briefly on what errand brings her on this journey. Then assign the story for in-class reading.

RETEACHING ALTERNATIVES As an alternative to the writing assignments on page 619, you may wish to have students talk about their responses to Phoenix Jackson. What makes her an admirable character? How does she meet the obstacles on her journey? How do people treat her? Ask students to tell about people they know—of any age—who remind them of Phoenix Jackson.

Responding to the Story   Text page 618

Answers to the questions in the Pupil's Edition appear in the Annotated Teacher's Edition.

Writing About the Story

Have students read and discuss "Primary Sources: 'Is Phoenix Jackson's Grandson Really Dead?'" (text pages 619–620) as preparation for the first three writing assignments. For help in revising their compositions, refer students to **Grammar, Usage, and Mechanics: A Reference Guide** on text pages 1183–1228 at the back of their books.

A CREATIVE RESPONSE
1. Extending the Story Divide the class into small groups and let each group brainstorm Phoenix Jackson's further adventures on this journey. They may address these questions: What will happen in the store? What will happen on the journey home? How will she find her grandson when she reaches home?

▶ CRITERIA FOR EVALUATING THE ASSIGNMENT The ending "works"; that is, the ending retains the characterization of Phoenix and the importance of her journey.

A CRITICAL RESPONSE
2. Analyzing the Journey In class discussion, with someone taking notes on the chalkboard, elicit examples for each category. Emphasize that the important part of the essay is the last question in the writing assignment—the mythic significance of Phoenix Jackson's journey.

▶ CRITERIA FOR EVALUATING THE ASSIGNMENT The essay cites at least one example for each category. Students should see that Phoenix Jackson is a hero who triumphs over difficulties large and small to fulfill an important obligation. She reaches her goal, like Odysseus, and her true worth is recognized.

3. Responding to a Comment Make sure students understand they are to discuss the phrase "the habit of love."

▶ CRITERIA FOR EVALUATING THE ASSIGNMENT The paragraph provides a reasonable explanation of Welty's term, "the habit of love." Students should recognize that the term implies a steady, long-term commitment filled with daily, often mundane, loving acts. The other images suggest recent or glamorous pathways.

4. Analyzing Character Most students will see that Phoenix is essentially timeless.

▶ CRITERIA FOR EVALUATING THE ASSIGNMENT Whether the essay presents Phoenix Jackson as someone who changes or as an essentially timeless character, it cites details from the story to support the position taken.

Primary Sources   Text page 619

"IS PHOENIX JACKSON'S GRANDSON REALLY DEAD?"

Welty wrote this essay after receiving many questions from students and teachers concerning "The Worn Path." Welty's favorite question is the one that provides the title. The essay gives students a rare opportunity to analyze a story in the light of the author's own explication of its origin and meaning.

With more advanced classes, you may want to discuss some of the schools of literary criticism that would not be interested in Welty's comments on her story. New critics, for example, would say that the story itself is all that matters and that you can analyze the elements of the story to derive its meaning. Other critics say that each reader brings his or her own experiences to the story and that the experience of reading the text is therefore unique for each reader; what Welty intended or sees in her story is of little importance. What do students think of these views?

This essay overcomes the misconception that slang is corrupt English or a "linguistic disease," and acknowledges it as "colorful, lively language." The first segment of the essay answers the question, "Why do people use slang?" and discusses theories about its origins. The second segment develops the idea that slang develops "in exactly the same ways as additions to standard English."

The final section discusses why some slang becomes standard English while most of it fades with time, or "hangs around" as slang.

This essay will prove entertaining to most students, who will doubtless appreciate several of the generalizations made in the piece.

Assign the essay as homework and have students work **collaboratively** on the Analyzing Language feature.

Analyzing Language

Text page 624

1. Students should collect as many slang terms as they can for the following words. They should then discuss the metaphors on which the slang terms are based. Sample answers might include the following:

   car: wheels, jalopy, buggy, limo, chariot

   failing: flunking, punting

   getting angry: blowing a fuse, blowing up, hitting the ceiling, having a cow

   going to sleep: catching some z's, hitting the sack, taking a cat-nap, drifting off, out like a light, zonking out

2. *chicken:* metaphor for cowardice

   stuffed shirt: metaphor for pomposity

   hit the ceiling: hyperbole for getting angry

   out like a light: simile for going to sleep

   to talk someone's ear off: hyperbole for garulousness

   tenderfoot: metaphor for inexperience

   rubberneck: metaphor for slowing down to look at an accident out of curiosity

   to put on ice: metaphor for postponement

   Student examples of other slang phrases based on the same figure of speech will vary.

3. *ad lib:* ad libitum   *cello:* violoncello   *lunch:* luncheon
   bus: omnibus   *flu:* influenza   *pep:* pepper
   car: cart   *gym:* gymnasium   *prop:* property

4. Students' speculations on the development of the current meanings of the words will vary. Here are the original meanings:

   bleachers: containers, like vats or tanks, used for bleaching

   bore: to make a hole with a sharp instrument

   club: a short spar on a ship

   freshman: a student in the first year of a course

   glib: slippery

   handsome: easy to handle

   kidnap: nab

   tidy: seasonable

   trip: step lightly

5. **a.** *winning streak:* series of consecutive victories
   snapped: interrupted

   b. *fast-break:* sudden offensive on the run

   c. *benched:* relegated to the player's bench and so not in the game
   hauled down: established

   d. *popped out:* hit a short fly ball that was caught for an out

   e. *punched:* struggled with force and vigor

EXERCISES IN CRITICAL THINKING AND WRITING   Text page 625

MAKING GENERALIZATIONS

In this exercise, students are asked to use the critical thinking skill of generalizing as they discuss in an essay the theme of either Faulkner's "A Rose for Emily," or O'Connor's "The Life You Save May Be Your Own." You might begin reviewing generalizations by discussing the five statements under the section Background, text page 625. Statements 1, 3, and 4 are matters of opinion. Statement 2 could be proved only if students knew the total number of both men and women who write poetry, statement 5 only if students knew the number of symbols used by all writers throughout time. In the prewriting stage, you might consider in class discussion especially questions 3 and 5 in the section Prewriting, text page 626.

▶ CRITERIA FOR EVALUATING THE ASSIGNMENT   The theme, as students discuss it in the essay, is a generalization about human nature and is not limited to the specific events and characters of the story. The theme expresses the complexity of human experience; it is not a moral lesson.

Further Reading

Works listed are suitable for both students and teachers unless the annotation ends with the note [Teachers].

Allen, Frederick Lewis. *Only Yesterday* (Harper & Row Perennial Library, 1964). A reissue of the classic social history of the 1920's, first published in 1930.

Bryer, Jackson R., ed. *Fifteen Modern American Authors: A Survey of Research and Criticism* (Duke University Press, 1969). An excellent resource. [Teachers]

Cowley, Malcom, ed. *The Portable Faulkner* (Viking, 1941). A critical introduction followed by a good cross-section of short stories and excerpts from novels.

Hemingway, Ernest. *The Complete Short Stories of Ernest Hemingway* (Scribner's, 1987). All of the stories with a very brief introduction by Hemingway's sons.

Hemingway, Ernest. *The Nick Adams Stories* (Scribner's, 1972). Hemingway's fictionalized account of his boyhood summers in Michigan. This edition has eight previously unpublished pieces and a preface by Philip Young.

Hoffman, Frederick J. *The Twenties: American Writing and the Postwar Decade* (Viking, 1955). Literary history and criticism, focusing on the 1920's.

Hughes, Langston, ed. *The Best Short Stories by Black Writers* (Little, Brown, 1967). Anthology of almost fifty stories written from 1899–1967. Writers include Ralph Ellison, Zora Neale Hurston, James Baldwin, Gwendolyn Brooks, and Richard Wright.

Kazin, Alfred. *On Native Grounds* (Harcourt Brace Jovanovich, 1942). A noted critic traces the development of American prose from the time of William Dean Howells. [Teachers]

O'Connor, Frank. *The Lonely Voice: A Study of the Short Story* (World, 1963). Discussion of the fundamental nature of the genre by the Irish short-story writer.

POETRY
VOICES OF AMERICAN CHARACTER

Text page 627

**Teaching the
Poetry Unit**

The strength and the limitation of the poets in this unit is that they wrote realistically about the lives of ordinary Americans. Their poems tend to be vignettes or anecdotes, comparable in power and intent to good short stories. Many of these poems are written in the third-person, and even those written in first-person are often about characters who are clearly external to the poet. These poems, then, might be considered a kind of "verse fiction."

The contrast with the American poetry that came afterward is stark. From the 1920's on, the best American poetry has been concerned mainly with advancing the art form itself—with making new explorations of technique and broadening the range of verbal effects available. The subject matter of this new poetry has consisted largely of introspection about the poet's most subtle feelings, or at least the feelings of a character (like Eliot's Prufrock) who is clearly a stand-in for the poet. This change was equivalent to the change that occurred in the visual arts at the same time, when painters became preoccupied mostly with technique and no longer thought it important to faithfully reproduce a representational subject.

With the exception of Frost, the poets in this unit may not seem, to some readers, as challenging or impressive as the poets in Unit Nine: Pound, Eliot, and Stevens. The poets in this unit represent, to many critics, an unexperimental, undaring period in American poetry, a fallow period before a period of tremendously exciting growth. Paradoxically, however, this makes them readily accessible to the high-school-age reader. In many respects, you can approach the poems in this unit almost as though they were works of prose fiction. Analyses of character and of social message will be of primary importance. Even the analyses of language will mainly involve discussions of characters' voices rather than of linguistic innovations. The purely formal discussions, meanwhile, will tend to involve conventional schemes of rhyme and meter, or, as in the case of Masters and Jeffers, a kind of free verse that seems secondary to the poet's message.

These qualities also create a resemblance between the poems in this unit and the lyrics of songs. The best contemporary rock lyricists (such as Bruce Springsteen, Suzanne Vega, Paul Simon, and Robbie Robertson) tend to write verse vignettes that are strong character studies of American lives. These lyrics are written in everyday language, usually in a simple, free verse, or with rhymes that range from the achingly obvious to the strikingly clever. Some of the poems in this unit are good candidates for musical settings. Paul Simon has recorded Robinson's "Richard Cory" as a song.

It is important to note that several of the poets in this unit had careers that were artificially and tragically stunted by the social conditions of their day. African American poets such as Paul Laurence Dunbar, James Weldon Johnson, and Countee Cullen were highly gifted, and yet their careers were filled with frustration. Even when they achieved some success, they found themselves in a kind of artistic ghetto, pressured to produce work that would not be threatening to the white intelligentsia: either stereotypical dialect poems, or verses in conventional schemes of rhyme and meter that tamed the anger and pain in their message.

All the poets in this unit did, however, produce some moving, lyrical expressions of the human condition. The characters they created still live, and their wisdom still impresses. We return to them for the reassurance that the pain of human life can be partially healed through song.

Objectives of the Poetry Unit

1. To improve reading proficiency and expand vocabulary
2. To gain exposure to notable poets and their works
3. To define and identify the elements of poetry
4. To define and identify significant literary techniques
5. To respond to poetry orally and in writing
6. To practice the following critical thinking and writing techniques
   a. Analyzing a poem
   b. Comparing and contrasting poems
   c. Analyzing imagery
   d. Responding to a poem's theme and to critics
   e. Comparing authors' attitudes
   f. Comparing sermons

Introducing the Poetry Unit

It's a good idea not to belabor the technical terms having to do with rhyme and meter at this point. Many students will have been exposed to them already, and while a certain amount of repetition is necessary to learning, an overemphasis on poetics is a sure way to turn your students against poetry forever. You will, however, probably want to discuss blank verse when you come to Frost's poems.

At the beginning of the unit, it might be best to stress the unit's rich geographical and ethnic variety and the interesting range of characters. You might give your students brief "coming attractions" about some of these characters: James Weldon Johnson's preacher, who orates beautifully on the death of Sister Caroline; Robert Frost's broken-down hired man, Silas, and the farm couple who discuss his fate; Edgar Lee Masters's tombstone-carver, Richard Bone, who tells us his thoughts from his own grave. Then go directly to the first poem.

Edwin Arlington Robinson

Robinson found his distinctive style early on, stayed with it throughout his career, and did not seem affected by changing trends or by the advances made by younger poets. His reputation today is neither much higher nor much lower than it was in his own lifetime. He is another of the great solitaries of American literature, belonging to no school, but solidly occupying his own niche.

After becoming known for brief character portraits of New Englanders, he produced a book-length poem, *Captain Craig* (1902), which is similar in subject and style to his earlier vignettes. Most critics agree that it is padded and would have benefitted from being held to the length of his previous vignettes. More successful were *Lancelot* and *Tristram* (1927), which retell the Arthurian legends, showing us heroes and lovers searching for light in a dark world. Robinson regarded *Tristram* as his masterpiece. Robinson seems to have been born, or at least early bred, to an introspective, sober temperament and a pessimistic but still hopeful view of the world. His work, as a result, is always intelligent and serious.

RICHARD CORY

Objectives

1. To respond to a character portrait in poetry
2. To recognize irony
3. To identify the speaker's tone
4. To state the moral
5. To identify the connotations of specific words

Introducing the Poem

"Richard Cory" uses the simple diction of small-town folk with a few expressions ("Clean favored," and "In fine") that seem dated. Have students notice that each stanza is a single sentence and that two begin colloquially with "And." The poem is written in iambic pentameter with an *abab* rhyme scheme.

BACKGROUND ON THE POEM This poem, like "Miniver Cheevy," was originally published in *The Children of the Night* (1897), the volume that can be considered Robinson's *Spoon River Anthology:* a collection of character portraits from his fictitious "Tilbury Town." Among his characters are a miser, Aaron Stark, who laughs at those who pity him; a butcher, Reuben Bright, who tears down his own slaughterhouse in grief over his wife's death; Annandale, a derelict, who is a victim of euthanasia.

THE LITERAL MEANING Richard Cory was rich and envied by all the townspeople, but one summer night, he committed suicide with a bullet through his head.

Teaching Strategies

PROVIDING FOR CULTURAL DIFFERENCES The vocabulary may cause some problems. Explain the phrases "from sole to crown," "fluttered pulses," and "schooled in every grace." You might also ask students how they would define the word *gentleman.*

PROVIDING FOR DIFFERENT LEVELS OF ABILITY This poem is easier to read than "Miniver Cheevy" both because it lacks the historical and literary allusions and because it is written in the first-person, plural voice of an ordinary American community.

READING THE POEM Give four students advance notice and time to practice. Assign each one a stanza to read aloud.

Have students reread the poem to see if Robinson gives any hint about why Richard Cory committed suicide.

Responding to the Poem   Text page 634

Answers to the questions in the Pupil's Edition appear in the Annotated Teacher's Edition.

Analyzing Language and Style

CONNOTATIONS
1. *Crown, imperially, arrayed, glittered, grace.*
2. *Hair, undeniably, dressed, was neat, skill.* The poem loses interest and color.

3. A titled person; a well-educated person.
4. Its assonance; the effect of Cory's ''descending'' to a lesser place.

Primary Sources   Text page 635

ROBINSON ON "RICHARD CORY"

These few excerpts from Robinson's letters give us a quick but revealing glimpse of the poet. He calls ''Richard Cory'' a ''nice little thing''—he is obviously pleased with it and wants people to respond positively to it. His style of letter writing is informal. In fact, he makes it clear that elegance does not suit him. That he would crack a vaude-ville-style joke certainly reinforces this notion, but leaves us with the somewhat disconcerting realization that the author of ''Richard Cory'' has a sense of humor.

MINIVER CHEEVY   Text page 636

Objectives

1. To respond to verse character portrait
2. To describe a change in tone
3. To write a letter using another point of view
4. To write a letter to the speaker in a poem
5. To write an essay responding to the poems
6. To write an essay comparing and contrasting the characters in these two poems

Introducing the Poem

Robinson packs a surprise ending into this poem, which is a long series of statements about Miniver. Note that each stanza begins with the name Miniver and contains two separate statements. The bouncy iambic tetrameter rhythm bumps to a short stop with a half-length (iambic dimeter) line at the end of each stanza. The rhyme scheme is *abcb* with feminine rhymes (the last syllable is unaccented) on the b lines.

BACKGROUND ON THE POEM   While the poem is not autobiographical, Robinson, who was later to write three books based on Arthurian legends, must have empathized with Miniver, who ''dreamed of Thebes and Camelot.'' The mocking humor aimed at Miniver seems less harsh if we understand that the poet is being to some extent self-deprecatory.

The name ''Miniver'' is a strong dactyl (an accented syllable followed by two unaccented ones) but most of the bulk of the poem is iambic. This combination produces a bouncy rhythm.

THE LITERAL MEANING   Miniver Cheevy day-dreams about many bygone eras and wishes he had lived in the medieval world of knights, ancient Greece, or Renaissance Italy. He scorns the money that he seeks, mourns his fate, and drinks.

Teaching Strategies

PROVIDING FOR CULTURAL DIFFERENCES   Many students will need help translating the allusions. Some students may not be able to relate to Miniver's plight, thinking it a case of a misty-eyed misfit. A modern-day analogy would be with a teenager of the 1990's who wishes he or she had been a teenager in the 1960's.

PROVIDING FOR DIFFERENT LEVELS OF ABILITY   The literary allusions and Romantic trappings make this poem difficult, and the bouncy rhythm makes it easy for the hasty reader to overlook the fact that this is a poem about a distressed person. Tell students that the last stanza serves as a kind of summation. After discussing it with the class, go back and reread the whole poem aloud.

READING THE POEM   You might begin by asking your students if they have ever wanted to live in a different time or place. Which ones? You might make a list on the chalkboard, and conduct a preference poll. You can then point out that a longing for other times is an almost universal human phenomenon, and Miniver Cheevy is the classic example in American literature. Read the poem aloud.

RETEACHING ALTERNATIVES   Have students write the numbers 1 through 8 on a sheet of paper and state, in one simple sentence for each stanza, what character trait of Miniver's each stanza depicts.

Responding to the Poem   Text page 636

Answers to the questions in the Pupil's Edition appear in the Annotated Teacher's Edition.

Writing About the Poems

For help in revising their compositions, refer students to **Grammar, Usage, and Mechanics: A Reference Guide** on text pages 1183–1228 at the back of their books.

A CREATIVE RESPONSE
1. Using Another Point of View   Students may also want to have Cory reveal the reasons for his suicide.

▶ CRITERIA FOR EVALUATING THE ASSIGNMENT Whether in verse or in prose, the first-person account fits the character of Richard Cory as revealed in the poem. It reports, especially, what Cory thinks of the people who look up to him.

2. Answering a Speaker   Have students list some suggestions they could give Cheevy. What hobbies, volunteer

work, travel, books, relationships might they suggest to help him accept the "here and now"?

▶ CRITERIA FOR EVALUATING THE ASSIGNMENT The letter gives Miniver Cheevy some practical advice on how to be happy with who he is.

A CRITICAL RESPONSE
3. Responding to the Poems   Note that the writing assignment outlines five specific aspects students might write about. Discuss all five areas but let students choose the areas that interest them most.

▶ CRITERIA FOR EVALUATING THE ASSIGNMENT The paper responds to "Miniver Cheevy" and "Richard Cory" and uses quotes from the poems to support its comments on one or more of the following areas: characterization, tone, verse forms, use of irony, or view of life and human nature.

4. Comparing Characters   Have students review the passages from Emerson (text pages 187–203) and Thoreau (text pages 204–225) to find comments on human nature suitable to this assignment. Write on the board quotations that students suggest.

▶ CRITERIA FOR EVALUATING THE ASSIGNMENT The essay shows how Robinson's characters—Richard Cory and Miniver Cheevy—are distortions of an ideal proposed by Emerson or Thoreau. The essay also shows how Richard Cory and Miniver Cheevy are similar to and different from each other.

Extending the Poems

Robinson, whose career began in the 1890's, has certain affinities with the Naturalists, though he is not usually classified as one of them. You might have students compare and contrast his bleak view of human life with that of Stephen Crane, using Crane's poem, "War Is Kind" (text page 463) as an example. Robinson was only two years older than Crane.

Edgar Lee Masters

Like Robinson, Masters is remembered mostly for character portraits in verse. The differences between the two artists in other respects, however, are great. Robinson was a stylist and prosodist of the highest caliber who managed to infuse conventional forms with a degree of new life at a time when they were on the wane. Masters was an indifferent stylist whose attempts at traditional verse were undistinguished and whose free verse has a prosy plainness. Robinson was first and foremost a poet, and his single-minded pursuit of poetry left him impoverished through much of his life. Masters was a lawyer who worked at poetry as an avocation. Masters's one notable

book of poetry, *Spoon River Anthology*, can be compared with Robinson's long roster of distinguished, if little read, volumes.

In his single great book, however, Masters produced one of the landmarks of twentieth-century American literature. It is more a thematic landmark than a poetic one. It did not influence the art of writing verse. But it did serve as a touchstone for later works—often works of prose, like Sherwood Anderson's *Winesburg, Ohio*—that show the unhappiness beneath the façades of ordinary small-town Americans.

RICHARD BONE

Objectives

1. To respond to the poem's message
2. To identify analogy
3. To invent names for fictional characters that reflect their traits

Introducing the Poem

This is a free verse poem in the plain-spoken voice of a Spoon River resident. Have students note the absence of figurative language and Masters's use of dialogue. The people standing round the shop speak of the dead in clichés.

BACKGROUND ON THE POEM ''Richard Bone'' can be considered the keynote poem of *Spoon River Anthology*, since it is about a carver of epitaphs and Masters himself is writing epitaphs on the lives of his characters. Here we find the crucial idea of the pleasant façade that conceals the unpleasant truth about people's lives. Here, too, we see the plainness of Masters's free-verse style in contrast with the more flowing styles of Whitman and Jeffers or the more highly charged style of Dickinson. An interesting exercise might be to have students rearrange the line breaks so that the lines end on different words.

THE LITERAL MEANING Richard Bone makes a living carving epitaphs to order, though he knows he is carving falsehoods.

Teaching Strategies

PROVIDING FOR CULTURAL DIFFERENCES Depending upon your region, students may or may not be very receptive to the idea that conventional small-town life hides a multitude of hypocrisies. The important point here is that although Masters is writing about a single fictitious town, his unveiling of the façade of society has universal applications.

PROVIDING FOR DIFFERENT LEVELS OF ABILITY The last five lines of the poem are the most challenging. Many students will need help understanding, ''And made myself party to the false chronicles / Of the Stones,'' and the idea of a historian writing without really knowing the truth. Advanced students may want to discuss the difference between being hypocritical and being unable to know the full truth.

READING THE POEM Have a student volunteer read the poem aloud. If the poem puzzles students, you might want to reread it aloud yourself, stopping to answer questions at points where they arise.

RETEACHING ALTERNATIVES   If some students still have trouble understanding the poem, you might ask them to write their own paraphrase of it, in one or two brief sentences.

Responding to the Poem   Text page 639

Answers to the questions in the Pupil's Edition appear in the Annotated Teacher's Edition.

Writing About the Poem

For help in revising their compositions, refer students to **Grammar, Usage, and Mechanics: A Reference Guide** on text pages 1183–1228 at the back of their books.

A CREATIVE RESPONSE
Inventing Names for Characters   Discuss the examples given in the writing assignment to be sure students grasp the point.

▶ CRITERIA FOR EVALUATING THE ASSIGNMENT   The surnames invented by the students somehow suggest the characters' traits. Ask students to explain their thinking.

LUCINDA MATLOCK   Text page 640

Objectives

1. To enjoy a famous character poem about a strong woman
2. To explain the poem's theme
3. To analyze the poet's attitude toward the subject

Introducing the Poem

The characterization in this poem is much stronger than in the preceding one. Where the voice of Richard Bone primarily expresses a theme, without providing details of the speaker's private life, the voice of Lucinda Matlock bursts with energy. In line after vividly detailed line, she tells us of the specific pleasures and duties of her ninety-six years. Because of the cataloguing of events and scenes, this poem moves at a much more energetic pace than the shorter "Richard Bone." "Lucinda Matlock" is written in free verse.

THE LITERAL MEANING   A woman reminisces about her ninety-six years and scolds the younger generation.

Teaching Strategies

PROVIDING FOR CULTURAL DIFFERENCES   Students new to American culture will need help with terms such as playing *snap-out*, spinning, weaving, gathering medicinal herbs. Some of your students have had this kind of nostalgic past in their family backgrounds. All students should be able to relate to Lucinda Matlock's vigor and optimism in her old age.

PROVIDING FOR DIFFERENT LEVELS OF ABILITY   Some students may be less excited by the characterization than others. The poem is not difficult, however, and the essential facts of Lucinda Matlock's life should not pose a comprehension problem.

READING THE POEM   This poem is a natural for an energetic female student to read aloud.

RETEACHING ALTERNATIVES   You might ask your students to think of their own grandmothers or great-grandmothers. How were they similar to Lucinda Matlock? How were they different? You might then ask them to write a brief description of Lucinda's character in a short paragraph.

Objectives

1. To respond to a poem about a character

2. To identify simile and irony

3. To describe tone

4. To write a paragraph comparing two poems

Introducing the Poem

It is important for students to understand that Butch Weldy's industrial accident took place at a time when workers' compensation laws, safety codes, and the laws of liability in general did not exist. Few industrial workers were protected by unions as we know them.

Masters uses two similes in this free-verse poem. The fried eggs simile is both horrifying and startling because of its contrast to Butch's plain speech and matter-of-fact tale.

THE LITERAL MEANING "Butch" Weldy tells of how he was horribly burned, blinded, and injured in an accident in the canning works. Because a fellow worker was at fault, the judge ruled the factory did not have to pay him anything.

Teaching Strategies

PROVIDING FOR CULTURAL DIFFERENCES You might ask students to express their views on the justice available in courts today, based on their own experiences and those of friends, family, and members of the community.

PROVIDING FOR DIFFERENT LEVELS OF ABILITY Some students may require a rereading and a paraphrase before they can accurately visualize the accident and comprehend the trial verdict. Students with legal ambitions may be particularly interested in this poem, and helpful in discussion.

READING THE POEM Have a student read the poem aloud.

RETEACHING ALTERNATIVES Ask your students how they would feel if they suffered an accident like Butch's. (They would probably feel anger, bitterness, despair.) Have them reread the poem to see whether Butch expresses any of these emotions directly.

Responding to the Poem

Text pages 640, 643

Answers to the questions in the Pupil's Edition appear in the Annotated Teacher's Edition.

Writing About the Poems

For help in revising their compositions, refer students to **Grammar, Usage, and Mechanics: A Reference Guide** on text pages 1183–1228 at the back of their books.

A CRITICAL RESPONSE

Comparing and Contrasting Poems Discuss both " 'Butch' Weldy" and "Mrs. George Reece," especially in terms of characters and message.

▶ CRITERIA FOR EVALUATING THE ASSIGNMENT The paper shows both similarities and differences between the two poems. (Both recount a personal tragedy that they did not cause; both describe injustice. "Butch" shows anger and self-pity; Mrs. Reece, a sense of her own accomplishments and integrity. The message of "Mrs. George Reece" is that one cannot control tragedy and injustice—only one's response to events.)

Extending the Poems

Some of your students might be interested in collaborating to create their own "Spoon Rivers" about their community or about fictitious towns they make up. They can create a set of characters from contemporary America—whether small-town or not—and write brief portraits in simple free verse. They need not imitate Masters's ironic, bitter tone.

Primary Sources

Text page 643

THE GENESIS OF SPOON RIVER

The fictitious small town has a long and honorable tradition in American literature: Masters's Spoon River, Anderson's Winesburg, Faulkner's Jefferson, Robinson's Tilbury Town, Bret Harte's Poker Flat, Updike's Olinger, Crane's Whilomville. Then there are the real towns that have been raised to almost mythic status by individual writers: Steinbeck's Salinas, Twain's Hannibal. Based on the readings by these authors that students have done, they might glean details about the towns and then write descriptions of one or more of them.

Paul Laurence Dunbar

Dunbar was the son of a fugitive slave who had fought on the Union side in the Civil War. He won high academic honors in an all-white high school. But because his skin was very dark, he was subject to further discrimination even within the boundaries of those jobs available to African American men at the time and could only find work as an elevator operator. Later, at the age of twenty-one, he was more fortunate in landing a job as Frederick Douglass's assistant at the Haiti Pavilion at the 1893 Chicago World's Fair. (Douglass was then the American consul of Haiti.) Dunbar benefitted from the inspiration of being near the great man, but perhaps more, he desperately needed the five dollar weekly wage from this temporary job.

William Dean Howells, who had championed Twain, James, and Crane early in their careers, was largely responsible for bringing Dunbar's work before the public. But he did so in a rather patronizing manner. His introduction to *Lyrics of Lowly Life* praises Dunbar for depicting the emotional and intellectual limitations of African Americans. It's not surprising, then, that Dunbar felt considerable ambivalence about his popular success.

THE HAUNTED OAK

Objectives

1. To respond to a poem about racial injustice
2. To analyze symbolic meanings and tone
3. To explain the use of meter, rhyme, and repetition
4. To set the poem to music
5. To write a paragraph analyzing imagery
6. To analyze the use of archaic diction

Introducing the Poem

This poem deals with lynching in the form of a traditional ballad, with old-fashioned poetic diction and the deliberate use of archaic words like *trow*. It raises the interesting question of whether the poetic technique is suited to its subject. On one hand, the form creates a certain mood of timeless outrage that expresses the poet's feelings. On the other hand, the reader may be left with a sense that Dunbar has decked the subject out in inappropriate garb. For many readers, Dunbar seems to have prettified his subject for a genteel audience by presenting the symbolic utterances of a personified hanging tree rather than depicting the realistic horror of a lynching.

Note that the ballad stanza has alternating lines of iambic tetrameter and trimeter with an *abcb* rhyme scheme. Have students notice the two questions in the poem and the use of repetition toward the poem's end.

THE LITERAL MEANING A passer-by asks an oak bough why it is bare, and the oak replies. It tells the story of the lynching of a guiltless man, who was hanged on the oak tree bough. The dying man cursed and the bough felt his pain. The judge rides by, cursed by mortal fear. The oak tree bough is haunted and bears no leaves.

Teaching Strategies

PROVIDING FOR CULTURAL DIFFERENCES Students in different parts of the country may react to this poem in different ways. Among African American literary critics, there is disagreement about whether to honor Dunbar as a forerunner or reprehend him for indulging in highly stereotyped dialect depictions of African American life. While "The Haunted Oak" is not in dialect, and does express anger at injustice, students may feel that it is a rather tame protest because of its conventional, ballad form.

PROVIDING FOR DIFFERENT LEVELS OF ABILITY Many students will have difficulty penetrating the deliberate antiquity of the poem's style. Careful attention to Analyzing Language and Style (text page 646) should help them substitute modern words for the archaic ones.

READING THE POEM In order to emphasize the speaker change after the first stanza, you might want to have one student read that stanza aloud—or read it aloud yourself—and another student read the rest of the poem.

RETEACHING ALTERNATIVES   Divide the class into nine groups—one for each stanza—and have each group paraphrase its stanza into simple language. Then have each group share its paraphrase with the class.

Responding to the Poem   Text page 645

Answers to the questions in the Pupil's Edition appear in the Annotated Teacher's Edition.

Writing About the Poem

For help in revising their compositions, refer students to **Grammar, Usage, and Mechanics: A Reference Guide** on text pages 1183–1228 at the back of their books.

A CREATIVE RESPONSE

1. Setting the Poem to Music   Students may wish to collaborate with a partner or small group; the assignment is optional. Students of music may be able to suggest an existing tune to which the poem can be set.

▶ CRITERIA FOR EVALUATING THE ASSIGNMENT   The student (or group) should sing the song or have another student sing it for the class. Give extra credit for any effort in this optional assignment.

A CRITICAL RESPONSE

2. Analyzing Imagery   Have students list and discuss the images they find in "The Haunted Oak," and draw some conclusions about the imagery, before they begin to write.

▶ CRITERIA FOR EVALUATING THE ASSIGNMENT   The essay comments on the use of imagery in "The Haunted Oak" and cites examples of images that involve sight, hearing, and touch.

Analyzing Language and Style

ARCHAIC DICTION

1. *Pray* (line 1), *trow* (line 5), *sore* (line 11), *smote on* (line 19), *nigh* (line 20), *throe* (line 23).
2. Let us *pray* (speak to God). My broken arm is *sore* (it hurts). The others are rarely used.
3. *Please* (line 1), *believe* (line 5), *severely* (line 11), *struck* (line 19), *near* (line 20), *agony* (line 23). The effect is to modernize the poem, but only in part, leaving expressions (such as line 14) sounding as if they come from another era (as they do).

Primary Sources   Text page 646

DUNBAR AND DIALECT POETRY

The comparison between Dunbar's dialect poems and James Weldon Johnson's folk poems is interesting. Using stereotyped dialect, Dunbar achieved results that can be seen as demeaning. Using standard English filled with the rhythms and idioms of African American speech, Johnson produced moving and authentic, though sometimes somewhat watered-down, folk poems with engaging characters and stirring depictions of African American religious life. Refer students ahead to Johnson's "Go Down Death" (text page 681) so they can understand Johnson's position.

Edna St. Vincent Millay

Text page 647

Nowadays Millay's name is better known than her work. Overshadowed by the more powerful, more original poets of the generation that followed her, she is now regarded as a minor lyricist. It would be a mistake, however, to view her as a prissy or genteel poet. She was in the vanguard of her age in matters of women's rights, took public stands on many issues of the day, and led a life that was free-spirited and eventful. The contrast with Emily Dickinson is interesting: The recluse of Amherst was a dazzlingly original poet, while Millay, the Greenwich Village personality, was quite conservative in her literary efforts.

Despite her lack of depth and complexity, Millay was a highly accomplished craftsman with a knack for simple, evocative descriptions of nature and the emotions of love. She was particularly adept at the sonnet form, and her 1931 volume of sonnets, *Fatal Interview*, helped revive that form in her time. She was a favorite poet of young people in an era when it was widely believed that young people could solve the problems of injustice and change the world for the better.

RECUERDO

Text page 648

Objectives

1. To respond to a famous memory poem
2. To identify metaphor
3. To describe meter and rhyme scheme
4. To analyze the connotations of images

Introducing the Poem

This poem is a model of simplicity in its use of language. In the entire poem there are only two words of more than two syllables: *underneath* and *bucketful*. The same two lines are used to begin each stanza. And the reiteration of very common words—*we, very, and*—gives the poem rhythm and melodic charm. Not every poem on every subject, of course, can be quite so simple. But "Recuerdo" provides a good lesson for students, showing that poetic description does not necessary imply difficulty or over-blown effects.

You might ask your students to think of good times they've had with people they've loved—very simple activities like taking a walk or a ride, looking at nature or buildings or people. This is exactly the kind of experience, and emotion, Millay is evoking.

The Literal Meaning   The speaker recalls a happy youthful experience with a friend—riding a ferry back and forth all night till sunrise, lying on a hilltop looking at the moon, buying apples and pears and a morning paper.

Teaching Strategies

Providing for Cultural Differences   There is a certain air of slumming in this description of two young lovers on a ferry, bestowing kindness on a poor woman by purchasing her apples and pears. Students from some backgrounds may identify more with the old woman than with the young lovers. You might point out that the young lovers themselves are only of modest means, as the remark in the last line implies.

Providing for Different Levels of Ability   All students will be able to undersand this poem. You may encounter some resistance in persuading your more advanced students of the virtue of its simplicity.

Reading the Poem   Play the audiocassette recording that accompanies this poem. Or have three students divide the lines for an oral interpretation.

Reteaching Alternatives   You needn't belabor the poem, but you might ask students to locate the specific, straightforward descriptions of lying on a hilltop, eating fruit, and so forth.

Analyzing Language and Style

IMAGERY AND FEELINGS
1. *Shrieking, shrilling.*
2. "An overripe orange," "a putrid lemon," "a damaged coin."
3. "A stringy-haired head."
4. She could have snarled or spat at the people and snatched at the apples and pears instead of thanking them.

DIRGE WITHOUT MUSIC

Objectives

1. To respond to a poem about death

2. To analyze the use of rhythm and rhyme

3. To write an imaginary conversation between two speakers

4. To write an essay responding to the poem's attitude toward death

5. To compare and contrast two poems

Introducing the Poem

In stark contrast to "Recuerdo" (a still-young poet's memories of past joys), "Dirge Without Music" is the meditation of a mature person on sorrows to come. During her own later years, Millay was in poor health and drank excessively, perhaps to numb the grief she felt after the deaths of several friends and relatives. After her husband's death in 1949, she was alone for the remaining year of her life.

The poem is written in a variable meter with an *abab* rhyme scheme. Much of the poem's sad music comes from repeated phrases and words. Millay also uses slant rhymes, internal rhymes, and long, irregularly syncopated phrases. The three short sentences in the last line give the poem a strong ending.

THE LITERAL MEANING The speaker repeatedly voices her refusal to be resigned to death, to the loss of loved ones. She expresses her disapproval—that all the life is suddenly "gone to feed the roses."

Teaching Strategies

PROVIDING FOR CULTURAL DIFFERENCES Students from all cultures will relate to the speaker's profound sense of loss. The poem suggests no hope of immortality, but students from strongly religious backgrounds may want to express more optimistic views of death, and some may believe in reincarnation.

PROVIDING FOR DIFFERENT LEVELS OF ABILITY Some students may have trouble appreciating the quiet mournfulness of the poem's tone. You might point out that despite its lack of verbal pyrotechnics, this is a poem of

strong grief rather than resignation: Indeed, the phrase, "I am not resigned," is used three times.

READING THE POEM Read the poem aloud, and ask for students' responses. How does it make them feel? What does it make them think about? What would they say to comfort the speaker?

RETEACHING ALTERNATIVES In discussion, ask students to find those phrases where Millay most specifically characterizes the qualities of the people she misses. Then have them find the phrases where she most specifically expresses her own reaction.

Responding to the Poem

Answers to the questions in the Pupil's Edition appear in the Annotated Teacher's Edition.

Writing About the Poems

For help in revising their compositions, refer students to **Grammar, Usage, and Mechanics: A Reference Guide** on text pages 1183–1228 at the back of their books.

A CREATIVE RESPONSE

1. Writing a Conversation Topics that allow the speakers to show contrasting attitudes toward life would include the meaning of life or the value of small joys. Have students brainstorm other topics that would work.

▶ CRITERIA FOR EVALUATING THE ASSIGNMENT The conversation reveals attitudes appropriate to the speakers in Millay's "Recuerdo" and "Dirge Without Music."

A CRITICAL RESPONSE

2. Responding to the Poem Discuss both sides of the issue in class until reasons have emerged for each side of the question.

▶ CRITERIA FOR EVALUATING THE ASSIGNMENT The essay gives reasons in support of its contention that "Dirge Without Music" expresses either an immature or a mature attitude toward death.

3. Comparing and Contrasting Poems Since students have reviewed "Thanatopsis" for other comparative essays, they may be able to complete the chart with no lengthy review of that poem. Have students work together to discuss and complete the chart on the chalkboard. Students should use the chart as they write their essays. (Bryant's poem expresses a totally opposite view from Millay's. Bryant finds comfort in the thought that each dead person joins all others to "mix with the elements." Millay rages and is not in any way resigned to death. Bryant's tone is peaceful, serene; Millay's is angry and mournful. Bryant uses blank verse—iambic pentameter but no regular rhyme; Millay uses rhymes, but a variable rhythm and pattern of stresses.)

Primary Sources   Text page 651

"THE BRAWNY MALE SENDS HIS PICTURE"
Though Millay may not have deliberately tried to hide the fact that she was a woman when she entered the poetry contest, it can't be denied that literary critics and judges have in the past been known to respond more favorably to the works of men. As a result, some female writers have used male pen names. Ask students to name some of them. (George Eliot, Isak Dinesen, the Brontë sisters.)

Robert Frost Text page 652

Frost's poetry invites interesting comparisons with some of the poets students have already studied. Like Emerson, Frost was a New England nature poet, but unlike Emerson, he was not a mystic. Frost found beauty in nature, and sought repose there, but did not seek in it an intimate contact with a transcendent spiritual force. While he makes rich use of nature in his imagery, his fundamental concern is with the choices and predicaments that make for happiness or unhappiness in human lives.

In his use of dramatic monologues and character studies, Frost resembles Masters and Robinson, but his style is much more skillful than the former's, and yet his language is much less "literary" than the latter's. In addition, unlike Masters and Robinson—and also unlike Sherwood Anderson, Erskine Caldwell, William Faulkner, and a good many other regionalists—Frost has no specific, unified location for his work. He has no "Spoon River" or "Tilbury Town" or "Yoknapatawpha County." Most of his poems take place within a New England landscape, but exact locations are left vague, and the poems do not contain cross-references to each other. Frost's farms, hills, pastures, woods, are universal settings, regionally accented but not parochial.

In the rhythms of his poetry, Frost tried to capture the rhythms of ordinary talk: what he called "sound-posture." He made this task more difficult for himself by refusing to write in free verse, at a time when most of the important new American poets were turning to that form. But Frost attempted to harmonize the rhythms of speech with the traditional meters of English verse. When successful, this produced a highly sophisticated, complex, and supple versification with a simple vocabulary.

Frost's poems generally "grow" in theme from beginning to end, imitating the process of human observation and thought. They often begin with a deceptively quiet description of a natural phenomenon or a situation, then proceed to develop it in such a way that we begin to see symbolic applications. The last line or two of a Frost poem often states, sometimes obliquely, a piece of wisdom gained from thought or experience.

DESIGN Text page 654

Objectives

1. To respond to a poem
2. To analyze similes, rhyme scheme, and tone
3. To write an essay responding to a critic's comment
4. To contrast the use of the spider image in three selections
5. To write an essay comparing two poems

Introducing the Poem

This short poem follows the strict conventions of the Petrarchan or Italian sonnet. The iambic pentameter lines are grouped into an octave with an *abbaabba* rhyme scheme and a sestet with an *acaacc* rhyme. Note that the poem uses only three rhymes. The octave contains four startling similes, and the sestet poses three unanswerable questions and ends with a wry comment.

BACKGROUND ON THE POEM   This poem was originally printed in an anthology in 1922, yet Frost himself did not include it in any of his own volumes until 1936.

The poem deals with the most serious theme of cosmic design versus cosmic accident, yet it also contains sparks of Frost's quirky humor. The description of the spider in the first line, especially the word *dimple*, makes it sound somewhat like a baby. Line 5 clearly echos breakfast food advertisements. Frost may have been implying a correspondence between what he finds appalling in nature and in humanity.

THE LITERAL MEANING   The speaker describes seeing a white spider holding a white moth atop a white flower, and wonders about the philosophical implications of what made them the way they are and what brought them together.

Teaching Strategies

PROVIDING FOR CULTURAL DIFFERENCES   Colors have different meanings in different cultures. (White, for example, is the color of mourning in some eastern cultures; in western cultures, mourners wear black.) The poem emphasizes the color white (the word is used five times in fourteen lines). Ask students to discuss what the color suggests or "means" in their ethnic or racial backgrounds.

PROVIDING FOR DIFFERENT LEVELS OF ABILITY
Though the poem's vocabulary is not difficult, it is an intellectually challenging piece at any level. In the octave, Frost describes a delicate but gruesome scene of a white spider gripping a white moth on a white flower. In the sestet, he asks what force brought them there, and whether cosmic design works on even such a small scale as this, and why the universe is so often appalling. These questions are similar to those Blake asks in "The Tyger."

READING THE POEM   You might ask your students whether they have ever looked at small, seemingly innocent plants or animals (insects, birds, small animals) and been appalled by the cruelty that occurs in apparently peaceful backyards and fields. Tell them that this is precisely the kind of experience Frost is writing about. Play the audiocassette recording that accompanies this poem.

RETEACHING ALTERNATIVES   The first eight lines paint a picture, and it might help some students if you actually draw a quick picture of the spider, moth, and flower, on the chalkboard. Ask students to reread the poem and paraphrase the questions the speaker asks about these three white things.

Answers to the questions in the Pupil's Edition appear in the Annotated Teacher's Edition.

Writing About the Poem

For help in revising their compositions, refer students to **Grammar, Usage, and Mechanics: A Reference Guide** on text pages 1183–1228 at the back of their books.

A CRITICAL RESPONSE
1. Responding to a Critic   Read and discuss Perrine's comment on Frost's "Design," checking for understanding. Ask students what in the poem might suggest "the problem of evil."

▶ CRITERIA FOR EVALUATING THE ASSIGNMENT   A clearly stated thesis statement agrees or disagrees with Perrine's comment. If students disagree, they state their idea of the theme. Students give reasons for the stance taken.

2. Contrasting Three Selections   Note that the assignment calls for attention to the *differences* in use of spider imagery by Taylor, Edwards, and Frost. Turn to the appropriate pages (text pages 39 and 46), and discuss the use each writer makes of the spider.

▶ CRITERIA FOR EVALUATING THE ASSIGNMENT   The essay cites details from Taylor, Edwards, and Frost to support points made about differences among the three writers in their use of the spider image. (For Taylor the spider represents Hell attempting to trap and destroy humans. Edwards uses the spider to represent humans in a cruel image—a spider being held over a fire as humans dangle over Hell. Frost's spider is an insect with no symbolic meaning although it has negative overtones. Frost uses the spider incident to pose a profound question.)

3. Comparing Poems   Briefly review what each of the five listed poems is "about" before students make their selection and begin to complete the chart.

▶ CRITERIA FOR EVALUATING THE ASSIGNMENT   The essay briefly states similarities between Frost's "Design" and one of the other poems in terms of rhyme, rhythm, figures of speech, tone, and message.

NEITHER OUT FAR NOR IN DEEP

Text page 656

Objectives

1. To respond to the irony and symbolism in a poem

2. To recast the poem into the second person

3. To write a paragraph comparing the messages in literary works

4. To write a paragraph comparing two poems

Introducing the Poem

Frost wrote this poem in the simplest diction; few words are more than one syllable. A series of very short statements make up all but the last two lines, which pose another unanswerable question. The poem has a basic iambic trimeter rhythm with an *abab* rhyme scheme.

BACKGROUND ON THE POEM This is a poem critics disagree about, so you may expect your students to disagree also. Randall Jarrell considered it a profound statement, in a restrained tone, of the essential limitations of mankind. William H. Pritchard feels that Jarrell himself may have gone out too far and in too deep in interpreting it, while Richard Poirier sees it as a comic indictment of human conformity. Rolfe Humphries complains of its lack of "lyric" quality. The poem invites lively discussion by being carefully suspended between tones.

THE LITERAL MEANING The speaker describes people on a beach, watching the ocean.

Teaching Strategies

PROVIDING FOR CULTURAL DIFFERENCES Students from all cultures can relate to the poem's theme.

PROVIDING FOR DIFFERENT LEVELS OF ABILITY As in many of Frost's poems, the words of this poem, taken one by one, are not hard to understand; the difficulty lies in discerning what is beneath the placid surface. The last stanza is the most thematically explicit part of the poem, and the final two lines will probably require some paraphrasing.

READING THE POEM Frost himself, during his numerous public readings, enjoyed reading the same poem aloud two or three times to make sure the audience "got

it," and you may want to do that with this poem, as well as with some of his other short, cryptic lyrics, such as "Design," "Once by the Pacific," and "Nothing Gold Can Stay." Play the audiocassette recording that accompanies this poem.

RETEACHING ALTERNATIVES Ask students who are still having difficulty understanding the poem to restate the poem in a short prose paragraph.

Responding to the Poem

Text page 656

Answers to the questions in the Pupil's Edition appear in the Annotated Teacher's Edition.

Writing About the Poem

For help in revising their compositions, refer students to **Grammar, Usage, and Mechanics: A Reference Guide** on text pages 1183–1228 at the back of their books.

A CREATIVE RESPONSE

1. Revising the Poem Make the change to second person in the first stanza, asking students to supply other changes needed for smoothness, and discuss the effect on the tone of the poem. Assign use of the final stanza for the essay.

▶ CRITERIA FOR EVALUATING THE ASSIGNMENT The essay changes the final stanza of "Neither Out Far . . ." to second person and makes other changes necessary for smoothness. The essay explains how the stanza differs from Frost's in tone. (The change makes the poem's message more immediate and personal. The tone becomes almost accusing; Frost's tone is that of wry observer.)

2. Setting the Poem to Music Students who try this assignment deserve some extra credit. Have each composer perform the musical version.

A CRITICAL RESPONSE

3. Comparing Literary Works Briefly review Ishmael's reflections and discuss their similarity to Frost's.

▶ CRITERIA FOR EVALUATING THE ASSIGNMENT The paragraph states similarities between Ishmael's reflections on the human response to the sea in *Moby-Dick* and Frost's views in "Neither Out Far nor In Deep." In both, the sea is a comfort to those wearied by life on land. It is a source of renewal and "truth."

4. Comparing Poems Review Whitman's poem "On the Beach at Night Alone" in a brief class discussion.

▶ CRITERIA FOR EVALUATING THE ASSIGNMENT The paragraph notes similarities between Frost's and Whitman's messages, their poetic forms, and the overall effect of their poems. (In both poems people search for meaning in nature. In Whitman's poem the speaker finds meaning—the unity of all things in the universe. In Frost's the speaker merely reports other people's search without answers. Whitman's poem is free verse with a passionate tone; Frost uses regular rhyme and meter and a nonemotional, wry tone.)

BIRCHES

Text page 658

Objectives

1. To enjoy one of Frost's most popular poems

2. To find examples of metaphor, simile, and onomatopoeia

3. To summarize the poem's message

4. To write a paragraph or poem using an everyday sight to comment on a larger subject

5. To write a paragraph comparing Frost's poems with Puritan and Romantic attitudes

6. To write a paragraph of a Puritan's response to Frost's scene

7. To write an essay responding to the poem

Introducing the Poem

It is important for students to keep in mind that the birches Frost speaks about have not in fact been swung by a boy. That is merely what he says "I should prefer" (line 23). In fact, they have been bent by an ice storm.

BACKGROUND ON THE POEM Frost wrote this poem during his stay in England, when he was feeling homesick for New England. The critic John Kemp, in *Robert Frost and New England,* identifies "Birches" as the first poem in which, rather than describing nature impersonally and realistically, Frost adopts the voice of a Yankee sage purveying wisdom—a trend Kemp regrets.

THE LITERAL MEANING Seeing birches bent by an ice storm, the speaker wishes a boy has swung them. He dreams of becoming a birch-swinger himself.

Teaching Strategies

PROVIDING FOR CULTURAL DIFFERENCES Students who are not from rural New England may have a hard time visualizing, or even believing in, the idea of a young person swinging a birch tree, but it is a realistic fact. Students from many regions, however, will have had the experience of climbing trees.

PROVIDING FOR DIFFERENT LEVELS OF ABILITY The major difficulty in this poem is the shift from fact to fantasy. On seeing the bent birches, the speaker first enjoys imagining that a boy has swung them, but in lines 5–20, he returns to a factual description of an ice storm. He then whisks reality aside in favor of his preference for imagination: from line 43 to the end of the poem, he makes birch-swinging a metaphor for life, death, and rebirth.

READING THE POEM You'll probably want to preface the reading of the poem with a discussion of the practice of birch-swinging Frost describes. For purposes of reading the poem aloud, you can divide the poem into parts: lines 1 to the middle of line 5 (which you might want to read yourself to get things started), from there through line 20, line 21 to the middle of line 32, from there through line 40, from line 41 through line 49, and from line 50 to the end.

RETEACHING ALTERNATIVES Discuss question 6 in class. Then have students break into small groups to summarize the poem's "story" and its message.

Responding to the Poem

Text page 659

Answers to the questions in the Pupil's Edition appear in the Annotated Teacher's Edition.

Writing About the Poem

Assignments 1, 2, and 3 relate Frost's work to earlier traditions. You may wish to allow students to choose one as an essay topic. Assignment 4 analyzes Frost's poetic theory.

For help in revising their compositions, refer students to **Grammar, Usage, and Mechanics: A Reference Guide** on text pages 1183–1228 at the back of their books.

A CREATIVE RESPONSE

1. Reading Nature   By now students have read many selections that move from observing nature to moral or philosophical comment. They should need no further models. Many students will feel more comfortable with this assignment if they can collaborate with a partner or small group.

▶ CRITERIA FOR EVALUATING THE ASSIGNMENT   The paragraph or poem moves from an everyday sight or event to comment on a much larger subject. If students have written a poem, call on volunteers to read their poems aloud.

A CRITICAL RESPONSE

2. Comparing Writings   Discuss how the Puritans find moral significance in nature, how Romantics read philo-sophical observations in nature, and how Frost may fit into one of these traditions.

▶ CRITERIA FOR EVALUATING THE ASSIGNMENT   The essay defines the tradition to which Frost seems to belong and offers cogent reasons in support of that position.

3. Comparing Attitudes   Review the Puritan tendency to see moral or religious lessons in natural events.

▶ CRITERIA FOR EVALUATING THE ASSIGNMENT   The paragraph explains how a Puritan would relate the bending of birches to human moral attitudes or behavior.

4. Responding to the Poem   Clarify Frost's meaning as necessary, especially the words *delight* and *wisdom*. Ask students to refer to specific lines to support their statements.

▶ CRITERIA FOR EVALUATING THE ASSIGNMENT   The essay defines *delight* and *wisdom*. "Birches" clearly fits the model. Lines 41–59 are "wisdom"; the beginning of the poem "delight."

MENDING WALL

Text page 660

Objectives

1. To enjoy another famous Frost poem

2. To explain a simile

3. To interpret the symbol of the wall

4. To write an answer, changing the speaker in the poem

5. To write a paragraph comparing two poems

Introducing the Poem

Frost's famous refrain, "Good fences make good neighbors," contains several possible levels of ironic meaning in this poem. As is pointed out in question 10 (text page 662), the character who needs the wall less is the one who initiates the yearly mending. Critic Richard Poirer suggests that even if good fences don't make good neighbors, good fence-*making* does.

The poem is also notable for its wonderfully flexible use of blank verse. A line-by-line scansion of at least part of the work would be appropriate for teachers and classes who are interested in that aspect of technique.

THE LITERAL MEANING   Each spring, two neighbors mend the stone wall separating their property, after the freezing of the ground has displaced some stones.

Teaching Strategies

PROVIDING FOR CULTURAL DIFFERENCES   As in many Frost poems, students from rural or New England backgrounds are likely to be quickest to respond to the setting of this poem. Fences and walls, however, are important features of urban and suburban settings as well. Students who have never seen a stone wall should look at the photo on page 661. Note that such low hand-built walls are not meant to be decorative but to mark a property boundary or to fence in a field.

PROVIDING FOR DIFFERENT LEVELS OF ABILITY

There are no words of more than two syllables in this 45-line poem, but Frost's simplicity of diction sometimes creates its own kind of difficulty. ESL students especially may require a paraphrase of the key line 35.

READING THE POEM   You might begin by asking your students what kinds of walls—tangible or intangible—separate them from their neighbors. Some students may live in apartments or houses surrounded by fences; others may lack fences around theirs. Why are walls especially important in apartment houses? (Neighbors' noises can annoy.) What effects do fences, or the lack of them, have on their daily lives?

RETEACHING ALTERNATIVES   You might ask your students to retell the poem in the form of a short prose paragraph. Have the voice of the speaker describe wall-mending and tell how he feels about wall-mending and about his neighbor.

Responding to the Poem   Text page 662

Answers to the questions in the Pupil's Edition appear in the Annotated Teacher's Edition.

Writing About the Poem

For help in revising their compositions, refer students to **Grammar, Usage, and Mechanics: A Reference Guide** on text pages 1183–1228 at the back of their books.

A CREATIVE RESPONSE

1. Changing the Poem's Voice   Discuss the possible responses a neighbor might make to the speaker's spoken and unspoken thoughts on walls. Since we know little about the neighbor, students are competely free to invent details. They can write either prose or poetry.

▶ CRITERIA FOR EVALUATING THE ASSIGNMENT   The first-person paragraph or poem has the neighbor responding to the poem's speaker.

A CRITICAL RESPONSE

2. Comparing Poems   Briefly call to mind Dickinson's main point in "The Soul selects . . . ," and discuss any connections the students see with "Mending Wall." (They should note that the neighbor's devotion to maintaining walls is like shutting the door in Dickinson's poem—a walling out.)

▶ CRITERIA FOR EVALUATING THE ASSIGNMENT   The paragraph clearly states what "Mending Wall" has in common with Dickinson's poem and cites details to support the points made. If students say the two poems have nothing in common, their position is also supported with references to the poem.

ONCE BY THE PACIFIC   Text page 663

Objectives

1. To respond to a poem about an approaching storm

2. To identify personification

3. To interpret symbolism

4. To write an essay comparing two poems

Introducing the Poem

BACKGROUND ON THE POEM   This is a poem of vague prophecy, and Frost himself used it as evidence that he had prophesied a wide variety of unhappy events in his own and his friends' lives. His manuscript of the poem bore the notation, "as of 1880," possibly indicating that the poem's mood sprang from an experience on the California coast when Frost was six years old. Technically, the poem is a sonnet in rhymed couplets.

THE LITERAL MEANING The speaker describes a frightening storm seen once on the Pacific coast, and compares it to the end of the world.

Teaching Strategies

PROVIDING FOR CULTURAL DIFFERENCES Students who have lived near a seacoast may be able to share their personal experiences of ocean storms.

PROVIDING FOR DIFFERENT LEVELS OF ABILITY Some students may need help with the simile in lines 5 and 6, with the progression shore-cliff-continent in lines 8 and 9, with the meaning of lines 10 and 14.

READING THE POEM The poem is short enough to be read aloud by a well-prepared student. Or play the audiocassette recording that accompanies the poem.

RETEACHING ALTERNATIVES Ask students to compare this poem with Frost's "Neither Out Far nor In Deep" (text page 656). Have them discuss the tone, scene, and symbolism in each poem.

Responding to the Poem Text page 663

Answers to the questions in the Pupil's Edition appear in the Annotated Teacher's Edition.

Writing About the Poem

For help in revising their compositions, refer students to **Grammar, Usage, and Mechanics: A Reference Guide** on text pages 1183–1228 at the back of their books.

A CRITICAL RESPONSE
Comparing Poems Reread Whitman's poem, and have students work together to complete the prewriting chart. Direct them to use at least three of the items from the chart in their essays.

▶ CRITERIA FOR EVALUATING THE ASSIGNMENT The essay compares Frost's "Once by the Pacific" with Whitman's "On the Beach at Night" in terms of the following: message, use of symbols, tone, use of rhythms and rhymes, or use of imagery.

THE DEATH OF THE HIRED MAN
Text page 664

Objectives

1. To respond to a narrative poem

2. To identify and interpret imagery

3. To analyze irony

4. To state the poem's message

5. To write a paragraph setting the poem in contemporary surroundings

6. To write an essay analyzing the three characters in the poem

7. To analyze the use of blank verse

Introducing the Poem

The poem includes two of Frost's most quoted lines (the two definitions of "home" in lines 118–120). One school of criticism, typified by Richard Poirer and Louise Bogan, views Frost's pose as "Yankee sage"—a regrettable concession to the tastes of the mass audience. These critics wish he had stuck with impersonal nature realism. However, William H. Pritchard asserts that Frost considered it "a challenge . . . to bring out an interplay of sympathy and judgment by setting in motion the contrasting voices of man and woman." Frost also enjoyed the challenge of writing a long poem consisting mostly of the sounds of plain speech, but with passages of more elevated diction to prevent monotony.

Analyzing Language and Style (text page 669) helps students examine the poem's blank verse.

THE LITERAL MEANING A farm couple discuss Silas, an old, worn-out hired hand who has returned to their farm for shelter. They talk about his life and his relationship to them. Warren, the husband, does not want to take him in, but Mary convinces him that Silas has come home to die. When Warren goes to check on Silas, he finds him dead.

Teaching Strategies

PROVIDING FOR CULTURAL DIFFERENCES Ask students what would happen to an elderly and/or homeless person like Silas if he were a member of their cultural group or community. Where would he go? Who would be responsible for his care?

PROVIDING FOR DIFFERENT LEVELS OF ABILITY The sheer length of this poem may daunt less advanced students, but they will enjoy reading it aloud. Point out that it is essentially a short story in verse, and not long by those standards.

READING THE POEM Given its length, you might want to assign this poem as homework. If you have it read aloud, you might have one student read Mary's dialogue, another read Warren's, with a third student reading the narration.

RETEACHING ALTERNATIVES This poem is about relationships of duty and of emotion, and about how both elements enter into the creation of a home. While the hired man's relationship to the farm couple is the subject of the poem, Mary's and Warren's relationship to each other is at least as important. Ask students to discuss what the hired man's arrival reveals about the couple.

Responding to the Poem Text page 669

Answers to the questions in the Pupil's Edition appear in the Annotated Teacher's Edition.

Writing About the Poem

For help in revising their compositions, refer students to **Grammar, Usage, and Mechanics: A Reference Guide** on text pages 1183–1228 at the back of their books.

A CREATIVE RESPONSE
1. Extending the Poem Write on the chalkboard "city," "rural area," "suburb," "modern farm," and "migrant camp," and brainstorm for each heading some of the changes that would have to be made in conflict, characters, and resolution to accommodate the altered setting.

▶ CRITERIA FOR EVALUATING THE ASSIGNMENT The paragraph selects a new setting for "The Death of the Hired Man" and explains changes that would have to occur in conflict, characters, and resolution.

A CRITICAL RESPONSE
2. Analyzing Characters Discuss the writing assignment fully. Note that it lists the characters to be analyzed (one paragraph each) and the aspects of characterization to be covered.

▶ CRITERIA FOR EVALUATING THE ASSIGNMENT The essay devotes one paragraph each to Silas, Mary, and Warren. It analyzes each character's values, the character's conflict and handling of it, the effect the character has on others, and any changes the character undergoes.

Analyzing Language and Style

BLANK VERSE
1. Students are to recite the first ten lines aloud.
2. In the first ten lines, lines 4, 6, 7, 8, 9, and 10 scan as iambic pentameter; lines 1, 2, and 5 vary the meter.
3. At times Frost ends a sentence in mid-line or breaks a line into dialogue between two speakers. These seem to be deliberate "stops" rather than examples of Frost's "tripping" himself.
4. Lines chosen will vary. Some rearrangement of words and number of lines might occur, as in this revision of lines 78–81:
    He mentally associates Harold with Latin.
    He asked me what I thought of Harold's claim
    To study Latin because he likes it,
    As he likes the violin—
    What kind of argument is that?
5. Students will vary in agreeing or disagreeing with Frost. Ask them to try to provide reasons or examples to support their opinions.

NOTHING GOLD CAN STAY Text page 670

Objectives

1. To respond to a brief lyric about loss

2. To analyze symbolism

3. To analyze sound, rhythm, and tone

4. To write a paraphrase of the poem

5. To write a paragraph comparing two poems

Introducing the Poem

This little gem of a poem is written in iambic trimeter with variations in the first and last line. The poem has rhyming couplets. Question 6 alerts students to the poem's alliteration, slant rhyme, and assonance.

BACKGROUND ON THE POEM   Some of your students may already know this poem from S. E. Hinton's popular ''young adult'' novel *The Outsiders,* or from the successful movie that was made of it. In *The Outsiders,* when Ponyboy Curtis and Johnny Cade are watching a sunset, Ponyboy recites this poem, which becomes a repeated motif in the story. When Johnny dies, he tells Ponyboy to ''stay gold.''

The poem was part of a section of short lyrics, called ''Grace Notes,'' in Frost's 1923 volume, *New Hampshire.* The section included several of his best poems, such as ''To Earthward'' and ''Stopping by Woods on a Snowy Evening.''

THE LITERAL MEANING   Spring greenery, flowers, Eden, and dawn are four ''gold'' things that cannot stay.

Teaching Strategies

PROVIDING FOR CULTURAL DIFFERENCES   Students from eastern cultures may need a brief explanation of the story of the loss of Eden and the Greek myth of the Golden Age.

PROVIDING FOR DIFFERENT LEVELS OF ABILITY   The fact that the word *gold* is used here metaphorically may give some students trouble at first. The word is used to mean anything precious; thus, Eden is, metaphorically, ''gold.''

Note that the logical form of the poem is based on inductive reasoning. From statements about spring buds, Eden, and dawn, the speaker makes a generalization in the last line of the poem. The thinking process (moving from specific statements to generalization) involves an ''inductive leap.'' (See ''Making Generalizations,'' an **Exercise in Critical Thinking and Writing,** text page 625.)

READING THE POEM   This poem is not only short enough to be read by one student in less than a minute, but it is also short enough to memorize, if you feel your class would benefit. Play the audiocassette recording that accompanies this poem.

RETEACHING ALTERNATIVES   You might ask students to write a paragraph about something they have experienced and enjoyed that has not stayed. Or have them list some other ''gold'' things that cannot stay.

Responding to the Poem   Text page 670

Answers to the questions in the Pupil's Edition appear in the Annotated Teacher's Edition.

Writing About the Poem

For help in revising their compositions, refer students to **Grammar, Usage, and Mechanics: A Reference Guide** on text pages 1183–1228 at the back of their books.

A CREATIVE RESPONSE
1. Paraphrasing   Discuss questions 1–5 before students try to paraphrase the poem. Students will soon discover that a paraphrase in fewer words is difficult to impossible. Frost's poem is compressed and succinct.

▶ CRITERIA FOR EVALUATING THE ASSIGNMENT   All key ideas of the poem are present in the paraphrase.

A CRITICAL RESPONSE
2. Comparing Poems   Briefly review use of ''gold'' as a symbol in ''Eldorado'' and ''Miniver Cheevy.'' Suggest that students chart the elements for ''Nothing Gold Can Stay'' and either ''Eldorado'' or ''Miniver Cheevy'' before writing.

▶ CRITERIA FOR EVALUATING THE ASSIGNMENT   The paragraph tells how Frost's poem is similar to or different from Poe's or Robinson's poem in terms of use of gold as an image and symbol, message, tone, and poetic form and technique.

Extending the Poem

The statement, ''Nothing Gold Can Stay,'' invites the rejoinder, ''What about great poetry?'' You might discuss with your class the idea that literature, and all art, disproves Frost's assertion. Read aloud W. B. Yeats's ''Sailing to Byzantium'' for a comment on the timelessness of art.

Primary Sources   Text page 671

''**I MUST HAVE THE PULSE BEAT OF RHYTHM . . .**'' Frost's comments would make a good basis for discussion or for a brief essay on your students' own views of free verse compared to metered verse. You might ask whether they feel Frost was contradicting himself. In the first paragraph, he praises Whitman and castigates the American literary world for being slow to accept him. Isn't Frost showing the same kind of fearfulness in his reluctance to accept the free-verse of his own time? You might want to save a full discussion of this question until after students have read the free-verse poets in Unit Nine. They can then determine for themselves whether free verse is largely a momentary effect without staying power.

Ransom's *Selected Poems,* published in 1945, contains only forty-two poems: Ransom weeded out from his early work everything he considered less than first-rate. The critic Willard Thorp says, ''It would be difficult to name a single volume by an American poet in which the quality is so consistently high.''

Ransom was part of a great Southern renaissance in American writing that began in the 1920's and had affiliations with the Modernist movement in art throughout the Western world but retained an identity of its own. Most of the participants in this Southern renaissance were descendants of landowning families that had suffered reversals in the Civil War and Reconstruction but had regained enough prosperity to send their children to college. Before that generation, literature among the Southern gentry had been an amateur pursuit—admired, but practiced as a pastime like sports, rather than as a profession. The generation of the Fugitives, as they were called, deliberately set out to become professional writers in opposition to the traditions of their families. Among them were William Faulkner, Robert Penn Warren, Tennessee Williams, Thomas Wolfe, Katherine Anne Porter, Margaret Mitchell, and many others.

BELLS FOR JOHN WHITESIDE'S DAUGHTER

Text page 673

Objectives

1. To respond to a poem about the death of a young person

2. To identify a simile

3. To analyze the poem's tone

4. To write an essay comparing two poems

Introducing the Poem

The duality of Ransom's tone has often been noted by critics: He combines wit and tenderness, amalgamating the two into an irony that distances itself from feelings without denying them.

The poem's basic meter is iambic tetrameter with a trimeter line at the end of each stanza, but there are many variations in the feet. The *abab* rhyme scheme has some slant rhymes. Students can find alliteration, assonance, and internal rhymes as well.

THE LITERAL MEANING   The speakers, in first-person plural, recall the frolicsome behavior of a young girl whose funeral they are attending.

Teaching Strategies

PROVIDING FOR CULTURAL DIFFERENCES   Although Ransom is very much a Southern poet, there is nothing specifically Southern about the setting of this poem. Some students may be puzzled at the lightness of the tone for such a melancholy subject. Note that some of the lightness comes from the image of the girl chasing geese (lines 5–16) and the wry humor of lines 12 and 16.

PROVIDING FOR DIFFERENT LEVELS OF ABILITY The meaning of the poem is simple enough for all students to grasp. LEP students will need some help in seeing ''brown study'' as a metaphor for death.

READING THE POEM   Warn your students that they are about to read a rather light-hearted poem about the death of a child. The poem requires a good reader; plan to read it yourself.

RETEACHING ALTERNATIVES   You might ask your students to visualize who is speaking the poem. It is not an ''I''; it is a ''we.'' Who are they? What are they doing? What is the occasion?

PARTING, WITHOUT A SEQUEL

Objectives

1. To respond to a poem about loss
2. To analyze conflict and symbols
3. To evaluate the use of rhyme
4. To write an essay interpreting ambiguities in the poem
5. To respond to a critic's commentary
6. To study the multiple meanings of words

Introducing the Poem

This is a more difficult poem than "Bells for John Whiteside's Daughter," which presents a clear situation toward which the speaker has a complex reaction. In "Parting, Without a Sequel," the situation is ambiguous: A woman sends a man a letter of rejection, but we can sense her grief in the very act of sending it. Also, "Bells for John Whiteside's Daughter" gives us a picture of what has been lost, but "Parting, Without a Sequel" gives no details at all about the quality of the relationship that is being ended.

Ransom uses a variable meter, though basically iambic, in lines of varying length. The rhyme scheme is *abba*.

THE LITERAL MEANING   A woman sends an angry rejecting letter to a lover, but even as she sends it, she hopes the letter will be lost. Grieving, she stands under her father's oak and seems to hear it reproach her.

Teaching Strategies

PROVIDING FOR CULTURAL DIFFERENCES   Students from all backgrounds will relate to the poem without difficulty.

PROVIDING FOR DIFFERENT LEVELS OF ABILITY   Since much of the story of the poem is "written between the lines," many students will need some help in understanding the poem. Close attention to the Analyzing the Poem questions (text page 675) should help.

READING THE POEM   You might want to read and study both Ransom poems in the same lesson.

RETEACHING ALTERNATIVES   Ask each student to write a one- or two-sentence synopsis of the poem.

Responding to the Poems

Text pages 673, 675

Answers to the questions in the Pupil's Edition appear in the Annotated Teacher's Edition.

Writing About the Poems

For help in revising their compositions, refer students to **Grammar, Usage, and Mechanics: A Reference Guide** on text pages 1183–1228 at the back of their books.

A CRITICAL RESPONSE

1. Comparing Poems   Review both Ransom's poem and Lowell's "She Came and Went." Note that students are to compare speakers' emotions and views on death. Students should note that Lowell's poem expresses quiet resignation and remembered joy; Ransom's seems more angry and astonished. Neither poet suggests a life after death; both suggest that the dead "live on" in memory.

▶ CRITERIA FOR EVALUATING THE ASSIGNMENT   The essay cites examples from the two poems to support comments on similarities.

2. Filling in Meanings   Read the assignment aloud and have students silently jot down the first answers to the questions that come to mind. Then read the answers aloud and discuss them until students know the positions they wish to take in their essays.

▶ CRITERIA FOR EVALUATING THE ASSIGNMENT   The essay cites details from the poem to support its interpretation. (Line 11 suggests that the woman is older. The oak tree seems to speak though she does not talk to it. The poet's tone seems sympathetic.)

3. Comparing Poems   Briefly review Dickinson's poem. Students may wish to chart its similarities with Ransom's poem as they have done for similar assignments.

▶ CRITERIA FOR EVALUATING THE ASSIGNMENT   The essay cites similarities between Dickinson's "Heart! We will forget him" and Ransom's "Parting, Without a Sequel,'' in terms of messages, speakers, authors' tone, and imagery.

4. Responding to a Critic Discuss Young's comment and students' first impressions in terms of Ransom's poems. They should review both poems before writing the essay.

▶ CRITERIA FOR EVALUATING THE ASSIGNMENT Most students will agree with Young's evaluation and cite evidence from both poems to support their view. Students who disagree with Young also cite evidence from the poems.

Analyzing Language and Style

MULTIPLE MEANINGS OF WORDS

1. Letters of the alphabet. Ransom is also revealing the letter writer's anger.

2. Bridegroom, stable hand, manservant. ''Manservant'' applies to line 7, with ''bridegroom'' echoed also.

3. Sickly and pale. Both the archaic and the modern meanings are appropriate for line 19.

4. A *seer* is a visionary or prophet. The pun is likely.

5. *Vaunting* (line 13) means ''prideful'' or ''boastful.'' It may suggest a slight mockery of the tree's advice.

Robinson Jeffers
Text page 676

Jeffers worked in isolation throughout his career. He belonged to no poetic school or movement, and lived in and wrote about a region of the country that seemed quite remote at the time. He became well known for the experimentalism of his free verse, the unrelieved bleakness of his view of human life, and the lurid plots of his long narrative poems, many of which were taken from Greek myths. Today he is still admired as someone who took Whitman's brand of free verse and developed out of it a strong, majestic line of his own. Jeffers is best known for his moving, well-observed lyrics about the California coast. In general, however, critics today see Jeffers's bleakness as a symptom of a gloomy personal temperament rather than a convincingly thought-out view of life. They also tend to agree that the gore and horror in the plots of his long narrative poems is not a sufficient substitute for dramatic skill, and that his insistent preaching of pessimism often weighs down his verse.

SHINE, PERISHING REPUBLIC
Text page 677

Objectives

1. To respond to the poem's message

2. To interpret implied metaphor and tone

3. To write an essay responding to the poem

Introducing the Poem

Although this poem is pessimistic in its view of American society, Jeffers spoke more optimistically about democracy in 1940, during the only speaking tour of his life:

''Our democracy has provided, and still provides, the greatest freedom for the greatest number of people.'' He went on to say that democracy meant tolerance and the recognition of each person as an equal. Also, it involved ''no snobbery, and no flunkyism'' and a disregard for social classes.

The poem is written in free verse with very long lines. For its sound effects, the poem relies on alliteration, assonance, and repetition.

THE LITERAL MEANING The speaker, disgusted with human society, counsels his sons to live far from the cities' corruption and to love their fellow humans in moderation.

Teaching Strategies

PROVIDING FOR CULTURAL DIFFERENCES This poem is apt to stimulate a variety of emotional responses. Students from working-class backgrounds may see Jeffers's bitterness as the fruit of privilege; some other students may share his dissident views. The best approach is probably to welcome all views as making for lively discussion.

PROVIDING FOR DIFFERENT LEVELS OF ABILITY Jeffers is one of the more difficult poets in this unit, and you'll probably have to go through the poem slowly, stopping to define words and explain ideas and images.

READING THE POEM You may need to go through the poem twice. First, read the poem aloud, or have a student read it, in its entirety. Then read it once more with pauses for discussion whenever there are questions.

RETEACHING ALTERNATIVES This poem presents an idea that will challenge idealistic high school students: One should retreat from humanity rather than try to help it. At the same time, Jeffers is not recommending hedonism. You might want to use the novelty of his message as a focus for discussion. If students had a chance to speak directly to Jeffers, what would they say in response to this poem?

LOVE THE WILD SWAN

Text page 678

Objectives

1. To respond to a poem about nature and poetry
2. To interpret symbolism and extended metaphor
3. To rewrite the poem in the form of a dialogue
4. To identify exact rhymes and slant rhymes

Introducing the Poem

The poem is a sonnet in the form of an interior monologue. It thus presents a different side of Jeffers, who was known primarily for his experiments in free verse. ''Love the Wild Swan'' shows him as a highly competent technician in traditional rhyme and meter. The sonnet's meter is iambic pentameter, but the final line has seven feet. The rhyme scheme is *ababcdcd, efefgg*.

THE LITERAL MEANING In the octave, the poet bemoans the inadequacy of his verse to capture the beauty of the world. In the sestet, he corrects himself, saying that the beauty of the natural world is not to be captured but to be loved.

Teaching Strategies

PROVIDING FOR CULTURAL DIFFERENCES The poem makes use of the thematic traditions of Western literature: the wild swan as a symbol of beauty, the hunt as a metaphor for the poetic act. Students from other cultural backgrounds may be accustomed to thinking of poetry in different ways: poetry as ritual or celebration, perhaps.

PROVIDING FOR DIFFERENT LEVELS OF ABILITY Despite its beautiful sensory images, this is very much a poem of abstract ideas. More advanced students may relish the chance to make the connections between Jeffers's images and his message; others may need help, particularly with lines 2–3, 5–6, and 10–13.

READING THE POEM Since the poem is in the form of a statement and response, have one student read the first eight lines aloud and another student read the last six lines.

RETEACHING ALTERNATIVES The poem is about the frustration of being unable to achieve all that one hopes to achieve in one's work, and the consolation that one is able to achieve part of it anyway. Ask students to discuss experiences of this kind that they have had.

Answers to the questions in the Pupil's Edition appear in the Annotated Teacher's Edition.

Writing About the Poems

For help in revising their compositions, refer students to **Grammar, Usage, and Mechanics: A Reference Guide** on text pages 1183–1228 at the back of their books.

A CREATIVE RESPONSE

1. Rephrasing a Poem   Identifying Details questions 1 and 3 (page 679) clarify parts spoken by the two different speakers. Help students to see that the first speaker is artistic and passionate, perhaps even high-strung. The second speaker seems calmer, more objective, less self-centered.

▶ CRITERIA FOR EVALUATING THE ASSIGNMENT   The paper includes a brief description of each speaker, and rewrites the poem as a dialogue between them.

A CRITICAL RESPONSE

2. Responding to the Poem   Identifying Details questions 1, 2, and 3 (text page 679) will help students summarize Jeffers's view of America. Have students suggest

contemporary issues (environment, racism, homelessness, crime, and some positive issues). Each student should feel completely free to be optimistic or pessimistic (or something in between) about America today.

▶ CRITERIA FOR EVALUATING THE ASSIGNMENT   The essay summarizes views expressed in Jeffers's poem and clearly states whether or not these views are still valid. Students' opinions are supported with facts.

Analyzing Language and Style

RHYMES
1. Breast/least, can/swan.
2. Catch/wax.
3. Word/bird.

Extending the Poem

Encourage students to organize a panel discussion or informal debate to extend the questions raised in writing assignment 2. One member of the panel or debate team could present facts about a contemporary American problem. Students can further discuss or debate ways to solve each problem.

James Weldon Johnson
Text page 680

GO DOWN DEATH
Text page 681

Objectives

1. To respond to a moving poem that imitates a funeral sermon

2. To identify similes

3. To write a speech that Death might make

4. To write an essay comparing sermons

5. To compare and contrast two poems about death

6. To identify the influence of Whitman on the poet's style

Introducing the Poem

Johnson's free-verse poem uses repetition and parallel structure and the simple, everyday language of the preacher's audience. (See Analyzing Language and Style, text page 684.)

BACKGROUND ON THE POEM   In an anthology he edited in 1922 called *The Book of American Negro Poetry,* Johnson wrote: "What the colored poet in the United States needs to do is . . . find a form that will express the racial spirit by symbols from within rather than by symbols from without, such as the mere mutilation of English spelling and pronunciation. He needs a form that is freer and larger than dialect . . . a form expressing the imagery, the idioms . . . of the Negro, but which will also be capable of voicing the deepest and highest emotions and aspirations, and allow for the widest range of subjects and the widest scope of treatment.''

To a considerable degree, he succeeded in finding such a form in *God's Trombones,* his book of poetic sermons in the voices of African American preachers.

THE LITERAL MEANING   The preacher, speaking at Sister Caroline's funeral, tells how God called Death to come for Sister Caroline so that she could attain rest.

Teaching Strategies

PROVIDING FOR CULTURAL DIFFERENCES   Ask African American students how realistic this sermon in verse is. Students from all backgrounds will easily be able to enjoy the richness of its expression and characterization, and the solemn power of its emotion.

PROVIDING FOR DIFFERENT LEVELS OF ABILITY The important point for students to understand is that this is an oration in the voice of a preacher, not a narration in the voice of an impersonal narrator. The preacher, who knew Sister Caroline, is speaking to a church audience who also knew her.

READING THE POEM   To gain the full impact of this powerful oration, have your students read silently along with the audiocassette recording.

RETEACHING ALTERNATIVES   You might ask students to tell whether they think this is a good funeral sermon or not, and why. Would it comfort the mourning relatives? What does it teach about Death?

Responding to the Poem   Text page 684

Answers to the questions in the Pupil's Edition appear in the Annotated Teacher's Edition.

Writing About the Poem

For help in revising their compositions, refer students to **Grammar, Usage, and Mechanics: A Reference Guide** on text pages 1183–1228 at the back of their books.

A CREATIVE RESPONSE
1. Extending the Poem   Interpreting Meanings question 5 (text page 684) can help students refine their picture of Death as drawn by Johnson. Suggest that students read their papers aloud and revise them before making the final copy.

▶ CRITERIA FOR EVALUATING THE ASSIGNMENT   The paper reads well as a speech. It is appropriate to the character of Death as drawn by Johnson in ''Go Down Death.''

A CRITICAL RESPONSE
2. Comparing Sermons   Note that students are to seek both similarities and differences between Edwards's sermon and Johnson's poem in terms of imagery, figures of speech, message, tone, audience, and purpose.

▶ CRITERIA FOR EVALUATING THE ASSIGNMENT   The essay compares and contrasts Edwards's and Johnson's sermons in terms of imagery, figures of speech, message, tone, audience, and purpose. The essay cites examples to support points made.

3. Comparing and Contrasting Poems   Briefly review Millay's ''Dirge Without Music.'' Direct students' attention to the questions contained in the writing prompt.

▶ CRITERIA FOR EVALUATING THE ASSIGNMENT   Students should note fundamental differences. The speaker in Johnson's poem welcomes death as a rest from hardship, a union with Jesus in heaven. Millay's speaker, in contrast, rages against death that has cut off life's loves and pleasures, confining the dead in their graves in the earth.

Analyzing Language and Style

FREE VERSE AND THE ORATOR'S STYLE
1. For example: Line 1 uses repetition (Weep not, weep not); and lines 2, 3, and 7 each begin with ''She is'' or ''She's.''
2. For example: ''Left-lonesome daughter'' (line 4); ''She's only just gone home'' (line 5); ''But they didn't make no sound'' (line 29).
3. For example: Lines 16 (long) and 17 (very short); and lines 47–49 (short/long/short).

Primary Sources   Text page 685

GOD'S TROMBONES
The passage describes one kind of community leader, one kind of preacher. You might ask students to describe community and religious leaders they have known in their own experience.

Claude McKay

McKay, born in Jamaica, spent much of his life traveling. He emigrated to the American heartland to go to college, and then lived and worked in New England and New York. He visited England (where he met George Bernard Shaw), then the Soviet Union and France. Though his creative drive waned in his later years, he still produced important work in nonfiction, particularly his autobiography, *A Long Way from Home.*

AMERICA

Objectives

1. To respond to a poem about an African American's feelings about his country
2. To interpret images
3. To analyze a paradox
4. To capture the poet's feelings in a phrase
5. To compare and contrast two poems

Introducing the Poem

"America" is a sonnet in iambic pentameter, with the rhyme scheme *abab cdcd efef gg.*

THE LITERAL MEANING   The speaker says that he loves America although he feels its racist cruelty and injustice. He looks into the future and envisions America destroyed.

Teaching Strategies

PROVIDING FOR CULTURAL DIFFERENCES   Students from various cultures may have a wide variety of reactions to the bitterness expressed in this poem. You may want to act as moderator in the airing of views from all sides.

PROVIDING FOR DIFFERENT LEVELS OF ABILITY   Some students may be somewhat daunted by the richness of the poem's imagery. Virtually every line contains a simile or metaphor; you might work with students on creating paraphrases.

READING THE POEM   After reading the poem aloud the first time, go over it with students on a line-by-line basis.

RETEACHING ALTERNATIVES   Question 1 under Writing About the Poem (text page 687) provides a creative way of paraphrasing McKay's message.

Responding to the Poem   Text page 687

Answers to the questions in the Pupil's Edition appear in the Annotated Teacher's Edition.

Writing About the Poem

For help in revising their compositions, refer students to **Grammar, Usage, and Mechanics: A Reference Guide** on text pages 1183–1228 at the back of their books.

A CREATIVE RESPONSE
1. Capturing the Poet's Feelings   Brainstorm some possible slogans (for bumper stickers) and some poster illustrations. When ideas die down, go back and evaluate the appropriateness of each idea to McKay's intent.

▶ CRITERIA FOR EVALUATING THE ASSIGNMENT   The bumper sticker or poster captures the main idea expressed in the poem.

A CRITICAL RESPONSE
2. Comparing and Contrasting Poems   Read and discuss Shelley's "Ozymandias." Note that both are sonnets, though they use different rhyme patterns. Shelley's poem uses the image of a great work of civilization sunk in the sand, conveying the disappearance of a once-powerful past civilization. McKay uses a similar image to predict what will happen to America. The speaker in "America" expresses patriotic love and awareness of racism. The speaker in "Ozymandias" is not emotionally involved with the lost civilization.

▶ CRITERIA FOR EVALUATING THE ASSIGNMENT   The essay compares and contrasts Shelley's and McKay's poems in terms of form, subject, point of view, and emotion. The essay cites examples to support points made.

Langston Hughes

Text page 688

Hughes was the most famous African American poet of the first half of this century. The story of his discovery by Vachel Lindsay in a Washington, D.C., restaurant where Hughes bused tables became something of a literary legend. During the 1940's he created the fictional character of Jess B. Semple, who came to be called Simple. In the view of many critics, Simple's humorous urban wisdom is Hughes's most enduring achievement.

HARLEM

Text page 689

Objectives

1. To respond to a poem about hardship and injustice
2. To write a news report based on the poem
3. To write an essay comparing two poems

Introducing the Poem

The poem is written in free verse with short, forceful lines in colloquial speech. It is about African American life in Harlem, New York City, during the Great Depression. Explain that a penny increase in the price of bread (line 10) was significant.

THE LITERAL MEETING   The speaker describes Harlem and expresses the economic hardships and emotional response of its residents.

Teaching Strategies

PROVIDING FOR CULTURAL DIFFERENCES   Ask students from other ethnic backgrounds to comment on whether the poem's statements apply today to ethnic neighborhoods they know. Is the poem dated or still relevant?

PROVIDING FOR DIFFERENT LEVELS OF ABILITY   This straightforward poem should pose few problems of literal comprehension. More advanced students may enjoy discussing what makes this a poetic rendering of colloquial speech rather than a mere prose transcription (sentence rhythm and line length).

READING THE POEM   You might want to combine this poem in the same lesson with Hughes's "I, Too" (text page 690).

RETEACHING ALTERNATIVES   Students might enjoy analyzing how this poem manages to combine a light, humane tone with social protest in the space of a few short lines. What is the speaker in the poem protesting? How angry is he?

Responding to the Poem   Text page 689

Answers to the questions in the Pupil's Edition appear in the Annotated Teacher's Edition.

Writing About the Poem

For help in revising their compositions, refer students to **Grammar, Usage, and Mechanics: A Reference Guide** on text pages 1183–1228 at the back of their books.

A CREATIVE RESPONSE
1. *Writing a News Report*   Suggest that students choose a specific newspaper or television show (for example, "Sixty Minutes").

▶ CRITERIA FOR EVALUATING THE ASSIGNMENT   The paragraph is suited to the medium chosen by the student and reflects at least one point made by Hughes in "Harlem."

A CRITICAL RESPONSE
2. *Comparing Poems*   Discuss the questions given in the writing assignment, and direct students to structure their essays around answers to the questions. Students should recognize a difference in tone: McKay's poem is angry and bitter; Hughes's, much quieter, more resigned.

▶ CRITERIA FOR EVALUATING THE ASSIGNMENT   The essay states each poem's response to oppression and states which poem the writer finds more effective as protest, and why.

UNIT EIGHT: Poetry   201

I, TOO

Objectives

1. To respond to a poem about overcoming racism
2. To identify details
3. To analyze tone

Introducing the Poem

This brief poem of only sixty-two words, in eighteen very short lines of free verse, is a powerful expression of hope for the end of racism.

THE LITERAL MEANING The speaker says that although he is "the darker brother," he too is part of America and will "be at the table" in the future.

Teaching Strategies

PROVIDING FOR CULTURAL DIFFERENCES Students of various cultural backgrounds may wish to tell how their forebears felt about being included in American society.

PROVIDING FOR DIFFERENT LEVELS OF ABILITY Be sure the students understand that the kitchen referred to in the poem is a metaphor for American society with its abundance.

READING THE POEM You may want to combine "I, Too" in the same lesson with "Harlem" (page 689).

RETEACHING ALTERNATIVES Students may wish to write poetic or prose responses to the speaker of the poem.

THE WEARY BLUES

Objectives

1. To respond to a poem about blues
2. To identify alliteration, onomatopoeia, and similes
3. To create a melody for the poem
4. To write an essay comparing two speakers' attitudes
5. To write an essay comparing two poems

Introducing the Poem

The poem freely adapts the rhyme scheme of the typical blues lyric, based on rhymed couplets. In lines 19–22 and 25–30 there is a poem-within-the-poem: a blues lyric sung by a fictitious musician.

THE LITERAL MEANING The speaker describes hearing a black piano player sing the blues in a Harlem cafe.

Teaching Strategies

PROVIDING FOR CULTURAL DIFFERENCES Blues music has penetrated into many different areas of American popular culture, including rock music, country and western, and soul music. You might ask your students what kinds of music they like and whether there's any blues influence in it.

PROVIDING FOR DIFFERENT LEVELS OF ABILITY Some students may need help identifying the changes of speakers in the poem.

READING THE POEM Play the audiocassette recording of the poem as a culmination for a lesson beginning with the previous Hughes poems. Or have a small group of students rehearse and present a choral reading of the poem.

RETEACHING ALTERNATIVES The last line of the poem is a subtle counterpoint to the more upbeat, joyous lines. You might ask students to read that concluding line again and discuss what it says about the singer's life.

Responding to the Poems

Text pages 690, 693

Answers to the questions in the Pupil's Edition appear in the Annotated Teacher's Edition.

Writing About the Poems

For help in revising their compositions, refer students to **Grammar, Usage, and Mechanics: A Reference Guide** on text pages 1183–1228 at the back of their books.

A CREATIVE RESPONSE

1. Creating Music for a Poem   Music students or a music teacher may be able to suggest an existing tune. Or let students work individually or in groups to create original music. Be sure to have them perform or record their musical versions.

▶ CRITERIA FOR EVALUATING THE ASSIGNMENT   The music is appropriate to the mood and content of Hughes's lines.

A CRITICAL RESPONSE

2. Comparing the Voices in Two Poems   Refer students back to the Responding to the Poem questions on Hughes's "Harlem" and "I, Too."

▶ CRITERIA FOR EVALUATING THE ASSIGNMENT   The essay briefly compares the speakers in Hughes's "Harlem" and "I, Too," stating how they are similar and how they differ.

3. Comparing Poems   Given a quick review of Whitman's poem, students should readily see how Hughes's "The Weary Blues" emulates Whitman's style but updates his content.

▶ CRITERIA FOR EVALUATING THE ASSIGNMENT   The essay briefly explains how Hughes's "The Weary Blues" echoes and comments on Whitman's "I Hear America Singing."

Extending the Poems

You might read aloud to students the following poem by Langston Hughes and have them compare it with the work of Whitman.

The Negro Speaks of Rivers

I've known rivers:
I've known rivers ancient as the world and older than
the flow of human blood in human veins.

My soul has grown deep like the rivers.

I bathed in the Euphrates when dawns were young.
I built my hut near the Congo and it lulled me to sleep.
I looked upon the Nile and raised the pyramids above
it.
I heard the singing of the Mississippi when Abe Lincoln
went down to New Orleans, and I've seen its
muddy bottom all gold in the sunset.

I've known rivers:
Ancient, dusky rivers.

My soul has grown deep like the rivers.

Countee Cullen

Cullen's career paralleled Hughes's in many ways: They both worked in similar genres at similar times. But Cullen was more ambivalent about race than Hughes, who wrote about it all his life. For instance, Hughes's play, *Mulatto,* had a long, successful Broadway run during the Depression, while Cullen's play, *The Medea,* was about the ancient world and not meant to be acted on the stage.

TABLEAU

Objectives

1. To respond to a poem with a racial theme
2. To identify metaphors
3. To interpret the poem's meaning

Introducing the Poem

The poem is in three quatrains, the lines alternating between iambic tetrameter and iambic trimeter. The rhyme scheme is *abab cdcd efef.*

THE LITERAL MEANING An African American boy and a white boy walk arm in arm down a street, drawing stares and indignant talk from the townspeople. The boys are oblivious and see nothing strange about their friendship.

Teaching Strategies

PROVIDING FOR CULTURAL DIFFERENCES The poem speaks of a time when boys of different races walking together would draw stares. You might ask your students how such a sight would be greeted in their localities today, and how it might have been greeted two generations ago, when this poem was written.

PROVIDING FOR DIFFERENT LEVELS OF ABILITY The scene described is very simple, but some attention to vocabulary study will probably be necessary, and the brilliant metaphor about lightning and thunder, lines 11–12, may need paraphrasing for some students.

READING THE POEM The two very short Cullen poems can be discussed in a single lesson, each read by one student.

RETEACHING ALTERNATIVES Ask students to describe the incident in the poem, the "folks'" reactions, and the metaphors in stanzas 1 and 2.

INCIDENT

Objectives

1. To respond to a poem about racism
2. To interpret irony
3. To write a dialogue between two characters in a poem
4. To write a list of camera shots for a screenplay of the poem
5. To write an essay comparing the language of two poems

Introducing the Poem

The poem is in three quatrains, the second and fourth lines of each quatrain rhyming with each other. Iambic tetrameter alternates with iambic trimeter, creating a sing-song rhythm appropriate to the children described in the poem.

THE LITERAL MEANING The speaker recalls an incident in Baltimore when he was eight. In response to a friendly smile, another child stuck out his tongue and called him "Nigger."

Teaching Strategies

PROVIDING FOR CULTURAL DIFFERENCES   If students in your class have been exposed to racial or ethnic slurs, they may be willing to talk about the experience.

PROVIDING FOR DIFFERENT LEVELS OF ABILITY This poem is written in a deliberately nursery-rhyme-like style befitting the subject and making the racial slur stand out in stark contrast. Its easy vocabulary and syntax make it accessible to all students.

READING THE POEM   Choose a good reader to read the poem aloud, or read it yourself. It should be read simply and straightforwardly, so that the racial epithet will have the proper unsettling effect.

RETEACHING ALTERNATIVES   Have students reread the poem to focus on its economy. What does each stanza contribute to the poem's total effect? Could any one stanza be omitted?

Responding to the Poems

Text pages 695, 697

Answers to the questions in the Pupil's Edition appear in the Annotated Teacher's Edition.

Writing About the Poems

For help in revising their compositions, refer students to **Grammar, Usage, and Mechanics: A Reference Guide** on text pages 1183–1228 at the back of their books.

A CREATIVE RESPONSE

1. Writing Dialogue   Clarify the writing assignment: The two boys walking together in ''Tableau'' are discussing what happened to the African American child in ''Incident.'' The child on the bus may or may not be the child (of ''Tableau'') himself.

▶ CRITERIA FOR EVALUATING THE ASSIGNMENT   The dialogue reveals the friendship between the boys, their feelings about the incident, and their growing awareness of prejudice.

2. Planning a Screenplay   Technical phrases that might assist students include: ''Panoramic shot of . . . ,'' ''closeup,'' ''tight closeup,'' and ''camera follows as. . . .''

▶ CRITERIA FOR EVALUATING THE ASSIGNMENT   The sequence of shots covers the entire content of ''Incident''—old Baltimore, the people on the bus, the children on the bus, the faces and reactions of the two children.

3. Setting the Poem to Music   Music students may be able to suggest an existing melody to which ''Incident'' can be set, or to create an original tune for it.

▶ CRITERIA FOR EVALUATING THE ASSIGNMENT   The music is appropriate to the mood and content of Cullen's poem.

A CRITICAL RESPONSE

4. Comparing Poems   Students may wish to copy the two poems and place them side by side. They should notice the easy vocabulary, very simple syntax, lack of figurative language, and rollicking rhythm of ''Incident.'' The nursery-rhyme effect contrasts strongly, almost ironically, with the racial slur. In ''Tableau'' the metaphors, more complicated syntax, and calmer rhythm create a loftier tone.

▶ CRITERIA FOR EVALUATING THE ASSIGNMENT   The essay briefly shows how Cullen used word choice and sentence structure to create different effects in ''Tableau'' and ''Incident.''

Extending the Poems

Interested students may want to compare the works of the African American writers in this unit with those of contemporary African American writers. Robert Hayden and Gwendolyn Brooks are African American poets included in Unit Thirteen. In addition to Andrea Lee and James Alan McPherson (Unit Eleven), prominent contemporary fiction writers include Toni Morrison, Alice Walker, Gloria Naylor, Ishmael Reed, and John A. Williams.

The essay treats the phenomenon of dialects, and their abrupt flourishing in the mid-nineteenth century. The essay opens with Twain's claim to have used "no less than seven dialects" in his novel *Huckleberry Finn*. The essay suggests that admitting the existence of this diversity amounted to social discord—contrary to the image of America as a unified nation. Even Webster considered it an "infection," while Twain saw local speech as an expression of local color.

The next section answers the question, "What is dialect?" In its broadest sense, it is the "characteristic speech habits of a particular speech community." Dialects differ from each other in pronunciation, vocabulary, and grammar.

After identifying three major dialect regions, the essay concludes that writers use dialect as an excellent technique of creating both an individual character and member of a class.

You may wish to assign the essay as homework but have students work collaboratively to complete the Analyzing Language activities on text page 702.

Analyzing Language

Text page 702

1. Answers will vary. If some students choose different words from their classmates, ask if they have grown up in a different area of the United States or a different country. Note that these words are characteristic of regional dialects.

2. **a.** In the first passage, examples include *holt, sich, k'n, preachin's, workin',* and *missionaryin.*

    In the second passage, examples include *settin', theayter, gettin', w'ile, openin',* and *aw de cologne.*

    In the third passage, examples include *axin, talkin, bout,* and *goin.*

    In the fourth passage, examples include *comin, O,* and *em's.*

   b. Students may suggest slight inconsistencies. For example, in the Twain passage, the final "g" of the present participle is sometimes indicated with an apostrophe and sometimes not. Reasons for inconsistencies will vary.

   c. Sample answers: In the first passage, the speaker uses "considerable" (a lot), "line" (occupation), and "missionaryin" (attempting to convert people to a religious faith or creed).

    In the second passage, the speaker uses "settin' " (sitting), "come" (came), "my right first name" (my actual first name).

    In the third passage, the speaker uses "axin" (asking), "to figure" (to calculate), "run" (ran), "stare" (stared), "goin rip" (going to rip).

    In the fourth passage, the speaker uses "copy" (connection), "10-4" (O.K.), "handle" (name), "copy you clear" (hear you clearly), "Smokey Bear" and "Smokies" (police).

   d. Students should be able to furnish numerous examples: See the answers under item c above.

   e. Examples of eye-dialect include "aw de cologne" in the second passage, and perhaps "O" (for *old*) in the fourth passage. Students' reasons will vary. In general, a writer might use eye-dialect to imitate pronunciation or to hint that the speaker might lack enough formal education to know the correct spelling of a word.

   f. The last passage reproduces the dialect of truckers.

Interpreting and Responding to a Poem

For some students the poem "Only the Polished Skeleton" may be difficult to interpret. You might review the biographical material on Countee Cullen (text page 694), and have students reread "Incident" (text page 697). With this background, point out that many critics see racial themes in "Only the Polished Skeleton." According to these critics, Cullen expresses racial bitterness in his statement of what is necessary for the body ("heart") and mind to survive and that only in death can the individual "rest at ease." Help students to understand the contrast in the poem by pointing out the word *only* at the beginning of the last stanza. Discuss each of the questions under "Guidelines for Interpreting a Poem."

▶ CRITERIA FOR EVALUATING THE ASSIGNMENT   Although students' essays do not necessarily have to follow the plan suggested in the "Writing" section, the essays should indicate, through paraphrase, students' literal comprehension of the poem. Students' interpretations of the poem's meaning should be supported with details from the poem and should be consistent with the literal meaning of the poem.

Further Reading

Works listed are suitable for both students and teachers unless the annotation ends with the note [Teachers].

Adoff, Arnold, ed. *The Poetry of Black America* (Harper & Row, 1973). A big anthology of poems by twentieth-century African American poets. The first section contains poems by Johnson, Dunbar, McKay, Cullen, and many other poets of the Harlem Renaissance.

Baker, Houston A., Jr. *Modernism and the Harlem Renaissance* (University of Chicago Press, 1987). A thorough history and criticism of the movement. [Teacher]

Frost, Robert. *A Pocket Book of Robert Frost's Poems* (Washington Square Press, 1967). More than one hundred of Frost's poems with an introduction and commentary by Louis Untermeyer.

Gregory, Horace, and Marya Zaturenska. *A History of American Poetry 1900–1940* (Harcourt Brace, Jovanovich, 1946). A historical survey of American poetry. [Teachers]

Hughes, Langston. *Selected Poems of Langston Hughes* (Vintage, 1957). Hughes's own selection of the best poems from his entire career.

Masters, Edgar Lee. *Spoon River Anthology* (Macmillan, 1944). More than 240 residents of Spoon River summarize their lives in verse portraits.

Robinson, Edwin Arlington, ed. by Morton Zabel. *Selected Poems of Edwin Arlington Robinson* (Macmillan, 1965). More than a hundred of Robinson's best poems with an introduction by the American poet James Dickey.

Vendler, Helen, ed. *Voices & Visions* (Random House, 1987). This richly illustrated text published as a companion to the PBS documentary series contains excellent essays on Robert Frost by Richard Poirier and Langston Hughes by Arnold Rampersad, with biographical and critical information as well as many poems.

White, Hilda. *Truth Is My Country: Portraits of Eight New England Authors* (Doubleday, 1971). Informative, readable biographical essays on Robinson, Millay, and Frost.

Williams, Oscar, and Edwin Honig. *The Mentor Book of Major American Poetry* (New American Library, 1962). A compact anthology of poems by twenty American poets, including Robinson, Millay, Frost, and Ransom.

IMAGISM AND SYMBOLISM

Text page 705

Teaching the Imagism and Symbolism Unit

The Imagist movement, proclaimed by Ezra Pound, lasted less than ten years, from 1909 to 1917, but it had significant consequences. Imagism expanded the subject matter of poetry, emphasized the exact word over the decorative word, and helped to make free verse respectable. Imagism was part of a broader movement, Symbolism, which had started in France in the late nineteenth century and began to influence American poetry in the early decades of the twentieth century. Symbolists stressed the importance of the sound, or music, of verse and like the Imagists believed that any subject matter is suitable for poetry.

Since the poems are so often cryptic or ambiguous, Imagism and Symbolism make real demands on the reader. To students in search of the one right answer for every question, such poetry can be a revelation (if multiple interpretations are accepted) or an ordeal (if hard-and-fast answers are demanded). During the study of this unit, your students may be comforted to learn that some critics have called Imagism "the cult of unintelligibility" and Symbolism a haven for the "rimed rebus." For this reason, the text material (the unit introduction, author biographies, and special features) are important to an understanding of the poetry. A brief review of Romanticism and Realism (students might review the introductions to units Three and Six) will help remind students of what poets in the early twentieth century were reacting to and rebelling against.

Many of the poems in this unit will be more understandable and enjoyable to students if read aloud. Poets have often asserted the importance of oral reading, especially for free verse. Amy Lowell, a leader of the Imagist movement, was one such poet, as critic Richard Benvenuto noted:

> [O]ne of her deepest convictions . . . is that poetry is an oral art, that poems are a form of speech and must be heard to be completely understood. . . . "To understand *vers libre* [free verse]," she said, one must "allow the lines to flow as they will when read aloud by an intelligent reader. Then new rhythms will become evident—satisfying and delightful. For this poetry definitely harks back to the old oral tradition; it is written to be spoken."

In this unit, students gain a working knowledge of the meanings of the terms *Imagism* and *Symbolism*, but they should also keep in mind that poets and poems are more important than labels. Each poet is a creative individual, not just a representative of a particular *-ism*. Since great poets can seldom be slotted into neat categories for analysis, students will find far more diversity than uniformity in the seven poets who appear in this unit.

Objectives of the Imagism and Symbolism Unit

1. To improve reading proficiency and expand vocabulary

2. To gain exposure to notable poets and their works

3. To define and identify elements of poetry

4. To define and identify significant literary techniques

5. To respond to poetry orally and in writing

6. To practice the following critical thinking and writing skills:
   a. Explaining poetic images
   b. Comparing a poem with a prose text

c. Comparing and contrasting poems
d. Evaluating a character
e. Comparing characters
f. Responding to a critic
g. Interpreting a poem
h. Analyzing a poem

Introducing the Imagism and Symbolism Unit

To show students graphically what poets of the early 1900's were trying to achieve—and to show the interrelatedness of the arts—you might introduce the unit with a series of prints or color slides showing the progression of modern painting. Begin with the impressionists of the late nineteenth century—Renoir, Seurat. Go on to the post-impressionists—Gauguin, Toulouse-Lautrec. Conclude with the abstract artists of the twentieth century—Mondrian, Miró. Point out to students (although they will surely see it for themselves) that the paintings in this sequence become increasingly more difficult to interpret. Indicate to them that a parallel situation developed in poetry during this period.

Rather than art, or in addition to art, you might want to play recordings of some of the music of Debussy and Stravinsky—music that Amy Lowell claims is "an immediate prototype of Imagism." She even attempts to prove it poetically in her poem "Stravinsky's Three Pieces 'Grotesques,' For String Quartet" (from Lowell's *Men, Women and Ghosts*). If you can obtain both the poem and the recording, you might want to see if students feel she has succeeded in reproducing "the effect," as she says, of Stravinsky's music.

Ezra Pound

Text page 711

THE RIVER-MERCHANT'S WIFE: A LETTER

Text page 712

THE GARDEN

Text page 716

Objectives

1. To respond to two Imagist poems

2. To identify images, a simile, and a pun

3. To analyze the mood of a poem

4. To create a single concrete image that indirectly expresses a feeling

5. To write a paragraph explaining three images as objective correlatives

Introducing the Poems

Significant techniques in these poems include the clear images conveying emotions and meanings, such as "on bamboo stilts," "climb the lookout," and "skein of loose silk blown against a wall." Both poems are written in free verse.

BACKGROUND ON THE POEMS Your students may be interested in this description by Richard Aldington, a British Imagist, of how the movement began:

[T]he Imagist movement was born in a teashop—in the Royal Borough of Kensington [England]. For some time Ezra had been butting in on our studies and poetic productions, with alternate encouragements and the reverse, according to his mood. H.D. [Hilda Doolittle] produced some poems which I thought excellent, and she either handed or mailed them to Ezra. Presently each of us received a ukaze [an order from the Czar of Russia; an official decree] to attend the Kensington bunshop. Ezra was so much worked up by these poems of H.D.'s that he removed his pince-nez and informed us that we were Imagists.

THE LITERAL MEANING   *The River-Merchant's Wife*
In the first stanza of this poem, the speaker remembers when her husband and she were children. In the next stanza, at the age of fourteen, they are married. By fifteen she is devoted to him. In the third stanza, when he is sixteen—and evidently a river-merchant, judging by the title of the poem—he goes by river to a distant region. He has been gone for five months. The images in the last stanza show her to be sad. She says she will go to meet him if she knows when he is coming.

The Garden   A woman, dying of "emotional anemia," is walking in Kensington Gardens. She feels surrounded by a rabble of poor infants, who will inherit the earth. She is bored and lonesome, wants someone to talk to, and is almost afraid the speaker in the poem will talk to her.

Teaching Strategies

PROVIDING FOR CULTURAL DIFFERENCES   Most students will find marriage at fourteen and business travel at sixteen rather unusual. Ask them in what century they think the events in the poem occur. (A good guess would be the eighth century.) Ask them why they think the girl married the young river-merchant. (Apparently it was an arranged marriage.) You might want to discuss the matter of arranged marriages. Do they ever occur today? How do students feel about having their families choose their husband or wife for them?

PROVIDING FOR DIFFERENT LEVELS OF ABILITY
"The River-Merchant's Wife," which deals with young love and loss, should be comprehensible to students at all levels. "The Garden," which, broadly interpreted, seems to concern social classes in England, is not so easy. While you may want to have students read the first poem on their own, you will probably want to work through the second poem with them in class.

READING THE POEMS   Read or have a student read each poem aloud in class. An audiocassette recording accompanies "The River-Merchant's Wife." Go back through the poem, asking questions about each event in the girl's life and about her relationship to her husband.

Before reading "The Garden," you might want to discuss social classes (especially the titled gentry) as they existed in their heyday in England prior to World War I. Students may not be aware of the rigid class distinctions of that time and place.

RETEACHING ALTERNATIVES   Have one or more interviewers ask questions of the river-merchant's wife and the well-bred lady in Kensington Gardens. The student playing each part should respond to questions in a way consistent with the content of the poem. The interviewer(s) should try to bring out as much information as the poems contain.

Primary Sources   Text page 714

"A FEW DON'TS BY AN IMAGIST"
Take the time in class to read and discuss Pound's advice to the Imagists. Ask students which advice they think is most important. Which rules do they think apply to prose as well as poetry? As they read other poems in this unit, ask them whether the poet has followed Pound's directions.

THE ELEMENTS OF LITERATURE   Text page 715

THE OBJECTIVE CORRELATIVE
Discuss this page in class, asking two or three students to explain the term *objective correlative* in their own words. Some students may feel that interpreting objective correlatives requires the ability to read the poet's mind. How can a reader know what emotion the poet believes a particular object or action represents? In the most abstruse Imagist poetry, the reader may not know. But in Pound's "The River-Merchant's Wife" there are many contextual clues. You may want to have students work in pairs or small groups to find the objective correlatives in the poem.

Responding to the Poems
Text pages 714, 716

Answers to the questions in the Pupil's Edition appear in the Annotated Teacher's Edition.

Writing About the Poems

For help in revising their compositions, refer students to **Grammar, Usage, and Mechanics: A Reference Guide** on text pages 1183–1228 at the back of their books.

A CREATIVE RESPONSE

1. Creating an Image Brainstorm a list of topics, both negative and positive, likely to arouse strong feelings—recent events or local issues that make your students happy, angry, elated, or frustrated. Elicit images for a few of these—a baby's rattle in a mud puddle, for example, to express sorrow about a burnt-out home—and then let students continue on their own.

▶ CRITERIA FOR EVALUATING THE ASSIGNMENT The sentence or phrase presents an image that evokes feelings, but does not directly state the feeling intended.

A CRITICAL RESPONSE

2. Explaining Images Have students go through both poems and list all the images that seem to be objective correlatives, perhaps working in pairs and discussing the images until they know which three they wish to write about.

▶ CRITERIA FOR EVALUATING THE ASSIGNMENT The paper presents three images from Pound's ''The River-Merchant's Wife'' or ''The Garden'' and offers an appropriate explanation of how each image is used as an objective correlative to convey emotion indirectly.

Extending the Poems

Ezra Pound felt that Walt Whitman was the one significant poet of the late nineteenth century. In Pound's poem, ''A Pact,'' published in 1913, he acknowledges his debt to Whitman, but with certain reservations. Ask students to interpret ''A Pact,'' which appears on text page 325.

William Carlos Williams

Objectives

1. To respond to four Imagist poems
2. To identify sensory images
3. To summarize the speaker's main idea
4. To interpret a paradox
5. To retitle poems
6. To write an essay analyzing a poem's use of concrete objects

Introducing the Poems

All of the poems are written in free verse.

BACKGROUND ON THE POEMS The first half of the twentieth century was a time of experimentation in poetry. Some poets, like Picasso in painting, went through various phases and were involved in more than one movement. Williams is one such poet. You might point out to students that, as a consequence, he may seem to be an Imagist in one poem and not an Imagist in another. As a young man and a traditionalist, Williams came under the influence of Pound and Imagism. Later, believing that Imagism had "dribbled off into so-called 'free verse,' " he embraced what he called Objectivism, a movement that one unsympathetic critic saw as a "craze for actuality."

THE LITERAL MEANING *The Red Wheelbarrow* The speaker sees an image on which "so much depends"—a rain-glazed wheelbarrow and white chickens.

The Great Figure At night the speaker sees a gold figure 5 on a fire truck whose gong is clanging, siren howling, and wheels rumbling.

Tract The speaker tells the townspeople how to perform a funeral. The hearse should not be black or white, but instead should be weathered like a farm wagon, with gilt wheels or no wheels. It should have no glass, no upholstery—no frills. There should be no wreaths. The driver should not wear a silk hat or sit high up on the wagon. He should walk beside the hearse. The mourners should walk behind it, or if they ride, they should not protect themselves from the weather.

Spring and All A cold wind blows near the contagious hospital. Bushes and trees along the road look brown and lifeless. With spring, the grass and leaves begin to awaken.

Teaching Strategies

PROVIDING FOR CULTURAL DIFFERENCES The poem "Tract" concerns American funerals—specifically the hearse and cortege—in the early 1900's. Apart from the time difference, funerals differ considerably from culture to culture. If you have students from different cultural backgrounds in your class, you may want to see if they can describe the funeral customs that are particular to their culture.

PROVIDING FOR DIFFERENT LEVELS OF ABILITY At all levels you may hear the objection, "But this isn't poetry!" Point out that good free verse is very carefully crafted. Williams, like Pound and other poets in this unit, had little use for "pseudo-poets" who thought that free verse removed barriers, lowered standards, and, in general, made randomly reformatted prose into poetry. With some students, you will have to explain what Williams is trying to do.

READING THE POEMS All the poems will be more comprehensible if you read them aloud in class. (An audiocassette recording accompanies "Spring and All.") Before reading the first two, have students close their eyes and try to visualize the scenes: (1) morning on a farm, with a light rain falling; from the kitchen window, they see a wheelbarrow and chickens; (2) a city at night with rain falling; a fire truck passes.

Before reading "Tract," discuss the introductory note. Have students suggest some of the ways in which a modern limousine hearse resembles a horse-drawn hearse and some of the ways in which it differs.

Introduce "Spring and All" with a few questions about spring. What does spring bring? How is spring usually treated by poets? Why might spring be less significant in some areas than it is in New Jersey, where the poet lived? Be sure that students mention rebirth, genesis, and awakening in connection with spring.

RETEACHING ALTERNATIVES Assign a capable student to each of the four Williams poems. Have each student read the poem in class and explain what it means to him or her. Since this assignment follows detailed discussions of both the poems and the accompanying questions and other material, students should have something meaningful to say. If not, suggest that they do some library research to obtain further information on Williams and his poetry.

A Comment on the Poem Text page 718

Whatever the level of your students, you may want to read and discuss this comment in class. William Carlos Williams is a pivotal figure in modern poetry, and "The Red Wheelbarrow," despite its brevity, is a major poem. If students are to appreciate the free-verse forms being written today, they need to understand why Williams's poem is neither a trick nor a fraud.

Responding to the Poems
Text pages 719, 721, 723

Answers to the questions in the Pupil's Edition appear in the Annotated Teacher's Edition.

Writing About the Poems

For help in revising their compositions, refer students to **Grammar, Usage, and Mechanics: A Reference Guide** on text pages 1183–1228 at the back of their books.

A CREATIVE RESPONSE
1. Retitling Poems Have pairs or small groups of students select images and argue their appropriateness before students individually submit titles for the poems.

▶ CRITERIA FOR EVALUATING THE ASSIGNMENT The new titles apply unmistakably to one poem or the other: for example, "No Upholstery" (line 27) for "Tract"; "Enter Naked" (line 16) for "Spring and All." It's all right if more than one student suggests the same titles.

2. Analyzing a Poem   You may wish first to ask students what they perceive Williams's beliefs ''about people, art, or life in general'' to be, and then ask which images from the poems support their opinions.

▶ CRITERIA FOR EVALUATING THE ASSIGNMENT   The essay is at least one paragraph long. It names a poem by Williams, identifies three or more concrete objects from the poem, and explains how Williams uses these objects to make statements about people, art, or life in general.

Extending the Poems

Since many of Williams's poems are short and visually striking, you may want to choose a few additional ones to read and discuss in class. Among the most appropriate and most frequently anthologized are ''Classic Scene,'' ''The Crowd at the Ball Game,'' ''Drink,'' ''Pastoral,'' ''The Yachts,'' ''This Is Just to Say,'' ''The Dance,'' and ''The Poor.''

Lezlie Laws Couch gives a detailed account of how she combines Williams's poems and a reader-response approach in '' 'So much depends' . . . on how you begin: A Poetry Lesson,'' *English Journal,* November 1987.

Primary Sources   Text page 723

WILLIAMS TALKS ABOUT POETRY
This excerpt from Williams's *Autobiography* demonstrates his own doubts about the value of his poetry, the responses of critics of the time, and the difficulty involved in creating genuine Imagist poetry—not just chopped-up prose. Suggest that students read it for insight into the poet and his craft.

Marianne Moore   Text page 724

THE STEEPLE-JACK   Text page 725

Objectives

1. To respond to a poem with many visual images, unconventional meter and rhyme

2. To identify sensory images

3. To describe the poem's tone

4. To describe a place using specific sensory images

5. To compare a poem to a prose text

6. To use a dictionary to check precise meanings

Introducing the Poem

Significant techniques in this poem include Moore's use of vivid visual images, such as ''waves as formal as the scales/on a fish'' and ''a sea the purple of a peacock's neck.'' The poem is also noted for its unusual ''syllabic'' meter and rhyme. There is a fixed syllable count for each line; the second and fifth lines of each stanza have end rhymes. Students familiar with Japanese verse forms, such as haiku, will appreciate Moore's method of versification.

BACKGROUND ON THE POEM   Marianne Moore created three versions of ''The Steeple-Jack.'' The first published version contains twelve stanzas. When Moore prepared the poem for publication in *Selected Poems* (1935), she cut it to eight stanzas. Three decades later, for *A Marianne Moore Reader* (1961), she restored the cut stanzas and added another. This last version, containing thirteen stanzas, is the one included in the text.

THE LITERAL MEANING   The poem pictures a pleasant northern coastal town in which Dürer might have liked to live. A note of fantasy is sounded with the ''eight stranded whales.'' The second stanza portrays the flight of seagulls, while the third describes the color of the sea and pictures fish nets and a huge lobster. A storm is shown, followed by a virtual catalogue of local plants, then a shorter list of fauna. Next, the poem introduces Ambrose, a college student who knows the town well, including the church steeple on which C.J. Poole, a steeple-jack, is working. The town has the church portico as a haven. It also has a schoolhouse and other buildings, along with a schooner. This is a safe town, despite the steeple-jack's danger sign below him on the sidewalk.

Teaching Strategies

PROVIDING FOR CULTURAL DIFFERENCES Most students will have seen photographs of old New England towns in which the church steeple is a focal point. If you think anyone in your classes may be unfamiliar with such a scene, bring in photos of some New England coastal towns and discuss their principal features. Many will have a tall-spired church, often Congregational; a cemetery, usually near the church; a schoolhouse; a village green or common, typically with public buildings facing it; and a harbor with boats. A few towns will have, as Moore's does, a nearby lighthouse.

PROVIDING FOR DIFFERENT LEVELS OF ABILITY
All levels should be able to relate to the concrete images in the poem: the seagulls, the lobster, the flowers, the student, the boats, the steeple. Only minimal interpretation is called for, and more advanced students should have little difficulty handling the poem. With other students you may want to provide help with paraphrasing and interpreting.

READING THE POEM You may want to show prints or slides of Albrecht Dürer's (1471–1528) work. A variety of subjects is ideal, with each picture showing the intricate detail for which the German painter and engraver is famous. Ask students why Dürer might ''have seen a reason for living'' in a particular kind of town. (Presumably because of its richness and variety of subject matter for his art.) Then ask what a poet, like Marianne Moore, might admire in the work of an artist like Dürer. (The exact and detailed representation of what the artist observed.) This introduction could lead to a review of earlier discussions about the Imagists' passion for vividness and exactness. Point out to students that Imagists must be highly skilled at writing description—it is their *modus operandi*.

RETEACHING ALTERNATIVES Rather than rereading the poem, try having students paraphrase it orally in class. Go through the poem phrase by phrase, image by image, having students ''translate'' the poem into conversational language and explaining whatever in it may be unclear. (For example, the references to Dürer, the fantasy quality of eight stranded whales, the primitive-art aspect of waves that look like fish scales).

Responding to the Poem   Text page 728

Answers to the questions in the Pupil's Edition appear in the Annotated Teacher's Edition.

Writing About the Poem

For help in revising their compositions, refer students to **Grammar, Usage, and Mechanics: A Reference Guide** on text pages 1183–1228 at the back of their books.

A CREATIVE RESPONSE
1. Imitating the Poet's Technique Note that students are to concentrate not on Moore's syllable count and rhyme pattern, but on her catalogue of sights, sounds, and smells. Elicit a list of local places (perhaps a farmer's market, a junkyard, a mall) with vivid sights, sounds, and smells.

▶ CRITERIA FOR EVALUATING THE ASSIGNMENT The poem or paragraph catalogues sights, smells, and sounds evocative of a specific place.

A CRITICAL RESPONSE
2. Comparing the Poem to a Prose Text As preparation for writing this paragraph, have students skim pages 511–516 and list a number of concrete items that prove Zenith's perfection to Babbitt. They should next compare this list with the list of images found in response to question 4.

▶ CRITERIA FOR EVALUATING THE ASSIGNMENT The paragraph states how Babbitt's and Moore's views of the ideal town differ, and cites specific details or categories of details from the speech and the poem (for example, appliances versus flowers) to demonstrate that difference.

Analyzing Language and Style

PRECISE MEANINGS
Tyrol: region of the eastern Alps in western Austria and northern Italy
salpiglossis: a Chilean herb with strikingly colored, trumpet-shaped flowers
lichens: plants made up of algae and fungi growing together on a solid surface, such as a rock
bracts: modified small leaves at the base of a flower
banyan: large tree with branches that have shoots growing down to the soil and forming secondary trunks
portico: a covered walk or porch at the entrance of a building
fluted: marked by grooves

Extending the Poem

Have a number of volunteers do library research on Marianne Moore's poetry, locating some critical comments, if they can, on ''The Steeple-Jack.'' Ask the researchers to read in class the critical commentary they have found. See whether other students agree or disagree with the comments.

You may want to go over Marianne Moore's statements in class to make sure that students understand them. Point out that not only was Moore a baseball fan, but she wrote a number of poems about baseball, including ''Baseball and Writing.'' The Imagists, by opening up the subject matter of poetry, brought baseball and other sports a literary respectability they had not had before. Ernest Lawrence Thayer's ''Casey at the Bat'' appeared in 1888, but it is a comic poem. William Carlos Williams's ''The Crowd at the Ball Game''—to take one example—appeared in 1923 and is a serious work of art.

Carl Sandburg
Text page 729

CHICAGO
Text page 731

LIMITED
Text page 733

Objectives

1. To respond to two free-verse poems

2. To recognize and interpret epithets

3. To identify the central image of a poem

4. To identify examples of parallelism

5. To analyze paradox and irony

6. To write an apostrophe to a place

7. To write an essay comparing and contrasting two poems

Introducing the Poems

In the 1950's and 1960's college students lined up to get tickets to Sandburg's touring performances. He recited his own poetry and sang his songs, strumming the guitar. One of his best-known poems, ''Fog,'' is mentioned in the introductory biography. To introduce Sandburg's work, you may want to read the poem aloud to your students.

Fog

The fog comes
on little cat feet.

It sits looking
over harbor and city
on silent haunches
and then moves on.

This poem caused quite a stir when it was published, many people claiming it was not a poem at all. You might ask your students to answer the question, ''Is 'Fog' a poem?'' Why or why not? What comparison is Sandburg making? How effective do your students find this comparison?

Like ''Fog,'' ''Chicago'' and ''Limited'' are written in free verse.

BACKGROUND ON THE POEMS   Sandburg ends his ''Notes for a Preface'' in his *Complete Poems* with a one-paragraph biographical sketch. Students may appreciate his observations on writing:

> I am still studying verbs and the mystery of how they connect nouns. I am more suspicious of adjectives than at any other time in all my born days. I have forgotten the meaning of twenty or thirty of my poems written thirty or forty years ago . . . All my life I have been trying to learn to read, to see and hear, and to write . . . It could be, in the grace of God, I shall live to be eighty-nine, as did Hokusai, [an eighteenth- and nineteenth-century Japanese artist], and speaking my farewell to earthly scenes, I might paraphrase: ''If God had let me live five years longer I should have been a writer.''

THE LITERAL MEANING   *Chicago*   The poet addresses the city in a series of apostrophes. He then notes the unfavorable things that people say about Chicago. He accepts the arguments of these critics, but gives ''them back the sneer'' by picturing the city as vibrantly alive and constantly in motion. He ends by saying that Chicago is proud to be all the things he names it in the first stanza.

Limited   The speaker is on one of the nation's best trains, crossing the prairie. There are fifteen cars with a thousand people in them. He says in parentheses that the train will become scrap and the passengers will die. A man, asked where he is going, answers, ''Omaha.''

Teaching Strategies

PROVIDING FOR CULTURAL DIFFERENCES Many students will benefit from a brief discussion of Chicago in the early twentieth century. By 1900, Chicago's population made it the "Second City" after New York (a title it can no longer claim), with more than a million and a half people. It was also, as the poem says, a meat-packing and food-processing center, a railroad hub, and a city of heavy industry. In 1900, New York, with more than twice the population of Chicago, was the financial and publishing capital of the nation; Chicago was a younger, rawer, brawnier city.

If there are students in your class who have lived in or visited cities in other countries, ask them to describe those cities and to compare them with their impressions of American big cities.

PROVIDING FOR DIFFERENT LEVELS OF ABILITY Students should not have much difficulty with "Chicago," but LEP students may need some help with "Limited." In teaching "Limited," focus on the multiple meanings of the word *limited*. Ask for a definition. Have students name things that are limited. In the broadest sense, everything except infinity has limits.

READING THE POEMS You will want to read aloud, or have students read aloud, both "Chicago" and "Limited." In "Limited" make sure that students see the point at which the speaker's mind takes a philosophical turn (the sentence in parentheses). What is the speaker thinking about when he asks, "Where are you going?"

Note that a significant technique in "Chicago" is the use of epithets to convey meaning, such as "Hog Butcher of the World," "Stacker of Wheat," and "City of the Big Shoulders." The central image of "Chicago" is indirectly expressed through these epithets, which express a tough, active man, and the participles (*flinging, shoveling, bragging*) that suggest someone boisterous. The images near the end of the poem—an unbeaten fighter, youthful laughter—indicate a young man.

In "Limited," the main idea of the poem is implicit through that one word: the *limited* life of manufactured products (the train); *limited* life of human beings (men and women on train; man in smoker); *limited* perception of man on train ("Omaha").

RETEACHING ALTERNATIVES Consider asking students to suggest (or perhaps bring in recordings of) songs about various cities in the United States. See how many the class can find. From the familiar "New York, New York" to less well-known songs, such as "Gary, Indiana" from *The Music Man*, there are a great many possibilities. Have students compare what they learn about each city from its song with what they learn about Chicago from Sandburg's poem.

Responding to the Poems

Text pages 732, 734

Answers to the questions in the Pupil's Edition appear in the Annotated Teacher's Edition.

Writing About the Poems

For help in revising their compositions, refer students to **Grammar, Usage, and Mechanics: A Reference Guide** on text pages 1183–1228 at the back of their books.

A CREATIVE RESPONSE

1. Writing an Apostrophe Clarify the meaning of *epithet* (a characteristic word or phrase replacing the name of a person or thing), and ask students to identify the city meant by the epithet "The Big Apple" (New York). Do promotional epithets already exist for their city? What epithets could they propose? Guide students to focus on key geographical, sociological, political, or industrial features of the city.

▶ CRITERIA FOR EVALUATING THE ASSIGNMENT The five or more epithets listed are appropriate for the intended city, and they could be used like Sandburg's five opening lines.

A CRITICAL RESPONSE

2. Comparing and Contrasting Poems Have students work in pairs or small groups to complete the prewriting chart on Whitman's and Sandburg's poems. Then discuss the chart with the whole class.

▶ CRITERIA FOR EVALUATING THE ASSIGNMENT The essay is well organized, states both similarities and differences between Whitman's "I Hear America Singing" and Sandburg's "Chicago," and cites specific details from each poem to support its major points.

Extending the Poems

Carl Sandburg's *Complete Poems*, published in 1950, contains many excellent poems. If you can obtain the book, you might want to read in class "When Death Came April Twelve, 1945." Ask students what kind of poem it is. (An elegy) See if anyone knows who died on April 12, 1945. (President Franklin D. Roosevelt) If not, see if they can discover the answer from context, pointing to the clues that helped them. (For example, "frontline tanks nearing Berlin," "The Commander," "battle stations over the South Pacific")

"RHYMES ARE IRON FETTERS"

Since some students are likely to feel that "real" poetry demands rhyme, you may want to have a class discussion about Sandburg's and Holmes's view of rhyme. Does the passage suggest that good poetry *cannot* be written in rhyme? (It may seem to, but surely neither Sandburg nor Holmes would have maintained that position.) Does it mean that better poetry can be written in free verse? (Again, it seems to; and Sandburg, if not Holmes, probably would have taken that position.) What do your students believe? Some will undoubtedly agree with Robert Frost that writing free verse is like playing tennis with the net down. Others may think that Sandburg, with Holmes's help, has made a convincing case for free verse and against rhyme.

E. E. Cummings   Text page 735

NOBODY LOSES ALL THE TIME   Text page 736

WHAT IF A MUCH OF A WHICH OF A WIND

Text page 738

Objectives

1. To respond to two unconventional poems
2. To identify images
3. To describe the rhyme scheme
4. To imitate the poet's style
5. To compare and contrast poems by two different poets
6. To write a paragraph comparing two poems
7. To apply a poet's comments to his poems
8. To analyze the poet's diction

Introducing the Poems

Cummings's poetry is known for its "thought groups" unmarked by punctuation or line endings, such as parenthetical-phrases not set off ("to use a highfalootin phrase," "to wit") and sentence endings not indicated by periods. As students will quickly note, the poems are also marked by unusual capitalization and punctuation and by parts of speech used as other parts of speech.

BACKGROUND ON THE POEMS Since many of your students are likely to question Cummings's eccentricities of style, you may want to present a critic's defense of them. Norman Friedman, author of a critical biography of Cummings, writes:

> To break lines and words on the page, to use capitals and lower case letters where they don't belong, to insert parentheses anywhere and everywhere, to scatter punctuation marks apparently at random—what uses can these serve? There is . . . the "feel" of the poem as it lies on the page. To me at least there is a pleasurable tactility in these devices, a sense of visual structure as in a painting . . . [T]he best reason [is] that typography may not be pronounceable but it does affect the way we read. Pause and emphasis are supported by these devices; the meaning of words and lines is underscored; but most importantly of all, meanings are created as the reader's mind is slowed in its progress through the poem and forced to go back and forth. . . . This is what any good poem asks of the reader and Cummings is simply extending this request by making it explicit.

THE LITERAL MEANING *nobody loses all the time* The speaker's Uncle Sol foolishly went into farming. He failed at raising vegetables, chickens, and skunks, because the chickens ate the vegetables, the skunks ate the chickens, and the skunks died. Sol then drowned himself. At the impressive funeral, everyone cried. Finally, Uncle Sol went into the earth and started a worm farm.

what if a much of a which of a wind If the universe is destroyed, "the single secret will still be man." If the world freezes over, the stouthearted will survive to "cry hello" to spring. No matter how many people are destroyed, the human spirit will prevail.

Teaching Strategies

PROVIDING FOR CULTURAL DIFFERENCES
Explain the vaudeville references (lines 5–6) and Victor Victrola (lines 27–28) before you read "nobody loses all the time."

PROVIDING FOR DIFFERENT LEVELS OF ABILITY
Most students will understand the sequence of events in "nobody loses all the time" and will appreciate the humor of the ending. Many students will find "what if a much of a which of a wind" confusing and perhaps annoying. Probably the best approach with these students is to read the poem to them—it is lyrically beautiful—and not press for much interpretation.

READING THE POEMS   Play the audiocassette recording of "what if a much of a which of a wind." Have students look at the poems before reading them. Ask: Do these look to you like poems? Why or why not? What punctuation and capitalization do you find in the poems? How does it differ from ordinary punctuation and capitalization? Do you see any logic in the line breaks? Why do you think a poet would write this way?

When students read the poems, have them pay attention to tone. Ask them what kind of poet seems to be revealed by the two poems. Use the questions to work through each poem's meaning. Do not try to analyze the meaning of every word or every line in "what if a much of a which of a wind." Knowing the general idea of the poem, appreciating its lyricism, and experiencing the feelings being conveyed are the desirable outcomes.

RETEACHING ALTERNATIVES   Ask students to re-read both poems and choose one or two words to express how each poem makes them feel. When you discuss students' responses, see if they can identify what in the poems caused their reactions.

NOBODY LOSES ALL THE TIME
Text page 736

Responding to the Poem   Text page 737

Answers to the questions in the Pupil's Edition appear in the Annotated Teacher's Edition.

Writing About the Poem

For help in revising their compositions, refer students to **Grammar, Usage, and Mechanics: A Reference Guide** on text pages 1183–1228 at the back of their books.

A CREATIVE RESPONSE
1. Writing in Cummings's Style   To demonstrate the idea, you might take a short "human interest" story used as a filler in a recent newspaper, and have students direct you in breaking lines and omitting punctuation as you rewrite it on the chalkboard or overhead projector. Have students write their finished poem to look like a poem on the page.

► CRITERIA FOR EVALUATING THE ASSIGNMENT   The material falls into reasonable thought groupings which suggest, by context, the omitted punctuation. Display students' work on a bulletin board.

A CRITICAL RESPONSE
2. Comparing and Contrasting Poems   Note that students are asked to compare and contrast "nobody loses all the time" and "Richard Cory" not in terms of message, but in use of rhyme, meter, and tone. Clarify the term *tone* by referring students to the **Handbook of Literary Terms** (text page 1182).

► CRITERIA FOR EVALUATING THE ASSIGNMENT   The paper states that the poems are similar in use of an ironic tone, but different in rhyme and meter. Specific details from the poems are used to support the points made.

WHAT IF A MUCH OF A WHICH OF A WIND

Responding to the Poem   Text page 739

Answers to the questions in the Pupil's Edition appear in the Annotated Teacher's Edition.

Writing About the Poem

For help in revising their compositions, refer students to **Grammar, Usage, and Mechanics: A Reference Guide** on text pages 1183–1228 at the back of their books.

A CRITICAL RESPONSE

1. Comparing Poems   With so many points of comparison to be drawn, students may wish to construct a prewriting chart similar to that on page 732. This time the poets are Whitman and Cummings, and the left-hand headings are (1) theme or message, (2) imagery, (3) tone, (4) form and structure. Draw the chart on the chalkboard and complete most of it (make notes) from class discussion.

▶ CRITERIA FOR EVALUATING THE ASSIGNMENT   The essay cites how the poems are similar in the five areas listed above. Specific details from both poems are used to support the points made.

2. Comparing the Poems to a Statement   Have students read and discuss Cummings's points in ''Miracles are to come'' and select statements that relate to the messages of his poems.

▶ CRITERIA FOR EVALUATING THE ASSIGNMENT   The paper mentions Cummings's statement that his poems ''are for you and for me and not for mostpeople'' and

relates it to the unconventional aspects of his poetry. The paper also mentions Cummings's joyful celebration of the miracles and mystery of life in both his prose and poems.

Analyzing Language and Style

DICTION
1. Pretentious, pompous
2. Deceptively splendid
3. Answers will vary; *pompous* and *glittering* are apt.
4. ''Wept a river of tears'' is one of many possibilities.
5. The diction, including the frequent alliteration (line 17) and internal rhyme (line 9), suggests a down-to-earth person who is playful despite danger. This contributes to a tone that is, overall, positive.
6. Answers will vary on what the words mean when used as nouns. Some possible answers are given in parentheses: *seem* (emptiness); *ago* (oblivion); *blind* (blindness); *soon* (immediate future); *never* (annihilation); *isn't* (non-life, death); *was* (a thing of the past).

Primary Sources   Text page 739

''MIRACLES ARE TO COME''
Students will need to analyze this excerpt by Cummings in order to respond to the second writing assignment. Read these paragraphs aloud in class and ask students to respond to Cummings's views. Do they agree or disagree with what he says about being alive, about what's important in life?

THE LOVE SONG OF J. ALFRED PRUFROCK

Text page 742

Objectives

1. To respond to one of the most famous poems of the twentieth century

2. To interpret an extended metaphor

3. To analyze setting

4. To paraphrase lines

5. To write a dialogue between the speaker and another person

6. To write an interior monologue, imitating the poet's writing style

7. To write an essay evaluating a character

8. To write an essay comparing two characters

9. To write an essay responding to a critic's comments on the poem

10. To analyze the poem's rhythms, rhymes, metaphors, and allusions

interest your students. Conrad Aiken, an American poet and fiction writer, showed a manuscript copy of the poem to people he thought might be interested in it. Aiken was enthusiastic. Pound called it "as good as anything I've ever seen." But Harold Morris, owner of Poetry Bookshop in London, dismissed "Prufrock" as "absolutely insane."

THE LITERAL MEANING   The speaker in the poem, Prufrock, invites the reader to go through half-deserted streets with him. Immediately, Prufrock interrupts the journey with an observation about women who speak of Michelangelo. Then he describes the evening fog and introduces his obsession with time. After another mention of the women and Michelangelo, he conveys a picture of his self-consciousness, his boredom, and his apparent fear of women. He laments that he should have been a silent sea crab. Next, he illustrates, through an incident after tea, his inability to communicate with another person. He wonders if he should, like Lazarus, arise from the dead, but he cannot. He compares his irresolution to Hamlet's. He laments growing old. Although he wants to be able to live a full, romantic life, he is unable to do so.

Introducing the Poem

In addition to the many literary and Biblical allusions, this poem also has many memorable figures of speech, such as the simile comparing the evening sky to "a patient etherized upon a table" and the metaphor comparing the yellow fog to a cat. In addition, students might note the many images that reveal the character of the speaker: Prufrock's fear of his bald spot; Prufrock "pinned and wriggling on the wall"; and Prufrock wondering if he dares to eat a peach.

Analyzing Language and Style (text page 748) helps students examine the poem's rhythms, rhymes, metaphors, and allusions.

BACKGROUND ON THE POEM   Eliot wrote "The Love Song of J. Alfred Prufrock" in 1911, when he was a student at Harvard University, but it was not published until 1915 in the June issue of *Poetry* magazine. The reactions that readers had to it before its publication may

Teaching Strategies

PROVIDING FOR CULTURAL DIFFERENCES   Use the side notes and Comment (text page 745) to help students through the poem's literary and Biblical allusions. Students who still feel they are missing a lot can concentrate on the poem's sound and imagery and on the character of Prufrock.

PROVIDING FOR DIFFERENT LEVELS OF ABILITY   You may simply want to tell students about "Prufrock," read the poem to them, and explain some of the major parts. Tell them that they will notice how Prufrock's thoughts seem to skip around. You should probably not expect all students to answer all the questions at the end of the poem. If you want to reduce that number, the following five questions are among the easiest: 1, 3 (first two parts), 5, 13, 20. All students will benefit from the commentary on text page 746, the side notes, and the questions. Remind them that Eliot expected readers to have to work to understand his poetry.

READING THE POEM After you have talked about Eliot and "Prufrock," read the poem aloud in class. For homework, you might have students review the poem and the side notes, read A Comment on the Poem, and think about the responding questions. Begin the next day with a second oral reading of the poem, this time perhaps by a well-prepared student. Go over the side notes before proceeding to the questions at the end.

RETEACHING ALTERNATIVES As a last approach to the poem, ask students just to enjoy the lush, haunting music of the poem as you read it aloud. Or play a recording of Eliot reading the poem (Harvard Vocarium, Spoken Literature Series, recorded for the Poetry Room, Harvard College Library, 1930 and 1945).

Responding to the Poem   Text page 748

Answers to the questions in the Pupil's Edition appear in the Annotated Teacher's Edition.

Writing About the Poem

For help in revising their compositions, refer students to **Grammar, Usage, and Mechanics: A Reference Guide** on text pages 1183–1228 at the back of their books.

A CREATIVE RESPONSE
Your most able students should be able to handle assignment 1; others may prefer assignment 2.

1. Writing a Dialogue If you want your students to make the dialogue between Prufrock and Emerson, review Emerson's advice in "Self-Reliance." Students might also enjoy having Prufrock talk with a counselor or psychologist, an old friend, his mother or father, a woman he once almost asked for a date.

▶ CRITERIA FOR EVALUATING THE ASSIGNMENT The conversation reveals the self-consciousness and inadequacy Prufrock feels, as conveyed by the poem, and perhaps paraphrases or uses specific lines from the poem. The second speaker is completely in character as Emerson or the speaker of the student's choice.

2. Imitating Eliot's Style As data for the assignment, discuss the thoughts that go through a person's mind when he or she thinks an invitation may not be accepted. Have students review the Interior Monologue section on text page 589.

▶ CRITERIA FOR EVALUATING THE ASSIGNMENT The interior monologue uses the stream-of-consciousness technique and reveals the thinker's feelings and fears. It begins with the words, "Let us go then, you and I."

A CRITICAL RESPONSE
Assignments 3 through 6 all evaluate Prufrock's character, but do so in different ways. You may wish to discuss all four assignments, but allow students to choose one on which to write.

3. Evaluating a Character The writing assignment outlines the contents of the essay. Elicit some immediate reactions to the three aspects suggested.

▶ CRITERIA FOR EVALUATING THE ASSIGNMENT The essay cites details from the poem in order to explain (a) how Prufrock sees himself, (b) how he thinks others see him, and (c) how he wants others to see him. The essay concludes with a statement of whether or not the student can sympathize with Prufrock.

4. Comparing Characters Students will need to have read the Walter Mitty story in order to complete this assignment. Although the prompt suggests that either answer is all right—that Prufrock is or is not a Mitty type—note that it directs students to make lists of similarities and differences and to choose the more persuasive list.

▶ CRITERIA FOR EVALUATING THE ASSIGNMENT The essay shows insight into the fact that Prufrock never imagines his own greatness, despite comparisons with John the Baptist and Hamlet, whereas Mitty constantly does so.

5. Responding to a Critic Read and discuss Pound's comment, together with directions preceding and following it. Note that students are to comment on whether it is possible to interpret the poem as ending on a note of triumph, and to give an opinion of the stanza on Hamlet.

▶ CRITERIA FOR EVALUATING THE ASSIGNMENT The essay offers cogent reasons for believing the poem does or does not end on a note of triumph, and states the student's opinion on the stanza referring to Hamlet.

6. Supporting a Premise Clarify the assignment: have students write an essay arguing in favor of only one of the ages listed.

▶ CRITERIA FOR EVALUATING THE ASSIGNMENT The essay offers cogent details from the poem to support its interpretation of Prufrock's age.

Analyzing Language and Style

RHYTHMS, RHYMES, AND METAPHORS
1. Metrical feet per line vary from 3 to 4, 5, or 6. The lines easiest to scan are lines 1 and 12 (trochaic tetrameter) and 11 (iambic trimeter).
2. Repetition within stanzas unifies stanzas (for example, "time" in lines 26–34) ; repetition of "In the room the women come and go/Talking of Michelangelo" serves as a refrain and warning of scene change.

3. Rhyme is used throughout the poem. Some examples of end rhyme: Stanza one uses *I/sky, streets/retreats, hotels/shells, argument/intent, is it/visit.* Lines 41–44 repeat one rhyme, *thin/chin/pin/thin.* Internal rhymes are far fewer but include "decisions and revisions" (line 48), "days and ways" (line 60).

4. Choices will vary. Some probabilities include "When the evening is spread out against the sky / Like a patient etherized upon a table" (lines 2–3); "I have measured out my life with coffee spoons" (line 51); "And when I am . . . sprawling on a pin, / . . . wriggling on the wall" (lines 57–58).

5. Answers will depend on responses to question 4. The figures of speech quoted above use "things" from modern life rather than elements from the world of nature.

ALLUSIONS

Students' interpretations of the meaning of the allusions in the poem will vary. Here are some sample answers:

1. The speaker lives in his own kind of hell.

2. Knowledge of the great Italian Renaissance sculptor and painter suggests sophisticated, "cultured" women.

3. There will be a time for philosophical considerations.

4. The speaker feels as if he's been dissected but will never really suffer such a prophet's fate.

5. Would it really matter if one could grasp the meaning of the universe?

6. These blasé people wouldn't be interested even in the observations of someone who came back from the dead.

7. The speaker does not see himself as wrestling with the meaning of existence so profoundly as Hamlet did.

8. The speaker knows how to play up to somebody important.

Extending the Poem

Your students might enjoy discussing a possible historical parallel between modern poetry and rock music. Many early readers of Imagist poetry and free verse were convinced that it was a fad, and a most annoying fad at that. They assumed that such poetry would quickly wither away. Much the same thing happened with rock music. Traditionalists disliked early rock and predicted its rapid demise, but here, too, the critics were wrong. Just as today's poetry shows the continuing influence of Imagism and Symbolism, rock music now dominates the popular music scene. You might want to find out whether your students regard this Imagist/rock parallel as valid.

Students undoubtedly will enjoy exploring the lighter side of T. S. Eliot by reading *Old Possum's Book of Practical Cats* or listening to a recording of the Broadway musical *Cats,* which is based on these poems.

Wallace Stevens

Text page 750

THE DEATH OF A SOLDIER

Text page 752

ANECDOTE OF THE JAR

Text page 753

Objectives

1. To respond to poems with images used as symbols

2. To recognize the nature of an elegy

3. To write an essay comparing what two poems say about art

4. To write a paragraph analyzing a poem's message

5. To determine the precise meanings of words

Introducing the Poems

In these poems students should note the use of images as symbols to stand for abstract ideas. Autumn, with its falling leaves, might represent falling soldiers. The jar is often seen to stand either for anything made by humans or for art. The wilderness, on the other hand, probably symbolizes untamed nature or possibly, even, chaos. In addition, you might want students to consider the poet's precise word choice to convey intentionally ambiguous meanings.

"The Death of a Soldier" is a free-verse poem; but in each stanza the first line has four accented beats, the second has three, and the last line one.

"Anecdote of the Jar" is basically iambic tetrameter with internal rhymes and an unusual rhyme scheme (*abcb defg ggha*).

BACKGROUND ON THE POEMS "Anecdote of the Jar" was first published in *Poetry* Magazine in October 1919 along with thirteen other poems under the general title of "Pecksniffiana." Stevens sent "Anecdote" to Harriet Monroe in August 1919. He added "The Death of a Soldier" to the second edition of *Harmonium* in 1930 along with thirteen other new poems.

THE LITERAL MEANING *The Death of a Soldier* A soldier dies. No pomp is called for; death has no memorial. The autumn wind may stop, but the clouds keep moving.

Anecdote of the Jar The speaker placed a round jar on a hill in Tennessee. The "slovenly wilderness" surrounded the jar, but the jar won out—it "took dominion everywhere."

Teaching Strategies

PROVIDING FOR CULTURAL DIFFERENCES Different cultures place different values on the lives of soldiers and on the encroachment of things human-made on the natural—the subject matter of the two poems by Wallace Stevens. Even in classes without significant cultural differences, you may want to have students discuss these two topics. The United States builds a monument listing the name of every soldier killed in Vietnam. How do other nations and cultures—the North Vietnamese, for example, or the Iranians—memorialize their war dead, if at all? Environmentalists in the United States worry about the encroachment of development on the natural environment. How do other nations and cultures view such development?

PROVIDING FOR DIFFERENT LEVELS OF ABILITY The broad ideas in the poems are not hard to grasp, although the poems do permit a range of specific interpretations and speculations. Encourage more advanced students, or ones especially interested in poetry, to read more of Wallace Stevens's poems.

READING THE POEMS The two Stevens poems can be handled in one class period. Before beginning, you might point out to students that highly symbolic poetry can have more than one interpretation. Symbols can be slippery. There is seldom one "right" answer for what a symbol means. For this reason, it is wise to accept any student's interpretation not absolutely inconsistent with the text of the poem.

You will probably want to spend more time on "Anecdote of the Jar" than on "The Death of a Soldier." If students cannot interpret the "jar" as a symbol, tell them that it seems to be a human creation—whatever it may be, leaving the interpretation of the "wilderness" open. There are varying interpretations of "slovenly" as well. In one interpretation, nature is already slovenly; in the other, nature becomes slovenly only after the "jar" is placed there. This difference is important in deciding what the poem "means." Also, have students think about the various literal definitions of the word *jar*. Could its various meanings as a verb ("to be out of harmony" is one meaning) have anything to do with the interpretation of the poem?

RETEACHING ALTERNATIVES You might ask two students who have differing interpretations of each poem to debate their ideas informally. If they can find support for their views in the interpretations of critics, that will help bolster their position. A number of critical studies of Stevens's poetry have been published.

Responding to the Poems

Text pages 752, 754

Answers to the questions in the Pupil's Edition appear in the Annotated Teacher's Edition.

Writing About the Poems

For help in revising their compositions, refer students to **Grammar, Usage, and Mechanics: A Reference Guide** on text pages 1183–1228 at the back of their books.

A CRITICAL RESPONSE
1. Comparing Poems Have students review both Melville's "Art" (text page 319) and Stevens's "Anecdote of the Jar" before they summarize either poet's views.

▶ CRITERIA FOR EVALUATING THE ASSIGNMENT The paragraph or brief essay cites Melville as commenting on the powerful, paradoxical forces that meet and meld in poetry, and Stevens as commenting on the power of poetry to serve as the focal point of everything around it.

2. Analyzing the Poem's Message Two legitimate interpretations of the poem are given in the writing assignment. You may wish to have students who strongly favor the different views conduct a sort of mini-debate for the class.

▶ CRITERIA FOR EVALUATING THE ASSIGNMENT Whether the essay argues that the jar symbolizes the way art gives order and meaning to nature or that the jar symbolizes human interference with nature, cogent reasons and details from the poem are used to support the argument.

Analyzing Language and Style

PRECISE MEANINGS

1. *Contracts* means "shrinks, draws together." "Life contracts" suggests a shriveling up as contrasted with death, which is conveyed by "life is extinguished."
2. Answers will vary. Possibilities include *vase, stone, monument,* etc. Another meaning of *jar* is "disharmony."
3. *Slovenly* means "lazily slipshod." It is usually applied to people and therefore does personify nature.
4. *Port* can mean "harbor, haven, gate, door, passageway," or "hole."

Extending the Poems

Have students discuss the following critical comments about "Anecdote of the Jar" from Susan B. Weston's *Wallace Stevens: An Introduction to the Poetry.*

1. "True, there are allegorical dimensions to the two images, with the jar suggesting man, imagination, and art, and the wilderness suggesting nature, reality, and unordered chaos."
2. "The poem's first line—'I placed a jar'—suggests the importance of the gesture to the speaker: the placing, focusing activity of mind organizing the 'wilderness.'"
3. "In spite of the ease with which we label Stevens's particulars, though, the poems are rarely adequately summed up by a single abstract assertion, for Stevens's ambiguous syntax and his titles generally create a richness not apparent at first glance."

Primary Sources Text page 754

POETRY AND MEANING

In this excerpt Stevens explains why it is difficult to say what a poem means. You may wish to compare the "man walking" with the literal words of a poem and the "shadow" with the deliberately ambiguous, multiple meanings a poem may imply.

EXERCISES IN CRITICAL THINKING AND WRITING Text page 755

ANALYZING A POEM

In this exercise, students are asked to analyze either of two poems, an Imagist poem by Wallace Stevens or a Symbolist poem by Marianne Moore. If time is limited, you might want to narrow the focus of the assignment to one or two of the elements that contribute to the poem's meaning, rather than to all of the elements.

During the prewriting stage, you might discuss with students the images of "Disillusionment of Ten O'Clock," pointing out that the words *haunted* and *dream* both indicate that the poem is about the imagination (or lack of it). With "Poetry," you might point out the importance of reading the poem for its literal meaning about the speaker's attitude toward poetry. In fact, she makes statements throughout the poem with which students should readily identify, such as "we do not admire what we can not understand." It might help students to know that the reference to "business documents and school-books" refers to the poet's belief that it is difficult to distinguish between poetry and prose. "Literalists of the imagination" refers to poets such as W.B. Yeats, who believed that his poetic visions and symbols represented divine ideas that should not be obscured with too much attention to style.

▶ CRITERIA FOR EVALUATING THE ASSIGNMENT   Students should demonstrate in their essays, through paraphrase, that they understand the literal meaning of the poem. In addition, essays should analyze one or more elements significant to the poem by illustrating how that element contributes to the overall meaning and effect of the poem. Finally, students should discuss their affective response to the poem.

Further Reading

Works listed are suitable for both students and teachers unless the annotation ends with the note [Teachers].

Allen, Gay Wilson, et al. *American Poetry* (Harper & Row, 1965). An excellent anthology that includes many poems by Pound, Williams, Moore, Sandburg, Cummings, Eliot, and Stevens.

Callahan, North. *Carl Sandburg: Lincoln of Our Literature* (New York University Press, 1970). Brief, readable biography, a good introduction to Sandburg's life and works.

Coffman, Stanley K., Jr. *Imagism: A Chapter from the History of Modern Poetry* (University of Oklahoma Press, 1951). A study of modern poetic forms that begins with a chronology of the Imagist movement and then presents an account of the movement's history, values, and deficiencies.

Doyal, Charles. *William Carlos Williams and the American Poem* (St. Martin's Press, 1982). The development of Williams's poetry from *Poems* (1909) through his Imagist and Objectivist phases to his culminating work, *Paterson.*

Friedman, Norman. *E. E. Cummings: The Growth of a Writer* (Southern Illinois University Press, 1964). Literary biography of Cummings and a guide to some of his best-known poems.

Goodwin, K. L. *The Influence of Ezra Pound* (Oxford University Press, 1966). Pound's influence on Eliot, Williams, Cummings, and others.

Gregory, Horace, and Marya Zaturenska. *A History of American Poetry 1900–1940* (Harcourt Brace Jovanovich, 1946). A systematic history of major developments in American poetry. [Teachers]

Hall, Donald. *Marianne Moore: The Cage and the Animal* (Pegasus, 1970). An appealing and informative study of the life, character, and art of Marianne Moore, based in part on personal interviews, written by a noted American poet.

Kidder, Rushworth M. *E. E. Cummings: An Introduction to the Poetry* (Columbia University Press, 1979). A poem-by-poem analysis of each of Cummings's twelve collections of poetry. A good one-volume source for help with a specific poem.

Matthews, T. S. *Great Tom: Notes Toward the Definition of T. S. Eliot* (Harper & Row, 1974). A good introduction to Eliot's life, with brief comments on some of his poems. Students may appreciate a number of parodies of Eliot in the appendix, including one by James Joyce.

Matthiessen, F. O. *The Achievement of T. S. Eliot: An Essay on the Nature of Poetry,* Third ed. (Oxford University Press, 1958). A classic study assessing Eliot's poetic method. One chapter deals with the objective correlative. [Teachers]

Matthiessen, F. O. *The Oxford Book of American Verse* (Oxford University Press, 1950). A standard anthology that includes many poems by Pound, Williams, Moore, Sandburg, Cummings, Eliot, and Stevens.

Nitchie, George W. *Marianne Moore: An Introduction to the Poetry* (Columbia University Press, 1969). A straightforward introduction to Moore's poetry, concentrating on her themes of adaptation and endurance.

Perkins, David. *A History of Modern Poetry* (Harvard University Press, 1987). Criticism and analysis of important modern poets. Chapters on Eliot, Cummings, and others in Part One, ''The Age of High Modernism''; chapters on Pound, Williams, and Stevens in Part Two, ''The Resurgence of Pound, Williams, and Stevens.'' [Teacher]

Rosenthal, M. L., ed. *The William Carlos Williams Reader* (New Directions, 1966). Prominent literary critic's selection of the best of Williams's poetry, fiction, autobiography, drama, and essays.

Sandburg, Carl. *Always the Young Stranger* (Harcourt Brace Jovanovich, 1953). Autobiography of Sandburg's childhood and youth in Galesburg, Illinois, revealing much about small-town Midwestern life of the nineteenth century.

Stevens, Wallace, ed. by Milton J. Bates. *Opus Posthumous* (Knopf, 1989). A collection of poems, plays, and prose published after Stevens's death.

Voices & Visions (Annenberg CPB Project, 1988). This series of thirteen videocassettes first broadcast on PBS has separate, fifty-minute documentaries on Pound, Williams, Moore, Eliot, and Stevens. Each videocassette contains biographical information, readings of important poems, and interviews with critics.

Wagner, Linda Welshimer. *The Poems of William Carlos Williams: A Critical Study* (Wesleyan University Press, 1964). A clear, readable account of Williams's poetic interests and development.

AMERICAN DRAMA

Teaching the American Drama Unit

The unit introduction covers the principles of drama and the history of American drama. Whether you use individual reading, teacher-led discussion, or small-group discussions with the unit material, students should note the following points:

1. Playwriting differs from other genres of writing in that a play is not finished until the words and gestures the playwright has imagined come to life on stage. This process also involves a director, actors, set and costume designers, stagehands, musicians, and electricians (The Elements of Drama, text page 758).

2. Good plays make dramatic use of conflict, a struggle that has the viewer rooting for someone, usually the protagonist (the major character who drives the action). Conflict may be external (coming from the side opposing the protagonist) or internal (within the protagonist). Exposition or the giving of background information must enable the viewer actively to *participate* in the performance (The Basic Principles of Drama, text pages 758–760).

3. It is almost a miracle if a new play is produced in the United States today because only Broadway plays earn enough to allow a playwright to remain dedicated to writing, and the route to Broadway is difficult. Involved are the playwright, his or her agent, a producer's ability to raise half a million dollars or more to finance the play, a director, actors, tryouts of the play off Broadway, and finally success—or failure—on Broadway (How a Play Is Produced, text pages 760–761).

4. Historically, Eugene O'Neill (1888–1953) is considered the first important American playwright. Before him, American drama consisted of shows, entertainments, melodramas, and farces, often presented by touring companies (The History of American Drama, text page 762).

5. "Drama travels in the caboose of literature" (Robert Sherwood). That is, it is slow to adopt new attitudes and methods, perhaps because drama is a social art. People may stalk out of a theater when presented with something they would read—even enjoy—in private (Theater as a Social Art, text page 763).

6. European drama, which greatly influenced American drama, matured earlier. Of special importance were the Norwegian Henrik Ibsen (1828–1906), who tackled subjects like guilt, sexuality, and mental illness; the Swede August Strindberg (1849–1912), who brought psychological complexity to his characters; and the Russian Anton Chekhov (1860–1904), who focused on the inner emotions and concerns of daily life (The Influence of Ibsen, Strindberg, and Chekhov, text page 763).

7. Early twentieth-century American drama was dominated by realism: the illusion that watching a play is looking at life through a missing "fourth wall." Eugene O'Neill tried to reveal more than realism can by experimenting with masks and asides. His plays were performed by the Provincetown Players in New York's Greenwich Village, formed in 1916 to produce plays the commercial theater would not touch. A similar group was the Washington Square Players, formed in 1917 (American Realism and Eugene O'Neill, text page 764).

8. The dominant American dramatists since World War II have been Arthur Miller (born 1915) and Tennessee Williams (1911–1983); both combine realism with poetic expression. Miller focuses on society's impact on his

characters' lives, while Williams probes his characters psychologically. Miller's great plays include *Death of a Salesman* (1949), *All My Sons* (1947), and *The Crucible* (1953). Williams's include *The Glass Menagerie* (1944), *A Streetcar Named Desire* (1947), and *Summer and Smoke* (1948) (Arthur Miller and Tennessee Williams, text pages 764–766).

9. Realism was originally a revolt against mid-nineteenth century theatricalism. There is currently a swing back to theatricalism, which emphasizes stage effects and imaginative settings. Expressionist (Theater of the Absurd) playwrights aimed not so much to tell a story as to reveal their characters' inner consciousness. They include Samuel Beckett and Eugene Ionesco of Europe, and the American, Edward Albee (born 1928). Thanks to such experimental drama, playwrights now have considerable freedom (The Revolt Against Realism, text pages 766–767).

Objectives of the American Drama Unit

1. To improve reading proficiency and expand vocabulary

2. To gain exposure to notable playwrights and their plays

3. To define and identify the elements of drama

4. To define and identify significant literary techniques

5. To interpret and respond to drama, orally and in writing, through analysis of its elements

6. To practice the following critical thinking and writing skills:
   a. Responding to conflict
   b. Responding to "biographical criticism"
   c. Evaluating versions of a play
   d. Analyzing the use of light
   e. Comparing a play with memoirs
   f. Predicting a character's development
   g. Evaluating a play

Tennessee Williams

THE GLASS MENAGERIE

Objectives

1. To enjoy and respond to one of the great plays of modern American theater

2. To analyze the use of basic dramatic elements

3. To interpret the symbolism in the play

4. To write a letter from one character to another

5. To write an essay responding to the conflict between freedom and responsibility

6. To write an essay responding to the ''biographical criticism''

7. To evaluate different versions of the play

8. To write an essay analyzing the use of light

9. To write an essay comparing the play to the memoirs

Introducing the Play

The major elements of the play are listed here in outline form. Review the section on The Basic Principles of Drama (text pages 758–760). Note that a case can also be made for Amanda Wingfield as protagonist. Her ''want'' is the desire to have her intensely shy daughter Laura settled in life with a job and a husband.

- **Protagonist:** Tom Wingfield
- **Conflicts:** person vs. person; internal
- **Significant techniques:** episodic (''memory'') structure, symbolism
- **Setting:** tenement apartment, Midwestern city (St. Louis, Missouri) in the Depression era of the early 1930's
- **Theme:** illusion versus reality; duty vs. individual freedom

BACKGROUND ON THE PLAYWRIGHT Williams was born March 26, 1911, as Thomas Lanier Williams, in the rectory of his grandfather's Episcopal church in Columbus, Mississippi. Both of his parents—Edwina Dakins and Cornelius Coffin Williams—came from proud American lineages. Because Cornelius traveled for the phone company, young Tom, his mother, and his sister Rose (two years his senior) lived with Edwina's parents in a warm, genteel environment rich in status (''the minister's family'') if not wealth. Tom's childhood case of diphtheria led to eye and kidney problems, delicate treatment as a child, and life-long hypochondria.

In 1919 Tom, Edwina, and Rose moved to St. Louis to join Cornelius, who had been promoted to a management position with the International Shoe Company. Relocation to a noisy industrial town where other children (and their own father) ridiculed their accents and quiet ways devastated the shy Tom and Rose. Meanwhile, Edwina was often ill after the birth of another son, Dakin, in 1919; and Cornelius's unsettled behavior pattern led to violent arguments. The family also moved repeatedly (Tom had lived in 16 places by age 15) because Edwina was constantly seeking a properly ''aristocratic'' home.

Tom reacted to his traumatic environment by turning to an imaginative inner life—he graduated 53rd in a high school class of 83. But his grandparents and father sent him to the University of Missouri at Columbia, noted for journalism and obligatory ROTC training. Classmates found the slim, five-foot-six-inch Tom shy, but enjoyed his wit and good humor, and ribbed him about an absent-mindedness that arose from his preoccupation with writing. Again, however, Tom let his grades slide. After three years, his father cited Tom's *F*'s in ROTC as a reason to pull him out of college (the real reason appears to have been money).

During the next two or three years, Tom worked for the shoe company days and wrote feverishly at night. Meanwhile his beloved sister Rose, who had already been institutionalized twice, grew more and more emotionally unbalanced. But it was Tom who collapsed—from too little sleep, too much smoking and caffeine, and turmoil about personal feelings he could not yet handle. He recuperated rapidly with his grandparents (then in Memphis), and began to view himself as a new kind of Williams—one that flourished in Tennessee.

After a brief stint at Washington University in St. Louis, Tom was associated with a writing group at the State University of Iowa. It was during this period that his parents solved Rose's problems by agreeing to her having a prefrontal lobotomy—an irreversible operation that left her calm but irrational the rest of her life. Tom finally earned his B.A. and left college in 1938, but the horror of his sister's fate never left him. He devotedly visited her and saw to her needs all his life.

For Tennessee Williams, as Tom renamed himself, the next six years were a precarious mix of odd jobs, small writing prizes, little theater productions of a few plays, and itinerant movement—New Orleans, southern California, Mexico, New York. A cararact on his left eye (he later had four surgeries) kept him out of World War II.

BACKGROUND ON THE PLAY   Williams's first professionally produced play, *Battle of Angels* (1940), was not a success, but a six months' screenwriting job in the MGM movie mill enabled him to complete *The Gentleman Caller,* soon retitled *The Glass Menagerie* (1944)—his first success. Surprisingly, critics kept the play alive in its three-month Chicago debut, and its longer New York run established Williams's name and fortune at the age of 34. As the noted critic Brooks Atkinson observed, *The Glass Menagerie* glowed with ''pity for people, coolness of perspective [and] poetic grace.'' Other successes followed, notably, *A Streetcar Named Desire* (1947), *Summer and Smoke* (1948), *Cat on a Hot Tin Roof* (1955), and *The Night of the Iguana* (1961). All of these plays were made into movies. But as biographer Donald Spoto notes, ''. . . nothing Tennessee Williams ever wrote after *The Glass Menagerie* has its wholeness of sentiment, its breadth of spirit and its unangry, quiet voice about the great reach of small lives.'' A 1980 recipient of the highest American civilian honor, the Medal of Freedom, Williams remains the foremost American dramatist of the post-World War II era.

SUMMARY   A summary of each scene appears in the Annotated Teacher's Edition.

Teaching Strategies

PROVIDING FOR CULTURAL DIFFERENCES   The ''Southern belle'' concept that figures strongly in the characterization of Amanda may need explanation. Students from other cultures may never have heard of this genteel way of life where the social graces and hospitality are of the utmost importance, social life revolves around the front parlor, and young men and women play elaborate flirtation games conducted with exquisite politeness.

PROVIDING FOR DIFFERENT LEVELS OF ABILITY   Vocabulary should be studied before each set of scenes. Complete the response questions at the end of each group of scenes before moving on.

READING THE PLAY   You might want to assign parts to your best readers and read the play aloud. Group Scenes 1 and 2, 3 and 4, 5 and 6. Take Scene 7 by itself. If you have many good readers, assign alternate casts for different sets of scenes. Briefly check comprehension of each set of scenes before moving on. After correcting misconceptions, begin to discuss the response questions from the text or assign them as homework. At the beginning of the next class period, briefly discuss this work before continuing the play.

RETEACHING ALTERNATIVES   If possible, audio- or videotape the in-class reading of the play. Use this tape to help students interpret the play as they follow in their texts.

Responding to the Play
Text pages 777, 785, 796, 809

Answers to the questions in the Pupil's Edition appear in the Annotated Teacher's Edition.

Writing About the Play

The six writing assignments differ in the critical thinking and writing skills demanded of the student. All should be discussed even if students write only one or two of the essays. Writing assignments 3 and 6 are the most similar, in that both use biographical data, but only the first analyzes the relevance of biographical information to a literary work.

For help in revising their compositions, refer students to **Grammar, Usage, and Mechanics: A Reference Guide** on text pages 1183–1228 at the back of their books.

A CREATIVE RESPONSE
1. Extending the Play   Discuss the probable contents of such a letter—Laura's and Amanda's feelings? their household worries? appearance of some new benefactor? concerns about Tom? Emphasize, however, that students are completely free to choose whatever details and tone they think are appropriate.

▶ CRITERIA FOR EVALUATING THE ASSIGNMENT   Whatever the letter's contents, it echoes Laura's attitudes and phrasing, and at least hints at the home situation without Tom.

A CRITICAL RESPONSE
2. Responding to the Play   This assignment deals with the internal conflict faced not only by Tom, but also by many grown children. Plausible arguments can be made for either side of the issue. Note that students should discuss the issue in general, and also state whether they believe Tom was right or wrong in leaving for the Merchant Marine.

▶ CRITERIA FOR EVALUATING THE ASSIGNMENT   Whatever stance is taken, the student offers cogent reasons or arguments in favor of the stance, and judges the rightness or wrongness of Tom's action in a manner consistent with the stance.

3. Commenting on ''Biographical Criticism''   Read and discuss Brendan Gill's remarks and the entire writing assignment. Clarify the dual issue: Is such biographical criticism *necessary*? Is it *helpful*? With your guidance, students should come to see that a work of art is an entity that can be understood without knowing about the author's life. Nevertheless, enjoyment or appreciation of a work can be enhanced by awareness of events in an author's life.

▶ CRITERIA FOR EVALUATING THE ASSIGNMENT The essay clearly states the student's opinion on both the necessity and the helpfulness of biographical criticism. These opinions are clarified by references to Tennessee Williams and *The Glass Menagerie,* or to the lives and works of other authors.

4. Evaluating Different Versions of the Play You may wish first to elicit from the class explicit statements of the theme and mood of the play. Then focus on how theme and mood would change if Laura's emergence from her fragile world were *not* left in doubt, or if the narrative lines spoken by Tom, in uniform, were omitted.

▶ CRITERIA FOR EVALUATING THE ASSIGNMENT The essay shows a grasp of the theme and mood of the play and clearly expresses an opinion on the changes in the TV and film versions and their effects.

5. Describing the Use of Lights Discuss a few of Williams's explicit comments on lighting (for example, pages 772, column 1; 778, column 2; and 779, column 1). Have students locate and analyze additional examples before they begin to write.

▶ CRITERIA FOR EVALUATING THE ASSIGNMENT The essay cites specific passages from the play to support its explanation of how lighting creates mood and contributes to the theme of illusion versus reality.

6. Comparing the Play to the Memoirs Have students read Primary Source: The Model for Laura (text page 811), and discuss it as a class or in small groups before they fill out the prewriting chart.

▶ CRITERIA FOR EVALUATING THE ASSIGNMENT The essay identifies similarities in characters, setting, and conflict between Williams's play and his real life as revealed in the excerpt from his *Memoirs.* The essay cites specific details to support its points.

Extending the Play

Consider having students research and report on the life of Tennessee Williams and his importance to American drama (see reading list) or read another famous American play and compare and contrast it with *The Glass Menagerie.*

Students who are musically inclined may wish to prepare the tape of "background music" for selected scenes, play the tape for the class, and explain their choice of music.

You may wish to have students compare and contrast a movie version of the play with the printed version. (The 1950 movie, which changes the ending, stars Jane Wyman, Kirk Douglas, Gertrude Lawrence, and Arthur Kennedy; the 1987 version, which omits some of Tom's narration, features Joanne Woodward, John Malkovich, Karen Allen, and James Naughton.)

Students might also read and/or view other prize-winning Williams plays: *A Streetcar Named Desire* (Pulitzer Prize, 1947)—a 1951 movie with Vivien Leigh as Blanche DuBois, and Marlon Brando as Stanley Kowalski; a 1984 TV movie with Ann-Margaret as Blanche. *Cat on a Hot Tin Roof* (Pulitzer Prize, 1955)—a 1958 movie with Burl Ives, Elizabeth Taylor, Paul Newman, and Judith Anderson.

Primary Sources   Text page 811

THE MODEL FOR LAURA

Williams's heartfelt portrait of his sister Rose sheds some light on the character Laura. Have students discuss the similarities between Rose and Laura, as well as the differences. Then have them consider why a playwright would choose to portray a character who is so like a close family member.

Lorraine Hansberry

Text page 812

A RAISIN IN THE SUN

Text page 813

Objectives

1. To respond to an important play about an African American family

2. To analyze the use of basic dramatic elements

3. To analyze the reversals in the plot and the use of suspense

4. To interpret the symbolism in the play

5. To identify dynamic and static characters

6. To analyze the play's theme

7. To write an essay projecting a character's development

8. To write an essay responding to the characters

9. To write an essay evaluating the play

Introducing the Play

Here are the major elements of the play:

- **Protagonist:** Walter Younger
- **Antagonist:** Karl Lindner and the Clybourne Park Improvement Association
- **Conflicts:** person vs. person; person vs. society; person vs. self
- **Significant techniques:** foreshadowing and reversals
- **Settings:** a rundown apartment, Chicago's Southside, between 1945 (''the end of World War II'') and 1959
- **Theme:** the triumph of courage over character flaws and social injustice

BACKGROUND ON THE PLAYWRIGHT You might comment on Hansberry's awareness that to her siblings (seven, ten, and twelve years older) she was a nuisance, so she learned to play alone. In *To Be Young, Gifted and Black* she writes, too, of childhood games (''Captain, may I?''), the whole family sleeping in the park on sweltering Chicago summer nights, and the howling mob that surrounded their house when they moved into a hostile white neighborhood. She recalls how other children at school beat her up when her mother sent her to kindergarten in the midst of the Depression wearing a white fur coat—an

experience that gave her a lasting hatred of symbols of wealth. Hansberry was from a middle-class home and remembers envying the latch-key ghetto children the yellow door keys they wore on strings around their necks.

In her twenties, attending the Art Institute in New York, Hansberry shared an apartment on the lower East Side with three women—because, she explains, it was too crowded in Harlem, even for those who *wanted* to move there. She was earning $31.70 a week as a typist-receptionist, attending Civil Rights meetings many nights, ushering at rallies, going for long walks in Harlem just to talk to people, and—always—writing and dreaming about making a contribution to American theater. By 1954 she was married to Robert Nemiroff, a songwriter and music publisher, and living with him in a small Greenwich Village walk-up apartment. They were still there when *A Raisin in the Sun* proved a phenomenal success.

Later Hansberry and Nemiroff moved to the country, and Hansberry continued the rest of her life to write and to speak for the Civil Rights movement. In January 1964 she was excited about her play *The Sign in Sidney Brustein's Window* (1964); by July she knew something was seriously wrong with her health. James Baldwin reports having seen Hansberry in the hospital as she was dying: ''She did not seem frightened or sad, only exasperated that her body no longer obeyed her; she smiled and waved.''

After her death in 1965, Hansberry's husband arranged a collection of her letters, poems, and dramatic scenes into a seven-and-a-half hour radio presentation, *Lorraine Hansberry in Her Own Words* (WBAI, 1967). Then the collection was produced as a play, *To Be Young, Gifted and Black* (Cherry Lane Theatre, New York City, January 2, 1969), which ran for twelve months. Finally it was published as a book with the same title (1970)—a work offering insight into the African American experience of mid-century America.

BACKGROUND ON THE PLAY In his introduction to *To Be Young, Gifted and Black,* James Baldwin talks about meeting Lorraine Hansberry in Philadelphia in 1959, when *A Raisin in the Sun* was opening. He calls it ''an historical achievement. . . . I had never in my life seen so many black people in the theater. And the reason was that never before, in the entire history of the American theater, had so much of the truth of black people's lives been seen on the stage. Black people ignored the theater because the theater had always ignored them.''

Students will also be interested in an interviewer's questions about *A Raisin in the Sun* and Hansberry's response:

INTERVIEWER: The question, I'm sure, is asked you many times—you may be tired of it—someone comes up to you and says: "This is not really a Negro play; why, this could be about anybody! It's a play about people!" What is your reaction? What do you say?

L.H. Well, I hadn't noticed the contradiction because I'd always been under the impression that Negroes *are* people. But actually it's an excellent question, because invariably that has been the point of reference. And I do know what people are trying to say. People are trying—what they are trying to say is that this is not what they consider the traditional treatment of the Negro in the theater. They're trying to say that it isn't a propaganda play, that it isn't something that hits you over the head; they are trying to say that they believe the characters in our play transcend category. However, it is an unfortunate way to try and say it, because I believe that one of the most sound ideas in dramatic writing is that in order to create the universal, you must pay very great attention to the specific. Universality, I think, emerges from truthful identity of what is.

In other words, I have told people that not only is this a Negro family, specifically and definitely culturally, but it's not even a New York family or a southern Negro family. It is specifically Southside Chicago . . . that kind of care, that kind of attention to detail. In other words, I think people, to the extent we accept them and believe them as who they're supposed to be, to that extent they can become everybody. So I would say it is definitely a Negro play before it is anything else . . .

When *A Raisin in the Sun* opened in New York City, critics praised it enthusiastically. Walter Kerr of the *New York Herald Tribune* called it "an honest, intelligible, and moving experience." Frank Ashton of the *New York World-Telegram & Sun* wrote, "It is honest drama, catching up real people. . . . It will make you proud of human beings."

SUMMARY A summary of each act appears in the Annotated Teacher's Edition.

Teaching Strategies

PROVIDING FOR CULTURAL DIFFERENCES Students need to grasp the enormity of a $10,000 check in the 1940's and 1950's. A salary of $6,000 to $10,000 a year was an extremely good salary, comparable to $25,000 or $35,000 in the 1990's. You may also wish to remind students that the language spoken by the characters in the play is a dialect that differs from standard English in grammar, pronunciation, and vocabulary.

Writing assignment 2 gives students a chance to write and talk about cultural and ethnic identity vs. assimilation. Before they write, have students meet in small groups to discuss their personal experiences and concerns. They might talk about language, customs, housing, stereotypes, etc.

PROVIDING FOR DIFFERENT LEVELS OF ABILITY If the play is presented well, it will be accessible to students at all levels of ability.

READING THE PLAY You might begin by reading and discussing the Langston Hughes poem (text page 813) from which the title comes. Then read the Hansberry biography (text page 812).

Depending upon your class, you will probably want students to read the play aloud. If possible, arrange to have students listen to the audiocassette recording of the final scenes in Act Three.

RETEACHING ALTERNATIVES Have students talk about their personal responses to the play as a whole and to each character. Focusing on one character at a time, ask students what they think: Is the character believable? sympathetic? Does the character remind you of anyone you know?

Responding to the Play
Text pages 834, 855, 865

Answers to the questions in the Pupil's Edition appear in the Annotated Teacher's Edition.

Writing About the Play

The three assignments differ in focus. Discuss all three, even if students write only one essay.

For help in revising their compositions, refer students to **Grammar, Usage, and Mechanics: A Reference Guide** on text pages 1183–1228 at the back of their books.

A CREATIVE RESPONSE
1. Extending the Play Discuss the depth of Walter's realization of new values, and brainstorm some possibilities for his future, depending on how well those values have "taken."

▶ CRITERIA FOR EVALUATING THE ASSIGNMENT The essay consists of at least three paragraphs that plausibly describe what happens to Walter after the family moves to Clybourne Park.

A CRITICAL RESPONSE
2. Responding to the Characters The questions in the writing assignment move from the concerns of Beneatha and Asagai to the basic issue of cultural identity versus assimilation. If your students are quite diverse in background, encourage those from minority cultures to speak on the issue. Note that at least three stances are possible:

(1) total commitment to ethnic identity; (2) total assimilation; and (3) adaptation in some ways but retention of key cultural values as well.

▶ CRITERIA FOR EVALUATING THE ASSIGNMENT   The essay clearly states the student's opinions on (1) Beneatha's and Asagai's feelings about heritage, (2) the importance of retaining cultural identity, and (3) assimilation as a goal for all Americans. Cogent reasons are offered in support of positions taken.

3. *Evaluating the Play*   Read the writing assignment with your students, but before they make decisions about the universality of the play, read also Primary Sources: A Letter from the Playwright at the bottom of text page 866.

▶ CRITERIA FOR EVALUATING THE ASSIGNMENT   The essay clearly states the writer's belief that Hansberry has or has not succeeded in saying something universal about human beings, and cites reasons or details from the play to support that belief.

Extending the Play

If possible, arrange a viewing of the perceptive film version of *A Raisin in the Sun* (1961) with its cast of Sidney Poitier, Claudia McNeil, Ruby Dee, Diana Sands, Ivan Dixon, John Fiedler, and Louis Gossett. Have students explain its effect on their interpretation of the play.

A number of African people and leaders are cited in footnotes to Act Two (see especially text page 837). Have students research these people and their accomplishments. Students might also research and present brief oral reports on the Pan-African movement that led to the independence of Nigeria and many other African nations around the time

A Raisin in the Sun was first produced. Another relevant movement was known as *négritude*, which was espoused by such influential writers as Léopold Sédar Senghor, the first president of Senegal, and the Martiniquan poet and politician Aimé Césaire. In Hansberry's play, Asagai embodies all of those aspects of African culture.

Students might also compare and contrast selected portions of Hansberry's autobiographical collection, *To Be Young, Gifted and Black,* with autobiographical works by James Baldwin, Alex Haley, or Richard Wright. Others may compare and contrast *A Raisin in the Sun* with fictional works by Alice Walker or Richard Wright.

For students who are interested in South Africa, suggest a study of Alan Paton's novel *Cry, the Beloved Country* (1948) or John Briley's novelization (1987) of Richard Attenborough's film of the Stephen Biko story, *Cry Freedom* (1987).

Primary Sources   Text page 866

A LETTER FROM THE PLAYWRIGHT
Inform students that New Haven was (and still is) the city where many plays open before going to Broadway in New York City. Hansberry's letter from New Haven shows just the slightest bit of anxiety about how good her play is; but it mainly exudes confidence, excitement, and a sense that this is the start of something big.

Ask students to respond to Hansberry's comment on "the very essence of human dignity." Do they know any real people like that? Have they met any other fictional characters who embody the essence of human dignity? How would they define or explain the phrase "human dignity"?

EXERCISES IN CRITICAL THINKING AND WRITING   Text page 867

EVALUATING A PLAY
The assignment here is for students to write an essay analyzing and evaluating one of the plays in this unit. In preparation, you might want students to read sample reviews of either stage or television plays from magazines or newspapers. As students discuss the reviews, have them point out which comments seem objective, based on criteria listed under Guidelines for Evaluating a Play (text page 867) and which comments seem more subjective. Also, if time and resources permit, a good preparation for this assignment is a class viewing and discussion of a videotaped production of a play. During discussion of the two plays in this unit, students will probably have reviewed the elements of drama that appear in the chart on text page 867; if not, you may want them to do so now.

▶ CRITERIA FOR EVALUATING THE ASSIGNMENT   Students' essays arrive at an overall evaluation of the play through an analysis of the elements of drama—characters, plot, setting and theme—as they contribute to the overall effectiveness of the play. Throughout the essay, specific examples are used to support the overall evaluation stated in the first paragraph. The essay concludes with the student's subjective response to the play. The response is supported with reasons.

Further Reading

Works listed are suitable for both students and teachers unless the annotation ends with the note [Teachers].

Albee, Edward. *The American Dream and The Zoo Story* (New American Library, 1961). Two examples of absurdist drama.

Esslin, Martin. *The Theatre of the Absurd,* Rev. ed. (Overlook Press, 1973). The authority on Absurdist drama. [Teachers]

Gassner, John. *Masters of the Drama,* Third ed. (Dover Publications, 1954; reprint of Random House, 1940). A comprehensive history of world drama. [Teachers]

Gassner, John, and Morris Sweetkind, eds. *The Reader's Encyclopedia of World Drama* (Crowell, 1969). Alphabetically arranged entries on playwrights, plays, and dramatic movements, through the mid-1960's. [Teachers]

Gilman, Richard. *The Making of Modern Drama* (1974). An influential work by a noted critic. [Teachers]

Hansberry, Lorraine. *The Sign in Sidney Brustein's Window* (Random House, 1965). A play in which a middle-class Jewish protagonist renews his sense of integrity after serious disillusionment.

Hansberry, Lorraine. *To Be Young, Gifted, and Black* (New American Library, 1969). A montage of letters, journal entries, speeches, and play excerpts, with an introduction by James Baldwin.

Hewes, Henry, ed. *Famous American Plays of the 1940's* (Dell, 1967). Includes Thornton Wilder's *The Skin of Our Teeth,* Arthur Laurents's *Home of the Brave,* Arthur Miller's *All My Sons,* Maxwell Anderson's *Lost in the Stars,* and Carson McCullers's *The Member of the Wedding.*

Nicoll, Allardyce. *World Drama from Aeschylus to Anouilh,* Second ed. (London: Harrap, 1976). An overview of world drama. [Teachers]

Rasky, Harry. *Tennessee Williams: A Portrait in Laughter and Lamentation* (Dodd, Mead, 1986). Perceptive account of Williams's life and works, based on the Canadian filmmaker's interviews and ten years' acquaintance with Williams.

Rasky, Harry. *Tennessee Williams's South* (Canadian Broadcasting Corporation, 1973). A 90-minute documentary on Williams's life, works, beliefs. Contains scenes from his plays and Williams reading some of his own work.

Spoto, Donald. *The Kindness of Strangers: The Life of Tennessee Williams* (Ballantine, 1985). A thorough, well-documented, and balanced biography.

Williams, Tennessee. *Memoirs* (Doubleday, 1975). Disorganized impressions of family and friends; source of "Primary Sources" excerpt on text page 811. [Teachers]

FICTION—1945 TO THE PRESENT

Teaching the Fiction Unit

The stories in this unit are most notable for their diversity of style, form, technique, artistic philosophy, and subject matter. Reading them will give students a good idea of the many alternative modes of narrative that are now available to the fiction writer. More advanced students will find these stories springboards from which they can explore more widely the world of postwar fiction. For instance, after reading Donald Barthelme's "Game," they might read not only other stories of his, but also stories by fellow experimentalists such as John Barth, Vladimir Nabokov, and William H. Gass. After reading stories by Isaac Bashevis Singer and Bernard Malamud, interested students may wish to make the acquaintance of other Jewish writers, such as Philip Roth, Saul Bellow, and Bruce Jay Friedman.

Among the postwar trends students might find interesting are "metafiction" and "magic realism." Both of these depart from the traditional form of realistic storytelling. Metafiction is a style of experimental fiction in which narrative form is itself part of the subject matter of the story. A metafictional story comments not only upon its ostensible subject matter, but also upon the art of fiction itself. Many of Donald Barthelme's stories are allegorical fragments in which Barthelme comments upon what he believes to be the exhaustion of realistic modes of storytelling. His story "The Tolstoy Museum," for instance, explicitly pays homage to the traditional realists, represented by Leo Tolstoy, but implies that their approach to fiction is now suited only to museums—to a memorialized past. The Barthelme story in this unit, "Game" (text page 920), does not make an explicit metafictional statement, but it continues Barthelme's investigation of the absurdity of modern life, the fragmenting of personality, and the breakdown of old belief-systems. In many respects it resembles a traditional type of science fiction story about the threat of nuclear war. However, Barthelme's sophisticated style and parodying use of banal figures of speech make it a comment not only on the possible destruction of the world but also about its ongoing mode of existence.

Metafiction is directly descended from the modernistic experiments of writers such as James Joyce, Gertrude Stein, and Samuel Beckett. But magic realism, in contrast, tries to infuse new vigor into storytelling by using the age-old devices of fable, fairy tale, and legend. Works of magic realism are usually set in a recognizably "realistic" setting rendered with skillful detail, but within which the laws of realism are occasionally suspended to create a dreamlike effect. In Isaac Bashevis Singer's story "The Key" (text page 877), the setting is an absolutely authentic New York City tenement apartment building, but a supernatural element, which in turn is a convincing outgrowth of the protagonist's state of mind, expands the dimensions of the story at the end. Mark Helprin's "Tamar" (text page 926) takes place in a lovingly detailed London before World War II, but a dreamlike air pervades the piece in marked contrast to the seriousness of the narrator's mission. In Bernard Malamud's "The Magic Barrel" (text page 886), nothing occurs that defies the laws of nature, but an air of allegorical improbability, perhaps partly influenced by Hawthorne, lends both charm and meaning to the work.

Other writers in this unit deal with a more straightforward kind of reality, and in their works we find a variety of American ethnic experiences that enrich our literature and our national life. John Updike's "Son" (text page 898) shows us three generations of white Protestant males in the space of a few short pages, transmitting love from one to the other at the same time that they experience conflict. Though the story is realistic, it makes use of metafiction devices in its shifting time scheme and somewhat ambiguous way of identifying characters. Julia Alvarez's "Daughter of Invention" (text page 903) and Amy Tan's "Rules of the Game" (text page 912) both deal with generational conflicts between immigrants and their children. Anne Tyler's "Your Place Is Empty" (text page 954) is about culture clash between an American woman and her Middle Eastern mother-in-law. In "Why I Like Country Music" (text page 943), James Alan McPherson contrasts the attitudes of Northerners and Southerners in the past, while Andrea Lee's "New African" (text page 968) is about a middle-class African American family in Pennsylvania.

After your class reads the stories in this unit, you may want to review the many kinds of narrative technique and the different approaches to storytelling that they have sampled. You may ask students to compare and contrast the effects, strengths, and limitations of these forms of narration.

Objectives of the Fiction Unit

1. To expand vocabulary and increase reading proficiency

2. To gain exposure to notable authors and their works

3. To define and identify elements of fiction

4. To define and identify significant literary techniques

5. To respond, orally and in writing, to fiction through analysis of its elements

6. To practice the following critical thinking and writing skills:
   a. Analyzing theme and the writer's method
   b. Comparing and contrasting literary works
   c. Responding to literary criticism and to a title
   d. Analyzing humor
   e. Analyzing and forming generalizations
   f. Evaluating a story's ending

Introducing the Fiction Unit

You might want to give your students a preview of the many worlds, both cultural and stylistic, they will find in this unit. There will be continuity with previous units—the African American experience, the Vietnam War, the immigrant experience, the Hispanic experience, the Anglo-Saxon Protestant experience all appeared in works previously studied—but what is new in this unit is a freedom in the authors' handling of the techniques of narrative. Authors such as John Updike have availed themselves of the entire range of techniques of modern fiction, from the most conventional realism to the fragmentations of metafiction.

You might pose this to your students as an imaginative exercise: Have them imagine that no one has ever written stories before, and that they are inventing the art of fiction. If they could start from scratch, what kind of structure would they provide for stories? What kind of narrative would do justice to the complexity of American life today? Would it be the conventional story form with a clearcut beginning, middle, and ending? Or would a story begin anywhere and end anywhere? Or is there some third alternative? Your students will doubtless not be able to arrive at final answers to these questions, since writers and literary critics through the past two generations have not arrived at final answers either. But you can inform them that all writers in this unit have striven, in their different ways, to arrive at a way of storytelling that does justice to the increasing complexity of contemporary life.

THE KEY

Objectives

1. To respond to a story about isolation and integration into society

2. To describe a story's setting and conflicts

3. To analyze foreshadowing

4. To write an episode from a different point of view

5. To write an essay analyzing the story's theme

6. To write an essay applying the writer's statements to his story

7. To write an essay comparing two stories

8. To analyze the story's imagery

Introducing the Story

Here are the major elements of the story:

- **Protagonist:** Bessie Popkin

- **Antagonist:** "Human tormenters . . . demons, imps, Evil Powers"

- **Conflict:** person vs. irrational fear and mistrust of environment

- **Point of view:** third-person limited (omniscient narrator)

- **Significant techniques:** foreshadowing, figurative language, irony

- **Setting:** Upper West Side of New York City, the present

BACKGROUND ON THE STORY Students may be interested to know that Singer spoke and wrote fluent English but preferred always to write his fiction in the language he spoke as a youth. Although Singer wrote in Yiddish (a language spoken by eastern European Jews), he took an active interest in the translations of his stories into English, usually as a collaborator. That situation, which is quite unusual, means that Singer's stories in English have, in the words of one critic, the author's "fortifying approval." The novelist Saul Bellow has acted as one of Singer's translators.

THE PLOT Bessie Popkin, an elderly, reclusive widow who is suspicious of her neighbors and afraid of supernatural forces, gets dressed and walks a short distance to a supermarket on Broadway. It is dusk when Bessie returns home, puts the groceries down by the door to her apartment, and starts to unlock the door. The key breaks. Bessie, desperate, does not dare turn to anyone for help. She leaves the grocery bag by the door and goes outside. Not knowing what to do, she wanders the streets. At last she falls asleep on the steps of a church. During the night, she sees miraculous signs from another world. In the morning, she feels "no longer alone." People seem friendlier, even the Irish super, supposedly "her deadly enemy." The super opens the door for her. A woman in a nearby apartment has kept Bessie's perishable groceries in her refrigerator. Bessie lies down in her apartment and has a vision of her dead husband, Sam. She hears the words spoken many years ago by a hotel owner on her honeymoon, "You don't need no key here." The ending suggests that Bessie may have had a heart attack and dies, though this is ambiguous.

Teaching Strategies

PROVIDING FOR CULTURAL DIFFERENCES Be sure students understand the reasons for Bessie's fears, exaggerated as some of these fears are. She is old and alone in a neighborhood that is no longer familiar to her. Her pocketbook has been stolen three times. She is Jewish, perhaps an immigrant, in a section of New York City that once had many Jewish residents, nearly all of whom have now moved away. Discuss in class what it would be like to be old and alone, living in a high-crime area of a large city.

PROVIDING FOR DIFFERENT LEVELS OF ABILITY Some readers may need help in understanding the third-person limited point of view in the story. Have a student or students read the first three paragraphs in class. Discuss with them how much of what Bessie views as fact really *is* fact. Point out that Singer is giving his readers Bessie's perceptions of reality, not reality itself.

READING THE STORY This story implicitly raises the question of what families and society should do for their senior citizens. You may want to discuss the question in class before students read the story. Should children provide a home for their aged parents? Are retirement communities a good idea? Is rent control or subsidized housing—which may permit older people to remain in familiar surroundings—a good idea? Have the students read the story as homework or in class.

RETEACHING ALTERNATIVES   Have students search for examples of foreshadowing in the story. One instance of foreshadowing is identified in Interpreting Meanings, question 7 (text page 883), and there are a number of others. Students should look particularly for examples indicating that Bessie's surroundings are not so grim and unfriendly as she thinks and that Bessie may die at the end of the story.

Responding to the Story   Text page 883

Answers to the questions in the Pupil's Edition appear in the Annotated Teacher's Edition.

Writing About the Story

For help in revising their compositions, refer students to **Grammar, Usage, and Mechanics: A Reference Guide** on text pages 1183–1228 at the back of their books.

A CREATIVE RESPONSE

1. Adopting Another Point of View   List with the class the other characters and briefly review the kinds of observations each might make about Bessie. (Students might choose from the grocery boy, superintendent, neighbor woman, the cashier, rats, mice, the black cat.)

► CRITERIA FOR EVALUATING THE ASSIGNMENT   The paper is two or three paragraphs long and remains consistently in first-person point of view as a character of the story. Observations made about Bessie and her problems are appropriate for the character.

A CRITICAL RESPONSE

2. Analyzing the Theme   As preparation for writing, elicit from the class the meaning of *reckoning* (a settling of accounts), how Bessie has lived without a reckoning, the confession she makes, the meaning of the story's title ("The Key"). Elicit also some possible statements of theme (on the lines of reawakening and/or reintegration into the community) and write these on the chalkboard as a springboard for students' own statements.

► CRITERIA FOR EVALUATING THE ASSIGNMENT   The essay interprets the proverb about reckoning and confession in terms of Bessie's experiences, the symbolic meaning of the story's title, and the story's overall theme of redemption or reawakening to community.

3. Relating the Speech to the Story   Have students read and discuss the excerpt from Singer's Nobel Prize Acceptance Speech (text page 884), restating some of his major points—for example, "True art uplifts the spirit," "Modern man has lost faith in everything," "Literature is capable of offering new perspectives to the reader." Have each student select three points that seem especially relevant to the story "The Key."

► CRITERIA FOR EVALUATING THE ASSIGNMENT   The essay shows a grasp of Singer's main points and accurately applies three points from the Nobel speech to the story, "The Key." The essay cites elements of the story that illustrate Singer's points.

4. Comparing Stories   Similarities between the stories should leap to the students' minds, beginning with the characters themselves—old women who are somehow journeying. Have them list from memory the similarities they see in (a) character, (b) perilous journey, (c) triumphant resolution, and (d) theme involving love; and then turn to the stories for supporting details.

► CRITERIA FOR EVALUATING THE ASSIGNMENT   The essay cites significant elements of both stories to illustrate the stories' similarities in character, perilous journey, triumphant resolution, and theme involving love.

Analyzing Language and Style

IMAGERY
1. Some images appeal to more than one sense. Here are some examples:

   Sight: torn newspapers, cigarette butts, hopping pigeons, blazing sky, golden dust, artificial grass, carved coconuts, black and white children
   Smell: stink of asphalt, gasoline, rotten fruit, excrement of dogs
   Hearing: truck blaring shrill songs, deafening campaign information
   Taste: papaya and pineapple juice
   Touch: crush of passers-by, sweated shirts, children splashing in water, hair that stood up like wires
2. Answers will vary. Some students will find the scene exhilarating; others will empathize with the sensory overload for a recluse like Bessie.
3. Answers will vary, although most students will see how Bessie could perceive her surroundings as dangerous and degenerating.

Extending the Story

Isaac Bashevis Singer is not the only important writer in Yiddish. In fact, Singer's older brother, I. J. Singer, is also a notable writer in the classical Yiddish tradition. Sholom Aleichem was for many years better known than either of the Singers. A committee of experts may do some research on Yiddish literature and present their findings orally in class.

NOBEL PRIZE ACCEPTANCE SPEECH, 1978

Singer's speech warrants some classroom time and discussion, if your teaching schedule permits. Here are a few questions for students to discuss:

1. What does Singer believe in? What do you think are the "eternal truths" for him?
2. What role does he see for the writer?
3. Is he a pessimist?

Bernard Malamud

Text page 885

THE MAGIC BARREL

Text page 886

Objectives

1. To respond to a story about love and self-discovery
2. To interpret a paradox and relate it to the story's theme
3. To interpret the story's ambiguous ending
4. To write a paragraph extending the story into the future
5. To compare similar elements of two stories
6. To respond to critical comments about the author and his work

Introducing the Story

Here are the major elements of the story:

- **Protagonist:** Leo Finkle
- **Antagonist:** Pinye Salzman
- **Conflict:** person vs. ambivalence of human nature; person vs. self
- **Point of view:** third-person, omniscient
- **Significant techniques:** realistic dialogue, paradox, ambiguity
- **Setting:** uptown New York City, not long ago

BACKGROUND ON THE STORY   Your students may find this critical commentary by F. W. Dupee helpful to an understanding of the story.

> . . . Malamud's Jewish community is chiefly composed of people of Eastern European origin . . . [T]hey tend to retain, morally speaking, their immigrant status. Life is centered at home and in the workshop and remains tough and full of threats. The atmosphere is not that of the 1930's Depression alone . . . but that of the hard

times immanent in the nature of things. His people may prosper for a while and within limits. But memories and connections continue to bind them to the Old World, in some cases to the world of the Old Testament where Jacob labors for Laban and Job suffers for everyone.

THE PLOT   Leo Finkle, a twenty-seven-year-old rabbinical student, calls in a matchmaker, Pinye Salzman, to find him a suitable wife. Leo rejects all six possibilities that Pinye suggests. Dismissing Pinye, Leo thereafter feels miserable. Soon the matchmaker reappears, recommending Lily Hirschorn, a schoolteacher Finkle had already turned down as too old. She is only twenty-nine, Pinye lies. They date, Lily presses Leo about becoming a rabbi, and he admits that "I came to God not because I loved Him, but because I did not." After rejecting Lily, Leo once again sinks into despair. Pinye next leaves a packet of photographs that Leo refuses to look at for months. Finally, he does, and falls immediately, hopelessly in love with the woman in one of them. He seeks out Pinye, who tells him that it was a mistake to have included this picture of "my baby, my Stella, she should burn in hell." Stella is "dead" to Pinye. Leo persists, and a meeting under a street lamp is arranged. Leo approaches Stella "with flowers outthrust." Salzman, hiding around the corner, chants prayers for the dead.

Teaching Strategies

PROVIDING FOR CULTURAL DIFFERENCES   When Pinye Salzman says of his daughter Stella that "to me she is dead now," non-Jewish students may not know exactly what he means. He does not mean (as we soon learn) that she is physically dead. She is "dead" only in the sense that Pinye has completely severed relations with her. He does not see her, does not talk to her, and in no way acknowledges her existence. For Salzman's daughter to be "dead" to him, she presumably has done something that he regards as very bad—something seriously offensive to his religious beliefs or principles. The offense is never specified. Since the ending of the story depends on this meaning of "dead," you will want to discuss the word briefly before students begin to read.

PROVIDING FOR DIFFERENT LEVELS OF ABILITY

This is a sophisticated story, but most students should be able to handle it. With some students, you may want to assign the reading in two parts, so that you can review the first part and answer any questions or clear up any misunderstandings before students reach the end. A good place to break is at page 891, after Leo's date with Lily.

READING THE STORY   Use the headnote on page 886 to prepare students for reading. Ask them if they have ever come across a fictional (or real-life) matchmaker before. Some may mention computer dating services. Others may suggest oversolicitous relatives or friends who try to "fix up" one person with another. Probably some will mention Yente, the matchmaker, who plays an important role in the 1960's Broadway musical *Fiddler on the Roof*.

RETEACHING ALTERNATIVES   The following scenes in the story are excellent for dramatizing:

- The first meeting between Leo and Pinye (pages 887–889)
- The second meeting between Leo and Pinye (pages 889–890)
- Leo and Lily's date (pages 890–891)
- The third meeting between Leo and Pinye (page 892)
- The conversation between Leo and Mrs. Salzman (pages 893–894)
- The first meeting between Leo and Pinye concerning Stella's picture (page 894)
- The final meeting in the cafeteria between Leo and Pinye (pages 894–895)

Choose one or more of these scenes and have selected students present them as stage dialogue. Although the text in the book can be used as a script (if students have practiced), the assignment will go more smoothly if the excerpts are retyped in the form of a script. If they are, be sure to leave in descriptions that serve as stage directions—for example, "He shook his head." If more than one scene is presented, you will want to follow the plot sequence of the story.

Responding to the Story   Text page 896

Answers to the questions in the Pupil's Edition appear in the Annotated Teacher's Edition.

Writing About the Story

For help in revising their compositions, refer students to **Grammar, Usage, and Mechanics: A Reference Guide** on text pages 1183–1228 at the back of their books.

A CREATIVE RESPONSE
1. Extending the Story   Note that in twenty years the characters will be in their forties—usually a strong, settled period in an adult's life. Brainstorm possibilities for Leo and Stella, but caution students then to think critically and to choose one they can justify in terms of qualities of character revealed in the story.

▶ CRITERIA FOR EVALUATING THE ASSIGNMENT   The future predicted for Leo and Stella is reasonable in terms of the problems encountered in any marriage and in terms of Malamud's characterizations of Leo and Stella.

A CRITICAL RESPONSE
2. Comparing Two Stories   Discuss the manner in which each story uses the four elements listed in the writing assignment. Encourage students to base their essays on the two elements for which they find the strongest degrees of similarity.

▶ CRITERIA FOR EVALUATING THE ASSIGNMENT   The essay cites two similarities and supports all generalizations with details from the stories. The essay is clearly organized, dealing with one element at a time.

3. Responding to a Critic   Read both comments and elicit comments on how they could apply to "The Magic Barrel." Direct students to choose the comment which they can most clearly relate to the plot, characters or theme of "The Magic Barrel."

▶ CRITERIA FOR EVALUATING THE ASSIGNMENT   The paragraph deals with either Lelchuk's comment about moral purpose or Roth's comment about being human and humane. It cites specific details of plot, character, or theme to show that the comment does or does not apply to "The Magic Barrel."

Extending the Story

You might ask students to collaborate with a partner to write and read aloud the dialogue that occurs as soon as Leo gives Stella the bouquet of flowers. Do violins and lit candles continue to revolve in the sky? Does the meeting go well? Do Leo and Stella find it easy to talk to each other? Students should make their dialogues and the accompanying text show the outcome of this first conversation.

John Updike

SON

Objectives

1. To respond to a story about relationships between fathers and sons

2. To state the story's theme

3. To describe tone

4. To write episodes imitating the story's structure

5. To write an essay analyzing the writer's attitude toward his subject

6. To analyze the writer's pictorial style

7. To rewrite a prose passage as a poem

Introducing the Story

Here are the major elements of the story:

- **Protagonist:** the narrator

- **Antagonist:** the narrator's son

- **Conflict:** fathers vs. sons

- **Point of view:** mainly first-person; one section third-person limited

- **Significant techniques:** shifting times and points of view; pictorial style of writing

- **Setting:** various places and times: begins and ends at home in the present

BACKGROUND ON THE STORY You may want to emphasize a point made in the brief biography of John Updike on text page 897. One of the most prolific of contemporary authors, Updike writes not only superb short stories but also highly regarded criticism, poetry, and novels. While a number of modern writers have established comparable reputations in one or two of those fields, few have achieved Updike's high repute in so many.

THE PLOT Instead of a traditional plot, the story is a series of vignettes. The first section takes place in 1973, as a father talks in the first person about his sixteen-year-old son.

The second section involves action occurring nearly twenty-five years earlier (in 1949) and is written with a limited, third-person point of view. The main character is in high school: it is implied that this student is the narrator of the first section as a young man.

The third section, which reverts to first-person narration, concerns a boy who returns from his paper route in the year 1913 or so. This boy is the narrator's own father, seen when young.

In the fourth section, also written in the first person, there is a discussion of letters written by the narrator's grandfather, when he was a young man in the late 1880's.

The events in the fifth section occur in approximately the same time period as those in the first section and have the same first-person point of view. The narrator discusses his son's physical vigor and success on the soccer team.

The sixth section concerns a trip that the narrator's parents take in order to hear their son, now a celebrated author, give a reading.

In the seventh section, the narrator's father recounts for his son a conversation about religious vocations that he had with his own father.

Finally, the eighth section reverts to a scene in the same time period as the opening of the story, with the narrator called upon to punish his son for bullying a younger brother.

Teaching Strategies

PROVIDING FOR CULTURAL DIFFERENCES Relations between generations are probably strained at times in all cultures. You may want to point out that Updike's fiction often comes close to being autobiographical. Since Updike is such a careful observer, with virtually total recall, he presents a very accurate picture of American middle-class life in the second half of the twentieth century.

PROVIDING FOR DIFFERENT LEVELS OF ABILITY This story requires thoughtful reading, but most students should be able to figure out its backward-moving chronology in the early sections. If you think students will have difficulty in following the sequences of events, point out that the eight sections of the story are shown by page breaks or by extra space. Advise them, too, to watch for the dates—1973, 1949, 1913, 1887–1889—for they provide useful keys. If you think it necessary, you may wish to read the plot summary to students as a preview, pausing to explain more fully the progress at each stage of the story.

READING THE STORY A brief discussion of genealogy makes a good introduction to this story. You might ask your students if they have read *Roots,* Alex Haley's fictionalized account of his African heritage, which became a tremendously popular television miniseries and caused an upsurge of interest in genealogy among Americans generally. Ask your students how much they know about their family history. As they will see in the story, Updike (or his narrator) has great curiosity about family history.

You may find it helpful to read this story in class, asking and answering questions after each of the eight sections. Emphasize to students that the narrator is in a familiar position—caught between the older generation, about which he knows some but not all, and the younger generation, about which he also knows some but not all.

RETEACHING ALTERNATIVES Have students write a one-paragraph critical review of "Son," modeled after reviews in such publications as *Book Review Digest, The New Yorker,* or even *Time* or *Newsweek.*

Responding to the Story   Text page 901

Answers to the questions in the Pupil's Edition appear in the Annotated Teacher's Edition.

Writing About the Story

For help in revising their compositions, refer students to **Grammar, Usage, and Mechanics: A Reference Guide** on text pages 1183–1228 at the back of their books.

A CREATIVE RESPONSE
1. Imitating the Story's Structure Success with this assignment depends on prior careful analysis of sections of

the Updike story and what they reveal about characters' private thoughts. With this background, students may wish to base their episodes on the first three paragraphs of the story.

▶ CRITERIA FOR EVALUATING THE ASSIGNMENT The story is titled "Daughters" and consists of three or more episodes that reveal the thoughts and feelings of three generations of women toward their mothers and daughters.

A CRITICAL RESPONSE
2. Analyzing the Writer's Method Question 10 on the believability of the relationships portrayed by Updike is good preparation for this assignment.

▶ CRITERIA FOR EVALUATING THE ASSIGNMENT The essay states whether Updike writes about parent-child relationships sentimentally or realistically, and uses details from two different parent-child relationships in the story in order to support this opinion.

Analyzing Language and Style

A "PICTORIAL" STYLE
1. Choices will vary. These are examples:
   a. The son playing soccer (text page 900).
   b. Town as sepia postcard (text page 900).
   c. The father's envy at his son's soccer playing (text page 900).
2. The simile is "burdock stalks like the beginnings of an alphabet." The words *holding* and *pondering* personify the apple tree.
3. Responses will vary. Allow students to move about in the paragraph, using nonconsecutive sentences which still make sense poetically. Students may be more successful with this assignment if they collaborate with a partner or small group. Suggest that groups exchange drafts to comment on each other's poems.

Julia Alvarez

Text page 902

DAUGHTER OF INVENTION

Text page 903

Objectives

1. To respond to a story about daughter-parent conflicts

2. To identify aphorisms

3. To interpret the story's title, theme, and climax

4. To evaluate characterization

5. To write a speech the narrator might have written

6. To write an essay analyzing the story's conflicts

Introducing the Story

Here are the major elements of the story:

- **Protagonists:** Cukita, the narrator; Mami, her mother
- **Antagonist:** Papi, the father
- **Conflict:** daughter vs. parent; immigrant parental values vs. second-generation values
- **Point of view:** first-person
- **Significant technique:** humor from mixed-up aphorisms
- **Setting:** New York City, 1961

BACKGROUND ON THE STORY Citing political and economic instability, the United States sent marines to the Dominican Republic in 1916, and stayed until 1934. The dictator Rafael Trujillo ruled from 1930 until his assassination in May of 1961. His son succeeded him, and popular unrest continued. Six months later, Rafael Trujillo, Jr., and members of hs family fled the Dominican Republic on hearing reports of a threatened military coup. After another year that saw a coup and a counter-coup, free elections were held, and Juan Bosch was elected president. This was not, however, the happy ending that the narrator's father hoped for. Civil war followed, and in 1965 the U.S. marines again landed, this time to prevent a feared Cuban-style Communist takeover.

THE PLOT The narrator's mother fancies herself an inventor, and indeed, she does have an inventive mind but never tries to market or patent her ideas. The narrator, a good student and a secret writer, is asked to deliver the teacher's day address at her Catholic school. She puts off writing the speech until the last minute. Inspired by some phrases from Walt Whitman, she writes a passionate speech that she reads to her approving mother. When she reads it to her father, he sees it as boastful and disrespectful to teachers. He forbids her to give the speech and tears it to shreds. Amid the anger and tears that follow, the narrator's mother takes control of the situation. She writes and types a new speech that says all the "right" things. The next day the speech is a big success. That night, the narrator's father brings her a gift—a deluxe electric typewriter, which she will use to carry on the tradition of inventiveness.

Teaching Strategies

PROVIDING FOR CULTURAL DIFFERENCES Students whose parents or other family members are first-generation immigrants will readily understand the mother's language slips (which are common even among many long-time native speakers), but some students may be inclined to laugh at the character and not with her. Many teen-agers are easily embarrassed by their parents' seeming lack of sophistication. Discuss the especially large generation gap between immigrants and their Americanized children, and encourage students to share their own stories.

PROVIDING FOR DIFFERENT LEVELS OF ABILITY Students who do not recognize the originals of the mixed-up sayings will fail to see the humor in them. Discuss a few of the aphorisms with the class as a whole. Have students provide the original saying and ask volunteers to suggest why the mixed-up version seems particularly funny.

READING THE STORY Students should have little difficulty understanding the selection. You might briefly review Whitman's joyful optimism and sense of self as represented in "Song of Myself" (text pages 332–341).

RETEACHING ALTERNATIVES Have students identify the narrator's rising and falling moods in relation to the story's events. Students should identify the main events and label each with the narrator's feelings about the event. For example, how does she feel about her mother's inventions? About writing poetry? About being asked to write the teacher's day speech?

Responding to the Story

Answers to the questions in the Pupil's Edition appear in the Annotated Teacher's Edition.

Writing About the Story

For help in revising their compositions, refer students to **Grammar, Usage, and Mechanics: A Reference Guide** on text pages 1183–1228 at the back of their books.

A CREATIVE RESPONSE

1. Writing a Character's Speech   Have students reread all of the Whitman selections, and then briefly discuss the kinds of phrases that the narrator might have borrowed from his work. Remind students that the narrator is in the ninth grade.

▶ CRITERIA FOR EVALUATING THE ASSIGNMENT   The speech addresses itself to the student body, is appropriate to teacher's day, and does not contradict the context of the story. It has the flavor of Whitman, even to the point of verbatim use of lines from Whitman's poems. The speech might be misinterpreted as boastful.

A CRITICAL RESPONSE

2. Analyzing Conflict   Help students complete the chart of the various conflicts found in the story.

▶ CRITERIA FOR EVALUATING THE ASSIGNMENT   The essay describes at least five conflicts in the story, providing details for each one that explain how the conflict is written into the story.

Extending the Story

Ask students to respond in an "inventive" way to the saying "Necessity is the mother of invention." They might describe an idea for an invention or a situation that "needs" an invention. Encourage them to use their imaginations. Students may get together in small groups to brainstorm ideas and collaborate on presenting their best ideas to the class.

For students who would like to learn what happens to Cukita and her family, recommend *How the Garcia Girls Lost Their Accents*. This collection of short stories moves backward in time, beginning with the Garcia daughters as thoroughly Americanized young women at a family reunion and goes all the way back to their childhood years in the Dominican Republic.

Amy Tan

Text page 911

RULES OF THE GAME

Text page 912

Objectives

1. To respond to a story about mother-daughter conflict
2. To analyze characterization
3. To identify and interpret conflicts and motivation
4. To write an essay applying a critic's comment to the story
5. To write an essay describing how characters from different stories might interact

Introducing the Story

Here are the major elements of the story:

- **Protagonist:** Waverly Jong
- **Antagonist:** Waverly's mother

- **Conflict:** authoritative mother vs. strong-willed daughter; traditional ways of parents vs. Americanized ways of children
- **Themes:** the relationship between mother and daughter; the assimilation of an immigrant family into American culture
- **Point of view:** first-person
- **Significant techniques:** Chinese-American dialect and culture, dream fantasy
- **Setting:** San Francisco's Chinatown, around 1960

BACKGROUND ON THE STORY   In 1960, when this story takes place, chess in the United States was getting a big boost from the play of Bobby Fischer, national champion from 1958–1961 and 1963–1967. Like Waverly Jong, Bobby Fischer was a child prodigy who learned to play chess from a sibling (his older sister). Fischer, the youngest player ever rated an international grand master, was the focus of many adoring articles in popular magazines such as *Life*. In 1972, when he defeated Boris Spassky of the Soviet Union for the world chess title, interest in the game skyrocketed throughout the world.

This story appears in Amy Tan's best-selling first novel, *The Joy Luck Club*. Have students read the biography on text page 911 before they read the story.

THE PLOT

Waverly's brother Vincent receives a chess set as a Christmas grab-bag gift, and he and Winston learn to play. Waverly's interest is piqued, and she sets out to learn all about the game. She succeeds so well that her brothers will no longer play against her. Waverly learns much about chess strategy from Lau Po, an old chess player whom she meets in the park. By the end of the summer, she is defeating all comers in regular outdoor chess exhibitions. She moves from there to local tournaments and becomes national chess champion at age nine. Waverly's mother proudly watches over her daughter's successes and shows her off as they walk through the market. One day Waverly confronts her mother, they argue, and Waverly runs away. She races through streets and alleys, finds a place to sit and think, and heads home two hours later. Her mother speaks briefly and coldly to her, and Waverly goes straight to her room. Lying on her bed, Waverly imagines a chess fantasy-dream with an opponent resembling her mother and ponders her next move.

Teaching Strategies

PROVIDING FOR CULTURAL DIFFERENCES

This story takes place in an ethnic community inhabited by members of a minority group who live there because of social, legal, or economic pressure. Students who have not lived in such an environment may nevertheless have heard of or visited a "Chinatown" or "Little Italy" or "Little Havana" or some other urban area. In such places, the cultural traditions are usually strongest among the older people, especially first-generation immigrants. Discuss with students why a young person who is influenced by the values of the dominant "mainstream" culture might feel stifled in such a traditional ethnic community.

PROVIDING FOR DIFFERENT LEVELS OF ABILITY

Most students will be able to identify with the emotions expressed in this story. Some students, however, may have difficulty with the scenes in which Waverly visualizes her thoughts. Have students read one of those scenes, such as the next-to-last paragraph in the first column on page 915. Lead them to see that the images represent Waverly's thoughts during a period of intense concentration. Assure students that they need not understand how to play chess to follow what happens in the story.

READING THE STORY

Students should read the story in one sitting. Before they read, have them talk about what they know about the game of chess—how it is played, how difficult a game it is, and so forth. You might bring a chess set to class and let a volunteer who knows the game briefly explain the pieces and moves (see Extending the Story on page 250).

RETEACHING ALTERNATIVES

From the beginning of the story to the end, Waverly progresses in regular steps. Have students summarize the plot by briefly describing each step of Waverly's progress as a chess prodigy. Then have them come up with an adjective to describe Waverly at each of those steps. For example, when she asks her brothers question after question about chess, some students might say she is curious; others might say bothersome. When she breaks free from her mother, she could be called either angry or willful. Have students discuss their descriptions, especially how they think she feels at the end of the story.

Responding to the Story

Text page 917

Answers to the questions in the Pupil's Edition appear in the Annotated Teacher's Edition.

Writing About the Story

For help in revising their compositions, refer students to **Grammar, Usage, and Mechanics: A Reference Guide** on text pages 1183–1228 at the back of their books.

A CRITICAL RESPONSE

1. Responding to a Critic Suggest that students review the conversations between mother and daughter in the light of the critic's observation.

▶ CRITERIA FOR EVALUATING THE ASSIGNMENT The essay interprets the critic's observation and offers a general opinion of its validity, using details from the story to make its case.

2. Putting the Characters in Different Stories Have students briefly review the character of the narrator's mother in "Daughter of Invention." You might wish to have them chart the characteristics of the mothers in each story and draw on that information as they develop their essay. Encourage students to write a dialogue for the two mothers and read their dialogues aloud with a partner.

▶ CRITERIA FOR EVALUATING THE ASSIGNMENT The essay introduces each mother into the other's story in some way. Each mother takes a side in the conflict (or offers some compromise) and gives advice.

THE "LANGUAGE" OF GAMES (A GROUP ACTIVITY)
Each group should choose a fairly well-known sport or game. Students should share responsibility for dividing up the task so that efforts are not duplicated. Each "expert" should contribute to presenting information to the class.

Extending the Story

Have students explore more about the game of chess. Groups of students might research the history of chess, teach those who are interested how to play the game, sponsor a schoolwide chess tournament, or invite a local chess expert to speak to the class.

Girls in the class might talk about how they felt at having a girl succeed in a traditionally all-male activity. Can they think of other examples? Are there any activities or professions that are still off-limits to women? To men?

Primary Sources   Text page 918

AN INTERVIEW WITH AMY TAN
In this brief excerpt from an interview, Tan suggests that aspiring writers must find their own voice, not try to imitate the people they admire. She is, in effect, suggesting that aspiring writers must practice their writing diligently to develop their own voice. Her answer to a question about her mother reveals a striking likeness with the story's mother character. Students might wish to discuss this similarity.

Donald Barthelme   Text page 919

GAME   Text page 920

Objectives

1. To respond to a satirical story

2. To identify narrator, setting, conflict, and resolution

3. To analyze the use of repetition as a literary device

4. To state the story's theme

5. To write a new beginning for the story

6. To write a paragraph extending the story into the future

7. To write an essay comparing the story to a poem

Introducing the Story

Here are the major elements of the story:

- **Protagonist:** narrator ("I")
- **Antagonist:** Shotwell

- **Conflict:** person vs. person; person vs. irrationality; person vs. bureaucracy
- **Theme:** the horrifying threat of nuclear war
- **Point of view:** first-person
- **Significant techniques:** fragmentary approach; repetition as literary device; sense of surrealism and absurdity
- **Setting:** underground control room in western state; the present

BACKGROUND ON THE STORY   Your students may be interested in critic Lois Gordon's description of the kinds of characters found in Barthelme's short stories:

If literature at one time presumably reflected life, Barthelme reverses the formula. His figures have in great part become the media, the art and slogans—the words—about them. They mouth technology, although they are utterly ignorant as to what it means; they explain everything and approach every experience with strategy and skill, with the statistics of management and survival, or the rationalizations of historical precedent. They accept roles—is it not one's greatest goal to be Mick Jagger or Blondie, the Brut man or the Breck girl?—and they admire expertise, as though it had divine authority. Indeed they give credence and praise to authorized texts and media personalities, as they once did to God.

Since Gordon's description was written in 1981, and since recognizable names change so fast in popular culture, you may want to ask students for suggestions on updating Mick Jagger, Blondie, "the Brut man," and "the Breck girl."

THE PLOT   The unnamed narrator (a first lieutenant) is annoyed becuse Shotwell (a captain) insists on keeping his jacks and rubber ball to himself. The two of them are in an underground missile-site control center, assigned to watch a console for "certain events" to take place. If the events occur, both men are to turn keys simultaneously in the appropriate locks, whereupon "the bird" flies—presumably a nuclear missile is launched. The two men were supposed to have been relieved after twelve hours ("twelve hours on, twelve hours off"), but they have now been underground for 133 days without relief. The bird has not flown; the men have suspended the rules of "normality"; and both are acting strangely. Shotwell plays with his jacks and studies a textbook on marketing; the narrator scratches long descriptions of natural forms (including, oddly, a baseball bat) on the walls with a large diamond. Each is armed with two guns, and each is authorized to shoot the other for acting strangely. Yet neither man can launch the bird by himself—the locks are too far apart for simultaneous turning. The narrator suspects that Shotwell, infantile and desperate, wants him to cooperate in turning the keys. The narrator may do it, he suggests, but only if he is allowed to play with the jacks. "That is fair," he says. "I am not well."

Teaching Strategies

PROVIDING FOR CULTURAL DIFFERENCES   Students from other cultures will need an explanation of jacks and of what an underground missile-site control center is. Most students have seen enough TV shows and movies about nuclear war scenarios to be familiar with the setting.

PROVIDING FOR DIFFERENT LEVELS OF ABILITY
With LEP students, you may want to read this story aloud in class. It is not very long, and the comparatively slow pace of oral reading (vis-à-vis even careful silent reading) is a plus. Moreover, you can stop and explain along the way, if necessary.

READING THE STORY   Some of your students have undoubtedly seen the movie *War Games*. Discuss the movie in class prior to assigning the story. Have students note the similarity of titles. Ask students particularly about the opening of the movie, which presents a situation that involves a decision to launch nuclear missiles. Students who have seen the movie, or heard it discussed, will have a clearer picture of what Shotwell and the unnamed narrator in "Game" are doing in their underground room.

RETEACHING ALTERNATIVES   You might have one student play the part of the narrator and another the part of Shotwell. Then have another student act as a psychologist who visits the underground room. The psychologist volunteers no information from the outside, but asks the two characters questions about their thoughts, behavior, and feelings. The psychologist/interviewer should prepare a list of at least ten questions probing the characters' thoughts and motivation. The narrator and Shotwell should base their answers on details from the story. Others in the class can challenge any answer that does not seem to be supported by the evidence in the story.

Responding to the Story   Text page 923

Answers to the questions in the Pupil's Edition appear in the Annotated Teacher's Edition.

Writing About the Story

For help in revising their compositions, refer students to **Grammar, Usage, and Mechanics: A Reference Guide** on text pages 1183–1228 at the back of their books.

A CREATIVE RESPONSE
1. Writing the Beginning   Discuss the probabilities—a world already destroyed? A simple paperwork foul-up? An experiment like the one the narrator hypothesizes? Students may write the paragraph as an omniscient statement of facts or in an absurdist style similar to Barthelme's.

▶ CRITERIA FOR EVALUATING THE ASSIGNMENT   The paragraph accounts for the characters' having been left underground for 133 days.

2. Extending the Story   Students need not be consistent with the explanation offered in the first writing assignment. Let them use their imaginations freely. Some may want to collaborate with a partner or small group to produce a joint story.

▶ CRITERIA FOR EVALUATING THE ASSIGNMENT   The extension is either plausible or imaginative. Point of view and tone are sustained throughout. If students have collaborated, have them share their stories with the class.

3. Comparing the Story to a Poem Discuss Auden's "The Unknown Citizen," focusing in particular on the coldness and inhumanity of the world described. You might ask students to read the "he" of the poem as "Shotwell" or "the narrator," and then ask how many lines still "work." (All fit except lines 7–8 and those on marriage, which cannot be deduced from Barthelme's story).

▶ CRITERIA FOR EVALUATING THE ASSIGNMENT The essay argues in a well-organized manner that Barthelme's and Auden's characters live in remarkably similar worlds—ones which ignore their humanity. The essay cites specific details from both the story and the poem to support points made.

Extending the Story

You might have students write a news article to fit this headline:

TWO OFFICERS GAIN FREEDOM
AFTER HARROWING 150 DAYS
IN UNDERGROUND CONTROL ROOM

Or play a video of Peter Sellers in the classic black-and-white satire *Dr. Strangelove, or How I Learned to Love the Bomb.*

THE ELEMENTS OF LITERATURE
Text page 924

SATIRE

This explanation of satire can be handled as if it were a literary selection. Ask students to be prepared to define in class the five literary terms included: satire, irony, hyperbole, incongruity, and fantasy. Also ask them to answer, orally or on paper, the two questions in the final paragraph. Answers will vary, but here are some sample answers:

1. A captain in the armed forces carries a set of jacks and a rubber ball in his attaché case. Both men are carrying supposedly concealed weapons that the other knows about. A twelve-hour stint underground has been extended to 133 days. Using a diamond, the narrator scratches a 4500-word description of the baseball bat on the south wall of the room.

2. Some students may point to elements of both types of response (the raftsmen's and Walter Mitty's) in the narrator and Shotwell. As military men with their fingers on the nuclear trigger, and with instructions to shoot the other in the case of strange behavior, they are presumably not timid, fantasizing men. The military must have regarded them as raftsmen types. On the other hand, their childish behavior after confinement suggests men who are cowed, if not by women, then by adversity. Like Mitty, they do not maturely face the reality of their situation.

Mark Helprin

Text page 925

TAMAR

Text page 926

Objectives

1. To respond to a story about a wartime interlude
2. To identify and interpret paradoxes
3. To write a journal entry based on the story
4. To write an essay interpreting a statement from the story
5. To write an essay responding to the title
6. To analyze metaphors, similes, and personification

Introducing the Story

Here are the major elements of the story:

- **Protagonists:** narrator, a 32-year-old British Jew; Tamar, a 17-year-old
- **Antagonists:** isolation of well-to-do British Jews from plight of Jews on the Continent; the approaching Holocaust
- **Conflict:** love vs. impossible reality
- **Point of view:** first-person
- **Significant techniques:** paradox, use of descriptive detail and figurative language; narrative seen in the larger context of world history
- **Setting:** London, just before Christmas, 1938

BACKGROUND ON THE STORY   Students should be aware that, at the time of the story, the modern state of Israel did not exist, and European Jews had no homeland to which they could flee. Although Jews had been struggling for a Jewish state in Palestine since the late nineteenth century, they had not achieved their goal prior to World War II. Jews and Arabs coexisted uneasily in Palestine during the period when the narrator of the story was living there.

THE PLOT   The narrator, a thirty-two-year-old British Jew, is in London before World War II, trying to set up a system so that Jews in Germany and Austria can sell their works of art in a way that will not seriously depress prices. One quarter of each sale is to go to help Jews escape the Nazis. Just before Christmas 1938, he attends a party given by a Jewish art dealer. Arriving very late, he is seated with the adolescents, one of whom is Tamar, a beautiful girl of seventeen with a brace on her upper teeth. They are attracted to each other, but the narrator feels that her youth allows him to talk openly with her, and he does. He tells tales of his exploits in Palestine. She, living "in a world of vulnerable beauty," talks blithely of studying art restoration in Brussels, or even possibly in Rome, "if Fascism flies out the window." Through the next six years of war, the narrator treasures the memory of this dinner party, a moment when the world, like Tamar, was fleetingly beautiful and "not quite real."

Teaching Strategies

PROVIDING FOR CULTURAL DIFFERENCES   Although the story of the Holocaust is well known, review it as important background for the story. Jewish students can probably provide information on the flight of Jews from Europe, the concentration camps, and the genocide. The narrator in the story, entranced by the beauty of Tamar, beguiled by the prosperity and complacency of British Jews, nevertheless sees quite clearly what they do not see—the horror to come.

PROVIDING FOR DIFFERENT LEVELS OF ABILITY   Some students may feel that not much happens in the story. Point out to them that good fiction can be a serious exploration of life. Tell them that in "Tamar" the hero discovers something of great importance to him—and, by extension, to everyone—in one apparently trivial conversation with a young girl at dinner. Suggest to them that a quiet story like "Tamar" can illuminate matters of great importance, often better than an action-packed adventure story.

READING THE STORY   In introducing the story, ask students if they can recall a moment of insight in their lives—a sudden realization of some truth of which they were previously unaware. Mention that many fine stories, including "Tamar," are based on such an experience. You may want to advise students to be aware of figurative language as they read the story. The author uses it so well, and it is so much a part of his style, that an inattentive reader can easily skip over the marvelous use of similes, metaphors, and personification.

RETEACHING ALTERNATIVES   In no more than four sentences, have each student summarize the main event in the story and tell why the narrator remembers it every day in the six years of war. What did the event mean to the narrator?

Responding to the Story   Text page 932

Answers to the questions in the Pupil's Edition appear in the Annotated Teacher's Edition.

Writing About the Story

For help in revising their compositions, refer students to **Grammar, Usage, and Mechanics: A Reference Guide** on text pages 1183–1228 at the back of their books.

A CREATIVE RESPONSE
1. Writing a Journal Entry   Questions 3 and 4 provide good preparation for this assignment.

▶ CRITERIA FOR EVALUATING THE ASSIGNMENT   The journal entries are consistent with the intelligence, sensitivity, and education of Tamar as revealed in the story.

A CRITICAL RESPONSE
2. Explaining a Statement   Question 2 also deals with the narrator's feelings about his time in London. This assignment requires additional discussion of what was happening to Central European Jews at the time and the degree to which a scheme such as the one the narrator was promoting could really help. Students should infer that the narrator, looking back, feels appalled and guilty at his blindness and pomposity—perhaps even at his pride.

▶ CRITERIA FOR EVALUATING THE ASSIGNMENT   The paragraph interprets the line, discusses the narrator's feelings and the reasons why he feels the way he does.

3. Responding to a Title   An earlier question that will help students examine the centrality of Tamar to the story is number 6. It may help them to evaluate the rightness of the title "Tamar" if you have them try out other titles, such as "Rescue Scheme" or "London Break."

▶ CRITERIA FOR EVALUATING THE ASSIGNMENT   The essay gives cogent reasons for citing "Tamar" as a good or poor title for the story. The reasons demonstrate an understanding of the point of the story.

Analyzing Language and Style

FIGURATIVE LANGUAGE
1. **a.** Sharply V-shaped valleys thick with pine trees
   b. It has military connotations—sleeve stripes.
2. **a.** Self-important manner
   b. It's a monster that needs clothing.
   c. Looking back, he is filled with guilt/dismay at his pride.
3. **a.** He feels that London is a happy fantasy land where nothing bad happens and everyone has fun.
   b. His purpose had to do with war and inhumanity.
4. **a.** A place of illusion
   b. A church is serious, subdued; a palace is elegant.
5. **a.** Sadness, melancholy
   b. Answers will vary.
6. **a.** Snakes suggests danger and/or evil.
   b. A yellow dog rubbing its muzzle against buildings The effect is tamer, friendlier.
7. The Jews of Central Europe were taken by surprise, hunted and killed like game or rounded up and slaughtered like cattle.
8. **a.** A miniature person being carried on a platter
   b. He feels like an exhibit about to be devoured.
9. They "spoke as seriously as very old theologians"; "pieced together their sentences with . . . care, the way new skaters skate"; "breathed in relief, not unlike students of a difficult Oriental language, who must recite in class." The narrator sympathizes with their lack of ease with him.
10. The extended simile describing the narrator's meeting with Tamar involves crosscurrented waves near a beach running into each other, then falling back in tranquility. This figure of speech suggests a sudden, natural meeting of elemental forces. In the most personal sense, it seems to suggest love at first sight. In a broader sense, it teaches the narrator an important lesson about life.

Extending the Story

Ask your students to assume that both Tamar and the narrator survive World War II. Have them meet by chance. Where would they be? What would they say to each other? How would they remember their first meeting? Have pairs of volunteers role-play a meeting.

SPEAKING OF COURAGE

Objectives

1. To respond to a story about the trauma of warfare

2. To interpret the meanings of symbols

3. To recognize irony

4. To analyze a character's internal conflict

5. To write dialogue for a television interview

6. To write an essay comparing and contrasting two stories

Introducing the Story

Here are the major elements of the story:

- **Protagonist:** Paul Berlin

- **Antagonist:** memories of the Vietnam war

- **Conflict:** person vs. self-image

- **Point of view:** third-person limited

- **Significant techniques:** use of symbolism; ironic dialogue; repetition to convey internal conflict

- **Setting:** small Midwestern town, recent Fourth of July

BACKGROUND ON THE STORY   At the height of the Vietnam war in 1969, there were 550,000 American troops there; consequently, there are a great many Vietnam veterans in the United States today. You may want to discuss the Vietnam war briefly before assigning the reading. However, as O'Brien implies, the incident in the clay tunnel, on which the question of courage turns, could have occurred in almost any war.

THE PLOT   On Independence Day, Paul Berlin, a Vietnam veteran, drives around a small Midwestern lake time after time, thinking about his early life in town, the present scene, and his wartime experiences. He received seven medals, none of them for valor, and he would like to tell someone how he almost won the Silver Star. As he circles the lake, he sees the same sights again and again—two boys walking, a stalled motorboat on the lake, and two mud hens. His thoughts keep returning to an incident in a tunnel in Vietnam in which Frenchie Tucker was shot

through the neck. It was then that Berlin missed his opportunity to be brave, refusing to advance in the same tunnel where Frenchie had been shot. Berlin keeps thinking about this, about other details of the war, and about how nobody cares or wants to listen. Finally, he goes to a drive-in. After honking his horn, he is told by an annoyed carhop that he has to order on an intercom. He does so, the order-taker using army jargon. He returns to the lake, drives around it some more, and then, when the Fourth of July fireworks start, stops near a picnic shelter, walks down to the beach, and watches them.

Teaching Strategies

PROVIDING FOR CULTURAL DIFFERENCES   As the controversial Vietnam war recedes into history, people in the United States think less about it than they once did, and some students may imagine that everyone now views the war in a similar way. But people who lived through the war—especially American military personnel—sometimes have continuing strong feelings about it. Ask your students if they have heard any such strong feelings expressed recently. What were those feelings? What was the occasion for expressing them? If there are Asian students in your class, ask them about their views. Vietnamese students may be able to add personal insights about relatives' experiences during and after the long war.

PROVIDING FOR DIFFERENT LEVELS OF ABILITY   Most students should be able to handle this story without difficulty. For ESL and LEP students, you might want to read aloud and discuss the long paragraph of Vietnam memories that begins at the bottom of page 938. This passage is difficult because of the stream-of-consciousness technique. Ask students to concentrate their efforts on the details of Paul Berlin's actions at the time Frenchie Tucker was shot. Tell them to view their search as a detective's investigation. The narrator presents the story in fragments, and is never totally clear about the specifics of the whole incident. Nevertheless, a careful search for clues will fill in most of the details. Ask students to point to sentences in the story that support their view of what happened.

READING THE STORY   Use the headnote on page 935 to prepare students for reading. Recall with students stories and poems about war they have read so far this year, and have them identify the various wars that were the subject.

Ask them to think about how this story is different from the others. Assign the story to be read as homework or in class.

RETEACHING ALTERNATIVES Paul Berlin insists that he wants to tell his story to someone. Have your students imagine that the town council, believing the Vietnam war to be inadequately understood, asks him to speak from the bandshell at next year's Memorial Day services. Have students talk about the speech that Berlin might deliver. What does he want to say?

Responding to the Story   Text page 941

Answers to the questions in the Pupil's Edition appear in the Annotated Teacher's Edition

Writing About the Story

For help in revising their compositions, refer students to **Grammar, Usage, and Mechanics: A Reference Guide** on text pages 1183–1228 at the back of their books.

A CREATIVE RESPONSE
1. Inventing an Interview Assuming that the interviewer is not a Vietnam veteran, brainstorm with the class some typical questions such a person would ask, and the points at which the interviewer would cut off Paul's responses, looking for brief, quotable sentences for TV.

▶ CRITERIA FOR EVALUATING THE ASSIGNMENT The dialogue reads like those typically seen on television news, allowing Paul scant time really to get at the meat of what it was like in Vietnam. The dialogue may use some actual quotes from the story.

A CRITICAL RESPONSE
2. Comparing Stories Briefly discuss the contrasts in setting, characterization, and tone used in both stories. Notes students have taken in answering the response questions for the stories will be helpful. It may also prove helpful for students to construct a prewriting chart of the elements.

▶ CRITERIA FOR EVALUATING THE ASSIGNMENT The essay explains that the stories are alike in the technique of using contrasts in setting, characterization, and tone. (For example, for setting, the essay points out that ''Tamar'' contrasts London with concentration camps, and ''Speaking of Courage'' contrasts Vietnam with a small Midwestern town.) The essay is arranged in a logical, coherent manner. That is, it either shows how contrasts are used for all three areas first in one story and then the other, or it moves from story to story for each element.

Extending the Story

Ask your students to suppose that Paul Berlin, still unhappy about his performance in the war, writes a letter to Stink Harris of his old platoon. He asks Stink to tell him what the rest of the platoon thought of his actions on the day Frenchie Tucker was shot. Were they disappointed in him? Did any of the other men dare to go into the tunnel? Did Stink dare? Have students write Stink Harris's reply to Paul Berlin. Stink can express any view he wishes that is not inconsistent with the story. In other words, he can add details to those given by Berlin, but he cannot change the details already in the story.

A committee of students might organize and present a panel discussion on war. Members of the panel could be characters from various war poems and stories students have read this year (e.g., some of the ''Voices from the Civil War,'' Fred Collins of Crane's ''A Mystery of Heroism,'' the narrator of Hemingway's ''In Another Country,'' Auden's Unknown Soldier, Stevens's soldier in ''Death of a Soldier,'' etc.). Let each character present his or her views on how to eliminate wars in the future.

Objectives

1. To enjoy a humorous story

2. To describe the conflicts in the story

3. To analyze the story's tone

4. To write a characterization using an anecdote

5. To write an essay analyzing a character

6. To write an essay analyzing the sources of humor

Introducing the Story

Here are the major elements of the story:

- **Protagonist:** the narrator, remembering himself as a boy

- **Antagonist:** Leon Pugh

- **Conflict:** a young boy in love vs. the rival for his girlfriend's affections and a clever teacher

- **Point of view:** first-person

- **Significant techniques:** conversational tone; mix of realism and romanticism; realistic dialogue

- **Setting:** small town in South Carolina, many years ago

THE PLOT   The narrator tells his wife Gloria that he likes country music. He remembers himself as a fourth-grade student in Mrs. Esther Clay Boswell's class in a small town in South Carolina. He is shyly enamored of Gweneth Lawson, a pretty, Brooklyn-born classmate. The teacher, a strict, perceptive woman, dominates her class, although lively Leon Pugh—the narrator's rival for Gweneth's attention—always manages to make his presence known. When assignments are made for the big square-dancing event on May first, neither the narrator nor Leon is in Gweneth's group. The narrator tries to get reassigned, and does, only to have Mrs. Boswell's further changes result in Leon and Gweneth being paired as square dancers. The narrator is disappointed, but nothing changes the arrangement until the last minute. Leon wears spurs to the square dance; Mrs. Boswell finds them dangerous and sends Leon off to the lunchroom to have them removed. With Gweneth standing alone, the narrator makes his move. He dances, smiles, and laughs with her. Now, years later, he thinks of Gweneth when he hears country music.

Teaching Strategies

PROVIDING FOR CULTURAL DIFFERENCES
Students from different backgrounds may have no idea what a Maypole is or what square dancing is like. Ask them to describe their festivals or rituals that celebrate spring.

You will want to impress on students that the story itself exemplifies a cultural difference. The narrator, who comes from the South, likes a certain kind of country music because of a childhood connection it has for him. His wife Gloria, a Northerner, cannot believe he likes it. Since popular music is close to the hearts of many students, you may be able to provoke a lively discussion of musical likes and dislikes. If you wish, have students try to discover what relevance, if any, musical taste has to where people live, how old they are, what they do in their leisure time, and other cultural factors.

PROVIDING FOR DIFFERENT LEVELS OF ABILITY
Most students should have no difficulty with this selection. It is relatively long, though, and ESL/LEP students may benefit if you make the story a two-day reading assignment, with discussion preceding their reading the second half of the story. A good place for a break is on page 948, with the paragraph that ends ''. . . Maypole and square dancing.''

READING THE STORY   Introduce the story by asking students to try to recall their own fourth-grade experiences. Who were their teachers? What subjects did they study? What were some seasonal activities? Who were the class leaders? Have them recall any specific experiences that they can. A discussion along these lines can provide a good lead-in for the story, which involves the narrator as a fourth-grader.

RETEACHING ALTERNATIVES   Ask students to list all the characters who play any significant part in the story, and then have them describe each character in a single sentence. (Lists should include the following people: the narrator; his wife Gloria; Gweneth Lawson; Mrs. Esther Clay Boswell; Clarence Buford; Leon Pugh; the narrator's father.)

Answers to the questions in the Pupil's Edition appear in the Annotated Teacher's Edition.

Writing About the Story

For help in revising their compositions, refer students to **Grammar, Usage, and Mechanics: A Reference Guide** on text pages 1183–1228 at the back of their books.

A CREATIVE RESPONSE

1. Writing a Characterization   Note that the time need not be the present—the student can write about someone who created a lasting impression when the student was a small child. Stress that essays should use an anecdote to reveal character. They should also include dialogue.

▶ CRITERIA FOR EVALUATING THE ASSIGNMENT   The essay consists of at least one well-developed paragraph. It creates a vivid characterization through use of an anecdote and contains dialogue.

A CRITICAL RESPONSE

2. Analyzing a Character   Point out that the writing assignment offers a way to organize notes for this essay. The student should look for details about the character's appearance, speech, and actions; about how others respond to the character; and any direct comments made by the writer. Clarify the word *credibility* (believability) if necessary.

▶ CRITERIA FOR EVALUATING THE ASSIGNMENT   The essay draws an accurate portrait of the character. Generalizations about character traits are supported by details on the character's appearance, speech and actions, the responses of others, and the writer's direct characterization. The essay ends with the student's personal response to the character and an assessment of the character's credibility.

3. Analyzing Humor   You may wish to divide the class into groups of six students each, with one student in each group seeking examples of one of the types of humor listed. Groups can then share the data and discuss which elements contribute most to the humor of the story.

▶ CRITERIA FOR EVALUATING THE ASSIGNMENT   The essay takes into account the six listed elements of humor (exaggeration, self mockery, comic irony, incongruity, comic descriptions, and understatement). Specific examples from the story support the student's major points.

Extending the Story

Imagine that the narrator, Leon, Gweneth, Clarence Buford, Queen Rose Phipps, and Mrs. Boswell attend the 10th reunion of their fourth-grade class. (The students will be twenty.) Have volunteers role-play their reunion.

Anne Tyler

Text page 953

YOUR PLACE IS EMPTY

Text page 954

Objectives

1. To respond to a story about conflict between cultures and generations

2. To interpret the meanings of flashbacks

3. To analyze the story's conflicts

4. To identify the gradual shift in tone

5. To state the story's theme

6. To write the events of an incident from another point of view

7. To write an essay comparing two stories

8. To write an essay responding to cultural differences

Introducing the Story

Here are the major elements of the story:

- **Protagonist:** Mrs. Ardavi

- **Antagonist:** narrowly: Elizabeth, and, to a lesser degree, Hassan; broadly: Western culture

- **Conflicts:** (cultural) between Iranian (Islamic) ways and American ways; (generational) between mother and daughter-in-law; between mother and son

- **Point of view:** omniscient for brief opening; third-person limited thereafter

- **Significant techniques:** flashbacks; changing tone as story progresses

- **Setting:** city in the United States, the present

BACKGROUND ON THE STORY Remind your students that Anne Tyler is married to an Iranian psychiatrist who was educated in the United States and now lives here. She is therefore writing from direct personal knowledge, rather than simply inventing this story wholly from her imagination. Since student writers are so often told, "Write what you know," you may want to use this opportunity to review the stories in this unit to see how many are either semi-autobiographical or based on direct personal knowledge.

THE PLOT Elizabeth, the American wife of an Iranian-American doctor, prepares for her mother-in-law's visit from Iran by fixing up a room for her and learning some Persian phrases. Elizabeth expects a three-month visit; her husband, Hassan, has said six months; and Mrs. Ardavi, the mother-in-law, plans on a year. From the very beginning, things go awry as Mrs. Ardavi makes a series of moves to revamp the "unclean" American household. During this time, flashbacks fill in details of Mrs. Ardavi's life in Iran. Relations between Elizabeth and her mother-in-law become increasingly strained, nearing the breaking point when the older woman blames Elizabeth for causing her granddaughter's ear infection. The end comes after less than five months when Elizabeth opens a box that Mrs. Ardavi had brought and is greeted by a cloud of insects. Hassan gently delivers an ultimatum, and Mrs. Ardavi prepares to leave for Iran, still "undeniably a foreigner."

Teaching Strategies

PROVIDING FOR CULTURAL DIFFERENCES This story is *about* cultural differences. You will want to indicate to your students that people tend to favor their own culture, in large part because they are familiar with it; to them, it inevitably seems "right." You may find it useful to write the word "Iran" on the board and ask students to characterize how Iranian culture differs from Western culture.

PROVIDING FOR DIFFERENT LEVELS OF ABILITY With LEP students you may want to read the plot summary in the manual before assigning any reading. You won't be giving away any real surprises, and you will be providing students with a framework on which to base their reading.

READING THE STORY In view of the Iran hostage crisis of 1979–81, and the subsequently unfriendly American relations with Iran, you might want to introduce this story with a look at other nations with which the United States has had both good and poor relations. Ask students to name as many such nations as they can. (Some possibilities: Great Britain, our enemy in the American Revolution and the War of 1812; Spain in the Spanish-American War; Germany, Turkey, Bulgaria in World War I; Germany, Japan, and Italy in World War II; the USSR in the Cold War; Cuba after Fidel Castro. Point out that the nature of international politics is that yesterday's enemy can be today's friend, and vice versa, as U.S. relations with Iraq prove.)

After students have read the whole story, you might play the accompanying audiocassette recording to spark a discussion of Tyler's use of foreshadowing.

RETEACHING ALTERNATIVES Elizabeth and Hassan have many conversations in English so that Mrs. Ardavi cannot understand them. A conversation of this kind is mentioned on page 959 following one of Mrs. Ardavi's big meals. Another occurs on pages 961–962 at the dentist's office. Have students playing the parts of Elizabeth and Hassan carry on a plausible dialogue that might have taken place on either (or both) of these occasions. Before beginning, have students review the story carefully up to the point of the dialogue. What they say should reflect the situation at the time they are talking.

Responding to the Story Text page 965

Answers to the questions in the Pupil's Edition appear in the Annotated Teacher's Edition.

Writing About the Story

For help in revising their compositions, refer students to **Grammar, Usage, and Mechanics: A Reference Guide** on text pages 1183–1228 at the back of their books.

A CREATIVE RESPONSE
1. *Taking Another Point of View* List scenes that lend themselves to this assignment—Mrs. Ardavi's arrival, assembling the clothes drying rack, Mrs. Ardavi's taking over the kitchen, going to the park, and so on. Discuss also Elizabeth's attempts to understand her mother-in-law.

▶ CRITERIA FOR EVALUATING THE ASSIGNMENT The narration keeps facts of the event the same, but focuses on Elizabeth, revealing her thoughts and feelings consistent with the story's characterization of Elizabeth.

A CRITICAL RESPONSE
2. *Comparing Two Stories* Note that the assignment focuses on parent-child tensions—in this story, Mrs. Ardavi and her son Hassan or even Ali or Babak; in Updike's story, more than one generation. Have students list the relationships from both stories so that they can make generalizations about common tensions.

▶ CRITERIA FOR EVALUATING THE ASSIGNMENT The essay consists of at least one well-developed paragraph which cites similarities in parent-child tensions between Tyler's and Updike's stories. Generalizations are supported by references to the stories.

3. *Responding to the Story* At first, students may see Mrs. Ardavi's ways as simply "foreign." Ask them to take another look at her diet, health concerns, relaxed pace of life, contact with relatives, etc. Remind students that they are to write about their personal response—there are no "right" answers.

▶ CRITERIA FOR EVALUATING THE ASSIGNMENT In at least one well-developed paragraph, the essay comments on two or three basic differences between the two cultures, and states the student's personal response to the differences.

Extending the Story

Have your students suppose that on the flight back to Iran Mrs. Ardavi sits next to another Iranian woman who is just returning from a six months' stay at *her* daughter-in-law's house. They converse. The other woman's stay may have been similar to Mrs. Ardavi's or totally different. Have students collaborate with a partner or small group to write the conversation between the two women in the form of dialogue for a play. You might then have two students do a dramatic reading of what you consider to be the best dialogue.

Primary Sources Text page 966

"STILL JUST WRITING"
Anne Tyler shares her doubts about her own work and her concern that she might one day run out of ideas for stories. Tyler tells how she began writing about everyday events and people and acknowledges her debt to Eudora Welty. Ask students to think about the people they know and the events they see around them. Are there stories waiting to be told? Ask each student to begin a writer's journal and jot down at least two *ideas* for stories—not the actual stories—based on everyday events and people in their own lives. You might ask students to get together in small groups to tell one story idea while others listen and give some feedback. Encourage students to write their stories but make this an optional assignment.

Andrea Lee

NEW AFRICAN

Objectives

1. To respond to a story about a young African American's conflict

2. To recognize and interpret conflict

3. To infer themes

4. To write a paragraph imitating the writer's style

5. To write an essay analyzing a character

6. To write an essay making generalizations about stories

Introducing the Story

Here are the major elements of the story:

- **Protagonist:** Sarah Ashley
- **Antagonist:** Aunt Bessie
- **Conflict:** person vs. family and community expectations
- **Point of view:** first-person
- **Significant techniques:** detailed description of setting; exploration of theme through childhood memory.
- **Setting:** New African Baptist Church, South Philadelphia, summer, 1963

BACKGROUND ON THE STORY   This is a story about the need to assert independence and find one's own identity. The theme is as old as the *Odyssey* and one with which students can readily identify. In preparation for reading this story, you might discuss with students the fact that a young adult asserting his or her independence might seem to be rejecting family and community values, but that, in reality, deeply ingrained values are seldom lost—often, in fact, they become even more meaningful in light of the new maturity. In "New African," a young girl has conflicting feelings about her church and asserts her independence from it. In doing so, she is supported by the love of her father, who is the minister, and the love of the congregation. At the end of the story, there is every indication that she, too, will find her "New African."

Although there are references in the story to the civil rights movement, your students may not realize just how important the movement was in the summer of 1963. At the time of the church service Lee describes, Dr. Martin Luther King, Jr.—a Baptist minister like Sarah Ashley's father—was at the height of his influence and prestige. On August 28, 1963, King delivered his famous "I have a dream" speech at the demonstration capping the massive March on Washington where two hundred thousand people heard his impassioned plea for equal rights. Because of the quiet, personal tone of Lee's story, students may not realize (any more than Sarah did at the time) how crucial the civil rights work of her father was in that activist summer of 1963.

THE PLOT   Sarah, the African American narrator, is in church in South Philadelphia, listening to a sermon given by her father, a Baptist minister. She is restless and vaguely resentful that her aunts and various members of the congregation keep encouraging her to be baptized. Matthew, Sarah's older brother, has been baptized and seems to have a sense of superiority as a result. As the sermon ends and the total-immersion baptism begins, Sarah sits on the lap of "Aunt" Bessie, a woman who often takes care of Sarah and Matthew when their parents are away. At the end of the baptismal ceremony, Aunt Bessie tells Sarah to step forward. Sarah refuses, a struggle ensues, and she flees to her mother's side. Neither her father nor mother ever insists that she accept baptism, and she continues to go to New African, grateful for the gift of independence her father has granted her.

Teaching Strategies

PROVIDING FOR CULTURAL DIFFERENCES   Some students may wonder about the ceremony of baptism as Lee describes it. There are two points about this view of baptism, both central to the story, that you may wish to discuss: the belief that the ceremony should not be performed on nonbelievers and the insistence on the body's total immersion during the baptism ceremony—thus the "pool" in the church.

PROVIDING FOR DIFFERENT LEVELS OF ABILITY   Most students should be able to read this story without difficulty. With LEP students, you might want to read the story aloud in class. Pause at the end of each section to have students discuss insights into Sarah and her attitude toward both the church and her father. Ask them to make predictions about Sarah's actions in the next section. More advanced students might discuss how the story would differ if it were told from the viewpoint of Sarah's father.

READING THE STORY As the headnote on page 968 suggests, it may be a good idea to review the section on Puritan beliefs in Unit 1 (text page 6). Ask students if they know what happened to the Puritans. (Puritanism as a political force died out in New England in the late 1600's, but Puritan churches, mainly Congregational at the outset—and, more importantly, Puritan beliefs and attitudes—still exist and exert great influence. Baptists gained attention early in American history when Roger Williams and his followers in Rhode Island rejected the Puritan/ Calvinist doctrine of infant baptism and established a church in 1639.) Tell students that they will be reading about a Baptist church service. Have them notice how it differs, if at all, from services with which they may be familiar.

RETEACHING ALTERNATIVES Have students compare the protagonist in ''New African'' with the protagonist in James Alan McPherson's ''Why I Like Country Music.'' What similarities and differences do they see between Sarah Ashley and the narrator in McPherson's story?

Responding to the Story   Text page 976

Answers to the questions in the Pupil's Edition appear in the Annotated Teacher's Edition.

Writing About the Story

For help in revising their compositions, refer students to **Grammar, Usage, and Mechanics: A Reference Guide** on text pages 1183 to 1228 at the back of their books.

A CREATIVE RESPONSE
1. Imitating the Writer's Style Analyze the opening paragraph with your students, leading them to note its attention to the season, the day of the week, the people present, the sensory details that make the reader feel everything that is happening.

▶ CRITERIA FOR EVALUATING THE ASSIGNMENT The paragraph identifies the situation; what the young person is wearing; what he or she sees, hears, and smells; and what the person thinks and feels about the event. All details work together to create a specific overall tone.

A CRITICAL RESPONSE
2. Analyzing Character This assignment lends itself to a prewriting activity done in small groups, with different members of groups seeking specific details that characterize either Sarah or her father, and the group then sharing information and agreeing upon key points of characterization.

▶ CRITERIA FOR EVALUATING THE ASSIGNMENT The analysis of Sarah or the Reverend Ashley makes generalizations about the character and supports them with details about the character's appearance, speech, or actions, how others respond to the character, the character's private thoughts and feelings, or direct comment from the writer.

3. Making Generalizations About the Stories Clarify the difference between theme (a statement or judgment about life) and subject (the topic of a story) before students begin to review the stories in terms of the three areas listed.

▶ CRITERIA FOR EVALUATING THE ASSIGNMENT The thesis statement or opening paragraph identifies areas the essay will explore or makes generalizations about the stories. The body of the essay explores use of family as a subject, use of generational conflict, and use of love as part of the theme, through references to specific stories in the unit. The essay need not refer to all ten stories, but does make use of several stories.

Extending the Story

Have students assume that Sarah Ashley, as a teenager, has recently joined your class. You have just assigned a topic for a brief (perhaps three-paragraph) essay: ''America's Greatest Hero.'' Ask your students to write, not their own essay, but Sarah Ashley's essay on the topic. They should base their conclusions on what they have learned about Sarah in ''New African'' and their style, insofar as possible, on Andrea Lee's.

Students will generally find this essay both amusing and informative. The introduction discusses the origin of euphemisms, and the first section discusses their original purpose: substitutions for taboo words. Euphemisms gradually became substitutes for vulgar or profane language. That's how many people still think of the euphemism today.

However, euphemisms are also used as "the language of anticipation," describing things as they are hoped to be in the future. "Linguistic optimism," otherwise politely called "inflated description," applies in American politics, social life, and the workplace.

The essay concludes that the euphemism can be used to demonstrate sensitivity to people's feelings, but also to obscure meaning. Students might enjoy watching for euphemisms in the mass media, particularly in the news.

Assign the essay as homework, and have students work collaboratively on the Analyzing Language activity.

Analyzing Language

Text page 981

1. Answers will vary. Sample answers are provided.

   hair designers: barbers
   face painting: makeup application
   custom bedding: mattresses

2. Answers will vary. Sample answers are provided.

   student: learning participant
   automobile: transport device
   baby sitter: infant custodian
   apartment house: residential cluster

3.

PLAIN	FANCY
eat (AS)	dine (L)
win (AS)	achieve (L)
pig (AS)	pork (L)
calf (AS)	veal (L)
spit (AS)	expectorate (L)
cheap (AS)	inexpensive (L)
cow (AS)	beef (L)
work (AS)	career (L)
father (AS)	parent (L)

4. Answers will vary. Sample answers are provided.

   armed conflict: war
   unlawful deprivation of life: murder
   dependent upon distilled spirits: drunk
   a controlled-substance abuser: a drug addict

EXERCISES IN CRITICAL THINKING AND WRITING

Text page 982

EVALUATING A STORY'S ENDING

This assignment asks students to evaluate the ending of one of the ten stories in the unit. It is important that students note a major point given in Background: A writer may deliberately choose not to provide closure on all conflicts, but leave some of them unresolved. You might list the ten stories on the board or give students a list of the authors and titles with spaces left for students to briefly recall and jot down the ending of each story. After choosing the story that most interests them, students can then continue, individually or in small groups, with the notetaking questions in the second column and the directions for organizing the essay.

▶ CRITERIA FOR EVALUATING THE ASSIGNMENT   The essay as a whole is coherent and well organized. The opening paragraph mentions the title, author, and subject of the story, and summarizes its ending. The second paragraph comments on the writer's use of foreshadowing in its explanation of why the student did or did not find the outcome logical or inevitable. The third paragraph evaluates how well the ending fits the story's theme and characters by showing how at least one alternative ending would have been more or less satisfying. The fourth paragraph discusses the student's emotional response to the story and brings the paper to a satisfying close.

Further Reading

Works listed are suitable for both students and teachers unless the annotation ends with the note [Teachers].

Allentuck, Marcia, ed. *The Achievement of Isaac Bashevis Singer* (Southern Illinois University Press, 1969). A collection of previously unpublished essays dealing with specific aspects of Singer's writings and with individual works. A good general introduction.

"Andrea Lee," *Contemporary Literary Criticism 36* (Gale Research Company, 1986). A brief, illustrated biography followed by critical comments of twelve reviewers.

Balakian, Nona, and Charles Simmons, eds. *The Creative Present: Notes on Contemporary American Fiction* (Doubleday, 1963). Essays on Baldwin, Welty, Malamud, Updike, and others.

Bloom, Harold, ed. *Modern Critical Views: Bernard Malamud* (Chelsea House, 1986). A collection of contemporary criticism on Malamud's work.

Chan, Jeffery Paul, and Frank Chin, Lawson Fusao Inada, and Shawn Wong. *The Big Aiiieeeee! An Anthology of Chinese American and Japanese American Literature* (Penguin, 1990). A comprehensive collection of poetry, prose, and drama, with a long introduction by Frank Chin.

Cisneros, Sandra. *The House on Mango Street* (Arte Publico, 1989). Brief stories told from the point of view of Esperanza, a young girl growing up in the Hispanic section of Chicago.

Courturier, Maurice, and Regis Durand. *Donald Barthelme* (Methuen, 1982). An 80-page introduction to Barthelme's writing. [Teachers]

Gardner, John. *On Moral Fiction* (Basic Books, 1978). A distinguished teacher's discussion of the need for moral vision in fiction.

Gass, William H. *Fiction and the Figures of Life* (Knopf, 1970). A leading fiction writer and philosophy professor discusses Barthelme, Updike, and others. [Teachers]

Gordon, Lois. *Donald Barthelme* (Twayne, 1981). A helpful discussion of specific stories; also contains a list of references.

Helprin, Mark. *A Dove of the East and Other Stories* (Random House, 1975). A collection of twenty short stories.

Hershinow, Sheldon J. *Bernard Malamud* (Frederick Ungar, 1980). Straightforward analysis of six of Malamud's novels and some of his short stories.

Hoffman, Daniel, ed. *Harvard Guide to Contemporary American Writing* (Belknap Press, 1979). Sections by ten distinguished critics on various aspects of fiction, poetry, and drama. [Teachers]

Jimenez, Francisco, ed. *The Identification and Analysis of Chicano Literature* (Bilingual Press, 1979). An anthology of readings about Mexican American literature, some in English, others in Spanish.

Karl, Frederick R. *American Fictions: 1940–1980* (Harper & Row, 1983). A comprehensive history and critical evaluation of four decades of American fiction. [Teachers]

Kiernan, Robert F. *American Writing Since 1945* (Frederick Ungar, 1983). A brief survey with chapters on realism, metafiction, and fiction by Southern, Jewish, and African American writers. [Teachers]

Kim, Elaine H. *Asian American Literature: An Introduction to the Writings and Their Social Context* (Temple University Press, 1982). Solid background for further study of Asian American literature, with extensive notes and bibliography. [Teachers]

Lee, Andrea. "A Funeral at New African," Chapter 12 in her novel *Sarah Phillips* (Random House, 1984). The final chapter of the novel concerns the death and funeral of Sarah's father. [Teachers]

Lincoln, Kenneth. *Native American Renaissance* (University of California Press, 1983). A wide-ranging exploration of Native American culture and literary history by a Native American author. [Teachers]

McMillan, Terry, ed. *Breaking Ice: An Anthology of Contemporary African American Fiction* (Penguin, 1990). A big anthology of stories by James Alan McPherson, Gloria Naylor, Alice Walker, Ishmael Reed, Al Young, and many new writers.

McPherson, James Alan. *Elbow Room* (Atlantic-Little, Brown, 1975). A collection of twelve warm, humorous stories.

O'Brien, Tim. *Going After Cacciato* (Delacorte, 1975). A novel combining reality and fantasy about an American soldier in Vietnam. Characters include Paul Berlin and Stink Harris. [Teachers]

O'Connor, Frank. *The Lonely Voice: A Study of the Short Story* (World, 1963). Discussion of the fundamental nature of the genre by the Irish short story writer.

Phillips, J. J., and Ishmael Reed, Gundars Strads, and Shawn Wong, eds. *The Before Columbus Foundation Fiction Anthology* (Norton, 1992). Selections from American Book Awards (1980–1990) with stories by James Welch, Louise Erdrich, Toni Morrison, Sandra Cisneros, Toni Cade Bambara, Ishmael Reed, and many others.

Singer, Isaac Bashevis. *Love and Exile: A Memoir* (Doubleday, 1984). A combination of three autobiographical memoirs about Singer's youth in Poland and his emigration to the United States.

Thorburn, David, and Howard Elland. *John Updike: A Collection of Critical Essays* (Prentice-Hall, 1979). A varied collection of essays on Updike's novels and short stories, with emphasis on the Rabbit novels. [Teachers]

Tyler, Anne. *Searching for Caleb* (Knopf, 1976). A lively and tender depiction of four generations of a family, described by one critic as the "sunniest" of Tyler's novels.

Uphaus, Suzanne Henning. *John Updike* (Frederick Ungar, 1980). Straightforward summaries of Updike's major novels and brief explications of his most frequently anthologized short stories. [Teachers]

Weaver, Gordon, ed. *The American Short Story 1945–1980* (Twayne Publishers, 1983). A good critical survey of both traditional and experimental writers. [Teachers]

MODERN NONFICTION

Teaching the Modern Nonfiction Unit

The essays and journalistic pieces of American writers since World War II have been notable for their high literary quality and for the new respect they have won for the genre of nonfiction, but this is not a wholly unprecedented phenomenon. In fact, nonfiction thrived in the United States before there was much fiction to speak of. The early flowering of nonfiction is probably the fruit of our pragmatic heritage. During the early development of our country, fiction was viewed as something of a frivolity, while nonfiction writers dealt with the most pressing issues of nation-building. Even such a great literary artist as Herman Melville came to prominence in the early years of his career not because of his bold imagination or his towering metaphysical insights, but because he reported to the American audience, with a memoirist's eye, what it had been like to live among a tribe of South Sea islanders. And Mark Twain was a great reporter, in *Life on the Mississippi* and *Roughing It*, before he flowered as the creator of Huckleberry Finn.

While you won't want to get bogged down in review work, this unit comes near the end of the year's work and might be a good place to cast a brief backward glance at some of the earlier nonfiction to help prepare your students for what is to come. They'll find that the rich vein of autobiographical writing in American literature proceeds—despite the differences in subject matter—from Benjamin Franklin to Richard Wright. N. Scott Momaday's observations on his own Native American culture can be compared and contrasted with the observations of Native Americans by writers of the Colonial period, such as William Bradford, Mary Rowlandson, William Byrd, and Benjamin Franklin. Michael Herr's reportage from Vietnam is descended from a long and honorable line of wartime writing not only in nonfiction like Walt Whitman's *Speciman Days*, but also in fiction such as Stephen Crane's "A Mystery of Heroism." Contemporary essayists who write personally about the natural world, such as Annie Dillard and Lewis Thomas, are the direct literary descendants of Henry David Thoreau. Richard Wright, James Baldwin, and Alice Walker, meanwhile, owe much to the writers of the Harlem Renaissance in Unit Eight.

At the same time, you'll want to direct students' attention to what is genuinely new in the nonfiction of recent decades. There is, for example, a brash willingness to place the individual writer's consciousness at the heart of the work, as in Jamaica Kincaid's "A Small Place," rather than maintaining a stance of objectivity. There is a willingness to try new forms—to mix fiction and nonfiction as Maxine Hong Kingston does, or expository prose and lyrical prose-poems as in the book-length version of *The Way to Rainy Mountain*. In the journalism of John Hersey and Michael Herr, there is a strong quality which writers at the beginning of the new nation's history had not had time yet to develop: There is a dry disillusionment with war—a cold but hopeful realism that replaces the naiveté of a belief in war's glories. And in the personal odyssey of William Least Heat Moon, we find another quality which, by definition, cannot be found in the infancy of a republic: nostalgia.

Because the contemporary essay is such a personal form, and because it doesn't require the imposition of an artificial structure—a plot—upon its material, it is particularly adaptable to student writing assignments. Some of your students may have already had experience writing articles for the school newspaper; all of them have had practice writing expository essays. In this unit more than in other units, they'll have the feeling that in writing about the selections, they are practicing the same skills as the writers of the selections themselves: observing, evaluating, criticizing, explaining, and stating their views.

Objectives of the Modern Nonfiction Unit

1. To expand vocabulary and increase reading proficiency
2. To gain exposure to notable authors of nonfiction and their works
3. To define and identify elements of nonfiction
4. To define and identify significant literary techniques
5. To interpret and respond to nonfiction, orally and in writing, through analysis of its elements
6. To practice the following critical thinking and writing skills:
   a. Analyzing an essay
   b. Analyzing style, atmosphere, character, and suspense
   c. Comparing and contrasting two works of literature
   d. Responding to a critical statement
   e. Imitating a writer's technique
   f. Evaluating fact and opinion in nonfiction

Introducing the Modern Nonfiction Unit

Nonfiction is part of all our lives even if we are not literary specialists. We come to know the outside world largely through the words of journalists and essayists. Some of those writers work in the print media, and many work in radio and TV. We learn about wars, elections, famines, economic upheavals, sporting events, without personally witnessing them. And we trust (or have to decide how much to trust) the writers and reporters who give us the information. In introducing this unit, you might ask students to try to visualize how their knowledge of the world would be different if they had never had any access to nonfiction writing or reporting. They'll probably agree that their knowledge of global and governmental affairs would be extremely limited. You might then inform students that nonfiction not only acquaints us with outside events, but it also acquaints us with the minds of the writers. If your students keep a journal, you might ask them to write and share entries expressing their personal reactions to public events that have affected their lives or to phenomena of nature or of family history that have been meaningful to them. The results will very likely be in the spirit of this unit.

E. B. White

DEATH OF A PIG

Objectives

1. To enjoy a humorous essay with a serious theme
2. To analyze the essay's theme
3. To write a recollection of an animal
4. To write an essay analyzing the essay's humor
5. To write an essay describing a character
6. To write an essay explaining an allusion

Introducing the Essay

White's essay has become a classic because of the poignant, universal themes he develops from a seemingly homely and perhaps even comical subject, the premature death of a pig he had been raising for meat. In the same sentence—for example, the last sentence in the essay— White pokes gentle fun at the antics of a pet dog and summons up the ache of grief at mortality. In examining this selection, you'll probably want to make your students aware of the subtlety and richness of these variations in tone, and the contrast between the barnyard subject matter and the sublime reflections it arouses.

Here are the major elements of the essay:

- **Characters:** the narrator; a sick pig; Fred, the dachshund
- **Conflict:** man vs. nature (the struggle to save the sick pig's life)
- **Themes:** empathy with suffering creatures; connection to all living things; inevitability of death
- **Significant techniques:** hyperbole, humor, metaphor, allusion

BACKGROUND ON THE ESSAY White's style and career are inseparable from the style and history of *The New Yorker* magazine, but "Death of a Pig," doubtless because of its subject matter, did not first appear in that publication. It was first published in *The Atlantic Monthly*. Nevertheless, you might want to tell your students briefly about the extraordinary influence *The New Yorker* has had on contemporary American nonfiction and fiction, publishing writers like J.D. Salinger, Truman Capote, John Hersey, John McPhee, John Cheever, John Updike, and many others. The magazine's nonfiction, in particular, is notable for its smooth, balanced, genteel style; its graceful fluency; and the nearly continuous irony that flows beneath the surface of impeccably researched and presented facts. You might want to obtain a recent issue of the magazine and read a few paragraphs of its nonfiction aloud to your class, so they can see that White's style is partly individual and partly generic.

SUMMARY White raised a pig in hopes of butchering it for meat, but it became severely constipated and died despite White's own efforts and those of a veterinarian.

Teaching Strategies

PROVIDING FOR CULTURAL DIFFERENCES Rural and urban students may react to this essay in different ways. Rural students may bring to it a fuller understanding of the livestock-raising processes involved, but because of familiarity with the mundane aspects of White's narrative, they may be reluctant to go along with the larger themes. Urban students, for whom the whole subject of pig-raising is only metaphorical anyway, may be more receptive to White's eagerness to philosophize. All students will probably need a brief explanation of the old crank-operated telephone with eavesdropping operator— now seen only in old movies.

PROVIDING FOR DIFFERENT LEVELS OF ABILITY White's style is fairly simple, but his wry stance and euphemistic style of humor may need some interpretation for LEP students. More advanced students will enjoy the pleasing flow of White's sentences, with their judicious variations in pace, tone, and diction. Almost any passage in the essay can be profitably used as the basis of a stylistic analysis.

READING THE ESSAY You might ask students whether they have ever been present at, or been affected by, the death of an animal. In certain circumstances, this can be a deeply poignant experience. You might ask whether these experiences made students feel that they were learning anything important about the nature of life.

RETEACHING ALTERNATIVES To help clarify the themes of the essay, you might ask students, individually, to write one-paragraph summaries of how White tended his sick pig and how he apparently felt about the experience.

Responding to the Essay   Text page 993

Answers to the questions in the Pupil's Edition appear in the Annotated Teacher's Edition.

Writing About the Essay

For help in revising their compositions, refer students to **Grammar, Usage, and Mechanics: A Reference Guide** on text pages 1183 to 1228 at the back of their books.

A CREATIVE RESPONSE

1. Imitating White's Technique   The assignment has a delightful latitude, allowing students to work with anything from their own pet to an imaginary unicorn, griffon, or creature of their own devising. Brainstorm a list of possibilities to give students this range.

▶ CRITERIA FOR EVALUATING THE ASSIGNMENT   The essay reflects White's influence in the way the animal is given a consistent, appropriate, human personality.

A CRITICAL RESPONSE

2. Analyzing Style   Have students work in groups to find and discuss examples of comic metaphors, comic images, irony, exaggeration, and puns. Ask how all of these help White to create his overall humorous effect. Direct them to cite specific examples in their essays.

▶ CRITERIA FOR EVALUATING THE ESSAY   In a well-organized manner, the essay cites specific details to demonstrate how White's humor makes use of the elements of comic metaphors, comic images, irony, exaggeration, and puns.

3. Describing a Character   Questions 3 and 4 provide data for this writing assignment on Fred the dachshund. Briefly review the appropriate paragraphs.

▶ CRITERIA FOR EVALUATING THE ESSAY   The essay describes the character of Fred the dachshund not as the student imagines it, but as White creates it. Generalizations are supported by details from the essay on Fred's appearance, interests, and responses to the pig's problems.

4. Explaining Allusion   Review questions 6 and 7 on the theme of White's essay, and lead students to recall that allusions usually enlarge upon, enhance, or ironically highlight an idea. If Donne's "Meditation XVII" is not readily available, give your students copies of these lines: "... all mankind is of one author and is one volume; when one man dies, one chapter is not torn out of the book, but translated into a better language; and every chapter must be so translated. ... No man is an island, entire of itself; every man is a piece of the continent, a part of the main. ... Any man's death diminishes me because I am involved in mankind, and therefore never send to know for whom the bell tolls; it tolls for thee."

▶ CRITERIA FOR EVALUATING THE ASSIGNMENT   The essay explains that the allusion enlarges upon the theme: human mortality and the common fate of all living creatures. It also is a humorous extension of the personification of the pig.

Extending the Essay

In his essay White finds universal echoes of mortality in the death of a farm animal. Here is a poem by Gerard Manley Hopkins, written in 1880, that finds the same echoes in the fall of a leaf, seen by a child. Have students compare and contrast the theme of mortality as it is expressed in the essay and the poem.

Spring and Fall:
To a Young Child

Margaret, are you grieving
Over Goldengrove unleaving?
Leaves, like the things of man, you
With your fresh thoughts care for, can you?
Ah! as the heart grows older
It will come to such sights colder
By and by, nor spare a sigh
Though worlds of wanwood leafmeal lie;
And yet you will weep and know why.
Now no matter, child, the name;
Sorrow's springs are the same.
Nor mouth had, no nor mind, expressed
What heart heard of, ghost guessed:
It is the blight man was born for,
It is Margaret you mourn for.

Lewis Thomas

Text page 994

CETI

Text page 995

Objectives

1. To respond to a science essay
2. To identify the essay's tone
3. To write an essay expressing a personal point of view
4. To write a paragraph evaluating the essay

Introducing the Essay

Thomas's essay resembles E. B. White's in the sense that both move from the particular to the general. White's "Death of a Pig" begins with some very specific memories of pig-raising and of discovering the pig to be ill, and moves on to become, by implication, a meditation on mortality in general. Thomas's "Ceti" begins with a description of a single scientific conference and goes on to discuss the nature of life and the self-image of the human race. This is a natural format for essays: The writer's attention is caught by a specific phenomenon, and he or she proceeds to muse upon that phenomenon until arriving at general conclusions, thus making the phenomenon seem larger and more meaningful than it was at first glance. The same kind of developmental structure is often used in poetry. Robert Frost was indirectly commenting on this when he said that a poem should "begin in delight and end in wisdom," and many of his poems, such as "Birches" and "Mending Wall," display this sort of structure.

This essay provides a good opportunity for your more scientifically oriented students to become interested in literature, and for your more literary-minded students to see the poetic side of science. Thomas himself is an excellent role model for young people, since his career has bridged the "two cultures"—science and the humanities—that the English novelist and physicist C. P. Snow described a generation ago.

BACKGROUND ON THE ESSAY   As is often the case in journalism, the form of this essay was dictated to some extent by the practical demands of a specific periodical. When Lewis Thomas began his career as an essayist by writing columns in *The New England Journal of Medicine*, he was required to produce an essay of a certain length, on a certain kind of topic, at regular intervals. Because readers responded well, and because the author's turn of mind suited the journalistic form, Thomas's writing career flourished.

Other excellent contemporary essayists in the sciences whom your students might be interested in reading are Stephen Jay Gould, Oliver Sacks, Richard Selzer, Arthur C. Clarke, Nigel Calder, Carl Sagan, Douglas Hofstadter, and Barry Lopez.

SUMMARY   In 1972 an international conference, intentionally called the Conference on Communication with Extraterrestrial Intelligence (CETI), was held to plan efforts to probe Tau Ceti and other stars for possible electromagnetic messages. Thomas discusses how the human race might react to the discovery of life elsewhere, and muses on what questions we might ask an extraterrestrial species and what artifacts of our civilization we might want to transmit to it.

Teaching Strategies

PROVIDING FOR CULTURAL DIFFERENCES   In his essay, Thomas assumes an unusual perspective. From outer space the people living on earth are simply human beings; their ethnic, racial, and religious differences are totally unimportant. Ask students what they think of this idea. Does it—or can it—apply to daily life on earth?

Play a bit of Bach's music and bring a book of Cezanne's paintings to class. Volunteers may want to extend Thomas's idea and make a tape of what they consider the best of the earth's music.

PROVIDING FOR DIFFERENT LEVELS OF ABILITY
Thomas uses a number of scientific terms in this essay (*anaerobic, pili, ganglions*) but they are defined in footnotes at the bottoms of the text pages. More advanced students will probably be excited by Thomas's speculations, particularly those in the second half of the essay, where he speculates on how we might present ourselves and our civilization to extraterrestrials. LEP students may find the beginning of the essay a bit dry, and they may need a paraphrase of his description of the "morphogenesis" of the earth (text page 996).

READING THE ESSAY   Though the essay is short, its scientific contents make it a bit thorny for oral reading. You might want to have your students read it for homework, and then have students read the most intriguing or most troublesome paragraphs out loud in class.

RETEACHING ALTERNATIVES   The most important part of the essay is the second half, where Thomas discusses what messages we might send to other species and what questions we might ask of them. Ask students to reread the second half (beginning with ''The immediate problem . . .'' on text page 996) and list all of the ways Thomas suggests for introducing ourselves as human beings to life forms in outer space.

Responding to the Essay   Text page 997

Answers to the questions in the Pupil's Edition appear in the Annotated Teacher's Edition.

Writing About the Essay

For help in revising their compositions, refer students to **Grammar, Usage, and Mechanics: A Reference Guide** on text pages 1183–1228 at the back of their books.

A CREATIVE RESPONSE

1. Expressing Your Point of View   Use Thomas's partial list of questions in his next-to-last paragraph as a springboard for further questions. Note that the writing assignment tells students how to organize their three paragraphs.

▶ CRITERIA FOR EVALUATING THE ASSIGNMENT   The first paragraph lists questions to be asked of intelligent

extraterrestrials. The second paragraph explains what ''news of ourselves'' to send. The third paragraph explains what ''harder truths'' (war, pollution, racism, etc.) we might need to tell these beings later.

A CRITICAL RESPONSE

2. Evaluating the Essay   Make sure students understand that they are to do two things: (1) state the main topic of Thomas's essay and tell what it teaches; and (2) evaluate the essay—make a judgment on its overall value or effectiveness.

▶ CRITERIA FOR EVALUATING THE ASSIGNMENT   The paragraph cites Thomas's topic (how to communicate with intelligent extraterrestrials) and what he ''teaches'' (the difficulty of establishing criteria for the information and questions to be sent). It offers a judgment on the overall effectiveness of the essay.

Extending the Essay

As a creative exercise, you might ask your students to bring to class some newspaper or magazine articles about recent scientific findings or science news of any kind. Students may also summarize a TV or radio report on science news. Have each student tell the class about his or her piece of science news, and let the whole class suggest what ''larger meaning'' the event has. What might a writer like Lewis Thomas say the event ''teaches''?

Russell Baker   Text page 998

LITTLE RED RIDING HOOD REVISITED   Text page 999

Objectives

1. To enjoy a satirical essay

2. To interpret irony

3. To rephrase slang, jargon, and pleonasm

4. To imitate the writer's technique

5. To analyze the use of jargon

Introducing the Essay

In the brief space of a newspaper column, Russell Baker pokes serious fun at the mutilation of the English language by the forces of institutional obfuscation. Starting with the phrase, ''Once upon a point in time,'' he weaves into the familiar fairy tale the stock pleonasms and linguistic barbarities of politicians, law enforcement officers (''alleged perpetrator''), social scientists (''attained interface''), lawyers, ("a third party, heretofore unnoted in the record"), advertisers ("dramatic relief for stomach discontent"), and the simply semiliterate ("What a phenomena!"). In addition to decrying the distortion of language, Baker implicitly criticizes the bureaucratic officiousness and widespread intellectual sloppiness that have made them possible.

BACKGROUND ON THE ESSAY   Russell Baker is one of a number of journalists who have in recent years raised alarms about the deterioration of our language at the hands of bureaucratic institutions and the mass media. Baker wrote this essay for his regular *New York Times* column, which is often satirical and sometimes merely hilarious. Another *New York Times* columnist, William Safire, regularly writes on this subject; and television commentator Edwin Newman has written several books on the subject, including *Strictly Speaking*. Tell students that for the most part Baker is not objecting to simple usage errors of colloquial speech, but to genteelisms—the kinds of mistakes committed by people who want to sound official, important, or impressive.

SUMMARY   Baker retells the folk tale of Little Red Riding Hood in the inflated rhetoric of the modern bureaucracy.

Teaching Strategies

PROVIDING FOR CULTURAL DIFFERENCES   In order to appreciate this satire, students will have to know "Little Red Riding Hood" in its original, simple language. If you have ESL students in your class, bring a copy of the original version and ask several students to read it aloud *before* students read Baker's retelling. Also, this satire of the jargon of contemporary institutions is likely to mean most to those who are familiar with those institutions. Students who may not hear standard English spoken in their homes may not "get" a satire of bureaucratic English.

PROVIDING FOR DIFFERENT LEVELS OF ABILITY
Some students may have to be shown the ways in which the language of this essay deviates from good English: for instance, that "a phenomena" is incorrect and that "residing at a place of residence" is redundant.

READING THE ESSAY   Although this piece is short, it will benefit from being read slowly, perhaps one paragraph per student if you are having it read aloud. Ask for paraphrases and definitions as you go; part of Baker's aim is to make us "translate" his pleonasms into clear English as we go along.

RETEACHING ALTERNATIVES   If oral paraphrasing of the essay leaves some students still confused, use question 1 of Analyzing Language and Style (text page 1001), which asks for a written paraphrase. You might divide the essay among small groups. Each group should collaborate on a written paraphrase of its assigned part. If you call on each group to present its paraphrase, you will have a paraphrase of the whole essay.

Responding to the Essay   Text page 1001

Answers to the questions in the Pupil's Edition appear in the Annotated Teacher's Edition.

Writing About the Essay

For help in revising their compositions, refer students to **Grammar, Usage, and Mechanics: A Reference Guide** on text pages 1183–1228 at the back of their books.

A CREATIVE RESPONSE
Imitating Baker's Technique   Brainstorm a list of other popular fairy tales (Cinderella, Snow White, Goldilocks, and such) that students might use.

▶ CRITERIA FOR EVALUATING THE ASSIGNMENT   Like Baker, the student uses a mixture of slang, jargon, verbosity and euphemisms in the retelling of a fairy tale. Have volunteers read their tales aloud.

Analyzing Language and Style

JARGON
1. Student choices will vary. The rewritten paragraphs should be entirely free of jargon. For example, the sentence used in this assignment might read, "Halfway to her grandmother's house, Little Red Riding Hood met a criminal." (See Reteaching Alternatives for suggestions on how to cover the entire essay as a collaborative exercise.)
2. *Jargon* is derived from a Middle French word meaning "a chattering of birds." The origin is appropriate because jargon seems meaningless, like birds' chatter, impossible to understand.

Extending the Essay

You might ask students to clip from periodicals, or write down from newscasts, examples of misused English that they read or hear. This can become an ongoing project, with all members of the class sharing their findings in a notebook or on a bulletin board, or sending their clippings to the school newspaper for publication. Refer students to **Grammar, Usage, and Mechanics: A Reference Guide** (text pages 1183–1228) if they are in doubt about usage.

SCHOOL VS. EDUCATION

Objectives

1. To respond to a satirical essay

2. To identify examples of comic hyperbole

3. To state the essay's theme

4. To write a "letter to the editor" responding to the essay

5. To support an assertion with examples

6. To interpret irony

Introducing the Essay

Part of the art of being a social gadfly consists of perceiving the obvious and calling attention to it in a more pungent way than has usually been done before. When Baker, for instance, says that from television, young children learn "how to pick a lock, commit a fairly elaborate bank holdup, prevent wetness all day long, get the laundry twice as white, and kill people with a variety of sophisticated armaments," he is saying, in an oversimplified way, what everyone already knows about the contents of television. But he is saying it memorably. The oversimplification, too, is part of the effect; the vivid rhetoric makes us stop and say, "Yes, that's the way it is."

BACKGROUND ON THE ESSAY Debates on the nature of American education have been raging for decades, and Baker is by no means the first to point out that schools teach students how to take tests rather than how to love knowledge. Nor does he propose specific solutions in this essay: that is the preserve of writers of books on education. Baker's role is limited to that of social gadfly, attempting to make us think, discuss, and perhaps come up with our own solutions.

SUMMARY Baker describes some of the deplorable things young children see and hear on television and in the home before they get to school. By six, he says, they have completed their basic education. When they get to school, children learn a number of lessons, including that the point of education is to take tests and that they can immediately be classified as either smart or dumb. Baker goes on to attack many other inequities and absurdities in the formal education system.

Teaching Strategies

PROVIDING FOR CULTURAL DIFFERENCES You may need to clarify the allusions to teachers' strikes and the violent demonstrations against school busing and integration in paragraph 5. Toward the end of the essay, Baker says that "the race is to the cunning and often, alas, to the unprincipled." This is an allusion to the common saying "The race is to the swift" from John Davidson's "War Song."

PROVIDING FOR DIFFERENT LEVELS OF ABILITY The essay refers to the fact that students are, indeed, at different levels of ability and experience different educational fates. All students should have a chance to respond personally to Baker's statements. Remind them not to take all of Baker's statements literally. He is saying things to be critical—satirical—of American education.

READING THE ESSAY Since the essay takes a swipe at the educational establishment, it might be a good idea for you—as the representative of that establishment—to read it aloud to the class. When you finish reading, ask students how they feel about the essay. Did they enjoy it? Do they agree (or disagree) with any of its statements?

RETEACHING ALTERNATIVES This essay is likely to spark lively discussion, since it touches upon an experience—school—in which all students are immersed. You may want to open up the discussion to students' views on what is right and what is wrong about American education as they've known it.

Responding to the Essay

Answers to the questions in the Pupil's Edition appear in the Annotated Teacher's Edition.

Writing About the Essay

For help in revising their compositions, refer students to **Grammar, Usage, and Mechanics: A Reference Guide** on text pages 1183–1228 at the back of their books.

A CREATIVE RESPONSE
1. Answering the Writer Have students look at the kinds and lengths of letters actually published in newspapers: they must be short and to the point.

ever the student thinks of Baker's essay, the paragraph
is appropriate for a letter to the editor and shows a
recognition both of Baker's serious intent and his satirical style.

A CRITICAL RESPONSE

2. Supporting an Assertion with Examples   Point out
several points in the essay such as ''Teachers show children you should belong to a union''; ''Television teaches
crime''; ''Parents teach prejudice.'' Ask students to think
of their own experiences which support or refute these
points.

► CRITERIA FOR EVALUATING THE ASSIGNMENT   The
essay cites at least one main point from Baker's essay
and goes on to support or refute that point with examples of personal experience.

Analyzing Language and Style

IRONY

1. One would expect parents to teach their children
   healthy, ethical behavior.
2. Formal education takes place outside the school and
   has nothing to do with academic subjects. Also, most
   of the formal education in this paragraph is made up of
   negative experiences and values.
3. Success means telling testers the answer they want to
   hear. Success has nothing to do with real learning.

Extending the Essay

You might want to give your students some practice writing newspaper-style columns by having them pick topics
of their own choice, from either current events or school
events, and writing brief essays in which they reveal the
foibles of the subject, in a style similar to Baker's.

Richard Wright

Text page 1004

FROM BLACK BOY

Text page 1005

Objectives

1. To respond to an African American personal narrative
2. To analyze imagery
3. To analyze character
4. To write a monologue from another point of view
5. To write an essay comparing and contrasting the styles
   and themes of two writers
6. To write a paragraph analyzing the use of dialogue

Introducing the Autobiography

Here are the major elements of the autobiography:

- **Protagonist:** Richard (the narrator as a boy)
- **Antagonists:** Richard's father; a gang of boys
- **Conflicts:** fear vs. the conquest of fear; deprivation
  vs. fulfillment; injustice vs. justice
- **Themes:** maturation through struggle; family strife as
  an outgrowth of poverty
- **Point of view:** first-person

- **Significant techniques:** naturalistic detail; vivid
  dialogue
- **Setting:** Memphis, Tennessee, early 20th century

BACKGROUND ON THE AUTOBIOGRAPHY   Wright
said that he hit upon the idea of writing his autobiography
after delivering a lecture about his life and about his people
at Fisk University in 1942, when he was newly famous
from the success of his novel *Native Son.* He found that
his honest words about the feelings of African Americans
startled the audience, simply because such things had not
often been publicly expressed till then. In *Black Boy,*
Wright memorably recounts how his discovery of literature helped him find his direction in life, and how a Catholic white man, who was also a victim of discrimination,
lent him his library card at a time when African Americans
were not allowed to use the public library.

SUMMARY   After Wright's father left home, his mother
tried to keep her family together, but their poverty was
such that there was often no food in the house. Finally she
had to send Richard to an orphanage, where conditions
were not much better. Richard ran away but was returned
and beaten. His father refused to provide for his children.
Wright describes seeing his father later in life, and forgiv-
ing him, but remaining aware of the unbridgeable distance
between them.

Teaching Strategies

PROVIDING FOR CULTURAL DIFFERENCES This selection will have special meaning for African Americans, and you might encourage them to share their responses. Bear in mind that such feelings may be too powerful for them to talk about comfortably. However, the power of Wright's narrative transcends race, and all students will empathize with the sufferings of a young boy who is hungry, confused about his parents' conflicts, frightened of neighborhood bullies, and tyrannized by a Dickensian orphanage director.

PROVIDING FOR DIFFERENT LEVELS OF ABILITY Wright's style is direct and forceful, though the passing of four decades may make it seem a trifle old-fashioned to today's students. More advanced students might be interested in comparing this selection to works of realism and naturalism studied in earlier units. Students will probably handle the dialogue sections more easily than the passages of narrative; the latter, you might briefly paraphrase in the normal course of discussion.

READING THE AUTOBIOGRAPHY Students will enjoy reading the selection aloud in class, especially the passages with dialogue.

RETEACHING ALTERNATIVES Despite deprivation, young Richard often displays pride and defiance in this narrative—for instance, on page 1008, when he doesn't want to eat his soup because the preacher is eating a lot of chicken. You might want to discuss how Wright dramatizes this character trait through specific incidents, and how he shows us the way his mother nurtured those traits in him by forcing him to be strong.

Responding to the Autobiography

Text page 1013

Answers to the questions in the Pupil's Edition appear in the Annotated Teacher's Edition.

Writing About the Autobiography

For help in revising their compositions, refer students to **Grammar, Usage, and Mechanics: A Reference Guide** on text pages 1183–1228 at the back of their books.

A CREATIVE RESPONSE

1. Experimenting with Point of View Remind students that an interior monologue should reveal what is happening as well as Richard's mother's feelings and opinions about the events. Richard's mother's interior monologue will take several paragraphs to develop. The second option

calls for a series of paragraphs of the "I remember him as . . ." type that you hear when people are interviewed after the death of a famous person.

▶ CRITERIA FOR EVALUATING THE ASSIGNMENT If the paper is an interior monologue, it believably interprets Richard's mother's memories and feelings about some of the same events Richard reports. If the paper is a series of comments from different people, the tone and content change appropriately for each speaker.

A CRITICAL RESPONSE

2. Comparing and Contrasting Two Writers Students might work in small groups to create and complete a pre-writing chart. Have students list the items to look for (theme, sentence structure, dialogue, use of detail, tone of voice, how the piece affected them) before they turn to Twain's *Huckleberry Finn* or Toth's *Ivy Days* to take notes. They should make similar notes on the Wright selection and draw conclusions about similarities and differences before they begin to write.

▶ CRITERIA FOR EVALUATING THE ASSIGNMENT The essay follows a coherent pattern of comparison/contrast, such as dealing first with similarities and then with differences, or going through the list of items point-by-point and stating whether the other writer and Wright are similar or different on each point. For each point made, details from both the other writer and Wright support the student's conclusion.

Analyzing Language and Style

DIALOGUE

Have students first list scenes that lend themselves to this assignment—for example, the mother-son discussion about hunger or the dinner with the preacher. Whichever incident the student chooses, the paper comments on the contributions of dialogue to the scene's total effect and the characterization of people involved. The paper also evaluates the use of dialogue by commenting on how effective the scene would have been without dialogue.

Extending the Autobiography

Interested students may want to read the rest of *Black Boy* and other works by Richard Wright: the novel *Native Son*, excellent short stories like "Long Black Song" and "Fire and Cloud," and works of nonfiction such as "Blueprint for Negro Writing" and "Joe Louis Discovers Dynamite." The latter is a fascinating and moving piece of reportage on the galvanizing effect Joe Louis's 1935 prize fight victory over Max Baer had on the self-image of African Americans. All of these short pieces are collected in the *Richard Wright Reader* (Harper, 1978).

N. Scott Momaday

FROM THE WAY TO RAINY MOUNTAIN

Objectives

1. To respond to a Native American personal narrative
2. To write an imagistic description
3. To write an essay evaluating the use of setting
4. To write a paragraph responding to a statement
5. To examine the use of poetic prose

Introducing the Essay

Here are the major elements of the essay:

- **Characters:** N. Scott Momaday; his grandmother; the Kiowa people
- **Themes:** the search for one's ethnic roots; the veneration of the past through memory
- **Point of view:** first-person
- **Significant techniques:** poetic prose, flashback
- **Setting:** Oklahoma, Montana, and points between

BACKGROUND ON THE ESSAY You might want to emphasize to your students that Momaday is talking about two distinct cultural transformations undergone by the Kiowa people at two different—though not widely separated—times in history. Until approximately the mid-seventeenth century, the Kiowa lived in the rugged mountains of western Montana, at the headwaters of the Yellowstone River. For some undetermined reasons, they migrated down from that terrain onto the plains, where they took up a new way of life, becoming expert horsemen, buffalo hunters, and warriors. This plains culture, the period of Kiowa predominance, lasted only a century. By then they had to undergo another transformation: battle against white soldiers and adaptation to the massive white presence.

SUMMARY After his grandmother's death, Momaday traces the heroic and ultimately tragic journey of his people, the Kiowa, from the headwaters of the Yellowstone River to Rainy Mountain in Oklahoma. He remembers details of his grandmother Aho, her house, and the Kiowa people when he was a boy.

Teaching Strategies

PROVIDING FOR CULTURAL DIFFERENCES This selection will have special meaning for Native American students, and for other students whose forebears were involved in the settling of the West. If your class includes such students, this will be a good chance for them to share their knowledge of such events. Other students may have a stereotyped or somewhat romanticized view of Native Americans, derived from Hollywood. This essay will serve to help them appreciate the reality and humanity of one particular Native American culture, and by extension, any culture that differs from their own.

PROVIDING FOR DIFFERENT LEVELS OF ABILITY More advanced students will savor Momaday's prose and his skillful way of handling shifts of time and place. LEP students will probably have trouble with precisely those aspects of the selection. Encourage students to ask about passages or sentences they don't understand, and let other students do the explaining.

READING THE ESSAY This brief, evocative selection, which winds in and out of various times and places, is perfect for reading aloud, one paragraph per student. Or play the audiocassette recording of an excerpt from this selection.

RETEACHING ALTERNATIVES If some students still find it hard to understand Momaday's flowing, poetic narrative, you might break the selection up into short passages and have a small group of students write a simple paraphrase of each passage. Then have each group share its paraphrase with the whole class.

Responding to the Essay

Answers to the questions in the Pupil's Edition appear in the Annotated Teacher's Edition.

Writing About the Essay

For help in revising their compositions, refer students to **Grammar, Usage, and Mechanics: A Reference Guide** on text pages 1183–1228 at the back of their books.

A CREATIVE RESPONSE

1. Writing a Description   Brainstorm some more places students might describe—the first place the student remembers living, a special park, a favorite relative's house, a friend's backyard, the zoo—until it is evident that students have a starting place. Recall Momaday's images (questions 8–9) to help students focus on mental pictures, sounds, smells, or sights associated with their special place.

▶ CRITERIA FOR EVALUATING THE ASSIGNMENT   The essay uses both direct description and specific sensory images to evoke what a remembered place looked like and what it meant to the student.

A CRITICAL RESPONSE

2. Analyzing Atmosphere   List major elements of setting (the mountain itself, weather, isolation) and recall also question 9 on the dominant images of the essay. Encourage students to list as many additional words and images related to setting as they can find. Then have them generalize about the mood the words and images suggest before they write.

▶ CRITERIA FOR EVALUATING THE ASSIGNMENT   The essay cites many details from the essay to support a concluding sentence, which states that the overall atmosphere is dark, elegiac, or meditative, but not despairing.

3. Responding to a Statement   You may wish to elicit one or two responses from your more outgoing students to suggest a starting point, but make it clear that the assignment asks for each student's personal response; there is no "right" answer.

▶ CRITERIA FOR EVALUATING THE ASSIGNMENT   The response consists of a few sentences or a paragraph explaining the student's personal response to the quotation from Momaday's essay.

Analyzing Language and Style

POETIC PROSE
1. **a.** Metaphor—the meadows are a stairway to the plain.
   b. The meadows must descend in step-like levels.
2. **a.** The earth is compared to a folded-up sheet of paper.
   b. Pieces of land extend farther and farther like a large sheet of paper opening into new sections.
3. **a.** "The great billowing clouds . . . are shadows"
   b. "shadows that move . . . like water"
   c. The shadows create dark patches between lighted areas.
4. **a.** The sun is "at home" like a person.
   b. To emphasize the words "character of a god"
5. **a.** Metaphors—"caldron of the land," "wean their blood from the northern winter"
   b. Answers will vary, but any revision is flat and dull compared with the original.

Extending the Essay

The complete book, *The Way to Rainy Mountain*, is only eighty-nine pages long, including illustrations. Interested students may read it and tell about their responses to Momaday's journey. Other students may want to read and report on other notable works by and about Native Americans; several are mentioned in the second paragraph of Momaday's biography (text page 1014).

James Baldwin

Text page 1021

AUTOBIOGRAPHICAL NOTES

Text page 1022

Objectives

1. To respond to an autobiographical essay by an important African American writer

2. To identify the essay's tone

3. To analyze the essay's main ideas

4. To write an essay responding to the writer

Introducing the Essay

This brief essay displays the sense of narrative movement, the ability to dip in and out of various portions of the writer's memory and intellect and establish connections among them, that your students have already seen in essays by White, Thomas, Wright, and Momaday. Baldwin begins with the most straightforward kind of autobiographical statement—"I was born in Harlem thirty-one years ago.'' After a short, impressionistic description of his up-bringing, he goes on to examine his literary influences, his views on the situation of the African American writer, and the role of the writer and citizen in general. You might discuss with your students the possibility that the special gift of a good essayist is to proceed inductively from specific facts to broader truths.

BACKGROUND ON THE ESSAY ''Autobiographical Notes'' appeared as a preface to Baldwin's first collection of essays, *Notes of a Native Son*. At that time the young writer, though not yet the preeminent spokesman he would become, was known in literary circles through a series of book reviews he had written for magazines such as *Commentary* and *The Partisan Review*. Though Baldwin's childhood had been quite miserable, he had the benefit of supportive teachers in the New York City public schools he attended, including the poet Countee Cullen (see Unit Eight) at Frederick Douglass Junior High School. Baldwin went on to edit the school magazine, *The Magpie*, at De Witt Clinton High School in the Bronx. A few years later, in 1944, he met his mentor, Richard Wright, who encouraged him and helped him get a grant to work on his first novel.

SUMMARY Baldwin grew up in Harlem, the son of a preacher. As a child, he was sustained by his love of reading and writing. He expresses his ambivalence about the problems of being an African American writer, asserts that one writes only out of one's own experiences, and says that his love for America causes him to insist on the right to criticize it.

Teaching Strategies

PROVIDING FOR CULTURAL DIFFERENCES This essay was written before the civil rights struggle of the 1960's, and therefore some of its statements—such as that neither African Americans nor whites are willing to face the past—may seem somewhat anachronistic. Students' reactions to the essay may be conditioned by the intervening history: Baldwin was a powerful spokesman for integration, but during the 1970's, some African American writers, such as Eldridge Cleaver, assailed him for this. The further passage of time, and Baldwin's death in 1987, will no doubt have led to further reassessment and an appreciation of what is enduring in his views.

PROVIDING FOR DIFFERENT LEVELS OF ABILITY The elegance of Baldwin's style may make the selection a challenge for some students, but the more factual, autobiographical passages should pose fewer difficulties. Some of Baldwin's key concepts will probably require detailed discussion, such as the problems of being an African American writer (text page 1023, paragraphs 1 and 2), his alienation from Western civilization (text page 1023, paragraph 4), and his suspiciousness of theories (text page 1024, paragraph 2).

READING THE ESSAY This short piece has a good deal of intellectual meat in it, so you might want to assign it as homework and then have it read aloud before discussing it in class.

RETEACHING ALTERNATIVES You might want to use the board to list Baldwin's major assertions about racial issues, about being a writer, about his attitude toward Western civilization, and about life.

Responding to the Essay   Text page 1024

Answers to the questions in the Pupil's Edition appear in the Annotated Teacher's Edition.

Writing About the Essay

For help in revising their compositions, refer students to **Grammar, Usage, and Mechanics: A Reference Guide** on text pages 1183–1228 at the back of their books.

A CREATIVE RESPONSE
Writing a Response Have students work in small groups to state in their own words Baldwin's major points about the dilemma faced by an African American writer, before they begin to respond to his points.

▶ CRITERIA FOR EVALUATING THE ASSIGNMENT The essay correctly identifies several points made by Baldwin and offers a response to each point.

Extending the Essay

If time permits, you might want to have your students write their own ''Autobiograhical Notes,'' in which they briefly describe their upbringing and how they feel it has affected their personalities, their goals, and their views of life.

Maxine Hong Kingston

Text page 1025

THE GIRL WHO WOULDN'T TALK

Text page 1026

Objectives

1. To respond to a personal narrative about childhood cruelty

2. To write a paragraph analyzing a character

3. To analyze descriptive images

Introducing the Memoir

Here are the major elements of the memoir:

- **Protagonist:** the narrator, Maxine Hong Kingston as a schoolgirl

- **Antagonist:** "the quiet girl"

- **Conflicts:** childhood anger and cruelty vs. helpless innocence; assimilation vs. Chinese American ethnic identity

- **Themes:** the cruelty of children toward each other; the insecurities that underlie that cruelty

- **Point of view:** first-person

- **Significant techniques:** ambiguity, imagery

- **Setting:** Stockton, California, early 1950's

BACKGROUND ON THE MEMOIR   In addition to being a powerful voice of the Chinese American experience, Maxine Hong Kingston writes specifically and forcefully as a voice for women. She emphasizes the emotional fortitude of Chinese women who endured lives of subordinacy through the ages. Her second book, *China Men*, begins with a fable about a man who crossed an ocean and came upon a Land of Women. He was captured by women who proceeded to inflict upon him the same pains that were routinely inflicted on women in traditional Chinese society: foot binding, ear piercing, and humiliation. The fable makes clear that forms of treatment which were scarcely given a second thought were in fact forms of torture.

SUMMARY   As a schoolgirl, Maxine Hong Kingston had a classmate who never spoke a word except to read out loud. The girl was protected by an older sister, but one day Maxine caught the girl alone in the school lavatory and tried to force her to speak through physical and psychological means. The girl cried piteously but didn't

speak. Soon afterward, Kingston says, she herself developed a mysterious illness that kept her bedridden for eighteen months.

Teaching Strategies

PROVIDING FOR CULTURAL DIFFERENCES   This selection will have special meaning for Chinese American students, but the basic story line (taunting and shyness and cruelty among children) will be recognizable to students from all cultures. Encourage students from other minority cultures to talk about their own experiences of childhood rejection from mainstream culture.

Non-Asian students and teachers should be cautious about making generalizations about Chinese Americans or any other Asian culture. Japanese Americans, Korean Americans, and Vietnamese Americans are separate cultures, and individuals within each group have different personalities and experiences.

PROVIDING FOR DIFFERENT LEVELS OF ABILITY
This is a very readable narrative written in relatively simple, though evocative, prose. The subject matter will be relatively easy for all students to handle. More advanced readers might want to delve into the question of whether every incident in the narrative is literally true, or whether some incidents might be a kind of poetic invention. You might want to discuss the strengths and weaknesses of this approach to memoir. LEP students may find the selection too long and will benefit from reading it aloud in class.

READING THE MEMOIR   You might want to assign the selection as homework and have some representative passages read out loud: perhaps the first two paragraphs (text page 1026), the two paragraphs beginning from, "I joined in at lunchtime," (text page 1027); the passage beginning, "I ran back into the girls' yard," and ending with, " 'Talk!' I shouted into the side of her head," (text page 1029); the passage beginning, "I looked right at her," and ending, " 'Say, "Stop it." ' " (text page 1030); the long paragraph beginning, " 'Why won't you talk?' " (text page 1031); and the passage from "Suddenly I heard footsteps" (text page 1031) to the end of the piece.

RETEACHING ALTERNATIVES   The core of the story line is the very dramatic confrontation between two schoolgirls, so you might want to have two female students act out the parts in front of the class for reaching purposes. (They should feel free to invent additional dialogue.) You might even have two male students act it out afterward, too, to show that with some very minor adjustments the same incident could have taken place between boys.

Responding to the Memoir   Text page 1032

Answers to the questions in the Pupil's Edition appear in the Annotated Teacher's Edition.

Writing About the Memoir

For help in revising their compositions, refer students to **Grammar, Usage, and Mechanics: A Reference Guide** on text pages 1183–1228 at the back of their books.

A CRITICAL RESPONSE
Analyzing a Character   Write across the chalkboard the headings ''Appearance,'' ''Speech,'' ''Actions,'' ''Private thoughts and feelings,'' and ''Responses of others.'' Elicit from the class—in any order—details from the essay that fit any category. Stop when responses slow down, and suggest that students skim the essay for additional details, and decide whether Kingston omits any of the categories.

▶ CRITERIA FOR EVALUATING THE ASSIGNMENT   The essay uses details from the essay to discuss the character of the narrator as actually portrayed by Kingston (not as the student thinks it should have been done). The essay ends with the student's response to the narrator.

Analyzing Language and Style

IMAGERY AND FEELINGS
1. Responses will vary. In general *ghosts* suggests beings which are not only pale in color, but perhaps also powerful, mysterious, or scary.
2. The images appear on text page 1029. Feelings revealed about the girl may be interpreted differently—perhaps the narrator's feeling of superiority and strength in comparison with the other girl's weakness. Students' responses will vary. Many may feel indignant or angry at the actions of the narrator.

Extending the Memoir

Ask students to talk about real or imagined incidents of cruelty between students that they think would make a good story. Some students may want to collaborate to write a story based on one of the ideas suggested.

Susan Allen Toth   Text page 1033

OUT EAST   Text page 1034

Objectives

1. To respond to a memoir about college life

2. To analyze character

3. To analyze stereotypes

4. To write a passage imitating the writer's technique

5. To rewrite an incident using a different point of view

6. To write an essay developing a statement

7. To write an essay evaluating the writer's objectivity

Introducing the Memoir

Here are the major elements of the memoir:

- **Protagonist:** the narrator, Sue Allen
- **Conflicts:** small-town Midwest vs. Ivy League; naiveté vs. sophistication; desire to belong vs. insecurity
- **Theme:** a wide-eyed college freshman's gradual adjustment to her new environment
- **Point of view:** first-person
- **Significant technique:** well-chosen detail
- **Setting:** Smith College, Northhampton, Massachusetts, the late 1950's

BACKGROUND ON THE MEMOIR   It's important that students understand the prestige and mystique attached to a Seven Sisters school such as Smith College. Admission to such a school represented a considerable achievement for a small-town girl. Sue Allen, in short, experiences a transition not only from one region of the country to another, and from high school to college, but also from one social grouping to another.

SUMMARY   Sue Allen looks back on her first week at Smith and the ordeal of taking "Posture Pictures." She talks about how she got her ideas of life "out east" and of "the Eastern look." By the time she is a senior, she feels she has the look just right.

Teaching Strategies

PROVIDING FOR CULTURAL DIFFERENCES   The essential underlying experience of this selection is the rite of passage between the high school years and the beginning of adulthood. All students will share this in varying degrees despite external differences that may exist in the classroom.

PROVIDING FOR DIFFERENT LEVELS OF ABILITY
The essay is about a very advanced student, so less advanced students may not recognize many of the references to the styles and behavior of the university elite. More advanced students, in contrast, may be positively eager to read about the kind of college experiences that—except for the differences between generations—may lie ahead of them. A discussion of styles of clothing, fads, and all-girls schools might be a good way to get non-college-bound students involved in the selection.

READING THE MEMOIR   You might assign the selection as homework and have a female student read a passage from it aloud as an introduction to discussion—not the passage about "Posture Pictures" at the beginning of the piece, but one of the passages about the "Eastern look" and clothes shopping, which can be found from the middle of page 1036 to the end of the selection.

RETEACHING ALTERNATIVES   If some students have trouble understanding the nature of Sue's anxieties, you might turn the discussion toward their own feelings about the prospect of leaving home and/or going to college. Help students see that the specific details of Sue's experience—Posture Pictures, choices of wardrobe—are not presented for themselves alone, but for what they reveal about the state of mind of a teenage girl eagerly but nervously facing imminent adulthood.

Responding to the Memoir   Text page 1038

Answers to the questions in the Pupil's Edition appear in the Annotated Teacher's Edition.

Writing About the Memoir

For help in revising their compositions, refer students to **Grammar, Usage, and Mechanics: A Reference Guide** on text pages 1183–1228 at the back of their books.

A CREATIVE RESPONSE
1. Imitating Toth's Technique   If students find it too painful or embarrassing to deal with a recent experience, suggest that they go back to early childhood—a time when they wanted to be included in an older sibling's games with friends, to be in the first-grade play, and so on.

▶ CRITERIA FOR EVALUATING THE ASSIGNMENT   The description clearly presents the "something" the student wanted to belong to, explains why he or she could not, and evokes the desperation of the student's feelings.

2. Changing the Point of View   Have students suggest some incidents that could be explored from another point of view, such as the one where the narrator receives her award. Remind students to think about the tone they wish to convey before they begin to write.

▶ CRITERIA FOR EVALUATING THE ASSIGNMENT   The narration consistently remains in the new point of view, and conveys a tone suitable for that speaker.

A CRITICAL RESPONSE
3. Developing a Statement   As background for this assignment, you might remind students that whole books exist on how to "dress for success." Question 7—how groups identify those who are "in" and "out"—will also prepare students to think of clothing as a langauge.

▶ CRITERIA FOR EVALUATING THE ASSIGNMENT   The essay is at least one paragraph long. It explains that clothes are a "language" in that they are often used to make statements about the wearer's personality, attitudes, and so on. Most students will conclude that people in general agree with this idea.

4. Evaluating Objectivity   The assignment in general focuses not on Toth's feelings, but on the facts she uses in her essay. Reading Primary Sources: "The Importance of Being Remembered" should help students make this distinction. The last question of the writing prompt does veer into feelings in that no matter how objectively facts are reported, one's personal feelings still dictate which facts to report.

▶ CRITERIA FOR EVALUATING THE ASSIGNMENT   The essay cites several facts Toth uses in her essay, such as the "Posture Pictures" of Orientation Week, and comments on the writer's apparent bias or lack of bias. The essay offers an opinion as to whether another person might report the same events differently, and explains this opinion by use of examples.

Extending the Memoir

You might ask your students to discuss what they anticipate their post-high-school experiences will be like. How similar to Sue Allen's will they be? How different?

Primary Sources   Text page 1039

"THE IMPORTANCE OF BEING REMEMBERED"
Toth relates some of the highs and lows of having to deal with public responses to her memoirs. She handles both the approving and the unbelieving readers with grace and honesty. Students may chuckle at the innocence of the young woman with the small-town sensibilities, but the article might help them realize that one day they will look back at their lives now and see their teenage years from a different perspective. What do they think they will remember most fondly? What incidents will they recall as having significant effects on their lives?

Alice Walker   Text page 1040

CHOICE: A TRIBUTE TO DR. MARTIN LUTHER KING, JR.   Text page 1041

Objectives

1. To respond to a speech about Dr. Martin Luther King, Jr.

2. To identify paradox

3. To analyze appeals to emotion

4. To give an oral presentation

Introducing the Essay

This tribute in memory of Dr. Martin Luther King, Jr., does not set out to list all his accomplishments or even the highlights of his career. It begins, in fact, with a bit of Alice Walker's own family history, to which she returns briefly at the end of the essay. In this way Walker establishes a connection with her audience and proceeds to link them all together with Dr. King.

Here are the major elements of the essay:

- **Characters:** the speaker (Alice Walker); members of her family; the Rev. Dr. Martin Luther King, Jr.

- **Conflicts:** love of home vs. the need to leave it; African Americans in a struggle for justice

- **Theme:** Dr. Martin Luther King, Jr., and the civil rights movement restore the South to young African Americans.

- **Point of view:** first-person

- **Significant techniques:** family details, repetition, parallel structure

SUMMARY   Walker relates the story of how her great-great-great-grandmother, who walked all the way from Virginia to her family's ancestral home in Georgia, was buried in a family plot. Yet even such sacred land could not belong to African Americans, who were not allowed to possess the land, even after Reconstruction. She tells how young African Americans were expected to forsake the South, which left them only with memories. The first time Walker saw Dr. Martin Luther King, Jr., on television, he was being arrested during a protest. Inspired by his courage, she knew she would have to become a resister too. Walker cites the aspects of King's life which are familiar to her audience: his public acts, his books, his preaching, his prizes and awards. She concludes her tribute by declaring that the most important thing King did was to give his people back their heritage, their homeland.

Teaching Strategies

PROVIDING FOR CULTURAL DIFFERENCES Students should be aware that after the Civil War, few African Americans owned land, and those who did were subject to terrorism by groups such as the Ku Klux Klan. Many farmers in the South were sharecroppers; they rented a plot of land to farm and gave the landowner a share of the crop at harvest time. Without the economic power that land ownership brings, African Americans could not hold on to political power once Reconstruction ended (1877). White political domination gave rise to the system of legal segregation that lasted until the time of Dr. Martin Luther King, Jr., and the civil rights movement.

PROVIDING FOR DIFFERENT LEVELS OF ABILITY There are several important keys to understanding Walker's essay. One is the concept of land, both the legal ownership of a piece of land and the general ownership of the South, as a homeland. Another is the idea that African Americans were forced to leave the South or to end up hating it; and those who went into exile were left only with memories of their homeland. Some students may benefit from a thorough discussion of paragraphs four through six of the essay.

READING THE ESSAY Before students read, briefly discuss how a tribute such as this is often an appeal to the emotions of the audience. Ask them for their ideas about who the audience was for this address. Students might then try to imagine themselves as part of Alice Walker's audience. Ask them to consider, as they read, how Walker links herself and her audience emotionally to the late Dr. King.

RETEACHING ALTERNATIVES Have students briefly outline the address, to see that it has a beginning (Walker's own family), a middle (Walker's and her family's relationship to Dr. King), and an end (the public acts of Dr. King). Help them see how Walker, an accomplished writer, organized her speech for the best effect.

Responding to the Essay   Text page 1043

Answers to the questions in the Pupil's Edition appear in the Annotated Teacher's Edition.

An Oral Presentation

Students are asked to give Alice Walker's speech as an oral presentation to the class. Be sure students know that they are to give their speeches as if the class were Walker's original audience. Assure students that they are free to interpret the speech in different ways. Their choice of emphasis, tone, and gestures should suit their understanding of content. Each student should have a chance to present the speech to a small group. Then have two or three of the best interpreters present the speech—or part of it— to the whole class.

▶ **CRITERIA FOR EVALUATING THE ASSIGNMENT** Students speak clearly and to the entire audience. Their tone, gestures, and phrasing are appropriate to the content of the speech.

Extending the Essay

Have groups of students research various aspects of Dr. Martin Luther King, Jr.'s, contributions to America. You might divide the class into several committees of experts. One committee might listen to and report on one or more of his speeches and present parts of some speeches to the class. Others can read and report on one of his books, such as *Why We Can't Wait*. Other committees can view and report on a video (if available) of one of his sermons or speeches; report on his prizes and awards; or research his work on behalf of poor Americans.

Sandra Cisneros

Text page 1044

STRAW INTO GOLD: THE METAMORPHOSIS OF THE EVERYDAY

Text page 1045

Objectives

1. To respond to a Mexican American writer's autobiographical essay
2. To identify images and figures of speech
3. To evaluate the use of metaphor
4. To write a paragraph identifying purpose and main idea

Introducing the Essay

Here are the major elements of the essay:

- **Protagonist:** the narrator, Sandra Cisneros
- **Theme:** transformation, through imagination, of everyday experiences into art
- **Point of view:** first-person
- **Significant techniques:** images and figures of speech; memories of feelings and important experiences

BACKGROUND ON THE ESSAY As indicated in the autobiographical introduction (text page 1044), Sandra Cisneros is the youngest writer represented in this book. By her early thirties, she had had the many experiences described in this essay and was already a recognized writer.

SUMMARY In a speech at Texas Lutheran College, Sandra Cisneros describes family experiences and other influences that shaped her as a writer. To make the point that everyday experiences, through imagination, can be shaped into fiction, poetry, and other forms of art, she uses the metaphor of the Rumplestiltskin fairy tale, in which the young maiden spins straw into gold.

Teaching Strategies

PROVIDING FOR CULTURAL DIFFERENCES Students who live in large cities with Mexican American populations or who themselves are Mexican American may already understand some of Cisneros's references to customs of that culture, such as expectations for the daughter in a family of males. An important point to be made with this essay is the cultural stereotypes that are revealed: Cisneros's hosts expected her to be able to cook Mexican food because she was Mexican.

PROVIDING FOR DIFFERENT LEVELS OF ABILITY Students who don't know Spanish will need some help with the Spanish phrases used in the essay. Point out that most of the phrases are defined within the context of the essay. *Provinciales*, for example, is identified in the next phrase as "country"; the meaning of *chilango* becomes clear when Cisneros writes that her father is from a large city.

READING THE ESSAY Since this essay was originally a speech, you might prefer to have it read aloud, perhaps with a little dramatic flair.

RETEACHING ALTERNATIVES You might want to divide discussion of the essay into a very brief summary of its four main parts: (1) childhood experiences and influences on Cisneros as a writer, (2) making tortillas in the south of France and the relationship of that experience to writing the essay for her MFA degree, (3) Cisneros's experiences as an adult writer, (4) Cisneros's "metamorphosis" theory.

Responding to the Essay Text page 1047

Answers to the questions in the Pupil's Edition appear in the Annotated Teacher's Edition.

Writing About the Essay

For help in revising their compositions, refer students to **Grammar, Usage, and Mechanics: A Reference Guide** on text pages 1183–1228 at the back of their books.

A CRITICAL REPONSE
Identifying the Main Idea Before students begin work on this assignment, you might review with them the meanings of the terms *purpose* and *main idea*. To help students imagine how the speech might have affected them as members of Cisneros's audience, you might want to have the essay read aloud by a talented student, perhaps one who contemplates being a writer.

▶ CRITERIA FOR EVALUATING THE ASSIGNMENT The paragraph states convincingly that the writer's purpose is to inform and/or to persuade her audience of the possibilities of transforming everyday experiences into art. The writer's main idea is the transformation, through imagination, of everyday occurrences into fiction, poetry, or another form of art.

John Hersey

A NOISELESS FLASH

Objectives

1. To respond to the retelling of an historical event in terms of individuals' experiences

2. To examine imagery and characterization

3. To analyze how the writer communicates his attitude

4. To write an essay analyzing the use of suspense

5. To write an essay classifying the history

6. To evaluate the writer's objectivity or subjectivity

7. To define Japanese terms through context clues

Introducing the History

Here are the major elements of the selection:

- **Characters:** Miss Toshiko Sasaki, a clerk; Dr. Masakazu Fujii, owner of a private hospital; Mrs. Hatsuyo Nakamura, a tailor's widow; Father Wilhelm Kleinsorge, a German Jesuit missionary; Dr. Terufumi Sasaki, a Red Cross doctor; the Rev. Mr. Kiyoshi Tanimoto, a Methodist minister

- **Themes:** the horror of atomic warfare; the arbitrariness of catastrophe

- **Point of view:** third-person omniscient

- **Significant techniques:** reportorial journalism; simple imagery; factual detail

- **Setting:** Hiroshima, Japan, on August 6, 1945

BACKGROUND ON THE HISTORY Before your students read "A Noiseless Flash," make sure they're familiar with the basic facts of the dropping of the atomic bomb on Hiroshima in the final month of World War II. You might ask them whether they've discussed that event in their history classes, or have read about it elsewhere. Students who are familiar with the history of the event can transmit their knowledge to their classmates during the course of discussion. If your students' knowledge on the subject seems thin, you might ask a volunteer to prepare a brief oral report and present it to the class. (The Hiroshima bomb killed more than 100,000 people, leveled four square miles, and destroyed the entire second Japanese army. A second atomic bomb dropped on Nagasaki three days later killed 36,000 people.)

SUMMARY Hersey presents the experiences of six survivors of the Hiroshima bombing, immediately before and after the blast.

Teaching Strategies

PROVIDING FOR CULTURAL DIFFERENCES The selection has particular meaning for Japanese American students. Encourage them to talk about their own family's experiences during World War II. Students from all backgrounds will find this selection moving and thought-provoking. You might want to discuss how Hersey's presentation of Japanese culture makes your students feel about the characters in the essay, in conjunction with question 7 (text page 1057).

286 UNIT TWELVE: Modern Nonfiction

PROVIDING FOR DIFFERENT LEVELS OF ABILITY
More advanced readers will probably be intrigued by the way Hersey achieves his intended tone (attitude toward his subject) despite a completely factual surface. (This is developed further in question 3 under Writing About the History, text page 1057). LEP readers may find it hard to keep up with the wealth of detail, particularly the Japanese names and customs. You might make a list of the characters' names on the board, and elicit from students a thumbnail description of each character. In addition, Hersey gives the distance and direction of each character from the blast center, and you might want to draw a simple diagram on the board that shows each character's approximate location.

READING THE HISTORY   The selection is too long to be read aloud in its entirety, so after having the students read it at home, you might want to have them read aloud one passage for each of the six characters: Mr. Tanimoto, the three paragraphs beginning, "Then a tremendous flash of light," bottom of page 1051; Mrs. Nakamura, the five paragraphs beginning, "As soon as the planes had passed," on page 1053; Dr. Fujii, the three paragraphs beginning, "Dr. Fujii had been relatively idle," on page 1054; Father Kleinsorge, the two paragraphs beginning, "After an alarm," on page 1055; Dr. Sasaki, the passage beginning, "He arrived at the hospital" and ending, "for a long, long time," on page 1056; Miss Sasaki, from "Miss Sasaki went back to her office," on page 1056 to the end of the selection.

RETEACHING ALTERNATIVES   Some students may find the narrative too "busy," in the sense that they have to keep track of the experiences of six characters in different parts of the city at the same moment. You might ask them to divide a sheet of paper into six horizontal columns, and briefly summarize the occupation, actions, and experiences of each of the six characters.

Responding to the History   Text page 1057

Answers to the questions in the Pupil's Edition appear in the Annotated Teacher's Edition.

Writing About the History

For help in revising their compositions, refer students to **Grammar, Usage, and Mechanics: A Reference Guide** on text pages 1183–1228 at the back of their books.

A CRITICAL RESPONSE
1. Analyzing Suspense   In discussion, most students will suggest that suspense is created because the reader knows something is coming that the people described do *not* know about (see also the definition of *dramatic irony*

in the **Handbook of Literary Terms,** text page 1175). This knowledge makes the reader wonder what is going to happen to each of these people.

▶ CRITERIA FOR EVALUATING THE ASSIGNMENT   The essay lists some questions Hersey plants in the reader's mind and cites the specific places where those questions are answered.

2. Classifying a Literary Work   Elicit from the students the criteria they associate with the word *literature* (perhaps "enduring value," "permanent interest," "universal themes," and so on). Guide them to a definition broad enough to include more than what we traditionally call "classics." They might also wish to consult a dictionary.

▶ CRITERIA FOR EVALUATING THE ASSIGNMENT   The essay offers a reasonable definition of the word *literature* and makes a good case for or against Hersey's *Hiroshima* fulfilling the criteria associated with the definition.

3. Evaluating the Report   Discuss carefully the distinction between objectivity and subjectivity made in the writing assignment. Most students will see that Hersey's report is objective, if only because even an extensive search fails to turn up passages stating his feelings.

▶ CRITERIA FOR EVALUATING THE ASSIGNMENT   The essay identifies Hersey's overall approach as objective and cites several passages to support that opinion.

Analyzing Language and Style

JAPANESE TERMS
1. *tonarigumi,* Neighborhood Association
2. *tansu,* a large Japanese cabinet
3. *Chugoku,* clearly the name of a newspaper from the context, "sat down to read that morning's Hiroshima *Chugoku*"
4. *Sankoku,* brand name for a sewing machine
5. *Suntory,* a Japanese brand of whiskey
6. *Murata-san,* Mr. or Mrs. Murata by analogy with *B-san* or Mr. B for the B-29 bomber
7. *Shu Jesusu, awaremi tamia,* Our Lord Jesus, have pity on us.
8. *gambare,* Be brave.

Extending the History

1. Interested students may want to read the entire book, *Hiroshima,* and report on it to the class.
2. As a creative exercise, you might have each student write a brief first-person account in the voice of any of the six characters, showing what the character was doing, thinking, feeling, and experiencing just before the blast and just afterward.

Objectives

1. To respond to dispatches from a Vietnam war correspondent
2. To respond to visual images
3. To write an essay assessing the impact of the dispatches
4. To compare and contrast two war reports
5. To write a paper analyzing the author's personality
6. To write an essay on the role of women in war

Introducing the Reports

These are the major subsections of the selection:

- **The Highlands:** A description of the highlands of Vietnam and the Montagnard villagers
- **"Tell My Folks . . .":** An anecdote about a Native American Green Beret who, having a presentiment of death, asks Herr to give a message to his folks, then survives
- **The Wounded:** A description of seriously wounded Vietnamese civilians and an Army surgeon who works in harrowing conditions
- **The Correspondents:** A description of an old war correspondent at work
- **Back Home:** A description of Herr's troubling dreams and memories after he returns to the States
- **Remembering the Dead:** A description of the unnerving experience of mistaking a living soldier for another who has died
- **The War Ends:** Herr's reactions to seeing scenes of evacuation and photographs of the war

BACKGROUND ON THE REPORTS You will want to avoid getting bogged down in a debate on the rightness or wrongness of the Vietnam War, but make sure students know something of the basic historical facts before they read this selection. You might ask your students what they already know about the war from other sources. Since this knowledge is likely to be fragmentary, you might recommend that they read about the Vietnam War in their history textbooks. Or assign a student volunteer to present an oral report on the subject.

SUMMARY Herr, a correspondent in Vietnam during the height of the war, presents a series of brief, sometimes enigmatic vignettes that depict the surreal, confusing quality of that war and of the country.

Teaching Strategies

PROVIDING FOR CULTURAL DIFFERENCES If there are Vietnamese students in your class, ask them to talk about what the long struggle in Vietnam meant to their families. You may need to explain these references: "triple canopies" (different heights of vegetation in the rain forests); "Cambodia (the Sanctuary!)" (the country directly west of Vietnam, where NVA troops sometimes retreated); and Viet Cong (Communist guerilla fighters in South Vietnam).

PROVIDING FOR DIFFERENT LEVELS OF ABILITY The collagelike nature of the piece and the interweaving of reality and weird unreality may be likely to intrigue advanced students and confuse less advanced ones. For instance, the image of the "chopper" flying out of Herr's chest (text page 1063) may need some explication; and the description of the Battle for Hill 875 (text pages 1060–1061) is presented in the tones of a tall tale even though the facts are apparently accurate. You might want to point out that this shifting sense of unreality was an important part of the psychological experience of fighting in Vietnam, and that Herr is deliberately trying to convey this.

READING THE REPORTS For purposes of reading aloud, you might divide the first section, "The Highlands," into two parts: the long opening paragraph, and the rest of the section. Each section after that is a good length to be read aloud by one student.

RETEACHING ALTERNATIVES You might divide your class into seven small groups, one for each section of the reports, and have each group prepare a short synopsis, including the facts of the report and an interpretation of the effect they feel Michael Herr is trying to achieve. Be sure they support their interpretations with examples from the text.

Responding to the Reports   Text page 1063

Answers to the questions in the Pupil's Edition appear in the Annotated Teacher's Edition.

Writing About the Reports

For help in revising their compositions, refer students to **Grammar, Usage, and Mechanics: A Reference Guide** on text pages 1183–1228 at the back of their books.

A CREATIVE RESPONSE
1. *Assessing the Impact of an Essay*   Response to this assignment will vary according to the student's view of war before reading the essay. Have students meet in small groups to discuss their personal responses before they begin writing.

▶ CRITERIA FOR EVALUATING THE ASSIGNMENT   The student explains what his or her feelings and attitudes were before reading the report, and tells how Herr either supported or challenged those feelings and attitudes.

A CRITICAL RESPONSE
2. *Comparing and Contrasting Two Writers*   Note that the assignment calls for students to seek both similarities and differences between the reports by Hersey and Herr. You may wish to suggest that they make a prewriting chart, using the four-point list as column one; notes on Hersey in relation to each point, column two; and notes on Herr, column three. They can fill in the chart through whole-class discussion or small groups.

▶ CRITERIA FOR EVALUATING THE ASSIGNMENT   The essay follows a coherent pattern of comparison/contrast, such as dealing first with similarities and then with differences, or going through the topics one by one and stating whether Hersey and Herr are alike or different on each item. Details from both Hersey and Herr support each of the student's conclusions.

3. *Analyzing a Writer's Personality*   First ask students for their impressions of Herr, and then send them back to the text to find passages documenting those impressions.

▶ CRITERIA FOR EVALUATING THE ASSIGNMENT   The paper is at least one paragraph long. It cites evidence from the report to support what the student thinks he or she knows about Herr.

4. *Analyzing Women's Roles*   Note that the essay asks for students' views on the role of women in war. They need not feel constrained to stick to Hersey's and Herr's reports. Encourage them to be as specific as possible and to support their views with reasons and facts.

▶ CRITERIA FOR EVALUATING THE ASSIGNMENT   Student's opinion is clearly expressed and supported with reasons and facts.

Extending the Reports

1. Interested students may want to read the rest of the book *Dispatches*, or other books on Vietnam, several of which are listed in the introduction to this selection (text page 1058). The class may want to compare and contrast the approaches of several different writers on the subject.
2. If you or your students have relatives, friends, or neighbors who fought in Vietnam, you might ask them to speak to the class about their experiences—bearing in mind that if they are reluctant to do so, their feelings should be respected.

Jamaica Kincaid   Text page 1064

FROM A SMALL PLACE   Text page 1065

Objectives

1. To respond to an ironic travel essay

2. To identify and interpret satire and irony

3. To express the theme of an essay

4. To write a paragraph with a particular tone

Introducing the Essay

This essay is biting, harsh, and angry, and it hits home. Students will be familiar with the beautiful, glamorous islands shown in TV ads and movies. In reality, these ads deceive by not showing the reality the islanders experience. Many of the islands have a bright, clean area reserved for tourists that is sometimes literally walled off, like a compound. Few tourists care to go inland to see where the real islanders live. After all, they are concerned with escaping such realities; they are "on holiday." Some students may be put off or offended by this satire; if so, Kincaid has done her job.

Here are the major elements of the essay:

- **Protagonist:** you (a tourist on vacation in Antigua)
- **Conflicts:** the privileged outsiders vs. the poor natives; illusion vs. reality
- **Theme:** The Antiguan government neglects the needs of its native people and prostitutes itself to attract tourists, who care only about their own pleasure.
- **Point of view:** first-person
- **Significant techniques:** satire, irony, second-person narrative
- **Setting:** Antigua, one of the Leeward Islands in the West Indies

SUMMARY Purporting to give a private tour of her home island of Antigua, Kincaid begins at the airport, which is named after the Prime Minister. She addresses her satire to *you* (the reader-tourist) and comments, in order, on the things that an arriving tourist experiences: the island's dry climate, customs, the taxi driver who tries to charge an exorbitant fare, the very bad roads, the expensive Japanese car with the "wrong (leaded) gasoline." We learn that the housing, schools, and hospital are no better than the roads. The library, damaged in The Earthquake of 1974, has still not been repaired. Kincaid offers some revisionist economic history and insists (unreassuringly) that we not feel uneasy about the exploitation, oppression, and domination of her people by Western imperialists. The tour continues with an exposé revealing who lives in Antigua's most luxurious mansions. Finally we reach our hotel; but Kincaid's insistent voice follows us into our room in order to force us to see and feel and think about all the contradictions on the small island she once called home.

Teaching Strategies

PROVIDING FOR CULTURAL DIFFERENCES Students who have never traveled to the West Indies should be assured of the authenticity of the beautiful setting and of the tourist attitudes that Kincaid describes. Encourage any students who have been to one of the islands or who have lived there to share their experiences with the class. American students may be unfamiliar with the oft-repeated British phrase "on holiday," which translates as "on vacation."

PROVIDING FOR DIFFERENT LEVELS OF ABILITY Some students may have trouble with the ironic tone of this essay. Help them develop a strategy for understanding it. Two related questions students must be prepared to ask themselves as they read this essay are, (1) Does she really mean that? and (2) What does she really mean? Students should review *verbal irony* (text page 1175) and *satire* (text page 1180) in the **Handbook of Literary Terms**.

READING THE ESSAY Assign the essay as homework. You might wish to tell students before they read that they are about to encounter an angry author. Students should consider, as they read, whether she has a right to be angry and what they think can or should be done about the conditions she describes.

RETEACHING ALTERNATIVES Have students write a paragraph summarizing the essay. They might begin writing by completing the following sentence: "Antigua is a small place, but . . ." They should include in their paragraph all the problems Kincaid reveals.

Responding to the Essay Text page 1069

Answers to the questions in the Pupil's Edition appear in the Annotated Teacher's Edition.

Writing About the Essay

For help in revising their compositions, refer students to **Grammar, Usage, and Mechanics: A Reference Guide** on text pages 1183–1228 at the back of their books.

A CREATIVE RESPONSE
Taking Your Readers on a Tour Discuss with students the different tones suggested in the writing assignment and any others you may think of. Encourage students to make up a sentence or two exemplifying each tone to help everyone get the idea.

▶ CRITERIA FOR EVALUATING THE ASSIGNMENT The paragraph gives the reader (addressed as *you*) a tour of a place the student knows well. The writing adopts a tone that is maintained throughout the paragraph.

Extending the Essay

The West Indies include many islands generally divided into three main groups: the Bahamas, the Greater Antilles (including Cuba, Puerto Rico, Jamaica), and the Lesser Antilles (Leeward Islands, Windward Islands, Barbados). Antigua is one of the Leeward Islands.

Take this opportunity to acquaint students with the culture of the West Indies—its art, music, dance, poetry, food. If you have students whose families have an island heritage, ask them to share some of the favorite parts of their ethnic heritage.

Students will enjoy reading Jamaica Kincaid's novel *Annie John* (Farrar, Straus & Giroux, 1985) about a girl growing up in Antigua, her conflicts with her parents, and her leaving home to study in England.

Objectives

1. To respond to a travel journal
2. To analyze characterization through dialogue
3. To write an essay about colorful place names
4. To write a description of the writer's character
5. To write an essay comparing and contrasting two journeys
6. To analyze metaphors

Introducing the Journal

Here are the major elements of the journal:

- **Characters:** William Least Heat Moon; a waitress; Madison Wheeler; Thurmond, Virginia, and Hilda Watts
- **Themes:** the enduring value of rural life; the search for the true America
- **Point of view:** first-person
- **Significant techniques:** regional dialect; metaphor; concrete detail; characterization through dialogue
- **Setting:** Nameless, Tennessee, and environs, 1977

BACKGROUND ON THE JOURNAL   William Least Heat Moon's other name is William Trogdon. One of his ancestors, an Englishman, emigrated to North Carolina and was killed by Tories for giving food to rebel Colonists during the American Revolution. The first leg of Least Heat Moon's journey, from Missouri to North Carolina, retraced in reverse the journey his forebears had made. He was thirty-eight at the time. His book about his journey was not published until five years later; it topped the best-seller lists for a considerable period.

SUMMARY   Least Heat Moon, reading an atlas, sees the name Nameless, Tennessee, and decides it will be the next stop in his odyssey. During his search he eats at a "three-calendar" cafe and asks directions of a man loading tools into a pickup truck. When he finally finds Nameless, he talks with the Watts family, owners of a very old-fashioned general store, who make him welcome with good food and conversation.

Teaching Strategies

PROVIDING FOR CULTURAL DIFFERENCES   Students new to America may be baffled by the writer's ranking of cafes by the number of wall calendars. Explain that these free calendars are given by businesses for advertising and good will. Usually they have a different color photograph or painting for each month.

PROVIDING FOR DIFFERENT LEVELS OF ABILITY   More advanced readers will enjoy Least Heat Moon's ability to record the various shadings of regional speech and individual speech patterns. LEP students may find the twists and turns of his journey a bit complicated and may wonder why so much time is spent asking directions. Some students may find the dialect an obstacle. Encourage them to read the dialogue aloud, pronouncing words as they're spelled. Explain that the writer has captured the way speakers in Tennessee pronounce and use words. *Holler* is a dialect variation of *hollow,* a valley in the mountains.

READING THE JOURNAL   The selection can be broken into sections fairly readily for the purpose of oral reading: from the beginning to "there were also mothers and children" (text page 1072); then to "You carry a dog?" (text page 1073); then to "the ones to ask you to dinner" (text page 1074); then to "how long he'd been in the store" (text page 1075); then to "It is for this I have come" (text page 1075); then to the end of the selection. Most of the dialogue is in a regional accent, and if your students don't share that accent or aren't unusually gifted actors, it might be best for them to read the lines in their natural voices.

RETEACHING ALTERNATIVES   You might have the students each divide a sheet of paper into three columns and list the places the author stops in the left-hand column. Next to that, they can list the people he meets at each stop, and in the right-hand column—the most important one—they can briefly state what he learns from each person. If you prefer, you can do this at the board, eliciting answers in discussion.

Responding to the Journal   Text page 1077

Answers to the questions in the Pupil's Edition appear in the Annotated Teacher's Edition.

Writing About the Journal

For help in revising their compositions, refer students to **Grammar, Usage, and Mechanics: A Reference Guide** on text pages 1183–1228 at the back of their books.

A CREATIVE RESPONSE

1. Writing an Essay Bring to class an atlas containing detailed maps of English-speaking countries, or ask students to bring travel maps from home. Discuss some usual sources of place names—words from languages of the early inhabitants of an area; names of explorers; and names derived from geographical features, historical events, or immigrants' origins. Give students time to browse through the maps and share discoveries before they select a specific area to write about.

▶ CRITERIA FOR EVALUATING THE ASSIGNMENT The essay identifies the state, county, or area under discussion, lists several names that appeal to the student, and offers reasonable explanations for the origins of those names.

A CRITICAL RESPONSE

2. Describing the Writer's Character Briefly discuss which scenes stand out in the students' minds, and what those scenes reveal about Least Heat Moon.

▶ CRITERIA FOR EVALUATING THE ASSIGNMENT The essay cites evidence from the journal to support a description of several aspects of Least Heat Moon's character.

3. Comparing and Contrasting Literary Journals Students might again construct a prewriting chart to make notes on similarities and differences. Have them list in the first column "purpose," "effect," and "other" (for elements that interest the student), and add columns for Momaday and for Least Heat Moon.

▶ CRITERIA FOR EVALUATING THE ASSIGNMENT The essay follows a coherent pattern of comparison/contrast, such as dealing first with similarities and then with differences, or going through the topics one by one and stating whether Momaday and Least Heat Moon are alike or different on each item. Details from both essays support conclusions drawn.

Analyzing Language and Style

METAPHORS

1. He's been wandering since the mid 1960's.
2. **a.** Ready to enter "yonder," the next life
   b. A creature is comfortable in its own environment.
   c. Supplies for the future

Extending the Journal

1. Interested students may want to read at least parts of the rest of *Blue Highways*. Since the book is episodic, you might have several students read a chapter apiece and report to the class. Students may also enjoy sampling parts of William Least Heat Moon's second "travel" book *PrairyErth* (Houghton Mifflin, 1991).
2. As a creative exercise, you might ask students to imagine that William Least Heat Moon is stopping in their community during his journey. Have them write down or act out his encounters with local residents.

THE AMERICAN LANGUAGE
Text page 1078

Students will enjoy this essay about how high technology (meaning "applied science") has influenced their language. The development of the steam locomotive and the application of steam technology led to an explosion of new terminology. Most of these terms were originally well-defined and highly scientific in their use. Gradually, however, many found a broader popularity and came to be used metaphorically, their meanings bent to suit new contexts. Space and computer technology have brought lively, new, and often whimsical additions to the language. Slang and acronyms also reflect popular, if fleeting, appreciation for technology's presence in daily life. Terms students use automatically today are obsolescing even as they speak.

Assign the essay for home reading. Then have students work collaboratively on the Analyzing Language activity on text page 1082.

Analyzing Language

Text page 1082

1. Answers will vary. Sample answers are provided.

   a. *A jerkwater town:* trains; an insignificant town off the main line, only important because steam locomotives would be supplied with water there by "jerking" or pumping the water into the boiler.

   b. *To sidetrack:* trains; to distract someone or digress, by analogy with moving a train from the main track to a siding.

   c. *A stopover:* trains; a brief stop on a journey to rest, visit friends, and so on; from the original meaning of being able to stop at one place and then proceed to one's destination using the original ticket.

   d. *The wrong side of the tracks:* trains; a socially undesirable neighborhood in a community; from the idea of getting off a train on the side next to another track rather than on the platform side.

   e. *A back-seat driver:* cars; an annoying meddler; from the idea of a person in the back seat confusing the driver with unnecessary comments or instructions.

   f. *A tailspin:* airplanes; a sudden, increasingly worse confusion or depression; from the idea of a plane going out of control.

   g. *To bail out:* airplanes; to abandon or give up on something; from the idea of jumping out of a plane with a parachute if the plane is going to crash.

   h. *A nosedive:* airplanes; a sudden plunge (as in spirits, profits, price); from the physical movement of a plane that is going to crash.

2. a. *allergic:* hypersensitive to an allergen; averse

   b. *obsessed:* abnormally dominated by one persistent idea or image; preoccupied

   c. *anemic:* deficient in hemoglobin (red blood cells that carry oxygen); weak

   d. *sanguine:* having blood as the predominating humor and thus ruddy-faced; optimistic

   e. *epidemic:* a disease affecting many persons at the same time in a community and spreading from person to person; large number

3. Answers will vary. Here are five examples:

   a. USA (pronounced as separate letters)

   b. UNESCO (pronounced as a word)

   c. IRA (pronounced either way)

   d. GOP (pronounced as separate letters)

   e. PTA (pronounced as separate letters)

4. Answers will vary. Here are some sample answers:

   a. Students may mention *bug* (an error in a program); *debugging* (removing such errors); *cursor* (the character or symbol that shows where the next character to be typed will go); *keyboard* (letter, number, and symbol keys); *software* (computer programs); *artificial intelligence* (computers that "think").

   b. Students may mention a variety of terms.

Exercises in Critical Thinking and Writing

Text page 1083

EVALUATING NONFICTION: FACT AND OPINION

This assignment asks students to evaluate any one of the selections from Unit Twelve. Key terms are *fact* and *opinion*.

Students often accept as a truism, "One opinion's as good as another." Stress that like many sayings, this one isn't accurate. As stated in the first paragraph of the section Background, without support an opinion does not have much substance. To explore the difference between fact and opinion, have students do the exercise included in the background section—stating three facts, deciding how each could be verified, and discussing this information with the class. (You may wish to use small groups so that everyone has a chance to speak.) After students have completed this activity, read and discuss with them the newspaper review (text page 1084) evaluating a biography of James Madison. Students should then be ready to read and follow the section Evaluating Nonfiction, the guidelines it contains, and the suggestions for prewriting and writing.

▶ CRITERIA FOR EVALUATING THE ASSIGNMENT   The opening paragraph of the essay cites the author and title of the piece being evaluated and contains the thesis statement. Subsequent paragraphs cite evidence from the selection to support the student's opinions on how the writer has used opinion, fact, and evidence in his or her work. Evidence is also given to support any comments on the writer's style and how well the selection held the student's interest. The concluding paragraph summarizes the student's overall evaluation of the selection.

Further Reading

Works listed are suitable for both students and teachers unless the annotation ends with the note [Teachers].

Haley, Alex. *Roots* (Doubleday, 1976). A well-known saga of the history of an African American family and the writer's search for his roots in Africa.

Hollowell, John. *Fact and Fiction* (University of North Carolina Press, 1977). Knowledgeable, readable study of the history and techniques of the ''new journalism.'' [Teachers]

Howard, Maureen, ed. *The Penguin Book of Contemporary American Essays* (Viking, 1984). More than two dozen fine essays—by Baldwin, Baker, Thomas, and others—introduced by a noted memoirist.

Kaplan, Justin, ed., with Robert Atwan, series ed. *The Best American Essays 1990* (Ticknor and Fields, 1990). Twenty or so outstanding essays selected by a different guest editor each year. The 1990 edition has essays by Ursula K. LeGuin, Tom Wolfe, Alan Dershowitz, Annie Dillard, James Alan McPherson, and others.

Kim, Elaine H. *Asian American Literature: An Introduction to the Writings and Their Social Context* (Temple University Press, 1982). Solid background for further study of Asian American literature, with extensive notes and bibliography. [Teachers]

Kinnamon, Kenneth, ed. *James Baldwin* (Prentice-Hall, 1974). A collection of critical essays in the Twentieth Century Views series. [Teachers]

Lincoln, Kenneth. *Native American Renaissance* (University of California Press, 1983). A wide-ranging exploration of American Indian culture and literary history by a Native American author. [Teachers]

Margolies, Edward. *Native Sons* (Lippincott, 1968). Critical survey of twentieth-century black male writers, with chapters on Wright and Baldwin. [Teachers]

Sims, Norman. *The Literary Journalists* (Ballantine, 1984). An excellent introduction on the ''new journalism,'' with examples by Tom Wolfe, Joan Didion, and others.

White, E. B. *The Second Tree from the Corner* (Harper & Row, 1954). White's classic collection of essays, including several on the writer's craft.

Wolfe, Tom, and E. W. Johnson, eds. *The New Journalism* (Harper & Row, 1973). Excellent anthology with an introduction by Wolfe.

Wright, Ellen, and Michael Fabre, eds. *Richard Wright Reader* (Harper & Row, 1978). Several of Wright's nonfiction pieces as well as poetry and fiction.

POETRY IN A TIME OF DIVERSITY

Text page 1085

Teaching the Poetry Unit

This unit presents a wide sampling of postwar American poetry, ranging in time from Theodore Roethke to Julia Alvarez, and in setting from a rural pasture to the Detroit ghetto, from a bomber over Europe in World War II to a Native American boarding school. The unit will give your students a taste of what American poetry is like today—a far cry from the traditional rhythms and rhymes of William Cullen Bryant and Ralph Waldo Emerson, though some of the underlying attitudes and emotional concerns are similar.

As the title of this unit implies, diversity is the keynote in American poetry written after World War II. A number of schools have flourished, and many individual poets have flourished without belonging to any stylistic school. No single poet has loomed so large as to provide an intimidating example, in contrast to the modernist era, when Pound and Eliot dominated the scene. Instead, more recognition has been given to poetry from outside the traditional mainstream— poetry written by women and by Americans of diverse ethnic and racial origins. In addition, "mainstream" poetry has become decentralized. It is written and published in places throughout the nation, and there is no single center of bohemianism—no Paris of the 1920's—to which poets feel they must flock. (The closest thing to it, today, is Iowa City, home of the Iowa Writers' Workshop.)

As the student introduction points out, the formalism (the view of poems as purely external esthetic objects), which dominated critical thought in the age of Eliot, has now largely been replaced by subjectivism. The poet Donald Hall, in his anthology *Contemporary American Poetry,* makes a distinction among several different kinds of subjective poetry currently being written. Probably most familiar is "confessional poetry," a direct, colloquial style in which the poet speaks of the most intimate emotional problems, usually in free verse. Sylvia Plath's *Ariel* is probably the most popular book of the confessional school, while Robert Lowell's *Life Studies* was an early book that inspired many followers. Confessionalism was at its height in the 1950's and 1960's. Later in that turbulent decade a new style of subjective writing that Hall calls "expressionism" or "neo-surrealism" became current. It is a poetry of wild imagery, where what is most important is neither the technical, prosodic skill of the poet nor the harrowingness of the poet's private life, but the originality of the poet's imagination. Alongside these two movements, African American poetry and the poetry of other ethnic Americans have developed in a manner marked by forcefulness, linguistic vigor, and above all, a sense of reality—sharply perceived external reality, in contrast to the painstakingly analyzed internal reality of the confessionalists.

While no poetic tradition that contained Emily Dickinson and Marianne Moore could have been said to lack a female voice, women poets in recent decades have come to the fore in a new way. Their poems make conscious statements about their identities as women and lend strength both to the confessionalist school and to the reality-oriented school. Adrienne Rich is perhaps the outstanding example of a poet who has at times worked in both styles. In contrast, Elizabeth Bishop deliberately steered her work away from identification with the concerns of women in any partisan sense. She was, however, an inspiration to female poets—and male ones as well—through the sheer quality of her work.

The biographical introductions to individual poets in this unit often emphasize stylistic developments during the course of the poets' careers. For the most part, this has been a development from a more formal verse early on to a less restrictive verse form later on. (Robert Lowell is the most obvious and perhaps most impressive such case.) This repeated pattern is as good evidence as any of the overall development of American poetry in this period: an opening up, a loosening of formal bonds, and a willingness to take on any subject and reveal any emotion, no matter how "unliterary" or "shocking" it may once have been considered. At the same time, however, it should be remembered that standards of craftsmanship have not declined. Quite the opposite. The average American poem published today, with its subtle use of internal rhyme, assonance, syllabic stresses, and varying line lengths, is undoubtedly more sophisticated and better crafted than the rather mechanically rhymed and metered American poem of a century ago.

Objectives of the Poetry Unit

1. To improve reading proficiency and expand vocabulary

2. To gain exposure to notable poets and their poems

3. To define and identify elements of poetry

4. To define and identify significant literary techniques

5. To respond to poetry, orally and in writing, through analysis of its elements

6. To practice the following critical thinking and writing skills:
   a. Comparing and contrasting poems
   b. Analyzing a poem
   c. Interpreting a poem
   d. Using another point of view
   e. Imitating a poet's technique
   f. Comparing and contrasting poetry and prose
   g. Analyzing an image
   h. Evaluating a poem

Introducing the Poetry Unit

You might briefly review with students poems they have read in previous units, and ask them to summarize what they did and didn't like about that older kind of poetry. You may find that the things they liked (for example, instances of powerful emotional expression) are the things most strongly present in this unit, while the things they didn't like (singsongy rhyme and meter, an old-fashioned quality) are for the most part not found here.

In introducing the various poetic "schools" of this period, you might point out that such labels are convenient for providing an overview of the poets of the period, but that they don't do justice to the diversity and scope of any individual poet's work. Theodore Roethke, for example, wrote traditional formal verse, free verse, confessional verse, and "deep image" poems (a type of poetry influenced by Pound's Imagist ideas). Allen Ginsberg, who started out as an outrageous Beat, is now a "grand old man" of American poetry. Stylistic labels are good teaching tools, but each poet and each poem must be considered individually.

Theodore Roethke

ELEGY FOR JANE

Objectives

1. To respond to a poem about a young person's death

2. To analyze the poem

3. To compare the treatment of death and mourning in two poems

Introducing the Poem

"Elegy for Jane" is filled with nature imagery, used by the speaker to develop Jane's personality and to come to an understanding of his relationship to Jane. You might have students pay particular attention to Roethke's use of metaphor in describing Jane. Suggest that they watch for variation or progressions of images. Have them also listen to the sound effects as the poem is read aloud. Alliteration, assonance, repetition, internal rhyme, and slant rhyme give this free-verse poem a rich melody.

BACKGROUND ON THE POEM In introducing the poem, you might first give a short history of the elegy as a literary form. An elegy is traditionally a meditation on the death of a person of particular importance to the poet or to the world. In the elegy, the poet seeks to invoke or bring to life the image of the dead person, usually to praise him or her. Point out to students that the speaker in the poem addresses the dead girl, a convention in the tradition of the elegy.

THE LITERAL MEANING In the first stanza, the speaker remembers his student's hair, her smile, her speech. He compares her speech and body language to a wren. In stanza 2, he describes her being lost in melancholy. She is compared to a sparrow and fern in stanza 3, and the speaker reveals his sadness over her death. In the final stanza, Jane is compared to a pigeon. The speaker stands over her grave, expresses his love for her, and qualifies that love.

Teaching Strategies

PROVIDING FOR CULTURAL DIFFERENCES Students from all backgrounds will relate to the poem's theme. Explain that a pickerel is a small, darting freshwater fish.

PROVIDING FOR DIFFERENT LEVELS OF ABILITY Some students may have difficulty with the central metaphors of this poem—the wren, the sparrow, and the pigeon. Discuss with these students the qualities of each of these birds and how the poet imparts those qualities to Jane.

READING THE POEM As students read, they should be mindful of the speaker's voice and the fact that each stanza reveals or describes his mood. What mood shifts does he undergo? How does the poem reveal these shifts? Have students consider why the poem begins with the lively description and closes with the declaration and qualification of the speaker's love. How would the poem read if the stanza order were reversed?

RETEACHING ALTERNATIVES The last two lines of this poem have received much attention. Ask students to observe their reactions to the lines when the poem is read aloud. Why do they think Roethke put in the lines? Perhaps he feels he has to qualify his feelings for his student, lest the poem be misinterpreted. An argument that contradicts such an interpretation is that the poet would be more likely to state his relationship at the beginning, rather than the close, of the poem. Or are the lines very much a natural part of the poem? They certainly convey the strength of Jane's character through her effect on a person not close to her. Perhaps the most acceptable and natural explanation is that the speaker discovers both his feelings for Jane and his role in her life through the poem. The poem is this discovery.

Responding to the Poem

Answers to the questions in the Pupil's Edition appear in the Annotated Teacher's Edition.

Writing About the Poem

For help in revising their compositions, refer students to **Grammar, Usage, and Mechanics: A Reference Guide** on text pages 1183–1228 at the back of their books.

A CRITICAL RESPONSE

Comparing Poems Briefly review Ransom's poem, checking for students' awareness of the affectionate tone, before they compare Ransom's poem with Roethke's "Elegy for Jane." Questions 2 and 3 (text page 673) and question 1 (text page 1089) call attention to figures of speech in the poems.

▶ CRITERIA FOR EVALUATING THE ASSIGNMENT   The essay cites phrases from both poems to identify simi-larity in warm, affectionate tone and use of figures of speech involving nature.

Extending the Poem

The critical response question asks students to compare the poem to another elegy. You might also have students compare Roethke's use of nature imagery with that of other poets in the unit. Ask them to look for the speaker's or poet's relationship with nature. In Plath they will find an antipathy, in Sexton a kind of otherworldly pact. In contrast, they will see that Roethke's relationship is inti-mate and basically joyful.

Robert Hayden
Text page 1090

"SUMMERTIME AND THE LIVING . . ."
Text page 1091

Objectives

1. To respond to a poem about memories of an African American urban neighborhood

2. To identify images in the poem

3. To analyze irony and tone

4. To give an oral reading of the poem

5. To write an essay analyzing the poem's use of ambi-guity

Introducing the Poem

Although the poem is written in free verse, Hayden does apply some formal restrictions. For example, many lines are iambic, though the number of feet varies from line to line, giving the poem a lilting, fluid rhythm. Another for-mal restriction is a consistency in stanza length. You can ask students to consider why the poet set the last line of stanza 3 apart, leading them to understand that the line is a causal transition from one stanza to the next. The line leads the reader from one time period or consciousness into another.

BACKGROUND ON THE POEM   As the headnote points out, the title is taken from *Porgy and Bess.* A very brief summary of that story would be helpful to a fuller understanding of Hayden's poem. You might simply tell students that the two characters lived in a ghetto and were in love, and that Porgy was crippled. Despite their circum-stances they did not give up hope.

THE LITERAL MEANING   In stanza 1, the speaker recalls sunflowers, tough as the children growing up on the streets. He remembers a circus poster of horses and his fantasy as a boy of riding them. In stanzas 2 and 3, he recalls that roses were bought only for the dead, that no one had vacations, and that life was hard and people were angry. He recalls people sitting on steps in the summer. He feels the "Mosaic eyes" of those people bearing down on him in the present. In the last stanza, he recalls grim street preachers, Elks parades, and the boxer Jack Johnson, who brought hope and dreams to the people of the ghetto.

Teaching Strategies

PROVIDING FOR CULTURAL DIFFERENCES   Ex-plain that Jack Johnson (line 29) lived from 1876–1946. He was the first African American boxer to win the world heavyweight title. Johnson defeated Tommy Burns in 1908 and knocked out Jim Jeffries, ''the great white hope,'' in 1910.

PROVIDING FOR DIFFERENT LEVELS OF ABILITY
With LEP students, you may want to emphasize the literal meaning of the poem, pointing out to them that the poem is a recollection and consideration of the speaker's past.

READING THE POEM   Before the class reads the poem, you might alert them to the use of flower imagery in the poem. As they read, they should note the purpose and meaning of each flower image, for the poem is, in the end, about the attempt to come to flower of a neighborhood, or, if extended, an entire people. Be sure to read this poem aloud.

RETEACHING ALTERNATIVES   You might give extra consideration to question 9, for these sections (stanza 1, stanza 5) tie together the major themes of the real versus the imagination. A more intensive study of the final lines also gives students time to reflect on the magnificent last lines of the poem, which echo the fantasy of the boy in stanza 1.

Responding to the Poem   Text page 1092

Answers to the questions in the Pupil's Edition appear in the Annotated Teacher's Edition.

Writing About the Poem

For help in revising their compositions, refer students to **Grammar, Usage, and Mechanics: A Reference Guide** on text pages 1183–1228 at the back of their books.

A CREATIVE RESPONSE
1. Giving an Oral Reading   If you cannot easily locate a recording of ''Summertime,'' ask a colleague who teaches music for help. You may wish to assign this activity to a few students or make it optional, because of the time it would take for all students to present the reading.

▶ CRITERIA FOR EVALUATING THE ASSIGNMENT   The reading captures the mood of the poem. The reader avoids rote end-stops and sing song, but groups ideas according to meaning.

A CRITICAL RESPONSE
2. Analyzing the Poem   To prepare students to deal with the ambiguity, mixed feelings, and mixed values of the poem, thoroughly discuss all nine questions. Then elicit comments on specific lines that point to values—for example, ''diamond limousine'' (material values) and ''Mosaic eyes'' (spiritual values).

▶ CRITERIA FOR EVALUATING THE ASSIGNMENT   The paper cites lines of the poem that reveal a mixture of fond and painful memories and of material and spiritual values. The paper may or may not comment on the irony of the poem's title.

Elizabeth Bishop   Text page 1093

FIRST DEATH IN NOVA SCOTIA   Text page 1094

Objectives

1. To respond to a poem about death

2. To identify and evaluate images

3. To analyze tone

Introducing the Poem

''First Death in Nova Scotia'' is a narrative poem in which the speaker relates her first experience with death. A way into this poem is to discuss with students how people often approach particularly painful and sad events by focusing on the objects around them. Bishop, through the voice of the child-speaker, does exactly that in the poem. Each stanza takes the speaker closer and closer actually to comprehending Arthur's death. The first stanza deals with the chromographs and the loon. The second stanza focuses on the loon, which becomes a metaphor for death, and therefore for Arthur. The third stanza physically moves the speaker toward her dead cousin in the coffin, but the speaker focuses on the strange beauty of the coffin and the loon who is able to look at it. The fourth stanza describes Arthur as a doll—unreal. It is not until the fifth stanza that the speaker, after imagining the warmth of the figures in the chromographs, tries to imagine Arthur's place with them, but cannot fully comprehend that her cousin must actually leave, and that in fact he has already gone into the cold and foreign place called death.

It may also be helpful to explore the use of repetition (line 1, lines 8–9, line 10, lines 21–22, lines 26–27, lines 34–35, and so on) in the poem, which often reflects a play on the meanings of the words repeated, while adding a musical element to the language. Each of the lines has three stresses, and many lines are strict iambic trimeter. Assonance, repetition, alliteration, and some end rhymes add to the poem's sound effects.

BACKGROUND ON THE POEM   Elizabeth Bishop is often considered an unemotional writer. While this might appear so in a dramatic comparison with Sylvia Plath and Anne Sexton, it is far from correct. As is evident in both poems included here, Bishop's poems certainly do contain deep feelings and a powerful understanding of human nature. Bishop's poems can be read and loved for their story line and their brilliant use of language. Or they can be explored as prisms: The reader can search for the irony, humor, sorrow, and wisdom that is almost always there, but almost always revealed beneath the surface.

THE LITERAL MEANING   The speaker's cousin Arthur is laid out in his coffin beneath chromographs of the Royal Family. Beneath the chromographs is a stuffed loon on a table. The child speaker observes the room, the objects in the room, and her cousin in his coffin. She speculates on Arthur's future as the ''smallest page at court,'' and then expresses her muddled understanding of what it means to die.

Teaching Strategies

PROVIDING FOR CULTURAL DIFFERENCES   As the headnote mentions, the practice of being ''laid out'' in a coffin at home was common during the time of Bishop's childhood in Nova Scotia, and is continued in some cultures today. Pictures of chromographs and loons may be helpful for students. The photography department of your local library will likely have books with such photographs.

PROVIDING FOR DIFFERENT LEVELS OF ABILITY
Some students may have difficulty realizing why the speaker does not refer directly to death, but, rather, to the objects around her. An approach to this aspect of the poem is suggested under Extending the Poem. More advanced students might do some research on the loon and consider why it is an appropriate symbol in this poem. A good explication appears in *Becoming a Poet* by David Kalstone (Farrar, Straus and Giroux, 1989). Kalstone also discusses the influence of Marianne Moore and Robert Lowell on Bishop's career.

READING THE POEM   Although the poem is narrative and the language is direct, the poem may be difficult for some students to fully comprehend after just one reading. It is the kind of poem that should be read several times, so that the many important and evocative details are not overlooked. Suggest that students read the poem two or three times to themselves and then have it read aloud in class.

RETEACHING ALTERNATIVES   Have students talk about their responses to the poem. Do they like it? How did reading the poem make them feel? Do they think other poems about death they have read are better, more moving poems? If so, which?

Responding to the Poem   Text page 1095

Answers to the questions in the Pupil's Edition appear in the Annotated Teacher's Edition.

Extending the Poem

You might have students relate an emotional event they have experienced by describing the physical surroundings within which the event took place. Suggest that they focus on details that mirror their emotional states and that they use a variety of similes and metaphors.

LITTLE EXERCISE   Text page 1096

Objectives

1. To respond to a poem about a storm
2. To identify similes and personification

3. To write a series of notes or a poem imitating the writer's technique
4. To write an essay comparing and contrasting two poems
5. To define words with multiple meanings

Introducing the Poem

This poem is divided into seven three-line stanzas. The language and images are clear and direct and include similes and personification. The music of this free-verse poem comes mainly from end rhymes (lines 4, 6, 10, 16), alliteration (lines 2, 3, 17), and repetition of the imperative form. Because the poem sounds as though someone were simply daydreaming aloud, it may at first appear simple, but the order of events is precise. You might discuss with students the effect on the poem if the order of events were reversed.

BACKGROUND ON THE POEM   This early poem appeared in Elizabeth Bishop's first book, *North and South* (1946). Within the poem are elements found in other Bishop poems: a description with qualities of the familiar and the unfamiliar, a slightly sardonic tone, clear and precise language, and a matter-of-fact voice. Many of the images are commonplace, yet described in a distinct and unusual manner that makes the observations memorable and haunting.

THE LITERAL MEANING   The speaker asks the reader to imagine a storm. She asks the reader to picture what the mangrove keys will look like, and the boulevard lined with palm trees. She describes the boulevard and the rain, and then describes the storm's departure. In the last stanza she asks the reader to imagine an uninjured and "barely disturbed" person asleep in the bottom of a rowboat.

Teaching Strategies

PROVIDING FOR CULTURAL DIFFERENCES   Have students who have never seen tropical foliage study the painting by Winslow Homer. The tall trees are palm trees. You may want to show photos of herons and red mangrove trees that have arched, above-ground prop roots that one can tie a boat to.

PROVIDING FOR DIFFERENT LEVELS OF ABILITY   Some students may have difficulty understanding that this is a poem about the mind wandering, about seeing things and imagining. You might suggest to these students that the poem is like a daydream and that perhaps each of them—the reader—is the person asleep in the bottom of the rowboat. For these students the activity suggested under Reteaching Alternatives might also prove helpful.

READING THE POEM   You may want to have four students read this poem aloud, with each of the four reading a "Think . . ." passage. The first students would read stanza 1; the second stanzas 2 and 3; the third stanzas 4–6; and the fourth stanza 7. To emphasize the variety of images in the poem, suggest that each of the students vary his or her pitch, tone, and voice quality.

RETEACHING ALTERNATIVES   The movement of this poem traces the way the mind can work—skipping from one image to another. To reinforce this concept, you might have students write a description of a scene, perhaps a sidewalk fair or soccer game. Have one student suggest an image that is a part of the scene, and then, without giving them time to think or to make connections between the images, have other students suggest additional images.

Responding to the Poem   Text page 1096

Answers to the questions in the Pupil's Edition appear in the Annotated Teacher's Edition.

Writing About the Poem

For help in revising their compositions, refer students to **Grammar, Usage, and Mechanics: A Reference Guide** on text pages 1183–1228 at the back of their books.

A CREATIVE RESPONSE
1. *Imitating the Writer's Technique*   Ask students to list some scenes of action or some settings that would lend themselves to a ''Little Exercise''—for example, a ball game, shoppers in a mall, a concert, a busy ski slope.

▶ CRITERIA FOR EVALUATING THE ASSIGNMENT   The student's paragraph or poem is titled ''Little Exercise,'' begins with ''Think of,'' and lists five or more vivid images which form part of an easily identifiable setting or scene of action.

A CRITICAL RESPONSE
2. *Comparing Poems*   You might suggest that students turn to the Moore poem first (text page 725) and list the details that strike them, and that they then choose the Bishop poem which seems to use details in a similar way.

▶ CRITERIA FOR EVALUATING THE ASSIGNMENT   The essay is at least one paragraph long. It names the Bishop poem being compared with Moore's ''The Steeple-Jack'' and, by citing specifics from both poems, shows how both poets use detail upon detail to bring a scene to life.

Analyzing Language and Style

MULTIPLE MEANINGS
1. *Frosted:* covered with ice crystals, iced as a cake is iced, touched with silvery coloring, killed (especially in the case of a young plant) by freezing. Several of these apply to ''First Death in Nova Scotia.''
2. *Exercise:* physical exertion, discharging a duty, practicing a drill, performance that demonstrates a skill. ''Little Exercise'' could be a performance or practice drill.
3. *Disturbed:* deranged, alarmed, inconvenienced, interrupted. ''Inconvenienced'' is the most appropriate meaning in the last line of ''Little Exercise.''

Randall Jarrell

Text page 1098

THE DEATH OF THE BALL TURRET GUNNER

Text page 1099

Objectives

1. To respond to a famous poem about war

2. To interpret the poem's meaning

3. To write a paragraph or poem from an imagined point of view

Introducing the Poem

In five powerful lines the speaker of this poem describes his grisly death in a ball turret. The poem is filled with womb and unborn child images that reinforce the innocence of the speaker—''my mother's sleep,'' ''hunched in its belly,'' ''my wet fur.'' In contrast, the gruesome images of the speaker's death emphasize the destruction of that innocence. Students should note how the repetition of the contrasting *s* sounds in line 1 and *k* sounds in line 4 reinforces the meanings of those lines.

In oral reading, students might note the five-stress rhythm of the first four lines, which approximates blank verse and moves the speaker, without pause for contemplation, from birth to death. The varying meter of the fifth line suggests the speaker's separation from birth and life. The prominent rhyme on the poem's last word rings with shocking finality.

Students with relatives who served in Vietnam may have heard firsthand about some of the horrors of war; for other students, the death in this poem may seem unnecessarily gruesome. At this point, you may want to review with students Walt Whitman's description of the ''real war'' (text page 351) or Stephen Crane's imagery in ''War Is Kind'' (text page 463). Both works illustrate the universal, timeless horrors of war.

BACKGROUND ON THE POEM The headnote tells students that the poem is perhaps the most famous World War II poem. You might also tell them that Jarrell's war poems taken together are considered to be some of the greatest war, or antiwar, poems ever written. In *Babel to Byzantium* James Dickey describes the effect of Jarrell's poems most eloquently:

The poems . . . put on your face, nearer than any of your own looks, more irrevocably than your skin, the uncom-

prehending stare of the individual caught in the State's machinery: in an impersonal, invisible, man-made, and uncontrollable Force. They show in front of you a child's slow, horrified, magnificently un-understanding and growing loss of innocence in which we all share and can't help: which we can neither understand nor help in ourselves in the hands of the State any more than can the children in *our* hands.

THE LITERAL MEANING There is contention over the literal meaning of this poem. Taking into consideration Jarrell's other work, the most accepted interpretation is that the speaker is taken into the army before he is fully conscious of himself, while metaphorically an infant. The State, or army, and literally the ball turret, becomes his new mother in the sense that the formation of his self continues in it. Hunched in the freezing turret, six miles from the earth, he wakes, or becomes conscious, under fire. This is his nightmare. He is killed in the air, his body literally torn apart. Nothing is left of him—the pieces of his remains have to be washed out of the turret.

Teaching Strategies

PROVIDING FOR CULTURAL DIFFERENCES Many students won't know what a ball turret gunner is. Have them read and discuss the Primary Sources: The Ball Turret at the bottom of the page.

PROVIDING FOR DIFFERENT LEVELS OF ABILITY Some students might have difficulty with the layers of literal and metaphorical meaning in this poem. For these students, you might discuss the fact that the ''State'' in this poem is sometimes seen to represent the faceless, nameless forces that seem to control us.

READING THE POEM After students have read the poem silently, read it aloud, and ask them to listen to its sound effects.

RETEACHING ALTERNATIVES If students have not already done so, have them read Primary Sources: The Ball Turret (text page 1099). With this information, have students describe, on a literal level, how the ball turret gunner dies.

Responding to the Poem
Text page 1099

Answers to the questions in the Pupil's Edition appear in the Annotated Teacher's Edition.

Writing About the Poem

For help in revising their compositions, refer students to **Grammar, Usage, and Mechanics: A Reference Guide** on text pages 1183–1228 at the back of their books.

A CREATIVE RESPONSE
Writing from Another Point of View   The assignment demands a thorough understanding of the poem, to be gained from completion of the nine response questions. Bring several newspaper articles about people who have died—celebrity notices are especially good—for students who are unable to locate one.

▶ CRITERIA FOR EVALUATING THE ASSIGNMENT   The poem or paragraph is as brief as Jarrell's, is written from the point of view of the person who died, and packs its message into metaphors in Jarrell's style.

Primary Sources
Text page 1099

THE BALL TURRET
In this comment, Jarrell explains what the ball turret was and how dangerous it was to be the ball turret gunner. His factual explanation does little to soften the images that are so powerful in his poem. If anything, his comment that the hose ''was a steam hose'' only enhances that gruesome image. Ask students to compare their personal responses to this prose explanation with their responses to the poem. Which gives them a clearer picture? Which do they find more powerful, more moving? Which do they think they will remember longer? See if they can express some reasons for their responses.

Extending the Poem

Have interested students locate one of the collections of Jarrell mentioned on text page 1098, *Little Friend, Little Friend* (1945) or *Losses* (1948). Students can then compare and contrast the war poems in this collection with ''The Death of the Ball Turret Gunner.'' In particular, students might look for themes of fantasy vs. fact and life vs. illusions about life.

Gwendolyn Brooks
Text page 1100

OF DE WITT WILLIAMS ON HIS WAY TO LINCOLN CEMETERY
Text page 1101

Objectives

1. To respond to a poem about a funeral procession
2. To interpret the poem
3. To describe the poem's tone
4. To perform a choral reading

Introducing the Poem

The clear imagery and direct language should make this an easily understood poem. You may want to emphasize the rhyme, meter, and repetition—all of which contribute to the poem's songlike quality. The meter is trochaic trimeter, and the basic rhyme scheme is *abab* with some variation. The refrain (lines 5–6) extends the *b* rhyme with *boy* and adds the slant rhyme of *chariot* and *casket*.

BACKGROUND ON THE POEM   This poem is a section of a longer poem titled ''A Street in Bronzeville,'' the title poem of Gwendolyn Brooks's first book. The entire poem consists of twenty sections, each of which focuses on different people and circumstances in a neighborhood.

THE LITERAL MEANING   Addressing the driver of the hearse in which the casket has been placed, the speaker requests that the body of De Witt Williams be driven by the landmarks of his life. The place of his birth, Alabama, and where he was raised, Illinois, are repeated in the poem, along with the refrain in lines 3–6.

Teaching Strategies

PROVIDING FOR CULTURAL DIFFERENCES This poem assumes a knowledge of the history of African Americans. You may want to make certain that students understand the symbolic importance of the song "Swing Low, Sweet Chariot" to this history. It has long symbolized a place of refuge in troubled times.

PROVIDING FOR DIFFERENT LEVELS OF ABILITY ESL students may have difficulty understanding the effect of the line repetitions. The choral reading, suggested under Reading the Poem, should help these students. More advanced students might benefit from writing an elegy of their own, imitating the songlike rhythm of the poem.

READING THE POEM You may want to have students prepare the choral reading suggested for A Creative Response (text page 1101).

RETEACHING ALTERNATIVES Focusing on question 3 (text page 1101), you might ask students what they think lines 3 and 4 mean. (The repetition indicates that it is an important line to the poem.) Have students discuss whether they believe there is any such thing as a "plain" person.

Responding to the Poem   Text page 1101

Answers to the questions in the Pupil's Edition appear in the Annotated Teacher's Edition.

Writing About the Poem

For help in revising their compositions, refer students to **Grammar, Usage, and Mechanics: A Reference Guide** on text pages 1183–1228 at the back of their books.

A CREATIVE RESPONSE

Preparing a Choral Reading   The poem is brief enough for as many as six or seven groups (of three to five students each) to present during a single class period. To get students started, you might ask if lines 4–6 call for single or multiple voices. Allow groups to compare interpretations before they formalize their own decisions, and, if they wish, to use "Swing Low, Sweet Chariot" or other music as background.

▶ CRITERIA FOR EVALUATING THE ASSIGNMENT   The reading conveys an interpretation of the poem in keeping with points discussed in response to the five Interpreting Meanings questions.

Robert Lowell   Text page 1102

FOR THE UNION DEAD   Text page 1104

Objectives

1. To respond to and interpret a challenging poem

2. To identify and interpret images and metaphor

3. To describe the poem's tone

4. To write a paragraph or a poem describing a building

5. To write an essay comparing and contrasting two poems

Introducing the Poem

The varying perspectives, or time points, in the poem are complex—the speaker seems to be everywhere at once. He is at the aquarium, then the Boston Common, then on Boylston Street, and, finally, in front of a television set. To simplify the shifts between both personal and historical time, you might tell students that it is likely the speaker is at the aquarium for the entire poem. The aquarium of his youth becomes the inspiration for this free-verse poem.

The tone in this poem shifts throughout from nostalgic to bitter and ironic, and figures of speech play a central role in establishing that tone. Students should note, for example, the effect on the poem's tone of such figures of speech as "my nose crawled like a snail on the glass," "yellow dinosaur steam shovels," and the monument that "sticks like a fishbone / in the city's throat." Alliteration also affects the tone, as students will especially note in the last three lines of the poem where the string of *s*'s mimics the silent flow of fish and grease. The somewhat bitter, ironic implication is that nothing sticks, nothing holds, not the speaker's treasured childhood aquarium nor the monument to African American war heroes. Both are forgotten and spiritually destroyed by the action of progress or history.

BACKGROUND ON THE POEM Judging from this poem, some students may question why Lowell is considered a confessional poet. You might tell students that this poem and the book in which it was first published were considered by critics as a move away from the loose lines and purely personal qualities of *Life Studies*.

THE LITERAL MEANING The comment at the end of the poem (text page 1106) provides a detailed paraphrase.

Teaching Strategies

PROVIDING FOR CULTURAL DIFFERENCES
Assure students unfamiliar with Boston and American urban life in general that they need not "catch" every reference to enjoy the poem. They'll need to know what an aquarium is (a building with exhibits of animals and plants that live in water).

PROVIDING FOR DIFFERENT LEVELS OF ABILITY
You may be able to motivate some students by explaining that the movie *Glory,* which many have seen on TV or video, is the story of the same Colonel Shaw and his African American regiment portrayed in St. Gaudens' monument and the subject of much of this poem. A photo of the monument appears on text page 1106.

READING THE POEM An audiocassette recording accompanies this poem. If possible, have students listen to the recording first, paying particular attention to the varying tones and emotions expressed by the performer. (An alternative might be for you or a talented student to prepare a reading.) Afterward, have students read A Comment on the Poem, text page 1106, so they will approach the poem itself with confidence. You might also suggest to students that the entire poem takes place in the speaker's imagination. In fact, his contemplation of the statue of Colonel Shaw becomes a kind of revery. In line 37, the colonel actually seems to come alive.

RETEACHING ALTERNATIVES Because the poem does have such shifting tones and emotions, you might have students look at word connotations. In line 9, for example, the poet uses the word *sigh,* a word that connotes nostaliga. In the same stanza, steam shovels are "dinosaur," the inference being that their work is thoughtless, archaic, and destructive. Students might also investigate the many ironies in the poem. The bulldozers, for example, work for "progress," but, in reality, are digging an underworld and undermining the Statehouse and statue, symbols of the city's heritage.

Responding to the Poem   Text page 1107

Answers to the questions in the Pupil's Edition appear in the Annotated Teacher's Edition.

Writing About the Poem

For help in revising their compositions, refer students to **Grammar, Usage, and Mechanics: A Reference Guide** on text pages 1183–1228 at the back of their books.

A CREATIVE RESPONSE
1. Writing a Description Discuss some local buildings the students could use—perhaps a restored "Old Town" area where banks have become boutiques, or a gas station that has become a convenience store.

▶ CRITERIA FOR EVALUATING THE ASSIGNMENT The paragraph or short poem describes a building as it is now and as it once was, and states whether the change reflects town events or wider changes in society.

2. Comparing and Contrasting Poems Discuss A Comment on the Poem (Lowell's poem, page 1106), and Timrod's poem (page 1107), before having students work in pairs to chart the similarities and differences between the poems. The first column of the chart should read (a) theme or message, (b) tone, (c) diction, and (d) form. The second and third columns should list appropriate comments for Timrod's and Lowell's poems.

▶ CRITERIA FOR EVALUATING THE ASSIGNMENT The essay cites specific details from both poems to demonstrate that they are similar only in commemorating war dead, and contrasted in every other way: word choice (Timrod's poetic language and Lowell's diction of daily life); message and tone (Timrod glorifies the dead, Lowell takes a grimmer stance); and form (Timrod uses four-line stanzas rhymed abab, Lowell uses free verse).

You might have interested students read (or read aloud to the class) a few poems from Lowell's earlier rhymed work and then a few lines from Part Four of *Life Studies*. After comparing these two examples of Lowell, students may acquire a greater appreciation for Lowell's progression into the more refined free verse of "For the Union Dead."

Richard Wilbur

Text page 1108

THE BEAUTIFUL CHANGES

Text page 1109

YEAR'S END

Text page 1110

Objectives

1. To respond to the images in a poem
2. To paraphrase the statement of a stanza
3. To identify the speaker's problem
4. To write an essay analyzing the poems
5. To analyze a poem's sound effects

Introducing the Poems

You will want to have your students think about the poetic uses of ambiguity as they study Wilbur's poems. In composition, students are often told to avoid constructions that can be understood in two or more ways. Poets, however, rely on ambiguity. Wilbur, for example, wants his readers to see multiple meanings in both the title and content of "The Beautiful Changes." He wants readers to realize that *downs* in line 1 of "Year's End" can have more than one meaning.

In "The Beautiful Changes," Wilbur uses a pattern of stressed lines (5, 4, 2, 3, 5, 5 stresses per stanza) with variable meter. The rhyme scheme is *abacdc*.

In "Year's End," the meter is iambic pentameter and the rhyme scheme *abbacc*. Analyzing Language and Style (text page 1111) guides students in an examination of this poem's sound effects.

BACKGROUND ON THE POET   If any of your students are familiar with the comic operetta *Candide,* based on Voltaire's classic satire, they may be interested to know that Richard Wilbur wrote the witty and memorable lyrics for Leonard Bernstein's music. *Candide* opened in New York at the Martin Beck Theater on December 1, 1956, and has been revived many times since then.

THE LITERAL MEANING   *The Beautiful Changes*
In the first stanza, the speaker walks through a meadow in autumn. Seeing the beautiful weed called Queen Anne's Lace (wild carrot), he compares it to lilies and the meadow to a lake. Its effect on him is somewhat the same as when the woman he loves makes him think of a lovely Swiss lake. In the second stanza, the speaker notes the changes in a forest and a leaf wrought by a chameleon (changing color to match the forest) and a mantis (appearing to be part of the leaf). In the third stanza, the woman, first mentioned in stanza 1, is said to hold roses in such a way that they are not hers alone. Other rose/beauty associations perhaps come to the speaker's mind. For a moment, he believes, beauty transforms everything it touches into beauty.

Year's End   In winter, the speaker notes the snow and the thinly frozen lake. He remembers seeing leaves partially frozen into the ice, fluttering all winter. The speaker then mentions ferns that became fossils, mammoths that froze in Arctic ice, and the little dog preserved in the volcanic ash of Pompeii. In the last stanza, the speaker ponders these sudden deaths, implying that our journey into the future is always uncertain. New Year's bells contend with the immediate but also timeless snow.

Teaching Strategies

PROVIDING FOR CULTURAL DIFFERENCES   Standards of beauty vary from culture to culture and from generation to generation. Since Wilbur's first poem concerns beauty, you may want to explore with students the nature of beauty. Why does beauty vary from one era to another? (You might mention the beautiful women in Rubens's paintings, who, by today's standards, are overweight.) Is beauty relative, or are there absolute standards?

Such a discussion is especially relevant to the poem "The Beautiful Changes," because it suggests still another meaning for the poem's title—one outside the poem—that also makes sense.

PROVIDING FOR DIFFERENT LEVELS OF ABILITY
With LEP/ESL students, read both of these poems aloud in class and paraphrase as necessary. The poems are lyrically beautiful, and all students should be able to appreciate their rhythm and euphony.

READING THE POEMS By now your students probably realize that beauty, love, and death are common themes in poetry. Point out that these themes recur because of their universality. The poet's challenge is to say something new about them, or else to say something familiar in a striking or different way. The two poems should be read aloud in all classes, at some point, either before or after the Responding questions have been assigned. (An audiocassette recording of "The Beautiful Changes" accompanies the text.)

RETEACHING ALTERNATIVES As students discuss their responses to the poems, make clear that poetry often *is* ambiguous, often *is* susceptible to more than one "right" reading or "correct" interpretation, but that an interpretation must be grounded in the poem itself. In class discussion have student volunteers summarize their interpretations of the poems, and then have the class attempt to agree on which of the interpretations, within the framework of the poem, seem most logical.

Responding to the Poems

Text pages 1109, 1111

Answers to the questions in the Pupil's Edition appear in the Annotated Teacher's Edition.

Writing About the Poems

For help in revising their compositions, refer students to **Grammar, Usage, and Mechanics: A Reference Guide** on text pages 1183–1228 at the back of their books.

A CRITICAL RESPONSE
Analyzing the Poems Discussing the questions on both poems will prepare students for this assignment. You may wish specifically to elicit from students what they think the poems say about beauty, love, and death, and whether any of these ideas seems to contradict the usual way people look at the subject.

▶ CRITERIA FOR EVALUATING THE ASSIGNMENT The essay cites details from the poems to demonstrate Wilbur's attempt to show us that beauty, love, and death blend into simple daily images which we often fail to notice as we "fray into the future." The essay contrasts Wilbur's views with more usual ways of addressing these topics.

Analyzing Language and Style

SOUND EFFECTS
1. abbacc
2. Internal rhymes include *allows/down* (line 6); *winter/into* (line 10).
3. Iambic pentameter
4. In stanza 1, the third line begins with an accented syllable; in stanza 2, the fourth and fifth lines do so; and so on.
5. Examples of alliteration incude "*d*owns the *d*ying" (line 1), "the *l*ate *l*eaves down" (line 8), "*f*ray into the *f*uture" (line 26).
      Instances of assonance include "fr*o*zen-*o*ver" (line 5), "*o*wn m*o*st" (line 12), "sh*a*pely thing th*ey*" (line 24).
6. Answers will vary. The sounds of "down(s)," "curled," "fray," and "wrangling" are especially evocative.

Extending the Poem

In "Year's End," Richard Wilbur makes a poetic statement about time. Ask students to write an original paragraph in which they, too, make a point about the nature of time. In their paragraphs, have students use appropriately at least one of the following quotations.

a. the "corridors of time"—Henry Wadsworth Longfellow
b. the "sands of time"—Henry Wadsworth Longfellow
c. the "scythe of time"—Napoleon Bonaparte
d. the "tooth of time"—Edward Young
e. the "whirligig of time"—William Shakespeare
f. "Time, the wisest counsellor"—Plutarch
g. "Time, the subtle thief of youth"—John Milton
h. the "inaudible and noiseless foot of time"—William Shakespeare
i. "Time, a maniac scattering dust"—Alfred, Lord Tennyson

SLED BURIAL, DREAM CEREMONY

Objectives

1. To respond to a free-verse poem about a dream

2. To analyze and interpret the poem

3. To interpret metaphor and simile

Introducing the Poem

This poem is an excellent example of a lucidly written, easy-to-read poem that nevertheless requires interpretation. As the headnote on text page 1113 indicates, the poem is exactly like a dream. The details are sharp and unmistakable, yet their meaning, like the meaning of a dream, is not obvious.

BACKGROUND ON THE POEM   There is a tradition in the English language of poetry about dreams and dreaming. In fact, one of the most famous poems in English—actually a fragment of a poem—was written not *about* a dream but *in* a dream. Samuel Taylor Coleridge's ''Kubla Khan'' was composed, according to Coleridge, while he was sound asleep. When he awoke, he started writing frantically, only to be interrupted after fifty-four lines by ''a person on business from Porlock.'' When the visitor left more than an hour later, Coleridge could not remember the rest of the poem. It was lost forever.

THE LITERAL MEANING   A dead Southerner is taken north by train in an open casket for burial. In a small, snowy village, warmly bundled men unload his body and put him on an old-fashioned, horse-drawn sled. They take him out of town, past barns, through woods, and between houses of ice-fishers on a lake. They go to the center of the lake, where they cut a coffin-sized rectangle in the ice. After lifting out the slab of ice, they take his body, holding the coffin by ropes, and lower him into the water.

Teaching Strategies

PROVIDING FOR CULTURAL DIFFERENCES   Students from tropical climates may be puzzled by the gunny-sacked bushes, which are covered with sacks made of a coarse fabric to protect them from the cold. Explain ice fishing—fishing through holes broken in thick winter ice—if some students don't know what it is.

PROVIDING FOR DIFFERENT LEVELS OF ABILITY   Students at all levels should be able to understand the events in this poem. With more advanced students, you will want to look into possible interpretations of the poem—that is, into interpretations of the dream. With less advanced students, you may wish to limit the discussion to what happens in the dream—the literal events.

READING THE POEM   To vary the presentation of the poem, you may want to consider appointing eight students to read it aloud in class, one student for each stanza. Give them some time to read their stanzas silently and, if necessary, to ask questions. Advise them to read aloud according to the way the poem is punctuated, not according to line breaks. (Line breaks should, of course, be acknowledged with a very slight pause, since they are there for a reason.) Tell students to allow a brief pause after the preceding stanza before beginning to read the next one. They should not need, or expect, a cue from you. If you choose good readers, and if they do their parts conscientiously, the poem can be handled very effectively in this manner.

RETEACHING ALTERNATIVES   If you did not use the eight-reader technique suggested under Reading the Poem, you may want to use it now. If you did use it, you can expand it when reteaching by having the same student who reads each stanza follow the reading with an interpretation of it in his or her own words. Then ask the class to discuss the stanza.

Extending the Poem

Although ''Sled Burial, Dream Ceremony'' is a poetic account of a dream, have students suppose that it really happened. Ask them to collaborate in small groups to write a brief local news article about the strange ''burial beneath the ice'' that a man from the South has just received on a snowy day, with resident pallbearers, in the middle of a nearby lake. Have your students invent details that will make the event plausible, or else have them report it without change in a deadpan-humorous way. Students can write their reports for a local TV broadcast. Have a spokesperson for each group share the article or broadcast with the whole class.

James Merrill

KITE POEM

Objectives

1. To respond to a narrative poem with a message

2. To identify internal rhymes, approximate rhymes, and alliteration

3. To analyze symbols

4. To write a response from another point of view

Introducing the Poem

This poem makes good use of both internal rhyme and approximate rhyme. Students will already be familiar with internal rhyme within the same line:

> The Northern Lights have seen queer sights (*Lights/ sights*)

They should be reminded that internal rhyme can also occur from line to line, as it does in "Kite Poem" (*port* in line 3 and *sport* in line 4). Merrill makes use of approximate rhyme, too; *person/parson, chair/chore,* and *kite/ coat* are examples. The variable meter is basically iambic with five stresses to the line.

BACKGROUND ON THE POEM As the headnote to the poem indicates, this poem apparently is set in the nineteenth century. Today the man in the parson's story could emulate the "sport of birds" by hang-gliding, which is the nearest approach to using a kite for manned flight. Hang-gliding can be almost as dangerous, however, as the doomed kite adventure of the man in the parson's "improbable" tale.

THE LITERAL MEANING A parson tells his daughters a cautionary tale about a man who tried to fly by climbing on a kite. The man was never seen again, although his coat was found two counties away. The parson's daughters are amused by this half-hour tale, which was meant to teach them a serious lesson. When the wind blows out the candles, and the moon entices the daughters, they flee to their boyfriends. They kiss repeatedly, "as though to escape on a kite."

Teaching Strategies

PROVIDING FOR CULTURAL DIFFERENCES Students from all cultures can relate to this poem about young love ignoring parental objections.

PROVIDING FOR DIFFERENT LEVELS OF ABILITY With some students you may want to go over the vocabulary before reading the poem in class. Make sure that students know the meanings of *parson* (line 2), *port* (line 3), *tittered* (line 7), *improbable* (line 12), and *wrought* (line 14). Encourage more advanced students, or ones especially interested in poetry, to read more of James Merrill's poems.

READING THE POEM Since much of the comic effect of this poem depends on its sound, you will want to read it aloud or have a student read it aloud. As the poem is read, have students listen especially for the internal rhymes, approximate rhymes, and alliteration. (An audiocassette recording accompanies this selection.)

RETEACHING ALTERNATIVES Ask students to write a one-paragraph prose summary, or paraphrase, of the poem. Remind them to concentrate on main points and not to try to include everything.

Responding to the Poem   Text page 1116

Answers to the questions in the Pupil's Edition appear in the Annotated Teacher's Edition.

Writing About the Poem

For help in revising their compositions, refer students to **Grammar, Usage, and Mechanics: A Reference Guide** on text pages 1183–1228 at the back of their books.

A CREATIVE RESPONSE

Taking Another Point of View Questions 5 through 7 prepare students for this writing assignment.

▶ CRITERIA FOR EVALUATING THE ASSIGNMENT The paragraph or poem is from the daughters' point of view and points out the moral of grasping joy (possibly also escape) when one can.

Extending the Poem

Ask students to find a poem in this text or in any standard collection of British or American poetry that expresses the viewpoint of the daughters in the poem. (Possibilities include Robert Herrick's "To the Virgins to Make Much of Time"; Edmund Waller's "Go, Lovely Rose"; and Ralph Waldo Emerson's "Give All to Love.") Have students share their poems, with the class as a whole deciding which poem makes the strongest case for the daughters.

Adrienne Rich

Text page 1117

POWER

Text page 1118

Objectives

1. To respond to a poem about women's power
2. To identify and interpret irony
3. To write an essay analyzing the poem

Introducing the Poem

Metaphor is extremely important in this poem. In fact, the movement of the poem depends on one metaphor (the uncovered bottle) leading into another (Marie Curie, uncovered from the obliterating dimness of history). In the final stanza Marie Curie becomes a metaphor for all famous women, famous women a metaphor for all women.

This powerful poem is written in free verse with very little punctuation. The spacing of the words on the lines and the line breaks create the rhythmical quality and the music of the poem. Although it may look somewhat unstructured, the poem is, on a closer reading, carefully organized and constructed. The last stanza ties in the title and Marie Curie.

BACKGROUND ON THE POEM According to some critics, this is a poem about women as the disregarded faction of society. Adrienne Rich herself, writing in *Blood, Bread, and Poetry,* acknowledges the need to treat women's issues as a serious theme in her poetry:

> Breaking the mental barrier that separated private from public life felt in itself like an enormous surge toward liberation. . . . To write directly and overtly as a woman, out of a woman's body and experience, to take women's existence seriously as theme and source for art, was something I had been hungering to do, needing to do, all my writing life. . . . It placed me nakedly face to face

with my anger; it did indeed imply the breakdown of the world as I had always known it, the end of safety . . . I felt for the first time the closing of the gap between poet and woman.

THE LITERAL MEANING The speaker describes a backhoe's uncovering of a 100-year-old amber bottle that might have contained a medicine. She then says that she was reading that day about Marie Curie, who suffered from and died from radiation sickness caused by the research that led to her crucial discovery of radium. The poem relates Curie's denial of the source of her illness and the irony of her death from her exposure to radium.

Teaching Strategies

PROVIDING FOR CULTURAL DIFFERENCES Depending on their cultural backgrounds, students may have varying degrees of familiarity with women's issues that have been raised in this country since the 1960's. It is important for students to understand the concern among many people in our society—both men and women—that women have historically lacked power.

PROVIDING FOR DIFFERENT LEVELS OF ABILITY To understand this poem, students need to know that unprotected exposure to radioactive materials can be fatal. (Review Hersey's "A Noiseless Flash," text page 1049, and Chernobyl.) Students should also know, as background for reading this poem, that the same elements that caused Marie Curie's death are used to save lives in radiation therapy for cancer and in many diagnostic procedures.

With LEP students, you might want to read the poem aloud, review the literal meaning, and then read the poem aloud a second time. If students are confused by the spacing of words in the poem, read the poem aloud a third time, emphasizing with pauses the many spaces between phrases. Students might also discuss reasons (such as emphasis or anger) that they might pause between words in their own speech.

READING THE POEM   For oral reading, have a different student read each of the first three stanzas and all three students read the last stanza together. Before reading, ask students to notice how the shift in voices parallels the shifts of meaning within the poem. Ask students to describe the effect of joining voices in the final stanza.

RETEACHING ALTERNATIVES   Have students reread the poem and meet in small groups to discuss the writing assignment. Ask them to try to figure out what lines 1–5 have to do with lines 6–17.

Responding to the Poem   Text page 1118

Answers to the questions in the Pupil's Edition appear in the Annotated Teacher's Edition.

Writing About the Poem

For help in revising their compositions, refer students to **Grammar, Usage, and Mechanics: A Reference Guide** on text pages 1183–1228 at the back of their books.

A CRITICAL RESPONSE
Analyzing the Poem   Ask students to identify the discoveries (a hundred-year-old bottle; radium) and to give one major similarity (from the earth) and one major difference (harmless; helpful/dangerous) before they begin to write.

▶ CRITERIA FOR EVALUATING THE ASSIGNMENT   The paper may be as brief as one paragraph, but correctly identifies the two discoveries, states one similarity, and explains an essential difference.

Extending the Poem

You might suggest that students read several other poems from Rich's collections and/or an essay from one of her other books. You may also want to suggest that students read more about the life of Marie Curie.

Sylvia Plath   Text page 1119

SPINSTER   Text page 1120

Objectives

1. To respond to a poem about love and rejection

2. To interpret the poem's symbolism and metaphors

3. To analyze the use of words with multiple meanings

Introducing the Poem

The orderliness of the poem's structure is important in that it mirrors the poem's content. A free-verse poem with five six-line stanzas, the line lengths in each stanza have the same pattern (short, long, short, long, short, shorter). Plath uses nature as a metaphor for the emotions of the young woman. Unlike many poems in which nature is a vision of comfort, the nature imagery here is disturbing and accosting. These feelings are evoked by adjectives and verbs

as well as the harshness of specific sounds. The resulting tone is one of anger, panic, and fear.

Some language may seem dated and therefore unfamiliar to the students, and you may need to clarify the meanings of *spinster* and *suitor*. Discuss with students that even though the word *spinster* is rarely used today, the feelings expressed in the poem are both universal and timeless. Most people have, at one time or another, felt the overwhelming power of emotion and the urge to retreat to a safer, more orderly existence.

BACKGROUND ON THE POEM   Plath has been dismissed by some poets, critics, and readers for being too emotional and too self-absorbed in her writing. Her direct language and exposure of the unpleasant, and her focus on mothering, her role as a wife, and her place as a woman in society have been regarded by some as inappropriate poetic material. Her poems are extremely important, however, for just those reasons—they have helped to extend the realm of "acceptable" subject matter.

THE LITERAL MEANING The poem describes a girl who, while walking with her suitor, is overwhelmed with tumultuous feelings. But she does not experience love as a comfort or a source of excitement; rather, love is a disordering and disturbing influence. The descriptions of riotous nature in spring mirror the girl's distressed psychological state. She longs for the orderliness of winter, retreats to her home, and sets up a barricade against all passion.

Teaching Strategies

PROVIDING FOR CULTURAL DIFFERENCES Encourage students to talk about their ideas about marriage. Does everyone expect to marry? What are their families' views?

PROVIDING FOR DIFFERENT LEVELS OF ABILITY The events in this poem are fairly straightforward, and students should have little trouble understanding that a young woman goes for a walk, becomes disturbed, and retreats to her home. Some students may need help interpreting the metaphors of winter and spring, although they have probably read many poems in which winter represents death or sterility, and spring represents rebirth and fertility. You might tell students that the symbolic meanings are essentially the same in this poem, but that it is winter that the girl finds desirable, rather than spring. Discussion can then focus on why the girl yearns for winter.

READING THE POEM Because Plath's language is so powerful and unusual, with such enormous attention paid to the sound and placement of words, this poem should be read aloud. As it is read, have students look for the nature imagery that reveals the girl's fright.

After a first reading, ask students if they noticed the poem's rhyme scheme (*abcbac*). Because Plath uses approximate rhymes, this subtle pattern of sounds may go undetected. Help students appreciate how carefully crafted free verse can be.

RETEACHING ALTERNATIVES In class discussion, have students paraphrase the poem twice, changing the point of view first to that of the girl and then to that of the suitor. Students can "fill in" details of thought and feeling that can be supplied by the new speaker.

Responding to the Poem   Text page 1121

Answers to the questions in the Pupil's Edition appear in the Annotated Teacher's Edition.

Analyzing Language and Vocabulary

MULTIPLE MEANINGS

1. *Burgeoning* refers both to the spinster's unruly feelings and the new spring growth around her.
2. Her "queenly," mentally disciplined senses are being overwhelmed with "vulgar," common emotions. The young woman feels debased and demeaned; she has become someone to laugh at.

Extending the Poem

Have interested students read some of Plath's poems in the collection *Ariel.* (Some particularly powerful poems are "Lady Lazarus," "Daddy," "Edge," and "Poppies in July.") Students can then compare and contrast these later poems with the earlier "Spinster." How, for instance, does the language differ? What similarities do they find in the ideas expressed in the poems?

Anne Sexton

RIDING THE ELEVATOR INTO THE SKY

Objectives

1. To respond to a poem that begins in fact and ends in fantasy

2. To interpret the images and symbols in the poem

3. To write a description of a painting of the poem's images

4. To write a comparison of two poems

Introducing the Poem

This free-verse poem begins with warnings about elevators and fires that may be interpreted as a warning that it is dangerous to be creative, to stretch oneself beyond one's perceived limits. The rest of the poem is packed with images that are vivid and mysterious. Students' responses to these images may vary widely.

BACKGROUND ON THE POET Anne Sexton discovered her talent for poetry relatively late in life. She was thirty when she attended a graduate seminar in poetry at Boston University in order to study under Robert Lowell, whom she came to regard as her "first real master." In a 1961 essay she wrote that Lowell didn't teach her what she should put into her poetry, but what she should omit. "What he taught me," she said, "was taste."

BACKGROUND ON THE POEM "Riding the Elevator into the Sky" originally appeared in *The New Yorker* in June 1974, four months before Sexton's suicide, and was published again in the collection *The Awful Rowing Toward God* (1975). That volume represented Sexton's best efforts to write poetry in order to find God. Some critics suggest that through her writing, she was instinctively getting ready for her own death.

THE LITERAL MEANING The speaker states dangers associated with reaching certain heights in buildings: firefighters refuse to climb higher than the fifth floor of a burning hotel; the elevator always seeks out the floor of the fire, where the doors open and won't shut. Yet, the speaker says, you must ignore these warnings if you are to climb out of yourself, as she has, but only once has she

gone all the way up. As she climbed, she experienced a variety of images, the last being the stars and a very large key at the six thousandth floor.

Teaching Strategies

PROVIDING FOR CULTURAL DIFFERENCES Everyone who has ever been in an elevator will be able to relate to this poem. The idea of an elevator "taking off" through the top of a building will delight students.

PROVIDING FOR DIFFERENT LEVELS OF ABILITY Most students will understand the warnings in the first part of the poem and be able to interpret the climbing idea in lines 13–14. Once the poem leaves reality behind, students will have to respond with their imaginations, which might be more difficult for those students who are inclined to literal interpretations. You might wish to discuss possible ways of arranging the information in the poem. As the elevator rises, how do the images change?

READING THE POEM For oral reading, you might wish to divide the poem into a number of parts: lines 1, 6, and 11—19 by one reader; lines 2–5 and 7–10 by two others; then each "floor's worth" of images by different students. Encourage them to interpret their parts freely.

RETEACHING ALTERNATIVES Have students reread the poem to choose the two or three visual images they find most striking.

Responding to the Poem

Answers to the questions in the Pupil's Edition appear in the Annotated Teacher's Edition.

Writing About the Poem

For help in revising their compositions, refer students to **Grammar, Usage, and Mechanics: A Reference Guide** on text pages 1183–1228 at the back of their books.

A CREATIVE RESPONSE

1. Describing Images Show students some paintings by Picasso and Dali to help them see what is meant by "nonrealist." Students may wish to describe one image at a time or a combination of images. Encourage students who enjoy painting and drawing to do a visual interpretation of lines 20–35.

▶ CRITERIA FOR EVALUATING THE ASSIGNMENT   The description refers to images in the poem, though the representation of those images is not realistic. The images may be distorted or rigorously geometric and they may be set in a surreal landscape.

A CRITICAL RESPONSE
2. Writing a Comparison   Make "who knows if the moon's," E. E. Cummings's poem, available to all students. You may wish to discuss some of the criteria by which the two poems can be compared.

▶ CRITERIA FOR EVALUATING THE ASSIGNMENT   The comparison cites similarities and differences between the two poems, quoting lines from the poems as needed to make each point.

John Berryman

Text page 1124

WINTER LANDSCAPE

Text page 1125

Objectives

1. To respond to a poem about the timelessness of art

2. To determine implications of words

3. To write a description using the poet's technique

Introducing the Poem

As the text introduction to the poem indicates, "Winter Landscape" has strict iambic rhythm. It is written in five five-line stanzas, all contained in a single sentence. The effect of the single sentence is one of tension that is further enhanced by the juxtapositions of stillness depicted in the actual painting, the movement of the characters in the first two stanzas, and the philosophy expressed in the final three stanzas. This is a poem about ideas as much as it is a poem about the images and characters that are its subject.

Because this poem does not directly speak about contemporary issues, it may seem slightly inaccessible to some students. You may want to emphasize that although the figures in the poem are greatly removed, the feelings conveyed are timeless. Students might relate the poem to their own experience viewing family photo albums or watching old newsreels that happen to capture people in the midst of activities and freeze them in time unknowingly.

BACKGROUND ON THE POEM   This is an early Berryman poem, written in a somewhat traditional form. Berryman's later work illustrates a departure from this traditional mode—vernacular language and provocative style.

You may enjoy reading some of the powerful *Dream Songs* to students to help them develop a fuller understanding of Berryman as a poet.

THE LITERAL MEANING   The speaker describes a famous Brueghel painting of three men returning from a day of hunting. He describes the surroundings—the trees, the burning straw, the snow drifts, the skating rink, the children. He describes men by the church and the appearance of the street. The speaker remarks these men will continue to exist throughout history when their peers have all been dead and lost forever. The speaker also remarks on how—unknown to the three men—they record a scene from a time long past.

Teaching Strategies

PROVIDING FOR CULTURAL DIFFERENCES   If you suggest that students find the images in the painting that Berryman mentions, they should have no problem caused by cultural differences.

PROVIDING FOR DIFFERENT LEVELS OF ABILITY
The last three stanzas may be confusing to some students. It may be helpful for you to stress that Brueghel's painting on text page 1125, which is described in the first two stanzas, is used by the poet in the final three stanzas to express his philosophical views on history and our place within it.

READING THE POEM   The steady iambic rhythm of this poem makes it pleasant to read aloud—for you or a student. Before reading, however, review the punctuation of the poem, pointing out that there is only one period and that the pause at the end of a line is only very slight, with a comma getting a slightly more pronounced pause.

RETEACHING ALTERNATIVES It may be helpful for students to list details that depict a sense of movement in the poem. The scene is frozen in time, yet Berryman's description of the scene through stanzas 1 and 2 is active. From reading these stanzas, the reader might guess that the characters are participating in an actual event witnessed by the poet, not that the poet is describing a painting. Ask students how the sense of ''reality'' affects their reading of the poem. By taking us into the scene, the poet makes the later emphasis on frozen time seem particularly accosting.

Responding to the Poem   Text page 1126

Answers to the questions in the Pupil's Edition appear in the Annotated Teacher's Edition.

Writing About the Poem

For help in revising their compositions, refer students to **Grammar, Usage, and Mechanics: A Reference Guide** on text pages 1183–1228 at the back of their books.

A CREATIVE RESPONSE
Imitating the Poet's Technique Give students the choice of looking for another painting that especially interests them or of continuing with Brueghel's winter landscape. Note that the assignment has two parts—what the student believes the original scene was like, and what will ''never happen'' in the painting.

▶ CRITERIA FOR EVALUATING THE ASSIGNMENT The poem or essay is clearly based on a specific painting, describes what the student believes the original scene was like, and describes what will ''never happen'' in the painting. Call on volunteers to share their poems. If they've written about a different painting, have students look at the reproduction of the paintings as readers read their poems aloud.

James Wright   Text page 1127

A BLESSING   Text page 1129

Objectives

1. To respond to a poem about a moment of intense joy

2. To identify the uses of anthropomorphism

3. To identify a metamorphosis

4. To write an essay comparing the poem with Emerson's *Nature*

Introducing the Poem

This beautiful lyric is written in clear and direct language. Various literary techniques create the gentleness, or softness, of the poem: assonance (*highway, twilight, eyes; munching, young, tufts*); alliteration (*body, break, blossom*); and rhymes. Similes (lines 11 and 21) enhance the mood.

BACKGROUND ON THE POEM ''A Blessing'' is one of Wright's most anthologized poems, and justly so, for the poem is representative of Wright on a profound level.

Many of Wright's poems carry a deep sense of human tragedy and vulnerability, yet these poems are never ugly. Instead, they exude enormous beauty and pathos, and there is often a sense of transcendence similar to the transcendence at the end of this poem.

THE LITERAL MEANING The speaker and a friend stop off the highway to visit two Indian ponies in a pasture in Minnesota. The speaker and his friend step into the pasture, where the ponies are pleased to have company. The ponies begin to feed, and the speaker relates his desire to hold one when she walks over to him. The speaker describes the pony's appearance and caresses her ear. He realizes suddenly that he feels an intense joy.

Teaching Strategies

PROVIDING FOR CULTURAL DIFFERENCES Urban students unfamiliar with the rural areas may not immediately relate to the scene that Wright carefully describes. You may want to describe to these students how the highways in areas such as Minnesota can be empty for mile upon mile. Students who are familiar with such sparsely populated countryside can describe its appearance at twilight during the spring.

PROVIDING FOR DIFFERENT LEVELS OF ABILITY
The poem is easy to understand and should be accessible to all students. Ask students who might have trouble visualizing the scene to describe exactly what they see in Wright's description. What is the twilight like? Describe the ponies—their eyes, their markings, their movements. How do the ponies behave together? Where is the speaker standing? What does he do?

READING THE POEM
Students who might otherwise be put off by the depth of emotion in the poem will probably best respond to an almost matter-of-fact reading. The sound effects and images in the poem will convey the speaker's emotion.

RETEACHING ALTERNATIVES
Have students assume the viewpoint of the speaker and write a journal entry about the encounter with the horses. The entry should describe the scene as well as the thoughts and feelings of the speaker.

Responding to the Poem   Text page 1129

Answers to the questions in the Pupil's Edition appear in the Annotated Teacher's Edition.

Writing About the Poem

For help in revising their compositions, refer students to **Grammar, Usage, and Mechanics: A Reference Guide** on text pages 1183 to 1228 at the back of their books.

A CRITICAL RESPONSE
Comparing Two Writers   Have students jot down brief notes on the major points of the extract from Emerson's *Nature* (text page 191) and Wright's "A Blessing" before they begin to write.

▶ CRITERIA FOR EVALUATING THE ASSIGNMENT   The essay cites details from Emerson's essay and Wright's poem that make the two works similar: for example, exhilaration, loss of egotism, and perfect harmony with nature.

Extending the Poem

Leslie Marmon Silko, a Native American poet and prose writer, corresponded with James Wright from 1978 until his death in 1980. In 1986, a book of their letters, *The Delicacy and Strength of Lace* (Graywolf Press) was published. In it, the two writers tell each other stories; discuss writing, language, and human nature; and talk about their own experiences. You may want to suggest that students read several of these letters. They are extremely beautiful—filled with wisdom, humor, and sensitivity—and are written in direct and unpretentious language that will be accessible and inspiring to students.

Louise Erdrich   Text page 1130

INDIAN BOARDING SCHOOL: THE RUNAWAYS   Text page 1131

Objectives

1. To respond to the poem
2. To analyze diction and imagery
3. To write an essay explaining a remark by the poet

Introducing the Poem

There is a deep sadness in this poem, but it is presented in a matter-of-fact way, through a steady series of declarative sentences. Occasional similes and metaphors poke up to let the reader know that something is happening beneath the surface, until the last five lines of the poem burst forth with images. The poem is written in blank verse.

BACKGROUND ON THE POEM   The text introduction provides helpful information about the Indian boarding schools. Of course, there are many more focuses working on the writer of this poem. Those schools are just one aspect of a historical concern of contemporary Native Americans—their dependent relationship with whites, mediated by the government's Bureau of Indian Affairs. For a better understanding of this relationship, you might wish to read ''Government Agencies,'' Chapter 6 of Vine Deloria's book *Custer Died for Your Sins* (Macmillan, 1969).

THE LITERAL MEANING   The speaker tells how the runaways hop the moving train, attempting to get home, and how they watch the rolling land through cracks in boards. They know that the sheriff is waiting for them at a stop ahead, that his car will take them back to the school. Returned in shame, the runaways wear green dresses as they scrub the sidewalks. They see faint images in the wet cement.

Teaching Strategies

PROVIDING FOR CULTURAL DIFFERENCES   Students should know that the boarding schools were established in the nineteenth century to assimilate Native Americans to the white man's ways. Children as young as four were taken far from their homes and forbidden to speak their native languages. Graduates of these boarding schools tell of feeling like strangers when they returned to their homes. Ask students to talk about how children from different cultural backgrounds become Americanized.

PROVIDING FOR DIFFERENT LEVELS OF ABILITY   Students' understanding of the poem might be enhanced by looking more closely at the mood established in the first stanza. Ask students why a Native American poet might refer to the rails as ''lacerations'' and ''scars.'' Literally speaking, the rails cut across the land, leaving visible wounds in the earth. One might also interpret the words to mean that the railroad inflicted figurative wounds by hastening settlement of the West. The settlers, among other things, killed off the buffalo and thereby destroyed the culture of the Plains Indians.

READING THE POEM   Give students time to read the poem silently. Then invite three students to read aloud one stanza apiece. As students read, the rest of the class should listen to the pleasing sound effects. They might point out examples of alliteration, assonance, and slant internal rhyme (*lost / cross*, line 7; *cold / clothes*, line 11; *midrun / dumb*, lines 12–13) that they may not have noticed when they read the poem silently.

RETEACHING ALTERNATIVES   Some students may wish to illustrate a stanza from the poem or perhaps a single image that is particularly striking to them. They should try to capture the mood of the poem in their illustration.

Responding to the Poem   Text page 1132

Answers to the questions in the Pupil's Edition appear in the Annotated Teacher's Edition.

Writing About the Poem

For help in revising their compositions, refer students to **Grammar, Usage, and Mechanics: A Reference Guide** on text pages 1183 to 1228 at the back of their books.

A CRITICAL RESPONSE
Responding to a Remark by the Poet   This is an easy assignment all students should be able to handle. Elicit a definition of *runaway* in its usual sense before students begin to write.

▶ CRITERIA FOR EVALUATING THE ASSIGNMENT   The essay examines the quotation in the context of the poem and comes to a conclusion about its meaning. Students should note that the speaker in the poem is a runaway and proud of it. Runaways flee from the school, trying to get back home again.

Primary Sources   Text page 1132

THE WELLSPRINGS OF CREATIVITY
In this excerpt from an interview, Erdrich says that it was difficult for her to write about the Chippewa side of her family until she learned not to fight the strong feelings that the writing brought out. She had to learn to let go so that her background or dreams could ''surface on the page.'' After students read this excerpt, you might wish to have them discuss how the poem reflects the spirit of ''letting go.'' Ask students if they have ever written in this way. If they could ''let go'' and let their truest, deepest stories come out, what stories would they tell? Ask everyone to make some notes about a story idea in his or her writer's journal.

Extending the Poem

Bring to class a copy of *Survival This Way* edited by Joseph Bruchac (University of Arizona Press, 1990). Bruchac, a Native American poet, interviews other Native American poets, who discuss their work and comment on one of their poems. Students will enjoy reading the poems and interviews.

Julia Alvarez

HOW I LEARNED TO SWEEP

Objectives

1. To respond to a poem about war
2. To analyze the use of rhyme and meter
3. To write an essay analyzing an image in the poem
4. To write an essay comparing and contrasting the imagery in two poems

Introducing the Poem

The language of the poem is relaxed, like everyday speech, but the meter and rhyme are carefully structured. The poem is written in iambic tetrameter, rhymed couplets (slant rhyme and many variations). You may want to have students look carefully at the poem's structure and its seemingly contrasting content—the chaos and disorder of war. What purpose does this contrast serve?

BACKGROUND ON THE POEM   The poem describes the speaker's first experience sweeping and her introduction to the realities of war. The poem is more than an antiwar poem, however, it is a poem about maturation—about growing up through increasing awareness of life and death. You might ask students how the speaker takes responsibility in the poem. Because this poem incorporates television, home life, and the world—in fact, the terrible world—outside the home, you should get an interesting response.

THE LITERAL MEANING   The speaker's mother asks her to sweep the floor. She begins, and as she sweeps the speaker watches the President talk about the Vietnam War on a TV news program. She sees news clips of helicopters being shot down and men falling from the helicopters through the sky, at which point she sweeps again. She sees a dozen men die and sweeps the floor harder, more thoroughly, as if by cleaning she can remove death from the room. The mother returns, turns off the TV, inspects the room, and admires the cleanliness. The mother doesn't see a sign of death.

Teaching Strategies

PROVIDING FOR CULTURAL DIFFERENCES   Have students recall other selections about the Vietnam War they've read this year (Tim O'Brien's "Speaking of Courage," text page 935; and Michael Herr's "Dispatches," text page 1059). Except for the mention of TV, helicopters, and jungle, the war could be any war, any time.

PROVIDING FOR DIFFERENT LEVELS OF ABILITY   Most students will have little difficulty understanding the literal events of the poem through line 20. LEP and ESL students, however, might have some difficulty with the interweaving of literal and metaphorical meaning that begins in line 21. With these students, you might lift lines 18–25 from the context of the poem and discuss how helicopters are being fired on as they attempt to land in the jungle. Discuss, also, the qualities of a dragonfly that make it an appropriate metaphor for a helicopter.

READING THE POEM   If you have students who are interested in dramatics, you might have a student do a dramatic oral interpretation of the poem.

RETEACHING ALTERNATIVES   Have students paraphrase the poem, substituting the Vietnam War metaphor with a more timely one, such as a horrible automobile accident or a terrorist kidnapping. Students can discuss how the substitution affects the poem.

Responding to the Poem

Answers to the questions in the Pupil's Edition appear in the Annotated Teacher's Edition.

Writing About the Poem

For help in revising their compositions, refer students to **Grammar, Usage, and Mechanics: A Reference Guide** on text pages 1183 to 1228 at the back of their books.

A CRITICAL RESPONSE
1. Analyzing an Image   Questions 4 through 7 should help students interpret the metaphoric meaning of the word *dust*, but opinions will vary as to why Alvarez chose *dust* rather than *dirt* or *grit*.

► Criteria for Evaluating the Assignment   The paragraph or brief essay identifies both the literal dust swept by the girl and the metaphoric dust of death she tries to scrub from her home. The writer offers a reasonable explanation for Alvarez's choice of *dust* rather than *dirt* or *grit*.

2. Comparing Poems   Lead students to recognize the imagery of *cleansing*. They should have no difficulty rec-

ognizing that Ginsberg's imagery comes from industry and technology while Alvarez's comes from war.

► Criteria for Evaluating the Assignment   The essay compares the Ginsberg and Alvarez poems, citing their similar use of images of cleansing; and contrasts them, citing the different aspects of modern life they tackle.

Allen Ginsberg

Text page 1134

HOMEWORK

Text page 1135

Objectives

1. To respond to a poem with an extended metaphor
2. To characterize the tone of the poem
3. To interpret the poem's title and main idea
4. To write a poem imitating the writer's technique
5. To write an essay evaluating the poem

Introducing the Poem

Although your students are well acquainted with metaphor by now, you may want to emphasize it again with this poem. Extended metaphors that comprise a whole poem are not uncommon, especially in short poems such as Emily Dickinson's or Edgar Lee Masters's. Even so, the one in Ginsberg's poem is striking enough to warrant students' attention. Nearly every laundry term imaginable appears in it.

While most students will favor environmental protection in theory, and will agree that nations ought to act honorably in international relations, some are almost sure to feel that Ginsberg's indictment of the current situation is overdrawn. It is probably best not to argue the point one way or the other, but simply to deal with this free-verse poem as a personal statement of what the poet thinks needs "cleaning."

Background on the Poem   To appreciate this poem fully, students need at least a passing acquaintance with environmental issues and international politics. Most

students should have some knowledge of these matters, since many of the poet's specifics are the continuing background items mentioned in the daily news. Among the lesser-known ones, perhaps, are Rocky Flats and Los Alamos—nuclear waste sites in the Southwest; Cesium-Love Canal—industrial pollution near Buffalo, New York; Neckar—polluted river in Germany.

The Literal Meaning   The speaker says that if he were doing his laundry, he would wash Iran and the United States, clean up Africa, the Amazon River, the Caribbean, and the Gulf of Mexico. He would get the smog off the North Pole, the oil off the Alaskan pipelines, the chemicals out of Love Canal. He would clean the acid rain off the Parthenon and the Sphinx, drain the sludge from the Mediterranean, put the blue back in the sky over the Rhine, and whiten the clouds. He would clean various rivers and get the pollutants out of Lake Erie. He would wash the blood and Agent Orange out of Asia, put Russia and China in the wringer, and squeeze the "tattletail Gray" out of some Central American police states supported by the U.S. Finally, he would put the planet in the drier and let it sit for twenty minutes, or indefinitely, until it comes out clean.

Teaching Strategies

Providing for Cultural Differences   Students who have come to America recently from other nations will need help interpreting the issues Ginsberg alludes to with place names. Let a committee of "experts" explain the issues and identify each place name before students begin reading.

PROVIDING FOR DIFFERENT LEVELS OF ABILITY

This is a poem that will be most effective for students with the greatest general knowledge. More advanced students should need little help with most of the references. LEP/ESL students on the other hand, will probably see few familiar names and ideas. Although it may take something away from the poem, you may want to go over the geographical and environmental references one by one.

READING THE POEM   The headnote to the poem suggests that students think of the poem as a series of exaggerated cartoons. As they read, ask students to think how they might sketch such cartoons, possibly having them do so after reading.

RETEACHING ALTERNATIVES   The Responding questions do not ask specifically for students to identify all the words and phrases that connote laundry. Try having students conduct a laundry-word search, going through the poem word by word in class, identifying (and putting on the chalkboard) every word and phrase commonly associated with laundry. This exercise will not only demand a slow, thoughtful rereading of the poem, but it will also show students graphically how well the poet has sustained the laundry metaphor. (*Blueing* in line 7 is a blue liquid or powder used as a whitener.)

A CREATIVE RESPONSE

1. Imitating the Writer's Technique   Elicit from the students additional things needing "washing" not listed by Ginsberg—perhaps local eyesores or issues in current headlines. Call attention to key elements of Ginsberg's technique: use of long lines, proper names, strong verbs, ampersands (&) for the word *and*.

▶ CRITERIA FOR EVALUATING THE ASSIGNMENT   The poem begins with the line "If I were doing my laundry, I'd wash . . ."; lists several "things" the student would wash; uses strong verbs, proper names, and ampersands.

A CRITICAL RESPONSE

2. Evaluating the Poem   Ginsberg's repetition of verbs and occasional rhymes ("Rub a dub dub") are easy to spot, but you may wish to suggest that students also review The Elements of Literature: Free Verse, page 333, which deals with imagery and such types of repetition as alliteration and assonance.

▶ CRITERIA FOR EVALUATING THE ASSIGNMENT   The essay cites examples of Ginsberg's repeated verbs, alliteration ("*c*lean the oily *C*arib"), assonance (dr*ai*n/Mediterr*a*nean/b*a*sin/m*a*ke in line 6), figurative language ("Flush that . . . Cesium out"), and rhythmic cadence.

Responding to the Poem   Text page 1135

Answers to the questions in the Pupil's Edition appear in the Annotated Teacher's Edition.

Writing About the Poem

For help in revising their compositions, refer students to **Grammar, Usage, and Mechanics: A Reference Guide** on text pages 1183–1228 at the back of their books.

Extending the Poem

You might have a number of volunteers do library research on the poets of the "Beat" generation, beginning with Allen Ginsberg, Lawrence Ferlinghetti, and Kenneth Rexroth. Have students do mini-oral reports on the approximate dates of the movement, the main ideas underlying it, the principal poets involved (in addition to the three named), and the reasons for its decline and relative insignificance today.

EXERCISES IN CRITICAL THINKING AND WRITING   Text page 1137

EVALUATING A POEM

This assignment asks students to evaluate John Malcolm Brinnin's "That Gull" or Simon J. Ortiz's "Washyuma Motor Hotel." The key term *evaluate* is explained under Background. Read and discuss both poems with the class. Consider also the model notes based on Ginsberg's "Homework" in the Prewriting section (text page 1138). Stress the fact that the guide questions demand *judgments* about the poem, and that each judgment must be backed up by citations from the poem. Another set of guidelines offers directions for setting up the final essay. You may wish to let students work either as individuals or in groups once they have chosen the poem to evaluate.

► CRITERIA FOR EVALUATING THE ASSIGNMENT The essay contains a thesis statement which expresses an overall evaluation of the poem. The rest of the essay supports that thesis statement strongly, presenting the most important point either first or last. All judgments made are supported by citations of word choice, images, figures of speech, or sound effects, with the line number for each citation included. The essay correctly observes the conventions (grammar, spelling, punctuation, capitalization) of written standard English.

Further Reading

Works listed are suitable for both students and teachers unless the annotation ends with the note [Teachers].

Brooks, Gwendolyn. *Selected Poems* (Harper, 1982). A selection from Brooks's many volumes.

Carruth, Hayden, ed. *The Voice That Is Great Within Us* (Bantam, 1970). An excellent anthology of modern and contemporary American poetry.

Cook, Bruce. *The Beat Generation* (Scribner's, 1971). An examination of the era of the ''beat'' poets. [Teachers]

Dickey, James. *Babel to Byzantium, Poets & Poetry Now* (Farrar, Straus, 1968). An American poet's impressions and analyses of his contemporary poets.

Ellman, Richard, and Robert O'Clair, eds. *The Norton Anthology of Modern Poetry* (Norton, 1973). An anthology of British and American poetry of the twentieth century.

Jarrell, Randall. *Poetry and the Age* (Ecco Press, 1979). A readable introduction to contemporary American poetry by one of America's most accomplished poets.

Kramer, Jane. *Allen Ginsberg in America* (Random House, 1969). An intensive look into the ''beat poets'' era. [Teachers]

Lowell, Robert. *Selected Poems* (Farrar, Straus & Giroux, 1977). Lowell's choices of his best poems from his life's work, selected the year before his death.

Malkoff, Karl. *Crowell's Handbook of Contemporary American Poetry* (Crowell, 1973). An overview and analysis of the poetic schools, theories, and poets since World War II. [Teachers]

Perkins, David. *A History of Modern Poetry,* (Harvard University Press, 1987). Criticism and analysis of major modern poets. Part Three, ''Postmodernism,'' has chapters on Roethke, Bishop, Lowell, Jarrell, Platt, Sexton, Merrill, and others.

Phillips, J. J., and Ishmael Reed, Gundars Strads, and Shawn Wong. *The Before Columbus Foundation Poetry Anthology* (Norton, 1992). A big anthology of contemporary poetry by multicultural poets, selected from American Book Awards (1980–1990).

Plath, Sylvia, *The Colossus and Other Poems* (Random House, 1968) and *Ariel* (Harper, 1981). Collections of Plath's early poems.

Sexton, Anne. *No Evil Star* (University of Michigan Press, 1985). Selected essays, interviews, and prose.

Wilbur, Richard. *The Poems of Richard Wilbur* (Harcourt Brace, 1963). Wilbur's choice of his best poems.

Part Two

RESEARCH
AND
REFERENCE
MATERIALS

BIBLIOGRAPHY

Works listed are suitable for both students and teachers, unless the annotation ends with the note [Teachers]. You will find the following general works helpful for more than one unit. An annotated bibliography of works for students and teachers also appears at the end of each unit in Part One of these Teaching Notes.

Contemporary Authors and its companion series, *Contemporary Literary Criticism* (Gale Research Company) Multi-volume, frequently updated source of information on current writers.

Dictionary of American Biography (Scribner's, 1927–1977) Ten volumes plus index and supplemental volumes added periodically. [Teachers]

Gottesman, Ronald, et al., *The Norton Anthology of American Literature,* First ed. (W. W. Norton, 1979) Two-volume, compendious anthology with good introductions on authors' lives.

Hart, James D., ed., *The Oxford Companion to American Literature,* Fifth ed. (Oxford University Press, 1983) Entries arranged alphabetically by author, title, or (sometimes) major characters.

Mainiero, Lina, and Langdon Lynne Faust, eds., *American Women Writers* (Frederick Ungar, 1981) Readable, informative two- to three-page articles on women writers from Colonial times through the 1970's.

Parrington, Vernon L., *Main Currents in American Thought: An Interpretation of American Literature from the Beginnings to 1920* (Harcourt Brace Jovanovich, 1927–1930, 1955) Still a valuable resource on earlier American literature. [Teachers]

Spiller, Robert, et al., *Literary History of the United States,* Fourth ed. (Macmillan, 1974) Substantial historical and critical reviews. [Teachers]

Urdang, Laurence, ed., *The Timetables of American History* (Simon & Shuster, 1981) Chronological, columnar entries from the year 1000 to 1980, paralleling events in literature and the arts in America and elsewhere with events in politics, technology, etc.

Integrating composition with the study of literature produces numerous benefits for both students and teachers. To write about a literary work, students must read it closely and formulate their thoughts clearly. By doing so, they gain a deeper understanding of what they have read and of how it applies to their own lives and values. At the same time, they practice essential critical thinking and composition skills as they use the basic aims and modes of writing: narration, description, persuasion, and, primarily, exposition. Exposition is the form students will use most frequently throughout their lives.

Having students write about their reading gives you advantages as well. When all students write on the same topic, you can evaluate their essays more easily, and when they write on different topics, their common knowledge of the literary work makes collaborative writing, evaluating, and revising especially fruitful. Students' written work can also alert you to individual problems in comprehension and sometimes, with more challenging works, to a general need for reteaching. If many essays show a similar confusion, you will know what needs clarifying.

Draw students' attention to the **Writing About Literature** section (text page 1148) early in the term. Explain that it provides strategies for answering the text's essay questions and for choosing and writing about their own topics for essays on literary works. Throughout the year, remind students to refer to this section when they are writing or preparing for an essay test.

You may want to devote one or two lessons to teaching this section. This is a good time to explain whether you will regularly set aside class time for writing, how often you will give timed essay tests, and how you will grade students' papers.

Writing Answers to Essay Questions

You probably cannot overemphasize to students the importance of understanding exactly what an essay question asks. What thinking tasks are required? What specifics of the literary work are to be dealt with? What kind of support, and how much, is asked for? Suggest that students reread a question more than once as they work, to make sure they are following all of the directions.

In discussing the key verbs listed in the text, whenever possible use examples from selections the class has already read.

As a further illustration of *analyze,* for example, you could ask students how they would proceed to analyze suspense in "Rappaccini's Daughter." As they answer, emphasize that they are *isolating* elements (foreshadowing, details that create ambiguity or doubt, vivid descriptions of physical and emotional states). In other words, they are "taking apart" the suspense in order to understand how it works to hook our emotions.

When you discuss *compare* and *contrast,* remind students of the two methods for organizing this type of paragraph or essay. In block organization, students write about all the features of one work (or element) and then the other. When they use point-by-point organization, they alternate between the two works or elements as they cover each feature of comparison or contrast. Be sure to emphasize that a direction to compare may mean to look for both similarities and differences. Suggest that students check with you when they are not sure whether *compare* means *compare and contrast* in a particular question.

Few students are likely to misinterpret a direction to *describe.* However, you might spend a few minutes reviewing spatial order as a method for organizing details in description. Also emphasize the importance of using precise words and a variety of sensory details.

Students may have difficulty with a question that requires them to *discuss.* Explain that even though *discuss* allows a broader response than some other key verbs, it does not permit superficiality or vagueness. Suggest that *examine* is a good synonym for *discuss* in an essay question, and also point out that in order to discuss, one must almost always first analyze.

When students *evaluate,* they are judging how well a literary element or technique "works"—how effectively it creates a desired effect. Emphasize that evaluation is not merely an expression of personal preference: It is a test against criteria, or standards. For evaluation questions, suggest that students first clarify the criteria they will use to judge a work. (For example, refer students to the Guidelines for Evaluating a Play, text page 867.) They can then judge how the work fulfills or falls short of those standards, citing evidence from the work to "prove" their evaluations.

For the next verb, *illustrate* (similar verbs are *demonstrate* and *show*), stress that students must always provide examples from the work (details, dialogue, figurative language, etc.) to support their ideas. Without supporting examples, even good ideas appear as mere opinions, lacking force.

Students should see that such support is especially important when a question asks them to *interpret* meaning or significance. Explain that the verb *interpret* implies that no single, or absolute, statement of meaning exists. Students must therefore carefully explain what has led them to their interpretation.

Finally, point out that a direction to *explain your response* allows students a purely personal reaction to a work. But once again, support is required in the form of reasons. Offer an example: The statement "Eudora Welty's 'A Worn Path' is the best story in the book" is acceptable—but not by itself; the student must tell why he or she thinks so.

Be sure students see that a question may contain or imply more than one key verb. For example, in *discussing* the use of irony in Jamaica Kincaid's "A Small Place" (text page 1065), a student might use both *illustration* and *description* to develop the essay's thesis. In every question, however, one key verb is usually emphasized.

The next step, item 2, is crucial for students. Stress that students write a brief, direct, and specific thesis statement. You could ask students to rephrase actual essay questions from the text as thesis statements. Then note that in gathering supporting ideas and evidence, students usually can draw from class discussion of a selection. In fact, class work on the Analyzing the Story questions can be thought of as prewriting. Explain that active participation in discussing these questions and note-taking will help students think of ideas and data for later writing.

In discussing items 3 and 4, be sure students see that an essay's main ideas will come from the information gathered to support the thesis statement. Emphasize that each paragraph should contain a single idea, supported by evidence, and suggest that students draft a thesis statement and a topic sentence for each paragraph before writing the complete answer. The final paragraph should bring the essay to a logical conclusion.

Emphasize that thinking, note-taking, and organizing are essential no matter what form the rough outline takes. It is not time wasted, *especially* when time is limited. If students begin writing without planning, their essays will tend to be incomplete and disorganized. Emphasize that, in timed writing, students must set a schedule for themselves, allowing time for all major stages of the writing process: prewriting, writing, evaluating and revising, and proofreading. (On occasions that seem to warrant it, you may want to consider allowing students who run out of time to turn in their prewriting notes along with their papers. The notes may demonstrate that a student understood the question and had planned a sound answer but simply did not have time to execute it.)

Writing and Revising a Research Paper

Students should learn to choose a limited topic narrow enough to cover in detail in a fairly brief essay. If they are afraid they won't find enough to say about a narrow topic, assure them that developing a limited idea is actually easier than thoroughly supporting a broad generalization. Suggest that they find limited topics to write about by asking themselves further questions about information discussed

in class. They might look at *why* a character changed in attitude, *which* conflict or conflicts revealed a major theme, or *how* word choice set a particular tone.

To write a research paper, students will have to use the library to find information from biographies about the author or from letters or essays by the author. They should also try to find books, essays, or articles that offer critical comments on the author and on the particular work they are writing about. Go over the second prewriting step in class and emphasize the importance of taking notes and keeping track of sources. Students will need this information when they document the source of a quotation and prepare a bibliography.

Go over each of the remaining prewriting steps with the students, illustrating how the wording of their thesis statement will control, or direct, the subsequent steps. Remind students to write an informal plan or outline.

Emphasize that students should write their first drafts by working steadily through to the end, referring as needed to their outlines and notes. Warn them against overusing direct quotations to pad the body of an essay. Students should get in the habit of asking themselves whether the precise wording of the quotation is important to their point or whether a shorter reference or paraphrase will suffice.

When you discuss revision, note that this final step is tied to evaluation. Students must first read a draft to evaluate its strengths and weaknesses; then they can make the changes—adding, deleting, replacing, or reordering words and phrases—that will improve the draft. Suggest that students go through their drafts once for content and organization, a second time for style (wordiness, monotonous sentence structure, etc.), and a third time for mechanical errors (spelling, punctuation, etc.). Unless students make corrections directly to the text on a word processor screen, learning the proofreader's symbols (text pages 1149–1150) can streamline this part of the process. Encourage the use of peer evaluation. As students revise their writing, refer them to **Grammar, Usage, and Mechanics: A Reference Guide** on pages 1183–1228 of their texts.

You might guide the class through the model essay (text pages 1150–1152) twice to focus attention on different aspects. First have students concentrate on content and organization, using the sidenotes that highlight development of the thesis. The second time, they can focus on the writer's revisions. Ask students why they think the changes were made and how each one improves the essay.

Documenting Sources

Read and discuss in class each section of Documenting Sources (text page 1152). For many students, this will be a useful review of information they've already used in previous research papers. For others, however, this may be new information, and LEP students may feel intimidated and overwhelmed. Give additional examples and some practice, and be very clear about the style of documenting sources you expect students to use. You may also want to make available a reference containing several examples of citations, whether a published style book, your own information sheet, or the students' composition and grammar text. Students could also use good essays from your previous classes as models of correct documentation.

Model Student Essays

The following papers were written by eleventh-grade students in response to three Writing About the [Selection] assignments and to one of the **Exercises in Critical Thinking and Writing** sections in *Elements of Literature: Fifth Course*. They are included here as samples of the writing you can expect from eleventh graders using the text.

ASSIGNMENT: WRITING A RESPONSE

On "Self-Reliance"

Text page 195

Often I find the ideas in nineteenth-century literary works to be outdated: they no longer seem to pertain to the world as we know it today. The ideas of one writer, however--Ralph Waldo Emerson--, do not fit into this category. In spite of having been born almost two hundred years ago, Emerson wrote pieces that can help us guide our lives in today's rapidly changing society. "Self-Reliance" is one such piece.

Emerson's main ideas in "Self-Reliance" revolve around individualism, the principle of independent thought or action, or as Emerson wrote, "whoso would be a man must be a nonconformist." This is valuable advice that can be applied in many contemporary situations. When dealing with school cliques, for example, these words are especially meaningful, since cliques are essentially made up of people who seem to feel a need to conform. In an effort to be accepted, members act, talk, and dress like others in the group. If a certain designer's blue jeans are the order of the day, then every member of the clique wears those jeans. If studying is "out," members would rather fail classes than be found with a book. Emerson felt that people are the best that they can be if they are themselves, and most teenagers who are "clique-concerned" would, in moments of honest reflection, admit that he is correct.

Another basic idea Emerson expressed in "Self-Reliance" that is still relevant today is that the way to succeed is for people to try their very best at whatever they do: "A man is relieved and gay when he has put his heart into his work and done his best; but what he has said or done otherwise shall give him no peace." This statement still stands true today, as the student who has put in hours of work to pass a difficult subject or an athlete who, after years of rigorous training, stands to hear the "Star-Spangled Banner" and receive an Olympic medal can attest.

In writing "Self-Reliance," Emerson did not, of course, have in mind school cliques or Olympic medals. His advice, however, still fits easily into today's society, and may, indeed, be a hook on which to hang our future hopes.

--Lyn Rutledge
Mrs. Barbara Freiberg, Teacher
University Laboratory School
Baton Rouge, LA

ASSIGNMENT: ANALYZING POINT OF VIEW (question 7)
Magic and Mystery
Text page 438

"An Occurrence at Owl Creek Bridge" is a captivating story written by Ambrose Bierce, a genius of unique, haunting fiction and a man deeply influenced by his own war experiences. In the story Bierce makes use of many literary tools, including evocative imagery and dramatic irony, but the one tool that Bierce uses most effectively is point of view.

"An Occurrence at Owl Creek Bridge" begins and ends with third-person, limited omniscient narration. With such narration, the narrator, who is not in the story, enters the mind of one character and focuses on his or her actions and thoughts. Thus, we are taken, in a limited way, into Peyton Farquhar's mind as he stands on the bridge about to be hanged and as the hanging takes place. Closer to Farquhar at this point, through first-person narration, or further away, through objective narration, and the dream vs. reality motif would have been destroyed. Only in the second section, when background information on Farquhar becomes important, does narration appropriately shift to third-person objective.

A crucial aspect of third-person narration is, of course, the withholding of certain information, with the result that the reader must constantly make inferences. Some important inferences in "Occurrence" deal with the war that is being fought and what Farquhar has done or tried to do to be dealt such a fate. For example, the narrator never states directly that the story takes place during the Civil War. Clues, such as the fact that Peyton Farquhar owns a plantation and that a Federal scout pretends to be a Southern soldier, enable the reader to make the inference. Another inference that the reader must make is what Farquhar did to get himself into such a predicament. From the text we draw the conclusion that Farquhar followed up on the scout's information and tried to burn down the bridge. Unfortunately, it was a trap and Farquhar was caught.

All of these inferences lead to the climax of the story. Here, once again, the narrator withholds information, this time until the very last moment. In a scene painted with vivid and realistic details, we see the exhausted Farquhar stagger toward his wife, his arms outstretched, reached to embrace her. It is with a jolt that we realize, for the last time, the effectiveness of our third-person, limited narrator. What we have not known until this moment is that Farquhar has died. His body swings from the railroad bridge.

--Rob Armstrong
Barbara Freiberg, Teacher
University Laboratory School
Baton Rouge, LA

ASSIGNMENT: WRITING A BRIEF ESSAY
Countee Cullen's "Only the Polished Skeleton"
Text page 703

What is the one idea that plagues a human being's deceitful life? This question is answered in Countee Cullen's "Only the Polished Skeleton," through the poet's description of three parts of the human body.

The first description is of the flesh, which is a machine fueled by deceit. The second part of the body described is the brain: the brain is trying to deceive itself into thinking it is immortal. The mind tries to "beat off the onslaughts of the dust." The final part of the human focused on is a quiet, polished skeleton. The skeleton is contemplating from the grave the life it once had.

In this manner, Cullen concludes that only the dead realize how humans waste their lives hating others. Alive, humans do not understand because their minds deceive them into thinking they are immortal and thus have time to waste in hating others. The first stanza, however, rationalizes this behavior, explaining that human lives are fueled by this deceit and hatefulness toward others. It therefore suggests that humans would not be happy knowing of impending death.

Even with this rationalization, the final attitude presented to the reader is one of almost helpless disgust for the human race. Humans live under the shadow of hypocrisy, deceiving themselves and wasting their lives with anger and hatred. The only one who realizes this ironic situation is the quiet, "polished" skeleton in the grave.

--Holly Bartels

Mr. Steve Delacroix, Teacher

University Laboratory School

Baton Rouge, LA

ASSIGNMENT: ANALYZING A CHARACTER

Leon Pugh: Someone I Have Known

Text page 952

Leon Pugh in James Alan McPherson's "Why I Like Country Music" is a character that everyone has met at one time or another. He is the brash, outspoken leader type who everyone else resents but tries to imitate. Possessing the poise and social grace that others only dream about, Leon gets what he wants. As he waits on the school bus in the afternoon, he loudly exclaims "Move off! Get away! This here seat is reserved for the girl from Brooklyn, New York." Of course, the other boys just sit, watching as their goddess, Gweneth Lawson, is taken in by Leon's charm. Everything about Leon, indeed, reflects his considerable flair. He is a "dancing fool," strutting proudly while the other males are awkwardly tumbling "over their own feet." When the big dance day comes, Leon's sharp outfit captures "the attention of all eyes." He proudly exclaims, "My daddy says it pays to look good no matter what you put on."

Leon is the classic romantic adversary. He is everything that everyone else wants to be. The catch, of course, is that he loses Gweneth (for one dance, anyway) to the narrator in the end. Presumably, Leon will wake up the morning after the dance and attack the new day just as vigorously as always, and in the end he will truly win Gweneth. When one reads the story, he or she may find it hard not to substitute some peer's name for Leon's. Leon is a very believable character. I know. I've met him before.

--Matthew Tomlinson

Mr. Frank Militano, Teacher

Jefferson Township High School

Oak Ridge, NJ

ASSESSING STUDENTS' MASTERY OF SUBJECT MATTER AND CONCEPTS

Students' writing is an excellent measure of their understanding of literary works and concepts. Whether writing compositions or answers to essay questions, students must organize and apply the knowledge they have acquired through reading, note-taking, and class discussion. They must demonstrate their understanding of particular selections as well as their understanding of literary genres and techniques.

With the aids in these Teaching Notes, you can plan your evaluation strategies carefully and reduce the time needed for grading or reviewing papers. For example, for each writing assignment in the text, the lesson plan in these Teaching Notes provides Criteria for Evaluating the Assignment, two or three major points to guide your assessment of students' work. In addition, the model responses and sample essays can serve as assessment aids. Finally, you can make use of the following evaluation methods.

Holistic Scoring

For some writing assignments, you may want to use holistic scoring, a method in which you read each paper quickly and respond to it as a whole, making no comments or corrections. With a carefully prepared scoring guide, holistic evaluation is an efficient and consistent means of judging students' work. Even though holistic evaluation does not provide students with your personal comments, it is not superficial or vague: Students receive an evaluation of key features of their papers. Two methods of holistic evaluation are the analytic scale and the general impression scale.

ANALYTIC SCALES   Using an analytic scale, you rank each of several features of a piece of writing from high to low. The following scale lists features common to all writing and uses a numerical ranking.

ANALYTIC SCALE				
	Low	Middle	High	
Ideas	2	4 6 8	10	
Organization	2	4 6 8	10	
Word choice	1	2 3 4	5	
Tone	1	2 3 4	5	_____
Usage, grammar	1	2 3 4	5	
Punctuation, capitalization	1	2 3 4	5	
Spelling	1	2 3 4	5	
Legibility	1	2 3 4	5	_____
			Total	_____

Adapted from Paul B. Diederich, *Measuring Growth in Writing* (Urbana, IL: NCTE, 1974).

In other analytic scales, the features are specific to a particular form of writing (description, narration, etc.). Such scales can be made specific for many different assignments.

The scales that follow cover four common writing tasks, each applied to a different genre. These examples use a yes-no scale.

FICTION : SUMMARIZING A PLOT ANALYTIC SCALE

	Yes	No
The story's title and author are cited.		
The summary includes the story's most important events.		
The events are summarized in the order in which they occur.		
The summary explains how one event causes or leads to another.		
The setting is briefly described.		
Extraneous details are omitted.		
The student primarily uses his or her own words.		
Word choice is precise and appropriate.		
Sentence structure is varied.		
Grammar, usage, and mechanics errors do not interfere with reading.		

POETRY : RESPONDING TO A POEM ANALYTIC SCALE

	Yes	No
The poem's title, author, and subject are stated.		
The student describes his or her general response to the poem.		
At least two details about the poem's content are used to explain the response.		
At least two details about the poem's construction are used to explain the response.		
Quotations from the poem are exact and are cited correctly.		
A concluding or summary statement ends the composition.		
Word choice is precise and appropriate.		
Sentence structure is varied.		
Grammar, usage, and mechanics errors do not interfere with reading.		

NONFICTION : ANALYZING A REPORT ANALYTIC SCALE

	Yes	No
The report's title and author are cited.		
The main idea of the report is stated.		
A sufficient number of the strongest facts supporting the main idea are cited.		
The facts in the report are distinguished from the author's opinions.		
Any appeals to emotion are identified and discussed.		
Significant narrative techniques are identified and discussed.		
Organization is clear and coherent.		
The conclusion summarizes main points of the analysis.		
Word choice is precise and appropriate.		
Sentence structure is varied.		
Grammar, usage, and mechanics errors do not interfere with reading.		

DRAMA : ANALYZING AND EVALUATING A THEME ANALYTIC SCALE

	Yes	No
The play's title and author are cited.		
A clear theme statement is presented.		
The theme statement is supported with at least three examples of action and dialogue.		
The student expresses an evaluation of the theme.		
The student presents at least two reasons for the evaluation, supported by evidence from the play.		
Quotations are exact and are cited correctly.		
The conclusion summarizes or restates the statement of theme and the student's evaluation.		
Word choice is precise and appropriate.		
Sentence structure is varied.		
Grammar, usage, and mechanics errors do not interfere with reading.		

GENERAL IMPRESSION SCALES A general impression scale is also keyed to the form of writing, but the individual features of the paper are not ranked separately.

(Continued on page 335.)

DESCRIPTIVE PARAGRAPH GENERAL IMPRESSION SCALE

Assignment: To write a subjective description of a person, place, or object

4 The topic sentence expresses a main impression of the topic.

Many concrete and sensory details create a vivid picture.

Each sentence supports the main idea in the topic sentence.

The organization is clear. Ideas flow smoothly with effective transitions.

Sentences are varied and the diction is fresh.

Errors in grammar and mechanics are minimal.

3 The topic sentence expresses a main impression of the topic.

Concrete and sensory details are used, but the description could be fuller and more vivid.

The organization is clear. Some transitions could be added or improved.

Sentences are varied and the diction is accurate but unoriginal.

Occasional grammatical and mechanical errors appear.

2 The topic sentence is vague or inexact.

Details are not specific or are insufficient.

The organization is flawed but can be followed.

Few transitions are provided between ideas.

Sentences are correct but often awkward or monotonous, with some inexact wording.

Occasional grammatical and mechanical errors interfere with reading.

1 The topic sentence is missing or does not clearly identify the topic.

Details are not specific and are insufficient to develop the description.

Organization is unclear. Ideas are missing or irrelevant.

Word choice is often inaccurate.

Frequent syntax and mechanical errors interfere with reading.

0 The paragraph does not develop a description.

COMPARISON AND CONTRAST ESSAY GENERAL IMPRESSION SCALE

Assignment: To compare and contrast the themes and tones of two stories

4 The essay addresses both similarities and differences.

The essay insightfully interprets the stories' themes and tones.

Main ideas are supported with appropriate details.

The essay is well organized (a clear thesis statement in the first paragraph, a main supporting idea in each body paragraph, and a concluding paragraph).

Ideas flow smoothly with effective transitions.

The essay contains few errors in grammar and mechanics.

3 The essay addresses both similarities and differences.

The essay interprets the stories' themes and tones thoughtfully.

The essay is well organized.

Main ideas are not adequately supported.

Some of the sentences are awkward or monotonous.

The essay contains occasional errors in grammar and mechanics.

2 The essay does not address (or does not address equally) both similarities and differences.

The essay interprets the stories' themes and tones sketchily.

Much necessary supporting detail is omitted.

In some places ideas are difficult to follow.

Errors in grammar and mechanics occasionally interfere with reading.

1 The essay does not address both similarities and differences.

The essay lacks insight into or misinterprets the stories' themes and tones.

The essay does not support main ideas with sufficient evidence.

The essay is disorganized and lacks clarity of expression.

The essay contains errors in grammar and mechanics that frequently interfere with reading.

0 The essay does not follow the assignment or does not develop its thesis.

(Continued from page 334.)

Instead, the paper as a whole is judged high, average, or low. In this case, developing a scoring guide entails outlining the general characteristics of high-, average-, and low-ranking papers for the assignment. For example, you could use the general impression scale in column 1 on the opposite page to evaluate a descriptive paragraph.

There is no one prescribed format for writing the general characteristics for this type of scale. What is important—whether you use complete sentences, a series of phrases, or even a list of items—is that you cover the key features of the writing assignment and that you address the same features in each ranking. The general impression scale in column 2 on the opposite page is for use in evaluating an essay comparing and contrasting elements in two stories.

When you use a general impression scale, be sure to provide students with your scoring guide before they write so that they know the specific criteria that determine their score. If possible, provide each student with a copy. Students with lower scores should use the guide to identify the errors and weaknesses in their papers, and all students should use the guide when developing similar papers in the future.

Remember that holistic scoring, while allowing you to evaluate many papers rapidly, does not preclude your giving more personal attention to students who need help. For example, you can invite students to consult with you individually when they cannot pinpoint the errors in their papers. You can also ask students to submit their revised papers. The revisions will show you exactly where they need further instruction.

Comments and Corrections

Some papers you will want to mark thoroughly, commenting on students' ideas and writing style and indicating errors. Many teachers prefer to do this in an oral conference; others prefer to write their comments on students' papers. You won't have the time and energy to do this for all assignments, but you should do it for some. Students respond to such personal attention and specific guidance.

Whether you are agreeing or disagreeing, praising or finding fault, your comments show that you are paying attention to students' ideas and that you care about students' skills. Always include some praise or encouragement. Even when a student has written poorly, you can often offer encouragement by referring to real strengths: ''You used some fresh, original words in last week's character sketch. I *know* you have the vocabulary to go beyond the trite expressions in this essay. I'll be looking for your vivid wording in the next assignment.''

Keep in mind that heavy marking of a paper is not a rewriting. Even if you suggest some specific content revisions, students must decide how to make the changes. Even though you isolate errors in grammar, usage, and mechanics, students must correct them. (Don't hesitate, however, to show students occasionally how to rework or correct a passage; students need models when they are acquiring skills.)

Using correction symbols will speed your marking of papers. You may want to distribute a list such as the following one with students' first marked papers. After students have worked with the list, you can ask for questions about particular symbols and writing problems.

	CORRECTION SYMBOLS	
Symbol	**Meaning**	**What to Do**
	CONTENT	
concl	conclusion missing, weak, or unrelated to main idea	Add or rephrase summarizing statement or paragraph.
irr	irrelevant detail	Delete or replace phrase or sentence.
spec	needs to be more specific	Clarify a detail, or add supporting details.
ts	thesis statement or topic sentence missing or not clear	Add or revise thesis statement or topic sentence to express main idea.

Symbol	Meaning	What to Do
ORGANIZATION		
org	organization not clear	Rearrange ideas in a more logical order.
tr	transition between ideas missing or confusing	Add or replace connecting words or phrases.
¶, no ¶	paragraphing problem	Begin new paragraph (¶), or join paragraphs (no ¶).
STYLE		
agr	agreement error	Make a subject and verb, or an antecedent and pronoun, agree in number.
awk	awkward sentence or passage	Rephrase sentence or section.
cap	capitalization error	Add capital, or lower-case letter.
frag	sentence fragment	Add subject or verb, or attach fragment to nearby sentence.
gr	grammatical error	Determine type of error, and correct it.
p	punctuation error	Add, replace, or delete punctuation.
pv	unnecessary shift in point of view	Eliminate shift in person.
ref	pronoun reference error	Clarify reference of a pronoun to its antecedent.
ro	run-on sentence	Correct with needed punctuation and capitals.
sp	misspelled word	Correct spelling.
t	tense error	Correct verb tense.
var	sentences lack variety	Vary structure and length of sentences.
wc	word choice problem	Replace with correct, more exact, or livelier word.

Grading

In grading students' writing about literature, you will want to focus on the quality of their ideas. Without diminishing the importance of mechanics and style, let students know that *what* they have to say is of first importance in their grades: An error-free paper that is either shallow or incomplete should not receive an *A.*

Some teachers use a double grade on papers, for example *B+/C,* to distinguish between content and mechanics. Whatever system you use, explain clearly to students how your marking relates to their grades. Sample papers are especially helpful for this purpose. From previous classes, accumulate a file of marked and graded papers that students may examine and review in class. Include a variety of papers that have earned *A, B, C, D,* and *F* grades on a typical assignment. These papers will illustrate for students exactly what you expect.

Self-Evaluation

Students help both themselves and you by evaluating their own papers. Good writers evaluate automatically, although usually not in writing. Most students, however, skip this essential step altogether. By assigning even brief and informal evaluations, you can show students the importance of evaluation and instill a habit of lasting benefit. You will gain not only improved papers but also insight into the students' ideas about writing. You may uncover misconceptions (a student is more concerned with correct spelling than with organization) and problems in composing (a student is a perfectionist and writes and rewrites an opening sentence). You can then help individual students or plan class sessions on particular aspects of the writing process.

One self-evaluation assignment is to have students rank the papers they are submitting as either high, average, or low and to explain their criteria for the ranking. Stress that you are not grading the evaluations and simply want honest, thoughtful responses to this question: What do you think of your paper and *why*? If you combine this self-evaluation with your own evaluation, students will see how their judgments compare to yours and can use the discrepancies to improve their evaluation skills. You can also use a simple form, such as the following one, for a self-evaluation.

SELF-EVALUATION COMMENTS

Name ——————————————— Date ———————————————

Assignment or Title of Paper ———————————————————————

1. I think one strength of this paper, or one thing that works well, is ———————————

———————————————————————————————————————

2. The weakest aspect of this paper is ———————————————————————

———————————————————————————————————————

3. One problem I faced and was not sure how best to solve was ———————————

———————————————————————————————————————

Students should evaluate and revise the first draft of every paper. Emphasize that no first draft is ever perfect. If students evaluate and revise for themselves—rather than submitting first drafts—they will take a great step toward improved writing and better grades. Students can use the following general checklist to evaluate and then revise their writing about literature. (If you use holistic scoring guides, also alert students that the guides may be reused as evaluation checklists for particular assignments.)

SELF-EVALUATION CHECKLIST FOR WRITING ABOUT LITERATURE	Yes	No
1. Have I followed all of the directions for the assignment?		
2. Have I understood the literary terms and used them correctly?		
3. Have I clearly expressed a main idea in a strong topic sentence or thesis statement?		
4. Have I included enough details from the literary work to support my ideas?		
5. Are all the details accurate and directly related to the main idea?		
6. Does my paper have a clear beginning, middle, and end?		
7. Have I used precise words and avoided clichés and repetitious phrases?		
8. Have I correctly punctuated quotations and dialogue?		
9. Have I checked other punctuation, spelling, and use of capitals?		
10. Have I read the paper aloud to listen for missing words and awkward phrasing?		

Peer Evaluation

When properly prepared for, peer evaluation can be highly rewarding and enjoyable for both writers and evaluators. It can produce new insights about the literary work and about the writing process. Unguided, though, peer evaluation can be ineffective or unpleasant. Irrelevant comments merely confuse, and heavy-handed criticisms wound. What is required is sensitivity, objectivity, and a common understanding of the evaluation criteria.

For successful peer evaluation, provide students with evaluation forms, and demonstrate constructive criticism. First conduct a class evaluation of a paper from a previous class. Explain the writer's assignment, read the paper aloud, and offer samples of the comments you would make. As students enter the discussion, point out off-target comments or negative comments that serve no purpose; help students redirect or rephrase these criticisms. Remind them always to point out a paper's good features: Evaluation identifies both strengths and weaknesses. You may want to go through two or three papers in this way before students work on their own.

At least for initial peer evaluations in small groups, use some type of prepared form. After students hear or read a paper, they can complete the form and then base group discussion on their written responses. Using a form need not limit discussion. Always encourage students to react to each other's comments and to brainstorm solutions for writing problems. After the discussion, the writer can use the completed forms for revising.

Depending on your students' abilities and maturity, you can either use a highly structured checklist or a form that elicits a more general impression. For example, you could adapt the preceding self-evaluation checklist for peer evaluation, providing room for the evaluator to explain every "No" response. A sample of a general impression evaluation form follows.

PEER EVALUATION COMMENTS

Reader ————————————————————— Writer —————————————————————

Assignment or Title of Paper ——————————————————— Date ——————————

1. What I liked best in this paper was ———————————————————————

——

2. The most effective sentence was ——————————————————————————

——

3. Good word choices were ———————————————————————————————

——

4. Ideas that I felt needed clarification or further support were ———————————————

——

5. Other positive comments are ——————————————————————————————

——

6. Other suggestions for revision are —————————————————————————————

——

USING PORTFOLIOS TO EMPOWER STUDENT WRITERS *Winfield Cooper and B. J. Brown*

For the past three years, we have been experimenting with student-writing portfolios, B. J. with her junior-high and Win with his high-school students. What is becoming especially interesting to us is the power of portfolios as teaching tools. Our research has shown us that, for students in an English language-arts classroom, the very act of compiling a portfolio can be a powerful process for many reasons, not least of which is that it helps students see themselves as writers, particularly when it involves many opportunities for self-evaluation and reflection.

The criteria involved in selecting work to include in a portfolio are both internal and external (Linda Rief 1990, "Finding the Value in Evaluation: Self-Assessment in a Middle School Classroom," *Educational Leadership* 47.6 [Mar.]:24–29). We set the external criteria by describing the kinds of writings that students must include; students choose the specific pieces they will include. The items our students include are quite similar because the external criteria were developed collaboratively by teachers at each grade level (7–12) to reflect the goals of the curriculum—

which had also been created collaboratively. Teachers in our district designed a portfolio format that emphasizes a process approach to writing in an integrated language-arts program. At the same time we take into account, on one hand, the implications of a statewide writing assessment that encourages students to become proficient in a variety of types of writing, and, on the other hand, the need for individual teachers to make decisions about how best to implement those goals in their own classrooms.

Our research is based on our work with the table of contents that has evolved in our district. (See the following box.) Each item in the portfolio has important implications for our teaching. We have found that selecting and preparing the various items provide students with many opportunities to reflect on their abilities as writers.

PORTFOLIO TABLE OF CONTENTS

1. **Introduction**

2. **Sample of timed writing**

3. **Different types of writing, one with evidence of process**

4. **Sample(s) of writing to learn**
   Possibilities include but are not limited to: copy change, dialogue, word-weaving, creating a persona, imitation of author's style, transition from author to student voice, dialectical journal, reading log, quickwrite, drawing inferences, note-taking, learning log.

5. **Creative writing sample**

6. **Student-selected best writing with rationale**

7. **Two pieces selected by student and/or teacher**
   Possibilities include but are not limited to: creative writing, special projects, evidence of collaboration, evaluation of oral presentations, evidence of listening, selections from other curricular areas, annotated reading list.

Introduction

In their introductions, students speak to the audience, the readers of their portfolios, by introducing themselves, describing their characteristic writing processes, and summarizing the contents of their portfolios. The introduction comes first in the portfolio but is written after students have assembled the body of their portfolios.

Diana, a twelfth grader, concludes her introduction by writing:

I am proud of the contents of this portfolio. It represents my hardest and best work, and I believe the three papers that get progressively more polished clearly track my progress as a writer.

Students' introductions are fascinating to read since they give insight into how students see themselves as writers. As Roberta J. Herter states (1991, "Writing Portfolios: Alternatives to Testing," *English Journal* 80.1 [Jan.]: 90), "Portfolios involve students in assessing the development of their writing skills by inviting self-reflection and encouraging students to assume control over their writing." In their introductions, students invite us to look at what they can do, not what they can't; at what they have instead of what they haven't.

Sample of Timed Writing

The way the portfolio is set up, students are asked to include at least one example of a timed first-draft writing. While a process approach is at the core of the district writing program, teachers also acknowledge that academic situations frequently require students to formulate, organize, and write their thoughts in limited time periods. Asking students to include one sample of such writing is a way of ensuring that the portfolio reflects that aspect of school writing.

When teachers first decided to include timed writings in the portfolio, we asked students to include two examples of the same type of writing, both completed in a forty-five-minute time period (thus simulating the California direct-writing assessment), one sample from the beginning of the year and the other from the end of the year. The assumption was that since the type of writing called for would be one of those that teachers had agreed to concentrate on at that grade level, the students would have had multiple experiences with that kind of writing during the year. We hoped that the later sample would demonstrate higher achievement than the earlier one.

The timed writings for the portfolio need not be thought of as artifacts that are produced simply for inclusion in the portfolio outside the context of the curriculum. It may be possible, even desirable, to design a timed-writing experience as an integral part of an instructional unit, thus achieving one of the goals of authentic assessment—that assessment be virtually indistinguishable from instruction.

For example, Win incorporated a piece of interpretive writing on John Cheever's short story "Reunion" into a unit on rites of passage. After they had read the story, students wrote their responses within a time limit. Their essays went into their portfolios for future reference. Near the end of the year, Win asked his students to respond to a similar prompt requiring them to read and analyze a short prose passage in the context of a different instructional plan. As part of compiling their final portfolios, students reread both papers and the scoring guide; they wrote comments about the differences they noted in their writing, speculating on what accounted for them and reflecting on the classroom experiences which had influenced the growth. The papers, as well as the self-evaluation and reflection, were included in the end-of-the-year portfolio. Advanced-placement students, who had been working on the kind of writing required for the AP literature exam, generally noted that the two samples showed they had become practiced at writing a focused essay using technical analysis; second-language students were able to point out dramatic evidence of their increased fluency in English; and other students often found that the comparison of the two papers offered concrete proof of their growth as writers.

Different Types of Writing, One with Evidence of Process

The statewide direct-writing test administered to eighth and eleventh graders by the California Assessment Program (CAP) identifies ten different types of writing. In our district, teachers have integrated these CAP writing types into our core literature units. It is from these writing types that we ask students to select three essays, one of which should be a packet including evidence of a complete process: prewriting, planning, writing, revising, editing, and rewriting. In most cases, students have several essays from which to choose their best three. They include their entire writing packet, for one essay of their choice, to show evidence of the writing process.

For example, before reading *Anne Frank: Diary of a Young Girl,* B. J.'s eighth-grade students interviewed someone who had firsthand experience in a war. James, an eighth grader, interviewed his father, who had been a child in London during World War II. His packet included notes from library research on WWII, his interview questions, the tape of his interview, his word-processed rough draft with revisions and corrections inked in, a response sheet completed by a classmate, and the computer printout of his final draft. As his other two choices, James selected an autobiographical incident he had written as a timed-writing sample for the NCTE Promising Young Writers' contest and a speculative essay written in response to "Flowers for Algernon." He chose not to include his short story, a tall tale, or his character analysis of Jeremy Finch in *To Kill a Mockingbird.* In order to make his selections, James had to reflect and evaluate the body of his work.

By showing examples of the whole process, the notion that it is the entire process that contributes to a satisfying finished product is reinforced. Since students include three essays in this section, they are able to show examples of writing for different purposes. These writing samples reflect the curriculum, the teacher's application of it, and the students' choices, making the portfolio inextricably tied to what goes on in the classroom.

Writing to Learn

One of the most valuable lessons that students can learn is that writing is a powerful tool for learning—that writing, far from simply being the product of thinking, can actually shape thinking, a phenomenon that James Britton calls "shaping at the point of utterance" (1982, "Shaping at the Point of Utterance," *Prospect and Retrospect: Selected Essays of James Britton,* Ed. Gordon M. Pradl, Upper Montclair, NJ: Boynton, 143). Through exercises such as double-entry literary journals, classroom quickwrites, conscious imitation of an author's style, and other activities common to a student-centered, integrated language-arts classroom, students come to find out what they know through the act of writing.

Recognizing the importance of this aspect of writing has certain implications for teaching. Teachers can reinforce the value of such writing in several ways: by designing such opportunities so that they build on one another, by providing students with the opportunity to clarify their thinking before discussing a text, by asking students to synthesize in writing their thoughts after discussion, and especially by encouraging students to go back to their "writing to learn" as they draft more formal papers based on ideas developed during their own discovery processes.

We have found that the process of sharing their choices with other students provides a valuable lesson. The reasons students give are varied:

> because I wrote about a really personal connection I noticed between Stephen's experience and my own
>
> because by the time I finished writing the different questions that the poem made me ask, I had already started to answer my own questions
>
> I wrote some questions which I took to my collaborative group and they were the beginning of a really good discussion
>
> this quickwrite was actually the inspiration for the final paper I wrote about the book

Seeing the uses others have made of such writing opportunities is often instructive to students, and it reinforces the importance of such writing more powerfully than our repeated assurances that such activities are good for them.

Creative Writing

We recognize that all writing that is not simple copying is creative, and we want our students to recognize that, too. The term springs from an unfortunate assumption that most academic writing is done according to some rigid formula or must somehow conform to strict guidelines that somehow constrain the writer. According to this thinking, all other writing in which the writer is not constrained is more spontaneous, more creative, more fun.

When we and our colleagues designed the first table of contents and looked at the kind of writing assignments we offered students, we recognized that some of our students' best work did not necessarily fit the other categories in the portfolio. We agreed that by requiring students to choose at least one creative-writing piece for the portfolio, we were implicitly providing more opportunities for students to do such writing.

Often the pieces chosen to fulfill the creative-writing requirement are written in response to a piece of literature or are written as a means of deepening understanding or appreciation of an author's technique or style. Win's students, for example, have chosen to include autobiographical pieces about early childhood written in the style of James Joyce's *Portrait of the Artist as a Young Man,* new chapters for *The Grapes of Wrath,* parodies of the style of Joseph Conrad, satires inspired by Jonathan Swift's "Modest Proposal," and "found poetry" based on *The Good Conscience.*

The creative-writing section might also contain a writing sample that was not written in response to a particular piece of literature or as a specific writing type. Students who write as a pastime can include their personal writing in this section. Poetry is a popular choice.

The creative-writing category reminds us that it is important to allow students the opportunity to write freely, to explore their ideas in their own way, thereby expanding the repertoire that they can present in their portfolios.

Student-Selected Best Writing with a Rationale

Requiring each student to select one piece of writing as a favorite allows the students additional personal choice, thus adding to their authority as writers. The best-writing selection might be something that is included in another category also, or it might be something the student has saved for the special designation of "my best writing."

Students have used their own criteria to evaluate each time they select a piece of writing for their portfolios; however, it is in the rationale that they specifically state their standards and show how the best-writing sample reflects those standards.

Andrea, an eleventh grader, near the end of her first year in this country, wrote:

> I chose the paper I wrote about *Glass Menagerie* because it was the first paper I am able to say in English exactly what I want to say. Even though it took me a lot of hard work to do it these are the ideas that I had in my head and I can say them. Before was frustrating because even with dictionary I knew I could not explain myself. When I finish this paper I know I have made a big step to learn English.

Carmen, an eighth grader, took a firm stance when she wrote her rationale:

I think that my best writing is my autobiographical incident because it's whole and pure. It was not anything I had to make up or lie about. All it says is the truth.

Tanya, an eighth grader, shows her enthusiasm for her best writing by commenting on her process:

> I feel it is my best piece of writing because it was exactly what I wanted to write. I just knew the poem was perfect when I finished. The first sentence of my poem says, "Starvation and misery pluck at my heart." That is the exact way I wanted those words to come out. I could scream, I think my paper is so great.

Brian Johnston says, "Students do not learn writing simply through having many experiences of doing it. To learn to control the medium they must also reflect, conceptualize and experiment" (1987, *Assessing English: Helping Students to Reflect on Their Work,* Milton Keynes, Eng.: Open UP, 105). Selecting their best writing allows students to evaluate their own work while the rationale asks them to internalize their own standards and to support that choice in writing.

Two Pieces Selected by Student and/or Teacher

The vague requirement that the last two items in the portfolio be "two pieces selected by student and/or teacher" is perhaps the most obvious example of how an agreed-upon set of portfolio contents can be flexible enough to allow for diversity. Among the possibilities for these pieces are creative writing, special projects, a collaborative piece, evidence of reflection on collaboration, evaluations of oral presentations, evidence of listening activities, an annotated reading list, or writing for other content areas. A teacher may define the criteria for choosing one or both of these items in order to ensure that the portfolios reflect an important aspect of the curriculum, or the choice of one or more items may be left up to the student so that the portfolio includes what the student believes to be most important.

Since collaboration in both the writing process and in the process of making meaning from a piece of literature is central to the way he teaches English, Win wanted his students' portfolios to reflect the importance of collaboration, so he required them to include in their portfolios an item labeled "evidence of collaboration." During the course of the year, students were frequently asked to reflect on the collaborative process in various ways. For each major paper they wrote a metacognitive piece about their process, including an analysis of how collaborating had influenced the changes in their writing at various stages. Sometimes, to encourage collaboration, they were asked to list all the sources from which they had gotten help.

Occasionally, after engaging in small-group discussions of literature, students would write notes to each other, commenting on what the others in the group had contributed to the discussion. They wrote self-analyses as well. At the end of the first semester and again at the end of the year, students looked over all this evidence, reflected on it, and attempted to synthesize what they had learned about themselves as collaborators and about the collaborative process.

A few examples of insights from their portfolio entries about collaboration serve to illustrate what happens when students are invited to engage in such reflection. Some students observed that collaboration had particularly influenced their understanding of literature:

> I am really grateful for those discussions in which the layers of my confusion are slowly peeled away by my peers. *Ronnie, twelfth grade*

> I like how my classmates can throw out their ideas, and how I can tell them mine, but then I can choose what I think is the "right answer." I also like collaborating because it is like figuring out a puzzle where you have to find the pieces first and later put it together. The most important thing I have learned is that there is no definite right answer, and that my answer does have the potential, if supported, to be correct. I also have learned that I am capable of analyzing literature, that I can figure it out, that I can be right. It is not some process that only English wizards can do. *Donna, twelfth grade*

Others came to understand the role of collaboration in the writing process:

> [A]lso an important skill is knowing when to listen to your own writing intuitions and when to yield to the suggestions of the group. Although there may be a degree of safety in numbers, you have to be wary of losing your voice or original intent under the well-intended, but not always healthy . . . suggestions of the group. *Gary, twelfth grade*

The Finished Product

Assembling their portfolios at the end of the semester or year is a way for students to celebrate their accomplishments. Students agonize over which pieces to select and ask their classmates for advice. As Herter points out, "authority as writers, editors, and audience is validated by their experience with one another's texts" (91). The time students spend organizing portfolios is valuable time to reflect and evaluate. When we allow time for students to assemble their portfolios, they often revise their work and share it informally before it "goes public" in the finished portfolio.

Students can present their portfolios to the class or a small group. B. J. asks students to show their parents the portfolio before presenting it to her. She includes a letter to parents that summarizes what the portfolio represents, and she encourages them to give positive, specific re-

sponses to their children. Sending portfolios home strengthens an important link between teacher, student, and parents.

Once students submit their portfolios, we read the introductions and rationales carefully and page through the rest, which we've seen before as assignments, stopping to read whatever strikes us. We add a final positive comment, then return the portfolios to the students. We continue to experiment with how to incorporate the portfolio into end-of-term grades. Once we have returned the portfolios to students, they are theirs to keep. And why not? They are the creators, the writers.

Portfolios can be a valuable source for summary evaluation by teacher and student; at the end of the year they can provide an accurate measure of what students have accomplished. By the same token, portfolios have potential for formative assessment. When students make tentative selections for portfolios and especially when they compile interim portfolios, evaluate them, and reflect on what they notice, they can reinforce their own learning processes and set goals for future learning. Often, writing about their reflections in such interim portfolios can help them see where they have come from and clarify where they want to go. For example, at the end of the first semester, Bruce, a twelfth grader, wrote:

> This year a combination of techniques has finally allowed me to expand my abilities, which is wonderful. But it also means that I feel like I've started over, and I found that it is like learning how to write again. These techniques have revolved around two areas—expanding my reading capabilities with more original, personal responses in the form of homework, and then, in class sessions involving the gathering of so many different ideas and opinions. With these new concepts of responding to literature, it is impossible that my writing abilities and attitudes wouldn't change.

After he explained how specific papers in his portfolio illustrated various stages in his struggles as a writer, Bruce concluded:

> Even though there are occasional pieces with discouraging results, the fact that I can finally write outside the boundaries of the five-paragraph essay is refreshing enough to keep my full interest and attention for what I'm sure will be all year.

We have come to believe that when students become more conscious of the many decisions they make in order to improve their writing, when they begin to be aware of the processes they must engage in to produce effective writing, and when they finally look over a body of their work, judging it against a set of criteria they have developed and internalized, they are engaged in the kind of thinking characteristic of writers.

Torrey Pines High School
Encinitas, California 92024

Earl Warren Junior High School
Solana Beach, California 92075

FROM WHAT I WISH I HAD KNOWN ABOUT PEER-RESPONSE GROUPS BUT DIDN'T

Ronald Barron

Forming Peer-Response Groups

How many people should peer-response groups have, and how should their composition be determined?

Trial and error has taught me that four people is probably the best size for a group. Assuming a fifty-five- to sixty-minute class period, an efficient peer group can provide useful feedback on four papers. Also, a four-member group seems to facilitate discussion of the paper. If a group gets too large, some students may be left out of the discussion, or a teacher may have to institute some "rule" to ensure equal participation opportunities. Neither alternative is desirable. On the other hand, if a group is too small, students do not get sufficiently diversified responses to their papers, thus limiting the value of peer response.

The membership of peer-response groups can be determined in a wide variety of ways, ranging from random assignment to balancing groups so that all of the best or all of the poorest writers do not end up together. Since rapport contributes to the effectiveness of a group, I allow students the option of setting up their own peer groups; however, I tell them I will rearrange the groups if they do not function effectively. After the peer-group practice sessions, my students select their own groups if they have a preference. Students who do not express a preference are randomly assigned to groups. One suggestion I offer students prior to selecting their groups is that they probably should not be in a group with their best friends since they would likely seek their responses anyway. They will derive the most benefit by getting additional responses from students they would not normally ask to read their papers.

Periodic teacher monitoring of groups is extremely important and enables teachers to recognize problems and to try to solve them before they become critical. If problems arise that cannot be resolved, I change the composition of the groups. Using response groups is not a "miracle method" which works equally well with all students. Teachers need to understand that there may be some students who do not function well with any group. In such cases, teachers have to work with those students to try to improve their group participation, but in the end they may have to be content with placing these students in groups where they do the least harm.

How often should peer groups meet, and what should they actually do?

I schedule peer groups to meet twice for each composition assignment. The first time the groups meet, they focus on such global components of the composition as the organizational pattern, additional material that may be needed, places where the paper could use emphasis or clarification, and unrelated or unnecessary material that may sidetrack the reader. These global components should be the subject of the first session because problems at the sentence and word level may change or disappear as the writers make large structural or conceptional changes during the revising process. To keep the focus on these larger components of a composition rather than on more limited items, I suggest that students read their papers to each other rather than exchange written drafts. However, I strongly recommend that students take notes during the discussion of their papers so that they will not forget the advice they receive from their peer group. When students revise their drafts, they decide which advice has merit and which advice doesn't match their goals for the composition.

For the second peer session, I require students to exchange drafts because the focus of this session should be on the word, sentence, or paragraph level—for example, sentence variety, word choice, punctuation, and the like. I also encourage students to provide copies of their papers to other group members prior to the day of the response group meeting. This practice allows other members of the group to provide a studied response rather than being restricted to a first impression.

Although I would like to devote more time to response groups, the time available in my composition course prevents it. However, my students are encouraged to convene their groups outside of class when and if they feel the need. As the course progresses and students learn the benefits of peer response, the groups meet more frequently on their own, or at least individuals exchange drafts of their compositions outside of class. I even see students going outside of their own group for additional feedback—probably the major testimonial to the value they place on peer feedback. Success with their first papers makes students believers in the technique.

(Continued on page 346.)

AUTHOR'S NOTE: I would like to thank Cindy Houlton, the writer of the paper, and her three peer editors (Amy Swanson, Mary Schultz, and Peter Gilbertson) for allowing me to use a sample of their work in this article.

A brightly colored ribbon tied back my shoulder length black hair. All around I could feel the excitement. The stands were filled with expectant coaches, family and teammates. The morning sun was still cool and slowly making its way to its peak. I looked over at my coach Kim Case. ~~and my best friend. Kim~~ *She* raised a ~~fist~~ *fist* and smiled, nodding her head. She stood by the finish line (near the outside lane.)

[delete] *[Unclear — is this the start of the race?]* With a burst of nervous energy I strided down the track towards the other girls in my race. My light weight ~~shoes~~ *Nikes* dug into the soft new red track. My energy pushed me forward with out my brain consciously ~~trying~~ *working* at each stride. ~~The~~ *A* mechanical voice called for us to line up in our lanes. One by one we were given our assignments. As the start neared the turning tenseness in my stomach tightened. By nature jumping around from foot to foot and up and down on both feet. I felt springs in my feet ~~legs~~ as I moved about to release my anxiety. The girl next to me tentatively wished me luck and I smiled only half hearing her voice.

[Too many adjectives]
[Good image but revise wording]
[All of these sentences are the same length.]

The starter raised his gun and all of us froze.

BANG!

The race had begun. ~~With a quick~~ In a matter of seconds we (filed) into a line. Many fought to keep up with the leader. I felt strong but I stayed back toward the back. I had run this race so many times yet regions was always different. This was my third year at regions even though I was only a sophomore in high school.

[filed?]
[Would it be better to mention when this happened earlier?]

~~The first lap~~ I had just finished my first lap with a good time even though I was in last place. ~~As I rounded the~~ *began* the second lap I ~~str~~ quickened my stride. I began to near the next runner in front and passed her with ease. I could hear the heavy breathing and pounding of the feet of the girls that had gone out too quickly. One by one I passed girls on the outside of the pack.

[Tell us more about you]

By the end of the third lap I managed to pass every girl but one. My legs began to feel tired. I had to push myself for each stride. My arms felt like dead weights. My head was pounding as the last lap loomed in front of me like another mile. I had never felt this before. I ran out of sheer will to finish. As I rounded the last turn with 200 meters left, the pounding of feet came up behind out of nowhere I fought but one by one they began to race ahead of me.

[cliche]
[Good sentence]
[good word choice]
[The short sentences give readers a sense of your lack of breath]

[I want to know more about the third lap. Try to build more tension.]

I crossed the finish line in seventh as I heard the timer yell 5:40.

The disappointment of being passed drained from my body.   In a rush Kim and my other team-

Sp

mates circled around me with hugs and congradulations.

The tired feeling had disappeared.   I had worked all season to get a 5:40 in the 1600 m, and I

← Write out

had done it.

The emotions you tell us about are interesting, but could you tell us more? It would help readers experience the event with you.

The conclusion is too quick. Work more on Bringing out the significance of the experience You have chosen a unique experience -- most people would only write about a race they won.

I like the subject you have chosen. Reveal more about what you were thinking. The little you tell us makes me want to Know more.

The introduction isn't very catchy. Tell us more about Kim. I expected to find out more about her.

Cindy's first draft

Where does the teacher fit into the writing process once students learn the importance of peer response?

First, teachers sit in on group sessions to determine how efficiently the groups are operating. During those observations, teachers can expect to be asked for advice about the drafts under consideration by the group. In these situations, I attempt to act as any other member of the group, giving my frank response to the draft but consciously resisting the temptation to take over the group. A second way teachers can participate is by making individual conference time available for students who request it. In other words, the use of response groups does not preclude teacher input, but it does change the nature of the input. Rather than the teacher determining when and what input is necessary, students determine when they need such input and what specific help they require. Sometimes students request a great deal of help with a particular assignment; at other times they feel quite content to proceed on their own with little or no teacher assistance. I consciously strive to become only one source of advice about how to write a composition, rather than trying to be a "writing seer" who knows all and tells all about how to complete

the assignment. This approach to composition closely resembles the way students will have to handle writing outside of school.

Prior to having students write a first draft, I have them study effective models, usually strong papers written by students during the previous year, but sometimes I also use professionally written examples. We then spend class time discussing the unique qualities of the types of writing students will be expected to do, as well as trying to reach a consensus about what makes the models effective. When students discuss what makes a piece of writing effective, they have a better understanding of how to write a composition of their own that incorporates those priorities. The discussion of quality papers can also lead to teacher- and/ or student-generated guide sheets that can be used both by the response groups in suggesting revisions of works-in-progress and by the teacher in evaluating final compositions. . . .

I encourage groups to set as a goal producing the four best papers in the class, not just one good paper. As one student said in her evaluation of my composition course this year, "When someone in my group got an *A* on a
(Continued on page 349.)

All around me I could feel the excitement of Regions.   The stands were filled with expectant

coaches, family, and teammates while runners moved about trying desperately to relieve their   *[These two lines are too similar.]*

anxiety.   Tears and pain along with joy and pride were evident in the expressions of those

~~already done~~   *Word choice*   while anxiety and fear raced through the minds of those ^of us^ who were waiting for their   *[arrow]*

chance.   *Would "our" be better?*

A brightly colored ribbon tied back my shoulder length black hair and my light-weight Nikes

dug into the new red track.   I slowly strided ~~down~~ towards the far end of the track to loosen my

tightly coiled leg muscles.   My mind replayed (fast forward) every race I had run since 8th grade   *Could these words be left out?*

as I tried to focus on today.

A (mechanical) voice called for us to line up in our lane assignments.   One by one we stood in   *good word*

our positions as the starter announced we had five minutes until the start.   I hopped from foot to

foot ~~releasing sore~~ as I did before every race.   I felt springs in my toes as I moved about to

release the pent up butterflies in the pit of my stomach.

"You can do it!" exclaimed ~~Mim~~ ^Kim^, my coach.   *You capitalize "Regions" in the first line, but here you don't.*

I looked over, and nodded ~~only half~~ smiling.   I had never worked so hard for anything as I had

for regions that year.   The long hot afternoons with Kim and that ever present stopwatch

reminded me of how prepared I was.   Together, Kim and I had planned nutrition, ^and^ worked to

improved my overall fitness.   ~~not just my~~   She had been there for me ~~when~~ through the good

days and bad days.   I had learned to depend on her support.   *← cliche*

I looked over at ~~her~~ Kim again to see her confident smile and her raised stopwatch.   I smiled

back, this time with strength and no doubt in my eyes.

The starter raised his gun and ~~all~~ everyone froze.

"BANG!"   *Was there any battle for position in the pack?*

The race had begun.   In a matter of seconds we filed into a line.   Many girls fought to keep up

with the leader, but I stayed back.   I had run this race so many times.   I unconsciously picked up a *combined*

rythym and strided along without thinking about each step.   *How did you feel about your pace?*

Before I knew it, I finished my first lap with a good time, even though I was in last place.   As I

I felt the excitement of Regions surround me.
Your second paragraph helps me understand what you were experiencing

rounded the ~~curve~~ first curve of the second lap I began to quicken my stride.   I neared the runner

in front of me and passed her with ease.   I could hear the pounding of my feet ~~of the girls who~~ *and the heavy breathing*

had gone out too fast.   My mind never focused except on the girl in front of me.   I felt nothing

except the natural pace of my stride as I passed girls one by one on the outside of the pack.

By the end of the third lap I managed to pass every girl but one.   My mind cleared as I could

sense victory.   I wanted to *win* more than anything else.   I pushed my body forward with all ~~as I~~ *my effort*

good lines began to feel the first signs of fatigue.   Every stride became a tedious effort as the last lap

loomed in front of me like another mile.   My arms and legs felt like lead weights as my mind

began to spin.   The sweat was dripping off my face in a constant flow as I gasped for every

breath.   I kept running ~~on the will to finish~~ only out on the sheer will to finish.   I rounded the last

curve with only 200 meters left.   My ears heard muffled tones of the crowd screaming as we

neared the finish.

I like this line → I pushed but my body resisted.   Pounding from behind pushed me forward ~~to yet once more.~~

The other runners passed me.   My last ounce of energy helped me reach the finish line in

seventh place as I heard the timer yell "5:40."   The disappointment of placing seventh drained

from my body as I processed what I had just heard.   *Didn't you start to react in the previous line?*

"You did it! You did it!" screamed Kim as she raced over to hug me before I could react.

In a rush my other teammates rushed over to congratulate me.   They all seemed very distant

though.   Everything was fuzzy except *for* Kim and her stopwatch.   She raised it slowly so I could see

the time.   Dark digital numbers read 5:40. ←

"I did it!" I said quietly with a grin.

One place you put it in quotes and in the other place you don't

I can imagine your emotional state much better after reading this draft. I also understand why you wrote about this event even though you didn't win the race.

Your new opening paragraph is more effective because it catches the excitement of the experience. Waiting until the second paragraph to focus on yourself is a good idea.

The conclusion is stronger now than it was in your earlier version. The importance of achieving personal goals rather than winning the race is clearer in this version.

I understand Kim's role in the experience better.

Cindy's third draft

(Continued from page 346.)

paper, I also felt like I had received an *A*." Although that ideal goal of producing the four best papers is not always attainable, how will students and, for that matter, their teachers know if it can be reached unless students try to accomplish it? Trying sometimes leads to pleasant surprises. A more realistic group goal should be to produce four papers that are all better than what individual writers could have produced on their own. That goal is within the capabilities of all students.

One of the purposes of a composition course should be to make students more confident and more independent writers. Peer-response groups help accomplish this purpose. In addition, good responders tend to become better writers. For most students, as their ability as responders improves, their ability to revise their own compositions also improves because they have a better sense of how to approach the task.

However, teachers should not expect all members of response groups to gain the same benefits from the experience. Teachers need to tolerate some partial failures even though they may have worked extensively with individuals trying to improve their performances. The important point to keep in mind is not to junk the technique because it does not work well with all students. Also, teachers may not experience as much success with peer-response groups as they wish the first time they try them. My own experience is a good case in point. Experience and modification of the technique to fit the individual personalities of teacher and students are necessary for success with peer-response groups, just as with almost every other effective teaching technique. However, teachers who devote time and effort to the use of response groups will be rewarded when students write better papers, feel more confident about their writing skills, and view writing as a positive experience rather than one to be avoided.

Richfield Senior High School
Richfield, Minnesota 55423

TWENTY (BETTER) QUESTIONS *Kris L. Myers*

Maybe you don't struggle getting your students to read literature assignments, but I do. Getting an edge on MTV, mall-walking, and girl- or boy-watching is difficult, but I am competing better since I've changed my tack in evaluating students' knowledge of literature and my view of what that knowledge should be.

Most of us have used the "pop quiz" as a quick check to see who has read last night's assignment. We rationalize that it is positive motivation—a reward for those who have read, rather than punishment for those who have not. We make quizzes "simple" so any fool who has skimmed the assignment can pass.

But do you remember *taking* one of those quizzes? I do. I remember heart palpitations, silent prayers that the teacher would ask what I'd remembered of the details (and they were always about details), and brain freeze. I couldn't remember the name of the main character, the author of the story, or even the setting. And I'd read it; I had!

Well, I'm guilty of having given those infernal quizzes, too. Why don't I give them any more? The influence of two people changed my approach to quizzing and my whole outlook on what is important to know about literature.

The first influence was a wide-eyed high achiever in my first-period class three years ago. Heidi was an eager student, willing to participate in all class activities. She went beyond what most students did. Needless to say, she always read her assignments, often more than once. Yet she would come in panic-stricken the day after a reading assignment, begging to know if we were going to have a pop quiz.

On the day we quizzed Thurber's "The Dog That Bit People," Heidi froze. It was a true/false quiz with "simple" questions, but Heidi missed them all. She left her paper totally blank; she didn't even record her name. But the agony for me was watching her face as I read each question. I saw various stages of panic, fear, agitation, and resignation, ending finally in silent tears.

She was silent the entire class period. As the classroom cleared at the bell, she came to my desk and stood for several moments. Then she apologized. She had read the story twice, she said, but didn't know the "important" parts; she would work harder, read again, do whatever I could suggest. But she didn't know how to figure out what I thought was important. That gave me pause. What *I* thought? Is this what I wanted her to do: psych out what *I* felt was important about Thurber's story? Is that what teaching literature should be?

The second influence was Maia Pank Mertz at Ohio State University. She introduced me to reader-response criticism by opening the worlds of Louise Rosenblatt,

David Bleich, Norman Holland, and Alan Purves. But, more importantly, her classroom procedures were response-centered theories in action.

So, do I still struggle to get my students to read their assignments? Well, yes, but less so. Do I still give pop quizzes? Not exactly. Instead, I have students keep response journals. I use David Bleich's response heuristic to help students define and refine their responses. In *Reading and Feelings* (Urbana: NCTE, 1975), Bleich suggests that readers respond first to their perception of the work (what it means to them), then to the connections and associations within them that caused the affective response.

Students are used to looking to teachers for answers. They are seldom asked to reflect on what they think about what they read, or even less so, why they think what they think. Bloom's Taxonomy levels of application, analysis, synthesis, and evaluation are still largely ignored in most classrooms. But my students are responding to literature on all of these levels. I give students the following list of questions at the beginning of the school year and ask them to keep the list in their response journals to use all year:

1. What character(s) was your favorite? Why?
2. What character(s) did you dislike? Why?
3. Does anyone in this work remind you of anyone you know? Explain.
4. Are you like any character in this work? Explain.
5. If you could be any character in this work, who would you be? Explain.
6. What quality(ies) of which character strikes you as a good characteristic to develop within yourself over the years? Why? How does the character demonstrate this quality?
7. Overall, what kind of a feeling did you have after reading a few paragraphs of this work? Midway? After finishing the work?
8. Do any incidents, ideas, or actions in this work remind you of your own life or something that happened to you? Explain.
9. Do you like this piece of work? Why or why not?
10. Are there any parts of this work that were confusing to you? Which parts? Why do you think you got confused?
11. Do you feel there is an opinion expressed by the author through this work? What is it? How do you know this? Do you agree? Why or why not?
12. Do you think the title of this work is appropriate? Is it significant? Explain. What do you think the title means?
13. Would you change the ending of this story in any way? Tell your ending. Why would you change it?
14. What kind of person do you feel the author is? What makes you feel this way?
15. How did this work make you feel? Explain.
16. Do you share any of the feelings of the characters in this work? Explain.
17. Sometimes works leave you with the feeling that there is more to tell. Did this work do this? What do you think might happen?
18. Would you like to read something else by this author? Why or why not?
19. What do you feel is the most important word, phrase, passage, or paragraph in this work? Explain why it is important.
20. If you were an English teacher, would you want to share this work with your students? Why or why not?

I am constantly revising this list, and students may use any of the questions when writing their responses, providing they answer all of the question fully. What is important about this list is not the specific questions on it but the nature of the questions, the attitude about literature that is fostered by the questions. The focus is constantly *on the students* and their perceptions, feelings, and associations that result from the work.

I still ''check up'' on my students' reading by randomly grading written responses, but students know what will be asked of them. Usually I require a minimum of half a page of writing but nearly always get more. Sometimes I ask students to include in their response a reaction to a specific question on the list, but most students tend to drop the crutch the list provides.

How do I grade responses? I use Bleich's suggestions again and grade on seriousness of intent and obvious knowledge of the story. Unlike answers on the objective pop quiz, responses are impossible to fake; the reader knows immediately whether the student has read and thought about the work. Also, I do not grade every response. I try to include my own written response to their writing occasionally as well.

I encourage students to take their journals with them and respond to the work while it is fresh in their minds. I am available to read and respond to their writing upon request. Sometimes they write, discuss the work, then write again. Or we discuss and then write. And the work doesn't end when the students leave the classroom. It becomes something they ''own'' and is forever a part of them.

Yes, more of my students are reading their assignments more of the time. They *do* see response writings as a positive reward. But more than that, they see themselves as critics and meaning-makers. They are less intimidated by and more intimate with the printed word. The mystery in the text has become the mystery in them. And that is a mystery they want to solve.

Granville Middle School
Granville, Ohio 43023

READING DEVELOPMENT IN THE *ELEMENTS OF LITERATURE* PROGRAM:
The Student as Reader / The Teacher as Facilitator
Nancy E. Wiseman Seminoff

Elements of Literature is a comprehensive program of literature study for grades 7–12. Each anthology includes a wide range of significant literary works, as well as supporting instruction that helps students become more responsive readers and more proficient writers. The anthology for the Fifth Course is organized chronologically, with a brief history of ideas for each time period given in the unit introduction. Often, selections are grouped to facilitate comparison and contrast of theme, structure, or style and technique.

The instructional materials in the student's text include background information for understanding the genres, the selections, and the writers' lives; factual and interpretive discussion questions; and creative and critical writing assignments. The questions and assignments, designed to stimulate critical thinking, emphasize reading and writing strategies in which students use their own experience and knowledge to comprehend and appreciate literature.

Additionally, exercises throughout the text use specific linguistic features of the selections as springboards to language and vocabulary instruction in numerous skills. The exercises cover literary terms and techniques, such as allusions and figures of speech, as well as word-study skills important in all reading, such as context clues, dictionary use, and word roots. For a listing of skills taught in the program, see the Index of Skills beginning on text page 1235, and the scope and sequence chart in the Annotated Teacher's Edition (Integrating the Language Arts, beginning on page A25).

Elements of Literature provides you with excellent materials and tools to help your students become better readers. Your role in the classroom is pivotal to students' success. By understanding the reading process and basing your teaching strategies on it, you can make use of the anthology's full potential.

Understanding the Reading Process

In the past, educators viewed reading as a series of discrete skills, sequential and hierarchical in nature. They increasingly found, however, that students who learned these skills in the elementary grades did not necessarily develop into proficient readers in the higher grades. Something was missing in the traditional view of the reading process: the interaction between the reader and the text itself.

According to recent research, reading is a dynamic process that involves the reader, the text, and the situation in which the reading takes place. The assumption behind previous reading theory was that the writer bore sole responsibility for conveying meaning. Educators now recognize that readers must actively seek meaning as they read and must be able to modify their approach to a text if the approach doesn't yield meaning. The reader's characteristics and background (linguistic, social, cultural, and psychological) and the writer's characteristics (as evidenced in the text) necessarily influence the reader's understanding.

Students actually *construct* meaning as they read; they do not simply absorb it. They bring prior experience and knowledge to the work. They draw tentative conclusions as they begin to read and modify those conclusions as they continue. The reading process is thus one of accumulating meaning.

The development of schema theory by cognitive psychologists has helped illuminate this process, showing how people approach new information by setting it against a known framework. In reading, schemata (frameworks) enable a student to recall relevant facts and experiences, to anticipate what will happen next, to fill in missing information, and to know when a writer's meaning is not clear. Important to a student's framework for understanding, therefore, is experience not only with the topic of a reading selection but also with the genre. In reading about spring, for example, a student's comprehension may be aided by prior knowledge of how plants form and grow, no matter what the genre of the writing. But a student cannot approach the reading of William Carlos Williams's "Spring and All" and the reading of a scientific discussion of the season in the same way. To construct full meaning from "Spring and All," the student must be familiar with poetic conventions and techniques, as well as with stylistic variations within genres; the student must have appropriate expectations against which to gauge understanding.

Teachers, in turn, must be alert to gaps in students' experiences and knowledge that will prevent them from being "active" readers, supplying (or guiding students in finding) necessary background. If students face a literary work that seems thoroughly unfamiliar, the reading will seem a difficult chore. Students will not read with interest—and interest is another essential element in the dynamics of reading.

The purpose for reading a selection, either self- or teacher-imposed, is an additional variable in the reading situation. A student uses quite different reading strategies to gain an initial impression of an essayist's position and to read a dramatic soliloquy. For the first task, the student reads in chunks, with wide eye sweeps. For the second, the student reads closely, ideally aloud, with attention to specific phrasing and detail. The section Teaching Students to Vary Reading Rates (pages 358–360 in these Teaching Notes) provides a discussion of different reading strategies as well as genre-specific guidelines for close reading.

The conscious awareness and control of cognitive processes is termed *metacognition*. In reading, metacognition is the adjustment of reading strategies to control comprehension. Encourage students to monitor their own comprehension as they read: to pause and raise questions when they do not understand, to reread a section to seek clarity, to use context clues to determine meaning, and so on. You should help students see, in short, that the response to difficult reading is not to stop reading. Students can learn reading techniques that will help them become flexible, responsive readers—a necessity if they are to participate in the experiences offered them in literature.

Before Reading—
Moving into the Selection

The instructional materials that accompany the selections in the anthology provide a framework for your classroom activities. These can be grouped into three phases: preparation for reading the selection, an encounter with the selection, and extension beyond the selection.

Students' preparation for reading a selection often determines the success of their reading. The unit and section introductions, the selection headnotes, and the Primary Sources features evoke responses, supply background information, relate the selection to contemporary life, and help students anticipate topics and themes. The Teaching Notes offer additional information and ideas for introducing the selections.

Also important are activities to bridge the gap between students' prior knowledge and an unfamiliar literary work, activities that will motivate them to want to begin reading. These notes present many hints for stimulating interest. Remember, however, that students do not need exhaustive introductions to begin reading, understanding, and appreciating a selection. Reading preparation should be stimulating and revealing, not oppressive.

During Reading—
Moving Through the Selection

The questions in Analyzing the Story are intended to assist students in responding to and understanding the literary work. The questions are offered for instruction, not testing,

and students should refer freely to the selection when answering them. (You may on occasion select some questions for closed-book reading checks or essay tests.)

Good questions help students to tap into their own experience and to engage more deeply with the text. The goal of the questions is to help readers to *accumulate* understandings of the text while encouraging them to think on their own. As students answer the questions, they are continually gathering information, interpreting, and raising their own questions in a process that causes them to refine their understandings and to confirm or reject their initial predictions. Cognitively, they move between and among the questions as they build comprehension and understanding.

Consequently, you should encourage students to answer questions as fully as possible but to be open to revising their responses in light of new evidence. In this process of deepening comprehension, other students' responses also play an important role. Small groups are particularly effective for discussing questions and comparing written answers. In this way, students can refine, reconsider, reject, revise, or confirm their understandings in response to the ideas of others.

Keep in mind that while questions should guide students to find meaning and to contribute their own ideas, the amount and type of guidance they need can vary. Debate exists among reading experts about how structured the guidance should be, but your students' needs should be the determining factor. For some students and in some situations, highly structured questions may be best. In other cases, you may be able to use open-ended questions and provide minimal guidance. For further discussion of questioning strategies, particularly to provoke critical thinking, see Using Literature to Teach Higher-Level Thinking Skills (pages 354–357 in these Teaching Notes).

After Reading—
Moving Beyond the Selection

Activities after reading serve two purposes: assessing students' understandings of a selection and helping students apply what they have learned to a new situation or selection. Forming small-group discussions—following your instruction and guided class discussion—is one simple but effective way for you to help students move beyond the selection. As students express and explain their final reponses to the work, you should move among the groups, listening for problems. You should determine how many students still have not read successfully and how best to help them.

Exercises in Writing About the Story and Analyzing Language and Vocabulary require students to demonstrate comprehension and to go beyond the selections. Many of the writing assignments encourage students to use their imaginations in response to or imitation of the literature selection. Other writing assignments require students to explore a literary element more deeply, to compare and contrast it with another selection, or to relate the work to other life situations. The language and vocabulary exercises, while assessing students' masteries of language and word-study skills, usually extend and apply the language study to other areas. Thus the students' understandings and abilities increase as they complete each exercise.

Discussing one or more of the selections in relation to each other is another successful technique. You may ask students to connect selections in terms of their theme, style, genre, historical period, or another element or combination of elements. You may ask them to create an original work. (The Teaching Notes provide many Extending the Selection suggestions.) In these activities, students are synthesizing. They analyze the selections, but they arrive at understandings (comparisons, contrasts, original works) that are external to the selections. In applying elsewhere what they learn from a literary work, students learn how to use past reading to approach new reading. They expand those frameworks for understanding that make them proficient, confident readers.

Further Reading for the Teacher

Alvermann, D. E. "Metacognition." *Research Within Reach: Secondary School Reading.* D. E. Alvermann, D. W. Moore, and M. W. Conley, eds. Newark, DE: International Reading Association, 1987. 153–168.

Armbruster, B. "The Problem of 'Inconsiderate Text.' " *Comprehension Instruction: Perspectives and Suggestions.* G. Duffy, L. Roehler, and J. Mason, eds. New York: Longman, 1984. 202–217.

Atwell, Nancie. *In the Middle: Writing, Reading, and Learning with Adolescents.* Portsmouth: Heinemann, 1987. 149–221.

Baker, L., and A. L. Brown. "Cognitive Monitoring in Reading." *Understanding Reading Comprehension.* J. Flood, ed. Newark, DE: International Reading Association, 1984. 21–44.

Langer, J. A. "The Process of Understanding: Reading for Literary and Informative Purposes." *Research in the Teaching of English* 24 (1990): 229–260.

———. "Understanding Literature." *Language Arts* 8 (1990): 812–816.

Meyer, B. J. F. "Organizational Aspects of Text: Effects on Reading Comprehension and Applications for the Classroom." *Promoting Reading Comprehension.* J. Flood, ed. Newark, DE: International Reading Association, 1984. 113–138.

Moffett, James, and Betty Jean Wagner. "Student-Centered Reading Activities." *English Journal* (Oct. 1991): 70–73.

Mosenthal, P. "Reading Comprehension Research from a Classroom Perspective." *Promoting Reading Comprehension.* J. Flood, ed. Newark, DE: International Reading Association, 1984. 16–29.

Paris, S. G., M. Lipson, and K. K. Wilson. "Becoming a Strategic Reader." *Contemporary Educational Psychology* 8 (1982): 293–316.

Pearson, P. D., and R. J. Spiro. "Toward a Theory of Reading Comprehension Instruction." *Topics in Language Disorders* 1 (1980): 71–88.

Rosenblatt, L. M. *The Reader, the Text, the Poem.* Carbondale, IL: Southern Illinois University Press, 1978.

USING LITERATURE TO TEACH HIGHER-LEVEL THINKING SKILLS

Because human life is its subject, imagination its method, and words its medium, literature is rich and subtle in both meaning and form. Critical thinking is inherent in its study. In order to discuss and write about literature, students must use the very skills that define critical thinking, including analysis, inference, interpretation, comparison and contrast, hypothesis testing, argumentation, evaluation, and synthesis. Moreover, they must use these skills on a subject matter that requires them, as few other subjects do, to confront ambiguity and relativity, to comprehend irony, and to arrive at moral and aesthetic judgments. They will also use critical thinking skills to make connections on many levels—concrete and abstract, personal and impersonal, literal and figurative. These sophisticated, but essential, mental processes are increasingly recognized as the realm of higher thinking.

Critical Thinking in the *Elements of Literature* Program

The *Elements of Literature* program thoroughly exercises students' critical thinking skills in the interpretive questions and composition assignments following each selection. It also uses literature to teach thinking skills. At the end of each unit or division of a unit, an **Exercises in Critical Thinking and Writing** isolates an important cognitive skill to be applied to a writing assignment. (For a complete listing of these exercises, see the Index of Skills on text page 1238.) In each **Exercises in Critical Thinking and Writing,** the Background material defines and explains the skill. Then the student is given detailed instruction—Prewriting, Writing, and a Checklist for Revision—on using the skill in writing.

Students are not simply being put through the paces of an exercise. They are being shown how to think, how to approach problems, how to transfer cognitive skills from one setting to another, and how to make critical thinking a habit of mind.

As you use the *Elements of Literature* program to develop students' critical thinking, the following teaching strategies, derived from educational theory and cognitive psychology, will assist you.

Three Basic Teaching Strategies

First, continually lead students to relate literature to their own lives. This approach has several benefits. It makes unfamiliar material less threatening or alien, and it helps students find ways to discover writing and project topics of particular interest. This approach also enables students to make connections between an external reality and their personal experience—an important criterion of higher-level thinking. The text and Teaching Notes demonstrate many ways to elicit these connections.

Second, take every opportunity to help students perceive the ambiguities, ironies, multiple meanings, and contrasting points of view that abound in literature. Emphasize exploration of a number of positions and supporting arguments, rather than the search for a single right answer. This attempt to see several sides of an issue is what philosopher Richard Paul calls dialogical, or dialectical, thinking. A related concept is Jean Piaget's ideal reciprocity, the ability to empathize with other people, ideas, and values.

Collaborative activities foster this kind of thinking, as do questions that require students to choose a position and assignments that concentrate on point of view. Especially important is the atmosphere you create in your classroom. When you communicate your willingness to accept students' responses and ideas, to consider different interpretations, students will respond positively. They will learn to listen more open-mindedly to their classmates' conclusions, as well as to examine their own more carefully.

Students' assessment of their own reasoning is the third basic teaching strategy. Make students *conscious* of their critical thinking; make them think about their thinking. (The term for this awareness is *metacognition*.) The text establishes this method in the critical thinking and writing exercises. You can extend it to daily classroom work in several ways. Call students' attention to their cognitive processes during discussion. Ask them how they arrived at an idea or opinion, and insist that they justify interpretations with textual evidence. Whenever they disagree with a classmate's conclusion, ask them to explain how the argument is flawed. When you increase students' awareness of how they think, their thinking improves.

These three teaching strategies—guiding students to relate literature to their own lives, to think dialectically, and to consider their own thought processes—underlie the questions and exercises in the text and Teaching Notes. Some additional teaching ideas follow.

Questioning Strategies

By planning the questions you ask and when you ask them, you will be rewarded not only with students' increased enthusiasm for literature but also with keener thinking about it.

INITIAL QUESTIONS   First, simply ask questions frequently. Use questions to stimulate discussion, not just to check comprehension. For example, begin the discussion of a selection with a question: Does John Hersey's historical essay ''A Noiseless Flash'' resemble fiction in any way(s)? How does the speaker in Anne Sexton's ''Riding the Elevator Into the Sky'' feel about the practical restrictions of life? Don't force-feed your ideas about a work; let students offer theirs first. An initial question immediately creates an atmosphere of inquiry. It frees students to form their own hypotheses or to voice feelings without reference to your ideas, and it provides focal issues around which they can organize new information (Meyers 59–60).

DIALOGUE QUESTIONS   Remember, too, that you can respond to students with questions, not statements. Meet a question with a question; turn a statement into a question; throw a problem back to the student who raised it or to the rest of the class. Whenever possible, do not ''give'' answers; help students find them.

A student may say, for example, that Donald Barthelme's ''Game'' isn't very realistic. Rather than disagreeing or agreeing and offering your own examples, draw out the student's thoughts: Why do you say that? Compelled to go beyond the vague statement, the student may reply, ''The government has all kinds of safeguards. Two guys would never be left alone that long with missiles they could launch.'' You can, of course, press the student further: What safeguards are you thinking of? But even at this point, the class has a specific judgment to explore (the government wouldn't let the situation continue), and other students may want to jump in.

As the discussion unfolds, continue probing with questions: What information from real life supports your opinion? What could cause the breakdown of those government or military safeguards? Could Barthelme have intended to create an absurd situation? Use these questions to help students define their criteria for judgments, offer examples and evidence, generate hypotheses to explain inconsistencies, and so on. Such questions create group dialogue and also put students in dialogue with themselves. Pushed to elaborate, reflect, or defend, students will learn to clarify what they ''really mean'' and to be aware of how they arrived at a position or response.

STRUCTURED QUESTIONS   When choosing or creating discussion questions, you can structure them to call forth particular types of critical thinking. Another approach is to focus on three areas: the literary work, the student's personal experience, and the external world (Christenbury and Kelly 12–15; Swope and Thompson).

About *A Raisin in the Sun,* for example, you could ask: Why doesn't the Younger family want to accept Mr. Lindner's offer? (The question elicits facts and inferences solely about the story.) What do people need, even more than money, to feel right about their lives? (The question calls for the student's personal opinion.) What social biases common to mid-twentieth century American life were hidden within the apparently generous offer? (The question seeks information external to the literary work.)

Each type of question can provoke critical thinking, but questions that combine two or three of the areas will lead students to more complex reasoning. A question that simultaneously elicits textual facts, opinion or personal experience, and outside information—what Christenbury and Kelly call a ''dense question''—can be the focus of a class discussion, presented to the students in advance. (For example: If you were Walter Lee Younger, couldn't you have used the money to solve all the family's problems in another way?) The single- and two-area questions that you ask during the discussion will help students approach the more complex question by clarifying its issues and guiding students to a more fully thought-out response. (For example: Is there any way in which Walter could both have accepted the money and retained his self-esteem? Could making successful investments and seeing Beneatha attend medical school balance out any blows to self-esteem involved in accepting the money?)

Classroom Activities

Experienced teachers report that students enjoy literature most when they actively participate in some way. The following sections suggest four kinds of activities that have worked successfully with eleventh-grade students.

COLLABORATIVE INTERPRETATION   Collaborative activities are especially conducive to critical thinking because they necessarily involve dialogue and exchange. Many teachers find, in fact, that lively whole-class discussions are greatly aided by initial small-group work. The following collaborative-learning activities can be used to discuss interpretive questions (Dragga).

Assign each group the same question, one that will generate different answers and require reference to the selection. Give each group about fifteen minutes to devise a collective answer, with supporting details from the text, to be reported by a group spokesperson. (Change speakers during the term so that each student serves in this role.) Because each group must arrive at a single answer, every group member is drawn into the discussion. Each student must offer, if not an original idea, at least a reasoned judgment of any suggested answer and evidence to support it. As the groups work, you can move among them, monitoring the content and process of the discussions and helping students through impasses.

When the time limit is reached, have each spokesperson report the group's answer, explaining reasons for main ideas and citing support from the text. (For early collaborations, speakers may report from notes. Later, you may want groups to write collective essays, which the speakers will read.) In the ensuing class discussion, students will challenge each other's interpretations, defend their own arguments, build on another group's position by offering overlooked evidence, and attempt an evaluation of the differing interpretations.

The critical thinking benefits of this kind of collaboration and discussion are numerous. Students model their thinking processes for one another, examine literary works closely to find logical supporting evidence, synthesize their thoughts into a coherent spoken or written answer, and evaluate different interpretations of a literary work.

COURTROOM TRIALS   A more structured collaborative activity is a courtroom trial about a compelling conflict in a literary work (Segedy). The trial format captivates students' imaginations as it challenges their reasoning power. It keeps students' interest high not only because of its inherent drama but also because of the variety of activities required: close reading, research, debating, role-playing, and composition.

For this project, choose a narrative containing a conflict appropriate to courtroom investigation. Plan how you will present the actual "case" (who is bringing suit against whom and for what), and decide the roles students will play. Stories, novels, and plays that focus on crimes are, of course, excellent choices. But any work that raises questions of social, ethical, or moral injustice may yield issues for prosecution and defense.

Generally, you will appoint a team of three or four lawyers for each side of the case and will choose students to play characters who must appear at the trial. For some cases, you might need to involve some students as expert witnesses, such as psychologists or scientists. The attorneys must work together to develop the best possible cases to represent their clients, without contradicting the literary work in any way. They must prepare strong logical arguments, support their arguments with compelling evidence, plan their questioning of witnesses, create persuasive rhetoric, and practice their public speaking. The students playing characters must do in-depth character analyses, gleaning from the text all facts about the characters and making inferences about feelings, motives, and experiences not explicitly described. The expert witnesses must research their areas sufficiently to be able to offer sound and relevant testimony.

Any students not playing roles are paired with either a lawyer or a character as research aides. They actively participate in case preparation or in character analysis and can thus substitute for their partners during the trial if necessary.

After both sides have presented their cases, every student prepares a written summation to the jury. Students should be preparing for this persuasive composition during all the pretrial work. They must also pay careful attention during the trial itself, for the proceedings may yield new ideas or arguments. For the essay, all students assume the persona of an attorney, address themselves to an imagined jury, and argue for conviction or acquittal as persuasively as possible.

Thus a courtroom trial project uses a variety of methods to improve students' critical thinking. As they work in small groups and pairs to prepare for their trial roles, students analyze, interpret, and synthesize many elements of a literary work. When they participate in the trial itself, students think on their feet as they present and defend logical arguments in dynamic, unrehearsed exchanges. Students listening to the trial observe and evaluate others' thought processes and refine their own positions accordingly. Finally, as they write the summations, students work individually to synthesize all of their experience into strong persuasive compositions.

EXPERT GROUPS   In addition to having groups of students research and report on particular aspects of a literary work, you can have an expert group take complete responsibility for teaching one of the text selections (Bonfiglio). This more sophisticated collaborative activity should be reserved for later in the term, after students have worked through many selections with you, and assigned only to students capable of independent work. The expert groups must devise an entire project plan, not simply follow directions, and must accomplish their plans without supervision.

Assign an appropriate text selection, and explain that the group is to serve as teacher for that selection. They must decide how to present the work (classroom methods and teaching focus), conduct necessary research, and decide how to divide the labor. Members of the group can use or create visual aids, and you can also require a written outline of the presentation. Encourage students to use their imaginations, to think of innovative ways to engage their classmates' interest while presenting sound insights into the literary work.

This activity requires critical thinking on two levels. First, students must analyze, interpret, and evaluate the literary work; then, they must propose, prepare, and execute a teaching plan. Throughout the project, they must make judgments both about the selection and about their presentation; they must solve problems of interpretation and of group interaction, compare and contrast teaching methods, organize their presentation into a coherent sequence, and so on. The task is challenging but extremely beneficial and satisfying, particularly for advanced students. They use higher-level reasoning not only to investigate literature, but also to communicate their findings to others.

ORAL COMPOSITION   Oral composition is a collaborative activity that specifically develops metacognition (awareness of one's thinking processes). Again, students need some preparation for this technique. You should attempt it only after students have completed several of the text's critical thinking and writing exercises or after you have accustomed students—through comments and questions during discussion—to reflecting on their own and their classmates' reasoning processes. Vinz describes an effective paired-student approach to oral composition.

Give each student in the pair a different interpretive essay question about a selection. Select or create questions that do not have clear right and wrong answers, such as those requiring decision making or problem solving. (For example: If Emerson had written a story similar to Crane's "The Open Boat," how might Emerson have changed the story? Do you think you would prefer Emerson's version or Crane's and why?) You may use the same questions for all pairs in the class.

For this open-book activity, students take turns as speaker-writers and listeners. The speaking-writing student is to compose *aloud* an answer to the question. The listening student is to take notes on the speaker's composition process. Explain that the speaker-writers are simply to say aloud exactly what they are thinking as they plan and draft their essays. Remind them of what they do normally during prewriting: brainstorm, consider and reject ideas, make up a possible thesis, look for supporting evidence, decide how best to arrange their main points. The point of oral composition is to get students to recognize and verbalize these processes. Speaker-writers should write down important prewriting notes and then begin to draft their essays.

The listeners are to observe, interpret, and record the composers' thought processes; they do not comment aloud. They might note how much time their partners spend on different processes (free-associating ideas, searching for supporting facts, evaluating their own thoughts, rereading and revising a draft paragraph). They should note how often good ideas come from chance associations and what seems most often to stop the flow of the composers' ideas. Listeners should also observe whether the composers are methodical, completing each line of thought before starting another, or more unstructured, willing to leave a difficulty unresolved and move on to something else.

You may want to set aside portions of two class periods for each speaker-writer to generate a first draft (students can work alone to write final versions of their essays). Then have the pairs exchange and discuss their listener-notes.

As a summarizing activity, both students should write, perhaps as a journal assignment, what they learned about their own thinking processes. The oral composition process itself, as well as the listeners' written observations, should lead to some insights for all students. They may ask themselves: Exactly how, and how well, do I think my way through problems? What could I change, improve? What did I learn from my partner's reasoning and composing process that I could adopt?

References and Further Reading for the Teacher

Bonfiglio, Joseph F. "Collection, Connection, Projection: Using Written and Oral Presentation to Encourage Thinking Skills." NCTE 93–96.

Christenbury, Leila, and Patricia P. Kelly. *Questioning: A Path to Critical Thinking*. Urbana, IL: ERIC Clearinghouse on Reading and Communication Skills and National Council of Teachers of English, 1983.

Dragga, Sam. "Collaborative Interpretation." NCTE 84–87.

Educational Leadership 42 (1984).

Lazere, Donald. "Critical Thinking in College English Studies." Urbana, IL: ERIC Clearinghouse on Reading and Communication Skills and National Council of Teachers of English, 1987.

Meyers, Chet. *Teaching Students to Think Critically*. San Francisco: Jossey-Bass, 1986.

Muldoon, Phyllis A. "Challenging Students to Think: Shaping Questions, Building Community." *English Journal* (April 1990): 34–40.

NCTE (National Council of Teachers of English) Committee on Classroom Practices, Chair Jeff Golub. *Activities to Promote Critical Thinking*. Urbana, IL: NCTE, 1986.

Parker, Walter C. "Teaching Thinking: The Pervasive Approach." *Journal of Teacher Education* 38.3 (1987): 50–56.

Segedy, Michael. "Adapting the Courtroom Trial Format to Literature." NCTE 88–92.

Swope, John W., and Edgar H. Thompson. "Three *R*'s for Critical Thinking About Literature: Reading, 'Riting, and Responding." NCTE 75–79.

Vinz, Ruth. "Thinking Through Dilemmas." NCTE 107–111.

TEACHING STUDENTS TO VARY READING RATES

The ability to read flexibly (that is, at different rates according to purpose and subject matter) is a valuable skill for students of literature. If students learn to adjust their reading rates and habits, they are likely both to improve their comprehension and to increase their enjoyment of literature.

To introduce the concept of reading flexibility, draw on students' experiences with recreational reading. Ask them to suppose they have just acquired a new novel by a favorite author. Ask what they would read first, how many times they might read all or part of the novel, and what they look for as they read. Responses might run along these lines: They first read the title and any other information on the cover and then may glance at any illustrations or chapter titles, all to get an idea of the subject and the plot. They may also read a few pages quickly to see whether the setting, characters, tone, and style are familiar. Then they probably settle on a comfortable pace to read the whole story, perhaps stopping occasionally to think about what a character says or does. Later they may come back to the story, rereading certain pages quickly to locate a character's exact words or more slowly to recapture the feeling of a favorite scene. They may even reread the whole story to see more clearly how early events led to the climax.

Use this example to show students that they (1) usually read something more than once to get the most out of it, (2) sometimes vary the speed at which they read, and (3) choose a reading speed based on their purpose for reading.

Setting a Purpose

Students often mistakenly believe that studying and enjoying literature are two mutually exclusive activities. Some may argue that their main purpose in reading a literature anthology's selections should be pleasure—having to "appreciate" each selection through study spoils the fun. These students don't realize that enjoyment increases with understanding, and that the mental struggle itself can be a pleasure. Readers will take more pleasure in the irony of a story when they recognize the technique of irony and understand how the writer uses it to manipulate our responses. Furthermore, students can better articulate a personal response to a work if they possess the terms to talk about it. Full enjoyment of literature, then, requires reading for several purposes: to get an overview, to respond to ideas and literary techniques, to locate important details, to refresh the memory, or to generate new ideas.

Naming one of these purposes for a particular reading is just the first step. An active reader takes another important step: formulating initial questions to be answered while reading. For example, to get an overview, a reader might ask the following questions: What type of work is it? What is the topic? When was it written, and by whom? To locate particular details, a reader might ask these questions: What key words or phrases will help me find the details? Am I likely to find them near the beginning, the middle, or the end of the work? Such reading-purpose questions not only further define the purpose but also provide an active reading plan.

With a definite purpose in mind, students should more easily identify a suitable reading rate. In general, they should use an average, or "most comfortable," rate when reading for pleasure. They should read faster when reading to get an overview, locate details, refresh the memory, or generate ideas. And they should learn to slow down when reading to respond to the writer's ideas and language. Students can apply this approach to literature by using the following reading techniques.

Skimming

Skimming is reading quickly for main ideas—just how quickly, in terms of words per minute, will vary from person to person. A rule of thumb is that the skimming speed should be twice as fast as the individual's average reading rate (Fry). To achieve the higher speed, the reader skips some sentences or details, concentrating instead on reading just enough of each paragraph to get its main idea. Since the reader does not consider every detail, the level of comprehension necessarily decreases somewhat. Some teachers like to describe skimming as a "prereading" or "rereading" activity; this distinction often helps students decide when to use the technique.

Perhaps most important is the use of skimming as a prereading activity. Explain to students that the common habit of simply opening the book to the right page and reading straight through once at an average rate is not the most efficient—or rewarding—reading approach. When they open the book to read a selection, they should first skim the title, the headnote, background information about the writer and the work, chapter or section titles, the questions and assignments that follow the selection, and their own notes from preliminary class instruction. The purpose of skimming a work before they read is to obtain an overview of the work. This skimming will help students prepare specific questions to be explored in a class reading.

As a rereading activity, skimming is an efficient way to review main ideas of a work and mentally summarize a personal response to it. A student might quickly go over a selection with questions such as these in mind: What does the writer say about life or about people? What literary devices does the writer use? Does the work end as I expected it to? How did it make me feel, and why? If skimming reveals a point of confusion, the student can slow down for a more careful rereading. Note that students may also use skimming to review their class discussion notes.

Skimming is useful, too, for generating writing topics. To questions like those above, a student searching for a topic might add these: Why am I drawn to a particular character, passage, or scene? Which literary element of the work seems most effective? Does this work have something in common with another I have read? How does the theme of the work relate to my own life?

Close Reading

A close reading is a slow and careful reading for the purpose of analyzing and evaluating a literary work. For class discussion and many assignments, mature readers may need to read at this "thoughtful" pace only once. When reading a difficult or lengthy work and when writing essays, almost all students should do two or more close readings, at least of portions of the work.

What all of your eleventh graders should begin to realize is that in reading literature closely, they are seeking three levels of understanding: literal, inferential, and critical. Put another way, they must read the lines, read between the lines, and read beyond the lines (Poindexter and Prescott). You no doubt have found students to be most comfortable, and most practiced, at the literal level—understanding directly stated details. They usually need more help at the inferential level—understanding implied ideas—and at the critical level—understanding a writer's purposes and making value judgments about a piece of literature.

POSING QUESTIONS   Before students begin a close reading, have them list a few questions about the selection to guide their initial reading. Use the text's headnotes and the teaching suggestions in the Teaching Notes to help them ask appropriate and specific questions. The headnote introducing each selection directs attention to a particular aspect of the work and ends by posing a reading purpose question. Several sections in the Teaching Notes (in particular, Introducing the [Selection] and Reading the [Selection]) will give you additional ideas for elements that students can look for and consider as they read. Posing initial questions sets a precise purpose for close reading, activates students' prior knowledge of both literature and cultural values, and arouses personal interest in a literary work.

PREDICTING OUTCOMES   For several selections, the textbook and the Teaching Notes suggest a stopping place in the reading, a point at which students are asked to predict what will happen and give reasons for their opinions. Take full advantage of this strategy, and use it for other selections whenever practicable. Many teachers have found that predicting outcomes encourages not only a rich exchange of ideas in the classroom, but also multilevel comprehension, more so than a traditional review of what has been read so far (Nessel). In order to predict the resolution of events, students must recall essential details, draw inferences about the situation and characters, and evaluate the writer's intent. Thus, the class gains a review as well as practice in critical thinking. Evaluate the predictions not on how close students come to the writer's conclusion but rather on how logically they form and support their hypotheses.

RESPONDING PERSONALLY   Suggest to students that their goal in reading closely is to understand their own intellectual and emotional responses to a literary work: what they liked or disliked and why, how the work affected them and why. They should think about their reactions as they read and when they discuss the work in class.

Alert students to the Responding sections following each selection in the text. The questions and assignments will help guide them, during a close reading, through the three levels of comprehension and will lead them, after the reading, to an organized expression of their personal responses through creative and critical writing.

Guidelines for Reading

Certain close-reading techniques apply generally to literature; others are important to particular types of literary works. You may want to duplicate and hand out the following guidelines, which are addressed to students.

GUIDES FOR READING LITERATURE CLOSELY

1. Write down a few questions you would like to answer as you read the selection. The skimming you did to get an overview of the work will help you pose questions, as will your teacher's introduction. Perhaps your questions will relate to the title.

2. Take notes as you read. Jot down answers you find to your initial questions as well as further questions that come to mind. Note your impression of the characters. Note passages that seem to hint at the writer's purpose or theme, passages that are particularly vivid to you, and passages that seem confusing. Identify how different parts of the work make you feel.

3. Stop occasionally to think about what you have read. Ask yourself these questions: What main ideas or

events have been presented so far? What do I think will happen next?

4. Look up unfamiliar words and allusions or use context clues to make educated guesses. Some definitions will be found in the textbook's Glossary. Keep your dictionary handy for words that seem important but that you can't figure out.

5. Keep in mind the type of literature you are reading. The questions you ask often relate to the literary form. Here are some specific hints:

Fiction. Look for the elements of storytelling: What is the point of view? The narrator's tone? What conflict or conflicts does the writer create? What complicates the problem? What are the main events of the plot? How does one event cause another to happen? How does the setting affect the story? What passage marks the climax? How is the main conflict resolved? What is the theme of the story?

Poetry. Read a poem several times, at least once aloud. (If the poetry is in an epic or a play, read each section or scene several times.) Pay particular attention to punctuation; it will help you follow the writer's ideas and help you ''hear'' the emphasized words. Paraphrase lines or passages that are not immediately clear. Which words or lines do you think are most important in the poem? Make a note of figures of speech, and look for the writer's main idea. Is a central thought or emotion expressed? Or is the poet telling a story? Try to state the main idea in one or two sentences.

Nonfiction. Be alert for the writer's attitudes toward the topic and toward the people described. Is the writer's tone humorous, serious, sympathetic, hostile, or some combination of these feelings? Is the work objective, or is it written from a subjective, or personal, point of view? Does the writer use narrative techniques, such as foreshadowing or suspense, to hold your interest? Decide what the writer's main purpose is: to tell a story, to explain or inform, to describe, or to persuade. Notice how the writer organizes information, and make an informal outline of the main points. Then determine the main idea of the work. Is it directly stated? Implied? How do you feel about the idea?

Drama. Who wants what, and what steps are taken to get it? What complications arise? Who drives the action? What feelings about life or people is the writer expressing?

Scanning

Scanning is reading very rapidly to locate details. Students unfamiliar with the term are likely to recognize the technique when it is explained. They use scanning to find a name and number in the telephone book, a listing in the television program guide, or a definition in the dictionary. Scanning is faster than skimming, because the reader is searching for key words rather than reading sentences or phrases to isolate ideas. The reader may focus the mind and eye by moving a finger rapidly across and down the page, not stopping until the key word or phrase is found.

In the study of literature, scanning is most useful as a rereading activity. When students have already read a work and know its organization, they can use scanning to answer certain kinds of follow-up questions, usually ones of literal comprehension (Who? What? Where? When?). For example, you may ask a student to identify Homeric similes that help describe a certain episode in an epic. The student would first locate the episode and then find the similes by scanning for key words such as *like* and *as*.

Two things are essential to scanning successfully: having a sense of a work's organization (Should I look first in the beginning, middle, or end? Didn't that scene close an early chapter?) and choosing key words or phrases appropriate to the search (Which words in the question are key? What key words are implied by the question?). When students think they have located the detail, they should stop to read the sentences around it to make sure they are correct. If they discover that they are frequently inaccurate when scanning, they should slow their pace for a while and check their choice of key words.

You can give the class a timed practice in scanning during your vocabulary exercises. List on the board ten vocabulary words, out of alphabetical order, that are defined in the Glossary. Tell students to write down for each one the word that follows it in the Glossary. Explain that you will start the stopwatch when they begin scanning and after one minute will begin putting the time on the board in ten-second intervals. When each student has finished the last item, he or she can then write down the last time given on the board. Check the answers and response times in class, and suggest further practice at home to increase speed or improve accuracy.

References

Fry, Edward B. *Skimming and Scanning, Middle Level.* Providence, RI: Jamestown, 1982.

Nessel, Denise. ''Reading Comprehension: Asking the Right Questions.''*PhiDeltaKappan*68(1987):442–444.

Poindexter, Candace A., and Susan Prescott. ''A Technique for Teaching Students to Draw Inferences from Text.'' *The Reading Teacher* 39 (1986): 908–911.

PROMOTING THE GROWTH OF STUDENTS' VOCABULARY

Many teachers have found that a concentrated effort on vocabulary during literature study results in great gains in students' active vocabularies. Often in such efforts you first must convince students of the value of a larger vocabulary. Besides continually sharing your own enthusiasm for words, you can easily demonstrate the necessity and power of language. Tell students to close their eyes for a few moments and to think thoughts for which there are no words. After a minute or so, the class will probably protest that it can't be done. This response is the point of the exercise: Words are essential to thought. Point out that the more words students know, the better they will be able to understand and communicate their ideas.

In guiding students through vocabulary for the selections, you will probably find that a multifaceted approach is most effective—a combination of dictionary use, context study, and structural analysis.

Dictionary Use

Here are a few ideas for encouraging the dictionary habit.

1. Have students turn to the Glossary (text pages 1229–1234) during your general introduction to the anthology. Go over the pronunciation key to review common symbols for sounds, and point out the abbreviations for parts of speech. Remind students that many words have multiple meanings, and note that the Glossary defines words according to their use in the selections.
2. Use a short, timed exercise to check students' basic dictionary skills. Provide dictionaries, and give the class five minutes to look up and write down the pronunciation and correct definition of three words from a selection. Check responses for the third word, asking about problems in following guide words, alphabetization, or pronunciation symbols.
3. Show students how to use dictionaries quickly and effectively when reading literature. Tell them to keep handy a supply of blank index cards. As they encounter unfamiliar words, they can jot down each one on a card, with the page number for reference, and later look up several words at once. Direct them to write the pronunciation under the word, say the word aloud, and, on the back of the card, write the part of speech and meaning that fit the context. Have students bring in their cards every week or two and compare their collections.
4. Pay special attention to words with interesting histories. Help students understand how to read an etymology and give them some in-class practice. Give examples that will help them discover that a word is borrowed from another language, for example, or that it derives from an old custom. Show students how to use special dictionaries of word and phrase origins.
5. Review usage labels in the dictionary when the class studies Americanisms, jargon, colloquialisms, and so on.
6. Be sure students understand that a dictionary's method of numbering definitions is significant. Some dictionaries begin with the oldest sense of a word, others with the most frequent usage. Have the class look up words such as *dashboard, temperance,* and *wardrobe* to see how the use of certain words has changed over time.
7. Emphasize pronunciation in your dictionary drills to help students "sound out" new words.

Context Study

The following activities will help students learn *and use* new words through recognizing context clues, making connections between words, and creating new contexts through original writing. The following suggestions are ways to reinforce students' use of context clues when they are reading or listening.

1. Before class begins, write on the board a sentence about the day's literary topic. The sentence should contain two or three new vocabulary words, with some clue to their meanings. Underline the vocabulary words. When students arrive, ask them to write a paraphrase of the sentence, without using the underlined words, while you call the roll. Discuss their responses, asking what context clues they used. Use the exercise as a springboard to your reading or discussion of the selection.
2. If you are reading a selection aloud, stop occasionally when you come to an unfamiliar word, and ask students for context clues to its meaning.
3. Use the vocabulary words in your comments to let students hear them in context.
4. When the vocabulary list for a selection is long, assign different words to different students. Ask them to find for each word a context clue, a synonym, and an antonym, and then share these in a class discussion.
5. Have students look for vocabulary words in contexts other than the text selection. For example, ask them to locate and paraphrase famous quotations in which the words appear. (Suggest that they look for quotations by using the index to *Bartlett's Familiar Quo-*

tations or another book of quotations. If a word does not appear in such an index, searching for a quotation with a vocabulary word will probably be futile.)

6. For quick reviews, write on the chalkboard the sentences from the selection that contain the vocabulary words, but replace the words with blanks. Ask students to fill in the blanks with the correct word from an alphabetized list, and discuss how they made their choices.

The next two activities emphasize word relationships.

7. Review synonyms or antonyms for vocabulary words by devising short matching quizzes. You might have students create them: Assign a small group to select ten words and put together a scrambled list of synonyms (or antonyms). Check the group's work, and have them write the two lists on the chalkboard, one list numbered, the other lettered. Ask the rest of the class to match the words.

8. Review any group of related words with a simple crossword puzzle using the words' definitions as clues. You may create the puzzle yourself or have students volunteer to do it. Give the puzzle a title that classifies the group of words, such as "Vivid Adverbs" or "Words That Describe [a character's name]." Some teachers also find such puzzles effective as a review of literary terms: "The Elements of Drama," "Sound Effects in Poetry," and so on.

The following activities require students to write new contexts for the words they are studying. Several suggestions also take advantage of the strategy of centering word study on a concept.

9. Have students create their own direct context clues for new words. Ask them to write sentences for vocabulary words, giving a clue to meaning by definition, example, restatement, comparison, or contrast.

10. Explain that some words have *connotations* (emotional associations) as well as *denotations* (dictionary meanings). To explore connotative meaning, have students use five vocabulary words in original sentences, and then substitute a synonym for each vocabulary word. How well does the synonym work in the same context? Does the synonym have exactly the same connotations? Ask students what difference in meaning or feeling is created.

11. Choose two or three vocabulary words that have distinctive multiple meanings, and ask students to write a sentence using each meaning.

12. If the vocabulary words for a selection number fewer than ten, offer students the challenge of writing one sentence using as many of the words as possible. However fanciful, the sentence must be intelligible.

13. When the vocabulary list for a selection is long, group the words by part of speech. Have students write a sentence using one word from each group and compare their sentences.

14. For a group of adjectives, ask students to create comparisons. For example, Sarah is more *disconsolate* than a lost kitten.

15. Encourage students' use of active verbs by having them write sentences in which they apply new verbs to a school situation.

16. When several vocabulary words for a selection relate to a particular geographical or cultural setting, introduce the words as a group. For example, *adobe, arroyo, mesa, mission* (church), and *tumbleweed* are words used in the American West or Southwest. Have students identify the common element through definitions and etymologies and then write sentences or a paragraph using the words.

17. If students are learning descriptive words that apply to a character in a selection, ask them to write sentences applying the words to other characters they have studied.

18. Assign different students, one or two at a time, to use vocabulary words in writing three or four quiz questions about a selection's plot, characters, or setting. At the beginning of class, the students can call on classmates to answer the questions, orally correcting the answers and clarifying the meanings of the vocabulary words when necessary.

19. For a review of words from several selections, group them according to an emotion or idea. Have students write new sentences using each word.

20. Encourage regular attention to new words by offering bonus points for the appropriate use of vocabulary words in the text writing assignments and in class discussions.

21. On Fridays, have students vote on their favorite new word from the week's vocabulary. Ask them to explain their choices.

Structural Analysis

Students can often learn and remember new words by breaking them into recognizable parts. Try these activities for an approach that focuses on roots and affixes. A list of common Greek and Latin word parts follows the activities.

1. Have students make a personal set of flashcards of Greek and Latin roots and affixes. Introduce a few roots, prefixes, and suffixes at a time, having students write each one on an index card. On the other side of the card, students should write the meaning of the root or affix, along with an example word that you provide—preferably a vocabulary word or literary term already assigned. Tell students to be alert throughout the term to vocabulary words (as well as words from other sources) that contain these roots and affixes and to add the words to their cards. Remind them that some words, such as *infallible,* will be recorded on more than one card.

Every week or two, ask students to bring in their collections of vocabulary flashcards. Divide the class into small groups for peer quizzing with the cards. Spot-check the cards and quizzing to evaluate students' progress and to decide on review strategies. (After you have introduced several groups of word parts, you may want the students themselves to begin presenting new roots and affixes from their assigned vocabulary or from other reading.)

2. In one lesson present prefixes that show position. Guide students in identifying and defining words with these prefixes. The examples might be vocabulary words from the selections, literary terms, or more familiar words encountered in the text.

3. Encourage students to recognize prefixes that create a negative or opposite meaning. Ask students to complete a list of ''not'' definitions with words they have studied.

4. To help students recognize the grammatical function of an unfamiliar word in context, show them how suffixes often—*not always*—signal a particular part of speech. Students can make a note on their suffix flashcards or list the groups in a vocabulary notebook, but remind them to watch for exceptions. In some words, the ending looks like a suffix but actually is part of a root or base word.

5. After you define a common Greek or Latin root in a new word, divide students into small groups, and, setting a time limit, have them list familiar words built on the same root. The group with the longest list could receive bonus points.

6. Occasionally review small groups of prefix, suffix, and root definitions with oral and written quizzes. For variety, you could create crossword puzzles or conduct a group competition on the pattern of a spelldown.

There are hundreds of roots and affixes, and the following lists contain only a selection of those that students may learn through their vocabulary study in literature. As you introduce the study of word parts, point out that the spellings of roots and affixes sometimes vary, that affixes almost always alter the root's meaning in some way, and that the meanings of some Latin and Greek roots have undergone slight changes over time.

ROOTS

Greek

-bio-	life (*biography*)
-chron-	time (*chronological*)
-crac-, -crat-	power, rule (*democracy, autocrat*)
-cris-, -crit-	separate, judge (*crisis, critical*)
-cycl-	circle (*Cyclops*)
-glos-, -glot-	tongue (*glossary, polyglot*)
-graph-	write, record (*biography, photograph*)
-log-, -logy-	speaking, study (*chronology, dialogue*)
-ops-, -opt-	eye (*Cyclops, optical*)
-phon-	sound (*phonetic*)
-stereo-	firm, solid (*stereotype*)

Latin

-aud-	hear (*audible*)
-cred-	believe (*incredulous*)
-dict-	tell, say (*prediction*)
-duc-, -duct-	lead, draw (*deduction, produce*)
-fac-, -fic-	make, do (*benefactor, fiction*)
-flect-	bend (*deflect, reflection*)
-ject-	throw (*projectile, reject*)
-leg-, -lect-	read (*legend, lecture*)
-loqu-	speak (*eloquent, soliloquy*)
-mis-, -mit-	send (*commission, noncommittal*)
-mort-	die (*immortality*)
-quer-, -quest-, -quir-	seek, ask (*query, quest, inquiry*)
-sci-	know (*omniscient*)
-scrib-, -script-	write (*describe, manuscript*)
-spec-, -spic-, -spect-	look at, examine (*circumspect, speculate, inspect*)
-tens-, -tent-	hold (*tenant, untenable*)
-vers-, -vert-	turn (*averse, invert, versatile*)
-vid-, -vis-	see (*videotape, visage, visual*)
-viv-	live (*vivacious, vivid*)

PREFIXES

Greek

a-	not, without (*atheist, atypical*)
ant-	against (*antagonist*)
auto-	self (*autobiography*)
dia-	through, across, between (*dialogue*)
exo-	out of, outside (*exodus*)
mono-	one (*monologue*)
poly-	many (*polytheism*)
pro-	before, first (*protagonist*)
syn-	with, together (*synthesis*)

Latin

a-, ab-, abs-	away, from (*abominable, abscond, abhor*)
ad-	to, toward (*adversary, advocate*)
ante-	before (*antecedent*)
bene-	well (*benediction, benefactor*)
circum-	around, on all sides (*circumstance*)
com-, con-	with, together (*complicity, connotation*)
contra-	against (*contrary*)
de-	from, down (*denotation, denouement, depress*)
dis-	apart, away (*dispel, disrepute*)
e-, ex-	out (*evade, exorbitant*)
extra-	outside of, beyond (*extravagant, extraordinary*)

il-, im-, in-, ir-	not (*incredulous, irresolute*) *or* in, into, on (*impetus, inversion*)	
inter-	between (*intermediary*)	
non-	not (*nonentity*)	
omni-	all, everywhere (*omniscient*)	
per-	through (*perpetual*)	
post-	after, behind (*postpone, postscript*)	
pre-	before (*prewriting*)	
pro-	forward (*projectile*)	
re-	again, back (*redress, reference, resolution*)	
soli-	alone, only (*soliloquy, solitude*)	
sub-, sup-	under, beneath, below (*subversive, support*)	
super-	above, over, outside (*superficial*)	
trans-	across (*translucent*)	

SUFFIXES

-able, -ible	able to (*formidable, infallible*)
-age, -ance, -ence, -ity, -ment, -ness, -ship, -tion	a state or condition (*atonement, calamity, carnage, gyration, indulgence, vigilance*)
-al, -ic, -ly	similar to (*acutely, cynical, heroic*)
-an, -ee, -eer, -er, -ian, -ist, -ite, -or	a person, one who (*barbarian, mountaineer, civilian, strategist, writer, actor*)
-ate	to act or do (*evaluate, perpetrate*)
-er, -est	degree (*shadier, shadiest*)
-ful, -ous	full of (*fearful, ominous*)
-less	without (*aimless, ruthless*)

VARYING TEACHING TECHNIQUES

Using a variety of teaching techniques keeps students' interest high and encourages their personal involvement with literature. A variety of approaches also allows you to accommodate individual learning styles. The following teaching suggestions make the study of literature an active, multifaceted experience for your class.

Collaborative Learning

To foster regular collaborative learning, you may want to assign students to groups (no more than five or six members) and pairs early in the year. Use a random-selection method such as counting-off. Then you will waste no time forming groups for each new activity. You may change the groups and pairs at some point, but do not change them too frequently. Students benefit from working with the same classmates for an extended period. They begin to appreciate different learning styles and abilities, and they develop a team spirit. The two group methods that follow have many applications in a literature course.

Expert Groups. In this technique, members of a small group become highly knowledgeable about one aspect of a topic or literary work and serve as experts for the other students. When you are reading Langston Hughes's poems, for example, one group might become experts on the Harlem Renaissance, another on Hughes's Simple stories, and a third on Hughes's life. The expert groups report to the class and answer whatever questions their classmates may have about their area of expertise. The benefit of this strategy is twofold: Group members gain experience in intensive research, and all students gain more information about a topic or a work.

Jigsawing. Jigsawing, which uses two levels of groups, is another method by which students become each other's teachers. This method is particularly effective for covering lengthy or complex material when class time is limited. For example, suppose you want your class to paraphrase five paragraphs of difficult prose. Divide the students into five groups, assign one paragraph to each group, and set a time limit for the paraphrase. (Whenever possible, use any standing groups for this first jigsaw level.)

When the students have finished, make a second-level group assignment. Within each group, have students count off (or designate themselves by letters, colors, etc.) and then move into their second groups—all 1's (A's, reds) together, 2's (B's, blues) together, and so on. Each student now becomes the "expert" for the paragraph paraphrased in his or her first group and presents the information to members of the second group.

Jigsawing also works well with lengthy vocabulary lists or an exercise containing many items. In those cases, divide the words or items equally among the first-level groups, and then proceed as before to the second-level groups.

Into, Through, and Beyond Techniques

Many teachers think of three distinct stages in teaching a selection: preparing students for it, guiding them through it, and offering them bridges from it to other works, ideas, and activities. Here is a summary of activities appropriate to each stage. Detailed descriptions of concept formation, imaging, debating moral dilemmas, journal writing, sensory recall, and Readers' Theater follow the summary.

To lead students *into* a work:

1. Use filmstrips, films, or recordings to arouse students' interest.
2. Invite lecturers to provide special background on a selection. The speakers may be knowledgeable about a particular work, author, or literary topic; or they may have experience that relates to a selection. Someone who has visited or lived in Boston, for example, could provide background for ''Old Ironsides.''
3. Introduce the work with a variety of background information (history, the author's biography, technical explanations), using the text's introductions and the supplementary information in these Teaching Notes.
4. Distribute plot summaries, study guides, or character lists for difficult or lengthy works.
5. Have students master vocabulary words before they begin to read, using a variety of strategies (see Promoting the Growth of Students' Vocabulary, pages 361–364 of these Teaching Notes).
6. Encourage skimming as a prereading step, and guide students in posing questions for a close reading (see Teaching Students to Vary Reading Rates, pages 358–360).
7. Use the techniques of concept formation, imaging, and journal quickwrites (see pages 365–366).
8. Read portions of the selection orally.

To guide students *through* a work:

9. Assign the questions following the text selections for discussion or writing. Assign the creative and critical writing exercises for individual or collaborative work.
10. Pause during in-class readings to allow students to predict outcomes.
11. Assign groups of students to dramatize and perform brief scenes from a story or novel.
12. Organize debates on issues and moral dilemmas raised by a work (see page 366).
13. Have students keep dialectical journals.
14. Schedule Readers' Theater presentations.
15. Lead imaging and sensory recall exercises (see pages 365–366).
16. Assign reports and projects for class presentation, encouraging forms of expression other than writing (creating maps, illustrations, charts, time lines; performing; composing original music; etc.).

To lead students *beyond* a work:

17. Encourage students to make connections between the work and other works they have read. The connections may be with works in the same genre or in a different one. Possible connections include subject, theme, major symbols, imagery, allusions, and historical setting. Students may present their comparisons and contrasts in compositions, reports, and projects.
18. Suggest further reading of works by the same author, of books and articles related to the selection's background, and of works in the same genre.
19. Have a group of students write and produce an original video play inspired by some aspect of the selection (a moral dilemma, a character, a striking element such as horror).
20. Have students create games based on literary selections.
21. Have a group of students assume the personae of characters from different works and engage in a panel discussion on a specific topic. Instruct students to prepare carefully for their roles so that they can respond in character and in a way appropriate to the time period portrayed in the work.

Concept Formation

When students use concept formation to approach a new work, they practice both classifying and predicting. To use this technique, present students—without any preliminary explanation—with a list of words, objects, names, or ideas taken from or related to the selection. (You may restrict the list to one category of information or mix several categories.) Ask the students to group items that seem related and then to formulate predictions about the selection based on the items and their common elements. For example, from the vocabulary list for ''Ahab'' from *Moby Dick,* students might isolate *vindictive, misanthropic, diabolical,* and *outlandish* and predict that Ahab has something to do with evil, that he's someone they wouldn't want to work for. From a list of words and phrases in the first three paragraphs of ''The Key,'' students can infer the kind of person Bessie Popkin is and how she views her world.

Concept formation, in addition to sharpening critical thinking, involves students actively in a work even before they begin reading. An unexplained list can be an intriguing puzzle, and once students have made predictions based on such a list, they may read a selection with more eagerness and more purpose.

Imaging

Imaging taps students' imaginations, leading them into a literary work through sensory awareness. Acting as guide, you ask students to close their eyes and then ''talk'' them into a specific time, place, or mental state. You may also play mood-setting or period music, and tell students to draw on their sensory memories as you give them a description rich in sensory detail.

Imaging is effective with image-rich poetry as well as with narratives; you may use it to introduce a selection as well as to focus on individual passages and sections. For example, you may want to set the stage for Mark Twain's ''Life on the Mississippi'' by guiding students in imagining the sights, sounds, and smells of the great river.

Imaging not only helps remove barriers to understanding of culture, time, and place but also shows students their own considerable power to evoke sensory experiences from words.

Moral Dilemmas

Examining moral dilemmas arising from conflicts within literary works is an approach that engages students' feelings and stimulates their critical thinking. You may use an actual situation from a selection (the moral dilemma Lena Younger faces in deciding what to do with her check in "A Raisin in the Sun") or an extrapolation from it. Whichever you choose, describe the situation in such a way that students are forced to take sides. (Some other provocative conflicts are those pitting individual conscience against law and those forcing a choice between loyalties.)

Have students articulate the opposing positions. Then write each as a statement on the board, and ask students to take sides by a show of hands. Divide students on each side into smaller groups for developing supporting arguments. Allow sufficient time, and then, taking one side at a time, have each group's spokesperson present one supporting argument. Go from group to group until supporting arguments are exhausted, and then allow a free exchange of rebuttals, guiding the discussion as necessary. Be sure each student comes to some formal closure about the moral dilemma, perhaps through a journal entry or a brief essay.

Journals

Journals are excellent tools for the study of literature: They encourage personal responses to literary works; allow freer, less formal writing; build a repository of writing ideas; and offer students a full year's record of their changing perspectives and thoughts. A loose-leaf notebook will allow students to make both private entries and assigned entries for your review. When you make journal assignments, specify those that must be turned in. Students should feel secure that no one has access to their private entries.

Two specialized uses of journals follow.

DIALECTICAL JOURNALS Sometimes called dialogue journals, dialectical journals are double-entry records in which students take notes about a literary work and then add their own reflections about the notes. Each page is divided into two columns, one labeled "Note-taking" and the other "Note-making." Notes about the work may include facts, passages, quoted dialogue, and significant plot developments. The students' recorded musings about

these notes will be personal, but occasionally you may want to direct a particular kind of response. (For example, you could direct students to "take" notes about a poem's imagery and then to "make" notes about their emotional responses to the images.)

A dialectical journal is valuable because students are forced to go beyond facts and think about what they read. Encourage students also to review all their entries for a selection, and then write a summary of their personal responses.

QUICKWRITES The aim of a quickwrite journal entry is an immediate, spontaneous, unedited response to a stimulus. Possible stimuli are many: a passage from a selection, an idea you supply, music, guided imaging and sensory recall, and so on. Quickwrites can be used in all three stages of teaching a selection (into, through, and beyond).

Sensory Recall

Literature presents all readers with emotions and situations far removed from their own experiences. Sensory recall, a technique by which professionals prepare for acting roles, is one means of making these unfamiliar experiences more understandable. An actress playing a character who, after extreme provocation, physically attacks someone may have no experience with such violence, for example. To help her "get in touch" with her character's feelings, the director may ask her to remember being driven crazy by mosquitoes and then act out the resulting scene. Under the director's coaching, the actress begins to understand her character's response to the provocation and can then build a believable series of emotions for her role.

An adaptation of this theatrical approach can help students identify with unfamiliar characters and understand emotions otherwise out of their reach. As an introduction, students may enjoy watching a classmate with acting experience demonstrate the technique, but all students can participate in sensory recall. First, isolate an experience in a selection, build an appropriate parallel situation (or brainstorm situations with students), and then have students put themselves in that situation and write their thoughts and feelings. You might use sensory recall, for example, to make accessible the bizarre events in "Rip Van Winkle." Ask students to recall awakening after a deep sleep in a strange room. Elicit from them memories of feelings of disorientation and momentary panic, and they will begin to feel more acutely Rip's feelings as he awakens from his long sleep.

Initially, you will have to lead students in using sensory recall, but after some practice, they will be able to create their own parallel situations and record their responses in their journals.

Readers' Theater

Readers' Theater is simply a group oral reading of a selection, whether the work is a play, story, poem, or essay. Effective Readers' Theater is not impromptu, however. Students are assigned roles, or passages, and practice their reading outside of class. Readers' Theater hones students' skills in oral interpretation and makes a work come alive for the whole class. It is a dramatic presentation with a minimum of production worries (you need only stools or chairs) and stage-fright problems (most students are much less frightened of sitting and reading than of acting).

Students may read whole plays or single acts or scenes; they may create their own scripts from short stories, novels, and epics; they may present poems and essays by alternating the reading of stanzas and paragraphs. One way to accomplish the latter is to count off the stanzas or paragraphs according to the number of readers. The first reader reads all the stanzas or paragraphs numbered one, the second reads those numbered two, and so on. Remember also that for scripts one reader should read aloud the scene setting, necessary stage directions, and any prologue or explanatory narrative.

You may want to assign roles for certain dramatic readings, but at other times students may form their own groups and choose roles. If students in a particular small group want to read a script in which the number of roles exceeds the number of members, some students can read more than one role. Whenever a student reads more than one role, he or she can indicate character changes with simple props (hats, glasses, shawls, etc.) or with name signs.

OBTAINING AUDIOVISUAL AIDS

Guides and Indexes

The following sourcebooks contain information about the wealth of educational audiovisual materials available.

AV Instruction: Technology, Media, and Methods. Ed. James W. Brown, Richard B. Lewis, and Fred F. Harcleroad. 6th ed. 1983. McGraw-Hill Book Co., 1221 Avenue of the Americas, New York, NY 10020.

Educational Film/Video Locator. 4th ed. 2 vols. 1990–1991. R. R. Bowker Co., 245 W. 17th Street, New York, NY 10011. (This reference contains 51,900 videos and films viewed and selected by 46 media library staffs across the country. It also contains 194,000 titles held by members of the Consortium of College and University Media Centers.)

Educational Media and Technology Yearbook. Ed. Elwood E. Miller. 17th vol. 1991. Libraries Unlimited, Inc. P.O. Box 3988, Englewood, CO 80155. (The yearbook is published in cooperation with the Association for Educational Communications and Technology.)

Educators Guide to Free Audio and Video Materials. Ed. James L. Berger. *Educators Guide to Free Films* and *Educators Guide to Free Filmstrips and Slides.* Ed. John C. Diffor and Elaine N. Diffor. Annual eds. Educators Progress Service, Inc., 214 Center St., Randolph, WI 53956.

NICEM Index Series. 1984, 1985, 1990 eds. in hardcover, monthly bulletins (separate multivolume sets for tapes, films, videotapes, slides, and transparencies). National Information Center for Educational Media, Access Innovations, Inc., P.O. Box 40130, Albuquerque, NM 87196. (The center works closely with the Library of Congress to update indexed titles.)

Suppliers

The following producers and distributors publish catalogs of their offerings.

Agency for Instructional Technology (formerly AITelevision), Box A, Bloomington, IN 47402.

AIMS Media, 9710 DeSoto Ave., Chatsworth, CA 91311.

Allyn and Bacon, Inc., 160 Gold St., Needham Heights, MA 02194.

Association Films, Inc., 866 Third Ave., New York, NY 10022.

Barr Films, Box 7878, 12801 Schabarum Ave., Irwindale, CA 91706.

Blackhawk Films, Inc., 12636 Beatrice St., Los Angeles, CA 90066.

Center for Humanities, Inc., Communications Park, Box 1000, Mount Kisco, NY 10549.

Churchill Films, 12210 Nebraska Ave., Los Angeles, CA 90025.

CRM Films LP, 2215 Faraday, Carlsbad CA 92008.

Encyclopaedia Britannica Educational Corp., 310 S. Michigan Ave., Chicago, IL 60604.

Epcot Educational Media (Walt Disney Co.), 500 S. Buena Vista St., Burbank, CA 91521.

Films for the Humanities, Inc., P.O. Box 2053, Princeton, NJ 08540.

Films, Inc. (also distributes Audio Brandon, Macmillan, and Texture Films), 1144 Wilmette Ave., Wilmette, IL 60091.

Great Plains National Instructional Television Library (GPN), University of Nebraska at Lincoln, Box 80669, Lincoln, NE 68501.

Grover Film Productions, P.O. Box 12, Helotes, TX 78023.

Guidance Associates, Communications Park, Box 3000, Mount Kisco, NY 10549.

Holt, Rinehart and Winston, School Division, 1627 Woodland Ave., Austin, TX 78741.

Indiana University Audio-Visual Center, Indiana University, Bloomington, IN 47405.

International Film Bureau, 332 S. Michigan Ave., Chicago, IL 60604.

Listening Library, Inc., Box 611, 1 Park Ave., Old Greenwich, CT 06870.

Lucerne Media, 37 Ground Pine Rd., Morris Plains, NJ 07950.

National Audiovisual Center, National Archives and Records Administration, 8700 Edgeworth Dr., Capitol Heights, MD 20743.

National Council of Teachers of English, 1111 Kenyon Rd., Urbana, IL 61801.

National Education Association, Audio-Visual Instruction, 1201 Sixteenth St. N.W., Washington, DC 20036.

National Film Board of Canada, 1251 Avenue of the Americas, New York, NY 10020.

National Public Radio, Educational Cassettes, 2025 M St. N.W., Washington, DC 20036.

National Video Clearinghouse, Inc., 100 Lafayette Dr., Syosset, NY 11791.

Phoenix/BFA Films and Video, Inc. 468 Park Ave. S., New York, NY 10016.

Public Television Library (Public Broadcasting System), 475 L'Enfant Plaza S.W., Washington, DC 20024.

Pyramid Film and Video, P.O. Box 1048, Santa Monica, CA 90406.

Silver Burdett Co., 250 James St., Morristown, NJ 07960.

Smithsonian Collection of Recordings, Division of Smithsonian Institution Press, Washington, DC 20560.

Society for Visual Education, Inc., 1345 Diversey Pkwy., Chicago, IL 60614.

Time-Life Video and Television, 777 Duke St., Alexandria, VA 22314.

Vineyard Video Productions, Elias Lane, West Tisbury, MA 02575.

INDEX OF AUTHORS AND TITLES